Understanding and Evaluating Research

This book is dedicated to my wonderfully intelligent husband, Peter. The idea and the book were conceived and written during the second two years of our retirement. Now we have the future together on our boat, without a computer in sight.

Sara Miller McCune founded SAGE Publishing in 1965 to support the dissemination of usable knowledge and educate a global community. SAGE publishes more than 1000 journals and over 800 new books each year, spanning a wide range of subject areas. Our growing selection of library products includes archives, data, case studies and video. SAGE remains majority owned by our founder and after her lifetime will become owned by a charitable trust that secures the company's continued independence.

Los Angeles | London | New Delhi | Singapore | Washington DC | Melbourne

Understanding and Evaluating Research

A Critical Guide

Sue L. T. McGregor

Los Angeles | London | New Delhi
Singapore | Washington DC | Melbourne

SAGE

FOR INFORMATION:

SAGE Publications, Inc.
2455 Teller Road
Thousand Oaks, California 91320
E-mail: order@sagepub.com

SAGE Publications Ltd.
1 Oliver's Yard
55 City Road
London EC1Y 1SP
United Kingdom

SAGE Publications India Pvt. Ltd.
B 1/I 1 Mohan Cooperative Industrial Area
Mathura Road, New Delhi 110 044
India

SAGE Publications Asia-Pacific Pte. Ltd.
3 Church Street
#10-04 Samsung Hub
Singapore 049483

Acquisitions Editor: Helen Salmon
Editorial Assistant: Chelsea Neve
Production Editor: Bennie Clark Allen
Copy Editor: Melinda Masson
Typesetter: C&M Digitals (P) Ltd.
Proofreader: Susan Schon
Indexer: Robie Grant
Cover Designer: Anupama Krishnan
Marketing Manager: Susannah Goldes

Printed in the United States of America

Library of Congress Cataloging-in-Publication Data

Names: McGregor, Sue L. T., author.

Title: Understanding and evaluating research : a critical guide / Sue McGregor.

Description: Thousand Oaks : SAGE Publications, [2018] | Includes bibliographical references and index.

Identifiers: LCCN 2017034708 | ISBN 9781506350950 (pbk. : alk. paper)

Subjects: LCSH: Research—Evaluation.

Classification: LCC Q180.55.E9 M34 2018 | DDC 001.4—dc23
LC record available at https://lccn.loc.gov/2017034708

This book is printed on acid-free paper.

MIX
Paper from responsible sources
FSC® C014174
www.fsc.org

17 18 19 20 21 10 9 8 7 6 5 4 3 2 1

BRIEF CONTENTS

DETAILED CONTENTS

PART III • ORIENTING AND SUPPORTIVE ELEMENTS OF RESEARCH

Chapter 4 • Orienting and Supportive Elements of a Journal Article

PART V • RESEARCH DESIGN AND RESEARCH METHODS

205

ATTENTION INSTRUCTORS!

The author has also provided editable PowerPoint slides for instructors to use with the book. Please find them available for download at **https://study.sagepub.com/ mcgregor.**

PREFACE

The inspiration for this book came while I was teaching graduate-level courses on research literacy (2010–2014). I could not find a book that contained everything I thought should be taught in a course about how to critically read and use someone else's scholarship. While teaching the course five times, I prepared a roster of detailed PowerPoint presentations about ideas not found in related texts. These topics especially included (a) the powerful link between research methodology and everything else in the research enterprise; (b) the far-reaching role played by conceptual frameworks, theories, and models in research; and (c) the criteria for judging argumentative essays and theoretical papers, which differ so much from a conventional research report. I could find "methods textbooks" in abundance (how to do research yourself), but less so textbooks about how to be research literate (how to critique someone else's research and the final report).

I remember thinking that if I, a seasoned academic with 30 years of experience, did not know this "stuff," then others might not either. With this in mind, I approached SAGE with an idea for such a book, and signed off on the project mere weeks later. Kudos to Acquisitions Editor Helen Salmon for her confidence in this idea. The publisher realized that a book like this was needed. The result is this book titled *Understanding and Evaluating Research*, focused on helping people learn how to read, critique, and judge research reports prepared by others. The assumption is that one cannot critically read a research report without being aware of the conventions that authors are supposed to follow when conducting and reporting their research. As a caveat, the book does not strive to teach people to do their *own* research, but readers may learn more about how to do research by appreciating research conventions as they vary by methodology.

PART I

The book comprises 18 chapters, divided into eight parts. In Part I, the **Introduction**, Chapter 1 ("Critical Research Literacy") begins by describing the approach I took to the book. Each chapter is prefaced with learning objectives, a sort of chapter abstract. To help readers engage with and apply chapter content, critical review questions, called *Review and Engagement*, are dispersed throughout each chapter. The premise is that after readers complete a critical assessment for each research component in a research report, they will complete the Appendix to help them decide if they can confidently use the study and its conclusions in their practice. The chapters all conclude with a wrap-up summary, followed with *Review and Discussion Questions*. I recommend you pose your own reflection and discussion questions as well. Your chapter takeaways will not be the same as mine. Chapter 1 then focuses on what it means to critically and uncritically read a research report. An uncritical reading means accepting the study without questioning it.

PART II

Part II is called **Philosophical and Theoretical Aspects of Research**. It begins with Chapter 2, which is the philosophical anchor for the book. Titled "Research Methodologies," it reinforces the point that the philosophical underpinnings of research determine everything from the research question to the reporting format, and everything in between. After describing philosophical axioms, positivistic and postpositivistic research paradigms, and empirical, interpretive, and critical research methodologies, I confirm that the book is organized using the qualitative, quantitative, and mixed methods approach to categorizing methodologies. The chapter concludes with a discussion of the importance of aligning research methodology and research questions, and with some basic conventions for writing the research methodology section of a research report.

Still in Part II, Chapter 3 is titled "Conceptual Frameworks, Theories, and Models." It makes the case that without frameworks, theories, and models, research is weakened. The chapter discusses concepts and constructs, the building blocks of all three, followed with (a) a detailed discussion of conceptual frameworks, (b) an extensive coverage of theories, and (c) a shorter overview of models. The chapter also covers the reporting conventions pursuant to writing the conceptual and theoretical framework or model sections of a research paper.

PART III

Part III is called **Orienting and Supportive Elements of Research**. These terms were coined for this book as a way to recognize the importance of their role in reporting research. They act as bookends for the major (primary) components of a research report (methodology, theoretical underpinnings, introduction and research questions, literature review, methods, results or findings, discussion, conclusions, and recommendations). The *orienting* elements bring the paper to people's attention (authors' names, credentials, and affiliations; article title; abstract; and, keywords). The *supportive* elements help authors acknowledgments, contributions to the research (references, footnotes and endnotes, appendices, acknowledgements, and biographies). Chapter 4 ("Orienting and Supportive Elements of a Journal Article") provides a rich discussion of each of these nine research elements, which are characterized as secondary, meaning they are important but for different reasons than the primary elements.

Chapter 5, titled "Peer-Reviewed Journals," focuses on the most common publication venue for research reports. Critical readers often use elements of the journal to judge the rigor of the scholarship, whether it is wise to do so or not. Starting with the role of journal editors, other types of editors, and editorial boards, the discussion shifts to the peer review process, acceptance rates, and journal impact factors. The discussion then turns to the journal's title; volume, issue, and pagination; year of publication and the paper's placement in the issue; and special or thematic issues. The chapter deals extensively with the new publication model of electronic journals, and discusses the possible threats to quality and rigor of open access journals, especially predatory journals.

PART IV

Part IV deals with issues pertaining to **Research Justifications, Augmentation, and Rationales**. Chapter 6 ("Introduction and Research Questions") distinguishes between opening points (six types) and an introduction. Opening points lead the reader into the introduction, and the introduction leads people into the paper. The chapter covers research problems, questions, purpose (statements), and objectives. These are all discussed in extensive detail (as they pertain to qualitative, quantitative, and mixed methods) because savvy authors and critical readers need a clear understanding of how they differ yet are inherently interconnected. Next comes an extensive overview of six approaches that authors can use to develop an argument supporting what they are doing in their study. These approaches help authors convince people of the merit of *their* study, namely by critically reviewing literature related to the research *problem*, identifying what is missing (justifying their research question), and explaining how their study will fill the gap (research *statement* and *objectives*).

Chapter 7 ("Literature Review") covers how the literature review section of a research paper differs with qualitative, quantitative, and mixed methods research methodologies. Quantitative studies do the review before collecting the data, and qualitative studies tend to wait and do the review after the data are collected and are being analyzed. The chapter covers what is involved in *critically engaging* with previous work done about the research question, and explains in detail the process of *synthesizing* insights gained from this critical engagement. Nine organizational strategies are identified and discussed, showcasing the many choices authors have about how to present their review of the literature.

PART V

The next part is titled **Research Designs and Research Methods**. It comprises three chapters. Chapter 8 ("Overview of Research Design and Methods") focuses on how the research methodology deeply affects the research design and the methods employed in a study. After distinguishing between methodology (philosophy, introduced in Chapter 2) and method (tasks to sample, collect, and analyze data), the discussion turns to how method and research design are different (but often used interchangeably). Readers learn the differences between qualitative and quantitative inquiries, followed with a general overview of the basic steps involved in each of qualitative and quantitative research designs. These steps are then used to organize the extensive, wide-ranging, comprehensive profile of both qualitative and quantitative methods, including seven qualitative research designs (Chapter 9, "Reporting Qualitative Research Methods") and seven quantitative research designs (Chapter 10, "Reporting Quantitative Methods and Mixed Methods Research"). Chapter 10 concludes with a discussion of the mixed methods approach, which involves using both qualitative and quantitative strands, informed by the principle of data integration. In addition to design rigor, mixed methods research has a criterion of interpretative rigor, concerned with the validity of the conclusions (strand-specific and meta-inferences).

PART VI

Part VI, **Results and Findings**, has three chapters. After addressing what it means for authors and critical readers to be statistically literate, Chapter 11 ("Statistical Literacy and Conventions") turns to the four main types of data (nominal, ordinal, interval, and ratio) and measurement scales, and then provides an overview of the nine most commonly used statistical variables. The chapter ends with the distinctions between experimental research designs (true, factorial, quasi, and single-case) and nonexperimental research designs (group comparisons, correlational research, surveys, and case studies). The criteria of randomization, variable manipulation, experimental and control groups, types of claims (causal and association), and types of research settings are used to differentiate between these two basic quantitative research designs.

Chapter 12 ("Descriptive and Inferential Statistics") starts with a discussion of the four types of measurements for descriptive statistics (i.e., central, variable, relative, and relationships), which includes a detailed overview of such basic conventions as standard deviation, the bell curve, contingency tables, chi-square, regression correlational coefficients, and scattergrams. The topic then shifts to inferential statistics, prefaced with a section on association and causation. Inferential statistics is concerned with (a) hypotheses and estimates, (b) p value and level of significance, (c) Type I and II errors, (d) statistical power (sample size and effect size), and (e) the most common inferential statistical tests.

Chapter 13 ("Results and Findings") discusses conventions for authors to follow when conducting and reporting the outcomes of their study. As with most other chapters in the book, it is organized by research methodologies: qualitative, quantitative, and mixed methods. Some challenges for qualitative research are balancing both describing and interpreting the data, providing supportive evidence for the existence of a theme, learning the protocols around using participants' quotations, and providing thick and rich descriptions (so as to ensure high-quality findings that can be trusted). The section on quantitative results deals with issues of comprehensiveness (when answering the research question or hypothesis), missing data and negative results, organizational strategies for presenting results, and conventions for reporting numbers (text, tables, and figures). The chapter ends with an overview of reporting protocols and conventions for mixed methods studies, especially the principle of data integration, and the steps/strategies researchers can take to ensure integration before data collection, during analysis, or both. The importance of moving from strand-specific inferences to meta-inferences is discussed as are barriers to integration in mixed methods studies. The importance of addressing the fit of data integration is followed with various organizational approaches and a discussion of how and where to publish the study to reflect the degree of data integration.

PART VII

Part VII, **Discussion, Conclusions, and Recommendations**, provides a chapter on each research element. Chapter 14 ("Discussion") begins by distinguishing between discussion points and concluding remarks, followed with an overview of the different conventions for relating results and findings to a discussion of their import. Then, the three main functions of a discussion section are addressed (summarize, explain, and examine), as are the topics of hedging and speculation. Discussion sections should address three basic questions, dealing with how the study (a) relates to existing understandings in the literature, (b) brings new understandings, and (c) makes new connections. After discussing these in some detail, the conversation turns to study limitations and how authors need to explain how threats to validity affect their conclusions and implications. The conversation then focuses on five major approaches to organizing a discussion section, shifting to an overview of strategies to keep the discussion section on track and focused. After explaining the importance of employing alternative interpretations of the results and findings, it ends with the role of critical and creative thinking when preparing discussion points.

Chapter 15 ("Conclusions") begins by advising authors of the need to appreciate how concluding comments differ from, but are related to, discussion points, and how concluding comments relate to a summary of the paper. The focus then turns to the four main purposes of a conclusion section: explore broader implications; suggest new research; relate study to existing literature; and identify policy, practice, and theoretical implications. Next, the chapter profiles eight closing strategies for a conclusions section, ranging from provocative questions to warnings and personal narratives. Things to avoid when creating concluding remarks are also discussed, especially apologies and new information. If done well, the concluding thoughts make the paper resonate with readers, increasing the likelihood they will engage with the study in the future.

Chapter 16 ("Recommendations") deals with the section of a research report where authors call people to action. After distinguishing between conclusions and recommendations (and the different roles they play), the discussion turns to the nine purposes that recommendations can serve, followed with an overview of the eight characteristics of effective recommendations. The chapter then turns to the topic of verbs when writing recommendations, with a special focus on the 10 modal verbs and on modal force (the writer's conviction when posing the recommendation). There are three modal forces (certainty, possibility, and obligation), and each is recognizable through the use of particular modal verbs. An extensive overview of strategies for crafting, presenting, and organizing a recommendation section is provided. The chapter ends with some basic grammatical conventions, especially the use of passive and active voice.

PART VIII

Part VIII, the final section of the book, is called **Argumentative Essays and Theoretical Papers**. The two chapters in this section are separated from the rest of the book because papers reporting research related to positions, opinions, think pieces, new conceptual frameworks, and new theories do not fit with the basic reporting conventions previously discussed in Parts II and IV–VII. Chapter 17 ("Argumentative Essays: Position, Discussion, and Think-Piece Papers") focuses on argumentative essays, which are judged by the ability of the author to develop a convincing and well-reasoned argument. The chapter begins by comparing and contrasting the three most basic forms of argumentative essays: position (opinion) papers, discussion papers, and think pieces. This clarification is followed with a detailed overview of the format for writing an argumentative essay: thesis, antithesis, and synthesis. The discussion then turns to the concept of persuasive writing and the key role played by Aristotle's rhetorical appeals: ethos (character), pathos (emotions), and logos (logic). The chapter then presents a very detailed discussion of both deductive and inductive argumentation, ending with a brief introduction to logical fallacies in argumentative essays.

Chapter 18 ("Conceptual and Theoretical Papers") is the last chapter in the book. Whereas Chapter 3 is about the role conceptual frameworks and theories play in the research design, and how to use and report on their use in a paper, this chapter is about how to write a paper that reports on a new conceptual framework or a new theory. They both require different formats. The chapter especially addresses the special role that the literature review plays in each paper. It is an *integrative* instrument in a conceptual paper and a *theoretical-step* instrument in a theory paper. The chapter then profiles the key structural elements in both types of papers, distinguishing between each one, explaining that they become the organizational subheadings in the published paper. What constitutes a good theory is addressed as well. The conversation turns to Lynham's idea of what to include in a theory paper, determined by how far along it is (ranging from the conceptual stage to being successfully applied in practice). The chapter concludes with a detailed discussion of what criteria to use to judge the rigor of a conceptual or a theoretical paper—mainly its supportive, red-thread argument—and the author's mode of reasoning (analytical and generative).

ACKNOWLEDGMENTS

First and foremost, I want to thank my husband, Peter, for his intellect, deep patience, powerful critical listening skills, and ability to make me reflect and accept things when I am in pushback mode—all part of the creative process. Thanks to my longtime friends Liz Goldsmith, Anne MacCleave, Felicia Eghan, and Vicki Jeans for lending supportive and critical ears during this creative process. Nearer to the end of the writing process came Frank Miccolis and Chrisanne Moffatt Miccolis, new boating friends who were incredibly patient with me while I unloaded my stress and expressed my excitement! My mom, Ethel Tweedie, has always been there for me during every life endeavor, as has my nephew, Connor Hunter Tweedie Morton.

This journey about research methodologies and their link to scholarship began with a doctoral student turned friend, Dr. Jenny Murnane. Our work formed the cornerstone of the book (see Table 2.1). It was followed with an opportunity to teach *Focus on Research Literacy* in our education graduate program. Thanks to Jim Sharpe, then the dean, for patiently waiting until I felt I was ready to teach it. And those students! They were something, approaching this overwhelming topic with anticipation, undaunted grace, and open-mindedness. I would not have written the book without them and their inspiration. Finally, thanks to the SAGE editors and their assistants.

SAGE gratefully acknowledges the following reviewers for their kind assistance:

Kristin Bodiford, *Dominican University*

Kadir Demir, *Georgia State University*

Scott Greenberger, *Grand Canyon University*

Tanya Kaefer, *Lakehead University*

Xyanthe Neider, *Washington State University*

Carole S. Rhodes, *Queens College, City University of New York*

Anita Rose, *New York University*

ABOUT THE AUTHOR

Sue L. T. McGregor (PhD, IPHE, Professor Emerita) is a Canadian home economist (nearly 50 years) recently retired from Mount Saint Vincent University in Halifax, Nova Scotia. She was one of the lead architects for the interuniversity doctoral program in educational studies, serving as its inaugural coordinator. She has a keen interest in home economics philosophy, transdisciplinarity, research methodologies, and consumer studies. She is a *TheATLAS Fellow* (transdisciplinarity), a Docent in Home Economics at the University of Helsinki, recipient of the *Marjorie M. Brown Distinguished Professor Award* (home economics leadership), a *Rhoda H. Karpatkin International Consumer Fellow*, and recipient of the *TOPACE International Award* (Berlin) for distinguished international consumer scholars, especially consumer educators. Affiliated with 16 professional journals, she has nearly 170 peer-reviewed publications, four books, 31 book chapters, and 12 monographs. She has delivered 39 keynotes and invited talks in 14 countries. Dr. McGregor is also the principal consultant for *McGregor Consulting Group* (founded in 1991). Visit www.consultmcgregor.com, or contact her at sue.mcgregor@msvu.ca.

INTRODUCTION

1 CRITICAL RESEARCH LITERACY

INTRODUCTION TO THE BOOK

This is an introductory-level text in the sense that *introduce* stems from Latin *ducere*, "to lead" (Harper, 2016). This book strives to *lead* people through the research process by using a critical lens—hence, the title *Understanding and Evaluating Research: A Critical Guide*. The book is intended to help people learn how to critique other people's research so they can use it with confidence. It is written in third person, explaining what authors should do at each stage of the research process while they respect the research conventions pursuant to the methodological (philosophical) approach used in their study (see Chapter 2). As readers gain a deeper appreciation of the expectations placed on researchers and authors to conduct and report research of high standards, they will concurrently learn how to critique the resultant study and the research report. In effect, the book is not intended to teach readers how to *do* research on their own. They will learn about it by way of osmosis, which is the gradual, often unconscious absorption of knowledge or ideas through continual exposure rather than deliberate learning (Anderson, 2014).

As a way to learn during this process, readers should choose a journal article or research report they want to critically read. As they read each chapter in this book, they should *engage* with its content by *applying* it to critique the research report. This book facilitates this critical reading process by providing *Review and Engagement* checklists, which are strategically positioned throughout the chapters, close to the respective content. For example, as people read and learn about the conventions authors should follow when preparing the Methods section of a research report (see Chapter 8), they would critically review the paper's Methods section to see if it meets the recommended standards for high quality. To help bring readers to this assessment, each chapter ends with a question such as "Taking *all* of the ***Review and Engagement*** criteria into account, what is your final judgment of the Methods section of the paper you are critically reading?"

Figure 1.1 summarizes the basic stages of critiquing a research report (often a journal article). These steps include reading it, identifying the elements used to organize it, rereading it while critically analyzing and judging each element, and then assessing (judging) the entire paper for its quality as scholarship. The Appendix (available for download at https://study.sagepub .com/mcgregor) contains a document developed to help readers track their critical judgment of each *separate* element of a research report, leading to a cumulative judgment of the quality of that entire study and its formal report. For example, if the keywords, title, and abstract were judged inadequate but the methods, the results, and their discussion were clearly and rigorously reported, it would make sense to confidently judge the paper as good quality. On the other hand, if the authors used a catchy title, chose keywords wisely, and had a solid reference list but the methods, the findings, and their discussion were inadequately documented, it would make sense to lower the judgment of the research report (and perhaps the research enterprise itself).

All chapters conclude with *Review and Discussion Questions*, another tool for *engaging* with the content of the specific chapter so as to better *apply* it when critically reading a research report. Furthermore, noting the etymological roots, origins, and meanings of the basic research terms adds linguistic flavor to each chapter. To illustrate, consider the phrase *critical research literacy*, the title of this chapter. *Critical* is Latin *criticus*, "to pass judgment on literature." *Research* is Old French *recercher*, "intensive seeking." *Literacy* is Latin *literatus*, "the quality or rank of being educated, or learned" (Harper, 2016). Being critically research literate thus means that someone has, through education, learned how to critically judge an effort to intensely seek and report something—in this case, new knowledge emergent from a study.

FIGURE 1.1 ■ Process of Critiquing a Journal Article

Critiquing a Journal Article

Note that you are **not just criticizing** the article, meaning you are not just trying to find fault with it (for there may indeed be errors).

To **critique** an article, you must *appraise it critically*, meaning you will conduct a detailed **analysis** of its structure and then conduct an assessment of it (**appraise it**).

Analyzing entails examining, in detail, the various elements of the structure of the paper (the main components of a research report: e.g., research question, literature review, and conclusions).

Assessing an article entails striving *to judge its worth* as research that you can confidently use in your practice, scholarly efforts, or both.

So, you are going to

1. Repeatedly **read** *the article* (at the surface and deeper levels)
2. **Identify the elements** used to organize and write it (e.g., method, results, and discussion)
3. **Analyze these elements** individually, passing judgment on **each** element as you read it (i.e., critically appraise it: good, bad, or not sure)
4. **Assess or judge the worth** of the *entire study and the article* (good, bad, or not sure)

This etymological example frames the main focus of this book, which is to help readers develop the ability to critically assess authors' studies and research reports. By association, authors reading this chapter can gain insights into how to ensure their research study and the report meet the expected rigor of a critical perspective. This approach mirrors contemporary definitions of research literacy, which include being able to function, respectively, as critical readers and critical producers of research (Dryden & Achilles, 2004; Ingham-Broomfield, 2008; Shank & Brown, 2007; Williams, Mulkins, Verhoef, Monkman, & Findlay, 2002).

To that end, this first chapter explains the concepts of (a) research literacy and (b) critical and uncritical readings of research. It serves as a preamble to separate chapters on each of the many elements of the research process—that is, what authors need to know and do when conducting and reporting research, and what critical readers need to know to judge its quality (see Figure 1.2). Separate chapters are provided for understanding the basics of *statistical literacy* (Chapters 11 and 12), for writing an argumentative essay (Chapter 17), and for writing a conceptual paper or a theoretical paper (Chapter 18). These types of papers do not follow the basic conventions for a research report.

FIGURE 1.2 ■ Basic Elements of a Research Report

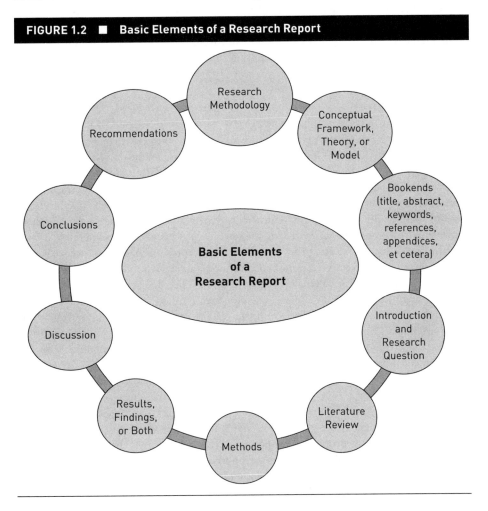

RESEARCH LITERACY DEFINED

The term *research literacy* comprises two concepts, research and literacy. *Research* is Modern French *rechercher*, "to examine closely, to see, to look for." As noted earlier, it also stems from Old French *recercher*, with *re*, "intensive," and *cercher*, "seeking." Research thus involves the intensive, concentrated search for knowledge. *Literacy* is Latin *literatus*, "educated, or learned." In the word *literacy*, the suffix *-cy* means "quality or rank" (Harper, 2016). Literacy thus means having the quality of being knowledgeable or educated and exhibiting the ability to recognize and understand ideas, in this case, about research. Taken together, research literacy can be defined as the ability to locate, understand, critically evaluate, and apply scholarly works—that is, to become discerning and knowledgeable about research (i.e., the search for new knowledge) (Dryden & Achilles, 2004).

Beyond these etymological definitions, research literacy is defined as understanding research language and conventions. It is a foundational block of *research capacity*, defined as "the ability to design and conduct [and report] research studies" (Williams et al., 2002, p. 14). Shank and Brown (2007) proposed that the term *research literate* refers to scholars being literate in how to conduct and report research. But it also refers to those who are reading the resultant reports. They need to be able to judge that scholarship before they use it.

BENEFITS OF RESEARCH LITERACY

Achieving research literacy is important for several reasons. Foremost, it helps alleviate the fear of not being able to access and assess research and scholarly publications. The more research literate people become, the more confidence they gain in judging others' work. Research literacy entails both criticizing and critiquing scholarship, privileging the latter. Both of these words have the same Latin root, *criticus*, "to pass judgment on literature" (Harper, 2016). But while (a) *criticizing* the research process means finding fault with it, (b) *critiquing* it means assessing the strength of arguments and their supportive evidence, including the authors' interpretations and conclusions drawn from their analysis and their discussion of the data. This accrued reader confidence is possible because, with experience, people build up knowledge of methodologies, theories, methods, and entire bodies of literature. Informed with this knowledge, confident readers are less inclined to erroneously rely on flawed scholarship.

Research literacy encourages (actually necessitates) people to become critical readers and thinkers of others' scholarly work (Kurland, 2000; Suter, 2012). Conversely, engagement with research enhances critical thinking and predisposes people to critique the scholarship. Indeed, critical readers of research both understand *and* engage with the research (Kattiyapornpong, Turner, Zutshi, Hagel, & Fujimoto, 2011). If people are engaged with something, they become involved with it, and it holds their attention (Anderson, 2014). This engagement means people go beyond merely reading the research report (superficial); rather, they dig deeper, holding the scholarship to high standards (Hart, Poston, & Perry, 1980; Shank & Brown, 2007). The next sections expand on this idea, in conjunction with being uncritical.

REVIEW AND ENGAGEMENT

Critical readers will

☐ Appreciate what it means to be research literate in general

☐ Appreciate what it means to be *critically* (and uncritically) research literate (see Table 1.2)

☐ Recognize the benefits of being critically research literate

☐ Distinguish between *being critical of* and *critiquing* research

☐ Understand that *critical engagement* with a study means paying attention to, and getting involved with, it (not just a superficial, lay reading)

☐ Have a fundamental understanding of the basic elements of a research report (see Figure 1.2) and the conventions involved in preparing it, appreciating that most elements contain some margin of error

CRITICAL RESEARCH LITERACY

Critical research literacy adds the dimension of judging the value of a study's contribution to theory, knowledge, and practice. Recall that *critical* is Latin *criticus*, "to pass judgment on literature" (Harper, 2016), so being *critical* means engaging in and expressing the merits and faults of literary works (i.e., formal writings) (Anderson, 2014). Being *critical of research* means carefully evaluating the scholarly work (i.e., looking for biases, unspoken assumptions, underlying ideologies, prejudices, quality, and rigor) and then judging the research, being able to defend one's position (see Figure 1.3). People cannot maintain a critical perspective when reading research unless they can unpack what it means to be critical and uncritical (Shon, 2015; Suter, 2012).

FIGURE 1.3 ■ What to Look for When Critically Reading Research Reports

Bias

- Unreasonable and undeserved preference or dislike for something or someone (i.e., favoritism, foregone conclusion, partiality)

Unspoken Assumptions

- Unmentioned beliefs (unarticulated, perhaps unexamined) that are thought to be true, without proof

Prejudice

- Inflexible and irrational attitudes and opinions held by someone about another (Beliefs are things considered true, without proof. Opinions are *personal* beliefs not founded on proof or certainty. In effect, people *prejudge* others with no evidence to the contrary.)

(Continued)

FIGURE 1.3 ■ (Continued)

- An inclination for or against something that inhibits impartial judgment (The latter is defined as a bias-free position arrived at by reasoning from premises or general principles.)

- Holding preconceived beliefs (i.e., beliefs formed without having evidence of truth or full knowledge)

Dominance of Particular Paradigms or Ideologies

- Dominance, or "superior and having power over" (Holding to a particular paradigm or ideology may preclude other valid points of view or perspectives.)

Quality and Rigor

- Standards and conventions for good scholarly work that may or may not be properly and consistently applied by the researcher when conducting the study

Balanced Appraisals

In more detail, Lunsford and Lunsford (1996) claimed that scholars and professional practitioners have a duty to critically review the literature and the research in their discipline and profession. Becoming "educated readers and interpreters of professional research literature" (p. 24) requires gaining the necessary skills and competencies to critically analyze research; that is, they have to learn to read research reports from a critical stance. Kurland (2000) agreed, claiming that readers have a responsibility to themselves and to others to monitor their reactions to a research report and to strive to understand the author's point of view. This understanding has to occur *before* the text can be critiqued.

The essence of the successful critique of a research paper is a balanced appraisal, meaning readers look for both merits and demerits (strength and weaknesses), achieved using logic and objectivity (Harris, 2014; Ingham-Broomfield, 2008). A balanced appraisal is accomplished via a logical and systematic assessment of the paper, grounded in *critical awareness* (see Figure 1.1). This means to strive to "be more questioning; try to see more than one side of an argument; try to be objective rather than subjective; weigh the evidence; make judgements based on reason, evidence or logic; look at the meaning behind the facts; identify issues arising from the facts; and recognise when further evidence is needed" (Ingham-Broomfield, 2008, p. 103).

Judging Chains of Reasoning

Once the research report has been critically assessed, readers are able to decide what to accept as true and useful. To do this, they must evaluate the evidence and the argument used by authors to reach their conclusions (Kurland, 2000). Kurland (2000) suggested that readers have to take control of the text they are reading (prepared by someone else) and become authors of their own understandings of the facts and their meanings as framed and argued by the authors. Only when readers fully understand a text can they truly critically evaluate the authors' assertions. This understanding entails unearthing the authors' purpose, persuasive arguments, and inherent biases. Authors choose content, language, writing styles, argumentative rhetorical styles, and logics for a reason. More than careful reading, critical reading of a research report involves actively recognizing and judging these linguistic elements (Kurland, 2000).

From another perspective, Kurland (2000) posited that critical readers of research will deeply appreciate that the report reflects just one person's portrayal of facts, one person's take on the topic. That author prepared an argument, and chose specific evidence to support it, for a reason. A critical reader will suss out those reasons, which are normally informed by research paradigms, assumptions, biases, values, prejudices, opinions, agendas, and interests. Upon recognizing what a text *says* on the surface, a critical reader goes further and deeper, discovering what it *means*. The latter process involves critical interpretation of the research report so as to offer alternative, possible meanings or to challenge the evidence and arguments used by the author to make points and to draw conclusions (Kurland, 2000).

A critical reading also entails stepping back and gaining distance from the research report. From this distance, readers can "launch into an intensive critical reading" (Knott, 2009, p. 1) of the document. They would be looking for (a) the authors' central claims or purpose, (b) the background context and intended audience, (c) the kinds of reasoning and appeals used by the authors to develop their argument, and (d) their selection of evidence to support their arguments. Readers culminate this intensive critical reading with their evaluation of the strengths and weaknesses of the arguments comprising the report (Knott, 2009) (see Figure 1.1 and the Appendix).

Once readers have critically assessed the research, they have to decide to what extent they will accept the authors' arguments, opinions, and conclusions. This involves uncovering the authors' (a) rationale for the evidence they selected and (b) construction of their arguments. Readers need to ask themselves several pertinent questions. "How well developed are the arguments leading to discussion points and conclusions? Is the author's interpretation of the data convincing? Are the author's conclusions supported by the preceding arguments? Does the author's line of reasoning (or logic) make sense and hold together? Might there be alternative interpretations of data other than those proposed by the author? Are there any hidden assumptions that have to be questioned?" These questions constitute an engaged, critical reading of a research report (University of Leicester, 2009).

Conscious readers of research will appreciate that all research contains a margin of error (an amount, usually small, that is allowed for) (Blackmore & Rockert, 2004). No study is perfect (Shank & Brown, 2007). Critical readers will acknowledge that these imperfections exist, accept this fact, and then determine whether these imperfections undermine the study's rigor, rendering the results/findings meaningless or even harmful (Croad & Farquhar, 2005). Critical readers will read between the lines, unpack the article, and pass judgment on it at many levels (Shank & Brown, 2007). They will look beyond the minor issues (like a weak title or irrelevant keywords) and take a broad view to ask the big questions. "Readers who are critically literate in . . . research never lose sight of this big picture, even when they are happily wallowing in the [method] and stylistic details" (Shank & Brown, 2007, p. 227) (see the Appendix).

Skeptical and Critical Scrutiny

Knowing that all studies are imperfect, critical readers would bring a healthy dose of skepticism to the process of critically reading research reports. Mitzenmacher (2010) suggested that critical reading requires people to be suspicious. But skepticism would likely be more productive and fair because suspicious means distrustful while skeptical means being inclined to inquire and to question (Anderson, 2014). Critical reading involves "harder, more positive thinking" than does suspicion, which tends to tear something down or apart (Mitzenmacher, 2010, p. 1). If people are skeptical, they can confidently resist ideas presented by others instead of uncritically accepting them. Their intent is to *inquire* into the scholarship in order to find unspoken assumptions, fallacies, dogma, and, yes, outright errors in the methods or analysis (McGregor, 2006; Suter, 2012). Harris (2014) urged readers to find a balance between naïveté and cynicism by thinking critically about research. Taking this stance, they can "intelligently appraise research" (p. 106). "A little skepticism provides healthy protection against [missing] mistakes" (Locke, Silverman, & Spirduso, 2010, p. 69).

Rather than getting bogged down by criticizing the minutiae, critical readers would focus on whether the scholarship is of high quality and meets the conventions for the research methodology employed in the study (Locke et al., 2010). For example, confirming long-held anecdotal assertions, Caldwell, Henshaw, and Taylor (2005) affirmed that people tend to use the quantitative criteria of reliability and validity to judge qualitative research (but not vice versa). They claimed the resultant criticism is unjustified because quantitative research should be judged using different criteria, including transferability, dependability, credibility, and confirmability. Critical readers would be able to evaluate and judge the quality of the evidence the authors presented, appreciating that different criteria are used for quantitative, qualitative, and mixed methods methodologies (Zardo & Pryor, 2012) (see Chapter 8, Table 8.5).

In a lighthearted example, Suter (2012) shared this anecdote. A quantitative researcher critically evaluated a qualitative study, taunting the researcher with "What? Your conclusion is based on only one participant?" The qualitative researcher aptly responded with "What? Your conclusion is based on only one experiment?" Suter affirmed that this rivalry and disrespect is unjustified because both research "'camps' . . . value rigorous data collection and analysis coupled with sound, logical arguments that characterize scientific reasoning, namely a compelling chain of evidence that supports the conclusions. Both camps are keenly aware of rival . . . and alternative explanations of their findings" (p. 345). Locke et al. (2010) concurred, acknowledging "the paradoxical fact that there are pervasive similarities" between quantitative and qualitative research paradigms (p. 80).

Wallace and Wray (2011) tendered a model for discerning readers that better ensures they critically scrutinize a study. They cautioned readers to remember that each study was conducted and the report written by particular authors, with a particular purpose and audience. These authors intentionally constructed an argument to convince that audience of the merit of their research. Critical readers have to try to discern what the authors were striving to achieve. They have to work out the structure of the argument and try to identify the main claims (see Chapter 6). As they do this, critical readers should adopt a skeptical stance, checking to make sure the evidence supports the claims. This involves considering any underlying values, assumptions, paradigms, or biases guiding the authors and influencing their claims. Throughout this whole critical process, readers have to keep an open mind and be willing to be convinced (but not cajoled).

REVIEW AND ENGAGEMENT

Critical readers will

☐ Recognize and understand the differences among biases, assumptions, prejudices, and agendas (see Figure 1.3)

☐ Appreciate that a critical reading of a paper necessitates a balanced appraisal (look for both strengths and weaknesses), doing so objectively and using logic

☐ Learn how to locate and evaluate the authors' argument and how to evaluate any evidence they used to make their claims (their conclusions)

☐ Practice stepping back from a paper to gain *critical distance*, and only then pass judgment on its merits and demerits, at many levels (see Figure 1.1)

☐ Bring a healthy dose of skepticism to the process of *critically reading* a research report (i.e., confidently resist ideas while remaining open to inquiry and to questioning)

UNCRITICAL READINGS OF RESEARCH

Short of stating the obvious, uncritical reading of research means people accept it without challenging anything. *Uncritical* means not using one's critical faculties (by choice or lack of ability). *Un* is Latin "not," and *critical* is "to judge." So, being uncritical means not judging, in that people accept something too easily because of being unwilling or unable to critique it (Anderson, 2014; Harper, 2016). People can be uncritical for several reasons (see Figure 1.4), to be discussed in more detail.

FIGURE 1.4 ■ Nuances of Uncritical Reading of Research

Being uncritical means accepting or approving something without analyzing or questioning it, or without discriminating between good and bad. People can be uncritical for several reasons:

Gullible

● Easily duped, tricked, or deceived

Naïve

● Not shrewd; lacking sophistication or critical judgment and analysis

Trusting

● Relying on or having confidence that something is good

Innocent

● Ignorant, having little knowledge of bad or evil

Unsuspecting

● Not suspicious or distrustful, unwary (not alert to dangers or deception)

Misplaced Trust

Some people may innocently approach research assuming it is true and valid. This misplaced trust is unfortunate because they may end up using a weak, flawed study (Locke et al., 2010). *Valid* is Latin *validus*, "strong" (Harper, 2016). It also denotes the condition of being true (Locke et al., 2010). Fundamentally, *internal validity* (strength) refers to whether the study truly dealt with what was being studied. The data gathered have to match the research question. *External validity* refers to the results being valid (i.e., remaining truthful or meaningful) beyond the confines of the study. Different research methodologies and traditions use different terminology for these two aspects of strength and truth/meaning (Hart et al., 1980; Locke et al., 2010) (see Chapter 8, Table 8.5).

Readers should also look for *logical validity*, meaning whether the report holds together and makes sense. Called *internal consistency*, it refers to whether each element of the research design logically flows from the others. For example, do the conclusions reflect the discussion points, which should be anchored in the results or findings and interpreted using the literature and any theory or conceptual framework underpinning the study (see Chapter 16, Figure 16.2)? If not logically valid, the report may be suspect and not usable (Wiersma & Jurs, 2009). At the crux of the matter is that authors must not deliberately insert falsehoods into their research reports; any errors or flaws have to be unintentional (Shank & Brown, 2007).

Overindulgent and Undiscriminating

Uncritically using flawed data, logic, or conclusions can have very negative consequences (Croad & Farquhar, 2005). Critical readers of research would know when to suspend their trust in a research report (Locke et al., 2010), but this is not always the case. Some people are relatively knowledgeable of the research process but are undiscriminating, meaning they do not consistently apply critical standards of analysis when reading studies. They run the risk of uncritically accepting the study as good research when it is actually compromised. They are too indulgent of the authors' claims and conclusions, overlooking flaws or being too tolerant of sloppy or shoddy scholarship. It is irresponsible, let alone uncritical, to disregard the requirement that authors should be held accountable to accepted standards and conventions of sound scholarship. Reading research is a collaborative event, with both writer and reader bearing responsibilities to ensure that communications do not break down. Every article is a conversation and a potential dialogue (Locke et al., 2010; Shank & Brown, 2007).

Surface-Level Reading

Locke et al. (2010) advised that if they are unable to detect a flaw yet *sense* something is amiss, critical readers should shift from reading for general content to examining details pertaining to the rationale for the study; variables or phenomena; settings, contexts, and samples; methods for data collection and analysis; discussion points; conclusions; and the logic used to present the study. Inadequacies in any of these basic research elements can set off alarms and warning bells.

If people persist in reading the article at the surface level while opting not to critique the research (or being unable to), their takeaways from the study will lack intellectual depth or thoroughness. They will end up using cursory, one-dimensional, and shallow interpretations of the study when actually their research or practice context demands more than a superficial, uncritical reading. Their naïveté hinders critical readings of studies. If they are also gullible (easily deceived), their unsuspecting demeanor may cause them to rely on scholarship without examining the authors' assumptions and any hidden agendas (see next section).

Reading Deeper for Ideologies and Paradigms

At a deeper level, uncritical readers may approach a research report unaware of the power of ideologies and paradigms. The consequences of this can cut two ways: (a) Readers may be unaware of which paradigm *they* bring to the exercise (or which ideologies are steeped into *their* psyche), and (b) they may not be able to discern the authors' worldview or appreciate that authors are favoring a particular ideology that is clouding their perspective. Indeed, some authors purposely promote an ideology dear to their heart rather than conduct an honest inquiry. On the other hand, readers may be very aware of the power of ideologies but choose to find fault with the research (criticize it) instead of critically reading it. Readers' unfounded suspicion that the author is harboring ideological motives may actually cramp their ability or inclination to read critically (Locke et al., 2010).

Ideologies

In more detail, ideologies (a system of ideas and ideals held by a group) are orientations to the world that characterize the thinking of a *group* or a nation. Paradigms (patterns) are *individual* thought patterns influenced by the ideologies. Ideologies come before paradigms. Ideologies are understood to be cultural blueprints, while paradigms are thought patterns for interpreting the world shaped by this blueprint. Ideologies are the ruling ideas of the times. They are assumptions about what is worthy of belief and attention, accepted as true, and valued. They pertain to how society should work and be arranged, and they provide the rules deemed most appropriate for achieving this ideal societal arrangement (see Table 1.1, which portrays only the dominant ideologies and paradigms, for illustrative purposes. There is a cadre of contending ideologies and paradigms, but their discussion is beyond the scope of this chapter) (see Donovan, 2010; Eaton, 1996; Elgin & LeDrew, 1997; Heuerman & Olson, 1998; McGregor, 2008, 2013; McGregor, Pendergast, Seniuk, Eghan, & Engberg, 2008).

TABLE 1.1 ■ Dominant Ideologies and Paradigms Seeping Into Research Agendas	
Dominant Ideologies (cultural blueprints of desired society)	**Attendant Paradigms (perspectives on a world shaped by the ideologies)**
Capitalism: an economic orientation that values profit, wealth accumulation, growth, production, and technological progress	• Control, mastery, management, and efficiency • Property ownership, dominance, profit, and competition • Mechanistic orientation, focused on parts (rather than holistic) • Transmissions and transactions
Patriarchy: a system that privileges and conveys power to men and marginalizes and disempowers women and other presumably weak people	• Dualism about every aspect of the world (One side of the binary pair is desirable because it is powerful; the other is undesirable and is in a powerless or marginalized position.) • Hierarchies that divide and separate human beings into categories such as gender, class, economic status, and political power

(Continued)

TABLE 1.1 ■ (Continued)

Neoliberalism: economic and political notions that favor business with nominal roles for governments	• Relativism (quick fix, no absolute truth) • Basic tenets: individualism, privatization, decentralization, and deregulation
Economic globalization (from the top down): corporate- and elite-led neoliberalism focused on integrating national economies into a global economy; concerned with the pace of integration	• Newtonianism (disconnected and fragmented) • Causal relationships, linearity, predetermination • Reductionism (reduce everything to categories, specializations, micro analysis) • Mastery over nature, resources, and marginalized people (exploitation, extraction, control)
Political ideology of conservatism: the idea that societies should maintain (*conserve*) the status quo of the ruling elites and accept change only reluctantly, at a very slow pace; things endure because they work	• Favors business with nominal roles for governments; minimal regulation of the market • Social hierarchy and social inequality viewed as inevitable, natural, normal, even desirable • Expansive military policies and spending are assumed to protect the country and, by association, the family
Social Darwinism: survival of the fittest; monies and support for elders, children, the sick, and people experiencing life transitions are considered to be wasted because these people are not economically productive members of society	• Scarcity mentality and competition for scarce resources • Evolutionism (natural selection—the strong survive and thrive) • Win–lose mentality • Elitism (privilege the wealthy and powerful, who should be rulers) • Division of labor based on gender
Fundamentalism: strong maintenance of and adherence to any set of ancient or fundamental doctrines and beliefs (moral codes), usually in the face of criticism or unpopularity (especially religious beliefs and social and political movements)	• Extremism (far outside the acceptable mainstream attitudes of society), especially religious extremism • Free-market fundamentalism (the market can solve social ills) • In-group and out-group distinctions must be maintained • Rejection of diversity of opinions • Moral intolerance and adherence to strict social conventions
Consumerism: inculcates the values of the western consumer lifestyle on a global scale; society's preoccupation with the accumulation of goods and the procurement of services formally self-performed	• Materialism (using *things* to measure success, with little concern for spiritual or ethical matters) • Material gains and possessions privileged over relationships • Conspicuous consumption that may be unethical and immoral • Popular culture postmodernism (novelty, commodification, entitlement, communication technologies)

Paradigms

Paradigms are habits of thinking in a particular way or of making certain assumptions (others call this a worldview or a mind-set). Paradigms profoundly affect the way people perceive reality as it is lived within society's dominant belief systems (i.e., its ideologies). Paradigms affect how people respond to their perceptions of the world, including those of a research report. Ensconced in their paradigms, people use them to make sense of their world by giving meaning to their lived experiences (see Table 1.1). A common metaphor used to explain this connection is an ideological camp where people live out their lives. When they climb up into an observation tower and view life below in the camps, they are seeing the world through their paradigms. The camps reflect the cultural blueprint by which all people are supposed to live, and the paradigms are the way people think about and make sense of that life (Donovan, 2010; Eaton, 1996; Elgin & LeDrew, 1997; Heuerman & Olson, 1998; McGregor, 2008, 2013; McGregor et al., 2008).

Example 1.1 A study inadvertently reinforcing patriarchy-informed policy Consider a study that explored the impact of social welfare policy on families. The policy said that once a man moves into a single woman's household, she no longer qualifies for welfare assistance because it is assumed that the man will be working and contributing money to the household. Even if he is not working, the policy still holds because a man is there. Under this policy, welfare assistance is automatically cut off. Researchers conducted focus groups and interviews with women receiving this assistance. They reported undue financial hardship because of this policy, which opponents called draconian, meaning excessively harsh. Despite the profound insights gained from these data, the researchers concluded that the policy was sound, in effect reinforcing the patriarchy ideology. It holds that the male is the head of the household and the main breadwinner. If a male is present (any male), it is assumed that women will be taken care of and do not deserve financial assistance using public tax dollars. Government bureaucrats cited the study as justification for maintaining the policy, and actually made it even harder for women to regain assistance once the man left. When opponents to this policy approached the researchers, challenging their assumptions and conclusions, the research team revealed they had simply not seen it from that perspective before (standing from their observation tower) and regretted drawing their conclusions. They had not intended to harm women with their study, but their unexamined ideological lens had the same effect.

In a research context, articles inherently reflect authors' assumptions about the phenomenon under examination and any surrounding contexts. Those assumptions are informed by ideologies and paradigms, which, for most people, go unexamined at the best of times. They are so ordinary in everyday life, even in research life, that they become invisible and go unchallenged. Despite that authors should be transparent about any assumptions underpinning their research, this often does not happen (Neuman, 2000). Critical readers would be aware of this and be prepared to suss out and question those assumptions. Actually, most authors *intend* to do good research and *intend* for readers to access their ideas so their work can be understood and used. Critical readers of research will respect these intentions, appreciating the insidious power of ideologies and paradigms (Locke et al., 2010).

Example 1.2 Dominant paradigm (thought pattern) in research A good example of a dominant thought pattern in research is the assumption that quantitative research is more valuable and legitimate than qualitative research because the former is empirical and positivistic, grounded in measurable numbers and verifiable statistics. Qualitative research is often maligned and called *soft* science, meaning it is *hard* to quantify, *assuming* that all data have to be quantified to be true. People's meanings, wisdom, and interpretations of their own lives are not *measurable*; hence, they do not matter. These assumptions reflect the deeply ingrained paradigms of Newtonianism and positivism. Newtonian thinking holds that objective reality comprises predictable, measurable, linear, cause-and-effect phenomena. Positivism assumes that the only way one can be positive that one has knowledge is if it is produced using the scientific method. Qualitative studies are often undervalued, minimized, and even dismissed as not good research because they cannot be judged as empirically valid and reliable, nor do they yield desirable proof of cause and effect (see Chapter 2).

REVIEW AND ENGAGEMENT

Critical readers will

- ☐ With practice, come to recognize when they are being gullible, naïve, too trusting, innocent, and unsuspecting (see Figure 1.4)

- ☐ Conversely, know how to check for the internal consistency in authors' logic, when to suspend their trust in the report, how to read beyond the surface level, and how to dig deeper to expose ideologies and paradigms

- ☐ Appreciate the persuasive power of ideologies and paradigms in research and learn to *critically recognize* when they are at play, affecting the authors' message (intentionally or not) (see Table 1.1)

- ☐ Examine their own research paradigms and ideological awareness, thereby becoming responsible partners in the *critical research conversation*

CRITICALLY AND UNCRITICALLY READING RESEARCH

In summary, "being a critical consumer of research is more than just reading academic papers; it involves thinking critically about the assumptions behind research, the methodologies [and methods] employed and the implications that research results [or findings] hold for practice" (Zardo & Pryor, 2012, p. 1). Suter (2012) compared the qualities of critical and uncritical readers of research (see pp. 10–11), summarized in Table 1.2.

A critical reader of research will be able to navigate or move with confidence and competence through research material and reports in order to critically evaluate and effectively use the information and new knowledge (Locke et al., 2010). Lacking this critical navigational ability can lead to a compromised knowledge base as well as compromised practice, policy, theory development, and future research (Zardo & Pryor, 2012).

Example 1.3 Uncritiqued research project shaping policy Croad and Farquhar (2005) took issue with an actual New Zealand study about the link between the quality of early childhood education and children's future learning. Touted as a significant study, it has influenced government policies and educational practice in New Zealand. The authors critically analyzed the study and found several issues that severely compromised its real contribution to the topic of competent children. They discovered shortcomings around "the sampling technique and the

TABLE 1.2 ■ Comparison of Critical and Uncritical Readers of Research Reports	
Critical Thinkers and Readers	**Uncritical Thinkers and Readers**
• Search for biases	• Accept information without scrutiny
• Recognize logical fallacies and inconsistencies	• Overlook, cannot recognize, or fall victim to fallacies (flaws in logic)
• Reason with clarity, precision, and relevance	• Fail to recognize disjointed or irrelevant reasoning
• Look to see if authors considered the context when reaching conclusions	• Accept stereotypes and overgeneralizations
• Confirm that conclusions are justified (supported by data) and well reasoned	• Accept conclusions without challenging the authors' reasoning and the evidence
• Assess the validity (strength and truth) of all claims	• Accept claims unchallenged, without questioning their validity
• Unearth and examine authors' assumptions	• Confuse assumptions about what is true (with no proof) with facts
• Discern whether authors accounted for complexity when judging import of study	• Upon reading a paper, come to snap judgments about the study (oversimplify things)
• Determine if authors considered alternative explanations (and come up with their own counter thoughts)	• Tend to confirm personal biases (i.e., favor only evidence that reinforces their own preexisting beliefs)

composition of the sample, the research design, data analysis, and interpretations of the data. Assumptions made in the research about children's competencies, quality in early childhood education and the measurement of quality therefore need to be questioned" (p. 18). They challenged the authors' and the media's uncritical claims about the study and admonished government officials, educators, and practitioners to critically examine and openly discuss it. They claimed that too much is at stake for people to uncritically use a study with so many unchallenged limitations. Both superficial reporting and using a study purported to be a significant policy resource are irresponsible and shortsighted. "Publically funded policy-driven research which is used to legitimate education policy and spending should not be exempted from scrutiny and critique" (p. 17).

On a concluding note, the rest of the book is focused on sharing detailed and nuanced discussions of accepted conventions and standards of conducting and reporting high-quality research. The intent is to help readers become better equipped at, and more predisposed to, being critical readers of research and scholarship. There are chapters on each of the basic elements of the research process (see Figure 1.2 and the Appendix), prefaced with a chapter that thoroughly discusses the main approaches to categorizing research methodologies (Chapter 2), which differ from yet inform research methods. Upon reading *Understanding and Evaluating Research*, readers should feel more comfortable assuming the mantle and deep responsibility of critiquing others' research.

REVIEW AND ENGAGEMENT

Critical readers will

☐ Be able to practice being a *critical thinker and reader* when critiquing research reports (see Table 1.2)

☐ Appreciate the necessity of being able to *critically navigate* a research report, with *critical awareness* and *critical prowess*

CHAPTER SUMMARY

This chapter introduced readers to the intent of the book, which is to help people critically read and evaluate other people's scholarship before they use it in their research or practice. Readers were introduced to the idea of research literacy and why it is important. The discussion then turned to the topic of *critical* research literacy, starting with what is involved in reading critically, followed with why some people may not critically read a research report (see Figures 1.1 and 1.2). The former included a discussion of the need for balanced appraisals, to judge the author's chains of reasoning, and to be skeptical

and engage in critical scrutiny. These strategies help critical readers deal with the author's biases, (unspoken) assumptions, interests, and prejudices (see Figure 1.3). People may fail to critically judge a research report for several reasons, including misplaced trust, being overindulgent and undiscriminating, reading at just the surface level, and failing to account for the power of ideologies and paradigms in research (see Figure 1.4 and Table 1.1). The chapter concluded with an overview of what constitutes critical and uncritical thinking and reading of a research report (see Table 1.2).

REVIEW AND DISCUSSION QUESTIONS

1. There are many reasons why it is important to be research literate. Identify three that are most important to you, and explain why they are so important.

2. How is criticizing a research report different from critiquing it? Are both skills needed? Which of these should be privileged, and why (see Figure 1.1)?

3. Compare and contrast what it means to be a critical reader and an uncritical reader of a research report (see Table 1.2).

4. What are five key things critical readers should look for when reading a research report (see Figure 1.3)?

5. What does someone have to do to be considered an uncritical reader of research reports (see Figure 1.4)?

6. Why is it important to critically understand a research report?

7. How do ideologies and paradigms differ? Explain how they are interconnected. What role do ideologies and paradigms play in research (see Table 1.1)?

PHILOSOPHICAL AND THEORETICAL ASPECTS OF RESEARCH

2 RESEARCH METHODOLOGIES

INTRODUCTION

Research and inquiry are about creating new knowledge (Habermas, 1984). Philosophy is the study of the fundamental nature of knowledge, reality, and existence—its truths, principles, and assumptions (Anderson, 2014). This book is premised on the assumption that everything in research hinges on philosophical underpinnings. But making this point is challenging because of the proliferation of methodology-related terms arising in the late 1970s and peaking in the early 1990s. Egon Guba is credited with initiating the paradigm dialogue about quantitative and qualitative research (Donmoyer, 2008). Since then, researchers have witnessed the emergence of a dizzying array of jargon used by scholars trying to address this thorny but imperative aspect of research. This scenario is exacerbated by the fact that "many researchers lack experience [or expertise] in deliberating about methodological issues, and the esoteric and unfamiliar language of philosophy can be intimidating" (MacCleave, 2006, p. 9).

This array of methodology-related terms includes *research paradigms, methodologies, methods, philosophical axioms, quantitative, qualitative, mixed methods, positivism, postpositivism, empirical, interpretive,* and *critical* (and one can add *postmodernism, poststructuralism, constructivism, naturalistic inquiry, critical realism,* and so on). Inconsistency in what these terms mean, alone and in relation to each other, is evident across all disciplinary literature (Cameron, 2011). Acknowledging this state of affairs, Locke, Silverman, and Spirduso (2010) sardonically noted that "the first tour through the research literature in your own area of interest is likely to reveal more variety than you would expect" (p. 80). They even coined the term *paradigmatic subspecies* (p. 80) to accommodate this diverse philosophical situation.

LEARNING OBJECTIVES

- Appreciate the history of key methodological terms

- Recognize the necessity of being able to defend any methodological choices made at the interface between philosophy and methods (methodologically responsible)

- Distinguish clearly between methodology and methods (as used in this book)

- Become familiar with the conceptual confusion, slippage, and clarity needed around three common terms: *research paradigm, research methodology,* and *research tradition*

- Appreciate the methodological approach used in this book (see Table 2.1)

- Explain the construct of philosophical axioms (epistemology, ontology, logic, and axiology)

- Distinguish between positivistic and postpositivistic research paradigms

(Continued)

Learning Objectives (Continued)

- Compare and contrast empirical, interpretive, and critical research methodologies

- Compare and contrast quantitative, qualitative, and mixed methods methodologies

- Explain why it is necessary to match research methodology with the research question

- Understand the conventions for writing the research methodology section of a paper

The result of such philosophical diversity is terminological soup or, as Buchanan and Bryman (2007, p. 486) called it, "paradigm soup." Actually, some of these terms have been in use for more than 400 years, adding to this linguistic and philosophical conundrum (see Figure 2.1) (Ary, Jacobs, & Sorensen, 2010; Denzin & Lincoln, 2011; Fox, 2008; Guba, 1990; Johnson & Christensen, 2012; Lockyer, 2008; Niglas, 1999; Paley, 2008; Smith, 1983). Nonetheless, researchers have the responsibility of explicitly identifying the methodological and paradigmatic underpinnings of their scholarship (Maxwell, 2013).

To address this conceptual slippage, this chapter explains and justifies the approach used in *this* book (see Table 2.1), knowing that not everyone will agree with it. Regardless, researchers and authors have to "acknowledge the paradigm debate" and rigorously defend any methodological choices "made at the interface between philosophy and methods" (Cameron, 2011, p. 101). This due diligence is necessary because, to academics, these words can mean different things. Without conceptual clarity, the integrity of any academic conversation about the interface between philosophy, methodology, and methods is compromised.

FIGURE 2.1 ■ History of Methodologically Oriented Terms

- *Scientific* and *empirical* (*quantitative*) go as far back as the 1600s (17th century), 400 years ago, with Descartes, Hume, Newton, and Comte; the classical concept of *quantity* can be traced back to Newton.

- *Qualitative-oriented* research (not named as such) emerged around the late 1700s with Kant's *Critique of Pure Reason* (introduction of *interpretive*).

- In the 1800s (19th century), the term *positivistic* was first coined, and *positivism* reigned supreme for more than 200 years.

- The term *postpositivistic* was coined in the mid 1960s (50 years ago). The legitimacy of *positivism* began to be questioned in the 1970s by those engaged in qualitative research (e.g., feminist researchers, those advocating for critical theory, and those engaged in postmodern critiques).

- The term *qualitative research* was coined in the late 1960s by Barney Glaser and Anselm Strauss.

- In 1970, Thomas Kuhn introduced and conceptualized the terms *research paradigm* and *paradigm shifts*.

- During the past 50 years, the discussion of *quantitative* and *qualitative* has been taken to a new level. Instead of focusing on how they are different due to methods, methodologists shifted gears to focus on their philosophical underpinnings.

- In the 1980s, it was agreed that first comes *philosophy*, then *methodology* (*axioms*), then *theory*, then *method(s)*.

- Also in the early 1980s, the discussion of *mixed methods* (mixing methodological assumptions) emerged, and continues strongly, with growing acceptance.

TABLE 2.1 ■ Overview of Main Research Methodologies, With Common Methods (used with permission) [Acknowledgment: Deep, deep thanks to Dr. Anne MacCleave, Professor Emerita (MSVU), for vetting and validating the core concepts contained in this table]

Research Paradigm	Positivistic	Postpositivistic	Critical (Power)
Research Methodology	Quantitative and Empirically Based Qualitative	Qualitative	
	Empirical (Scientific)	Interpretive (Humanistic)	Critical (Power)
Intent of Inquiry	Explore, describe, predict, control, and explain	Understand	Emancipate
AXIOMS Epistemology [What counts as knowledge and ways of knowing [criteria for evaluating knowledge]? How should we study the world? What is meaningful evidence or insights? How does knowledge arise?	– The *one* truth is out there waiting to be discovered via the scientific method – Strive for certainties, laws of behaviors, and principles that provide explanations leading to predictions and control of phenomena – Knowledge is objective (bias-free) – Knowledge is dualistic (fragmented and not connected); mind and matter are separate – Only knowledge generated using the scientific method is valid – Only things that can be seen (observed or experimented) are worthy of study – Knowledge comes from using the scientific method (experiments or nonexperimental methods)	– Truth is created, and there is more than one truth; knowledge relies on humans' interpretations of *their* world – Strive for confidence – Knowledge is constructed by people – Agreed-upon knowledge in one culture may not be valid in another culture – Takes into account social and cultural influences on knowledge creation – Knowledge is subjective or intersubjective and includes perspectives – Research is often perspective-seeking, not truth-seeking – There are many ways of knowing aside from the scientific method (e.g., stories, spiritual experiences, religion, the sacred, the mystical, wisdom, art, drama, dreams, music) – Knowledge can be cognitive, feelings, or embodied	– Truth is grounded in the context – Knowledge is grounded in social and historical practices – Knowledge is emancipatory, created through critically questioning the way things "have always been done" – Knowledge is about hidden power structures that permeate society – Knowledge is dialectic (transformative), consensual, and normative – Knowledge is about the world, the way things *really* are, and is subject to change

(Continued)

TABLE 2.1 ■ (Continued)

Research Paradigm	Positivistic	Postpositivistic	
Ontology (What should *be* the object of the study? What is human nature? What does it mean to *be* human? What counts as a meaningful statement about reality? How do people make choices? What is the nature of reality? How can reality be meaningfully portrayed?)	– Reality is *out there*; the world is a universe of facts waiting to be discovered	– Reality is *in here* (in people's minds and/or collectively constructed)	– Reality is *here and now* (it is material, actually of the world, not imagined)
	– There is a single reality made of discrete elements: When we find them all through the scientific method, we have a full picture of reality	– Social reality is relative to the observer, and everyday concepts need to be understood to appreciate this reality	– Reality is shaped by ethnic, cultural, gender, social, and political values, and mediated by power relations
	– A single reality exists that people cannot see	– The focus is on the life-world and shared meanings and understandings of that world	– Reality is constructed within this social-historical context
	– A fact is a fact; it cannot be interpreted	– Reality is socially constructed via the lived experiences of people	– Humans are *not* confined to one particular state or set of conditions; things can change
	– The true nature of reality can only be obtained by testing theories	– Human nature is determined by how people see themselves	– Human beings have the capacity to exercise control over social arrangements and institutions: They can create a new reality
	– Seeing is believing	– Humans are active and self-creating	
	– Laws of nature can be derived from scientific data	– Human beings can act intentionally (need capacity and opportunity)	– Humans who are oppressed are able to emancipate themselves and challenge the status quo
	– Human nature is determined by things people are not aware of and have no control over	– Reality can be a product of people's minds or the interactions of persons	
	– Humans are passive, malleable, and controllable	– Reality constitutes that which is constructed by individuals in interaction within their contexts and with other people	– Reality is never fully understood and is deeply shaped by power
	– Reality is determined by the environment, inherited potential, or the interaction of the two	– Reality is conditiona upon human experiences	– Seek to truly understand the real circumstances (i.e., the political, social, and institutional structures) in order to change the power balance
	– Reality is external to our consciousness (not a product of our minds)		

Research Paradigm	Positivistic	Postpositivistic	
Logic [How do people come to their understandings? What is acceptable as rigor and inference in the development of arguments, judgments, insights, revelations, or social action?]	– Deductive, rational, formal logic – Through objective observation, experts form research questions and hypotheses and empirically test them – Concerned with prediction, control, and explanation – Clear distinction between facts and values – Strive to generalize universal laws – The goal of research is replication and theory testing, leading to control, predictions, and explanations	– Inductive logic, attempting to find various interpretations of reality and recognize patterns that govern and guide human behavior – Assumes researchers can help people become aware of their unconscious thoughts – Concerned with meanings and understandings so people can live together; how people make sense of their world – Meaningful findings are more valuable than generalizations – The goal is to understand lived experiences from the point of view of those living them – The goal of research is a credible representation of the interpretations of those experiencing the phenomenon under study	– Inductive logic, aimed at emancipation – Attempt to reveal ideologies and power relationships, leading to self-empowerment and emancipation – Concerned with the relationship between meanings *and* autonomy and with responsibility as citizens – Concerned with critiquing and changing society – The intent is to create contextualized findings – The goal of research is to reveal power relationships leading to changes in the status quo and more autonomy, inclusion, and justice – Determine sources of oppression (whether internal or external) – Focus on complex generative mechanisms that are not readily observable (e.g., it is hard to *observe* consciousness raising)

(Continued)

TABLE 2.1 ■ (Continued)

Research Paradigm	Positivistic	Postpositivistic	
Axiology (What is the role of values and perceptions? The role of researchers and participants? How is what is studied influenced by the researcher and the participants? What is the relationship between the researcher and the participants?)	– Values-neutral (often ignored) – Moral issues are beyond empirical investigation – No place for bias, values, feelings, perceptions, hopes, or expectations of either researcher or participant – Researcher tries to control for anything that can contaminate the study – The relationship between researcher and participant is objective and dualistic (separate with no interchange)	– Values-laden – The intent is to uncover the beliefs, customs, and so forth that shape human behavior – Bias, feelings, hopes, expectations, perceptions, and values are central to the research process – Participants play a central role in the research, even instigating it – The perspective of the "insiders" supercedes that of the researcher – The role of the researcher is to uncover conscious and unconscious explanations people have for their life through dialogue with and among participants – The relationship between the researcher and participants is intense, prolonged, and dialogic (deep insights through interaction)	– Values-oriented and values-driven – Researchers' *proactive* values concerning social justice are central to the research – The intent is to critically examine unquestioned values, beliefs, and norms to reveal power – The researcher works in collaboration with citizen interlocutors as conversational partners in dialogue – The researcher seeks to understand the effects of power so as to help people empower themselves – The very participatory research process is grounded in terms of the insiders' perspective, respecting that researchers have contributing expertise (balance both) – The role of the researcher is to challenge insiders with expert research findings leading to self-reflection and emancipation – The intent is to create change in society by emancipating citizens to take action – The relationship between researcher and participants is dialogic, transactional, and dialectic (transformative)

Research Paradigm	Positivistic	Postpositivistic
Methods Common to Each Methodology (Appreciating the **mixed methods methodology**, which employs quantitative and qualitative approaches in the same study)	*Seeking causality, laws, and relations via:* **Quantitative:** Experiments Quasi-experiments Field experiments Surveys *Seeking relations and regularities via:* **Qualitative:** Quasi-experiments Field experiments Surveys Ethnoscience (new ethnography) Ethnography Phenomenology Case studies Content analysis	*Seeking theory, meanings, and patterns via:* Phenomenology Case studies Content analysis Grounded theory Natural/interpretive inquiry Discourse analysis Thematic analysis Document analysis *Seeking meanings and interpretations via:* Case studies Discourse analysis Ethical inquiry Life history study Narrative research Hermeneutic inquiry Heuristic inquiry *Seeking reflection, emancipation, and problem solving via:* Action research Discourse analysis Participatory research Critical analysis Feminist inquiry Reflective phenomenology

Sources: From McGregor & Murnane (2010) with permission from John Wiley & Sons. Sources used by the authors to develop the appendix included: Howe, 1992; Lather, 1994; Niglas, 2001; MacDonald et al., 2002; Khazanchi and Munkvold, 2003; Guba and Lincoln, 2005; Ponterotto, 2005; Salmani and Akbari, 2008). Acknowledgment and deep thanks to Dr. Anne MacCleave, Professor Emerita Mount Saint Vincent University (MSVU), for vetting and validating the core concepts contained in this table.

CONCEPTUAL CONFUSION, SLIPPAGE, AND CLARITY

This section attempts the near impossible, to distinguish between the terms *research paradigm*, *research methodology* (compared to *methods*), and *research traditions*. All three terms are used in the academic world, leading to confusion because *paradigm* means thought patterns, *methodology* is linked with philosophy, and *tradition* refers to long-standing customs (see Figure 2.2). In truth, they all have some merit when trying to distinguish between (a) collecting new information (data) to answer a research question and (b) knowledge creation using interpretations of those data. On the other hand, the diverse language used to refer to this aspect of research has created a quagmire. This complex and difficult situation makes it hard for one scholar to talk to and understand another. But talk to each other they must, so this section briefly explains how the literature understands these concepts, settling on *research paradigm* and *research methodology* for this book (they mean different things).

Research Paradigm

Paradigm is Latin *paradigma*, "patterns" (Harper, 2016). A paradigm is "a generally accepted explanation of things," with the dominant paradigm providing "the focal point and measuring stick" for inquiry (Rohmann, 1999, p. 296). Paradigms are thought patterns that help people make sense of their world, *regardless* of whether they are engaged in research or not. Paradigms are habits of thinking in a particular way or of making certain assumptions about the world (others call this *worldview* or *mind-set*) (Donovan, 2010) (see Chapter 1 for a discussion of paradigms and ideologies).

The term *research paradigm*, coined by Kuhn (1962), is understood to mean "patterns of beliefs and practices that regulate inquiry within a discipline, doing so by providing the lenses, frames and processes through which investigation is accomplished" (Weaver & Olson, 2006, p. 460). Johnson and Christensen (2012) defined a research paradigm as a "perspective about research held by a community of researchers that is based on a set of shared assumptions, concepts, values, and practices" (p. 31).

These definitions make sense. After all, disciplines are groups or communities of people, and paradigms reflect a *group's* commitment to a constellation of beliefs about viewing

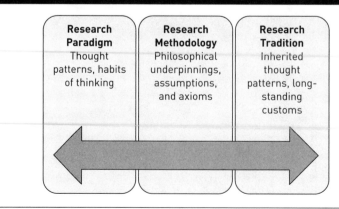

FIGURE 2.2 ■ Research Paradigm, Methodology, and Tradition

the world. They are a group-licensed way of seeing reality (Botha, 1989). Normally, the philosophical notion of axioms is reserved for the term *research methodology*, as is the case in this book. Some scholars, however, characterize research *paradigms* by distinctive axioms, namely *ontology, axiology, epistemology, rhetoric, causality* and *logic*, and *methodology* (by which is meant the identification, study, and justification of research methods) (Guba, 1990; Pruyt, 2006).

Research Methodology

In many disciplines, the term *methodology* is used to refer to the methods used to collect, analyze, and report data (see Schneider, 2014; Trochim & Donnelly, 2007). This usage eschews the real meaning of *methodology*. *Ology* is Greek for a branch of knowledge or science. Method is Greek *methodos*, "the pursuit of knowledge" (Anderson, 2014; Harper, 2016). Taken together, *methodology* means a branch of science that studies the pursuit of knowledge. "The misuse of *methodology* obscures an important conceptual distinction between the tools of scientific investigation (properly *methods*) and the principles that determine how such tools are deployed and interpreted (*methodology*)" (*American Heritage Dictionary*, 2000).

This chapter views methodology as the philosophical underpinnings of research intended to generate new knowledge and methods as tools and techniques to collect and analyze data (Lather, 1994; MacCleave, 2006) (see Figure 2.3). To that end, this chapter focuses on methodologies, and Chapter 8 focuses on methods (and research design). In particular, *methodology* refers to knowledge creation, including what counts as knowledge and knowing, reality, logic, and the role of values in knowledge creation (i.e., four axioms, to be discussed shortly). Two common approaches to describing research methodologies are (a) quantitative, qualitative, and mixed methods and (b) empirical, interpretive, and critical. These are discussed in more detail further on in the chapter. This book uses the former as its organizational framework.

Research Traditions

Actually, some academics skirt the contentious issue of whether to use the term *research paradigm* or *research methodology* and instead use the term *research traditions* (Jacob, 1987; Schneider, 2014). A tradition is an inherited pattern of thought and a specific practice of long standing (Anderson, 2014). Kuhn (1970) said any research tradition differs along three dimensions: (a) its assumptions about nature and reality, (b) the foci of studies and major issues of interest about the phenomenon, and (c) methodology (by which he meant methods). He also noted that a tradition can occur either as an entire discipline or as a school within a discipline (e.g., subdisciplines and disciplinary specializations). For example, Jacob (1987) applied this approach to profile three subdisciplines within the discipline of education.

The term *tradition* is the least commonly used in the literature, but it was important to acknowledge it in this chapter because authors may choose to use it when reporting their study, or they might encounter it when reading literature. Patton (2002) identified 10 qualitative research *traditions* including constructivism, symbolic interaction, semiotics, hermeneutics, systems, and chaos (nonlinear dynamics). This book views these as falling within qualitative and interpretive research methodologies (see Table 2.1).

FIGURE 2.3 ■ Methodology Compared to Method

Methodology	Method
• Philosophical basis for research (truth-seeking or perspective-seeking); determines methods	• Procedures or instruments used to collect and analyze data and report results or findings, determined by methodology
• Deals with axioms pursant to generating *new knowledge* (i.e., reality, knowing, logic, values)	• Deals with the technical steps taken to generate or produce *new data and information*
• Rational or philosophical assumptions that underlie approaches to research; analysis of principles, rules, postulates (assumptions), and axioms employed by a discipline to frame research	• Documented process for managing research project that contains procedures, definitions, and explanations of the techniques used to collect, store, and analyze data and write research report
• Leads to *new knowledge* that is eventually added to a discipline's cumulative body of knowledge	• Leads to *new data* and then new knowledge when interpreted using methodological assumptions
• Section in research paper should be called *Methodology*	• Section in research paper should be called *Methods*

Confusion Ensues

Despite this attempt to clarify how these three constructs differ, confusion ensues. Dash (2005) said there are two main research paradigms, positivism and postpositivism (to be discussed shortly). Others claim that quantitative and qualitative are the main research paradigms, with some calling them methodologies or worldviews (Creswell, 2009; Shank & Brown, 2007). Still others claim that quantitative and positivism are the same thing and that qualitative and postpositivism are the same thing (Lin, 1998; Williams, 1998). Some scholars believe it is possible to have "positivistic qualitative" research (Paley, 2008).

Some scholars use the terms *quantitative* and *qualitative* to refer to methodologies, while others use them to refer to methods (Creswell, 2009; Shah & Corley, 2006). Some assume that there is a diversity of research traditions *within* qualitative research. Others, like this book (see Table 2.1), present qualitative as a unified approach that spans several research traditions (e.g., narrative, phenomenology) (Jacob, 1987). Shank and Brown (2007) called the quantitative and qualitative approaches worldviews (while most scholars associate the term *worldview* with paradigms). There is simply *no agreement* in the literature about this fundamental aspect of academic scholarship (Cameron, 2011).

Theory and method choices

This issue becomes even more convoluted when trying to figure out how methodology is related to both theory and method choices. Schneider (2014) acknowledged that it is very easy for authors to get it wrong when it comes to finding balance and to discerning the conceptual distinctions among methodology (philosophical), theory, and method. Creswell (1994) said the choice of theory determines whether the research is qualitative or quantitative. This book assumes the opposite, that the qualitative or quantitative nature of the research determines the relevant theory. Creswell further said that theory is independent of, or separate from, the researchers' worldview. This may be true, but theory is not necessarily independent of the methodology; that is, the assumptions of a theory should reflect the basic assumptions of reality as understood by the different research methodologies.

Example 2.1 Methodology and theory choice A qualitative researcher, interested in the emancipation of oppressed peoples, is more likely to use critical theory than economic theory. The former *assumes* people are oppressed by dominant, hegemonic ideologies and need their consciences raised so they can free themselves and change the system. Economic theory, premised on scarcity, competition, a win–lose mentality, and wealth accumulation, is better suited to explain how the hegemony arose in the first place, rather than how to climb out from under it.

REVIEW AND ENGAGEMENT

When critically reading a research report, you would

- ☐ Determine if the authors actually included a separate section or subheading called *Methodology* (with another section or subsection called *Methods*)
- ☐ Determine if they appreciated the distinction between method (sampling, data collection, and data analysis) and methodology, likely referring to qualitative, quantitative, or mixed methods (see Figures 2.2 and 2.3)
- ☐ If they did not clearly articulate the research methodology underpinning their study, determine if they provided enough information for you to deduce it
- ☐ Determine if the authors referred to research paradigms or research traditions (see Figure 2.2), and judge if this was clear or caused confusion
- ☐ Ascertain if they explained how their theory choice was affected by their research methodology
- ☐ Check to see if they explained how their methods were affected by their research methodology

METHODOLOGICAL APPROACH USED IN THIS BOOK

Respecting the long-standing conundrum of how all of these terms are separate or related, an approach *had* to be developed as the anchor for this book. That approach is set out in Table 2.1 (adapted from McGregor and Murnane, 2010, used with permission). Several sources were used to compile Table 2.1 (Guba & Lincoln, 2005; Howe, 1992; Khazanchi & Munkvold, 2003; Lather, 1994; MacDonald et al., 2002; Niglas, 2001; Ponterotto, 2005;

Salmani & Akbari, 2008). In a nutshell, the rest of the book is organized using qualitative, quantitative, and mixed methods methodologies, assuming that qualitative is postpositivistic (and includes interpretive and critical) and that quantitative is positivistic (and includes empirical).

This book further assumes that positivism and postpositivism research *paradigms* are a different construct than quantitative, qualitative, and mixed methods research *methodologies* or empirical, interpretive, and critical *methodologies* (which differ on axioms). Overall, unlike paradigms, methodologies differ according to assumptions, basic tenets, and axioms (Kuhn, 1970; Weaver & Olson, 2006). The axioms were used to compare and contrast each methodology in Table 2.1 (see the left column), and the assumptions are used in Chapter 8 to contrast quantitative methods, qualitative methods, and mixed methods (see Table 8.2). Table 2.1 also includes *positivistic qualitative* research, when numbers are used, such as with a content analysis (Paley, 2008).

As a further caveat, some researchers view other "methodological" approaches as research *traditions*, including poststructuralism, postmodernism, constructivism (naturalistic), hermeneutics, and critical realism or critical theory (Lincoln & Guba, 1985; Neuman, 2000; Niglas, 2001; Paley, 2008). For the purposes of this book, these are construed as aspects of "qualitative postpositivism," especially interpretivism, which assumes there are many truths and many realities. Finally, in no way does Table 2.1 "imply a certain rigidity" (Paley, 2008, p. 649) in the idea of a paradigm or a methodology, giving a nod to the lack of disciplinary agreement on this idea. And, although the result of preparing and using Table 2.1 was an "oversimplification of the philosophical issues" (Paley, 2008, p. 649), it seemed justified in that this colossal topic could not be covered in sufficient detail in one chapter.

Methodological Responsibility in an Ideal World

Before explaining the components of Table 2.1, consider that, in an ideal world, researchers would live an examined life wherein they are aware of the paradigms shaping their life. They would also be aware of the different research methodologies and how they affect the entire research enterprise. With this paradigmatic and methodological awareness, researchers would consciously choose a research question while fully cognizant of which methodology is most appropriate to generate the information required to address it, leading to new knowledge. They would be able to reconcile any disconnect between *personal* worldviews and their assumptions about *research* (see Neuman, 2000; Schneider, 2014). For example, they might personally eschew the scientific worldview, favoring a life-oriented paradigm; yet, they would choose to conduct an empirical experiment because it was the best approach to answer their research question.

In particular, with methodological awareness, they would be able to consciously shift their point of view and see the world from a variety of paradigmatic stances (Donmoyer, 2008), choosing the approach that best answers their research question (Ary et al., 2010). On the whole, however, personal paradigms and research methodologies are usually unexamined, subliminal aspects of scholarship (Neuman, 2000; Tashakkori & Teddlie, 1998). For that reason, this book is focused on the deep importance of understanding how the philosophical underpinnings of research profoundly shape the choice of research question, research design, theory, methods, reporting of results or findings, and discussion and conclusions.

Each of the key building blocks of Table 2.1 is now addressed, starting with (a) the philosophical *axioms* (the left column) and moving to (b) research *paradigms* (positivism and postpositivism), followed with (c) each of two approaches to methodologies: (i) empirical, interpretive, and critical *methodologies* and (ii) qualitative, quantitative, and mixed methods *methodologies*. As a caveat, recognizing the confusion caused by the interchangeability of all of these terms, the rest of the book consistently uses these terms as clarified in the following text.

REVIEW AND ENGAGEMENT

When critically reading a research report, you would

☐ Confirm if the authors convinced you that they are reflexive about their research and are philosophically aware—hence, methodologically responsible

☐ Ascertain if the methodology they chose for their study best reflects their research questions

PHILOSOPHICAL AXIOMS

All research entails knowledge creation, generation, or production (depending on the methodology), meaning authors need to address issues of methodology (the study of knowledge creation) and relevant philosophical underpinnings (Dudovskiy, 2016). Methodology is a branch of philosophy that analyzes the principles and procedures of inquiry in disciplinary studies (Anderson, 2014). Philosophy has several fields of inquiry (Rohmann, 1999), with four branches of philosophy pertaining to the notion of *research methodology* (see Figure 2.4): (a) Metaphysics (ontology) studies the nature of reality and of being and becoming, (b) epistemology is concerned with the nature and the scope of knowledge, (c) logic involves the study of valid argument forms and truth claims, and (d) axiology studies values, especially the role of the researchers' values in research (Ryan & Cooper, 2007). These philosophical foundations are the crux of all research, whether or not authors acknowledge them in their paper (Neuman, 2000).

Paley (2008) defined the various approaches to research as an "encapsulated and rather rigid set of ontological, epistemological . . . beliefs" (p. 650). He was referring to the axioms of research methodologies. *Axiom*, a philosophical concept, is Latin *axioma*, "that which commends itself as evident" (Harper, 2016). In philosophy, an axiom is an authoritative statement about reality, knowledge, logic, or values. An axiom is regarded as established, accepted, or self-evidently true (Cicovacki, 2009; *Oxford American College Dictionary*, 2002). These four axioms were used to help profile the paradigmatic and methodological approaches used in this book (see Table 2.1).

As a caveat, most academics link the notion of philosophical *axioms* to the empirical–interpretive–critical model of research methodologies (Kim, 2003), rather than the qualitative–quantitative–mixed methods model, which is differentiated by *assumptions* (see Chapter 8, Table 8.2). These two ideas are quite different. An axiom is a self-evident truth that *requires no proof* (never needs to be questioned). An assumption is a supposition that

FIGURE 2.4 ■ Four Methodological Axioms

Ontology	**Epistemology**
Reality Greek *ontos* "to be"	Knowledge Greek *episteme* "knowledge" and *logos* "study of"
• What counts as nature, existence, feelings, reality, being, and becoming? • What is the ultimate nature of things?	• What counts as knowledge (is worthy of knowing)? • How do people know what they know? How did they come to know it?
Axiology	**Logic**
Greek *axi* "value, worth"	Greek *logike* "reasoning"
• What counts as fundamental values? What is their role in research? • What are consciousness (moral choices), ethics, and normative judgments?	• What habits of mind are acceptable for reasoning, inference, and arguing one's position? • What logic is acceptable for forming thoughts, conclusions, opinions, judgments, relevations, or insights?

is taken for granted *without questioning* or proof, when it probably should have been questioned (Anglika, 2008).

> ***Example 2.2 Axiomatic statement*** A researcher could say, "I hold as *axiomatic* that reality is out there waiting to be discovered. With enough value-neutral and objective studies using the scientific method, the truth about reality can be found using deductive logic." Such an authoritative statement reflects the positivistic, empirical research methodology. Despite that others (i.e., those who assume other things about knowledge creation) may not agree with this statement, this researcher assumes this authoritative statement cannot be challenged because it is *true*.

By acknowledging the axiomatic underpinnings of their research, authors tell readers that they are reflexive and philosophically aware. They are able to link the abstract ideas of philosophy to the concrete practices of research. By not questioning assumptions, researchers may not be able to justify or defend their research design to more discerning parties (Neuman, 2000).

REVIEW AND ENGAGEMENT

When critically reading a research report, you would

☐ Determine if the authors referred to one or more philosophical axioms (see Figure 2.4 and Table 2.3), ideally in concert with mention of empirical, interpretive, and/or critical methodologies

☐ Judge if the scope and depth of their discussion of philosophical axioms affected your critical assessment of the quality of their paper

POSITIVISM AND POSTPOSITIVISM

As noted, this book uses positivism and postpositivism as the two overarching research *paradigms* under which research *methodologies* can be categorized (Alaranta, 2006; Creswell, 1994; Gephart, 1999; Kim, 2003). Table 2.2 profiles their main assumptive differences (Lin, 1998; Ritchie & Lewis, 2003). Not everyone agrees with this stance of using these two labels for overarching paradigmatic constructs. For instance, Ponterotto (2005) proposed three key research paradigms, positioning (a) postpositivism as a *strand of positivism* but identifying (b) constructivism/interpretivism and (c) critical/ideological as the other two dominant paradigms (rather than methodologies). In a strange twist, Creswell (2009) used the term *postpositivism* to refer to what others call positivism (i.e., reductionism, determinism, empirical observation, and theory verification).

Historically, in the early 1800s, social scholars assumed they could study human behavior by copying or adapting the assumptions and methods used to study natural phenomena (i.e., positivism). Eventually, social scientists began to question the correctness of this assumption. They had discovered that positivistic assumptions do not hold when examining human behavior because humans are "qualitatively different" from nature. Humans can think, learn, and reflect, and they possess motives and reasons for their actions. Not so for stars, chemical compounds, objects, or other species. Eventually, qualitative research emerged because enough people accepted that "adjustments to the natural science approach" were not enough. Instead, "an entirely separate, special kind of science" was needed, which became known as postpositivistic (and qualitative) (Neuman, 2000, p. 96).

Positivistic Research Paradigm

The term *positivism* was coined 200 years ago by Auguste Comte (early to middle 1800s). Positivism is a strand of philosophy that recognizes only that which can be scientifically verified or logically proved (Anderson, 2014). The term stems from Comte's assertion that academic disciplines and the human mind progress through three stages: (a) theological preoccupations, (b) metaphysical speculations, and (c) their full and perfect development marked by the *positive* state. The latter stage confines itself to the study of experimental facts and their relations, representing perfect human knowledge. He felt that in the positive stage, people would "work for the progress of humanity by studying it (science and education), loving it (religion), beautifying it (fine arts), and enriching it (industry)" (Sauvage, 1913, p. 2). This would all be achieved by reducing human knowledge to "sense experiences [experiments] and empirical associations" (p. 2) (i.e., positivism).

TABLE 2.2 ■ Comparison of Assumptions of the Positivistic and Postpositivistic Research Paradigms

Positivistic Paradigm Assumptions	Postpositivistic Paradigm Assumptions
• The only way people can be *positive* that the knowledge is true is if it was discovered using the scientific method	• Denies positivism, assuming there are many ways of knowing aside from using the scientific method
• Empirical data derived from experiments and observations are interpreted using deductive reasoning	• Rather than testing hypotheses, the intent is to generate hypotheses through inductive reasoning
• Human knowledge is based on unchallengeable, rock-solid foundations	• Human knowledge is based on human conjecture (opinion based on incomplete evidence)
• The only authentic knowledge is that based on senses, experiences, and positive verification	• Authentic knowledge arises from the search for meaning, understandings, and power relations
• The intent is to discover general laws applicable to everyone (generalizability)	• The intent is to help people in specific cultural and social contexts better understand and/or change their world
• Individual *theories* must shift in the face of new evidence	• *Worldviews* must shift in the face of new insights
• Seeks to identify details with hypotheses that can be tested or identified in other cases	• Seeks to combine details into belief systems whose manifestations are specific to a case
• Does so by identifying general abstract patterns	• Does so by showing how the general patterns look in real life (in practice)
• Identifies the existence of causal relationships	• Produces detailed explanations of causal mechanisms
• Cannot explain how the causal mechanism works, only that there is one	• Explains how the causal mechanism works (how particular variables interact)

In the 1920s and 1930s, *logical positivism* emerged as a philosophical movement (also known as *logical empiricism*). It is associated with the Vienna Circle, comprising a group of mathematicians, scientists, and philosophers who banded together after the First World War. Intent on reducing human knowledge to logical and scientific foundations, they posited there are only two sources of knowledge, (a) logical reasoning and logical analysis and (b) empirical experience (experiments and observations). Logical knowledge includes mathematics, and empirical knowledge includes the natural sciences (e.g., physics, biology, and psychology). The main tenets of logical positivism are (a) the verifiability principle, (b) the logical structure of scientific theories (formal, deductive logic), and (c) probability (Folse, 2000; Paley, 2008). Eventually, Karl Popper eschewed the quest for verification, advocating instead the falsifiability of scientific hypotheses rather than their confirmation (Kemerling, 2011). If something is falsifiable, it can be proven false.

Although it began in Europe, logical positivism especially flourished in the United States, in the climate of the philosophy of *American pragmatism*. This strand of philosophy evaluates theories or beliefs in terms of the success of their practical application (Anderson, 2014; Folse, 2000; Paley, 2008). This philosophy holds that most philosophical topics are best viewed in terms of their practical uses and successes (e.g., the nature of knowledge, meaning, belief, and science) (Gutek, 2014). And, although the movement eventually broke down, five very strong ideas persist to this day: "first, that there are logical relations between theory and observation and second, that explanations consist of law-like generalizations from which the occurrence of specific events can be deduced" (Paley, 2008, p. 647). An enthusiasm for statistics is a third hangover of positivism (Paley, 2008). Fourth is the tendency for objective, value- and bias-free research and jargon (vocabulary), and fifth is the idea that humans are objects to be observed by detached scientists (Smith, 1983).

In contemporary times, the positivistic research paradigm assumes that the only way people can be *positive* that the knowledge is true is if it was created using the scientific method (see Chapter 9), which consists of generating hypotheses as explanations of phenomena and then designing experiments to test these hypotheses. This encompasses the empirical methodology, meaning numerical data are derived from experiments and observations (Rohmann, 1999). Science strives to discover universal laws for society (akin to universal laws for nature). And philosophical problems and paradoxes are assumed to be resolved using logical analysis, leading to more clear scientific theories.

As previously noted, positivism is best known for the principle of verifiability and its resultant penchant for quantifiability, especially using numbers and statistics (Paley, 2008). Not surprisingly, then, a wide range of statistical measures has been developed as a means of measuring reliability and validity, the two criteria taken as evidence of intellectual rigor (logically valid) in the positivistic paradigm (see Chapter 10). If all of the rules of the scientific method are followed, people should feel comfortable with their judgments, their conclusions, and any actions based on their interpretation of the results (Nahrin, 2015).

In this whole process, it is imperative that the entire exercise is objective (value free) so as to reduce researchers' biased interpretations of the results. Also, value neutral means the researchers' choice of what to study should be influenced not by their values, beliefs, or interests but by objective criteria. For example, they can study about values, but their values cannot influence the study. Also, science is viewed as isolated from human beings, who are seen as objects to be studied and controlled. Most empirical research is contrived, happening in a laboratory or a controlled setting. And reductionism is an important tenet of positivism, involving understanding problems by reducing them to their simplest elements, thereby negating any appreciation for life's complexities (Nahrin, 2015; Salmani & Akbari, 2008). By the 1970s, scholars were beginning to debate the merit and legitimacy of using positivism in social research (Neuman, 2000; Ritchie & Lewis, 2003), leading to a research paradigm that is now called postpositivism.

Postpositivistic Research Paradigm

Post is Latin, "afterwards" (Harper, 2016). Some scholars disagree with the term *postpositivism* because they think it incorrectly implies positivism is over. They advocate instead the term *nonpositivism* (Dash, 2005; Hunt, 1991). That being said, this chapter uses the well-accepted label of postpositivism as the overarching term for a research paradigm that denies positivism (Neuman, 2000; Niglas, 2001; Zammito, 2004), with justification.

In the late 1800s and early 1900s, Max Weber developed the concept of *Verstehen* (understanding); thus began the early stages of the postpositivistic movement. Weber believed that social realities need to be understood from the perspective of the person living them (the subject) rather than the person observing them (the object) (Fox, 2008; Smith, 1983). The actual term *postpositivistic research paradigm* was coined in the mid 1960s and assumes there are many ways of knowing *aside* from using the scientific method. There is a place for the voice and role of the researcher and of the study participants. Humans are seen as central to the research process, rather than isolated from it. This notion emerged when Karl Popper and Thomas Kuhn popularized the idea of thinking about science in ways *other than* positivism (Zammito, 2004).

The postpositivistic research paradigm generates hypotheses (for future studies) through inductive reasoning, striving to (a) understand why something or someone operates in the manner that it does (interpretation) or (b) reveal power relationships and structures (critical). It assumes that research is value laden, subjective (within a person's mind), and intersubjective (shared by more than one conscious mind), even value driven within the critical stance. Postpositivistic research usually happens in natural settings (i.e., communities and daily lives). The intent of the research varies, but it can include (a) seeking patterns and commonalities; (b) discovering underlying meanings and structures; (c) revealing beliefs, kinships, and ways of living; (d) placing experiences into words and narratives; and (e) uncovering ideologies and power relationships (Lather, 1994; Thorne, 2000).

Postpositivistic researchers strive for trustworthiness criteria by endeavoring to achieve rigor through credibility, transferability, dependability, and confirmability. Authenticity criteria (i.e., fairness, ontological, educative, catalytic, and tactical) become paramount when participants are involved in the research design (Guba & Lincoln, 2005; Koch, 1996; Shah & Corley, 2006) (see Chapter 8, Table 8.5).

REVIEW AND ENGAGEMENT

When critically reading a research report, you would

☐ Check to see if the authors knowledgeably used the term *positivistic* or *postpositivistic* (see Tables 2.1 and 2.2)

☐ Determine, if they did use these terms, if they used them correctly (given their historical and current meanings)

EMPIRICAL, INTERPRETIVE, AND CRITICAL METHODOLOGIES

In addition to qualitative, quantitative, and mixed methods methodologies (to be discussed shortly), this book embraced another approach to methodologies: (a) empirical (positivistic, scientific), (b) interpretive, and (c) critical, the latter two falling under the postpositivistic paradigm umbrella (Kim, 2003, Neuman, 2000; Weaver & Olson, 2006). Each of these three approaches to knowledge creation differs along the four axioms outlined earlier (see Figure 2.4 and Table 2.3). Much more detail is provided in Table 2.1. In essence, the interpretive and critical methodologies provide "nonpositivistic alternatives" to the long-standing positivistic (empirical) approach to knowledge creation (Neuman, 2000, p. 96).

TABLE 2.3 ■ Philosophical Assumptions (Axioms) of Empirical, Interpretive, and Critical Research Methodologies			
	Empirical Methodology	**Interpretive Methodology**	**Critical Methodology**
Ontology (reality)	Assumes reality is *out there* in the universe waiting to be discovered. Do enough studies and collect enough data, and eventually a full picture of reality will emerge	Assumes reality is *in here* (in people's minds, and collectively construed via lived experiences of a phenomenon); there are multiple realities	Assumes reality is material, here and now, shaped by ethnic, cultural, gender, social, and political values. It is mediated by power relations. Reality is constructed within this historical-social context
Epistemology (knowledge and knowing)	The one truth is out there waiting to be discovered, and knowledge is created using the scientific method	There is more than one truth because there are multiple realties; knowledge is constructed or created by people. Truth is based on people's interpretations and meanings of their world	Knowledge and truths are grounded in context; knowledge is dialectic; truth is liberating and in flux
Logic (arguments and claims)	Deductive logic (rational, formal, objective)	Inductive logic (patterns, meanings, multiple interpretations)	Inductive logic in hopes of revealing power and influence, leading to personal autonomy and empowerment
Axiology (values)	Values neutral; there is no place for the *researcher's* feelings, opinions, values, perceptions, or expectations	Values laden; bias, hopes, feelings, expectations, and perceptions of participants and researcher play a central role	Values driven and values oriented; the researcher's proactive values concerning social justice are key to the research

Habermas's Theory of Communication

Habermas (1984), a contemporary German philosopher, also addressed knowledge creation from these three approaches. His theory of communication posited three domains of human knowledge: (a) empirical-analytic (technical), (b) cultural-hermeneutical interpretive (practical), and (c) critical (emancipatory). These domains of human interest determine what people will accept as knowledge—respectively, (a) technical actions related to work, (b) social interactions related to intersubjective communications, and (c) critical self-knowledge and system knowledge related to emancipation (see also Brown & Paolucci, 1979).

First, the empirical-analytic approach to knowledge creation assumes that nature and society are possible objects of inquiry and new knowledge, based on prediction and control of natural and social environments. Second, the interpretive approach to knowledge creation assumes that features of everyday life and human interactions are possible objects of inquiry and new knowledge. Human societies depend on (a) action-oriented (inter)personal *understandings* that operate within cultural life and (b) the *interpretive* competencies that translate these understandings into the practical conduct of life (Habermas, 1984).

Third, the critical (emancipatory) domain assumes that social criticism, sociopolitical ideologies and power structures, and personal self-delusions (plus consciousness awareness) are possible objects of inquiry and new knowledge. Human emancipation involves critical self-reflection so as to overcome dogmatism, compulsion, and domination. Knowledge is emancipatory and transformative, created through critically questioning the way things are and have always been (i.e., power). Emancipatory knowledge deals with the power relationships between marginalized voices and mainstream hegemonic power brokers (i.e., the dominance of one group over others) (Habermas, 1984).

In short, *empirical* knowledge is objective, not influenced by the personal feelings or opinions of the researcher. This knowledge (gleaned from *one* study) is assumed to reflect other populations not included in the study (generalizable). *Interpretive* knowledge is subjective, gained by the researcher while interpreting the meanings and understandings expressed by participants in a study. That knowledge is context specific and likely inter-subjectively shared by other individuals or the culture under study. *Critical* knowledge is normative. Its creation frees people from inner compulsions and unnecessary social control by those in power, wielding hegemonic influence over society. This knowledge arises from discourse among people experiencing this control. Through this discourse, they are humanized, gain emancipation, and are empowered to change the situation (Brown & Paolucci, 1979; Habermas, 1984).

Matching Methodology With Research Intent

Each of these three research methodologies (empirical, interpretive, and critical) answers basic questions about research quite differently. Authors can "study the same topic from any of these approaches, but each approach implies going about it differently" (Neuman, 2000, p. 120). Table 2.4 provides an illustration of this idea, using consumer debt as an example. What researchers try to accomplish (their intent) will vary with the methodological approach chosen to underpin their study. Their ultimate research design is based on the axioms from each particular approach, and if done responsibly, their research report will share "the back-ground reasoning on which [the study] was originally based" (Neuman, 2000, p. 123).

REVIEW AND ENGAGEMENT

When critically reading a research report, you would

☐ Determine if the authors referred to one or more philosophical axioms (see Figure 2.4 and Table 2.3), ideally in concert with mention of empirical, interpretive, and/or critical methodologies

☐ Ascertain if they referred to knowledge creation as a reason for their research and if, by chance, they mentioned empirical, interpretive, or critical knowledge

☐ Comment on whether the authors linked their research question with their research methodology (see Table 2.4)

TABLE 2.4 ■ Examples of Research Intent Within the Empirical, Interpretive, and Critical Research Methodologies

Positivism Paradigm Quantitative Methodology	Postpositivism Paradigm Qualitative Methodology	
Empirical Methodology Intent is prediction, explanation, and control	**Interpretive Methodology** Intent is understandings	**Critical Methodology** Intent is power and liberation
Methodological Framings of Research Problem **Consumer Debt as Example**		
The intent is to *explain* or *predict* why people get in debt so the results of the study can be used to *control* human behavior, leading to less debt. The researcher will use the scientific method to design the research project (likely including a survey instrument), focusing on facts and/or objective assessment of attitudes. Seen as an expert, the researcher's results can be used to legitimize prescriptive policy or design consumer education curricula so as to *control* people's financial behavior, leading to less indebtedness, more solvency, and more credit savviness.	The intent is to *understand* what is happening (indebtedness), how people who are in debt feel about it, how these conscious and unconscious feelings came to be, and how these new, shared meanings affect their lives. The researcher designs the study in such a way that dialogue ensues with and among those in debt to identify patterns of behavior that lead to indebtedness, as explained by those experiencing this event. Methods could include case studies, storytelling, or content or thematic analysis of interview transcripts. Findings are used to help the indebted person gain a better understanding of his or her lived experiences with being in debt. With these new insights, humans are capable of intentionally changing their behavior, given the right circumstances, but behavior change is *not* the intent of the research.	The intent is to *reveal power* relationships in society that are embedded in existing societal institutions (e.g., consumer society, marketplaces, lending practices, government policies). This is achieved by facilitating participation and transactions with and amongst citizens in such a way that their consciousness is raised about the fact that they are oppressed (they also may know this but feel incapable of taking action). This emancipatory process leads to personal self-empowerment to take steps toward changing their own circumstances and the entire consumerism system. Research methods focus on social justice, inclusion, and liberation and can include action research, critical analysis, and reflective phenomenology. The intent is to give voice to the participants, leading to social change.

QUANTITATIVE, QUALITATIVE, AND MIXED METHODS METHODOLOGIES

The other popular approach to labeling research methodologies emerged during the 1970s and early 1990s and is used to structure the rest of this book. It is the "quantitative–qualitative–mixed methods" approach, so named by Guba (1990). Ary et al. (2010) explained that first came quantitative, then qualitative (see Figure 2.1). The emergence of qualitative led to "the paradigm wars" (p. 559), with people in agreement that these approaches to knowledge creation are distinct due to their philosophical underpinnings but in disagreement about whether they should (or could) both be used in the *same* study (see Donmoyer, 2008). Purists said no, and pragmatists said yes, leading to mixed methods, the third methodological approach in this triad (Guba, 1990; Tashakkori & Teddlie, 1998).

Quantitative and Qualitative Methodologies

Quantitative and qualitative methodologies differ on their assumptions about how to approach research. Fundamentally, the quantitative methodology originated in positivism, with qualitative arising as a push back to positivism (Ary et al., 2010; Wiersma & Jurs, 2009). This approach to distinguishing between the two methodologies is different from the axiom approach previously discussed (see Figure 2.4). Table 2.5 profiles the main assumptive differences between qualitative and quantitative research methodologies, with more detail available in Chapter 8, Table 8.2 (Johnson & Christensen, 2012; Shank & Brown, 2007; Suter, 2012; Weaver & Olson, 2006; Wiersma & Jurs, 2009).

Compared to quantitative researchers, qualitative researchers are "more concerned about uncovering knowledge about how people feel and think in the circumstances in which they find themselves, than making judgements about whether those thoughts and feelings are valid" (Cole, 2006, p. 26). Qualitative research is about meanings and understandings, as perceived and expressed by those living the phenomenon (Shank & Brown, 2007; Smith, 1983). Meaning is Old English *mænan*, "intent, a sense of, import"

TABLE 2.5 ■ Assumptions Underpinning Qualitative and Quantitative Research Methodologies	
Qualitative Methodological Assumptions	**Quantitative Methodological Assumptions**
• Research is best conducted in the natural setting (uninterrupted)	• Research is best conducted in a controlled environment (scientific method)
• A social phenomenon needs to be understood from the perspective of those living it	• Relationships and causal mechanisms (objectively) need to be determined
• Meanings derived from data are context specific (one setting)	• Meanings derived from data should apply to other settings (context free)
• Data are words (nonnumerical); phenomena are too complex to reduce to numbers	• Data are numbers; phenomena can be reduced to simplest parts (using numbers)
• Researchers can be observers or participants and are the key data collection instrument	• Researchers can and should distance themselves from the study
• Theory can emerge from the data (and research can be atheoretical)	• The study can be theory based from the onset
• Hypotheses must emerge from the data	• The study can start with hypotheses that are tested to find the truth
• Reality can be studied using exploration, observation, and interaction	• Reality can be studied using experimental and nonexperimental methods
• Conclusions can be drawn using inductive logic (specific to general)	• Conclusions can be drawn using deductive logic (general to specific)
• Findings can be presented using narrative	• Results can be presented statistically

(Harper, 2016). Meaning is defined as an explanation of what the words were intended to express when someone used them (Anderson, 2014).

Qualitative *meaning* differs from quantitative meaning (Locke et al., 2010; Shank & Brown, 2007; Smith, 1983), as shown in Table 2.6. In qualitative research, meaning is key to understandings, with researchers looking for patterns in the data in search of meaning (Shank & Brown, 2007). *Truth* also has different connotations in qualitative and quantitative work. Succinctly, quantitative scholars assume truth is out there waiting to be discovered while qualitative researchers assume truth is internal to people, either created or agreed to (Smith, 1983) (see also Table 2.1).

Mixed Methods Methodology (Mixing Assumptions)

Mixed methods is the term commonly used to refer to a study that combines assumptions *and* methods from both qualitative and quantitative approaches. Although a better term for this enterprise is *mixed paradigms* (Caracelli & Greene, 1997, p. 19), this chapter uses the term *mixed methods* (with hesitation). Indeed, people's definitions of what constitute mixed methods are "diverse and differentiated in terms of what was being mixed, the stage in the research process were [sic] the mixing occurred, the extend [sic] of the mixing, the purpose of the mixing and the drive behind the research" (Cameron, 2011, p. 96). In this book, Chapter 10 discusses what is involved in conducting a study using both types of methods (techniques and procedures to sample, collect, and analyze data). To complement

TABLE 2.6 ■ Meaning and Truth in the Qualitative and Quantitative Research Methodologies

	Qualitative Methodology	Quantitative Methodology
Meaning	• Meaning is the person • People hold meaning • People make meaning out of their own experiences or take meaning from others • The whole point of research is to examine the processes and types of meaning people might create in, or take from, their world (operationalized during research) • Observations are internal • People are an integral part of reality (and there are multiple realities that differ across time and space for a phenomenon)	• Meaning is the world • Things hold meaning • Meaning comes from abstract laws of nature or the operations of things in the world • Issues of meaning must be settled before testing hypotheses and theories (operationalized before) • Observations are external • Things are separate from reality (there is one reality for a phenomenon)
Truth	• Reality is created by people, meaning what is claimed as true about that reality is purely internal to people • Ontological truth: what is agreed to at any particular point and place in time • Coherent truth: because reality is created, truth has to be constructed	• Reality is out there waiting to be discovered • Truth exists independently of what is in our minds • Something is true if it corresponds with existing reality and false if it does not

this discussion, this chapter focuses on *mixing assumptions* and whether or not this is possible or desirable.

For the remainder of this section, the term *mixed methods* is hereby viewed as *mixed methodology*, defined as "the broad inquiry logic that guides the selection of specific methods [and research questions]" (Teddlie & Tashakkori, 2010, p. 5). The term *inquiry logic* refers to the problems and interests of those engaged in learning about and inquiring into phenomena (Mosier, 1968). Regarding this logic, the "*thoughtful* mixing of assumptions . . . can be very helpful" (Johnson & Christensen, 2012, p. 31). But not everyone agrees that mixing them is a good idea or even possible (see Figure 2.5).

Kim (2003) believed that *empirical, interpretive,* and *critical* can all be used to study a phenomenon but not in the *same* study because their axioms are at odds with each other. Platt (1986) used this logic: (a) *Positivism* and *postpositivism* are not compatible because they hold different assumptions; (b) *quantitative* and *qualitative* correspond to them respectively; thus, (c) the latter two cannot be used in one study because their fundamental assumptions

FIGURE 2.5 ■ Disagreement on Mixing Assumptions (Methodologies)

Cannot Use Methodologies in Same Study	• Cannot mix methodologies in the same study because they have mutually exclusive assumptions, but they can be used in separate studies to address the same research problem; however, this would necessitate different research questions
Can Use Methodologies in Same Study	• Can mix methodologies as long as researchers acknowledge they are combining different logics of inference to answer different research questions (different logics to arrive at conclusions - *reconstructed logic* for quantitative and *logic-in-use* for qualitative)
Be Pragmatic	• Do not wait for philosophers to settle this issue. Researchers can combine methodologies as long as they are accountable for all assumptions, and provide a justification for mixing assumptions, relative to their research questions
Desirable to Combine Positivistic and Postpositivistic	• Researchers should not privilege positivistic because they can be used to explain each other. Positivistic confirms there is a causal link (or an association), and postpositivistic helps explain the link (interactions or associations between variables)

differ too much. Shah and Corley (2006) and Niglas (2001) concurred that *qualitative* and *quantitative* cannot be mixed because they have mutually exclusive epistemological positions (i.e., what counts as knowledge and knowing).

From a more liberal and progressive stance, Lin (1998) believed that combining positivistic and postpositivistic paradigmatic approaches in one study is possible as long as researchers remember that they are combining two different *logics of inference*. This term refers to the act or process of deriving logical conclusions from premises known and presumed to be true (i.e., assumptions). To reach their conclusions, quantitative (empirical) researchers would use *reconstructed logic* while quantitative researchers would use *logic-in-use* (Maxwell, 2008) (see Chapter 8). Lin (1998) argued that it is "precisely because the logics of inference are different, and suited for answering different questions, that research combining both logics is effective" (p. 163) (see also Johnson & Christensen, 2012). Lin (1998) explained that positivistic work can find causal mechanisms, and postpositivistic research can help explain how the mechanism works.

In attempts to mediate this situation, Kim (2003) maintained that not all disciplines view research methodologies as incompatible; rather, some disciplines prefer or advocate for one over the other (see also Botha, 1989). Kim tempered this thought by cautioning authors to not favor the positivistic paradigm and associated methodologies to the exclusion of postpositivism. Niglas (2001) and Trochim and Donnelly (2007) advocated for pragmatism, meaning researchers can use whichever approach they want *as long as* they are accountable for any *assumptions* they bring to their work. At a minimum, authors reporting mixed methods studies must justify *mixing assumptions* and *logics of inference* and clearly articulate their philosophical positions on this still unsettled aspect of scholarship. This especially involves matching the research question with the methodology (see Table 2.4), as discussed in the next section.

REVIEW AND ENGAGEMENT

When critically reading a research report, you would

☐ Determine if the authors provided some level of discussion of the assumptions behind the methodology they chose for their research design (see Tables 2.3 and 2.5): qualitative, quantitative, or mixed methods

☐ Ascertain if they addressed the topics of meaning and truth and how they are understood within the methodology used in their study (see Table 2.6)

☐ Check to see if they justified using a mixed methods (mixed assumptions) methodology, providing a cogent discussion, ideally with some mention of logics of inference

☐ Ascertain if their research questions correlated with their research methodology (qualitative, quantitative, or mixed methods)

RESEARCH METHODOLOGY AND RESEARCH QUESTION ALIGNMENT

Research paradigms and research methodologies can become so ingrained that they influence the very choices of the questions deemed worthy of study, the methods used to conduct the study, and the theoretical lens for interpreting the results and findings

(Rohmann, 1999), knowingly or not. *When* the researcher should pose a research question is still under dispute, relative to the research methodology (see Figure 2.6).

First, Wiersma and Jurs (2009) suggested that researchers tend to pose their research question first. Only then do they identify the pertinent research methodology (philosophical assumptions) from the words they chose in their question and proceed to develop their research design using the appropriate methods. Similarly, Dudovskiy (2016) claimed that the underlying philosophy of a study will reflect the researcher's assumptions (and worldviews), intimating that the latter come first, followed with clarification of pertinent research methodology. In plain language, researchers will pick a research problem of interest to them and *then* align it with the appropriate research methodology. Only then do they create their research design logic and logistics (see Chapter 8).

Second, some scholars believe that researchers consciously choose a research methodology, from which the research questions will naturally flow (Ary et al., 2010). These scholars would know that the research methodology exists regardless of their own worldviews. Sometimes they align, and sometimes they do not. What matters is that the research question and the research methodology align (see Table 2.4). For example, if a scholar is concerned with power relations in society, it is a natural progression to the critical (emancipatory) research methodology. In another instance, a scholar may personally prefer empirical research but appreciate that she or he cannot answer a research question focused on what a phenomenon *means* to the people living it unless an interpretive (qualitative) research methodology is used to create the research design. The scholar's personal worldview would not get in the way of her or his research methodology.

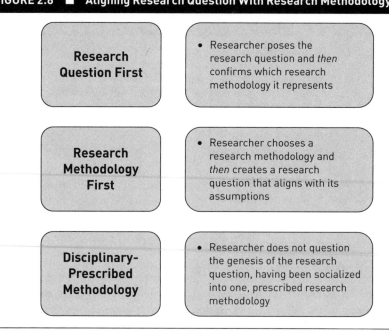

FIGURE 2.6 ■ Aligning Research Question With Research Methodology

Research Question First
- Researcher poses the research question and *then* confirms which research methodology it represents

Research Methodology First
- Researcher chooses a research methodology and *then* creates a research question that aligns with its assumptions

Disciplinary-Prescribed Methodology
- Researcher does not question the genesis of the research question, having been socialized into one, prescribed research methodology

Third, in other cases, researchers never question their research methodology or worry about the genesis of their research questions because they have been socialized into disciplinary blinders, with many disciplines adhering to specific methodologies, especially the empirical, quantitative, positivistic methodology (Weaver & Olson, 2006). In light of this, Weaver and Olson (2006) urged disciplines to avoid uncritically prescribing one mode of inquiry and knowledge creation. This would remove the paradigmatic blinders.

Regardless, the research methodology and the research question must be consistent (Wiersma & Jurs, 2009). Ary et al. (2010) concurred, advising that the research methodology must be suitable for what is being studied and what one wants to find out—that is, suitable for the research question (see Table 2.4).

REVIEW AND ENGAGEMENT

When critically reading a research report, you would

☐ Determine if the authors ensured that their research methodology and research questions were consistent—in other words, that the research methods (determined by the methodology) were appropriate to answer the research question (see Table 2.4)

☐ Ascertain if they explained *how* the research question was affected by their research methodology (see Table 2.4)

☐ Check to see if they commented on *when* they posed their research question (see Figure 2.6)

WRITING THE RESEARCH METHODOLOGY SECTION OF A PAPER

When writing their papers, authors rarely explicitly indicate which research paradigm or methodological approach(es) shaped their study. Nonetheless, this key aspect of research should be "candidly expressed [and] made explicit and shared" (Neuman, 2000, p. 122). It will likely comprise one paragraph (longer for a thesis or dissertation), which should include (a) identification of the specific research methodology used in the study; (b) the reasons for choosing this particular methodology; and (c) a discussion of how it informed the [research question], the research strategy in general, and the choice of methods in particular (Dudovskiy, 2016).

Because it usually prefaces the Methods section, which reports what *was* done to sample, collect, and analyze data, any discussion of methodological decisions should be written in past tense unless it is a research proposal (future tense), where the researcher is seeking approval of his or her research design, meaning the research has not yet happened.

Example 2.3 Reporting a qualitative research methodology (adapted from Murnane's 2008 doctoral dissertation, pp. 42–43, references in the original)

This research will be conducted through the **interpretive paradigm**, which views research as a way of better understanding reality, as well as the researcher him- or herself, within a given context (Koetting, 1984). Because of the contextual nature of **interpretive research**, it is imperative to better understand a particular setting and activities that are specific to the organization in addition to just gathering data. For that reason, appropriate ontological, epistemological, axiological, and rhetorical components were observed to achieve this understanding. **Ontologically**, there are many realities based on the researcher's interaction with the participants as well as the researcher's and participants' experiences occurring **naturally** (Khazanchi & Munkvold, 2003; Ponterotto, 2005). The research subjects develop the interpretive researcher's view of their reality, and the **nature of the knowledge** attained is conceptual with regard to the participants' **meanings** (Baranov, 2004; Berrell & MacPherson, 1995; Gephart, 1999). **Epistemologically**, the researcher and the study participants are completely dependent on one another as they work together to create knowledge throughout the study; therefore, **objectivity** is not a goal for this work (Khazanchi & Munkvold, 2003; Ponterotto, 2005). **Axiologically**, the researcher's and participants' **values** are integral to the research process and are incorporated into the study (Ponterotto, 2005). Lincoln and Guba (1985) define "values" as judges of preference or choice and include preferences grounded in assumptions, theories, perspectives, and social norms. The researcher's **biases** are also acknowledged as part of the axiology. From a **rhetorical** perspective, the narrative is personal and involved and written from the viewpoint of the researcher (Ponterotto, 2005), the desired reporting structure for a narrative presentation of the research findings. The **case study method** will be used because it is consistent with the **narrative** presentation of **findings**, where the description of a real situation and context is required (Stake, 1978; Yin, 2003).

Compared to the thoroughness of Example 2.3, in reality, what usually appears in a paper is a very truncated statement, something like "This *qualitative* study employed the case study *method* to address the *research question*." Although authors seldom use axiomatic terms (e.g., *epistemology* and *ontology*), the words *interpretive* and *critical* appear quite often, as do *qualitative*, *quantitative*, and *mixed methods* (less so *positivistic* and *postpositivistic*). Authors of empirical studies hardly ever self-identify as using a "positivistic, quantitative research methodology." They believe (subliminally, perhaps) that this clarification is unnecessary because all empirical studies follow the same research protocol (i.e., the scientific method), which is self-evident, needing no explanation or justification. The information in this chapter strived to foster responsible methodological decisions and reporting, as a precursor to the actual Methods section.

REVIEW AND ENGAGEMENT

When critically reading a research report, you would

☐ Confirm that the authors clearly explained which methodology they used, linking it with their theory and method choices

☐ Ascertain if they at least provided enough information for you to deduce their research methodology

FINAL JUDGMENT ON THE METHODOLOGY ELEMENT OF A RESEARCH PAPER

Taking *all* of the *Review and Engagement* criteria into account, what is your final judgment of the methodology element of the paper that you are critically reading?

CHAPTER SUMMARY

This chapter tackled the very challenging task of distinguishing between an array of methodology-related terms and how each relates to research questions, research design, and methods. After briefly describing the provenance of the most common terms (see Figure 2.1), the discussion turned to three overarching terms: *research paradigm*, *methodology*, and *tradition* (see Figure 2.2). This section acknowledged that there is simply no agreement in the academy about what these terms mean and how they should be used. What is agreed to is that they impact the research question, methods, and theory choices (see Table 2.4). This book, and this chapter in particular, also clearly distinguished between methodology and method (see Figure 2.3).

After clarifying the approach used in this book (see Table 2.1), all four key aspects of this approach were then discussed: (a) philosophical axioms (see Figure 2.4); (b) positivistic and postpositivistic research paradigms (see Table 2.2); and (c) empirical, interpretive, and critical research methodologies (see Table 2.3) (along with Habermas's three approaches to knowledge creation). After clarifying that the book uses (d) the quantitative, qualitative, and mixed methods methodology approach, each of these methodologies is described (see Tables 2.5 and 2.6 and Figure 2.5). The chapter concluded with a discussion of the importance of aligning research methodology and research question (see Table 2.4 and Figure 2.6) and some basic conventions for writing the research methodology section of a research report.

REVIEW AND DISCUSSION QUESTIONS

1. Had you ever heard of the idea of methodology before reading this chapter? Explain your reaction to this key research convention.

2. What are your thoughts about *the very idea* of "a methodology"? Does *the idea* make sense? What is your knee-jerk reaction to the concept? After reading this chapter, what is your mental image of the concept (how do you picture it in your mind)?

3. What is the difference between methodology and method, as explained in this chapter (see

Figure 2.3)? What is the connection between methodology and methods in a research design?

4. After reading this chapter, find someone who might be interested and explain to him or her the approach to methodology that is used in this book (see Table 2.1).

5. One approach to methodology is based on philosophy, including four axioms dealing with what counts as knowledge, reality, logic, and the role of values (see Figure 2.4). How comfortable are you with this *philosophical*

idea? How easy (ease of effort/no worries) or hard (anxiety and/or difficulty) was it to intellectually grasp this *philosophical* aspect of research? Explain your answer.

6. Explain in plain language the main differences between the empirical, interpretive, and critical research methodologies (see Table 2.3).

7. How new to you were the ideas of positivism and postpositivism? Are you more comfortable with these concepts after reading this chapter? Why or why not? (See Table 2.2.)

8. Another approach to methodology is quantitative, qualitative, and mixed methods. How do these three approaches differ on their assumptions about research? In particular, how comfortable are you with mixing assumptions in a research design (mixed methods)? (See Table 2.5 and Figure 2.5.)

9. How are positivism/postpositivism and qualitative/quantitative connected?

10. Methodologies are *supposed* to come first (be the axis of everything), then be *followed* by the research question, the logic used for research

design, the theory, and finally the method(s) (data collection, analysis, interpretation, and reporting). Do you agree with the role that methodologies are *supposed to* play in research? Explain your answer.

11. What is your opinion about the *many ways* of categorizing, labeling, and conceiving methodologies (there is no one, agreed-to approach)? Explain your thoughts on this topic and provide justifications for your arguments.

12. What impact do you think this range of approaches has on being able to understand and use the idea when critiquing research? Are there too many or too few? Is it too confusing or too obscure, or is there too much uncertainty? Is it very clear, straightforward, or clear as mud? Explain your thoughts on this topic, and provide justifications for your arguments.

13. Explain the intended relationship between the research question and the research methodology. Which do you think should come first? Justify your answer (see Figure 2.6).

3

CONCEPTUAL FRAMEWORKS, THEORIES, AND MODELS

INTRODUCTION

Chapter 2 focused on research methodologies, arguing that they are the crux of all scholarship. They especially determine the research question(s), the research design, and how to interpret the data. Aside from methodologies, authors and critical readers must be aware of the role that conceptual frameworks, theories, and models play in scholarship. "All knowledge is theory-laden and all methods are theory driven" (Tavallaei & Abu Talib, 2010, p. 574). This chapter is about *using* these framing and interpretive tools in research and how to report that aspect of research in a research report, including a journal article. As a caveat, this book does not address the process of theory *development* (see Jacard & Jacoby, 2010; Lynham, 2002a, 2002b; Steiner, 1988; Swanson, 2013; Swedberg, 2014). Readers can turn to Table 18.1 (in Chapter 18) for Steiner's (1988) overview of the basic steps to theory development.

Research and scholarship that is not undergirded by some sort of *framework* is considered weakened (Casanave & Li, 2015; Labaree, 2016). Conceptual frameworks, theories, and models all make research stronger, with theories holding the most weight. Respecting this tenet, the chapter starts with a general overview of the role of theory in research inquiries. It serves as a precursor for a richer discussion of theories in general (relative to conceptual frameworks and models), bridged with an introduction to concepts and constructs, the building blocks of all three research elements.

This order was chosen because conceptual frameworks do not have theory status (they have no propositions) but they often lead to new theories. Both are built using concepts and constructs. To clarify, when a conceptual framework is used, its concepts and constructs guide the study. When a theory is used, its percepts, assumptions, and

LEARNING OBJECTIVES

- Elaborate on the role of theory in research, as it pertains to the four stages of inquiry

- Distinguish among conceptual frameworks, theories, and models

- Compare and contrast concepts and constructs, and explain the characteristics of a good concept

- Explain the essence of a conceptual framework, and how it differs from a theory

- Explain the basic building blocks of a theory (types, purposes, formative elements)

- Describe the characteristics of good theory

- Explain the role of models in research

- Discuss the issues involved in choosing and using conceptual frameworks and theories in a study

- Understand the conventions for writing the theoretical or the conceptual framework section of a research report

propositions guide the study (Plakhotnik & Rocco, 2009). When authors need a powerful and memorable way to illustrate their thinking, they can use models. The chapter ends with a discussion of the conventions involved in writing a conceptual framework and a theory section of a research report. For clarification, Chapter 18 discusses what is involved in writing a paper reporting a new conceptual framework or a theory developed by a researcher.

ROLE OF THEORY IN RESEARCH INQUIRIES

Research relies on theory, and theory testing and development relies on research (Fawcett & Downs, 1986; Ellinger & Yang, 2011). Research tends to happen in four phases (i.e., the reasons for the inquiry): explore, describe, identify relationships (associations), and causally explain relationships (see Figure 3.1). There are three types of theory, which are related to the four reasons for an inquiry: (a) descriptive theory, using exploratory and descriptive research; (b) relational theory, using correlational research; and (c) explanatory theory, using experimental, predictive, and qualitative causal research (Berg, 2008; de Vaus, 2001; Gall, Gall, & Borg, 2015; Harvard University, ca. 2001; Lambert & Lambert, 2012; Maxwell & Mittapalli, 2008a, 2008b; Sandelowski, 2000; Suter, 2012; Yin, 1984; see also Table 3.1).

FIGURE 3.1   ■   Four Phases of Research (Related to Theory Development)

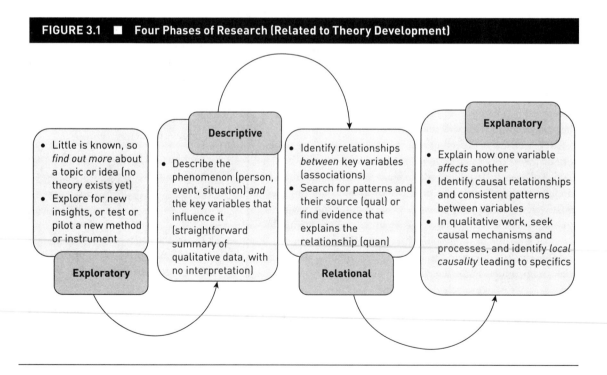

- Little is known, so *find out more* about a topic or idea (no theory exists yet)
- Explore for new insights, or test or pilot a new method or instrument

Exploratory

Descriptive
- Describe the phenomenon (person, event, situation) *and* the key variables that influence it (straightforward summary of qualitative data, with no interpretation)

- Identify relationships *between* key variables (associations)
- Search for patterns and their source (qual) or find evidence that explains the relationship (quan)

Relational

Explanatory
- Explain how one variable *affects* another
- Identify causal relationships and consistent patterns between variables
- In qualitative work, seek causal mechanisms and processes, and identify *local causality* leading to specifics

TABLE 3.1 ■ Relationship Between Research Purpose, Theory, and Research Design

Exploratory	Descriptive	Predictive	Experimental	Explanatory
Broad, initial understandings of reality	Deeper understandings of reality	Predicts reality	Changes reality	Explains reality
Lays the *groundwork* for future studies (rarely provides definitive answers)	Makes clear by careful, highly *detailed observations*	*Quantitative:* determines beforehand whether something *predicts future* behaviors or events *Qualitative:* does not predict but does *identify general processes* that are applicable to a given context	*Quan:* determines *the effect* of something on something else *Qual:* gains *information and wisdom* from lived experiences	*Quan:* determines whether something is *the cause of* something else *Qual:* determines *elucidation of meaning;* also, explicates processes and mechanisms that result in a particular occurrence in a given context
Identifies key aspects of practice to study	*Quan:* discovers problems in practice *Qual:* discovers processes and meanings in practice	*Quan:* solves problems in practice *Qual:* understands practice in a given context	*Quan:* makes practice more effective *Qual:* understands the lived process of practice	*Quan:* elucidates practice (causal processes) *Qual:* controls practice

Descriptive research design for when little is known about the phenomenon (no theoretical explanations available; qual and quan)

Correlational research design for when the phenomenon is adequately described but its relationship to other phenomena is not known

Experimental research design for when the phenomenon is adequately described and its relationship to other phenomena is well known

Qualitative research design for when the goal is to discern the participants' understandings of the phenomenon and what this means to them

53

Descriptive Theory

Descriptive theory helps researchers understand reality. Scholars ask, "What is this?" and "What are the existing characteristics of the real world relative to the specific research question?" Good descriptions of reality eventually provoke the *why* questions of explanatory research. As an example, linguistic descriptive theories provide adequate descriptions of *what* individual languages are like. Explanatory linguistic theories are about *why* languages are the way they are (Dryer, 2006).

Describe is Latin *describere*, "to write down" (Harper, 2016). Descriptive theories describe or classify specific dimensions or characteristics of individuals, groups, events, or situations by summarizing their commonalities. Typical research methods employed with descriptive theories are case studies, surveys, grounded theory, ethnographies, phenomenological studies, historic research, and philosophic inquiries. Familiar examples of descriptive research results are the census, social and economic indicators (such as household expenditure patterns), employment and crime statistics, and family demographics (Fawcett & Downs, 1986).

Descriptive research often yields typologies or taxonomies. They do not have theory status, but they can definitely lead to theories, and they can be used as stand-alone frameworks for research questions and studies (Fawcett & Downs, 1986; Johnson & Christensen, 2012).

Typology

Typology is Latin *typus*, "form or kind" (Harper, 2016). When the genesis of something is unknown, researchers can create a typology of its attributes. Typologies are general classifications of *types* of things that have common characteristics, attributes, features, or structures (Johnson & Christensen, 2012; Marradi, 1990). Any identified patterns exist in all features of the phenomenon and in the dependencies between these features (Croft, 2003). A typology "breaks down an overarching concept into component dimensions and types" (Collier, LaPorte, & Seawright, 2012, p. 223).

Example 3.1 Typology As an illustrative example, a popular typology is the *Myers-Briggs Type Indicator* (MBTI), with the actual word *type* in the name of the typology. It comprises four dimensions: (a) where people focus their attention (extrovert or introvert), (b) the way they take information (sense or intuit), (c) how they make decisions (think or feel), and (d) how they deal with the world (judge or perceive). Using these elements, this typology comprises a 16-cell matrix, leading to 16 personality *types*, each with names and descriptions. In a supportive diagram, the color of each "type square" represents the dominant function for each type—green for sensing, yellow for intuition, blue for thinking, and red for feeling (Kaplan & Saccuzzo, 2009; Myers & Myers, 1980).

One problem with typologies is that they do not accurately reflect anyone, and they provide oversimplifications of everyone (Lasley, 2008). Nonetheless, researchers can use typologies to organize their thinking as part of descriptive and exploratory research, facing the question "What is this?" To continue example 3.1, when I take the MBTI test, I am usually an *ENTJ*, which stands for extrovert, intuition, thinking, and judging. It is in a blue square, representing thinking as the dominant personality (which is correct for me).

People with this personality type typically see the big picture and think strategically about the future. They are able to efficiently organize resources in order to accomplish long-term goals. Conversely, they often overlook the contributions of others and can intimidate people with their take-charge attitude and energy. This really describes me but misses the mark on some aspects of my personality.

Taxonomy

When more becomes known about a phenomenon through research, it is possible for concepts and subconcepts, categories and subcategories, and sets and subsets to be formed and systematically arranged, creating a taxonomy. *Taxonomy* stems from Greek *taxis*, for arrangement, or putting things in order (Harper, 2016). It refers to several categories arranged and considered in succession, often using branch diagrams (Marradi, 1990). "When information is structured and indexed in a taxonomy, users can find what they need by working down to more specific categories, up to a more inclusive topic, or sideways to related topics" (Walli, 2014, p. 1). Taxonomies provide both "meaningful context and ideas for further exploration" (Walli, 2014, p. 1), which is why they are pertinent to exploratory and descriptive research.

> *Example 3.2 Taxonomy* Examples of taxonomies include those for biological plant and animal classification systems (Hunter, 2001), knowledge management (Nie, Ma, & Nakamori, 2007), and research practice (Ulrich, 2011). Most educators are familiar with *Bloom's Taxonomy of Educational Objectives.* Each of six categories (levels) of learning is labeled and contains subcategories (averaging five to six), all lying along a continuum from simple to complex, concrete to abstract, and lower to higher orders of thinking (Anderson & Krathwohl, 2001) (see Figure 3.2).

Relational Theory

Relational theories help explain reality, asking, "What is happening here?" and "To what extent are two things occurring together (or in *relation* to each other)?" Occurring together means happening at the same time or in close proximity. Called relation-searching theories, they seek to identify relationships between concepts and how they are associated with each other (but not if they caused each other). After descriptive theories have been developed and validated (establishing the essential characteristics of a phenomenon), relational theories are often developed to explain how parts of the phenomenon are related to one another and why—that is, how the change in one dimension of a phenomenon *correlates* with changes in one or more other dimensions (which is not the same as causing the change, requiring explanatory theory) (Fawcett & Downs, 1986).

> *Example 3.3 Relational theory* Sternberg (2003) developed what could be called a relational theory, the *duplex theory of hate.* His theory comprised three components (*concepts*), each with *subconcepts.* He clarified that he did not claim any statistical independence of the three theoretical concepts. Rather, using these concepts and subconcepts, Sternberg created a typology of seven types of hate, which he proposed *are related to* terrorism, massacres, and genocides along four degrees of danger. He then provided a list of 18 hypotheses (*propositions*) of how the types of hate and

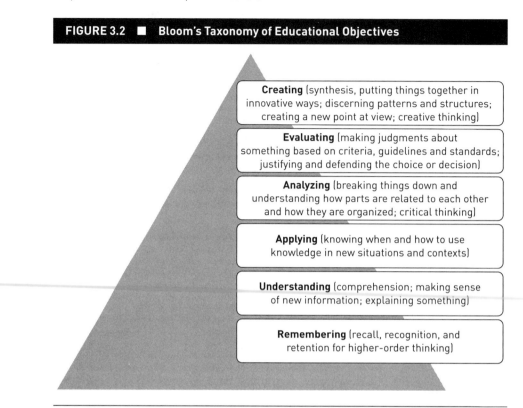

FIGURE 3.2   ■   Bloom's Taxonomy of Educational Objectives

Creating (synthesis, putting things together in innovative ways; discerning patterns and structures; creating a new point at view; creative thinking)

Evaluating (making judgments about something based on criteria, guidelines and standards; justifying and defending the choice or decision)

Analyzing (breaking things down and understanding how parts are related to each other and how they are organized; critical thinking)

Applying (knowing when and how to use knowledge in new situations and contexts)

Understanding (comprehension; making sense of new information; explaining something)

Remembering (recall, recognition, and retention for higher-order thinking)

Source: Adapted from Anderson and Krathwohl (2001).

degrees of danger are *related*. His theory attempted not to predict how they are causally related, only that they are *associated* with each other. He invited others to empirically test his theory, anticipating a future explanatory theory.

Relational research

Unlike descriptive research, which uses open-ended approaches, relational research uses surveys and interview instruments, which comprise fixed-choice observation checklists, rating scales, or standardized questionnaires. They yield either quantitative or qualitative data. The latter need to be categorized, with numbers assigned to the categories. These numbers are analyzed using descriptive or inferential statistics, by running correlation coefficients (i.e., creating a number that serves as a quality or a characteristic of the relationship between two or more things) (Fawcett & Downs, 1986) (see Chapters 11 and 12). Any resultant theory would posit associations among variables but stop short of making causal suggestions, which requires explanatory theory. In order to know if one *thing* caused another, researchers would need to know what would happen if *that* thing did not happen.

Explanatory (Predictive) Theory

Explanatory theories are used to predict and control reality (i.e., cause and effect). They answer the questions "What will happen if . . . ?" and "Is treatment A different from treatment B?" Moving beyond determining if there *is* a relationship, explanatory theory strives to determine the cause and effect of the relationship—that is, *why* there are changes in a phenomenon. Explanatory theories stem from association-testing studies that test relationships by manipulating variables (rather than seek relationships). It is not enough to simply find correlations (associations) between variables; explanatory theory and related research are focused on the *cause and effect mechanism* so they can predict and control reality (Fawcett & Downs, 1986) (see Chapters 11 and 12).

> ***Example 3.4 Explanatory theory*** The Health Belief Model (HBM) theorizes that people's readiness to take action to improve their health is predicted by (a) their belief about whether or not they are at risk of a disease or health problem and (b) their perceptions of the benefits of taking action to avoid it. This theory has four core constructs (concepts): perceived susceptibility and perceived severity, perceived benefits and perceived barriers, cue to action, and self-efficacy. This theory *predicts* that individual perceptions are modified by a collection of factors (demographics, sociopsychology, and cues to action [media, advice, illness]), which, combined, effect their perceived threat of a disease, *causing* a likelihood to take recommended preventative action to improve their health (Glanz, 2016).

> ***Example 3.5 Explanatory research*** In an exploratory study about addictions, a researcher conducted a thematic analysis of interviews and private diaries. Several themes emerged around coded concepts and constructs. The researcher created a new, untested grounded theory about teen-into-adult addictions. She discerned that using marijuana as a teen was linked with having more troublesome relationships in early adulthood. Comments pursuant to this finding were quite prevalent. To ascertain if there is an association between these two concepts, she next conducted a survey with pertinent subjects, focused on the link between using marijuana and the health of their adult relationships. A Pearson's *r* of +.90 confirmed a positive, strong, direct relationship, affirming that high teen marijuana usage and unhealthy adult relationships are related. As one goes up, the other goes up, but she still does not know if one *causes* the other.

Explanatory theory-generating and theory-testing research is conducted using the empirical, scientific method of controlled experiments or observations. Numbers are needed to quantify the cause and effect and to help researchers draw inferences about the data; hence, a wide range of inferential statistical methods is employed (see Chapter 12). Inferences are conclusions reached based on reasoning and judgments rather than just observations (like with descriptive research). To illustrate, a descriptive theory may identify 10 different parenting styles, one being an abusive parent, whereas the explanatory theory will tell *why* parents abuse their children. Using explanatory theory, researchers can predict precise cause-and-effect relationships between phenomena and groups (Fawcett & Downs, 1986).

> ***Example 3.6 Moving from descriptive to explanatory theory*** In example 3.5, a researcher reported an *association* between teens' marijuana usage and the health of their adult relationships, a word that conveys they seem to "go together, hand-in-hand," but there was no evidence in the data that one *caused* the other. Many other things were going on, which had not been controlled for in the relational study. To ascertain causation, a longitudinal, experimental study could be designed with

two teen groups, one using marijuana and one not. They could be followed over the years to see whether their marijuana use caused troubled relationships as adults (this is not ethical of course, but you get the point). Resultant data could lead to a new causal (explanatory) theory about teen-into-adult addictions.

Qualitative explanatory

Qualitative scholars can also conduct explanatory research, although this practice is considered to be controversial (because qualitative scholars conventionally eschew randomization, generalizability, and predictability). In qualitative work, an emphasis on explanation refers to the understanding of causal processes in specific cases. Instead of causality consisting of regularities in relationships between variables, it consists of real, causal mechanisms and processes arising from natural and social entities in a specific context. These mechanisms and processes produce particular outcomes, but may not produce regularities (Maxwell & Mittapalli, 2008a). Qualitative studies often strive for "'local causality'—the actual events and processes that lead to specific outcomes [in given contexts]" (Maxwell & Mittapalli, 2008b, p. 325).

Causal narratives are the most widely used qualitative approach to explanation. They were originally developed as an alternative to correlational methods. "[I]nstead of seeking regularities in the relationship between proposed explanatory factors and outcomes across cases, the goal is to elucidate the processes at work in one case, or a small number of cases, using in-depth intensive analysis and a narrative presentation of the argument" (Maxwell & Mittapalli, 2008a, p. 324). Case study research can also employ causal explanation, including narrative approaches. In these instances, researchers strive for analytic generalizability, meaning they generalize to a theory of a specific case instead of statistically to a defined population (Maxwell & Mittapalli, 2008b).

In summary, as noted in the chapter introduction, the previous overview of the role of theories in research inquiries is a precursor for a richer discussion of theories in general (relative to conceptual frameworks and models), bridged with an introduction to concepts and constructs, the building block of all three research elements. The takeaway from this first section is that the type of research inquiry determines the type (if any) of theory used in the paper. Exploratory and descriptive research both employ descriptive theory, if it exists. Relational research (searching for associations and patterns) uses relational theory. And explanatory research (quantitative [non]experimental) seeking causal effects uses experimental (predictive) theory. Qualitative explanatory research seeks local causality as well as causal mechanisms and processes (see Figure 3.1; see also Chapter 11).

REVIEW AND ENGAGEMENT

When critically reading a research report, you would

☐ Determine if the authors acknowledged the importance of having a theoretical or conceptual perspective in their research design (i.e., appreciated their purposes in research, especially how they help structure thinking)

☐ Ascertain if they intimated their knowledge of the link among the four reasons for an inquiry, the three types of theory, and their research design (see Table 3.1)

CONCEPTS AND CONSTRUCTS

Each of conceptual frameworks, theories, and models is based on the notion of abstract concepts and constructs, whether it is a stand-alone collection of concepts (framework), a set of propositions about how they are related (theory), or a representation of them (model). The ensuing discussion begins with concepts and constructs, the foundation of all three.

Concept is Latin *conceptum*, "something conceived" (Harper, 2016). First, people observe reality (objects and phenomena). Next, they draw ideas away from what they see (i.e., they abstract), and then, they give these ideas a name and meaning; that is, they conceptualize or conceive something new. When the abstracted idea is an observed fact, it is called a *concept* (e.g., dog, cat, chair). When people have to infer the idea from what they observe or think is going on, it is called a *construct* (e.g., happiness, leadership, morale, wellbeing) (Aswar, 2011; Nalzaro, 2012). *Infer* means they reasonably concluded that something is going on and then gave this construct a name.

In more detail, construct is Latin *consturere*, "to build" (Harper, 2016). Compared to concepts, constructs are higher-order abstractions that are difficult to observe, measure, sense, and interpret. Consider the statement "Women seek empowerment." It is easy to quantify the *concept* of a woman (sex) but less so the *construct* of empowerment (The Learning House, 2016). Constructs are subjective in nature compared to concepts, which are grounded in facts. Sometimes, constructs are clusters of concepts that form a higher unit of thought (Anfara & Mertz, 2006).

In effect, concepts and constructs are "intellectual representations of some aspect of reality that is derived from observations made from phenomena" (Nalzaro, 2012, p. 1). To clarify, phenomenon is Greek *phainomenon*, "a thing appearing to be viewed" (Harper, 2016). Botha (1989) described this abstraction process as ideas "linguistically projected into terminology" (p. 52). The subsequent terms and concepts help theorists organize their experiences of the world, and help facilitate their understanding of phenomena (Botha, 1989). Actually, all theories deal with abstractions (i.e., drawing ideas away from observed phenomena), so it makes sense that their building blocks are concepts and constructs (Aswar, 2011).

Castro-Palaganas (2011) proposed that concepts and constructs are *theoretical variables* that are not directly measurable. Authors need to distinguish between the theoretical definition of a concept or construct and the *operational definition* of the version used in a study, which is measured or discerned (quantitatively or qualitatively). Theoretical definitions state what the concept means in a *particular* theory. Indeed, concepts differ with context and from theory to theory. Operational definitions explain what the researchers did to find evidence of the concept in their study (Imenda, 2014; The Learning House, 2016; Wacker, 1998).

Example 3.7 Theoretical versus research variable A theory comprising three main concepts may propose that *socioeconomic status* and *academic ability* both affect *academic* achievements. When used in a study, the theoretical concept of socioeconomic status can be operationally expressed as *income and job prestige* (measurable research variables). Academic ability (a theoretical concept) becomes operationalized as *math and language skills* (research variables). Academic achievement (a theoretical concept) becomes operationalized as both *grades and level of schooling attained* (research variables) (Castro-Palaganas, 2011).

Harris (2014) cautioned that different researchers often propose divergent definitions for the same-named concept or construct, a practice leading to confusion and contradictions for those reading and employing their work. For example, Rhode and Packel (2011) observed that there are at least 1,500 definitions of the constructs of *leader* and *leadership* and their synonyms. It is imperative that authors distinguish between theoretical and operational definitions and cite relevant literature used for *their* conceptualizations (and operationalizations in a study).

Characteristics of a Good Concept and Construct

Authors can benefit from knowing that Gerring (1999) tendered eight characteristics of a good concept (and construct) (see Figure 3.3). Each concept should be *familiar* to the intended audience, and its chosen term or name should *resonate* with people. He called this a "cognitive click," which means the name sticks with people (p. 370). The name of the concept should be simple (*parsimonious*) as should the list of defining attributes (i.e., what it intends to capture or reflect about reality). The concept should exhibit *internal consistency*, meaning its attributes and the attendant aspect of reality are logically related. The concept should also be discernibly different from other existing concepts (i.e., *differentiated*).

Concepts should exhibit *depth*, which means they capture a rich bundle of characteristics of the phenomenon. The resultant theory thus needs fewer concepts and propositions. Most important, good concepts are actually useful for building theory (*theoretical utility*). And their definitions should be developed with full awareness of any spillover on existing and related concepts in the field of study or discipline, which may also have to be reconceptualized and redefined. This *field utility* maximizes the efficiency and clarity of theoretical language (Gerring, 1999).

Regarding field utility, Gerring (1999) stated people have to be cognizant of how their definition of a new concept affects, even rises from, existing concepts. This is important because every concept contains components (bits) originating from other concepts, and all concepts relate to other concepts. Also, all concepts have a history, meaning each one is created from something, rather than nothing. For these reasons, every concept must be understood "relative to its own components, to other concepts, to the plane on which it is defined, and to the problem it is supposed to resolve" (Deleuze & Guattari, 1991, p. 21).

Distinguishing Among Conceptual Frameworks, Theories, and Models

As noted earlier, each of conceptual frameworks, theories, and models comprises concepts, constructs, or both. Researchers have a choice of using conceptual frameworks, theories, and/or models in their research, appreciating that the relationship among the three is significant, yet deceptively simple (Tavallaei & Abu Talib, 2010). Succinctly, conceptual frameworks comprise a collection of concepts with their definitions and explanations of how they are related *to the phenomenon*. When scholars begin to propose relationships between and among these concepts (using propositions), couched in assumptions, or claims about the phenomenon in the world, they are moving toward a theory. When they strive to pictorially represent a conceptual framework or a theory using schematics, they are creating models (see Figure 3.4). The rest of the chapter discusses this progressive relationship,

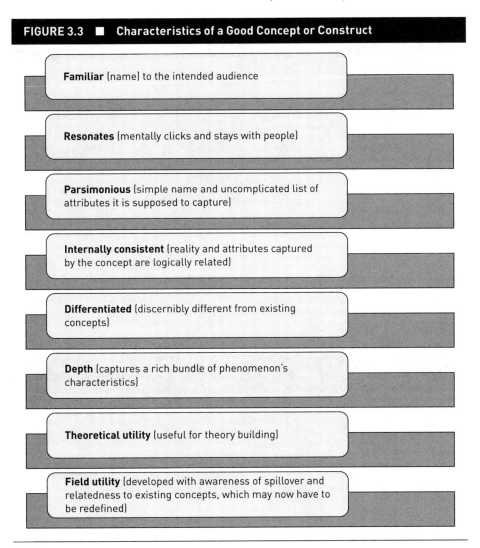

FIGURE 3.3 ■ Characteristics of a Good Concept or Construct

Familiar (name) to the intended audience

Resonates (mentally clicks and stays with people)

Parsimonious (simple name and uncomplicated list of attributes it is supposed to capture)

Internally consistent (reality and attributes captured by the concept are logically related)

Differentiated (discernibly different from existing concepts)

Depth (captures a rich bundle of phenomenon's characteristics)

Theoretical utility (useful for theory building)

Field utility (developed with awareness of spillover and relatedness to existing concepts, which may now have to be redefined)

appreciating that not all conceptual frameworks progress to theories and not all conceptual frameworks or theories are represented using models.

Terminology confusion

As a caveat, not everyone distinguishes so clearly between these three aspects of research. Unfortunately, these terms are used interchangeably, causing unnecessary confusion (Mosterín, 1996). Some people use the term *conceptual framework*, others use *theoretical framework*, and still others assume they are interchangeable, framing reference to them as a "theoretical (or conceptual) framework" or a "theoretical/conceptual framework/model" (Casanave & Li, 2015; Ellinger & Yang, 2011; Imenda, 2014; Jabareen, 2009; Sinclair, 2007). Others use the terms in reverse, with *model* meaning what others think is a theory and vice versa (Botha, 1989).

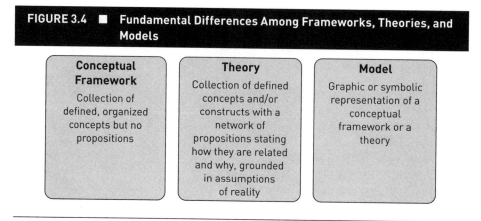

FIGURE 3.4 ■ Fundamental Differences Among Frameworks, Theories, and Models

Conceptual Framework	Theory	Model
Collection of defined, organized concepts but no propositions	Collection of defined concepts and/or constructs with a network of propositions stating how they are related and why, grounded in assumptions of reality	Graphic or symbolic representation of a conceptual framework or a theory

Judiciously careful authors would use these terms "in related but, slightly different, senses" (Mosterín, 1996, p. 72), appreciating they are different yet all concerned with conceptualizing or representing an abstract phenomenon. This chapter strives for conceptual clarity, arguing that each of the three ideas serves different roles in research; hence, there is a section on each one.

REVIEW AND ENGAGEMENT

When critically reading a research report, you would

☐ Ascertain if the authors seemed aware of the role of constructs and concepts in each of conceptual frameworks and theories

☐ Determine if they seemed to appreciate the distinction between a theory, a conceptual framework, and a model (see Figure 3.4), using appropriate and nonconfusing terminology in their paper

CONCEPTUAL FRAMEWORKS

As explained, a concept is an abstract idea that is given a name and a definition by a theorist or a researcher; that is, it is conceptualized. This conceptualization process involves forming basic ideas based on given facts, situations, and available examples (Nalzaro, 2012). It also means the theorist has expressed a mental image in words (and sometimes diagrams), enabling the theorist to communicate it with efficiency (Anderson, 2015). By pulling concepts together into one spot, researchers can create a conceptual framework. Frameworks are underlying structures that enclose and support something (Anderson, 2014), in this case, the framing of a collection of concepts around a given phenomenon.

In the realm of research, a conceptual framework is defined as a group of concepts and/or constructs that are broadly defined and systematically organized to provide a focus, a rationale, and a tool for the integration and interpretation of information and data. Usually expressed abstractly through word models, conceptual frameworks are the conceptual basis for many theories, but they can also successfully retain framework status (O'Toole, 2013; Smyth, 2004). A word model is a clear statement and description of each element (i.e., concept or construct) in the framework and any processes that link these elements to the phenomenon in question, but not to each other as does a theory (Kimmins, Blanco, Seely, Welham, & Scoullar, 2010). Although the concepts are placed in a logical and sequential design, conceptual frameworks are not as intellectually structured as a theory. Conceptual frameworks are not dependent on propositions to explain how the concepts are related to each other (Nalzaro, 2012). They are descriptive rather than predictive; thus, they are less amenable to hypothesis testing, prediction, or explanation as are theories (Ilott, Gerrish, Laker, & Bray, 2013).

The framework organizes the concepts and the constructs in a consistent way, making it easier to communicate the conceptualization to others. These frameworks are a conceptual apparatus (a complex structure) and a matrix of terminology (Botha, 1989). When developing them, researchers move through an intellectually creative process leading to a new conceptualization of a phenomenon, with supportive material. But they do not test the concepts, nor do they propose relations between them. The testing happens when scholars choose to use the concepts to create a theory, whereupon they or others validate the concepts and constructs through research (Hieke, 2015).

Conceptual frameworks creatively integrate bodies of knowledge from one or more substantive areas to generate new insights, theoretical stimuli, and research opportunities (Yadav, 2010). They emerge from the researcher's ability to "bridge existing theories [and concepts] in interesting ways, link work across disciplines, provide multi-level insights, and broaden the scope of our thinking. [The researcher creating the new framework faces the daunting task of] developing logical and complete arguments for [these] associations" (Gilson & Goldberg, 2015, pp. 127–128) (see Chapter 18). Most conceptual frameworks are accompanied with a pictorial representation, comprising simple diagrams and short summaries (word models) showing how the framework conceptualizes the issue or the process in question. These images help people make better sense of the conceptualization (Ilott et al., 2013) (see Figure 3.5 for an explanation of the essence of a conceptual framework).

Example 3.8 Conceptual framework McGregor (2014) created a conceptual framework for a phenomenon she called a sustainable life path leading to responsible, engaged, and sustainable consumption. She culled her concepts and constructs from a diverse collection of literature, culminating in the integration of seven constructs into a new conceptual framework, with a documented chain of reasoning. She conceptualized a sustainable life path as a pathfinder's lifelong, engaged journey where people consume in such a way that their examined decisions sustain all life. This pathfinder purposefully consumes with acumen in a complex world, fulfilling the role of a lifelong innovator and a moral leader. Perceiving consumers as pathfinders journeying along a life path is a new way to conceptualize consumer behavior, but her approach does not yet have theory status. The constructs are defined and logically interconnected (one builds on the other) and are related to the phenomenon, but there are no propositions (see also Box 18.1 in Chapter 18).

FIGURE 3.5 ■ Essence of a Conceptual Framework

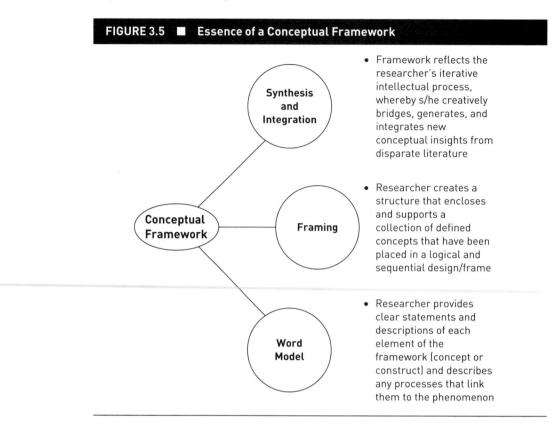

- Framework reflects the researcher's iterative intellectual process, whereby s/he creatively bridges, generates, and integrates new conceptual insights from disparate literature

- Researcher creates a structure that encloses and supports a collection of defined concepts that have been placed in a logical and sequential design/frame

- Researcher provides clear statements and descriptions of each element of the framework (concept or construct) and describes any processes that link them to the phenomenon

Example 3.9 Conceptual framework An excellent example of a conceptual framework is Bannister and Monsma's (1982) well-known consumer education classification system. It comprises 154 concepts organized along four levels. There are 3 broad, first-level concepts; 8 second-level concepts; 36 third-level concepts; and 107 fourth-level concepts. The authors provided a rationale for their framework, gave definitions for each concept/construct, and discussed in detail how they are related to the phenomenon (but not to each other); that is, they used a 22-page word model (pp. 14–36) as well as pictorial models (see Figures 3.6 and 3.7, used with permission). They did not propose propositions, meaning their contribution is not a theory. Regardless, their conceptual framework helps researchers make conceptual distinctions and organize their ideas about consumer education curricula. It captures the real world of consumer education and makes it easy to remember and apply. Their approach is the quintessential example of a conceptual framework. It is a group of concepts that are broadly defined and systematically organized to provide a focus, a rationale, and a tool for the integration and interpretation of information. Their approach is still widely used in consumer education research and practice, 35 years later (McGregor, 2010a).

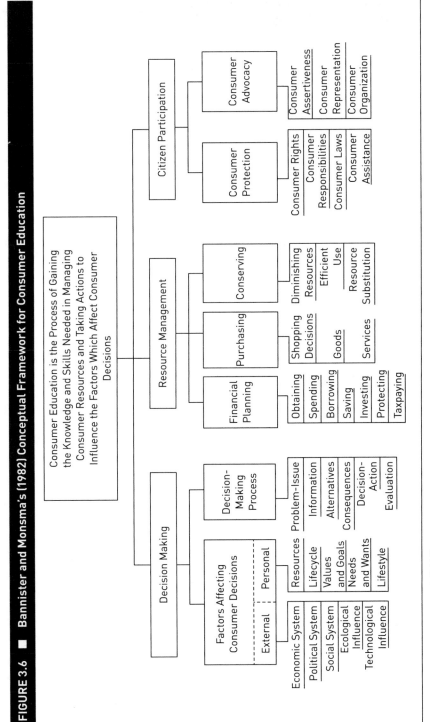

FIGURE 3.6 ■ Bannister and Monsma's (1982) Conceptual Framework for Consumer Education

Consumer Education is the Process of Gaining the Knowledge and Skills Needed in Managing Consumer Resources and Taking Actions to Influence the Factors Which Affect Consumer Decisions

Source: Bannister, R., & Monsma, C. (1982).

FIGURE 3.7 ■   **Bannister and Monsma's (1982) 154 Consumer Education Concepts**

CONCEPT NUMBERING SYSTEM

1.0   DECISION MAKING

1.1 External Factors Affecting Consumer Decisions

    1.1.1   Economic System*

        1.1.1.1   Mixed Economy

        1.1.1.2   Scarcity

        1.1.1.3   Supply and Demand

        1.1.1.4   Price

        1.1.1.5   Competition

        1.1.1.6   Economic Problems

            Unemployment

            Inflation

        *Additional economic concepts which are closely related to important consumer education concerns include: economic concentration, monetary policy, fiscal policy, productivity. economic growth, international trade, interdependence, and income distribution.

    1.1.2   Political System

        1.1.2.1   Government

        1.1.2.2   Public Policy

        1.1.2.3   Regulation

        1.1.2.4   Interest Groups

        1.1.2.5   Power

    1.1.3   Social System

        1.1.3.1   Roles

        1.1.3.2   Status

        1.1.3.3   Cultural Values

        1.1.3.4   Standard of Living

        1.1.3.5   Quality of Life

        1.1.3.6   Discrimination

        1.1.3.7   Social Change Household Composition
               Work Force Composition

        1.1.3.8   Advertising

    1.1.4   Ecological Influence

        1.1.4.1   Environmental Protection

        1.1.4.2   Conservation of Resources

        1.1.4.3   Energy Alternatives

    1.1.5   Technological Influence

        1.1.5.1   Communications Technology

        1.1.5.2   Computer Technology

        1.1.5.3   Scientific Innovation

        1.1.5.4   Engineering Advances

1.2 Personal Factors Affecting Consumer Decisions

    1.2.1   Resources

        1.2.1.1   Financial Resources

        1.2.1.2   Human Resources

            Time

            Energy

            Knowledge

            Skill

        1.2.1.3   Natural Resources

        1.2.1.4   Community Resources

    1.2.2   Lifecycle

        1.2.2.1   Age

        1.2.2.2   Income

        1.2.2.3   Household Composition

    1.2.3   Values and Goals

        1.2.3.1   Psychological Influences

        1.2.3.2   Societal Values

        1.2.3.3   Individual Values

        1.2.3.4   Value Clarification

        1.2.3.5   Goal Setting

    1.2.4   Needs and Wants

        1.2.4.1   Individual Needs

        1.2.4.2   Societal Needs

    1.2.5   Lifestyle

1.3 Decision-Making Process

    1.3.1   Problem-Issue

    1.3.2   Information

        1.3.2.1   Sources of Information

        1.3.2.2   Gathering of Information

        1.3.2.3   Availability of Information

        1.3.2.4   Costs of Information

        1.3.2.5   Evaluation of Information

    1.3.3   Alternatives

    1.3.4   Consequences

    1.3.5   Decision-Action

        1.3.5.1   Criteria

        1.3.5.2   Opportunity Cost

        1.3.5.3   Trade-Offs

        1.3.5.4   Consumer Behavior

    1.3.6   Evaluation

2.0 RESOURCE MANAGEMENT

2.1 Financial Planning

  2.1.1 Obtaining Financial Resources

    2.1.1.1 Employment Income

    2.1.1.2 Retirement Income

    2.1.1.3 Investment Income

    2.1.1.4 Public Assistance

  2.1.2 Spending Plan

    2.1.2.1 Record Keeping

    2.1.2.2 Budgeting

  2.1.3 Borrowing

    2.1.3.1 Credit Agreements

    2.1.3.2 Credit Sources

    2.1.3.3 Credit Costs

    2.1.3.4 Credit Rating

    2.1.3.5 Credit Cards

  2.1.4 Saving

  2.1.5 Investing

  2.1.6 Protecting

    2.1.6.1 Life Insurance

    2.1.6.2 Health Insurance

    2.1.6.3 Property Insurance

    2.1.6.4 Automobile Insurance

    2.1.6.5 Social Security Insurance

  2.1.7 Taxpaying

2.2 Purchasing

  2.2.1 Shopping Decisions

    2.2.1.1 Comparison Shopping

    2.2.1.2 Alternative Markets

    2.2.1.3 Contracts

  2.2.2 Goods

    2.2.2.1 Food

    2.2.2.2 Clothing

    2.2.2.3 Housing

    2.2.2.4 Furnishings and Appliances

    2.2.2.5 Transportation

    2.2.2.6 Recreation and Leisure

  2.2.3 Services

    2.2.3.1 Community Services

    2.2.3.2 Death Related Services

    2.2.3.3 Education Services

    2.2.3.4 Financial Services

    2.2.3.5 Health Services

    2.2.3.6 Legal Services

    2.2.3.7 Maintenance and Repair Services

    2.2.3.8 Government Services

2.3 Conserving

  2.3.1 Diminishing Resources

  2.3.2 Efficient Use

  2.3.3 Resource Substitution

3.0 CITIZEN PARTICIPATION

3.1 Consumer Protection

  3.1.1 Consumer Rights

    3.1.1.1 Redress

    3.1.1.2 Safety

    3.1.1.3 Information

    3.1.1.4 Choice

    3.1.1.5 Unfair Practices

  3.1.2 Consumer Responsibilities

    3.1.2.1 Ethical Behavior

    3.1.2.2 Effective Performance

    3.1.2.3 Environmental Protection

  3.1.3 Consumer Laws

    3.1.3.1 Informative Laws

    3.1.3.2 Protective Laws

    3.1.3.3 Enabling Laws

  3.1.4 Consumer Assistance

    3.1.4.1 Government Agencies

    3.1.4.2 Community Agencies

    3.1.4.3 Business Assistance

3.2 Consumer Advocacy

  3.2.1 Consumer Assertiveness

    3.2.1.1 Effective Communication

    3.2.1.2 Complaint Procedures

    3.2.1.3 Stress Management

    3.2.1.4 Conflict Resolution

  3.2.2 Consumer Representation

    3.2.2.1 Public Membership

    3.2.2.2 Regulatory Commission

    3.2.2.3 Public Hearing

    3.2.2.4 Consumer Advisory Panel

  3.2.3 Consumer Organization

    3.2.3.1 Organizing Strategies

    3.2.3.2 Action Strategies

    3.2.3.3 Consumer Groups

      State and Local Groups

      National Groups

      International Groups

      Cooperatives

Source: Bannister, R., & Monsma, C. (1982).

In summary, conceptual frameworks normally do not rise to the level of sophistication of a theory because no propositions are generated (Ellinger & Yang, 2011). They are less developed attempts at understanding phenomena than are theories, but they can serve as an organizing framework from which a more accurate theory may emerge or be derived (Castro-Palaganas, 2011; Nalzaro, 2012; The Learning House, 2016). Regardless, conceptual frameworks play a key role in research, helping scholars structure their thinking and actions around a phenomenon of interest (Ilott et al., 2013; Smyth, 2004).

Presenting a Conceptual Framework in a Research Paper

If a conceptual framework was used to help guide the study, authors have to include a section on this research element in their paper, with the appropriate heading or subheading. In this section, they should (a) identify the conceptual framework and its key architect(s). (b) If it is not well known, authors should provide the historical context for its formation, supporting its initiation and development. (c) If appropriate, authors should also identify competing frameworks and justify the use of the one they chose, relative to their research question. (d) Using present tense, they should specify any and all of the framework's concepts or constructs being used in their study to frame their work and to facilitate the analysis and interpretation of their data (Labaree, 2016). Finally, (e) they should make sure they actually *use* the conceptual framework in their study, connecting it to their literature review and to the analysis of their data (Casanave & Li, 2015; Labaree, 2016).

REVIEW AND ENGAGEMENT

When critically reading a research report, you would

☐ Determine if the authors had a separate section devoted to any conceptual framework that underpinned their study in its own titled (sub)section (e.g., *Conceptual Framework*)

☐ Ascertain if they elucidated the essence of the conceptual framework, including some combination of its architects, key concepts or constructs (their definitions), and how they are related to the phenomenon reflected in their research questions

☐ Using Table 3.7, critique their use of a conceptual framework in their paper

THEORIES

When scholars begin to discuss how the concepts and constructs in a conceptual framework are related to each other (using propositions), they have begun to theorize (i.e., form conjectures about the relationships between the concepts identified for a particular phenomenon). Theory is Greek *theoria*, "contemplation and speculation." A theory is basically a system of ideas or suppositions tendered by theorists after they have observed and contemplated a particular phenomenon that needs to be explained, understood, or predicted. Theory is also Greek *thorós*, "a spectator," someone who watches or observes (Harper, 2016). This etymological meaning reflects the fact that all theories are people's mental model of how *they* perceived reality when they *looked* at it (Aswar, 2011).

In effect, while developing a theory, someone looked at the world (i.e., observed reality or a phenomenon), *took away* some ideas (abstracted), gave these ideas names (concepts and constructs), defined them, and suggested how these ideas are related to each other (propositions) and why or how. The result is a network of propositions grounded in assumptions about the world. In combination with these assumptions, the networked relationships among the propositions form the new theory (Tavallaei & Abu Talib, 2010) (see Figure 3.8).

Overarching Types of Theories

An earlier section discussed three general types of theories as they relate to the reason for the inquiry (see Table 3.1). At a more abstract level, there are three overarching types of theories: scientific, philosophical, and mathematical (see Table 3.2). Scientific theories make testable predictions (leading to truth). Philosophical theories make verifiable or falsifiable truth claims (often used in qualitative work), and mathematical theories employ well-reasoned theorems, with proof of their truth.

Scientific theories

Scientific theories explain nature, namely "how the universe, nature, and life came to be, how they work, what they are made of, and what will become of them" (Schafersman, 1997, p. 8). Using the scientific method (see Chapter 10), researchers strive to support a scientific theory (verify it) or contradict it (falsify it) but not to prove it. A scientific theory cannot be proven; rather, it makes predictions about the natural world that are testable by experiments or observations. Any disagreement between prediction and experiment/observation

FIGURE 3.8 ■ Essence of a Theory

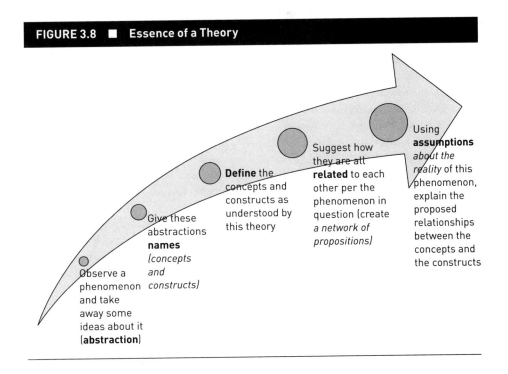

TABLE 3.2 ■ Three Overarching Types of Theory		
Scientific	**Philosophical**	**Mathematical**
Makes *predictions* about the world that are *testable* by experiments or observations of natural phenomena (empirical data); the theory works if reality behaves as predicted	Concerned with ideas and comprises philosophical statements and positions (*truth claims*) reflecting principles, laws, rules, and paradoxes	Made of *theorems* (purely abstract, formal statements, supported with a chain of reasoning) expressed as *proofs* (arguments attesting to the truth of the statements, the theorem)

demonstrates the incorrectness of the scientific theory (falsifies it) or at least limits its accuracy or domain of validity.

In fact, one of the tasks of science and research is to find out whether a theory works (is satisfied or realized) or fails. If a theory works, it means that what was studied behaved within the constraints imposed by the theory (i.e., its assumptions, tenets, and propositions). If the theory does not work, it means the phenomenon being studied did not behave as *proposed* by the theory. The phenomenon *is what it is*, whether humans understand it or not. Humans have to adjust their theories to the phenomena.

> ***Example 3.10 Scientific theories*** Examples include biology (cell theory, germ theory, evolution), physics (theories of relativity, quantum mechanics), and chemistry (collision theory, molecular theory). Other scientific theories include climate change theory and geology (plate tectonics) (Schafersman, 1997).

Qualitative theories

Compared to the scientific method (quantitative research), some qualitative research starts in the absence of theory, with the assumption that a deep comprehension of a real-world phenomenon, event, or experience cannot always be based on theory, nor does it need to be. Qualitative researchers can collect data about a phenomenon and then mine the data to see if a theory emerges. Such theories are said to be *grounded in the data*, rather than confirmed or falsified by the data. Once the new grounded theory emerges, others can then test it or apply it (Creswell, 2009; Denzin & Lincoln, 2011). In short, because the intent is to gain deep understandings of phenomena from those experiencing it, qualitative research really cannot be based on theory developed by someone who has not lived the experience (Tavallaei & Abu Talib, 2010).

> ***Example 3.11 Qualitative theories*** Grounded theory generates a new theory from the data, ethnographical data are interpreted with an existing theory, constructivists build toward a consensus rather than theory, and some phenomenological researchers set aside theory altogether (Paley, 2008; Tavallaei & Abu Talib, 2010).

Philosophical theories

Philosophical theories are concerned with ideas rather than empirical data. Their truth claims (assumptions and propositions) may or may not be empirical, but they are still statements that the theorist, and those who use the theory, accept as true. The definition of what is a theory is more hazy for philosophical than for scientific theories. Philosophical theories often comprise philosophical statements and philosophical positions, which reflect principles, hypotheses, rules, laws, even paradoxes (statements contrary to accepted opinion). These positions can be based on belief systems, ideologies, worldviews, religions, and schools of thought (Bothamley, 2004).

> ***Example 3.12 Philosophical theories*** Examples include critical theory, economic theories, sociology theories, psychology theories, ethical theories, and political theories, such as theories of justice. Regarding critical theory, it relates to a wide variety of political, literary, and philosophical positions that take at least some of their inspiration from the Frankfurt School of thought and its dialectic. Critical theory typically contests the possibility of objectivity or aloofness from political positions and privileges, believing instead that people must engage with and critique the privileged ideology so they can be emancipated from its oppressive regimes (Bohman, 2005).

Mathematical theories and theorems

Examples of mathematical theories include chaos theory, game theory, field theory, and set theory. They each have their own collection of concepts, propositions, and assumptions (Bothamley, 2004). Although not covered in this book, mathematical *theorems* are purely abstract formal statements, expressed in proofs, which are arguments trying to convince people that something is true. A theorem is a general proposition not self-evident but proved by a chain of reasoning, presented in a proof, which is Latin *preove*, "evidence to establish a fact" (Harper, 2016).

Rather than using experiments or other empirical evidence, the concept of a theorem is deductive. Proofs are expressed using mathematical symbols, formulas, or narrative scripts, and they comprise logically organized and clearly worded informal arguments. These well-reasoned arguments are intended to convince readers of the truth of the statement of the theorem beyond any doubt (see Figure 3.9).

FIGURE 3.9   ■   Example of a Mathematical Proof

Proof. Let λ be the linear transformation $Df(a)$. Then λ is non-singular, since det $f'(a) \neq 0$. Now $D(\lambda^{-1} \circ f)(a) = D(\lambda^{-1})(f(a)) \circ Df(a) = \lambda^{-1} \circ Df(a)$ is the identity linear transformation. If the theorem is true for $\lambda^{-1} \circ f$, it is clearly true for f. Therefore we may assume at the outset that λ is the identity. Thus whenever $f(a + h) = f(a)$, we have

$$\frac{|f(a+h) - f(a) - \lambda(h)|}{|h|} = \frac{|h|}{|h|} = 1.$$

Example 3.13 Mathematical theory Pythagoras's theorem has 370 known proofs, or approaches to proving the theorem, which states that, in a triangle, the square of the hypotenuse (the side opposite the right angle) is equal to the sum of the squares of the other two sides (Wikipedia Encyclopedia, 2016c).

Disciplinary Theories

Table 3.3 provides examples of popular theories organized by the disciplines that propagate and employ them. Normally, disciplines are focused on respectively different phenomena, meaning they tend to develop discipline-oriented, phenomenon-specific theories. Disciplines speak different languages and use particular concepts, meaning they do not look at (a) the world the same way, (b) the same phenomena, or (c) similar phenomena in the same way (Del Favero, 2005). However, every disciplinary, theoretical perspective suggests a reasonable explanation of a phenomenon, with these multiple theoretical orientations serving as the bedrock of social sciences (Tavallaei & Abu Talib, 2010).

Purposes of Theory in Research

Researchers need theories for several reasons: (a) They provide a framework for conceptualizing a study and for analyzing data, which derive significance from the theory. (b) Theories are fodder for research questions and hypotheses that individual researchers can explore or test in their study. (c) They help academic fields and areas of specialization develop and advance. This is possible when integrated theory is developed through consistent theory-building methods, contributing to the efficient creation of an integrated disciplinary body of knowledge about particular aspects of the world. (d) Theories also provide clear insights into some aspect of reality, which in turn makes practice more meaningful and effective (Ary, Jacobs, & Sorensen, 2010; Creswell, 2009; Wacker, 1998; Wiersma & Jurs, 2009). (e) As scholars integrate isolated knowledge into theoretical frameworks, further areas in need of investigation become evident. In this way, developed theories can stimulate new discoveries and insights. (f) Theories can be used to give old data new interpretations and new meaning. (g) They can provide members of a discipline with a common language and a frame of reference for their research and practice. (h) Finally, their use can inspire new responses to problems that previously lacked solutions (Labaree, 2016) (see Table 3.4). A conscientious author would speak to how theory is benefiting their scholarship for the particular study.

Deductive Versus Inductive Theory

When considering the role of theory in their research design, authors can benefit from knowing the difference between deductive and inductive approaches (see Figure 3.10). Deductive reasoning entails an author using an *existing* theory by proposing hypotheses to test or to modify the theory. Hypotheses are educated hunches about what is thought to be, as proposed by the theory (see Chapters 10 and 12). They are general statements derived from the theory's propositions and applied to a specific case. Results from the study are used to support or refute the theory (but not to prove it) (de Vaus, 2001; Ellinger & Yang, 2011).

TABLE 3.3 ■ Examples of Popular Theories, Organized by Discipline

Discipline (and Specific Phenomena)	Names of Discipline-Specific Theories
Education theories (practice of educating, teaching, and learning)	• Constructivist theory • Critical pedagogy • Multiple intelligence theory • Motivational theory • Cognitivism • Behaviorism • Conflict theory • Functionalism • Social mobility theory • Cultural theories of education (identity) • Progressive education theory
Economic theories (production, consumption, and transfer of income and wealth)	• Classical • Keynesian • Marxist • Market socialist • Behavioral • Feminist • Ecological • Rational choice • Public choice
Leadership theories (guiding, directing, or managing a group)	• Integral • Transformative • Servant • Transactional • Spiritual and ethical • Principle centered • Contingency • Situational • Behavioral
Sociological theories (development, structure, and functioning of human society)	• Symbolic interaction • Conflict • Systems • Structural-functional • Feminist • Social learning • Role • Social constructivist • Social constructionist

TABLE 3.4 ■ Purposes of Theory in Research

Theories

- Help conceptualize a study
- Provide fodder and inspiration for research questions and hypotheses
- Can be used to analyze data
- Give old data new interpretation or meaning
- Develop and advance a discipline and its specializations (body of knowledge)
- Make practice more meaningful and effective
- Stimulate new discoveries, insights, and lines of research inquiry
- Provide disciplines with a common vocabulary/jargon and a frame of reference for their research and scholarship

FIGURE 3.10 ■ Deductive Versus Inductive Approaches

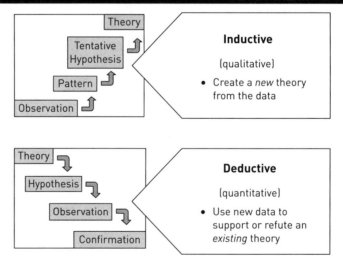

On the other hand, inductive approaches entail the author conducting a study to develop a *new* theory because of a lack of theory for a specific phenomenon. Inductive reasoning involves taking information that is gathered through research and deriving a general statement or a theory to describe the underlying principles of the observed phenomenon. The theory emerges from the data. This new theory will contain assumptions, concepts, and a set of relational statements (propositions) and normally arise from grounded theory research designs. Qualitative researchers usually use an inductive approach, but they can turn to deductive approaches by using existing theory to develop interview protocols or to aid in data analysis (de Vaus, 2001; Ellinger & Yang, 2011).

REVIEW AND ENGAGEMENT

When critically reading a research report, you would

☐ Take a moment to see if the authors referred to which type of theory they were using (Tables 3.2 and 3.3) or provided enough information for you to deduce it

☐ Per Table 3.4, ascertain if they commented on why they thought using a theory in their study would be beneficial

---

Elements of a Theory

Theories comprise several fundamental building blocks, namely (a) assumptions; (b) concepts and/or constructs and their theoretical definitions; (c) propositions that state how the concepts are related to each other and why; and, sometimes, (d) variables expressed in hypotheses, although the latter are usually posed by researchers for their study, not by a theorist (Botha, 1989; Wacker, 1998) (see Figure 3.8 and Table 3.5). In effect, "the three defining characteristics of a theory are that it (a) is 'a set of interrelated propositions, concepts and definitions that present a systematic point of view'; (b) specifies relationships between/among concepts; and (c) explains and/or makes predictions about the occurrence of events, based on specified relationships" (Imenda, 2014, p. 187). Qualitative theories emerge from the data and focus on meaning and interpretation rather than on predictions (Ellinger & Yang, 2011). When completed, qualitative theories also contain these basic elements (i.e., assumptions, concepts, and propositions). Each of assumptions, propositions, and hypotheses is now discussed.

Assumptions

Assume is Latin *assumere*, "to take" (Harper, 2016). If people assume something, they *take* for granted that it is true, without proof or evidence. Theories are based on a set of assumptions about reality, and these assumptions reflect the theorist's worldview (Ellinger & Yang, 2011). Assumptions are often called the basic tenets of a theory. A tenet is a central principle or belief also proclaimed as true without proof. Using these assumptions, theorists draw conclusions. Because assumptions are one of the key building blocks of a theory, the glue that holds everything together, the theorist must spell them out (Nkwake, 2013).

Indeed, most people believe that a theory is only as good as its assumptions, which must be true. Others are less concerned with truth, caring instead if the assumptions are useful for understanding the phenomenon in question (e.g., qualitative researchers). Either way, the assumptions made by a theorist about a phenomenon must be plausible (i.e., within the realm of possibility), or else the theory is rendered worthless (Arena, 2012).

TABLE 3.5 ■ Basic Elements of a Theory		
Element of a Theory	**Definition**	**Lay Questions**
Domain or phenomenon being considered	The exact setting or circumstance explained by the theory, and where the theory will be applied	When? Where?
Assumptions	A statement thought to be true without proof (taken for granted)	What?
Concepts and constructs	Ideas conceived and named by theorists after observing reality	Who? What?
Theoretical definition of concepts and constructs	What a concept or construct means in a *particular* theory	
Network of propositions: concepts and constructs arranged into a system using propositions that propose how they are related to each other	Propositions are statements expressing an opinion about how two concepts are related to each other, put forward for others' consideration (posed by theorists and/or researchers)	How? Why?
Variables related to each other, framed as hypotheses	A supposition based on limited information (hypothesis) about how something might change (variable) (posed by researchers)	
Predictive claims (if it is an explanatory theory)	A statement made now about a possible future event (no proof yet)	Could? Should? Would?
Associative claims	A statement made about how two concepts are *related* to each other but do not cause each other	Could? Should? Would?

Example 3.14 Assumptions Classic economic theory assumes that consumers have perfect information, are not affected by their values, know exactly what they want, and make rational choices (Colander, 2013) (see Box 3.1). In real life, these assumptions hardly ever hold up, meaning the theory *should* be deemed worthless; yet, inexplicably, classical economic theory remains a dominant theory informing marketing practice and public policy.

Propositions

To recap, concepts are the names or labels people use to identify an idea and bring it to others' attention. Each theory has a unique collection of concepts, which are defined especially for *that* theory. Concepts are the vocabulary that scholars use when employing a particular theory (Aswar, 2011). That theory is held together with a network or set of systemically ordered propositions. These are *relational statements* about how two or more

BOX 3.1

- Classical economic theory—all about the allocation of scarce resources (the **phenomenon**)

Assumptions (also called basic tenets):

- Rational man (people always make rational choices)

- Perfect information

- Scarcity of resources

- People are not influenced by values or beliefs

- Profit maximization

- Market equilibrium (supply equals demand)

- Self-interest and self-control (individualism)

- Liberate the market from any government intervention

Basic concepts/constructs, each with a definition specific to *this* theory, often differing from lay definitions:

- Profit

- Prices

- Competition

- Demand

- Supply

- Utility

- Marginal utility

- Diminishing marginal utility

- Opportunity costs

- Comparative advantage

- Elasticity

- Substitutes and complements

- Externalities

- Efficiency

Some key propositions:

- Law of supply and demand (the proposed relationship between these two terms is that the higher the demand, the lower the supply [because people will have bought everything]; the higher the supply, the lower the demand)

- Law of diminishing returns (the continuing application of effort or skill toward a particular project or goal declines in effectiveness after a certain level of result has been achieved)

- Price elasticity of demand (determined by the price of the item or service, availability of alternative goods, amount of time being measured, consumer income, and whether the item or service is considered to be a necessity or a luxury)

- Price and demand (the higher the prices, the lower the consumer demand for a product)

concepts are related to each other (Castro-Palaganas, 2011). Propose is Latin *proponere*, "to put forward" (Harper, 2016). In effect, when developing propositions, theorists put forward ideas about how one concept is related to another and why (Mosterín, 1996) (see Box 18.2 in Chapter 18).

Theorists can draw on three approaches to conceive and justify their propositions: (a) They can draw on previous research (empirical results, qualitative findings, or mixed methods integrated outcomes), using other people's ideas about how two concepts are connected. (b) They can draw on the practice literature or their personal experience to justify a proposition. And (c) they can use logical reasoning, leading to sound theoretical explanations for their propositions. The latter is the highest standard, the crucial part of theory development, but the other two approaches often provide valuable support, or at least inspiration (Webster & Watson, 2002; Whetten, 1989).

A theory's set of propositional statements is arranged in a logically (internally consistent) interrelated system (Castro-Palaganas, 2011; Imenda, 2014; Wacker, 1998). The proposed relationships can be positive or negative, direct or indirect; they can have a high or low magnitude; and some relationships are mediated by other concepts or variables (Creswell, 2009) (see Chapters 11 and 12). As a caveat, although each proposition flows from the basic tenets of the theory, no one propositional statement "encapsulates ALL that the theory entails" (Lynch, 2013, p. 11).

> ***Example 3.15 Proposition stated using two concepts*** In economic theory (see Box 3.1), a key proposition is that consumer demand goes down when prices go up. The *proposed* relationship is inverse, meaning when one goes up, the other goes down. The two theoretical concepts are *demand* and *price*. Price is usually defined as the amount of money required, expected, or given in exchange for something. In economic theory, price is the dollar figure (*asking price*) placed on a product by a seller. The actual price paid by the consumer is called the *transaction price*. In *this* theory, demand does not mean to insist on having something; rather, it means whether consumers want, can afford, and are willing to pay for a product or service. According to this theory, all three dimensions of demand have to present for consumer demand to exist. People may have lots of money and want something but are not willing to pay the asking price. Or, they may want something badly, are willing to pay the asking price, but do not have the money.

Hypotheses

Propositions explain the theoretical relationships between the concepts and are vital for hypothesis formulation and testing (Ilott et al., 2013). The set of propositional statements is arranged in a logically interrelated system that permits researchers to derive new statements in the form of hypotheses (Castro-Palaganas, 2011). Because each proposition is "a *single* potentially testable component of a theory," researchers can develop hypotheses for each empirical study they conduct (Lynch, 2013, p. 11). A hypothesis is a statement that can be falsified through research; in other words, it can be disproved. When stating hypotheses, researchers have to define their main concepts, which arise from the theory (see Chapters 10 and 12 for more on hypotheses). Normally, theorists create propositions, while researchers conducting studies form hypotheses (and state these using variables, as described in Chapter 11). A hypothesis is a prediction about why things happen the way they do, *as explained by the theory*.

> ***Example 3.16 Theory, proposition, and hypothesis***
>
> **Theory:** Durkheim's theory of modernization (it explains why modern societies hold together rather than fragment into chaos or anarchy)
>
> **Concepts:** Division of labor and anomie (a state of isolation and anxiety resulting from a lack of social control and regulations)
>
> **Proposition:** Societal development of a *division of labor* (concept) generates *anomie* (concept).
>
> **Hypothesis:** Societies with a more heterogeneous occupational structure will have members with higher levels of anxiety.

Note that this hypothesis operationalized the two theoretical concepts of *division of labor* and *anomie* as, respectively, heterogeneous occupational structure and anxiety (the measurable variables in this study) (Lynch, 2013).

When writing their journal article, authors can present the hypotheses used in their study by using one of three approaches: (a) They can present a series of if–then logic statements that explain why they expect one variable to influence another (citing appropriate literature). What they think will happen (*if* I do this, *then* this will happen) should be based on their preliminary research. They are not simply guessing or pulling the if–then statement out of thin air; instead, they are making an educated guess based on what they already know and what they have already learned from their research and their critical review and synthesis of the literature. (b) They can also present a listed series of hypotheses, prefaced or followed with a literature review.

Example 3.17 If–then hypothesis statement In his theory about consumer socialization from a life cycle perspective, Moschis (1986) presented 197 propositions. Each numbered proposition (usually an if–then statement of some manner) was prefaced with a several-paragraph-long supportive argument, citing relevant literature. As an example, after citing and explaining the contributory relevance of 18 different sources from his research and his literature review, Moschis offered "*Proposition 8.1: Consumer education courses at school are more effective when they teach skills relevant to present and immediate consumption needs than when they teach skills relevant to needs in the distant future*" (p. 194). In effect, this if–then logic statement says that *if* consumer education courses at school teach skills relevant to present and immediate consumption needs, *then* the courses will be more effective than when skills relevant to needs in the distant future are taught.

Example 3.18 Series (list) of hypotheses, prefaced with literature review After presenting a four-page review of literature about anticonsumption lifestyles, materialistic societies, and mortality salience (MS) (citing about 50 different pieces of literature), Nepomuceno and Laroche (2016, p. 127) listed two numbered hypotheses for their study, prefaced with three *given that/we expect* statements: "Given that worldviews are further endorsed when death is made salient, and given that high anticonsumption individuals do not endorse a worldview that consumption is desirable, we expect that high anticonsumption individuals should not have their propensity to consume changed after death is made salient. Conversely, given that worldviews are further endorsed when death is made salient and considering that low anticonsumption individuals support a worldview that more consumption is desirable, we expect that low anticonsumption individuals should increase their propensity to consume in a MS condition. Therefore, we test:

$H1_a$: Relative to the control condition, low-frugality individuals exposed to MS are less inclined to resist consumption, whereas high-frugality individuals are equally inclined to resist consumption in the MS and control conditions.

$H1_b$: Relative to the control condition, low-voluntary simplicity individuals exposed to MS are less inclined to resist consumption, whereas high-voluntary simplicity individuals are equally inclined to resist consumption in the MS and control conditions."

Third, (c) authors can use visual models that translate the variables and their proposed interconnections into a visual picture, called *causal modeling* (see Figure 3.11). These models illustrate the causal mechanisms of a system or a process. The causal modeling approach is especially useful when authors are concerned with intervening and mediating variables (see Chapter 11). These models (visual tools) use labels, lines, and arrows (Creswell, 2009).

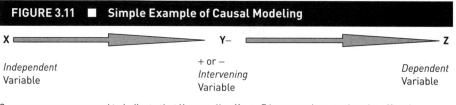

FIGURE 3.11 ■ Simple Example of Causal Modeling

X ⟶ Y– ⟶ Z

Independent
Variable

+ or –
Intervening
Variable

Dependent
Variable

One-way arrows are used to indicate that X normally affects Z in a negative way, but the effect is mediated by Y (can be positive or negative). An example might be that driving while drunk (X) effects ability to drive safely (Z), moderated by how many drinks are consumed, and in what time frame (Y–).

Characteristics of a Good Theory

Authors should be able to judge whether the theory they chose to undergird their study is a good theory (Johnson & Christensen, 2012). Table 3.6 profiles the fundamental virtues of a good theory (Cramer, 2013; Patterson, 1983; Wacker, 1998), with Wacker advising authors that any theory used for research should be weighed against these virtues. To err on the safe side, the theory, at a minimum, must meet the criteria of internal consistency and refutation (achieved via empirical riskiness). Regarding the latter, every study should be designed to disprove a theory. The harder it is to disprove, the better the theory is at explaining, predicting, understanding, or controlling some aspect of reality (Wacker, 1998).

Wacker (1998) also warned that "since theories tie together many concepts, it usually is not easy to identify internal inconsistency" (p. 366). This is because phenomena are

REVIEW AND ENGAGEMENT

When critically reading a research report, you would

- ☐ Determine if the authors chose to present a series of if–then logic statements, which explained the reasoning for their research questions or hypotheses, and used the theory's elements to justify them

- ☐ Ascertain if they chose instead to identify the research questions or hypotheses as a whole (in a list), prefaced or followed with an overview of the theory and the literature that informed them

- ☐ Determine if the authors effectively used causal modeling to present their hypotheses

- ☐ In a qualitative paper using a grounded theory method, determine if they placed the description of the new theory that emerged from the study after the Discussion section, in its own titled section. Did they comment on their use of inductive logic?

often complex, meaning it is a challenge to identify *all* propositions that form the network structure of a theory; nonetheless, authors should remain vigilant. They need to minimize their usage of theories that have not been legitimated, unless the intent of their study is to contribute to that cause. Chinn and Kramer (1998) added three additional criteria: clarity, empirical precision, and derivable consequences. Finally, Lincoln and Lynham (2007) contributed the two criteria of saturated and grounded in context (for grounded theory, which emerges from the data) (see Table 3.6).

TABLE 3.6 ■ Characteristics of a Good Theory	
Theory Traits	**Explanations**
Parsimonious	The fewer the assumptions, the better (simple and not overly complex)
Unique	Different from other theories
Conservative	Superior to existing theories (else the latter can be conserved)
Clear and precise	Easy to understand with a good logical flow, meaning all concepts are theoretically defined, relational propositions are provided, and a model pictorially illustrates the theory (the internal connections)
Internally consistent	Identifies *all* pertinent relationships (propositions), with explanations
Abstract	Integrates *many* internally consistent relationships (propositions) and variables at the highest level of abstraction (i.e., a grand theory instead of a middle or low theory, which are also essential to research)
Empirically precise	Concepts and constructs must be measurable so research can support the theory's premises and assumptions (also called operational)
Saturated	A grounded theory is saturated with exemplars of the phenomenon
Refutable	Can withstand questioning and be proven right or wrong. Also, its predictions must be risky rather than always certain
Generalizable	Able to explain phenomena in many domains
Fecund	Generates many rich hypotheses and research questions, expanding research into new areas and provoking new thinking and development of ideas
Practical	Useful to practitioners in informing and helping them understand their practice as well as useful in organizing their thinking and practice (provides a sensible application of principles)
Derivable consequences	Real-world applications informed by the theory should lead to social, political, and environmentally responsible practice; also, interpretivist theory needs to be grounded in the context or genesis of the theory

WRITING THE THEORETICAL OR CONCEPTUAL FRAMEWORK SECTION OF A PAPER

Johnson and Christensen (2012) cautioned that readers may not always see the word *theory* in a paper because they are simply not available for some phenomena, or those that exist are too underdeveloped to be used in a study yet. Goodson (2017) agreed, noting that not all authors discuss or even adopt a theory for their study. For those who do, the following conventions can be followed.

Theory in Quantitative Papers

If authors of quantitative papers *do* choose to underpin their study with a conceptual framework or a theory (with or without a supportive or a stand-alone model), they need to describe it in their article. Authors can (a) have a separate section with the appropriate title; (b) weave the theory's explanation into, or place it at the end of, the literature review section; or (c) place it after the hypothesis or research question (Creswell, 2009). If they choose a separate section, appropriate headings include *Theoretical Framework*, *Theoretical Perspective*, *Conceptual Framework*, *Theory*, and sometimes *Theoretical Model* (Labaree, 2016).

Theory in Qualitative Papers

In qualitative research, the theory can appear (a) early in the paper if an existing theory is being used as an orienting perspective or (b) at the end of the paper if a new theory is being reported from the data. In the latter, instead of being used to set up the study, the theory emerges *from* the study. In the former, authors choose an existing theoretical lens or perspective and use it to help frame questions, inform the research design, interpret results, and provide ultimate calls to action. Examples of such perspectives (theories) are critical, feminist, cultural/racial/ethnic, radicalized discourse, queer theory, and disability inquiry (Creswell, 2009). As noted earlier, grounded theory generates a *new* theory from the data, ethnographical data are interpreted with an *existing* theory, and some phenomenological researchers *set aside* theory altogether (Tavallaei & Abu Talib, 2010). Mixed methods researchers can use theory either deductively (quantitative) or inductively (qualitative) and should report it accordingly (Creswell, 2009).

Elucidate Essence of the Theory

"Theoretical and conceptual frameworks typically reflect the assumptions and world-views that the author is making about the phenomenon to be studied" (Ellinger & Yang, 2011, p. 119). These research methodologies are instrumental in framing the research question (see Chapters 2 and 6) and in helping authors choose a relevant theory. In their article, authors need to identify the theory and its architects, briefly explain its key assumptions pursuant to their research question, and identify any pertinent concepts or constructs (with their definitions), as well as propositions or hypotheses used in their study (Goodson, 2017). If using a conceptual framework, the same advice applies, except there are no propositions to report.

Explicating the theory or conceptual framework affirms the authors' familiarity with and understanding of any theories and concepts related to their research question(s) or hypotheses (Casanave & Li, 2015). It also shows that they are able to connect their study to the larger body of knowledge, both content and theory (Johnson & Christensen, 2012; Labaree, 2016; Wiersma & Jurs, 2009). As a reminder, when a theory is used, its percepts, assumptions, and propositions guide the study. When a conceptual framework is used, its concepts and constructs guide the study (Plakhotnik & Rocco, 2009).

REVIEW AND ENGAGEMENT

When critically reading a research report, you would

- ☐ Determine if the authors actually used a theory to guide their study
- ☐ Check to see if they discussed why they chose a particular theory to address their particular research question
- ☐ Determine if they, ideally, had a separate section devoted to the theory that underpinned the study, in its own titled section (e.g., *Theoretical Framework, Theoretical Perspective, Theory*)
- ☐ If they did not have a separate theory section, ascertain if they at least wove the theory's explanation into, or placed it at the end of, the Literature Review section, with a subheading (e.g., *Theoretical Framework*)
- ☐ If they used an *existing* theory to underpin a qualitative study, check to see that they placed the theory overview early in the paper, which may not have a formal Literature Review section
- ☐ Determine if the authors elucidated the essence of the theory used in their study, including some combination of its architects, key assumptions, key concepts or constructs, and any propositions or hypotheses used for *their* study

Justify Theory Selected for Study

Authors should include a discussion of why they chose a particular theory, conceptual framework, or model and explain why alternatives were rejected for this research question (Casanave & Li, 2015). In both instances, this entails identifying key theorists and noting relevant literature. They should explicitly link the theory, conceptual framework, or model *and* the topic of their study, instead of expecting readers to infer it. And authors should explain any limitations of the theory they selected for their study. If they adapted an existing theory to suit their purpose, they should describe the adaptation, including any new constructs developed for their study. If they developed a new conceptual framework or model for their study, its genesis should be laid out as well, or they should refer to previous publications that explained it (Goodson, 2017; Labaree, 2016).

Furthermore, any theory selected should reflect the reason for the inquiry (see Figure 3.1). Theories, in combination with research methodology, provide the basis for any research questions or hypotheses and for the author's choice of research methods (Goodson, 2017; Labaree, 2016). The final choice of a theory for a quantitative study may not be made until the literature has been fully reviewed, allowing that, sometimes, authors intend to test a particular theory. As noted before, in qualitative research, the intent of the inquiry is to understand a phenomenon through the eyes of those experiencing it. Any theory normally emerges *from* the data and is then added to the field's body of knowledge for others to test or apply (Labaree, 2016).

Use Theory to Interpret Data

Theories have a special role to play in interpreting the results of a *quantitative* study. A theory enables authors to "intellectually transition from simply describing a phenomenon [of interest] to generalizing about various aspects of that phenomenon" (Labaree, 2016). Then, during their Discussion and Conclusions sections, the theory helps authors "identify the limits of those generalizations" to populations beyond their sample (Labaree, 2016). Indeed, theories provide a foundation for quantitative research to be meaningful. They help authors attach meaning to their data and place the data in proper perspective as determined by the tenets of the theory (Ellinger & Yang, 2011).

Because data from a *qualitative* study can be used to inductively generate a new theory, the theory gains significance from the data (and the data gain significance and meaning from the researcher, who interprets data selectively chosen to build the theory) (Schram, 2006).

Conversely, data from a quantitative study "derive significance from the theory" (Wiersma & Jurs, 2009, p. 21). In fact, several people could approach a raw data set and come away with very different interpretations depending on the theory they use (Harris, 2014; Jacobs, 2011), as demonstrated in example 3.19.

> ***Example 3.19 Various theoretical interpretations of a phenomenon*** As an example, the research problem and the study's data pertain to a couple who are getting divorced. Different theories have different foci, meaning they bring different interpretations of this phenomenon. To illustrate, *exchange* theory explains change and stability in a relationship as a process of negotiated exchanges between parties. *Family systems* theory posits that individuals can be understood not in isolation from one another but rather as a part of their family, an emotional unit. *Symbolic interaction* theory holds that people are active in shaping their world, rather than being acted upon by society. And *structural-functional* theory looks at the social structures that shape society as well as the functions of society's main elements, including norms, customs, traditions, and institutions. Each of these theories assumes different things about this couple's reality, respectively: (a) They individually negotiated themselves into a divorce, (b) their divorce cannot be understood without referring to what is going on in their family, (c) they made their own mess (cannot blame society), and (d) their divorce can be explained in terms of society's norms about fidelity and its views on marriage and divorce as institutions. The interpretation of the data is greatly shaped by the theoretical lens.

Critiquing Theory in a Paper

On a final note, authors need to be aware of several issues pursuant to choosing and then using a theory to frame their research, and critical readers need to be aware of this when critiquing the theory element of a research report. These issues range from not having any theory at all, through choosing the wrong theory, to having a theory and not using it in the study (Casanave & Li, 2015) (see Table 3.7).

TABLE 3.7 ■ Issues With Choosing and Using a Conceptual Framework or Theory to Frame Research	
Issues When Choosing and Using a Conceptual Framework or Theory to Frame a Study	**Explanation**
No theory or framework	Because no theory or framework is used, readers are unable to clearly discern the author's assumptions underlying the study (methodological, theoretical, or conceptual); no theory is indicative of the author's inability to work within such a framing. It is possible that no theory exists to be used.
Inappropriate theory or framework	The chosen theory does not fit with the research question or the purpose of the study.
Framework or theory is not used to interpret data	The author fails to use the theory or framework to help interpret findings or results or to write a discussion (there is no further mention of theory after it was introduced earlier in the paper).
Imbalance between data and framework or theory	Either (a) there is a heavy focus on data interpretation with too little connection back to the theory or (b) the author has heavy discussion of theory and too little data reported.
Incomplete, superficial, or inconsistent treatment of theory or framework	The author either (a) leaves out pertinent parts of the theory or framework, (b) provides only surface-level coverage with no depth, or (c) focuses too narrowly on certain parts.
Misinterpretation of theory or framework	Due to unfamiliarity with the theory or framework, the author erroneously applies it, not fully understanding its assumptions.
Pay lip service to theory or framework	The author uses a popular or expected-to-use theory or framework without fully understanding it or fully using it to interpret the study (e.g., tossing in things, name dropping).
Inappropriate use of popular and attractive theory or framework	The author thinks that linking work to faddish theories and concepts (especially buzzwords) will attract people to a paper; this action misrepresents the study to readers.
Missing influential theory or conceptual framework	The author fails to draw on key, influential theories or frameworks (due to lack of familiarity with, or lack of understanding of, their theoretical and conceptual contributions).
Fail to link theory or framework to a specific research methodology	By not identifying a specific research methodology (e.g., critical, interpretive, empirical), the author conveys naïveté as a researcher; that is, the author's lack of appreciation for how methodology and theory choice is interlinked.

REVIEW AND ENGAGEMENT

When critically reading a research report, you would

☐ Determine if the authors revealed any adaptations they made to an *existing* theory to suit their particular research purposes, and then if they demonstrated that their adaptations met the characteristics of a good theory (see Table 3.6)

☐ Ascertain if they actually used their selected theory to interpret their data (i.e., did not explain it and then not use it)

☐ Discern if they commented on the notion that their data could be interpreted quite differently by using alternate theories

☐ Judge if they appreciated that, in quantitative research, the data derive significance from the theory (while a qualitative theory gains significance from the data)

☐ Using Table 3.7, critique their use of a theory in their paper

MODELS

Both theories and conceptual frameworks can be represented using models, which are symbolic representations that help theorists and researchers express ideas with minimal words (Castro-Palaganas, 2011; Nalzaro, 2012). Model is Latin *modulus*, "a small measure or standard" (Harper, 2016). Models have a lower normative status than theories because they are derived from theories (Klein & Romero, 2007). Actually, Goldfarb and Ratner (2008) called models "theory wannabes," acknowledging that some models *can* gain theory status. They explained that theories often include a model, but "a theory does not require a 'model' and a 'model' is not sufficient for a 'theory'" (p. 93).

Models are visible or tangible renderings of an idea that is difficult or impossible to display just in words. The actual image, as well as the attendant mental images (the mind's eye), better helps people access deep and complex phenomena. Models are very useful when people cannot directly observe a phenomenon yet it has been empirically (or otherwise) shown to exist (admin, 2015a; *Boundless*, 2016). Models serve to represent both complex theoretical formulations and interrelationships between multiple variables and constructs (Drotar, 2009; Johnson & Christensen, 2012). Often, a model leaves out some elements of the theory or selectively simplifies or expounds on them. In practice, authors may choose to represent only the elements of the original model that are relevant to the problem or issue being examined in their study (Castro-Palaganas, 2011; Macefield, 2006; Nalzaro, 2012; van Maarseveen & van der Tang, 1978).

Models can be viewed as a way to map out or visualize theoretical threads thereby forming diagrammatic representations of the interrelatedness of concepts expressed as propositions. The resultant model can be an inspiring mental image, with a good example being the pyramid usually used to represent Maslow's hierarchy of needs (Sinclair, 2007). Another familiar model, used by physicists, is the planetary model of an atom representing atomic theory, which comprises the constructs of proton, neutron, electron, and nucleus and how they are related and why (i.e., propositions tested and proven via hypotheses in scientific experiments) (see Figure 3.12).

FIGURE 3.12 ■ Model of Atomic Theory

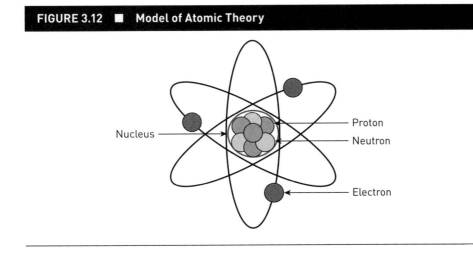

A third example is the model illustrating the basics of economic theory's circular flow of money (see Figure 3.13). The theory holds that firms hire people to build and/or deliver their products and services (paid with wages, salaries, commissions, tips). Laborers use that income within their household as consumers (spend, save, invest) via retailers and lending institutions. Firms and consumers pay money to governments in the form of taxes, and that money flows back to them in the form of public services, subsidies, and governments' procurement of services (Colander, 2013).

Models can be physical, symbolic (graphic), or verbal. Because they are devoid of unnecessary details, they can help clarify people's understandings of a theoretical notion; that is, models contain only the parts necessary to explain the essence of the concept or an idea. They are often depicted using diagrams such as maps, graphs, charts, balance sheets, circuit diagrams, and flowcharts using combinations of words, symbols, images, lines, arrows, and shapes (admin, 2015a; *Boundless*, 2016).

Aside from a pictorial format, models can be (a) mathematical or statistical formulas or algorithms whereby scholars capture a formal theoretical system using mathematical representation employing letters, numbers, and mathematical symbols (e.g., Einstein's relativity theory equation, $E = mc^2$), (b) physical miniatures of larger entities (e.g., a scaled model of the planetary system), and (c) computer simulations (e.g., an engineering model of the behavior of houses in earthquakes) (admin, 2015a; *Boundless*, 2016; Castro-Palaganas, 2011).

Phenomena are often intangible (i.e., people cannot touch or feel them). Models can make theoretical concepts tangible, an example being mathematical *manipulatives* so-called because people can actually hold and manipulate a model as they learn the mathematical concept (admin, 2015a; *Boundless*, 2016; Castro-Palaganas, 2011) (see Figure 3.14). From a slightly different perspective, Ford (2009) said that *visualization* models can be used to convey concepts and abstract ideas using diagrams, maps, and such. They help readers visualize the theorist's or researcher's approach to explaining a phenomenon or some aspect of it for the study.

FIGURE 3.13   ■   Model of Economic Circular Flow of Money

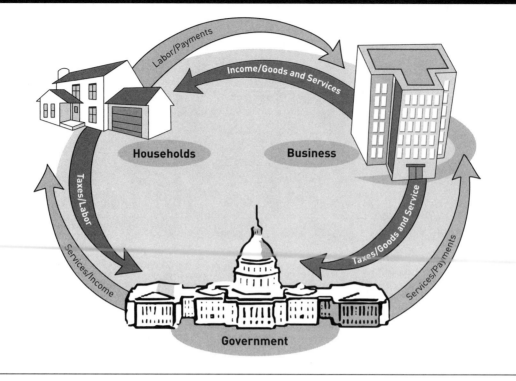

Source: Adapted from Microsoft clip art.

Finally, thanks to advances in statistical modeling tools, researchers can create simple or complex *statistical models* of reality using computer software packages. Examples include *multiple regression* equations or models that predict how a selection of variables will affect one key variable (e.g., effective staff meetings). Results are shown using scatterplots (see Chapters 11 and 12). *Path analysis* models help researchers create a network of correlations to show how various variables impact each other. *Factor analysis* models reveal whether the intercorrelations among many variables contain patterns or factors that link the variables to each other. *Structural equation* modeling (see Figure 3.11) helps determine the presence or absence of latent variables that cannot be measured directly but can be inferred from the interactions of other variables. "It is the researcher's job to translate the findings of the statistical modelling procedures into ordinary theoretical language. Such statistical procedures are only used to *support* the creation of theory; they do not *replace* the efforts of researchers to create theory" (Shank & Brown, 2007, p. 55).

In summary, there is an array of different types of models that can inform the research enterprise: physical miniatures, manipulatives, symbolic (graphic visualizations), verbal, computer simulations, mathematical formulae using symbols and word models, and statistical models. These models serve to help readers receive information, process this information, and respond accordingly while reading the research report. They do so by helping

FIGURE 3.14 ■ Mathematical Manipulatives (Models)

Source: Microsoft clip art. Used with permission.

people create internal mental models of the conceptualization of the phenomenon in question (Ford, 2009). It is incumbent on authors to clearly explain the model they employed and why, justifying it as the best one to address their research question.

REVIEW AND ENGAGEMENT

When critically reading a research report, you would

☐ Determine if the authors, ideally, had a separate section devoted to any model that underpinned the study, in its own titled section

☐ Ascertain if they shared the entire model or if they chose to represent just the elements germane to addressing their research questions. Was this a judicious decision?

☐ If they used statistical modeling procedures (e.g., structural equation, path analysis, or factor analysis), check to see that they translated their results into ordinary theoretical language

☐ Determine if they used their selected model to help interpret their data (i.e., did not explain the model and then not use it)

FINAL JUDGMENT ON CONCEPTUAL FRAMEWORK, THEORY, OR MODEL ELEMENT OF A RESEARCH PAPER

Taking *all* of the ***Review and Engagement*** criteria into account, what is your final judgment of the conceptual framework, theory, or model element of the paper that you are critically reading?

CHAPTER SUMMARY

Following on the heels of the chapter on methodology (Chapter 2), this chapter addressed the importance of undergirding a research project with some form of framework, be it conceptual, theoretical, or a model (see Figure 3.3). Lack of such a framework can weaken the scholarship. The chapter began with a general overview of the role of theory in research inquiries (see Figure 3.1 and Table 3.1). There are three main types of theory (descriptive [taxonomy and typology], relational, and explanatory), which are related to the four reasons for a research inquiry (i.e., explore, describe, identify relationships, and explain causation).

This rhetorical side trip served as a precursor for a richer discussion of theories in general (relative to conceptual frameworks and models), bridged with an introduction to concepts and constructs, the building blocks of all three research elements (see Figure 3.3). The rest of the chapter contained (a) a detailed discussion of conceptual frameworks (see Figure 3.5), followed with (b) an extensive coverage of theories (see Figure 3.8 and Tables 3.4, 3.5, 3.6, and 3.7), ending with (c) a shorter discussion of models. The chapter also contained information about the reporting conventions pursuant to writing the conceptual and theoretical framework sections of a research paper.

REVIEW AND DISCUSSION QUESTIONS

1. Identify the four phases of research (also called the reasons for the inquiry) (see Figure 3.1). Why do you think they occur in the order they do? Explain how the three types of theory are related to the four phases of research inquiry (see Table 3.1).

2. What is the difference between a typology and a taxonomy? Why do you think they are classified as descriptive theory?

3. How does a construct differ from a concept? What makes a good concept?

4. Explain in plain language the major distinctions among a conceptual framework, a theory, and a model. Why do you think people find it hard to differentiate between them?

5. Explain how the process of integration comes into play when developing a conceptual framework (see Figure 3.5).

6. What are the three or four major building blocks (elements) of any theory? Explain how they are related to each other (see Figure 3.8 and Table 3.5).

7. Explain the difference between an inductive and a deductive approach to using theory in research.

8. Theories serve several key purposes in research. Identify three of these roles (see Table 3.4).

9. Table 3.6 identifies 13 characteristics of a good theory. In your opinion, which five of these are the most important, and why?

10. People often mix up the terms *theory* and *model*. Explain how they differ, and then explain how they are related to each other.

11. Suggest five tips for how to write the theoretical or conceptual framework section of a research article. Explain how this is different for a quantitative and a qualitative paper.

12. What is the impact of not having a theory, having one but not using it, and/or having an incorrect theory to guide the research design process (see Table 3.7)?

ORIENTING AND SUPPORTIVE ELEMENTS OF RESEARCH

4

ORIENTING AND SUPPORTIVE ELEMENTS OF A JOURNAL ARTICLE

INTRODUCTION

The three previous chapters dealt with critical research literacy, research methodologies, and the role of conceptual frameworks, theories, and models in scholarship. Before delving into details about the many conventions pursuant to reporting research (see Figure 4.1), this and the next chapter focus on the more prosaic, but still important, topics of journal articles and journals as publication venues of choice.

Most authors choose a particular journal for their scholarship, with each journal having its own history, procedures, and reputation. Despite being beyond their control, authors need to appreciate that readers take cues from the actual journal, inferring scholarly excellence and research caliber and quality from the status of the journal. While Chapter 5 provides a basic overview of academic journals, this chapter focuses on the journal's articles. Just like the journal, most *articles* comprise discrete and specific parts, each having its own nature, characteristics, and purposes (Shank & Brown, 2007) (see Figure 4.1, which distinguishes between primary and secondary journal article elements). A savvy author will be skilled at preparing each research element, whether it be primary or secondary. A critical reader will be able to find, assess, and pass judgment on each element.

Primary is Latin *primarius*, "first" (Harper, 2016). If something is primary in nature, it is the ultimate constituent of something complex, in this case, a research report. This book contains separate chapters for each of the *primary* elements of a research report (Chapters 2, 3, 6–16) (Harris, 2014; Shank & Brown, 2007) (see Figure 4.1). This particular chapter addresses the *secondary* elements of the research process as reported in a journal article, called the bookends. *Secondary* is Latin *sequi*, "subordinate, to follow" (Harper, 2016). If something is secondary, it is minor or of lesser importance, but it still matters (Anderson, 2014). In a research report or article, secondary elements are important, but for different reasons than the primary elements. To be discussed shortly, the secondary elements include everything from the author's name and affiliation to the reference list (see Figure 4.1).

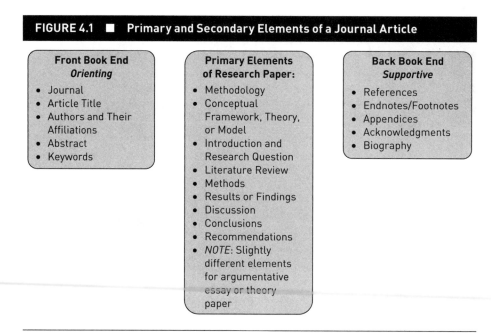

FIGURE 4.1 ■ Primary and Secondary Elements of a Journal Article

Front Book End
Orienting

- Journal
- Article Title
- Authors and Their Affiliations
- Abstract
- Keywords

Primary Elements of Research Paper:

- Methodology
- Conceptual Framework, Theory, or Model
- Introduction and Research Question
- Literature Review
- Methods
- Results or Findings
- Discussion
- Conclusions
- Recommendations
- *NOTE*: Slightly different elements for argumentative essay or theory paper

Back Book End
Supportive

- References
- Endnotes/Footnotes
- Appendices
- Acknowledgments
- Biography

Ideally, critical readers will reserve judgment of the research until reading the entire paper, but authors must be aware that this is not always the case (Lunsford & Lunsford, 1996). Some readers may stop short of the primary elements, focusing instead on the secondary ones. Readers take cues from all of these secondary elements, whether or not they are appropriate for inferring the rigor of the scholarship. Some secondary elements serve to *orient* people to the article, while others are *supportive* elements for the research enterprise (see Figure 4.1).

Orienting Secondary Elements

It is particularly important that authors adequately address three orienting elements: the title, the abstract, and the keywords. Not doing so "would almost be equivalent to leaving the accessibility of the research paper up to chance and lucky guessing of target words, indirectly making the effort and time expended on the research and publication process almost null and void" (Rodrigues, 2013). Despite being short and succinct in stature, these three orienting elements provide shortcuts and cues for readers so they can determine if the research meets their needs and merits further reading. They are instrumental in determining whether a study comes to the attention of potential readers (Locke, Silverman, & Spirduso, 2010). And their pivotal role in communicating research continues, triggering readers' interest and maintaining their curiosity (Rodrigues, 2013). She likened these elements to marketing tools that help to promote, sell, and disseminate the study's results or findings.

Supportive Secondary Elements

Supportive is Latin *supportāre*, "to provide assistance, to back up" (Harper, 2016). If something is supportive, it enables something (e.g., a research report) to fulfill its function and remain in operation by providing additional help and assistance (Anderson, 2014). At the end of the paper, authors always have a reference list (or bibliography), unless the citation style is bottom-of-page footnotes. Authors may also include other supportive elements such as footnotes, endnotes, appendices, acknowledgments, and their biography (journal permitting) (see Figure 4.1).

In essence, this back bookend serves to provide supportive material for the ideas presented in the paper, whether it is citations of relevant literature, additional results or findings, instruments, professional identity, or acknowledgment of contributions to ensure the research actually happened. These supportive elements amount to giving credit where credit is due, to those who deserve recognition for their direct or indirect contributions to the research project. This end-of-paper support is compared to the orienting front-end bookend, which draws the study to people's attention and makes them want to read and use it. Each of the nine secondary elements is now discussed, starting with the orienting elements.

AUTHORS' NAMES, CREDENTIALS, AND AFFILIATIONS

Each article is anchored with the authors' names, credentials, and affiliations. Journal editors normally place this information just below the title of the paper. This convention conveys the academic authorship of the paper. The name and affiliation can be together; the affiliation can be included in a footnote or a text box on the same page that the name appears; or the name can appear on the first page, with the affiliation at the end of the document. It is now common to include contact information for one or more of the authors, but usually just one author is designated "*Corresponding* Author," who is often the *lead* person, either conducting the study, preparing the manuscript, or both (see Figure 4.2).

If authors place their name on a manuscript, they are (a) asserting that they made an intellectual contribution to the research (substantial or tangential), (b) agreeing to be accountable for all aspects of the work, and (c) affirming that they have approved the final version to publish (i.e., they bear responsibility for its contents and interpretation) (Dickson, Conner, & Adair, 1978). Authors have to take into consideration several things when preparing this part of their paper. Discerning readers can draw many inferences from the arrangement of authors' names, their credentials (e.g., PhD, MA, Director, Dean, or President), and their institutional affiliation (see Figure 4.2).

There are many types of authors (see Table 4.1). If the author is responsible for the research and the paper, she or he is considered to be *sole* author. Papers regularly have multiple authors, and the order of their names can reflect several scenarios, with conventions varying by journals, institutions, and disciplines. Names may be listed alphabetically (with some journals and disciplines mandating this order), but normally the order indicates who did most of the work. *Lead* authors worked with others, but their name is first, normally meaning they took the lead on both the research and the writing. *Principal* authors worked with others but played crucial and essential roles in most aspects of the research process, writing the manuscript, or both. They may have conceived the research idea, conceptualized and formalized the research design, collected and/or analyzed data, drafted the manuscript, procured funding, supervised the study and/or researchers, and so on (Rennie, Yank, & Emanuel, 1997). Some journals explicitly identify the principal author, whose name may or not be first in the list.

FIGURE 4.2 ■ Example of Authors' Names and Affiliations, Title, Abstract, and Keywords

International Journal of **Consumer Studies**

International Journal of Consumer Studies ISSN 1470-6423

Paradigm, Methodology and Method: Intellectual Integrity in Consumer Scholarship

Sue L.T. McGregor[1]* and Jennifer A. Murnane[2]

[1]Faculty of Education, Director Graduate Education, Mount Saint Vincent University, Halifax, NS, Canada
[2]Human Capital Lab, Bellevue University, Omaha, NE, USA

Keywords

Consumer, methodology, positivism, post-positivism, interpretive, paradigm.

Correspondence

Sue L.T. McGregor, Faculty of Education, Director Graduate Education, Mount Saint Vincent University, 166 Bedford Highway, Halifax, NS, Canada B3M2J6.
E-mail: sue.mcgregor@msvu.ca

*Names are listed alphabetically. Please direct correspondence to Sue McGregor.

doi: 10.1111/j.1470-6431.2010.00883.x

Abstract

The intellectual integrity, trustworthiness and diversity of consumer scholarship depend on researchers accounting for the methodological (philosophical) underpinnings of their work. The discussion is predicated on the assumption that many scholars do not clearly differentiate between methodology and method. To address this issue, the paper distinguishes between these two concepts, identifies four axioms of methodologies, identifies and describes two overarching research paradigms (positivism and post-positivism), contrasts quantitative/qualitative with positivistic/post-positivistic, and positions consumer scholarship with three dominant research methodologies: scientific, interpretive and critical. Suggestions are offered about what various actors can do to better ensure responsible consumer scholarship through methodological accountability.

Source: Nielson, L., & McGregor, S. L. T. (2013).

TABLE 4.1 ■ Types of Authorship	
Author Type	**Explanation**
Sole	Only one involved; responsible for the research and the article
Lead	While working with others, took the lead (in charge) on the research and the article
Principal	Worked with others but played most important (crucial and essential) role relative to the research and the article
Coauthor	Worked in partnership and collaboration, whether even or uneven
Coordinating	Brought order to the research enterprise comprising a collection of contributors, ensuring its completion (research and/or article)
Contributing	Provided help and/or scholarly expertise (i.e., furnished works for a publication), knowing the enterprise would be coordinated by one author
Ghost	Made a substantial contribution, but name is *not* on the article
Honorary	Made *no* contribution at all, but name is on the article

Coauthorship indicates partnerships and collaboration, whether even or uneven. These partnerships can be very telling, in good ways and bad. Strong scholars can serve as mentors. Two strong scholars can partner and enrich the research and each other's reputation. Poor scholars can partner with and piggyback stronger ones. Two weak scholars can partner and appear (or actually be) stronger. PhD supervisors and master's or doctoral candidates can cowrite, with solidarity or tension. Readers can deduce much (correctly or incorrectly) from these collaborations. This is where the aforementioned order of multiple authors comes into play. The issue of collaboration hinges on whether a person is being credited for being involved or being identified as making specific, significant contributions (Biagioli, 2003).

Collaboration can also reflect associations within a university (intrauniversity), as well as between or among universities (interuniversity), universities and other sectors (intersectoral), and nations (international). And specific authors' affiliations can reflect prestige and their reputation. They can be affiliated with particular universities or colleges, research institutes, think tanks, nongovernmental (NGO) or nonprofit (NPO) organizations, or industry organizations. Readers can infer both the caliber of work and any partiality of the research enterprise (i.e., special treatment within special relationships).

In these collaborative partnerships, authors may wish to identify themselves and others as a *coordinating* author or a *contributing* author. A coordinator brings order to an enterprise and helps ensure that those who contributed are acknowledged (they provided help or their scholarly expertise). A contributing author furnishes works for a publication, knowing the enterprise will be coordinated by one author.

Regarding the latter point, two other approaches to authorship exist, ghost authors and honorary authors. *Ghost authors* reflect situations where the person made a substantial contribution to the research or the writing of the report, but is not listed as an author. Examples include paid researchers, statisticians, technical writers, and policy analysts (Gøtzsche et al., 2007). I personally worked for 18 months on a policy document, but my name is not on the final government white paper. Although readers will not know whether the paper involved ghost writing, authors have to decide whether or not to give credit to these contributors.

On the other hand, *honorary* authors are given credit although they played no significant role in the research or the preparation of the document. Examples include department heads, deans, institute directors, or project supervisors (who had no concrete role other than being the figurehead). Despite being an accepted practice, their inclusion in the roster of authors can dilute or mask the contributions of other legitimate contributors (Pearson, 2006).

In short, unless a footnote or text within the manuscript assigns responsibility for different parts of the paper to different authors, readers can assume that the authors whose names appear on the paper share responsibility for all of it. Whether formally defined or a disciplinary cultural custom or convention, authors have a lot of decisions to make when deciding how to reveal key contributions to their research and the authorship of the actual manuscript (Dickson et al., 1978).

ARTICLE TITLE

The title is the most frequently read part of a journal article (Locke et al., 2010), likely read by thousands of people (Day, 1998). Authors should use a title that orients readers to their topic and the approach they used (Shank & Brown, 2007). To *orient* means to find one's position relative to unfamiliar surroundings (Anderson, 2014). When people read an article title, they normally have not read the whole piece, meaning they are unfamiliar with its content. Respecting this reality, Shank and Brown (2007) identified five types of titles (see Table 4.2). They likened the title to a picture frame, which creates boundaries for the reader. These boundaries could include the topic, circumstances of the research, variables, participants or target groups, situations or contexts, processes, theories, methods, or treatments. Because indexing and retrieval systems depend on article titles for keywords, it is imperative that authors pay special attention to this deceptively simple research element.

TABLE 4.2 ■ Five Types of Titles, With Examples	
Type of Title	**Overview, With Examples (Shank & Brown, 2007)**
Descriptive	• Identifies the content to be covered in the paper
	• Identifies the topic, concepts, or phenomenon
	• Promises readers information about a phenomenon, and nothing more (nothing about cause and effect, relationships, or processes)
	• Can be used for both qualitative and quantitative studies
	Examples:
	1. *Rates of Practice and Midterm Grades **in** Four Eighth-Grade Magnet School Science Classrooms*
	2. *High-Protein Snacks and Quiz Grades **in** Afternoon High School Math Classes*

Type of Title	Overview, With Examples (Shank & Brown, 2007)
Equation	• Identifies a relationship that will be explored in the article • States proposed links between two or more phenomena, often specifying key variables, but the variables and their possible relationship are the real keys to the article • Word clues for this type of title include *impact of, role of, effect of, comparing, testing, correlates of* • Usually used for empirical, quantitative studies Examples, per above: 1a. **Comparing** *Rates of Practice and Midterm Grades in Four Eighth-Grade Magnet School Science Classrooms* 2a. **Testing** *the Effects of High-Protein Snacks and Quiz Grades on Afternoon High School Math Classes* 2b. *Testing the* **Relative** *Effects of High-Protein Snacks and Quiz Grades on Afternoon High School Math Classes* **Note** that adding the word *relative* opens the title to the possibility of several testing conditions in one study
Situation	• Names a particularly important situation or context for which critical details or explanations will be provided, to help understand the situation • The key situation is the focus of the article • Often used for qualitative research Examples: 3. *Situational Influences on Children's Beliefs About Global Warming* 4. *Analyzing the Web Blogs of Three School Shooters: Similarities and Differences*
Process	• Variables and relationships between them are an integral part of the process of reaching or achieving a goal or target, but the goal or target is the real focus of the paper • The title indicates a description and analysis of a process (i.e., the workings of something, like a community or classroom dynamics) • Often used for qualitative research Examples: 5. *Working With Parents on a Supplemental Character Education Program for Elementary School Children* 6. *Reflecting on a Teacher Research Study About Young Children's Sociodramatic Play*
Theoretical	• Identifies a theory or model that will be created and/or tested • Article will report a complex model or extended theoretical discussion • Can be used for both qualitative and quantitative studies Example: 7. *Critical Factors for Understanding Male Juvenile Offenders: Developing an Empirically Based Model*

Characteristics of a Good Title

A title does not validate or invalidate research, but readers may nonetheless take that perceptual leap (Ingham-Broomfield, 2008). A *good* title has "the fewest words possible that adequately describe the contents of the paper" (Day, 1998, p. 15). The title has to be clear, concise, accurate, and appealing, respectively, (a) easy to understand, creating no doubt or uncertainty; (b) expressed using few words (brevity); (c) correct in all details; and (d) interesting and attracting attention (Anderson, 2014; Locke et al., 2010). A title that meets these four main criteria instills confidence in readers that it is worth their time to move on to the abstract and hopefully the whole paper. Indeed, a bad title can convey a negative impression of the author's prowess as a thinker and a writer (Locke et al., 2010).

Example 4.1 Inaccurate title

> **Actual title:** *Insights Beyond Neoliberal Educational Practices: The Value of Discourse Analysis*
>
> **Better title for the actual content:** *Revealing Neoliberal Ideology's Power Over Educational Practices: The Value of Discourse Analysis*

Note: The *actual title* implies that the paper will provide insights into how educational practices might look if teachers can get beyond the neoliberal agenda. Instead, the *paper actually* discusses how teachers felt while experiencing a practice informed by an imposed neoliberal agenda (i.e., how they lost agency, power, and autonomy).

Along with abstracts, authors are advised to write their title last. After completing their entire article, they are in a better position to identify the key aspects of their research that they wish to communicate to potential readers (Bem, 2004; Shank & Brown, 2007). This task is so challenging that some authors actually acknowledge people who helped them come up with their title. Titles normally contain fewer than 12 words, making this task even more challenging (Bem, 2004; Johnson & Christensen, 2012; Rodrigues, 2013).

When creating a title, authors should choose those descriptive words that they most strongly associate with their paper (Anderson, 2015). They need to find a balance between an extremely long and convoluted title and one that is so short it is meaningless, and they should let the data guide them. They should use their most "instructive findings" and create multiple versions of the title until satisfied with one of them (Bem, 2004; Day, 1998). Authors are further encouraged to find a balance between providing enough information to describe the contents of the paper without getting so technical that only specialists can understand it. Said another way, the title needs to be appropriate for the intended audience (Chua, ca. 2003). Also, authors should minimize the use of waste words (excess baggage), such as *studies on*, *investigations on*, and *observations on*, which tend to appear at the beginning of the title. Word count can also be reduced by avoiding articles (*a, an, the*). Authors should not reduce word count by using abbreviations, formulas, jargon, or proprietary names (Day, 1998).

Although often done, Day (1998) recommended not using titles phrased as questions because they can become unintelligible. Dewey (2012) liked question titles because they tell readers exactly what will be covered. The question can draw in readers who have that thought in mind. Preferring literal questions, she cautioned that rhetorical questions can mask the real topic or be perceived as cynical. In an article in the American Psychological Association (APA) blog, Lee (2010) said style manuals normally require that the title give away the ending. She said question titles cannot fulfill this requirement. Ultimately, Haggan (2004) advised that this title convention varies by discipline.

Example 4.2 Question titles

Effective rhetorical question title: Consume Less to Be Happy? Consume Less to Be Happy! (**NOTE:** This title tells readers the paper will address this issue from two perspectives, a question and an imperative, which bodes well for an intriguing discussion and conversation about this topic.)

Effective literal question title: Why Does Consumer Behavior Matter? (**NOTE:** This title gives away the ending, that it *does* matter.)

Ineffective question title: Is Eating Vegetables Important? (**NOTE:** This title implies a yes or no answer.)

Better title: Eating Vegetables Is Important (**NOTE:** This title gives away the ending, which is a good thing.)

Day (1998) also addressed the merits of using hanging titles, meaning there are two sections separated with a colon. Hanging titles can appear pedantic (i.e., too narrowly focused on a minor thing). Some journals prefer these compound titles because they enable authors to get the most important words into the title. Day (1998) further advised authors to view titles as *labels* for the article, meaning they should not be sentences. The label accompanies the article. Despite not being sentences, word order (syntax) matters because faulty syntax is the most common cause of incomprehensible titles.

Example 4.3 Hanging titles

Antiharassment Programs: Implementation and Outcomes

Better title: Implementation and Outcomes of Antiharassment Programs

Learning in Small Groups: College Students' Perceptions

Better title: College Students' Perceptions of Learning in Small Groups

Spider Plant Metaphor: Integrating Human Ecology Into Home Economics

Better title: Integrating Human Ecology Into Home Economics

Example 4.4 Faulty syntax in title

"A paper was submitted to the *Journal of Bacteriology* with the title 'Mechanism of Suppression of Nontransmissible Pneumonia in Mice Induced by Newcastle

Disease Virus.' Unless the author had somehow managed to demonstrate spontaneous generation, it must have been the pneumonia that was induced and not the mice. (The title should have been 'Mechanism of Suppression of Nontransmissible Pneumonia *Induced in Mice* [emphasis added] by Newcastle Disease Virus.')" (Day, 1998, p. 17).

REVIEW AND ENGAGEMENT

When critically reviewing a research report, you would

☐ Determine which type of title the authors chose (see Table 4.2) and reflect on whether this choice affected your thoughts about the paper's quality

☐ Determine whether the title actually reflected the content of the paper

☐ Ascertain if the authors met the key criteria for a good title (e.g., clear, concise, accurate, and appealing)

ABSTRACTS

Abstract is Latin *abstrahere*, "to draw away." It is a smaller quantity containing the virtue or power of the greater whole (Harper, 2016). Abstracts are the articles in miniature, or a tiny version of the whole article (Day, 1998; Goodson, 2017; Shank & Brown, 2007). An abstract is "a snapshot that captures only the most vivid elements of a complex process. The picture it provides is devoid of the rich contextual details [of the research enterprise]" (Locke et al., 2010, p. 148). Abstracts highlight the essential characteristics of a study without the details (Johnson & Christensen, 2012; Lunsford & Lunsford, 1996). Sometimes they are the only thing a reader can obtain via electronic literature searches or in published abstracts, so it behooves authors to get this right (Anderson, 2015). "Usually, a good Abstract is followed by a good paper; a poor Abstract is a harbinger of woes to come" (Day, 1998, p. 31).

As an aside, although this chapter is focused mainly on abstracts for journal articles, there are other forms of abstracts, including (a) those that preface grant proposals, (b) executive summaries of technical reports or policy documents, and (c) conference presentations for proceedings or websites. Regardless of the type of abstract, its key role is to convince readers of the value of the research, enticing them to read further (Goodson, 2017). The features of a good journal article abstract are set out in Table 4.3 (Anderson, 2015; Day, 1998; Goodson, 2017; Locke et al., 2010; Michaelson, 1990; Shank & Brown, 2007). Abstracts are normally fewer than 300 words and confined to one paragraph. Some journals require authors to use a series of subheadings in their abstract (e.g., Background, Methods, Results, and Conclusions), but this is not common practice in all disciplines (Day, 1998; Harris, 2014; Rodrigues, 2013). In these instances, the abstract may reach a half to full page in length (Wiersma & Jurs, 2009).

"Artfully designed abstracts can display most elements that will concern readers . . . ordinarily a general statement of the research topic, a brief description of the study design and the methods involved, and the most important results" (Locke et al., 2010, p. 147). Authors can also explain any theoretical motivations for their study (Cole & Firmage,

TABLE 4.3 ■ Features of a Good Abstract

- *Accurate:* correct in all details, with nothing added that was not in the paper
- *Self-contained:* must stand by itself without having to resort to the article for clarification. This means no literature citations, abbreviations, acronyms, or any sort of table, figure, or diagram (or references to them)
- *Concise and succinct:* no more than 300 words (normal length is 150 words), usually in one paragraph (with exceptions, depending on journal styles); use clear, significant words (usually nouns), and avoid being abstruse or verbose
- *Nonevaluative:* report but do not judge the research (avoid adjectives such as *important, interesting, compelling, surprising*)
- *Coherent (quickly comprehensible):* present content in an orderly and logical manner, using active voice, past tense, and, normally, third person
- *Informative:* provide precise details about the main elements of the research (normally research question, method, results or findings, and main conclusions)

2006). On the other hand, Shank and Brown (2007) believed that abstracts are not standardized: "They can be simple or complex, very short or somewhat longer, linear or recursive" (p. 101). They further described abstracts as *foregrounding* tools that serve to bring some aspects of the research forward so people will pay attention to them, while pushing back or minimizing other aspects. What is deemed essential and worthy of being included in the abstract depends on the type of study, what the author wants to highlight, the intended audience, and journal protocols (Locke et al., 2010; Michaelson, 1990). The final abstract should reflect the *key* points of the research story (Day, 1998).

Employing the metaphor of article switches (like a light switch), Shank and Brown (2007) explained that authors can selectively turn on and off one or more of seven aspects of the research report as they prepare their abstract: purpose, problem, participants, design (methods), analysis, results, and conclusions (see also Creswell, 2009). This strategy enables authors to highlight the parts of the research they think are most important for a particular paper or audience. These foregrounded elements serve as cues so readers can decode the abstract. In effect, authors can custom design their abstract to suit their intended audience (appreciating that sometimes they have to follow the dictates of the journal publishing their paper). Also, professional journals often require authors to specify any practical implications of their results (Johnson & Christensen, 2012; Locke et al., 2010). And some authors may choose to provide general background on the topic, using these comments to identify the gap their study is addressing (Shon, 2015).

Example 4.5 Custom-designed abstract for qualitative research (the switches turned on are in [brackets] but do not appear in the actual abstract in a paper)

[DESIGN/METHOD] This action research study was conducted with [PARTICIPANTS] seven female business owners selling financial services [SITE] in the Greater Halifax area. [PROBLEM] This particular group of entrepreneurs was struggling with obtaining and maintaining its client base. [PURPOSE] The seven entrepreneurs decided that the best strategy would be to enroll in special courses offered by the Center for Women in Business and then reevaluate their business in one year. [FINDINGS] After a year and a half had lapsed, five of the seven women had increased their client base and maintained it for six months. [CONCLUSION] Follow-up data will be collected to see if these results persist over time, and the sample frame will be expanded to include more seasoned business owners.

The APA agreed that different kinds of articles require different kinds of abstracts. Empirical work usually contains the research problem, participants, methods, analysis, results, and conclusions. A discussion, position, or theoretical paper, or a literature review, would include topic, main thesis or purpose, sources that support the argument, and conclusions. A case study abstract could include the site(s), participants and their characteristics, the nature of the issue, and questions raised for future work (VandenBos, 2010).

Using another approach, Michaelson (1990) suggested that abstracts can be descriptive, informative, or informative-descriptive. A *descriptive* abstract, the shortest version (100 words), does not report the results, conclusions, or recommendations. Instead, it describes the general, broad nature of the subject matter of the study: study objectives, the scope of the work, and perhaps the methods. It is descriptive in nature, not substantive, meaning people will likely need to access and read the entire paper.

Conversely, an *informative* abstract is, by its nature, much more detailed (about 250 words) because it reports discoveries and results. For example, a quantitative abstract normally includes the purpose of the work, hypotheses, methods, primary results with statistics, and a summary of conclusions and/or recommendations. The *informative-descriptive* abstract includes both the broad nature of the study and information about the study design, results or findings, and conclusions (Michaelson, 1990). Because of their substantive nature, the latter two approaches actually supplant the need to read the full paper (Day, 1998).

Example 4.6 Informative abstract (with article switches turned on, but not part of the original quote)

[PURPOSE] The purpose of this study was to examine the influence of parenting styles on 8-year-olds' emotional and cognitive levels. [SAMPLE] Volunteer parents from an after-school program [STUDY DESIGN/METHOD] were observed on five occasions over a 6-month period, and [their parenting styles] were categorized as permissive ($n = 53$), authoritative ($n = 48$), or authoritarian ($n = 51$). The 8-year-old children were measured on four emotional variables (stress level, emotional distress, anger, and creativity) based on laboratory assessment and two cognitive variables (composite measures of verbal reasoning and quantitative reasoning). [ANALYSIS] Data were analyzed by MANOVA. [RESULTS] Comparisons among the parenting styles showed that the children of authoritarian parents had significantly more stress and anger ($p > .05$), whereas children of permissive parents were the most creative. There were no significant differences for any other variables. [CONCLUSION] These results indicate that parenting style might influence some measures of child development but have little impact on other developmental variables (Locke et al., 2010, p. 149).

Formatting Abstracts

Bottom line, abstracts help authors present the main purpose of their study, its methods of inquiry, and its major findings or results (Gall, Gall, & Borg, 2015). Regardless of the type of abstract, on the technical side, abstracts must contain full sentences, with no ellipses (. . .) or incomplete sentences. Also, authors should not cite other sources unless they are modifying a previously published method or theory (Day, 1998). These rules exist in case readers cannot access the full article. To ensure a tightly written abstract, authors should delete all unnecessary and repetitive words like *study of*, *investigates*, and *reports*. This recommendation may be hard to follow but worth trying if it makes the abstract more concise and clear (Rodrigues, 2013; see example 4.7).

Example 4.7 Deleting unnecessary words in an abstract

Original sentence: This *study* is a randomized trial that investigates whether X therapy improved cognition function in 40 dementia patients from six cities in Japan; it *reports* improved cognitive functions. (28 words)

Revised sentence: A randomized trial showed that X therapy improved cognitive function in 40 dementia patients in Japan. (16 words)

Authors are encouraged to use active voice in their abstracts when possible. Active voice explains who did something instead of what was done (passive) (see Chapters 14 and 16 for more information about active and passive voice). Abstracts are written in past tense. Normally, third person is used, but qualitative authors may opt to use first and second person. Authors may want to allot two or three sentences to each main element (or switch) in the abstract, respecting the rule of brevity. This strategy would yield about eight sentences (Anderson, 2015; Shon, 2015; see Figure 4.2). Finally, though not part of research reporting protocol, authors should write their abstract last (Goodson, 2017). Goodson (2017) estimated this task to take from 30 minutes to an hour, often spread over several days. The distance provides perspective.

REVIEW AND ENGAGEMENT

When critically reviewing a research report, you would

☐ Determine if the authors' abstract meets the six main criteria of an effective abstract (see Table 4.3)

☐ Appreciating that abstracts contain foregrounding article switches, ascertain if the authors turned on enough switches to convey the type of study being reported (combination of design, participants, sites, problem, purpose, method, analysis, findings or results, conclusions, and recommendations)

☐ Determine if the abstract stands alone (informative or informative-descriptive) or whether you would have to read the whole paper (descriptive)

☐ Check to see if the abstract follows the recommended conventions for length, tense, voice, and person, guided by whether it is a qualitative or quantitative study

KEYWORDS

Many journals now require authors to identify several *keywords* (between three and eight) that aid others in finding and retrieving the article using electronic search engines, databases, indexing and abstracting services, or journal website search engines (Panter, 2016). A *key* explains something, provides access to it, or opens it up (Anderson, 2014). Keywords reflect the significant content of an article, as judged by the authors. If judiciously selected, keywords reveal the internal structure of the authors' reasoning. They describe the essential content, subjects, or topics of an article. Keywords tend to be the most important *nouns* in the paper; other words are considered irrelevant as keywords. Keywords help others find articles that link like-minded research, and they also serve to separate papers from the non-related subjects. They are also useful for finding papers in journals not usually read by the person conducting the search (Bishop Library, 2016; Joshi, 2014; Panter, 2016).

All keywords should be relevant to the ideas in the paper. Authors must not choose keywords that are not in the article. Sometimes, authors choose particular words because they are popular, and if so, they must ensure that these actually reflect the paper's essence. Authors also have to find a balance between words that are too general or too specific, and they should try to avoid abbreviations and acronyms, unless deeply entrenched in the field (an example being CSR for corporate social responsibility). Authors are encouraged to think internationally, choosing country-specific terms for the same thing (e.g., *real estate* versus *property listing*). They may choose to imagine which words others would use to find the research topic. It is also a good idea to minimize the use of invented words because keywords should reflect a collective understanding of the subject or topic. *Key phrases* are also acceptable (e.g., instead of *business* and *ethics*, choose *business ethics*) (Emerald Group Publishing, 2016; Joshi, 2014; Panter, 2016).

There seems to be some controversy around whether the keywords should be repeated from the title or the abstract. Although keywords are *keys to information*, some sources encourage authors to use different keywords than the main nouns included in the title. They claim that because the words in the title are automatically indexed, the keywords supplement the title information (Joshi, 2014). Others believe that the paper's visibility is increased when the keywords, title, and abstract all share the keywords. This replication ensures more effective results from the algorithms used by most search engines. Algorithms are the processes or rules used in problem-solving operations (Panter, 2016). As a fallback, some journals offer guidance about keyword selection.

On a final note, relevant and descriptive keywords better ensure that the article can be easily found through Internet search engines (e.g., Google, Yahoo, Bing, and Ask), and library search engines. The complex algorithms used by Internet search engines determine what URLs (uniform resource locators, or World Wide Web [www] addresses) appear high on the list of results. Well-chosen keywords can improve search engine optimization (SEO), meaning the article has a better chance of showing up in an algorithmic search and appearing high on the list (Emerald Group Publishing, 2016; Gall et al., 2015).

Example 4.8 Keywords Per Figure 4.2, in their article titled "Consumer Morality and Moral Norms," Nielsen and McGregor (2013) identified six keywords: "*morality, consumption, moral norms, consumer behaviour, consumer society,* [and] *consumer morality*" (p. 473). These words reflected their main line of thinking—that is, the internal structure of their reasoning. They maintained that consumer behavior in a consumer society is rife with moral overtones, because consumption decisions can harm other humans, species, and ecosystems. To understand this phenomenon, they explored and integrated the constructs of morality, moral norms, and consumer morality. They developed a new conceptual framework, anticipating that consumer theorists could begin to develop a theory of consumer morality and moral norms.

REFERENCES

No academic enterprise is complete unless authors fully acknowledge the work of other scholars that informed the current piece of research. Authors have to provide either a reference list that contains everything cited (referred to) in the paper or a bibliography, which contains everything read but not necessarily cited (Ary, Jacobs, & Sorensen, 2010; Ingham-Broomfield, 2008). Citations in a research paper (a) help authors attribute prior work to the correct sources, (b) allow readers to independently assess whether the referenced material supports the author's arguments as claimed, and (c) help readers gauge the validity and strength of work cited by the author (Association of Legal Writing Directors & Barger, 2010).

Plagiarism and Paraphrasing

Citations also (d) help authors avoid plagiarism by making them intellectually honest. *Plagiarism* is Latin *plagiarius*, "kidnapper" (Harper, 2016). It entails authors taking someone else's work and claiming it as their own, with varying degrees of intention. It is appropriate and necessary that authors use other people's works. In those instances, they should either (a) paraphrase the original source (meaning express the same message using different words) with an in-paragraph citation or reference to the source or (b) quote the original source, placing the other author's words in "direct quotation marks" with the relevant page number(s) (Boudah, 2011).

Example 4.9 Plagiarism and paraphrasing

Original source: While there's uncertainty regarding the success rate of organizational change and improvement efforts, many reports show failure rates of 60%–70%.

Author's plagiarism: This study is concerned with diagnosis methods that can be used for preengagement organizational consulting. While there's uncertainty regarding the success rate of organizational change and improvement efforts, many reports show failure rates of 60%–70%.

Properly cited: This study is concerned with diagnosis methods that can be used for preengagement organizational consulting. "While there's uncertainty regarding the success rate of organizational change and improvement efforts, many reports show failure rates of 60–70%" (Hatley, 2017, p. 1).

Paraphrased version: This study is concerned with diagnosis methods that can be used for preengagement organizational consulting. The efficacy of these diagnostic approaches matters because efforts to improve organizations and to effect organizational change tend to fail upwards of 60% of the time (Hatley, 2017).

Citation Styles

Different disciplines prefer different citation models, with journals specifying which reference citation style they use. Authors have to follow these guidelines. The most common citation styles are set out in Table 4.4. Different citation systems and styles are used in scientific work, legal and medical work, and the arts and humanities (Ary et al., 2010; Wikipedia Encyclopedia, 2016a).

In-text citations usually entail mention of the author(s) and the date of the source, whether noted parenthetically or using a numbering system. As a basic convention, items in the reference list or the bibliography must contain enough information that readers can find the original source. Table 4.5 provides an overview of the types of sources authors may cite

TABLE 4.4 ■ Common Citation Style Manuals			
Citation Style	**Parenthetical (author and date in parentheses embedded in paragraphs, with an alphabetical list at the end)**	**Vancouver (sequential numbers in text, either bracketed, superscript, or both, with or without a list)**	**Citation-name (both name and superscript number, with a numbered list at the end)**
APA (American Psychological Association)	✓		
Chicago Manual of Style	✓	✓ footnotes or endnotes, may have a bibliography	
MLA (Modern Language Association)	✓		
Harvard Citation Style	✓		
ASA (American Sociological Association)	✓		
Bluebook (legal writing)		✓ footnotes, no list	
ACS (American Chemical Society)		✓	
CSE (Council of Science Educators)			✓
University of Oxford Style Guide		✓ footnotes in addition to an alphabetical list	

in their paper, roughly organized by paper-based or technology-based formats, appreciating significant overlap.

Each of these sources requires a different formula, but most citations will include, in some order and in some combination, author (or editor); date; title of paper or chapter; name of journal or book (with editors, if relevant); edition (if relevant), volume, and/or issue numbers; page numbers; and basic city and state/province for a book publisher. Citation styles differ on (a) the sequence of the entries in the list (e.g., alphabetical, order of use, or some other approach) as well as (b) conventions for preparing each entry, including the use of italics, underlining, bold text, parentheses, brackets, quotation marks, upper- and lowercase letters, commas, colons, and semicolons (see example 4.10). Authors must determine which style the journal prefers, learn it, and use it.

TABLE 4.5 ■ Types of Sources for Research Citations	
Paper-based	**Technology-based**
• Journal articles	• Websites
• Books (including e-books)	• Blogs
• Book chapters	• Videos
• Encyclopedia or dictionary entries	• Podcasts
• Government, corporate, or NGO publications (reports, briefs)	• Software
• Press releases	• Music or recordings
• Newspapers, magazines, or newsletters	• DVDs or film
• Dissertations or master's theses	• Artwork, photographs, or maps
• Court cases	• Broadcasts (television or radio)
• Conference proceedings or abstracts	• Archive material
• Personal correspondence	• Patents
• Lectures or presentations	• Interviews
• Monographs or supplements	• Newsgroup and electronic mailing list
• Unpublished documents or raw data	• Online forums
	• Emails

Example 4.10 Citation models

APA

Haroldson, A., & Yen, C. (2016). Consumer understanding of nutrition marketing terms: A pilot study. *Journal of Family & Consumer Sciences, 108*(3), 24–31.

Chicago

Haroldson, Amber, and Chih-Lun (Alan) Yen. 2016. "Consumer Understanding of Nutrition Marketing Terms: A Pilot Study." *Journal of Family & Consumer Sciences 108*: 24–31.

MLA

Haroldson, Amber, and Chih-Lun (Alan) Yen. "Consumer Understanding of Nutrition Marketing Terms: A Pilot Study." *Journal of Family & Consumer Sciences,* vol. 108, no. 3, 2016, pp. 24–31.

Authors are encouraged to pay special attention to the referencing aspect of their scholarship. Errors of omission, commission, or other inaccuracies not only are irritating to readers but also can compromise the integrity of the research report and challenge the integrity of the entire enterprise. Savvy readers will use the reference list and the author's citation prowess as code for the quality of the scholarship (Suter, 2012). Indeed, citing a source *implies* that the author has personally read and consulted it, looking for any ideas, theories, or previous research that might directly influence their own research. Authors have to be accountable for this foundational aspect of their scholarship (VandenBos, 2010).

REVIEW AND ENGAGEMENT

When critically reviewing a research report, you would

- ☐ Determine if there are keywords and then ascertain if they reflect the actual content and essence of the paper. Are there any keywords you would remove or add?

- ☐ Ascertain if the authors used a wide range of credible reference sources and followed the proper conventions for paper-based and technology-based sources (see Table 4.5)

- ☐ If they used a parenthetical citation style, check to see if all of the references in the list appear in the paper and if all of the references cited in the paper are in the reference list (for other citation styles, see Table 4.4)

- ☐ Determine if the authors followed the in-text citation conventions for their chosen style manual (see Table 4.4), thereby giving credit where due and avoiding plagiarism

FOOTNOTES AND ENDNOTES

As noted, some journal citation styles require authors to use footnotes or endnotes (e.g., Chicago, Harvard) instead of a parenthetical style (see Table 4.4). But sometimes authors may wish to add information that supplements a particular thought in their paper. This information is not needed to make their point. There are just times when authors want to designate some text that they wish to elaborate, augment, or clarify. In these instances, they can use *footnotes* (which appear sequentially, one at a time, at the bottom of each page), *endnotes* (which accumulate, and are printed collectively at the end of the document), or both (Anderson, 2014). Footnotes and endnotes serve several purposes in reporting research (Reilly, 2016; see Table 4.6).

Footnotes and endnotes are usually numbered sequentially (sometimes bulleted), using superscript numbers (i.e., small numbers placed at the end of a word, like this[1])

TABLE 4.6 ■ Purpose of Footnotes and Endnotes
• Give arguments in favor of a viewpoint
• Explain why the author used a piece of information
• Acknowledge the source of information
• Provide additional information or resources
• Add clarifying information
• Provide important details with which readers may be unfamiliar
• Explain a context or situation in more detail
• Provide a chronological history of a salient point
• Refer to supportive or contradictory documentation or perspectives
• Explain unfamiliar jargon, terminology, people, places, or sources

(Reilly, 2016). There are conventions for where to position the footnote or endnote number. "Whenever possible, put the footnote [number] at the end of a sentence, immediately following the period or whatever punctuation mark completes that sentence. . . . [If the footnote must be included] in the middle of a sentence for the sake of clarity, or because the sentence has more than one footnote (try to avoid this!), try to put [the note number] at the end of the most relevant phrase, after a comma, or other punctuation mark. Otherwise, put it right at the end of the most relevant word" ("What Are Footnotes?," 2014).

Word processing systems automatically format either approach (at the bottom of the page or the end of the document). Authors should add a separate heading called *Notes* or *Endnotes*. Some journals do not permit footnotes or endnotes because they are too expensive to format, so authors should check with the venue before going too far in their writing.

Example 4.11 Endnotes

Back et al. (2010) published a paper about how well Facebook profiles reflect a person's actual personality. They used an endnote to provide correlation details about the association between accuracy criteria and ideal-self ratings (at page 3). It was positioned just before the reference list (see Figure 4.3).

APPENDICES

Authors may have to seek permission from journal editors to include an appendix, defined as a collection of separate material at the end of a document (Anderson, 2014). Appendix is Old French *apendre*, "to be dependent upon" (Harper, 2016). The word *appendix* contains part of the word *depend*. Appendices are supplemental material that are not essential but do support some idea or process that is reported in the paper. They may be used to (a) validate a conclusion, (b) pursue a related point, or (c) support the method or the analysis. Various types of information can be placed in an appendix, including questionnaires,

> ## FIGURE 4.3 ■ Example of an Endnote in an Article
>
> **Declaration of conflicting Interests**
>
> The authors declared that they had no conflicts of interests with respect to their authorship and/or the publication of this article.
>
> **Note**
>
> 1. As expected, accuracy criteria and ideal-self rating were moderately correlated, mean $r = .28$ (neuroticism: $r = .08$; extraversion: $r = .36$; openness: $r = .33$; agreeableness: $r = .22$; conscientiousness: $r = .26$).
>
> **References**
>
> Ambady, N., & Skowronski, J. (Eds.). (2008). *First impression.* New York: Guilford.
>
> Boyd, D.M., & Ellison, N.B. (2007). Social network sites: Definition, history, and scholarship. *Journal of Computer-Mediated Communication, 13,*210–230.

surveys, research instruments, instructions, raw statistical data, interview transcripts, results of a pilot study, maps, drawings, figures, tables, charts, graphs, pictures, lengthy derivations of equations, letters or correspondence, technical specifications or data sheets, and computer program information (Labaree, 2016; Suter, 2012; UniLearning, 2000).

As is self-evident, these artifacts tend to be too cumbersome to be included directly in the body of the paper. Also, their inclusion may interrupt the narrative flow, clutter the presentation of significant information, or distract the reader from the main line of thought (Labaree, 2016). Furthermore, authors should not use appendices as a net to catch and hold semi-interesting information gathered during the research process; instead, the information must bear directly on the research problem or the report's purpose (Weaver & Weaver, 1977). Authors should limit appendix content to information that will help readers better understand and evaluate the research. Actually, readers should not have to read the appendix in order to understand the study. Appendices are supplemental, not essential (Labaree, 2016; Suter, 2012). Authors are encouraged to briefly summarize what is included in the appendix if this strategy would enhance the presentation of results or findings (Labaree, 2016).

Formatting Appendices

If authors do choose to use appendices, they must follow the proper reporting protocol. Each separate appendix should be identified with a letter or number (e.g., Appendix 1 or Appendix B). The specific number or letter (A, D, F) reflects the order in which an appendix is mentioned in the text. The first one is Appendix A, the second Appendix B, and so on. The order of appendices' arrangement at the back of the document must reflect this numbering or lettering system. Each appendix must be given a title, and only appendices referred to in the paper can be placed at the back of the document. They should not carry on any sequential numbering used in the paper for tables and figures. Finally, each appendix must be referred to in the paper, using accepted conventions (see example 4.12). Appendices are normally placed after the reference list, and their page numbering continues on from the last page of the text, unless they are stand-alone documents (Labaree, 2016; Weaver & Weaver, 1977).

Example 4.12 Referring to an appendix in a paper

Example 1: For the full intervention protocol, see Appendix B.

Example 2: Appendix B explains the full intervention protocol.

In this age of online publishing, many journals now allow authors to post large appendices at the journal's website, with the authors noting these as an endnote or an appendix in their paper. This option is especially appropriate for posting raw data so others can recheck results or findings or analyze the data themselves from a different perspective. It is also relevant for posting lengthy survey instruments, intervention protocols, and such (Labaree, 2016).

REVIEW AND ENGAGEMENT

When critically reviewing a research report, you would

- ☐ Determine if any footnotes and endnotes were used effectively, directing readers to only supplemental, nonessential information (see Table 4.6)

- ☐ Ascertain if any appendices were used effectively, directing readers to only supplemental, nonessential information

- ☐ If used, check to see if the authors avoided using the appendix for interesting but tangential and peripheral information

- ☐ Determine if the authors followed proper appendix formatting and reporting protocols (e.g., order, numbering, and pagination)

ACKNOWLEDGMENTS

There may be instances when authors want to (or are required to) give credit to those who provided support for their research. This support can come in many forms (see Table 4.7). Authors should tailor their acknowledgments to suit the situation, being selective yet inclusive. Readers may be especially interested in funding sources, which can convey impressions of (im)partiality (special treatment within special relationships). Written in first person singular or plural (*I, my, me, we, us*), this research element can range from one sentence to a

TABLE 4.7 ■ Examples of Whom/What to Acknowledge for Support During the Research Process

- Funding (grant, scholarship, fellowship, foundation, institute, corporation, or government)
- Collaborators
- Supervisors and committee members (if graduate research)
- Technical data input
- Data analysis
- Software expertise
- Expert review panels
- Graphic design or artwork
- Preparing and piloting research instruments or another apparatus
- Laboratory, research, or teaching assistance
- Library and literature search assistance
- Participants, subjects, and/or volunteers
- People responsible for gaining access to research sites or special equipment
- Reading earlier drafts, proofing, and editing
- Copyright permission
- Permission to use or adapt materials
- Emotional and personal support (with discretion)

paragraph or more in length. Appropriate expressive language includes *acknowledge, thank you, gratitude, appreciate, indebted, grateful, credit*, and *recognize*. Authors should be conscious of the tone, opting for academic and professional instead of informal. The writing should be concise, with minimal emotive language (Centre for Independent Language Learning, 2008a). Most journals place acknowledgments either on the front page in a footnote or text box or on the last page of the article.

> ***Example 4.13 Acknowledgments*** This research was funded by the XYZ Corporation, based in Atlantic Crest, Maryland (Grant #2009-14-887Q). My thanks to Dr. Fred Smith for copyright permission for Figure 5. I am grateful to Jane Flowers and Mott Lang for their statistical expertise. I appreciate the collegial collaboration of like-minded colleagues, who sustained me during this lengthy research project (five years). Many thanks to Sony Martin for reading and editing earlier drafts of this manuscript. Mary Thompson deserves credit for the creative title.

BIOGRAPHIES

On a final note (pun intended), aside from providing their name, credentials, and affiliation, authors may be asked to provide a brief (100- to 200-word) personal biography, which is normally placed at the end of the paper (Ingham-Broomfield, 2008). A biography is an account of the series of events that make up a person's life (Anderson, 2014). When publishing a research paper, authors normally include information about their scholarly and academic life. They often include their name, credentials, affiliation, and contact information (and perhaps a photograph and the URL for their personal and/or institutional website). They can also refer to professional positions held (past and present), research interests, major publications, and honorary appointments or other forms of professional recognition (Ingham-Broomfield, 2008).

This element of a journal article is a way for authors to showcase themselves. Moreover, readers often use this information to discern research expertise and then *infer* the quality of the scholarship (Ingham-Broomfield, 2008). Inference entails drawing conclusions from evidence deemed to be true (Anderson, 2014), meaning readers usually assume the biography is truthful. Authors should tailor each biography to the topic of the paper and to the targeted audience. Example 4.14 is a personal example.

Example 4.14 Biography for a journal article

Dr. Sue L. T. McGregor (PHD, IPHE, Professor Emerita) is a Canadian home economist (nearly 50 years) recently retired from Mount Saint Vincent University in Halifax, Nova Scotia. She was one of the lead architects for the interuniversity doctoral program in educational studies, serving as its inaugural coordinator. She has a keen interest in home economics philosophy, transdisciplinarity, research methodologies, and consumer studies. She is a *TheATLAS Fellow* (transdisciplinarity), a Docent in Home Economics at the University of Helsinki, recipient of the *Marjorie M. Brown Distinguished Professor Award* (home economics leadership), a *Rhoda H. Karpatkin International Consumer Fellow,* and recipient of the *TOPACE International Award* (Berlin) for distinguished international consumer scholars, especially consumer educators. Affiliated with 16 professional journals, she has nearly 170 peer-reviewed publications, four books, 31 book chapters, 12 monographs. She has delivered 39 keynotes and invited talks in 14 countries. Dr. McGregor is also the principal consultant for *McGregor Consulting Group* (founded in 1991). Visit www.consult mcgregor.com, or contact her at sue.mcgregor@msvu.ca.

Courtesy Sue L. T. McGregor

REVIEW AND ENGAGEMENT

When critically reading a research report, you would

☐ Determine if the authors acknowledged people who helped them with the research (see Table 4.7)

☐ If they did have an acknowledgment element, check to see if they avoided emotive language and wrote in a concise and respectful manner

☐ If they prepared a personal biography, determine if they followed the recommended conventions for length, tone, and the elements to include

FINAL JUDGMENT ON ORIENTING AND SUPPORTIVE ELEMENTS OF A RESEARCH PAPER

Taking *all* of the **Review and Engagement** criteria into account, what is your final judgment of the secondary orienting and supportive elements of the paper that you are critically reading?

CHAPTER SUMMARY

This chapter introduced the idea of orienting and supportive bookends for a research report. Orienting elements include the authors' names, credentials, and affiliations; the article title; an abstract; and keywords. Each of these is discussed, followed with the supportive elements of a journal article (i.e., references, footnotes and endnotes, appendices, acknowledgments, and biographies). Taken together, these comprise the *secondary* elements of a research report, scaffolding the *primary* elements, discussed in their own respective chapters (i.e., methodology, theoretical underpinnings, introduction and research question, literature review, methods, results or findings, discussion, conclusions, and recommendations) (see Figure 4.1). Secondary elements serve two main purposes. First, the *orienting* elements bring the article to people's attention and make them want to read it. Second, the *supportive* elements give authors a chance to acknowledge all previous work and people involved in bringing the research enterprise into being and to completion.

REVIEW AND DISCUSSION QUESTIONS

1. How receptive were you to the idea that the front and back ends of a research paper can be used to judge the quality of the research?

2. Do you think just using the author's name and affiliation to judge the quality of the research is an acceptable practice? Explain your answer.

3. How important is *collaboration with others* as a criterion for judging the quality of a research report? What should this criterion be combined with to reach a better judgment?

4. There are many types of titles that authors can choose for their paper (see Table 4.2). Which of these do you prefer, and why? What are the four main criteria for a good title for a research paper? What can happen if the title does not meet these criteria?

5. Abstracts play a key role in finding a paper, but can they also be used to judge the quality of the scholarship? Explain. Identify the six key features of a good abstract that make it a good foregrounding tool for the paper (Table 4.3).

6. Explain the main functions of keywords in a journal article. Do you ever use these as a tool to judge scholarship, or do you use them just to find the paper?

7. Readers use references to judge the caliber of the scholarship. Explain why this is an acceptable practice, and then suggest why it may not be.

8. Explain the concept of plagiarism and how it differs from paraphrasing. Why do you think the latter is the preferred convention when writing up research reports?

9. How can errors of omission, errors of commission, or other inaccuracies in the reference list or text citations affect perceptions of quality and rigor?

10. Do you ever turn to an appendix when reading a research report? Did you realize they are not required reading, just supplemental? Will knowing this change your approach to using appendices to discern the caliber of a research report?

11. How important do you think an acknowledgments section is when judging a research report? What about the author's biography? Are these just frill pieces, or do they play a role in your assessment of a paper? Should they? Explain your answer.

PEER-REVIEWED JOURNALS

INTRODUCTION

Most scholars eventually publish some aspect of their research in peer-reviewed journals (in addition to conference proceedings, books, chapters, and other scholarly venues). This chapter provides a general discussion of academic journals (see also Chapter 4 for other elements of journal articles). Critical readers of research can draw many inferences about the quality of the scholarship from key aspects of a journal and the peer review process. However, they must do so with their eyes wide open because using journal elements and features as proxies for quality and rigor can be a misleading exercise, fraught with erroneous assumptions and logical fallacies. Done with judicious caution, assessing the actual journal venue can be eye-opening.

Harris (2014) referred to "the complex world of academic journals" (p. 15), with their editorial reputations, peer review process, acceptance rates, and impact factors. To complicate matters, some journals publish quantitative research, some qualitative, some mixed methods, and some all three (Ary, Jacobs, & Sorensen, 2010). Authors need to become fully cognizant of the relevant conventions and criteria for each of these research methodologies before preparing a manuscript for submission. Likewise for critical readers.

JOURNAL EDITOR, EDITORIAL BOARDS, AND FACILITATING EDITORS

The editor's identity can provide authors and readers with clues about the quality of a journal. The editor's personal and professional status and reputation in the field can lend a journal prestige and respect. Each journal has an editor (or editor-in-chief), whether paid or unpaid. An editor is someone who prepares text and written material for publication (Anderson, 2014). Editor is Latin *edere*, "put out" (Harper, 2016).

Journal editors' role is to *put out each issue of* the journal under their care. To do this, they have to ensure there is a clear statement of the journal's policies and standards, which entails describing, regularly reviewing, and implementing those policies. Editors are expected to consistently apply these policies to *put out* each volume of the journal (Scott-Lichter & Editorial Policy Committee, Council of Science Editors, 2012).

To aid in this intense process, editors can turn to some combination of associate editors, assistant editors, coordinating editors, section editors, book review editors, statistical editors, special issue editors, and managing editors. In varying capacities (indicated by their title), people in these roles help the editor manage and lead the journal (Holland, Duncombe, Dyas, & Meester, 2014). In this chapter, they are called *facilitating* editors.

Guidelines for Authors

Editors have a special relationship with authors in that they guide them through the submission and peer review process and the acceptance or rejection of their manuscript. Editors have to prepare, provide, and apply a document titled *Guidelines for Authors*, explaining how to prepare manuscripts for submission and peer review (Scott-Lichter & Editorial Policy Committee, Council of Science Editors, 2012). These guidelines contain basic information about referencing style (e.g., APA, Chicago, or Harvard, introduced in Chapter 4); word counts and page length; preferred word processing program (e.g., Word or Word Perfect); document format (e.g., RTF or PDF); formatting (e.g., spacing, pagination, pitch, font, line numbering, headers, endnotes, and footnotes); how to deal with tables and figures; title page format; where, how, and to whom to send the submission; and the review process with timelines. *Guidelines for Authors* are normally found in the front or back of a journal or at the journal's website (Ary et al., 2010; Plakhotnik & Shuk, 2011).

Roster of Peer Reviewers

To help with the flow of manuscripts, editors have to assemble and manage a roster of peer reviewers, who are usually collectively acknowledged in the journal or at its website (with their name, academic rank, and institutional affiliation). This roster can range from 50 to hundreds of reviewers (Locke, Silverman, & Spirduso, 2010). As each paper comes in, editors decide if the topic fits the remit of the journal. *Remit* means a task or area of activity officially assigned to an individual, organization, or other entity (Anderson, 2014). If the paper does not fit the remit of the journal (and for other reasons), the editors can *desk reject* it. If it does fit, they (or their associate editors) turn to the journal's roster of peer reviewers and decide who is best suited to review the topic and/or method or methodology of the paper (ranging from one to four reviewers). In practice, associate editors often play a crucial role in determining if an author's submission is ready for peer review (Holland et al., 2014; Sugimoto, Larivière, Ni, & Cronin, 2013).

Editorial Board

Most journals also have an editorial board (appointed or elected) comprising a collection of established scholars (ranging from five to more than 20 board members). Editors work with their boards to varying degrees of intensity in order to set and review journal policies, missions, visions, goals, foci, objectives, and topics. Some boards are more active than others, meeting in real time, electronically, or some combination. These meetings are usually prefaced or scaffolded with the editor's annual report and the journal publisher's annual report (see next section) (Holland et al., 2014; Locke et al., 2010).

Journal Publishers

Journal publishers use the material sent to them by the journal editor and print and/or distribute the actual journal; that is, they make the journal available to the public. More than half of all journals are published by the following six publishing firms: John Wiley & Sons (Blackwell), Kluwer Academic, Reed Elsevier, SAGE, Springer, and Taylor & Francis (listed alphabetically). Some journals are published by university presses, and others are self-published, with the editor reporting to a professional association or an institution. Regardless of who is publishing, editors (not publishers) play the crucial role of stewarding a discipline's body of knowledge. They solicit and promote scholarship in their specific field and its specializations. They are the gatekeepers of what does and does not get published in a discipline (Hargens, 1988; Holland et al., 2014).

REVIEW AND ENGAGEMENT

When critically reading a journal article, you should

- ☐ Discern the identity, then assess the reputation, of the editor. Do you think the editor has the requisite experience to lead *this* journal? Are you fairly confident the editor is a good steward for the discipline's body of knowledge?

- ☐ Per the above, do the same for the editorial board, the associate editors, and the peer reviewers. If this information is not available, how did its absence affect your judgment of the journal or paper?

- ☐ Access then judge the *Guidelines for Authors* (prepared by the editor). Are they straightforward and thorough?

- ☐ Determine the publisher and explain whether the publisher's identity (e.g., big player, university press, or self) affected your judgment of the journal.

PEER REVIEW PROCESS

Authors and critical readers can also judge a journal's quality by the nature of its article review process. Before being published, most academic writing undergoes a review by peers (those of equal standing), which entails leading experts anonymously judging its rigor (Tamburri, 2012). Journals that use the peer review process are called *refereed* journals (Locke et al., 2010). The reviewers critically appraise the submission, professionally judging its intellectual contribution to the discipline (Kriegeskorte, 2012; Plakhotnik & Shuk, 2011).

A conscientious editor will provide reviewers with review criteria, which usually include the significance of the research question, quality of writing, appropriateness and implementation of the research design and analysis, robustness of discussion and conclusions, organization of the manuscript (logic and argumentation), and adherence to referencing and style conventions. Reviewers are asked to write a report relative to these criteria, which (ideally) the editor then shares with the authors when communicating the decision about the submission, with normal options being accept as is, accept with minor revisions, accept with major revisions, or reject. The time frame between submission, peer review, and editorial decision varies substantially among journals, averaging three to four months and sometimes much longer (Ary et al., 2010; Locke et al., 2010; Wiersma & Jurs, 2009).

Types of Peer Review

Peer review is an *external quality control* benchmark for papers submitted to a journal (Editage Insights, 2014). It is presumed to lend credibility to the research and enhance visibility for the journal because it constitutes self-regulation and quality control (Harris, 2014; Locke et al., 2010). There are several types of peer review, differing on the transparency of the identity of the authors and the reviewers in the prepublication stage (see Table 5.1).

TABLE 5.1 ■ Types of Review for Scholarly Submissions (Prepublication Stage)	
Type of Review	**Explanation**
Double Blind	Neither the authors nor the reviewers know each other's identity, and they are not in contact with each other. Only the editor knows all of the names. This is considered the most rigorous type of review. Authors revise their paper according to the reviews, providing justifications for accepting or rejecting their peers' critique and suggestions.
Single Blind	The reviewer knows the author's identity, but the author does not know who is reviewing (the editor knows all names) (see above for process and degree of direct contact).
No Blind	Both authors and reviewers know each other's identity, as does the editor who acts as the go-between (i.e., the authors and reviewers are not in direct contact with each other).
Editor Reviewed	There are no peers involved, but both the editor (in effect a peer) and the author know each other's identity.
Committee Reviewed	Often used for conferences with an editorial program committee reviewing many submissions. This approach has varying degrees of *blindness* among peers.
Paid, In-House Staff Reviewed	The editor pays for external professional reviewers (not academic peers of the author) or uses in-house reviewers (staff).
Open Review	This approach rejects the blind peer review process entirely, replacing it with open, transparent, direct communication between authors and their peers. An open review before publication involves a colloquy (dialogue and exchange) among peers, assuming this collegial process leads to better scholarship.
Extended Peer Community Review	Rather than using just academics (peers) to review manuscripts before publication, editors *extend* the process to include people and groups from the community who have *extended* insights and knowledge about the topic. This approach ensures robustness of knowledge in societal terms.

Open and Extended Peer Reviews (Prepublication)

There is agreement within the academy (i.e., the university system) that because of some fundamental flaws, the traditional peer review process is not a gold standard. It is just a *good enough model* that has sustained the academy so far (Kriegeskorte, 2012; Locke et al., 2010; Tamburri, 2012). An emergent conversation is challenging the holy grail of the closed, peer review process. People are calling instead for open reviews and for extended peer reviews. *Open review* means just that; it is open peer commentary. The article is posted (prepublication) at a journal's website or blog, where self-identified people can post comments about it. Using this format, moderated feedback "unfolds publically and in real time . . . like a public conversation" about the paper (Tamburri, 2012, p. 22). Extended peer review opens the manuscript review process to include those nonacademics who are living with the research issue and may use the study's results or findings. Society-based reviewers can access the knowledge in the paper, and "legitimately verify its relevance, fitness for purpose and applicability in societal contexts, contributing with 'extended insights and knowledge'" (Pereira & Funtowicz, 2005, p. 76).

Postpublication Peer Review

Another new approach is called postpublication peer review. Instead of just the double-blind review of two to four peers (and the editor) *before* a paper is published, this approach advocates for ongoing peer review *after* the paper is published. Rather than just editors determining the direction of the field (by deciding what gets published), postpublication reviews would involve peer-signed ratings and reviews of published papers (also called *Open Evaluation*). This way, researchers themselves can help costeward the body of knowledge in a discipline. By transparently providing a plurality of perspectives on an already published paper, postpublication reviews can "usher in a new culture of transparency, constructive criticism, and collaboration" (Kriegeskorte, 2012, p. 1).

REVIEW AND ENGAGEMENT

When critically reading a journal article, you would

☐ Determine if the journal is peer reviewed (or uses some other form of review) (see Table 5.1). How did this information affect your judgment of the journal or paper?

☐ If peer reviewed, you would discern then judge any articulated review criteria. If this was available, were you satisfied with the array of criteria? If this was unavailable, comment on how its absence affected your impression of the journal.

ACCEPTANCE RATES

Readers can also use acceptance rates to superficially judge the quality of scholarship in a journal. For indeed, not every paper submitted to a journal is published. Plakhotnik and Shuk (2011) observed that up to 50% of revised and resubmitted manuscripts are rejected by editors. Others place this rejection rate much higher. A quick glance at the 2011 *Cabell's directory of journals* (nearly 1,000 business, education, and psychology journals) showed an average acceptance rate of 10%–20%, meaning 80%–90% of all submitted papers were rejected by editors. This number reaches 90% for high-ranking journals (Agarwal, Echambadi, Franco, & Sarkar, 2006).

For clarification, although peer review is an external quality control benchmark for papers submitted to the journal, *acceptance rates* (rejection rates) are *internal benchmarks* for quality that are set by the editor (and/or the editorial board). Few journals publish this information, although it is normally available on request. Editors and editorial boards monitor *acceptance rates* (the percentage of submissions they accept), based on several assumptions. The lower the acceptance rate (e.g., 10%–15%), (a) the higher the caliber of the papers (i.e., more rigorous), (b) the more prestigious the journal, and (c) the more competitive the journal (i.e., if it's hard to get published, it must be a good journal) (Editage Insights, 2014; Harris, 2014). Editors assume that people will trust the journal's scholarship if they see a low acceptance rate, because they can infer (correctly or not) that any low-quality papers were rejected or that only the best of the best were published.

In reality, acceptance rates can reflect many factors having nothing to do with quality, thereby challenging these assumptions. Acceptance rates vary widely by discipline (Hargens, 1988). For example, business and computer science have much lower acceptance rates than health, education, or psychology. Acceptance rates are also affected by the number of reviewers for each paper (the more reviewers, the more likely one is to be rejected), as well as the editor's country affiliation (North American editors had the highest rejection rates, and African editors had the highest acceptance rates) (Sugimoto et al., 2013). Hargens (1988) further explained that rejection rates can be good indicators of the quality of scholarship, in that if reviewers come to a consensus that a paper is not of high caliber, it probably is not, and merits rejection. Put another way, readers should be able to trust the scholarship of a paper that has been accepted, although "the guarantee of quality provided by most journals is something less than absolute" (Locke et al., 2010, p. 36).

To complicate matters, smaller specialty journals have higher acceptance rates (above 50%) than larger journals, because the pool of authors is so small. Rejecting too many could mean insufficient papers to complete an issue. On the other hand, larger journals usually receive too many quality papers that cannot be accommodated by the publisher, meaning editors have to reject good papers (intimating that larger journals have higher-quality papers). There is also the possibility that a faulty review process may mean a flawed or defective paper is accepted (Hargens, 1988; Locke et al., 2010; Wiersma & Jurs, 2009). Electronic journals (e-journals) tend to have higher acceptance rates because page length is not an issue (this affects the cost of publishing). Open access journals (see end of chapter) in all disciplines have much higher acceptance rates than non–open access journals (Editage Insights, 2014; Sugimoto et al., 2013; Wiersma & Jurs, 2009).

REVIEW AND ENGAGEMENT

When critically reading a journal article, you would

☐ See if you can obtain the acceptance rates for this journal

☐ Determine whether having this information affected your judgment of the journal and the paper

JOURNAL IMPACT FACTORS

Aside from the reputation of the editor and the editorial board, the journal's peer review process, and its acceptance rates, another common means of judging the quality of a paper and a journal is its impact factor. Although the idea of impact ratings has been in existence for over half a century (since the mid 1960s), it only recently gained significant prominence, with most journals now having, or striving for, a number or score (metric) that allegedly measures the impact of their published articles. These metrics (Greek *metron*, "measure") (Harper, 2016) *assume* that the more often a paper is cited, the more important the paper or the journal must be, meaning it is having an impact. This numerical evidence is supposed to prove that a paper is making a difference in the field, influencing the body of knowledge and research agendas. Impact factors "estimate the relative influence exerted by the average article in a particular journal [or discipline] over scholars working in the same or adjacent areas of inquiry" (Locke et al., 2010, p. 32).

An array of metrics has emerged during the last decade. These metrics strive to "appraise the relative quality of journals [thereby making it easier for readers to] figure out which journals deserve greater respect and trust" (Locke et al., 2010, p. 37). They are summarized in Table 5.2, each with its own advantages and criticisms. It all started in the early 1960s, when Eugene Garfield invented the *journal impact factor* concept for Thomson Scientific (now Thomson Reuters), thereafter published in the *Journal Citation Reports* (JCR) (Garfield, 2005). As of October 2016, the JCR is no longer affiliated with Thomson Reuters, published instead by a new company called Clarivate Analytics (Clarivate Analytics, 2016).

TABLE 5.2 ■ Examples of Ranking Systems for Journals and Individuals	
Index (with date of inception)	**Explanation**
Journal and Its Articles	
Clarivate Analytics (2016) *Journal Citation Reports* (*impact factor*) (formerly Thomson Reuters)	Assigns an impact factor (IF) score to a specific journal (from 0.0 to 30), which is recalculated every year. If journals do not meet the criteria to be accredited, they are deleted from Clarivate Analytics' system. A score of 2.0 or higher out of 30 is considered a *good* ranking.
Eigenfactor (2007)	The average journal has a score of 1. Journals are compared, and their influence is measured by their score relative to 1 (similar to how Google ranks websites). The score considers the origin of who is citing the paper and reflects how frequently an average researcher would access content from that journal.
Tiered journals	Rating agencies create a hierarchy of several tiers and place peer-reviewed journals in one of the tiers or levels. The lower number or first alphabet letter (e.g., Tier 1 or Tier A) is considered the top level (prestigious journal), although second- and third-tier journals are still respectful (see Harzing's 2016 list of tiered journals).

(Continued)

TABLE 5.2 ■ (Continued)	
Index (with date of inception)	**Explanation**
Individuals and Their Articles	
h-index (Hirsch index) (2005)	This author-level metric attempts to measure both the actual productivity and apparent citation impact of the publications of a scientist or scholar. An h-index of 10 means the researcher has 10 papers, each cited 10 times or more. Desirable scores vary according to academic rank and experience. An h-index of 12 would be good for a tenured associate professor, with full professors expected to score 18 or more.
Other indices for individual scholars	*Google Scholar's* self-tracked and self-created h-index (2011) *Scopus* (2004) *Web of Science* (previously *Web of Knowledge*) (1990) *ResearchGate* (2008)
Altmetric (2011)	This index collects *qualitative* data from social media sites (online *attention*, mentions, and shares) and assesses a paper's wider impact. It is a noncitation metric (no number or score), measuring instead what people are saying about the article.

The metric convention is very controversial but has become entrenched in the psyche and practice of most journal editors and editorial boards. McGregor (2007) provided a very detailed overview of 10 key concerns about assessing an article's impact using a number or a score for the journal (see Table 5.3 for a summary). Despite these pervasive and lingering issues, people persist in judging the quality of a paper (and the caliber of the author) by the journal's impact factor (or another metric). To address this flawed logic, metrics have been developed that try to measure an individual scholar's impact (e.g., the h-index) or how the public is reacting to the ideas in the paper as expressed through social media (e.g., Altmetric) (see Table 5.2). Some say these alternative approaches are necessary because "most published work is rarely if ever cited. Only a small percentage of what is published is ever heard of again in the literature" (Harnad, 1996, p. 111).

Another issue is whether or not people actually understand the number they are reading. To illustrate, Clarivate Analytics' *journal impact factor* (IF) is calculated by assigning journals a number from *0.0 to 30* (people erroneously assume the range is 0–100). The system calculates indices for more than 9,000 journals. Any number over 2.0 is considered to be a good ranking in this system, a convention that contravenes the inclination to assume that a number of 15 or higher (midway to 30) would be a *good* ranking. In reality, using 2012 impact factor data, 93% of journals (virtually all of them) scored using this system scored lower than 2.0. More than half of the journals scored 1.0 or lower. Only 5.5% scored higher than 10, and only 23 journals had an IF of 30 (0.3%) (Sisson, 2012). Unfortunately, if a journal has an IF of 1.9, people see this *very low* number and erroneously assume the journal

TABLE 5.3   ■   Issues With Impact Factors and Journal Rankings

- Accreditation processes usually do not measure the scientific merit of the ideas (they measure only the perceived level of interest in the topic, determined by counting citations)

- People are unable to tell if the citation cast the paper in a positive or negative light

- These indices ignore the fact that publication rates, citation rates, and peak impact vary widely from field to field (ignoring context and the fact that many papers remain uncited for three years at a minimum, if ever cited)

- The system is subject to inflation (through either selective citations or editorial policies and choices) (e.g., the first issue of any year (volume) receives the most citations)

- Most indices include only recently published papers, meaning seminal, deeply influential works that are frequently cited by scholars are not counted when the journal's index is calculated

- If a journal is not in the database used to develop the index, any frequently cited papers from that journal are not included in the count (i.e., missing data)

- Those calculating the index assume that a relatively small number of high-quality journals publish the core of disciplinary research, justifying exclusion of *all* journals in a discipline when calculating the score

- Some disciplines cite each other more often than other disciplines, so people should always compare ranking value with journals in the same discipline

- Topics that cross disciplinary boundaries complicate the calculation of indices, skewing the actual meaning of the metric (score) for a journal

and its papers are not of high caliber, when in fact this number corresponds to 93% of the database. Very few journals in Clarivate Analytics' stable (only 7%) have an IF of 2.0 or higher. It behooves authors and critical readers to learn about *each* index being used to judge the caliber of the author, paper, or journal.

REVIEW AND ENGAGEMENT

When critically reading a journal article, you would

☐ See if you can obtain any impact factors or ratings for the journal (see Tables 5.2 and 5.3)

☐ Determine whether having this information affected your judgment of the journal and the paper?

JOURNAL TITLE

Authors and critical readers can use other criteria to judge the quality of a journal, starting with its title. There are literally thousands of journals currently in operation around the world (Harris, 2014). The title of a journal can be revealing, providing clues to its focus, scope, and intended audience (see Table 5.4). Titles can reflect the topic, country, discipline, and whether the journal is international in scope. While many titles contain the noun *journal*, just as many use other nouns such as *forum*, *quarterly publication*, *yearbook*, *review*, *digest*, or *bulletin*. Some journal titles start with the article *The*, followed with a noun. Other journal titles simply name a specific topic, like *Arts*.

TABLE 5.4 ■ Common Titles for Journals

• Journal of . . .	*Journal of Family & Consumer Sciences*
• International Journal of . . .	*International Journal of Home Economics*
• Specific country . . .	*Canadian Journal of Education*
• Specific discipline . . .	*Global Education Journal*
• . . . Quarterly	*Economic Quarterly*
• . . . Forum	*Kappa Omicron Nu FORUM*
• . . . Yearbook	*National Business Education Association Yearbook*
• . . . Research	*Family and Consumer Sciences Research Journal*
• . . . Review	*Computer Science Review*
• . . . Bulletin	*Bulletin of the Chemical Society of Japan*
• . . . Letters	*Ecology Letters*
• . . . Papers	*Oxford Economic Papers*
• Digest of . . .	*Digest of Middle East Studies*
• The . . .	*The Lancet*
• Name of specific topic	*Radical Pedagogy*

If the journal's content actually reflects the intent of the noun in its title, readers can cautiously infer what to expect from it. The word *journal* means a written document dealing with a particular subject. *Forum* refers to a meeting place or a medium for an exchange of views. The term *quarterly publication* has been in use since the 1830s and refers to a publication that comes out every three months. The word *yearbook* technically means an annual publication providing current information about, and listing events of, a previous year. When used to name a journal per se, it normally means the journal is published once a year (Anderson, 2014; Harper, 2016).

Review means a critical appraisal or summary of a literary work or body of literary work. A *digest* is a compilation or summary of material or information. *Bulletin* means a short official statement or summary, but the term is also used to refer to a regular report or newsletter. The latter two formats often include peer-reviewed articles, technical notes, correspondence, and official news of the sponsoring association. *Letters* and *papers* connote scholarly correspondence in the form of peer-reviewed papers (Anderson, 2014; Harper, 2016). Drawing inferences of quality from the journal's name is not recommended, but authors and critical readers may be able to gain a sense of its essential intent and the scholarly tone of the articles.

REVIEW AND ENGAGEMENT

When critically reading a journal article, you would

☐ Appreciate that the journal title is a proxy indicator of quality, discern the type of title, and then comment on it (see Table 5.4)

☐ Determine whether the topic of the paper seems appropriate for the journal's title

JOURNAL VOLUME, ISSUE, AND PAGINATION

Some critical readers and authors infer quality of a journal by how long it has been in existence. Most journals have both a volume and an issue number. In most instances, the volume number indicates how many *years* the journal has been published. For example, Volume 17 would mean 17 years. There are exceptions. For example, a very recent issue of *Nature* is numbered Volume 539, Issue 6727. *Nature* was first published in 1869, meaning 2016 should be Volume 147. As a general rule of a thumb, a journal with a volume number of 50 or higher would be considered extremely well established. Thirty years or more would be well established, with Volumes 10–29 indicating moderately established. A journal with a volume number of 5–10 would be a relatively "new kid on the block," and anything with a volume number of 1–4 would be totally untested. The latter two examples now tend to constitute electronically based journals (see end of chapter).

Although not really a useful criterion for quality assessment, it is helpful to know that instead of releasing one large collection for the whole year, most journals have several issues per year. An issue normally contains 5–20 individual articles. By long-standing convention, journals tend to publish either two or four issues per year, but some publish an issue every month. Journals that publish twice a year usually release an issue in the winter (Issue 1) and the summer (Issue 2). Indeed, some journals do not use numbers, opting instead for seasons or months. Quarterly issues are published every four months (Issues 1, 2, 3, and 4). To illustrate using the previous examples, *17*(3) means Volume 17, Issue 3, or the third issue of that year. In the *Nature* example above, Issue 6727 means this journal numbers issues from its inception (not a common convention).

Journals can also vary on pagination conventions. Some journals start the first issue in the year's volume with page 1, with the numbers growing steadily until year's end. An example for a paper would be Volume 77, Issue 4, pp. 992–1005. Some journals start each

TABLE 5.5 ■ Journal Pagination Conventions

Pagination Approach	Example
Page range	McGregor, S. L. T. (2008). Ideological maps of consumer education. *International Journal of Consumer Studies, 32*(5), 545–552.
Paper or article number, with URL	MacCleave, A. (2006). Incommensurability in cross-disciplinary research: A call for cultural negotiation. *International Journal of Qualitative Methods, 5*(2), Article 8. Retrieved from https://ejournals.library.ualberta.ca/index .php/IJQM/article/view/4389/3515
URL for article	McGregor, S. L. T. (2010). Historical notions of transdisciplinarity in home economics. *Kappa Omicron Nu FORUM, 16*(2). Retrieved from http://www .kon.org/archives/forum/16-2/mcgregor.html
DOI	Cheryan, S., Master, A., & Meltzoff, A. N. (2015). Cultural stereotypes as gatekeepers: Increasing girls' interest in computer science and engineering by diversifying stereotypes. *Frontiers in Psychology, 6*. http:// dx.doi.org/10.3389/fpsyg.2015.00049

issue within a volume with page 1, an example being Volume 77, Issue 4, pp. 1–16. Many online journals do not have page ranges. Instead, there is the volume number, usually an issue number, and then some combination of (a) the paper or article number along with the uniform resource locator (URL or web address), (b) the URL for the article or its portable document format (PDF) file name, and/or (c) a digital object identifier (DOI) (see Table 5.5). These conventions become relevant when citing journal articles in research papers. Editors and peer reviewers sometimes judge the perceived quality of a paper based on the author's attention to referencing conventions and can even reject a good paper for failure to adhere to these conventions. They assume that if the authors cannot even follow the citation style requirements, maybe their scholarship is irresponsible as well.

YEAR OF PUBLICATION AND ARTICLE PLACEMENT IN ISSUE

Aside from the other elements of a journal discussed in this chapter, the year a paper is published in a journal can provide clues about the currency of its ideas. The paper could be old and outdated or old and seminal (meaning other works were inspired by it). And, while seminal papers have long-lasting currency, recent papers may contain leading-edge ideas or innovative interpretations of previous ideas. This assertion is tempered with the reality that it can take years for a paper to be published (relative to when the author submitted it to the journal), and the data are usually older than that. This is less of an issue with conference papers or online journals (Ary et al., 2010). With the latter, the editor can ask the publisher to post the paper as soon as it is accepted, rather than placing it in a queue for a paper-based version of the journal, which only has so many pages per issue.

Where the editor choses to place a paper in the issue's lineup also can be perceived as a clue about the merits of the scholarship, the author's reputation, or both. (a) *Lead articles* (first in the issue) can be indicative of the currency of the ideas. (b) Article placement could be a political decision by the editor because the first paper is always the most cited (and more citations mean higher IFs). (c) The editor may want to grab readers' attention with an interesting idea (with no guarantee that it is the *best* paper in the collection). (d) An article's placement could be as simple as alphabetical by author name or article title (Coupe, Ginsburgh, & Noury, 2010; Ginsburgh, 2012).

SPECIAL TOPIC AND THEMED ISSUES

Editors and editorial boards will often select themes for specific issues. These are thought to lend prestige to the journal and raise its profile. Thematic issues serve a key role of agenda setting for research and policy (Avison, Fitzgerald, & Powell, 2001). Editors choose specially selected scholars to serve in the role of *guest editors*. These academics are experts in the topic or discipline, and they can use their network to invite others to contribute articles (although normally, anyone can respond to the *call for papers*). These thematic issues are usually prefaced with an introductory essay (by the guest editor), followed with five to seven peer-reviewed papers (Avison et al., 2001; Olk & Griffiths, 2004).

Journal editors use thematic or special topic issues for several reasons. They can (a) capture state-of-the-art thinking in the field about a particular topic, (b) stimulate enriched conversations about an important topic, (c) profile emerging topics in the field, (d) develop a topic the editor thinks fellow scholars should engage with, or (e) be used to publish a collection of papers from a conference (Avison et al., 2001; Olk & Griffiths, 2004).

Sometimes, editors create a special issue by pulling together a collection of articles from their own archives, presenting them as a theme. These editor-selected thematic collections highlight just a portion of the high-quality content published by the journal in a particular area. Of relevance to how aspects of a journal imply quality of scholarship, papers in a special issue tend to be cited more often than regular articles, and authors are perceived to be recognized experts in the field. Normally, special topic issues are very competitive and elite (Avison et al., 2001), meaning critical readers should be able to assume high-caliber scholarship.

REVIEW AND ENGAGEMENT

When critically reading a journal article, you would

☐ Determine what year the paper was published in the journal and then explain how this information affected your judgment of the paper

☐ Determine how old the journal is (check the volume number), infer its quality (totally untested, well established?), and explain how this information affected your judgment of the journal

☐ Determine where the paper was positioned in the issue (lead article, last paper) and explain how this information affected your judgment of the paper

☐ Comment on how its being in a journal's special issue affected your judgment of the quality of the paper

ELECTRONIC JOURNALS

Academic journals have been published on paper for centuries. But since the early 1990s, there has been rapid movement toward electronic journals (*e-journals*), using various business and distribution models, which can take one of four basic forms. E-journals can (a) be online only, with no paper version; (b) be online with limited paper distribution; (c) have the same online and print versions, with extra online papers; and (d) have the same online and paper versions but no extra online material (Kling & McKim, 1999). As a side note, electronic publishing of scholarly works can also use other media, including PDF files, e-books, CD-ROMs, blogs, file sharing (e.g., Dropbox, LinkedIn SlideShare, Scribd), mobile apps, videos (e.g., TED Talks, YouTube), podcasts, and tablet reading devices (e.g., Amazon Kindle).

There was initial resistance to the electronic publishing format, grounded in concerns around quality control and the fairness of the peer review process (Armstrong, 1997; Tenopir & King, 2000). In the meantime, most e-journals have followed Harnad's (1996) advice and implemented a peer review quality hierarchy that mitigates scholars' concerns for the quality of e-journal publications (see the next section for the exception of predatory open access journals). E-journals now abound, with some people claiming they are becoming the norm. Five years ago, Lamothe (2012) reported the existence of nearly 60,000 e-journals, representing exponential growth in that there were only 16 in 2000.

The scholarship posted at these media sites may or may not be peer reviewed, but when a paper *is* peer reviewed by a journal, it is the publisher (not the editor) who assigns a DOI when making a paper available electronically (on the Internet). The DOI is a number (digits) that identifies an object (e.g., the journal article). When readers click on this *live* number, they are taken directly to the online article (or to the journal's site where they can retrieve it for free or a fee). A related trend is editors and publishers posting journal articles online before the paper-based version is released. In those instances, the *Early Online*, *Ahead of Print*, or *Advance Online* paper is assigned a DOI, which it retains when published.

OPEN ACCESS JOURNALS

A recent trend is *open access* journals, wherein anyone can access articles for free (i.e., *access* is *open* to the public), but authors have to pay to have their work published (ranging from $500 to $5,000 per paper). Prior to this technological innovation, only people or libraries with subscriptions to the journal or members of a sponsoring professional association (membership benefit) could access published papers (Suber, 2015).

Open access to journal articles is provided through two avenues. *Gold* access is via the journal's website. *Green* access is (a) through the researcher's institutional depository (e.g., a university's research commons) or (b) by self-archiving at one's own website or at central depositories like *Academia.edu*, *ResearchGate*, and *PubMed Central*. Authors pay to have their work published at Gold access venues, but not at Green access. Some publishers allow for an embargo period after which authors can post their Gold access document at a Green access depository. Open access is compatible with every form of peer review and does not presuppose any particular peer review model (Suber, 2015). But the caliber of that peer review process for open access journals is another matter (Williams-Jones, Pipon, Smith, & Boulanger, 2014).

The principle of open access challenges the reader-pay-to-access model by asserting that people beyond universities must be able to access academic research (i.e., policy makers, industry actors, practitioners, and the public at large). A concurrent concern driving open access was that excessive fees were precluding scholars in "developing countries" from accessing their peers' research. This lack of access severely compromises their scholarship and resultant knowledge dissemination for their context (Suber, 2015; Williams-Jones et al., 2014). Despite open access journals being a relatively well-established publishing model (first created in the early 1990s), critical readers are cautioned to remain wary of drawing conclusions about scholarship caliber and quality when reading open access papers.

Predatory Open Access Journals

Although wide access to scholarship is desired, the juggernaut of predatory open access journals (via Gold access) is a mounting concern (Williams-Jones et al., 2014). A predator is someone or something that preys on others and exploits their vulnerabilities (Anderson, 2014). In the case of research, this often means new, novice, or otherwise disadvantaged scholars who must publish their work in order to get tenure (job security), be promoted, obtain funding, or some combination. These scholars may be charged exorbitant fees by the journal to get their paper published, but predatory journals do not provide the review, editing, or publishing services rendered by legitimate journals (Williams-Jones et al., 2014).

As a side note, an academic librarian, Jeffrey Beall, had identified criteria for categorizing predatory publications and had listed publishers and independent journals that met those criteria. In an unexplained move, in January 2017 he unpublished his list, which at that time contained over 1,100 predatory journals (Silver, 2017). The loss of this valuable information is unfortunate because these predatory journals have "spurious or no editorial boards, poor or absent scientific [peer] review, and little to no ethical and/or publication guidelines" (Williams-Jones et al., 2014, p. 1). Indeed, open access journals in all disciplines have extremely low rejection rates (Sugimoto et al., 2013). Also, predatory publishers do not account for "digital preservation," meaning the journal could disappear at any moment (Beall, 2010, p. 15). Another issue is the inability of many authors to pay the excessively high Article Processing Fee (APF) or Article Processing Charge (APC) (regardless of whether they are predatory or legitimate journals). This financial obstacle in effect bars them from publishing what might be valuable research (thwarted by the open access business model) (Fischman & Tefera, 2014).

REVIEW AND ENGAGEMENT

When critically reading a journal article, you would address the following questions:

☐ Did knowing it was an e-journal affect your confidence about future access? How did this publishing format affect your judgment of the journal and/or the paper?

☐ Did you access the e-journal paper directly through the publisher (Gold access) or at an outside depository (Green access)? How did this access affect your judgment of the paper?

☐ If it is an e-journal, determine if it is an *open access* journal. Then, try to determine if it is a reputable or predatory journal. How did this information inform your judgment of the journal and the quality of the paper?

CHAPTER SUMMARY

This chapter provided an overview of peer-reviewed journals, describing many key aspects of their management and distribution. Starting with the role of journal editors, editorial boards, and other types of editors, the discussion shifted to the peer review process, acceptance rates, and journal impact factors. It was recognized that people reading journal articles may use these aspects of journals as proxy evidence of the quality of the scholarship in the article itself. The discussion then turned to other facets of a journal that could be used to infer scholarly rigor including journal title, year of publication, volume and issue number, paper placement in the issue, and special issues. The chapter dealt extensively with the new publication model of electronic journals and discussed the possible threats to quality and rigor of open access journals, especially predatory journals. Critical readers are cautioned to use these journal elements judiciously because the superficiality of some of them may lead to erroneous judgements of research quality.

FINAL JUDGMENT ON PEER-REVIEWED JOURNAL

Taking *all* of the **Review and Engagement** criteria into account, what is your final judgment of the quality of the journal and respective paper that you are critically reading?

REVIEW AND DISCUSSION QUESTIONS

1. Were you aware of the key role that journal editors play in building a discipline's body of knowledge (their decisions about what gets published)? How did this information make you feel?

2. Had you ever given any thought to the impact that a journal's provenance has on scholarship in a field? Explain.

3. What was your reaction to the power and influence of the peer review process in shaping the rigor of scholarship in a research paper? Explain your reaction to the idea of extended peer review and community review for shaping the rigor of a published paper.

4. In your opinion, should journal articles even undergo a review by disciplinary peers? Explain your answer.

5. Should critical readers of scholarship put much weight on acceptance rates? Is this criterion too overrated? Justify your position.

6. The contentious issue of journal impact factors is not going away anytime soon. Discuss your point of view on this criterion for judging a paper's quality (see Table 5.3).

7. In your opinion, should metrics have this much power when judging the quality of a research project and its report? Explain your answer.

8. Do you agree with the idea of giving authors a score on their publishing record and then using that score to judge their paper? Explain your answer.

9. Have you ever been swayed to read a paper because it is in a special issue? Do you think it is reasonable to assume that these papers tend to be of better quality?

10. Does the nature of the publishing venue (paper or electronic) affect your decision about the quality of the research? Explain your thoughts.

11. Do you like the idea of open access journals? Do you think this publishing format will affect the quality of papers in the future? Why or why not?

12. Had you ever heard of predatory journals? Given what you know now, would this influence your decision to read a paper from such a journal? Explain your answer, as it relates to the perceived quality of the scholarship therein.

RESEARCH JUSTIFICATIONS, AUGMENTATION, AND RATIONALES

6 INTRODUCTION AND RESEARCH QUESTIONS

INTRODUCTION

Just as the abstract is the foreground of a paper, the introduction is the background (Shank & Brown, 2007). All research articles begin with an introduction to the study being reported in the *particular* paper. The lay meaning of the word *introduce* is to present for the first time (Anderson, 2014). In a scholarly research paper, *introduce* means to present to readers the context and significance of *the* study (Labaree, 2016). The introductory segment of a paper sets up the literature review, methods, results or findings, discussion, and conclusions. Although not all papers follow the same reporting formats, they all have an introduction of some sort (Goodson, 2017). As a caveat, this chapter distinguishes among and discusses broad areas of interest, topics, issues and problems within the topic, research problems, research questions, research statements, and research objectives. It also distinguishes between opening points and introductions, conventions that are not always evident in every research paper. They are compartmentalized here to show their uniqueness coupled with their interdependence.

In brief, *opening points* (one to three sentences) tell the reader why the author thinks the *research topic* is important. The lengthier *Introduction* section (several paragraphs or pages) explains what the author is attempting to accomplish in a *particular paper*. The research problem is the *author's topic of interest* within a larger area of interest, and the research question and the research statement reflect what will be addressed in a *particular study*. In other words, authors move from the general to very specific as they set up their paper. The Introduction section can be viewed as an inverted triangle or cone (see Figure 6.1). Authors begin by presenting the more general aspects of the topic, narrowing their discussion to more specific information that provides context and significance to *their* research problem within that topic, ending with a purpose statement and research questions for *their* study (Annesley, 2010; Creswell, 2009; Labaree, 2016).

Learning Objectives (Continued)

- Differentiate between a research statement and a research objective, and demonstrate the difference between qualitative, quantitative, and mixed methods research statements

- Recognize each of six approaches to writing Introduction sections, being able to judge when each has been executed properly

- Compare and contrast delimitations and limitations to a study (and explain why delimitations matter in the Introduction section)

Papers often have headings for all of these elements, but just as often, they do not. And if they do, not all authors use the same labels (often mixing up *research problem, question, purpose, statement,* and *objective*). Nonetheless, authors have to make sure readers can find each of these elements because they are the context and the anchor for the entire paper. Introductions create initial impressions about the logic of the author's argument and approach to the research problem. Negative first impressions can put off readers, especially if the Introduction section is disorganized, vague, and illogical (Creswell, 2009; Labaree, 2016). A well-written Introduction section "lays out the itinerary of an article's path of logical travel" (Shon, 2015, p. 41).

Although only a few paragraphs in length (sometimes a few pages if some aspect of the literature review is included), the Introduction section plays a crucial role in presenting research to readers for the first time. The research question becomes significant and compelling if authors can place it in the context of a very focused and current research area and a topic within that general area. Without this context (i.e., a historical and contemporary backdrop), or if the context is unfocused and

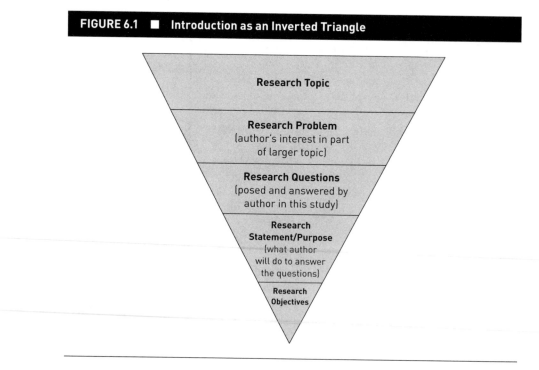

FIGURE 6.1 ■ Introduction as an Inverted Triangle

Research Topic

Research Problem
(author's interest in part of larger topic)

Research Questions
(posed and answered by author in this study)

Research Statement/Purpose
(what author will do to answer the questions)

Research Objectives

rambling, the research question becomes lost, both literally and significantly. It will seem like it is not worthy of consideration and stop readers in their tracks (Creswell, 2009; Wong, 2006).

The Introduction section comprises, in some combination, opening points, reference to past and current literature, and an argument that justifies the specific research question being examined (Rocco & Plakhotnik, 2009). These elements were used to organize this chapter (but not in that order), appreciating that the ultimate format used in a paper differs according to the author's writing style, the research methodology, the journal's style, the field of study (discipline), or some combination (Goodson, 2017). Because the entire research project hinges on a clear articulation of the research problem and attendant questions, this chapter starts with this topic, ending with a detailed discussion of how to write an Introduction section for each of quantitative, qualitative, and mixed methodologies (especially how to develop an argument that provides a strong rationale for the study). This chapter ends with a discussion of delimitations (i.e., placing boundaries around the study).

ETYMOLOGICAL ROOTS

Introduce is Latin *introductionem*, "a leading in" (Harper, 2016). A good introduction uses *leads* or statements that draw people in and along to a predetermined destination (Anderson, 2014). These leads make readers want to delve further into the paper. They are often called signposts, pointing the way to what is to come and why (Goodson, 2017; Shank & Brown, 2007). The Introduction section leads readers into a research paper, which reports efforts to find the answers to research question(s).

Research is Latin *recercher*, "to search" (Harper, 2016). Researching means using a systematic effort to find, discover, or create data, information, or answers to something of interest (Booth, Colomb, & Williams, 1995). *Question* is Latin *quaerere*, "to ask or to seek" (Harper, 2016). In general, questions are a linguistic convention wherein people make a request for information or data. The response is an answer, whether researched or not.

Lay Versus Research Questions

A research question is different from a regular lay question. Answering *research questions* involves using a systematic effort to search for data and information (Booth et al., 1995). This entails quantitative, qualitative, or mixed methods research protocols (see Chapter 8) as well as sophisticated argumentation and/or conceptualization yielding position papers, discussion papers, think pieces, or theoretical papers (see Chapters 17 and 18, respectively). Lay questions are posed on a daily basis, while research questions are specific to the *scholarly* research process, project, or inquiry (i.e., serious academic study). The answers are presented in a research report (e.g., a journal article), which is "a written document that gives the history of a research study from start to finish" (Locke, Silverman, & Spirduso, 2010, p. 15).

REVIEW AND ENGAGEMENT

When critically reading a research report, you will

- ☐ Determine if the authors created an organized, positive first impression of their paper

- ☐ Determine if they, ideally, presented the more general aspects of the topic, then narrowed their discussion to more specific information that provided context and significance to *their* research problem within that topic, ending with a purpose statement and research questions for *their* study

- ☐ Ascertain if they included *headings* for all of these aspects of the Introduction section, making them easier for you to find and judge

RESEARCH TOPICS, PROBLEMS, QUESTIONS, STATEMENTS, AND OBJECTIVES

As noted earlier, this chapter distinguishes among a broad area of interest, topics within that broad area, issues and problems within the topic, research problems, research questions, research statements, and research objectives (see Figures 6.1 and 6.2). Whether they use these terms or not (they are used to organize this chapter), authors have to provide evidence that they moved from the general to the very specific when they wrote the Introduction section of their study. Readers have to be able to follow the authors' logic and thinking, and be able to discern any arguments posited by authors to support their reasons for the study (Labaree, 2016).

FIGURE 6.2 ■ Moving From a Topic Through a Research Problem to a Research Statement

General to the Discipline   **Specific to Authors and Their Study**

| Broad and general **area of interest** | **Narrower topics** of interest *within the broader area* | **General issues and problems worthy of research** *within a topic* (known by way of practice or reading the literature) | **Research problem:** *authors' interest* in what they believe to be an important issue around which they take a stand (reflects gaps, puzzles, or inconsistencies in the literature or practice) | **Research question or hypothesis:** *posed and answered by authors* to understand the problem (others may pose different questions) | **Research statement:** authors' *purpose statement of what will happen in the study* to answer the research questions; may be further drilled down to **research objectives** (things to be done to collect data relevant to the research question) |

In more detail, researchers and authors usually have existing expertise in several broad areas of interest (for me, that is home economics philosophy, consumer education, studies and policy, and transdisciplinarity). They continually read the literature from these areas to stay current. This process inevitably leads to a narrowed focus on particular aspects of the broad area of interest, called topics. Within those topic areas, researchers will eventually decide that there are important issues or problems that have not received adequate attention. This insight leads them to further narrow their own interest to problems *they* perceive to be important and worthy of further investigation. This in turn leads them to pose a research problem of special interest to *them*, which may lead to an actual study wherein they pose specific research questions or hypotheses to be answered by their study. These are then expressed explicitly, in any paper reporting the study, as research statements and research objectives (Booth et al., 1995; Boudah, 2011; Handley & Oakes, 2016; Jacobs, 2011) (see Figure 6.3).

Example 6.1 Moving from broad to very specific Hypothetically, Dr. Rattray is a researcher in the *field* of consumer studies. She regularly reads from more than 15 professional journals in this *broader area of interest*, in addition to attending conferences and reading books and related documents. Over the years, she has developed her *own area of expertise* around the *topics* of consumer finances and consumer education. Recently, she has noticed a *new issue* emerging in the literature, that of the possible relationship between consumers' level of education and their consumer indebtedness. No one else has explicitly identified this as an issue, so she coined the phrase *consumer literacy* and identified it as a new *research problem* worthy of investigation. She wrote a position paper on the topic (re: the need to conceptualize consumer literacy) and then designed a mixed methods study that explored both quantitative and qualitative aspects of this new problem. She posed different *research questions* for each phase or strand of the study (qualitative and quantitative), and she developed *specific research objectives* for each research question. Her Methods section then reflected the steps she took to gather data to answer the research questions.

The next part of this chapter purposefully separates the research topic from the research problem, question, statement, and objective. This demarcation is not always found in authors' papers, but it serves to help distinguish the very different role each plays in the Introduction section of a research paper. When appropriate, the discussion differentiates these basic elements of an Introduction section in quantitative, qualitative, and mixed methods research (see Chapter 8).

Research Topics

Broad, general areas of interest include disciplines, subdisciplines, and subfields, as well as specializations within these areas. These broad areas of interest comprise *topics*. A topic is a situation, phenomenon, or event that is thought about (Anderson, 2014). Research topics are narrow enough that researchers can master a reasonable amount of information about them (i.e., gain expertise, even notoriety) while continually thinking and posing questions about them until they find something of interest to them personally. This interest arises from their engagement with gaps, puzzles, or inconsistencies in the literature, which they

FIGURE 6.3 ■ Example of General Area of Interest Through to Research Statement and Research Objectives

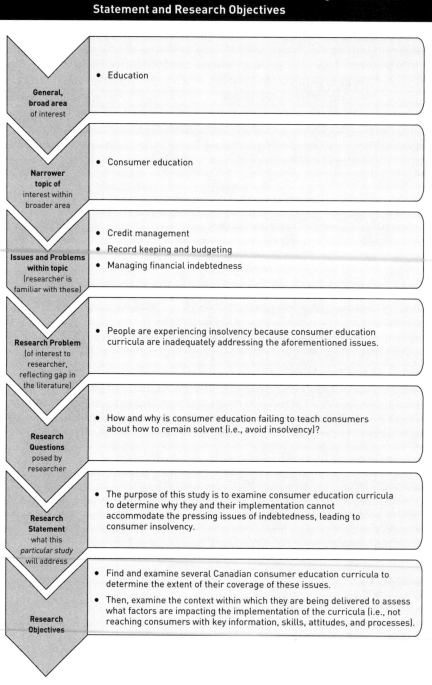

General, broad area of interest

- Education

Narrower topic of interest within broader area

- Consumer education

Issues and Problems within topic (researcher is familiar with these)

- Credit management
- Record keeping and budgeting
- Managing financial indebtedness

Research Problem (of interest to researcher, reflecting gap in the literature)

- People are experiencing insolvency because consumer education curricula are inadequately addressing the aforementioned issues.

Research Questions posed by researcher

- How and why is consumer education failing to teach consumers about how to remain solvent (i.e., avoid insolvency)?

Research Statement what this *particular study* will address

- The purpose of this study is to examine consumer education curricula to determine why they and their implementation cannot accommodate the pressing issues of indebtedness, leading to consumer insolvency.

Research Objectives

- Find and examine several Canadian consumer education curricula to determine the extent of their coverage of these issues.
- Then, examine the context within which they are being delivered to assess what factors are impacting the implementation of the curricula (i.e., not reaching consumers with key information, skills, attitudes, and processes).

eventually turn into *their own* research questions (Booth et al., 1995; Labaree, 2016). For clarification, a topic is an area within a specific field of study or a discipline. It is the context for the paper, while an issue or problem is what the author takes a stand on and turns into a research question and, ultimately, a research report (Handley & Oakes, 2016, who provided the following example of a research topic).

> ***Example 6.2 Topic, issue, research problem, and question*** Nuclear waste is one *topic* within the *discipline* of chemistry (the broader area of interest). Whereas nuclear waste is the topic, a pressing *issue* (*problem*) within this topic is the safe and economic disposal of nuclear waste. With a passion for this issue (problem), a researcher may pose a particular *research question*, such as "Why has the nuclear waste energy industry failed to find safe and economic means to dispose of such products?"

In example 6.2, the *disposal of nuclear waste* is the focus of the study, instead of the broader topic of nuclear waste or the even broader discipline of chemistry. The topic is manageable and achievable. A good research topic is broad enough for researchers to find plenty of material but narrow enough to fit within the constraints of their research resources. Also, the scope of information dealing with a topic must be reasonable, and the sources containing this information must be accessible. The topic must be adequately focused from broad to specific. For example, authors may want ensure that their study avoids long time frames, the complete works of a prolific author, or topics that are too general (e.g., the topic of the *price of urban housing* is preferred to the broader topic of *urban housing*) (Booth et al., 1995; Handley & Oakes, 2016).

REVIEW AND ENGAGEMENT

When critically reading a research report, you will

☐ Ascertain if the authors convinced you they appreciate the difference between research topic, problem, question, statement, and objective (see Figures 6.2, 6.3, and 6.8 and example 6.2) (If they did not, you will be very confused and likely frustrated.)

☐ Ensure that their Introduction section included *at least* (a) opening points (one to three sentences), (b) references to past and current literature (normally more fully developed in the Literature Review section), and (c) an argument justifying their specific research question (threaded throughout the Introduction section)

Research Problems

A *topic* is something to think about whereas a *research problem* is something to be solved or framed as a question, which is raised for inquiry, consideration, a solution, or an explanation (Labaree, 2016) (see Figure 6.2). Research problems are posed by researchers. They "do not exist in nature just waiting to be plucked out by some observant researcher (Guba, 1981). Instead, they are artificial entities that come together only through the intense efforts of the researcher" (Jacobs, 2011, p. 127). Which problem is actually identified by the researcher determines everything that follows in the research process (Gall, Gall, & Borg, 2015). Some scholars argue that focusing on the topic as a problem limits the framing. For example, those using the appreciative inquiry method look at what is working, not what is broken (a problem that needs to be fixed). They pose *affirmative topics* rather than research questions. To illustrate, instead of focusing on low staff morale (research problem), they might focus on what is involved in becoming a place where people want to work (Bustos Coral, Ortiz Jiménez, & Voetmann, 2015). That being said, there are quantitative, qualitative, mixed methods, casuist, theoretical, and practical research problems.

Quantitative research problems

In quantitative research, authors can identify one of three types of research problems. *Relational* problems focus on investigating the relationship between variables (cause and effect, or associative). *Difference* research problems are concerned with identifying differences between two or more phenomenon (e.g., treatments, groups). *Descriptive* research problems focus on understudied, underresearched, or undertheorized issues, striving to describe a situation, event, state, or condition (Labaree, 2016). In studies anchored around these three types of problems, authors typically frame the problem as a question, followed with hypotheses that examine relationships between variables (Ary et al., 2010).

Qualitative research problems

Qualitative research problems are sometimes called a *research phenomenon* (Boudah, 2011). They are concerned with *exploring and understanding* phenomena from the perspective of those living the problem (Johnson & Christensen, 2012). These problems tend to reflect a lack of previous research and a need for relevant theories (Creswell, 2009). Indeed, with qualitative research, authors may not know the precise problem at the onset of their study. They tend to initially frame problems as general topics of interest, prefaced with *why* or *how* (e.g., How do high school students feel when they become alienated from their peers?). *How* and *why* questions invite deep research and lead to more interesting answers (Booth et al., 1995). Also, qualitative *why* questions do not have to refer to causation as do quantitative questions (Yin, 1984) (see Chapter 12).

Actually, qualitative authors tend to have a hunch that a problem situation exists. This hunch inspires them to choose sites and participants, involving them in the problem identification process. As a result, the formal research problem often becomes an outcome of the study and is not stated until or during data collection and analysis (see Chapters 8 and 9 for a discussion of emergent research designs). This problem can then become part of the intellectual cache of a discipline, prompting further research (Ary et al., 2010; Babor, Stenius, Savva, & O'Reilly, 2004; Jacobs, 2011).

Johnson and Christensen (2012) suggested that a good *qualitative* research problem comprises four elements. It stems from a general topic area, it arises from a key research problem pursuant to the topic, and there are sound reasons why this is an important problem (relative to other issues related to the topic). Finally, authors will clearly state that they intend to design a study that will either (a) *explore* some process, event, or phenomenon; (b) seek *understandings* of the inner world of a particular group at a particular site experiencing this problem; or (c) both (see their paraphrased example below from p. 72):

Example 6.3 Qualitative research problem statement The authors opened with a statement about the value of education, especially for women [general topic area]. They followed with the point that women are less likely to receive an education than men [the main research problem]. They then pointed out that educated women benefit society and themselves but are held back for various reasons [why this problem is important], ending with a statement that the study will focus on *understanding* these women and *exploring* the education and cultural process.

Mixed methods research problems

Mixed methods research is a new type of research intended to address research questions that require both qualitative and quantitative data (Johnson, Onwuegbuzie, & Turner, 2007). Discussed in more detail in Chapters 2, 8, 10, and 13, the term *mixed methods* "applies only to studies that employ both quantitative and qualitative methods" (Gall et al., 2015, p. 479). And the term refers only to instances when qualitative and quantitative methods are used within a *single* research project or study (Driessnack, Sousa, & Mendes, 2007b). Mixed methods research problems

(a) can be similar to a quantitative research problem (because mixed research can add perspective to a quantitative study), (b) can be similar to a qualitative research problem (because mixed research can add perspective to a qualitative study), or (c) can be a hybrid of the quantitative and qualitative approaches (in which ideas associated with quantitative and qualitative research are explicitly included in the single problem statement). (Johnson & Christensen, 2012, p. 71)

Casuist, theoretical, and practical research problems

Neither qualitative nor quantitative in nature, *casuist research problems* deal with determining the right and wrong of conduct or conscience by analyzing moral dilemmas. Casuistry (Latin *casus*, "case") is reasoning used to resolve moral problems by extracting or extending theoretical rules from particular instances and applying these rules to new instances. Philosophical, ethical, and jurisprudence (law) researchers would be interested in these types of research problems (Labaree, 2016). To answer these research problems, authors would use a special form of a *case* method to solve moral disputes and quandaries (Kopelman, 1994). The solution of these research problems leads "to the formulation of expert opinion about the existence and stringency of particular moral obligations, framed in terms of rules or maxims that are general but not universal or invariable, since they hold good with certainty only in the typical conditions of the agent and circumstances of action" (Jonsen & Toulmin, 1988, p. 297).

Authors may also be interested in *theoretical* research problems as well as *practical* problems. The former involves either developing new and refining existing theories or testing theories by deducing hypotheses. Authors would preface these problems with "What is it? Why [or how] does it occur?" *Practical research problems* reflect problems people encounter in their day-to-day work activities, at the actual level of practice. These problems are often prefaced with *how* and *what* and tend to be concerned with effectiveness. Authors hope to use their study results to improve practice (Ary et al., 2010).

REVIEW AND ENGAGEMENT

When critically reading a research report, you would

☐ Determine if the authors clarified which of three quantitative research problems (relational, difference, or descriptive) they addressed (if any)

☐ Determine if they clarified which of two qualitative research problems (explore processes or seek understanding) they addressed (if any)

☐ Ascertain if they justified using mixed methods to address their research question, which needs both numbers and participants' words to be answered

☐ Determine if they clarified whether they were answering a casuist, theoretical, or practical research problem, prefaced with the appropriate journalistic W

Research goals

Shank and Brown (2007) argued that any research problems selected by researchers reflect their overall *research goals*, of which there are eight (see Table 6.1) and possibly more, including exposing power relationships, creating persuasive arguments, and developing new theories and conceptual frameworks. They explained that authors often do not expressly articulate their research goals, but these are inductively evident in the arguments they use to justify their methodological approach and their method choices to solve the research problem, indicated by the bolded action verbs in Table 6.1.

TABLE 6.1 ■ Eight Possible Research Goals

- **Explore** relationships and phenomena that are not well understood
- **Predict** results by manipulating and controlling important factors
- **Explain** or **describe** some previously unstudied setting, context, or situation
- **Bring together** facts and information not previously connected to see how they interact
- **Compare** important processes or factors to gain new understandings of how they relate to each other
- **Replace** a current understanding, theory, or model
- **Understand** change within a complex setting or situation
- **Reflect** on the impact of research on self and others

Basic versus applied research

Shank and Brown (2007) further suggested that research problems can reflect either basic or applied research. Basic research is focused on creating new knowledge through theoretical understandings of fundamental processes and structures that underlie observed behavior. Applied research strives to use basic knowledge in practice to solve immediate and practical issues and problems (Gall et al., 2015; Smith, 2008; Suter, 2012).

It also leads to further understanding of theory employed in basic studies (Wiersma & Jurs, 2009). Table 6.2 compares these two fundamental approaches to knowledge discovery and creation.

Authors should be aware of prevailing myths around which approach (basic or applied) is the best. With this awareness, they will not inadvertently eschew one approach over another when it would have been the most relevant one for their research purpose. Basic research is often viewed as complex, precise, exacting, and performed by scientific thinkers. Applied is seen to be simple, imprecise, sloppy, haphazard, and carried out by unsophisticated practitioners. These grave misconceptions need to be acknowledged and challenged. Both approaches are important, with neither being better than the other. They "are differentiated not by their complexity or value, but by their goals or purposes" (Wiersma & Jurs, 2009, p. 12).

Authors tend to be intuitively aware of which type of research is informing their work—basic or applied (especially what they consider to be a research problem). Infrequently, they explicitly state this in their paper. Including this information would contribute to the provenance of the research problem because it helps clarify the impulse that drove the authors' investigation, the origins of their interest, and what shaped their research problem and subsequent questions or hypotheses (Locke et al., 2010).

TABLE 6.2 ■ Basic Versus Applied Research	
Basic Research	**Applied Research**
Example: In 1895, Dr. Wilhelm Röntgen's study of the **nature** of electricity led to the inadvertent discovery of X-rays (X stands for an unknown form of radiation).	*Example:* **X-ray technology is now used** and **applied** in surgery and medicine (the first X-ray was a picture of Dr. Röntgen's wife's hand and her wedding ring).
• Motivated by intellectual curiosity (i.e., people want to learn more about something)	• Motivated by desire to answer specific questions and to solve practical problems
• Using empirical research, the intent is to acquire knowledge for knowledge's sake, adding to the growing pile of knowledge (with no concern for if or how it will be used); the intent is to expand humanity's knowledge of the world	• Using empirical, interpretive, and critical research, the intent is to innovate, enhance practice, and augment development so as to address and solve today's practical problems by using new applications, often based on basic science
• Strives to study the laws of nature, assuming this will lead to new fundamental understandings	• Strives to improve the human condition and make the world a better place (via treatments, interventions, products, processes, strategies, programs, and policies)
• Assumes that basic research lays down the foundations for applied science (if basic is done well, applied spinoffs will eventually result)	• Assumes it can turn to basic science for inspiration for new applications
• Leads to revolutions (drastic changes in thinking and behaving)	• Leads to reform (changes leading to improvements)

Sources of research problems

Unlike the research question, the provenance of the research problem is not normally reported in a research paper (Locke et al., 2010), although readers often can deduce this information. Research problems can come from personal experience and interest, professional research agendas, professional literature, practice, policy debates, engagement with colleagues within and outside a discipline, theories, current social issues, and social movements (Ary et al., 2010; Gall et al., 2015; Jacobs, 2011; Labaree, 2016; Suter, 2012; Wiersma & Jurs, 2009).

Characteristics of a good research problem

Regardless of their source, in order to prepare good research questions, authors must be confident that they have a good research *problem* (i.e., significant, researchable, suitable to their expertise, and ethically appropriate) (see Table 6.3) (Ary et al., 2010; Gall et al., 2015; Johnson & Christensen, 2012; Wiersma & Jurs, 2009). Ill-defined research problems compromise the integrity, and the perceived significance, of the entire research enterprise (Creswell, 2009).

TABLE 6.3 ■ Characteristics of a Good Research Problem

Criteria for a Good Research Problem	Explanation of Each Criterion
Significant	A research problem should be extensive or important enough to merit scholarly consideration (i.e., serious academic study). Its worth is judged by the strength of the author's rationale for the study and its contributions to knowledge, practice, or theory.
Researchable	The problem must be capable of being studied carefully, thoroughly, and in detail. It must be possible and feasible to gather data that answer the question, an exercise that depends on resources (especially time and money), sample availability and accessibility, and researchers' expertise.
Original or replicable	Good research questions are original, but they can also lead to replication and extension of existing scholarship. Both are valuable ways to construct a cumulative body of knowledge, theories, and practice innovations.
Suitable for researcher	Problems must match the researchers' expertise and resources and be meaningful and interesting enough to sustain their commitment to addressing the problem.
Ethically appropriate	Researchers must be able to investigate the problem without violating ethical principles of conducting research with humans (see Chapter 8).
Considerable potential for new research trajectories	Addressing the problem will create new questions and sustain wider interest in the issue. Answers found when addressing a good research problem will change ways of thinking (conceptual problems) and acting (tangible problems) and/or tender new strands of research and inquiry.

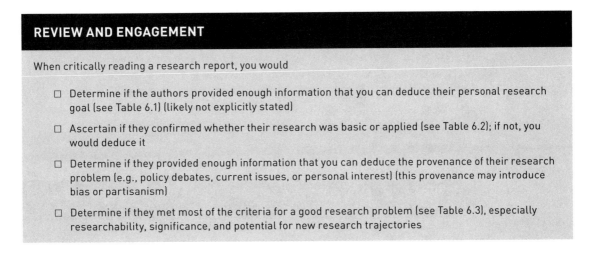

REVIEW AND ENGAGEMENT

When critically reading a research report, you would

☐ Determine if the authors provided enough information that you can deduce their personal research goal (see Table 6.1) (likely not explicitly stated)

☐ Ascertain if they confirmed whether their research was basic or applied (see Table 6.2); if not, you would deduce it

☐ Determine if they provided enough information that you can deduce the provenance of their research problem (e.g., policy debates, current issues, or personal interest) (this provenance may introduce bias or partisanism)

☐ Determine if they met most of the criteria for a good research problem (see Table 6.3), especially researchability, significance, and potential for new research trajectories

Research Questions or Hypotheses

Authors often confuse the research problem with the research question (Creswell, 2009). This confusion can be mitigated by appreciating that a *problem* can be solved by asking and answering *questions* using the data collected in the study (Labaree, 2016). So, once a good research problem has been identified (see Table 6.3), researchers have to pose questions for *their* particular study. A *research question* reflects what *the author* wants to know about the problem. Other scholars may be interested in the same problem but pose very different research questions. This is because controversial research topics (which are the geneses of research problems) tend to generate multiple points of view from different sectors (Brenner, 2001).

Example 6.4 Varying research questions to address a problem

Research problem: Education professionals profess the value of a systems approach but fail to employ it when developing training programs.

Possible research questions:

• Why do education professionals who value the use of a systems approach to develop training programs seldom follow through?

• What is it about the systems approach that precludes education professionals from actually using it in their practice?

• What is unique about education training programs that prevent education professionals from using a systems approach in their development?

Table 6.4 profiles the general characteristics of a good research question (Wilfred Laurier University Library, ca. 2009), including being specific, subtle, and focused on one issue. Figure 6.4 shares a modest example of applying one criterion to judge a selection of research questions around the topic of juvenile delinquency.

TABLE 6.4   ■   General Characteristics of a Good Research Question

- Focused on just one issue that can be examined or explored in great detail
- Specific, precise, and clear (not too broad or too narrow)
- Subtle, requiring analysis and thinking (no simple or obvious answer)
- Prefaced with one of the journalistic *W*s: why, how (with what), what, when, who, or where
- Verbs accurately reflect the research methodology (exploratory qualitative or deterministic quantitative and mixed methods)

FIGURE 6.4   ■   Examples of Too Broad and Too Narrow Research Questions (Handley & Oakes, 2016)

Juvenile delinquency is a *topic* that can be found within the *broader field* of sociology. The following three examples illustrate the author's *research questions* intended to address a *research problem*. The questions are designed to gather data to solve the problem.

Research Problem: *Juvenile delinquency and recidivism are a persistent problem in Canada.*

Research question that is too narrow (it can be answered with a number, a datum):

- *What is the 2016 rate of juvenile delinquency in Canada?*

Research question that is too broad (it requires nationwide canvassing to obtain data):

- *What is being done to reduce juvenile delinquency in Canada?*

A better research question (focused enough for in-depth research):

- *What role can public school education play in reducing juvenile delinquents' return to crime?*

The discussion now turns to what authors need to know about posing good qualitative, quantitative, and mixed methods questions, summarized in Table 6.5 (Creswell, 2009) and discussed in the following text.

Qualitative research questions

Actually, a common failure of qualitative papers is that the research question is so embedded in the introductory text that readers cannot find it. Authors can mitigate this happening by actually have a subheading called *Research Questions* (Babor et al., 2004). Creswell (2009) explained that authors of qualitative papers should pose questions but not hypotheses. And those questions should comprise one or two central research questions, perhaps in conjunction with a set of five to seven subquestions. The broadness of the central question(s) enables authors to collect a wide range of data from participants and other sources. The questions posed by the author must reflect the particular qualitative method employed in the study (for examples, see Table 6.6). Babor et al. (2004) concurred, arguing that authors should ensure that their question reflects the ambition of the study. Articles can *explore* a topic, *discover* a new social phenomenon, *present* a new perspective, *seek* to raise consciousness, *evaluate* a project, or *create* a new theory. The characteristics of good qualitative research questions are set out in Table 6.5.

TABLE 6.5 ■ Characteristics of Good Qualitative, Quantitative, and Mixed Methods Research Questions		
Good Qualitative Research Questions	**Good Quantitative Research Questions**	**Good Mixed Methods Research Questions**
• Designed in expectation that they will change and evolve during data collection and analysis • Usually prefaced with *what* or *how* because these words convey an open and emerging research design • Employ *exploratory verbs* that reflect the emergent nature of the research design (e.g., *discover*, *seek to understand*, *explore a process*, *describe experiences*, *report stories*)	• Designed to remain fixed during the study • Usually prefaced with *why, when, where, who,* and *do* • Use *directional verbs* that reflect the deterministic nature of the research design (e.g., *affect, influence, impact, determine, cause, relate*) • Instead of research questions, authors may develop hypotheses (null or alternative, directional or nondirectional) that specify variables and either compare, relate, or describe the impact of one variable(s) on another	• Questions can be advanced at the beginning or emerge during later quantitative or qualitative phases of the research • First-phase questions should be posed first followed with second-phase questions (e.g., pose quantitative then qualitative questions) • In a single-phase study, order the questions according to which strand received the most weight (qualitative or quantitative) • Authors can pose an *integrated (hybrid) question*, either at the beginning, when it emerges, or in between discussions of the results and findings from the two earlier phases

TABLE 6.6 ■ Examples of Qualitative Questions Corresponding With Method		
Qualitative Method	**Intent of Study**	**Focus of Questions**
Grounded theory	Discover	Direct questions toward generating a new theory of a process
Case study	Explore or describe	Questions may address a description of a case and the themes that emerge
Ethnography	Seek to understand	Questions can focus on gaining understandings of cultural processes and events
Phenomenology	Describe experiences	Questions ask what is it like for someone to experience something in a particular context
Narrative	Report stories	Questions can focus on gaining information used to recount people's life stories

Quantitative research questions and hypotheses

Quite simply, a quantitative research question is "an interrogative sentence that asks a question about the relationship that exists between two or more variables" (Johnson & Christensen, 2012, p. 74). The most common forms of questions are (a) causal, (b) predictive, and (c) descriptive, which serve two functions. Descriptive questions can be posed either to seek answers to how much, how often, and what changes or to identify the degree of relationship that exists between variables (see Table 6.5 for characteristics of good quantitative research questions).

Authors of quantitative papers may opt to report hypotheses rather than specific research questions (see Chapters 12 and 14 for more details about writing hypotheses). Hypotheses constitute a supposition that is not yet verified but, if true, would explain certain facts or phenomena. They are based on limited evidence and are used as a starting point or the foundation for further investigation. Indeed, *hypothesis* is Greek *hupothesis*, "foundation" (Anderson, 2014). In a research context, they replace questions and constitute "the formal statement of the researcher's prediction of the relationship that exists among the variables under investigation" (Johnson & Christensen, 2012, p. 77).

Example 6.5 Quantitative research question versus hypothesis (Johnson & Christensen, 2012, p. 77):

In this example, help-seeking behaviour is the dependent variable, and the type of setting is the independent variable.

Research question: *Does* the type of setting (ego-involving or task-solving) affect children's propensity to request help? There is no prediction in a research question.

Hypothesis: Children in ego-involving settings *will be less likely* to request help than children in task-solving settings. There is a prediction in a hypothesis.

Mixed methods research questions

Authors can pose three types of mixed methods research questions. First, they can pose separate quantitative questions and/or hypotheses and separate qualitative questions. Second, they can pose separate qualitative research questions (or hypotheses, but not both), separate quantitative research questions, and then mixed methods questions. Third, authors can use just mixed methods research questions, with no separate quantitative or qualitative questions. This approach can focus on procedure, content, or both and intimates some degree of integration of the data from both strands. Procedure questions mention a particular method and wonder how it can explain a result from the other strand. Content questions refer to a particular form of finding from one strand (e.g., themes) and wonder how that can help enrich interpretation of results from the other strand (e.g., how can qualitative text [themes] help explain quantitative numbers [statistics]?) (Creswell, 2009, 2010; Tashakkori & Creswell, 2007). See Table 6.5 for characteristics of good mixed methods research questions.

Example 6.6 Mixed methods research questions

Separate quantitative and qualitative questions: A study investigated students' grade level (junior versus senior high) and attitude toward truancy. Researchers first *hypothesized* that there would be no significant difference between junior and senior high school students' attitudes toward truancy. At the same time, they framed qualitative research questions that *explored the issue in more depth* after the quantitative phase was completed. Through qualitative interviews and thematic analysis, they *explored* the relationship between parents and the police to better *understand* the latter's response to student truancy. They wanted to know *how students felt* about their parents' reactions to their truancy. And what did it *mean* to junior versus senior high students that their future was impacted by their truancy?

One mixed methods question (procedure): How do data from *interviews* with students, their parents, and police help to explain any quantitative differences in *number and frequency* of junior versus senior high school students' truancy?

One mixed methods question (content): How do the *themes* mentioned by the parents help to explain the frequency and intensity (*numbers*) with which the police engaged with truant students?

REVIEW AND ENGAGEMENT

When critically reading a research report, you would

- ☐ Determine if authors distinguished between a research problem they are personally interested in and the *research questions* they posed in this particular study (so the problem can be addressed using their new data and insights)

- ☐ See if they met most of the criteria for a good research question, whether qualitative, quantitative, or mixed methods (see Tables 6.4 and 6.5)

- ☐ Ascertain if they appreciated that *quantitative* studies do not usually have both a research question and hypotheses, usually just the latter

- ☐ Determine if they made sure their mixed methods research questions reflected either procedure or content

Research Statements

It is one thing to identify a research question and another to formally state it in the paper. Any statement expresses something clearly and definitively in writing (Anderson, 2014). A *research statement* is the author's clear declaration of what a particular study will address. The research statement follows both the research problem (something to be solved) and the research question (something requiring data and information). Research statements are also called *overall objectives* of the study (Konradsen, ca. 2016) and are often introduced by saying, "The purpose of this study is to . . ." Authors can present their research statement (a) explicitly in a question or (b) implicitly by using a declarative or descriptive statement (Goodson, 2017; Suter, 2012; Wiersma & Jurs, 2009).

Example 6.7 Declarative and question form research statements

Declarative statement: The researchers conducted *a study of* the effects of three teaching techniques on science achievement of senior high students.

Question form: *Do* three different teaching techniques have differing effects on science achievement scores of senior high school students?

Regardless of which form is used, the research statement must provide a focus and direction for the research and clarify the context. Also, authors should provide adequate definitions of any concepts inherent in the statement, placing them after the statement (Wiersma & Jurs, 2009). In example 6.7, this would include the teaching techniques and the concept of achievement in science. Because it reveals the gap that will be investigated, the research statement usually appears just before the Literature Review section (Suter, 2012).

On a technical and grammatical note, authors are advised to use active verbs rather than nouns when writing their research (purpose) statements (e.g., *describe, understand, develop, present, discover, examine the meaning of, analyze, argue*). This strategy keeps the statement active rather than nebulous (Creswell, 2009; Goodson, 2017). Goodson (2017, pp. 157–158) tendered the following two examples, explaining that, in example 6.9, it is not clear what the authors intended to do in the study, just that they agreed with a previous approach found in the literature.

Example 6.8 Research statement using active verbs (in italics)
The purpose of the paper is to argue for an alternative approach to *analyzing* data on adolescent sexual activity. We *present* four arguments supporting Jones's (2015) proposal to analyze data from a dynamic systems perspective, instead of applying an individual-level approach.

Example 6.9 Research statement using nouns
A proposal to analyze adolescent sexual activity data from a dynamic systems perspective is offered by Jones (2015). Jones's proposal is against applying individual-level analyses to these data. In this paper we are in agreement with Jones's position and rationale.

Quantitative research statements

Quantitative research statements identify the type of relationship investigated (i.e., causal, explanatory, or descriptive) between a set of variables (expressed using hypotheses or research questions but not both). Creswell (2009) provided scripts for posing quantitative research statements (see Figure 6.5), which authors can use and adapt. Research statements are supposed to be one sentence and should include the variables, the proposed relationship among the variables (e.g., causal), the participants or subjects, and the site or locale for the study. Any theory should be mentioned as well. Once the statement is made, it does not change during the study. Authors may want to follow up the research statement with

---

FIGURE 6.5   ■   Proposed Scripts for Quantitative Research Statements (Creswell, 2009)

- The purpose of this study is to test _____ theory [name the theory] by **relating** _____ [independent variable] to _____ [dependent variable] for _____ [participants] at _____ [research site].

- The purpose of this study is to test _____ theory [name the theory] by **comparing** _____ [group 1] and _____ [group 2] in terms of the _____ [dependent variable] for _____ [participants] at _____ [research site].

- The purpose of this study is to **describe** the effect of _____ [independent variable] on _____ [dependent variable] for _____ [participants] at _____ [research site].

Source: Creswell, J. W. (2009), p. 118.

definitions of their main variables (*conceptual* and *operational*) (Johnson & Christensen, 2012; Wiersma & Jurs, 2009).

Qualitative research statements

Authors of qualitative papers deal with a much broader research statement than that used in quantitative work. Qualitative research statements reflect the general purpose of the inquiry, anchored in an overall focus on the way people interpret and make sense of their world and their experiences. It is often called the *focus of inquiry*, appreciating that this initial broad focus may change and become more specific as the research unfolds (i.e., emergent research design, discussed in Chapters 8 and 9). "As the researcher gathers data and discovers new meanings [and insights], the general problem narrows to more specific topics and new questions may arise" (Ary et al., 2010, p. 53). When reporting their study, authors should seriously consider accounting for the evolution of their research statement, starting with the initial broad framework question and ending with the more specific and much narrower research statement (Ary et al., 2010).

To reflect the dynamic nature of emergent qualitative research designs (see Chapters 8 and 9), authors should include three key elements in their research statement: (a) They should include words such as *describe, understand, develop, explore,* or *discover* when they say "the focus or purpose of this study is to . . ." (b) This phrase is usually followed with a declaration of the central idea to be *described, understood,* or *discovered,* appreciating that the idea will become more focused as the study unfolds. (c) Authors should state the specific data collection and analysis methods, including reference to the participants and/or the research site (Johnson & Christensen, 2012). Creswell (2009) provided a script for posing qualitative research statements (see Figure 6.6), which authors can use and adapt.

Example 6.10 Qualitative research statement

The *purpose of this study* (its focus) was to *explore* distressing and nurturing encounters of institutional caregivers with patients and *to ascertain the meanings* that are engendered by such encounters. This *narrative* study was conducted *in* Maryville, Nova Scotia, *at* a local 34-bed community care hospital *during* the fall of 2013.

FIGURE 6.6 ■ Proposed Script for Qualitative Research Statements (Creswell, 2009)

The purpose of this _____ [strategy of inquiry such as ethnography, case study] study is to _____ [understand, describe, develop, explore, discover] the _____ [central phenomenon] of/for _____ [the participants] at _____ [research site]. At this stage of the research, the _____ [central phenomenon being studied] will be generally defined as _____ [provide general definition].

Source: Creswell, J. T. (2009), p. 114.

Mixed methods research statements

Creswell (2010) suggested that when presenting their mixed methods research statement, authors should articulate several key reasons for using mixed methods and then, if appropriate, indicate that lack of integration was a deficiency in previous studies. Creswell (2009) provided a basic script for posing mixed methods research statements (see Figure 6.7), which authors can use and adapt. He advised that the scripts can be adapted to reflect one of five main research design approaches for mixed methods studies: convergent, explanatory sequential, exploratory sequential, transformative, or multiphased (see Chapter 10 for more details).

Mixed methods research statements should contain (a) information about the overall intent (purpose) of the study (see Table 6.6), (b) followed with information about both the qualitative and quantitative strands of the study. (c) They should also include a rationale for combining both strands in one study. More details are provided in Chapters 2 and 10, but the main reasons for combining the two methodologies and their methods in one study are to gain a more complete understanding of the problem, to understand the data from one strand at more detailed levels, or to develop a research instrument or protocol (Creswell, 2009).

FIGURE 6.7 ■ Proposed Script for Mixed Methods Research Statements

The intent of this mixed methods study is to _____ [state content or procedural objective of the study]. In the study, _____ [identify quantitative instrument] will be used to measure the relationship between _____ [independent variable] and _____ [dependent variable]. At the same time, the _____ [central phenomenon] will be explored using _____ [state qualitative data collection strategy] with _____ [participants] at _____ [research site]. The reason for combining both quantitative and qualitative data is to better understand this research problem by converging quantitative (identify broad numeric trends) with qualitative (identify detailed views) data.

Source: Creswell, J. T. (2009), pp 122–123.

REVIEW AND ENGAGEMENT

When critically reading a research report, you would

☐ Determine if the authors provided a *research statement* that clearly explained what this particular study addressed (either in question form—"Does . . . have an effect?"—or in a declarative statement—"The purpose of this study is . . .") (they should have used active verbs)

☐ Check to see if they followed Creswell's (2009) recommended conventions and scripts for each of quantitative, qualitative, and mixed methods research statements

Research Objectives

Per the progression depicted in Figures 6.1 and 6.2, research objectives are at the micro level, compared to the general, broader area of interest (field of study and discipline). Whereas research questions pose the standard journalistic *W* questions of who, what, when, where, why, and how (Booth et al., 1995; Brenner, 2001), *research objectives* drill this down to measurable, actionable tasks. Authors form and state research objectives for their study so they can answer the research questions from their unique perspective. A set of *specific research objectives* should follow the *overall objective*, also called the research statement (i.e., "The purpose of this study is . . .") (see previous section). Specific research objectives are often the last thing stated in the Introduction section before leading readers into the Literature Review (perhaps Theory) section and then the Methods section (Konradsen, ca. 2016; Suter, 2012).

They are precise investigative questions that help authors answer the overall objective or research question. Specific objectives operationalize the questions by stating precisely what needs to be researched in a particular study (see Rojon and Saunders, 2012, p. 58, for the following examples).

> *Example 6.11 Overall research questions and specific research objectives*
>
> **Research question (overall objective) 1:** *Why* have organizations introduced coaching programs for senior managers?
>
> **Specific research objective 1:** *To identify* organizations' objectives for creating coaching programs targeted to senior managers
>
> **Research question (overall objective) 2:** *Can* the effectiveness of coaching programs targeted to senior managers be explained?
>
> **Specific research objective 2:** *To determine* the factors associated with the effectiveness criteria for senior managers' coaching programs being met

Good research objectives clarify what specific things will be *done* to collect and/or analyze data to answer the question(s). They are transparent (comprehensible), specific, measurable, achievable in an identified time frame, realistic, and timely. They are usually presented in a numbered, itemized, interconnected list. The objectives should not sound like an activity, which belongs in the Methods section (Derese, ca. 2015; Konradsen, ca. 2016; Rojon & Saunders, 2012). For example, authors should say "*to assess* the correlation of levels of pesticides with rainfall season" instead of "*to measure* the changes in pesticides with rainfall season." Authors can draw on Bloom's taxonomy of learning for appropriate verbs to state objectives related to understanding, analysis, evaluation, and creation (see Anderson & Krathwohl, 2001).

Objectives are active statements about how the study is going to answer the specific research question (Farrugia, Petrisor, Farrokhyar, & Bhandari, 2010). Technically, authors should present their specific research objectives as an infinitive sentence or phrase (Konradsen, ca. 2016). *Infinitive* is Latin *infinitus*, "not finished" (Harper, 2016). In grammar, it refers to placing the word *to* before the simple or base form of a verb (meaning the verb is unfinished, with no *ed*, *s*, *ing*, or *ly*). The infinitive verb (e.g., *to analyze*) is followed with the main clause, which usually contains objects or modifiers that provide detail (Simmons, 2016).

> *Example 6.12 Research objectives* (adapted from Konradsen, ca. 2016)

> **Research problem:** Teenage students engaged in sports activities tend to lack knowledge about nutrition and sports, which can impact their health status and performance.

> **Research statement (i.e., overall research objective):** *The purpose of this study is* to analyze the association between nutritional knowledge and the nutritional status of teenage students engaged in sports activities.

Specific research objectives:

1. *To assess the knowledge level* of teenage students on recommended nutritional practices for sports activities

2. *To determine* the nutritional status of teenage students engaged in sports activities

3. *To analyze* the statistical association between knowledge level and nutritional status of teenage students engaged in sports activities

In summary, these clearly set-out tasks (research objectives) help organize the study into distinct but related parts or phases (numbered in a sequence) and help researchers collect only data that are related to the research problem (i.e., avoid irrelevant data).

REVIEW AND ENGAGEMENT

When critically reading a research report, you would

☐ Ascertain if the authors articulated research objectives (what will be done to collect data to answer the research questions) and presented them in a numbered list (using an infinitive verb, prefaced with *to*)

☐ Check to see if they met most of the criteria for a good research objective (e.g., measurable, realistic, timely)

OPENING SENTENCES AND OPENING POINTS IN AN INTRODUCTION

The previous section detailed the nuanced and not always transparent relationships among research topics, problems, questions, statements, and objectives. Although this chapter discussed them before focusing on introductions, they are in fact the nuts and bolts of introductions. In the spirit of this out-of-sequence approach, this section addresses the importance of opening points in an Introduction section. These points are used to draw people into the Introduction section, and the Introduction section is used to draw people into the paper. Authors use opening points to connect with readers and make them want to keep reading. Without this connection, the article will not be read. The opening sentences (points) help authors clarify why they think their research question and study are important. Ideally, authors would introduce their opening point(s) within the first three sentences or first paragraph of the paper (Shank & Brown, 2007).

Shank and Brown (2007) offered six different points or perspectives that authors can draw upon as they introduce and lead readers into their paper: crisis, important, gap, depth, commitment, and synopsis. First, authors can try to convince readers of a state of urgency, with supportive argumentation that a *crisis* is looming. Readers are warned of possible fallouts if the problem discussed in the paper is not addressed. Another approach, short of a warning, is to convince readers that the problem is a critically *important* and extremely significant issue. A third approach is to reveal a *gap* (lacuna) in existing theories or practical understandings of the problem. Filling this gap is the intent of the study reported in the paper.

Fourth, authors can claim that more *depth* is needed in order to gain deeper insights into the phenomenon (i.e., penetrating, vigorous, intense). Their study will dig deeper to reach better understandings of the problem. Some authors may feel it is sufficient to tell readers of their personal *commitment* to and involvement with the issue or the problem. They assume that this intimate perspective (i.e., their opening segues to the study) will compel readers to engage with the paper. Finally, authors can just dive right into the paper, assuming that the issue is so central to the field that it needs little justification given the context shared in the opening points. It just makes sense to study this problem. Shank and Brown (2007) called this the *synopsis* opening point, explaining that it often leads to importance, gap, or depth perspectives in tandem.

Example 6.13 Opening points

Crisis: Children's futures are *doomed* if we do not "get school right."

Important: Research has shown that "getting school right" is very *important* for ensuring that children have a strong start on their futures.

Gap: Having a good start in life is key to a successful and hopeful future. Despite that research has shown "getting school right" is crucial to ensuring that children have a strong start on their futures, existing theories do not adequately reflect this fact. Research is needed to fill this theoretical *gap*.

Depth: How do some children leave the U.S. school system fully prepared for the future, while others do not? This study intends to explore this question in some *depth*.

Commitment: In this action research study, I was invited by the school board to help design new "getting school right" curricula that reflect input from students. I welcomed this opportunity because of my long-standing *commitment* to a promising and sustainable future for children.

Synopsis (with depth): Members of the workforce with a high school diploma earn four times that of dropouts. Graduates of community college and trade schools hold down jobs much longer than those with a high school diploma. University graduates are most financially successful in life because they have a higher education degree. Given these facts (*synopses, the context*), one has to wonder why governments and public school boards do not pay more attention to "getting school right." This issue needs to be studied in more *depth*.

Labaree (2016) concurred that authors must use their opening points to engage readers and make them *want* to read the paper. He said that the best way to grab their attention is to use a narrative. Authors can begin by using keywords from the title in the first few sentences of the Introduction section. They can also choose to open with a compelling story, include a vivid or strong quotation or anecdote, pose a provocative or thought-provoking question, describe a puzzling scenario or incongruity, or cite a stirring example or case that convinces readers of the importance of the research problem. See Chapter 15 for a richer discussion of these strategies, which can also be used in a Conclusions section.

REVIEW AND ENGAGEMENT

When critically reading a research report, you would

- ☐ Try to discern if the authors effectively used one or more *opening points* to help readers connect with the paper (i.e., crisis, importance, gap, depth, personal commitment, and synopsis)

- ☐ Reflect on how easy or hard this was for you to find, and if this affected your judgment of the quality of the research

SIX APPROACHES TO WRITING INTRODUCTIONS

As noted, the opening points *are* part of the Introduction section of the paper (Shank & Brown, 2007). But, while opening points grab readers' attention and draw them into the Introduction section, the full Introduction section takes them further into *the paper*. As authors present a *particular piece* of research, they have to embed several key elements into their Introduction section. "It must engage the reader quickly; it must clearly lay out the road map for the reader's journey; it must state the purpose unambiguously; it must provide enough historical background on the topic [which is later supplemented in the literature review]" (Goodson, 2017, p. 148). Not surprisingly, authors are encouraged to use the conjunction *because* frequently in their Introduction section because it primes readers to look for a rationale, a reason, an explanation, or a justification for the study (Goodson, 2017).

Creswell (2009) confirmed that most introductions do not contain a complete literature review; rather, authors should refer to large groups of studies in the Introduction section (focused on broad areas of research), leaving reference to individual studies for the longer, formal Literature Review section. He further recommended that, to avoid the risk of appearing nonscholarly, authors should cite a minimum of 12 references in their Introduction section (the coverage of which can be expanded and augmented in the formal Literature Review section).

Example 6.14 Broad literature in introduction Earlier studies focused on some broad aspect of the research problem (e.g., Author A, 199X; Author B, 200X; Author C, 201X).

Specific citations in the literature review Author A (199X) found Q. In contrast, Author B (200X) discovered Y. Author C (201X) took both of their ideas further, and suggested Z.

There are no hard and fast rules for writing introductions (Wong, 2006). This lack of agreement has led to many models that authors can examine and adapt. Six approaches are discussed in this section (see Table 6.7 for a summary of respective models, followed with a discussion of each one). Each approach includes three to four separate elements, which overlap considerably from one approach to another; yet, each approach offers a somewhat

TABLE 6.7 ■ Overview of Six Possible Models for Writing Introductions					
5W framing	**Three phases (niche)**	**Five-paragraph model**	**Four-paragraph model**	**Four research arguments**	**Four propositional statements**
Purpose of the study (what)	State the research area and relevant literature	State the research problem, with related issues	Summary of previous research	Set up an argument (provide context and then state the problem)	Principle proposition (facts about the topic)
Rationale for the study (why)	Identify a niche within this area (problems)	Identify studies that have addressed the research problem	Critique of previous research	Support the argument (state the problem and then provide an argument for study)	Interacting proposition (juxtapose contradictory facts)
Background literature about the problem (when and who)	Place research questions and purpose statements within this niche	Note deficiencies in these studies	Gaps in previous research	Set up the context, state the problem, and then develop a supportive argument	Speculative proposition (why it is important to resolve any contradictions)
Theory (how, or with what)		Explain the significance of the current study	Rationale for current study, with research questions stated	Make a grounded argument (state the research question with no argumentation)	Explicative proposition (explain how the current study will address contradictions)
		Research the purpose statement			

unique flavor to the Introduction section. Authors can take inspiration from any of these models as long as they include some semblance of an argument that justifies their approach to providing answers to a research problem by using specific research questions and a specific research design. At the minimum, they *must* (a) identify the research problem and attendant question(s) or hypotheses, (b) refer to and critique relevant literature, and (c) develop a logical, convincing rationale and argument for *their* particular approach to addressing the problem (see the last section of this chapter on delimitations).

5W Framing of an Introduction

In this approach, the Introduction section serves to *frame* the study and the resultant article by telling readers what to expect. This frame comprises a combination of the journalistic *W*s: the purpose of the study (what), the rationale (why), the background literature (when and who), and any theoretical support (how). Answers to these questions help authors formulate the remaining *W*s, the where (site selection and participants) and the how (with what?) (data collection and analysis) (Goodson, 2017; Labaree, 2016).

This 5*W* framework becomes the readers' blueprint for the paper, telling them what to anticipate in the Methods, Results or Findings, and Discussion sections. Readers can expect authors to justify why the topic and this particular study are important and why they chose particular methods and theories (if any) (Goodson, 2017). This information is an inherent part of stating the delimitations of the research design (see the last section of this chapter).

Continuing with her advice, Goodson (2017) explained that the rationale follows, or is integrated into, a brief review of the literature or the full literature review (the format differs according to research methodology, journal style, or field of study) (see Creswell, 2009). If the rationale is separate from the literature review, Goodson (2017) recommended providing enough literature in the Introduction section to provide context for the study. To achieve this, authors can cite studies that (a) *support* and *validate* their problem, purpose, or research question. (b) They can also identify studies that *contradict* and *refute* the importance of their problem, purpose, or research question and then say that these alternative perspectives merit examination "because . . ."

(c) Authors can also cite sources that *carry the most authority* on their topic, issue, research problem, or research question and then tell readers why they are the most authoritative sources. (d) Finally, they can use a combination of *recent and dated sources* that address their problem, justifying their inclusion. As noted, authors may truncate their coverage of literature in the Introduction section (using citations as leads), or they may choose to move on to a separate section called *Literature Review*, where they add more depth and critical analysis of the sources used to ground and frame their research problem and question(s) (Creswell, 2009; Goodson, 2017) (see Chapter 7).

Finally, if relevant, authors may choose to wrap up their Introduction section with mention of a relevant theory or theories. This brief mention may be sufficient, or they may need to add a separate section on theoretical frameworks (see Chapter 3). Appreciating that "some manuscripts are atheoretical," a theoretical perspective, when appropriate, helps make "the argument, the rationale, and the proposed topic stand out" for readers (Goodson, 2017, p. 166). As well, insights gained when authors use the theory to interpret their results or findings may contribute to theoretical development and refinement in the field. Again, authors should clearly explain why they chose a specific theory or theories for this particular study and not other theories, using the conjunction *because*. They should present the theory logically, sufficiently, and clearly, using diagrams, models, or figures when appropriate and available (Goodson, 2017).

Three-Phase Approach (Niche) to Introductions

Goodson's (2017) aforementioned 5*W* approach to preparing an Introduction section involved four elements: purpose, rationale, literature (context and significance), and theory. Labaree (2016) offered a three-phase approach to writing an Introduction section. Authors can (a) establish an area to research, (b) identify a niche within this area, and then (c) place their work within this research niche. The first phase involves authors highlighting the importance of their topic and presenting a general overview of current research on the subject. The second phase involves creating a niche, which is a recess or small space set aside within the larger area. This niche may indicate opposing assumptions, reveal a gap, reflect a new research question, or continue an existing, or create a new, research trajectory. Within this niche, authors state the intent or purpose of *their* study and then provide a layout of their research design and a general overview of the paper.

Five-Paragraph Model for Introductions

Contrary to Wong's (2006) assertion that there is no one way to write introductions, Creswell (2009) claimed that "there is a model for writing a good, scholarly . . . introduction" (p. 100). It comprises five stages, each presented in its own paragraph, under the heading *Introduction*: (a) the research problem, (b) studies that have already addressed the problem, (c) deficiencies in those studies, (d) the significance of the particular study for specific audiences, and (e) the research (purpose) statement (see Table 6.8). This approach should yield about two pages of introductory text for the paper. Creswell (2009) provided a good example of this approach in pages 100–102 of his book.

TABLE 6.8 ■ Creswell's (2009) Five-Paragraph Model for Writing Introductions

Five Paragraphs	Examples of Expected Content in Each Paragraph
Research problem (not the same as a research question)	Using a narrative hook, state the research problem in the first sentence. Then, clearly identify issues pursuant to the problem that leads to a need for another study. For example:
	Since home economics was founded more than 100 years ago, it has been concerned with how a focus on home benefits humanity. Unfortunately, this focus has become diluted over time, ironically to the detriment of humanity [narrative hook]. *This dilution of the profession's mission is a problem because it deeply impacts our ability to be effective in the 21st century* [cite X; Y; Z].

(Continued)

TABLE 6.8 ■ (Continued)	
Five Paragraphs	**Examples of Expected Content in Each Paragraph**
Studies that have already addressed the problem	Identify large groups of studies that have examined various aspects of this issue, distinguishing them from the proposed study. Place these references at the end of the paragraph. After summarizing these previous works, state a need for current work. For example: *Several studies have examined possible reasons for why home economics has lost its focus on humanity. The most common reasons were . . . [cite X; Y; Z]. Due to the vagaries of the complex 21st century, it is imperative that contemporary home economics practitioners examine their philosophical base.*
Deficiencies in those studies	Identify any possible shortcomings, gaps, or failings of previous works, explaining how the current study will address or remedy them. For example: *Previous studies have examined possible reasons for why home economics has lost its focus on humanity. Collectively, ideological shifts were deemed to be the main reason for this phenomenon, in that families and homes are now only valued as consumers and laborers. What remains to be explored is how home economists themselves feel about this issue. Do they think the most pressing issue is ideological hegemony and imperatives?*
Significance of the study for specific audiences	Convey the importance of the problem for specific groups (in effect, a rationale for the study and why people need to read it). For example: *This study will especially benefit curriculum planners at the higher education level, those professors and instructors who are socializing the next generation of professional home economists. It behooves them to sensitize young professionals to the fact that the philosophically-based mission of the profession needs to be continually monitored and adjusted, especially from an ideological perspective.*
Purpose statement (leads to more specific research questions for this study)	Wrap up the Introduction section with a clear statement about what this particular study intends to accomplish. For example: *The purpose of this exploratory study is to gain home economists' perspectives about the link between ideological imperatives and the profession's mission, especially as it pertains to our focus on the home to benefit humanity. The following research questions were addressed.*

Source: Creswell, J. T. (2009).

Four-Paragraph Model for Introductions

Authors may want to use Shon's (2015) approach for writing their introduction section, which involves the four-paragraph model (with some elements requiring more than one paragraph and some thoughts requiring elements to be merged): (a) a *summary* of previous literature; (b) a *critique* of previous literature; (c) a *gap* in the literature (i.e., shortcomings, failures, or conspicuous absences) that serves as a rationale for the study; and (d) the rationale for or justification of the study (i.e., why the gap matters), followed with the research question(s). Authors can combine *summary, critique, and gap* in one sentence or in three or more consecutive sentences. The Introduction section may well include a rich sequence of these synthesized critiques of the literature, building a case for the current study. Shon (2015) explained that not all introductions are "structurally elegant" (p. 43), but they all should result in the emergence of a full argument in favor of the current study. He tendered sentence or phrase templates for each stage of the model (see Table 6.9 for some examples).

Research Argument Model

Shank and Brown (2007) took a different approach to writing introductions, focused on where the argument for the study is placed relative to the actual research question being stated. An argument is a set of reasons given in support of something (Anderson, 2014)

TABLE 6.9 ■ Sample Phrases for Shon's (2015) Four-Paragraph Model	
Four-Paragraph Model	**Sample Sentence or Phrase Templates**
Summary of previous literature	• *Scholars have found that . . .* • *Previous research showed that . . .* • *Earlier work illustrated that . . .* • *Other researchers discovered that . . .* • *Recently, researchers examined . . .*
Critique of previous literature	• *Previous studies failed to . . .* • *Earlier studies lacked . . .* • *Brown examined X but neglected to include . . .* • *White studied this phenomenon; however, she did not . . .* • *Earlier studies overlooked the importance of . . .* • *Few studies have seriously considered . . .* • *Research has not kept pace with . . .*
Gaps in the literature (and why they matter)	• *Despite that . . . , a theoretical or practical void remains. This gap is unfortunate because . . .* • *Many previous studies have examined this topic; nonetheless, this particular aspect deserves more attention because . . .* • *To date, few studies have examined this idea. This gap matters because . . .* • *Scholarly understandings of this topic matter because . . .* • *Although particular aspects of this problem have received considerable attention, this part is underresearched.* • *Existing scholarship has undertheorized this phenomenon.*
Rationale for the study (leading to research question)	• *This paper will contribute to theory development in three ways.* • *This paper is important for several reasons.* • *This study brings several new perspectives to the topic.* • *The proposed study is warranted because others have not addressed the gaps identified in the literature.*

(see Chapter 17 for more information on argumentation). There are four types of research arguments: (a) setup, (b) support, (c) setup and support, and (d) grounded (in the author's convictions). "Sometimes arguments come before the question to help *set up* the question. Other times, the argument comes after the question in order to *support* the question. In more complex cases, the research question is both set up and supported [sandwiched between the two]" (Shank & Brown, 2007, p. 113). Authors may choose to provide no argumentation, instead letting an observed anomaly speak for itself. This is called a *grounded* research question, arising from the researcher's experience with the phenomenon; that is, it is grounded in the researcher's convictions (Shank & Brown, 2007).

The bottom line is that when authors present their research question(s), they must provide a supportive argument. A good argument logically and clearly pulls together what is already known and what is missing. Because a good argument both lays the foundations for the research design and methods and provides the anchor for interpreting the data, research arguments also help readers critique the paper. Table 6.10 explains these four approaches, with examples of patterns that authors can use to present their argument (Shank & Brown, 2007). Discerning these arguments is a very difficult task for most readers, behooving authors to pay special attention to this aspect of writing introductions (Creswell, 2009; Shank & Brown, 2007).

TABLE 6.10 ■ **Four Types of Research Arguments, With Sample Scripts**

Type of Argument	Explained	Sample Script
Setup	Authors provide a context and conceptual support for the question *before* stating it; that is, they set the scene by making a series of points (citing and critiquing relevant literature) and then state the question (setup)	*The literature said . . .* [**cite and critique previous studies**]. *The* **gaps** *identified in the literature review justify this research because . . . Consequently, this study will address two* **questions**.
Support	Authors first state the research question and *then* refer to previous work to support the question already posed; the argument comes *after* the question. This approach is often used in qualitative studies, which have no hypotheses.	*How do people go from having a home to being homeless? The study intends to explore this* **question** *in depth. Cite and critique previous studies,* **making the case** *that they were insufficient to answer the question, meaning the posed question is justified (supported).*
Setup and Support	Authors sandwich the question in between the setup (i.e., the justification) and the support. The setup arguments provide the context (grounding the study in existing work and thought on the topic) leading to the statement of the question. The supportive arguments follow logically from the setup. This approach is often used in quantitative studies.	**Research has shown** *that . . .* **Given that** *. . .* [share some pertinent insights or concerns from the previous literature], **state the question. The purpose of the study** *is to . . .* [this indicates support for the question].

Type of Argument	Explained	Sample Script
Grounded (in the author's convictions)	This research question does not require setup or supportive arguments; instead, authors state research questions that are grounded in their observed experiences of the real world. In these instances, an observed anomaly is justification for the study. Anomalies are states of affair that deviate from the normal way of doing things. The need for an answer to the question is patently obvious to the author. This approach is often used in qualitative, field-oriented research.	*State an observed anomaly, which must be so compelling that it alone is sufficient argument for the need for the study. Then, **state the research questions**.*

Problem Statement (Propositional) Model for Introductions

Akin to Shank and Brown's (2007) focus on research argumentation when writing an Introduction section, Jacobs (2011) framed this logical process as the development of a *problem statement*. By this, he meant what is involved in authors preparing and presenting *their argument* in favor of their particular approach to addressing a research problem. He maintained that this *statement* is, in fact, a collection of four specific propositional statements, which, taken together, develop a case for the research problem. These four statements reflect both the author's deep familiarity with the topic and the author's specific interest in *one aspect* of the topic. To adequately develop their argument, authors have to "peel away the extraneous clutter of understandings to reveal [their] core scholarly interest. [This process is] an intellectual activity governed by [logic and] system thinking" (Jacobs, 2011, p. 139).

From this perspective, an Introduction section must reflect the authors' appreciation that discontinuities exist in the literature. This means that two facts can exist at the same time; yet, when juxtaposed against each other, they create a tension that begs to be addressed. This intellectual tension inspires (compels) authors to pose specific research problems and then related research questions (Jacobs, 2011).

Example 6.15 Discontinuity inspiring a research problem

Fact 1: *Philosophically,* education professionals *consistently profess* the value of using a systems approach to develop training programs.

Fact 2 (contradicts Fact 1): However, in *actual practice*, education professionals *seldom use* aspects of a systems approach to develop training programs.

Research problem: Education professionals profess the value of a systems approach but fail to employ it when developing training programs.

Possible research questions:

- Why do education professionals who value the use of a systems approach to develop training programs seldom follow through?

- What is it about the systems approach that precludes education professionals from actually using it in their practice?

- What is unique about education training programs that prevent education professionals from using a systems approach in their development?

Table 6.11 summarizes the four statements (propositions) that collectively comprise Jacobs's (2011) problem statement approach to writing introductions. He clarified that this approach is not a singular statement, as the term *problem statement* suggests: "Instead, they represent a series of statements that should form the logical flow of understanding" (p. 137).

TABLE 6.11 ■ Jacobs's (2011) Problem Statement (Propositional) Approach to Introductions

Proposition	Explanation	Examples From Jacobs (2011, pp. 134–136), bolded emphasis added
1 Principal	These sentences establish a baseline of true facts about the topic. Citing relevant literature will ensure their credibility.	*Historical records suggest* that central Ohio typically has a relatively mild winter weather pattern. As a result, over the years, local **newspapers have reported** few disruptions on daily life caused by the weather.
2 Interacting	These sentences provide a contrast to the principal proposition and have to be convincingly argued. Start them with a connecting adverb or a conjunction such as *but, however, yet, although, rather, conversely, in contrast,* or *instead.*	*However,* the past five winters in central Ohio have been especially harsh, with temperatures ranging well below the daily averages. As a result, most schools have been closed more days than their allotted number.
3 Speculative	These sentences juxtapose the principal and interacting propositions, illustrating their contradictions, failings, gaps, or shortcomings. Authors speculate why it might be important to resolve the apparent contradiction.	*If* central Ohio has had relatively mild winters in the past based on historical information, **and if** the recent winter weather patterns suggest a new weather pattern, **which may** have detrimental effects on daily life, **then more must be known** about the most current winter weather patterns of central Ohio.
4 Explicative	This final statement (proposition) explains how *this study* will address the contradiction between two true facts that have been juxtaposed by the author.	*The purpose of this study* is to investigate the recent winter weather pattern and its effects on daily life in central Ohio.

REVIEW AND ENGAGEMENT

When critically reading a research report, you would

☐ Determine if the authors chose an approach to writing their Introduction section that made it easy for you to find and follow their argument for their study (rationale, reason, justification) (see Tables 6.7, 6.8. 6.9. 6.10, 6.11)

☐ Ascertain *which* approach they did use and judge if they employed it correctly and completely

☐ Determine if they, at the minimum, (a) identified the research problem and attendant question(s) or hypotheses, (b) referred to and critiqued relevant literature, and (c) used that critique to develop a logical, convincing rationale and argument for *their* particular approach to addressing the problem (see Figure 6.8)

In summary, the Introduction section is a series of progressive statements. The *opening points or statements* grab readers' attention and draw them into the Introduction section. The *Introduction section* is a set of statements that draws people further into the paper. These statements pertain to, in some manner, (a) the authors' rationale and argument supporting the *research problem* (i.e., identifying gaps in the literature and explaining why it is important that they be addressed). This argument leads to (b) a set of *research questions* (or hypotheses) posed by authors to obtain answers to solve the problem. These questions lead to (c) a *research or purpose statement* setting out what the authors intend to do in this particular study to collect the data to answer the questions and may include (d) statements setting out *research objectives*.

The entire Introduction section is a series of progressive statements leading readers to the Literature Review section, a possible Theory section, and the Methods section (see Figure 6.8). These introductory statements constitute the author's attempt to set boundaries around the study, called delimitations.

DELIMITATIONS

Interestingly, authors often include a section in their paper about limitations but seldom formalize *delimitations* as such. Both terms refer to boundaries or limits pursuant to the research enterprise but mean different things. *Limitations* (see details in Chapter 14) are beyond the researcher's control. They refer to aspects of the research design that place constraints on the interpretation and application of results or findings, as well as the generalizability of quantitative results and the transferability of qualitative findings. In this case, *limit* refers to a point beyond which one cannot go. In contrast, *delimitations* are within the researcher's control and refer to earlier decisions pursuant to setting the scope of a research project *before* it starts. In this case, *limit* refers to placing a boundary around something, keeping some things in and others out (Anderson, 2014; Baltimore County Public Schools, 2015; Eftekhar, 2015; Simon, 2011).

In more detail, *limitations* are potential weaknesses of the study that are usually out of the researcher's control and become an issue *during* the study, especially when interpreting and discussing findings and results and drawing conclusions. Limitations include instrument

FIGURE 6.8 ■ Introduction as a Series of Progressive Statements

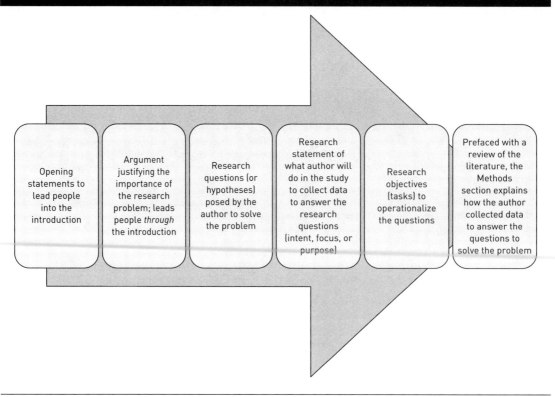

failings or inadequacies, sampling issues, data collection constraints (e.g., attrition, missing data, or low return rates), analytical challenges, and changes in the research context. Authors have to identify and explain how these limitations influenced the outcomes of the study and what they can conclude after analyzing and interpreting the data collected to answer the research questions (Baltimore County Public Schools, 2015; Eftekhar, 2015; Simon, 2011) (see Figure 6.9).

But authors should also report or acknowledge the *delimitations* to their study. These are conscious, intentional judgments about what to include and exclude in the study. Authors have to make decisions about research questions and objectives, literature to review, site selection or geographic location, participants or subjects, instruments or apparatus, phenomena or variables of interest, treatments, methods, alternative theoretical perspectives, and analytical approaches—in effect, the research design (see Chapter 8). These aspects of a study are within the researcher's control and should be accounted for in the paper, either explicitly in a separate section or implicitly in the articulation of research questions, research statements, objectives, methods, or theoretical frameworks underpinning the study. In other words, authors can weave these decisions throughout the Introduction section of the paper (the most common approach), or they can clearly articulate them in a separate section headed *Delimitations* (Baltimore County Public Schools, 2015; Eftekhar, 2015; Simon, 2011).

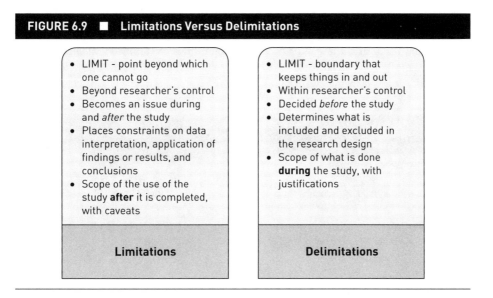

FIGURE 6.9   ■   Limitations Versus Delimitations

- LIMIT - point beyond which one cannot go
- Beyond researcher's control
- Becomes an issue during and *after* the study
- Places constraints on data interpretation, application of findings or results, and conclusions
- Scope of the use of the study **after** it is completed, with caveats

Limitations

- LIMIT - boundary that keeps things in and out
- Within researcher's control
- Decided *before* the study
- Determines what is included and excluded in the research design
- Scope of what is done **during** the study, with justifications

Delimitations

Delimitations are not good or bad; they are simply descriptions or articulations of the scope of the study, with justifications. Respecting that delimitations set boundaries around the study, authors should also discuss what is not going to be covered in the study and why. What participants, sites, theories, literature, and methods were not used to design the study? In this section of the paper, authors should confine their delimitations to things that a reader might reasonably expect to see but, for reasons clearly explained, were not done in the study. Possible reasons for exclusion include practicality, interest, relativity to the study at hand, and the researcher's expertise and access to resources (Baltimore County Public Schools, 2015; Eftekhar, 2015; Simon, 2011).

Example 6.16 Delimitations and limitations

Delimitations (researcher had control): This cross-sectional design study was conducted three years ago using a five-point Likert scale survey instrument. Data were collected from women affected by the government's policy for social welfare recipients. At the time, the government was being challenged about its policy, with charges that women were being harmed and marginalized. A survey was used because it was the most expedient way to collect data, respecting the researcher's resource constraints. The participants were randomly selected from a large metropolitan area in New York State. This geographic region was chosen because participants from this area were the most boisterous in their complaints around the policy. Data were analyzed using Minitab because the researcher did not have access to the most recent version of SPSS software.

Limitations (researcher had no control): This study had several limitations that constrain the generalizability of the results. Future studies should include men as well as women because results intimated that gender may be more of a factor than anticipated. This study employed a cross-sectional design (data were collected once, at one site, the most vocal on the issue). Future studies may want to employ a repeated cross-sectional design whereby they collect data once from many sites at the same time (differing degrees of vocalness). Finally, these data were collected three years ago before government policy around this issue changed. Others may want to do follow-up research in the new policy context.

REVIEW AND ENGAGEMENT

When critically reading a research report, you would

☐ Ascertain if the authors implicitly or explicitly set out the *delimitations* (scope) of their study in their Introduction section (i.e., their decisions about what to include and exclude in their research design) (see Figure 6.9)

☐ Judge if they provided enough information regarding the scope of their study

CHAPTER SUMMARY

Although not presented in this order, this chapter distinguished between opening points and the Introduction section. Opening points lead the reader into the Introduction section, and the Introduction section leads people into the paper. Six kinds of opening points serve to help the author connect with readers, making them want to read further. The opening points tell readers why the author thinks the research topic is important. Once into the Introduction section, authors entice people to read the paper by progressively moving through a presentation of what they intend to accomplish in the paper. This involves articulating their research problem, questions, purpose (statement), and objectives. The chapter discusses all of these in extensive detail (as they pertain to qualitative, quantitative,

and mixed methods) because critical readers need a clear understanding of how they differ yet are inherently interconnected when writing the Introduction section.

The chapter then provides an extensive overview of six approaches authors can use to develop an argument supporting what they are doing in their study. These approaches help authors write an Introduction section that convinces people of the merit of their study, namely by critically reviewing literature related to the research problem, identifying what is missing (justifying their research question), and explaining how their study will fill the gap (research statement and objectives). The chapter concludes with an explanation of delimitations (author has control) versus limitations of a study.

FINAL JUDGMENT ON INTRODUCTION AND RESEARCH QUESTIONS

Taking *all* of the **Review and Engagement** criteria into account, what is your final judgment of the Introduction section and the research questions of the paper you are critically reading?

REVIEW AND DISCUSSION QUESTIONS

1. The opening points are related to the topic and the Introduction section is focused on the paper itself. How are these two aspects of research interconnected?

2. Using an inverted triangle, explain how research topic, problem, question, and purpose are related. Why do you think it is easy and common for authors to mix up or mislabel these key aspects of reporting research?

3. What is the result of an unfocused introductory section?

4. Explain how a research question is different from a lay question. Why is it so important that researchers properly articulate their research question(s)? What roles do these questions play in the research design?

5. Discuss and elaborate on how research *problems* differ for qualitative, quantitative, and mixed methods research.

6. Regardless of the type of research problem, what are several key characteristics of a good research problem?

7. Compare the characteristics of a good research problem with those of a good research question. What insights did you draw about how they are different?

8. Examine Table 6.5 and related text and then describe the basic differences between a good qualitative, quantitative, and mixed methods (methodologies) research question.

9. How do research *questions* and *hypotheses* differ, and when should either be used in a research design?

10. Research *statements* flow from research problems and questions. What special role do these purpose statements play in the research design? How do declarative and question form research statements differ? Review Creswell's (2009) sample scripts for quantitative, qualitative, and mixed methods research statements (Figures 6.5, 6.6, and 6.7).

11. Research *objectives* are the smallest (micro) level of the progressive connection between research topic and research statement (see Figure 6.8). Explain their very concrete role in a research project (see also Figure 6.3).

12. Shank and Brown (2007) tendered six types of opening points. Briefly explain each one, and then identify the point that resonated the most with you and why.

13. There are many ways to organize (write up) the introductory section (see Table 6.7). Which two resonated with you the most, and why?

14. One of the roles of the Introduction section is to present the author's arguments that support the research questions. What was your reaction to the idea that an Introduction section is actually a well-developed argument? Why is it so difficult for critical readers to actually *find* the author's research argument? Why is it important that they persevere and find it?

15. What is the minimum information that must be included in an Introduction section?

16. What role does synthesis play in writing and presenting an Introduction section to a research paper?

17. Explain the difference between delimitations for a study and the study's limitations.

LITERATURE REVIEW

INTRODUCTION

This chapter focuses on the traditional literature review that prefaces and/or scaffolds a particular research initiative and research problem. It is imperative that authors conduct a thorough literature review because, in some way or form, it is the foundation for their eventual discussion and interpretation of their findings or results. As a caveat, although freestanding literature reviews are a form of research in their own right, they are not the focus of this chapter. Examples of freestanding reviews include integrative, historical, argumentative, theoretical, systematic, scoping, conceptual, and methodological literature reviews (Gall, Gall, & Borg, 2015; Imel, 2011; Labaree, 2016). These are "a distinctive form of research" (Torraco, 2005, p. 356) and "a recognized genre of scholarly writing" (Kennedy, 2007, p. 139).

ETYMOLOGY AND DEFINITION OF LITERATURE REVIEW

The word *literature* is Latin *literatura*, "a learning, a writing." It originally meant "writing formed with letters" and now means "a body of writings from a period or people." *Review* is Latin *revidere*—*re-*, "again," and *videre-*, "to see." It is also Middle French *reveeir*, "to go to see again" (Harper, 2016). Put simply, a *literature review* entails looking back at a body of writings from a period or people.

In the case of academic research (the topic of this book), the word *literature* does not refer to novels, plays, poems, fiction, or other works of literature (unless that is the genre being studied). It refers instead to studies, research, and scientific findings on a specific topic that are published in scholarly venues such as academic journals, conference proceedings, and books (University of Guelph Writing Services, 2006).

A literature review is defined as both an assessment and a critical, evaluative report of information found in the literature related to a selected area of study (Fink, 2004). The rest of the chapter addresses various aspects of this important component of research, as it appears in quantitative, qualitative, and mixed methods scholarship.

PURPOSES OF A LITERATURE REVIEW

Generally speaking, a literature review "positions the research problem within the context of the literature as a whole" (Wiersma & Jurs, 2009, p. 51). It "relates the study to the larger, ongoing dialogue in the literature" (Creswell, 2009, p. 25). Authors need to tell others what has already been done or not on their topic. Another purpose of a literature review is to build a picture or portrait of prior knowledge that has accumulated around a topic, thereby bringing the author and readers up to date on the current state of knowledge. Literature reviews help authors find studies that are closely related to their research question. Authors use this knowledge to make a case for their *particular* research question and research design (see Chapter 6) (Boote & Beile, 2005; Creswell, 2009; Shank & Brown, 2007). Literature reviews help authors (a) prepare the background for their study and (b) create support and a rationale for their area of proposed research. Authors then use the literature review at some point to aid in interpreting their quantitative results or qualitative findings (Boudah, 2011; Creswell, 2009).

REVIEW AND ENGAGEMENT

When critically reading a research report, you would

☐ Check to see if the authors effectively positioned the research question within existing literature by painting a picture of what has been done so far, then critiquing this work relative to the research question (e.g., what is missing, underdeveloped)

☐ Ascertain if the authors used their critique of existing literature to make a case (develop an argument) for their particular research question

☐ Determine if they then used that same (perhaps additional) literature to interpret the data collected and analyzed for their study

WHEN TO CONDUCT A LITERATURE REVIEW

In essence, reviews of the literature occur before, during, and after a study. By way of explanation, researchers are always reading literature in their field to stay current (Gall et al., 2015; Harris, 2014). Once embarked on a *particular* research topic, however, the author's ongoing level of knowledge in that topic is fine-tuned and focused. But *when* an author should conduct a literature review for a particular study differs for quantitative and qualitative research and for mixed methods (Creswell, 2009; Johnson & Christensen, 2012; Wiersma & Jurs, 2009) (see Table 7.1).

TABLE 7.1 ■ When to Conduct the Literature Review		
Quantitative Study	**Qualitative Study**	**Mixed Methods Study**
• Occurs *before* the study • Authors draw on it at the end of the study to interpret their results; no new literature can be added	• Usually occurs *after* the data are analyzed (authors first have to "hear the data" and then read the literature to interpret the data) • Can prepare a nominal orienting review *before* the study, with a larger review happening *after* the data are collected and *while* they are being "heard" and analyzed	• *Before* the study, do a detailed literature review; then, collect and "hear" the data; next, go to *different* literature and then *weave* that together with the first review to inform the discussion

Quantitative Literature Review Conventions

In a quantitative study, the literature review occurs *before* the study is conducted (with some refinement at the writing-up stage). It serves to (a) introduce a problem, (b) describe in detail the existing literature about the problem, and (c) provide direction for the research questions and hypotheses, and it may (d) introduce any theory being used to interpret the results. It usually follows the Introduction section as a stand-alone section with its own title, but it can be part of the Introduction section without a separate heading (see Chapter 6). Quantitative reviews often contain sections focused on the dependent and independent variables and previous work relating them to each other. In addition to serving as a logical point of departure for research questions, hypotheses, and the Methods section, at *the end of the study*, the authors revisit the literature to help explain and interpret their results (Creswell, 2009) (see Chapter 14).

Qualitative Literature Review Conventions

In quantitative work, the existing literature serves as a contextual and theoretical background and guide; however, many qualitative scholars view literature reviews as a "constraining exercise rather than a guiding one" (Ramalho, Adams, Huggard, & Hoare, 2015, p. 1). In truth, the issue of when to conduct a qualitative literature review is one of "ambiguous character" (Hallberg, 2010, p. 1). There is disagreement among qualitative researchers about the role and purpose of the literature review and when it should happen (Gay, Mills, & Airasian, 2006).

Overall, the general consensus seems to be that qualitative authors should do some preliminary reading before the study begins (reported in their paper as a truncated literature review) and *then* return to that, as well as new literature, to interpret and discuss their findings (Hallberg, 2010; Ramalho et al., 2015). This initial foray into the literature serves to ensure that the work being done has not been done before. It also stimulates authors' sensitivity to previous theorization about the topic, stimulates questions, and may help them learn more about their chosen population (Gay et al., 2006; Johnson & Christensen, 2012).

Qualitative data are normally represented using words (especially quotes to provide evidence of themes or new constructs) (see Chapters 8 and 9). The second approach to conducting a qualitative literature review is to collect and "hear the data" in the words and *then* go to the literature to find previous works that help discuss what they mean. In a nutshell, from this approach, a qualitative literature review tends to happen *after* the data are collected and *as* they are analyzed, not before. This means the author sets aside any preconceived notions about the topic and uses a fully exploratory, revelatory approach (Johnson & Christensen, 2012).

This exploration is necessary because qualitative work strives to *listen* to the participants instead of getting them to answer prescribed research questions. Usually, not much has been written on the topic, so the researcher *has* to listen to the participants (Creswell, 2009). Hallberg (2010) described this approach to conducting a literature review as "listen and look with an open mind" (p. 1). By this, he meant that if a hypothesis, model, or theory can be discerned in qualitative data, authors should *then* conduct a literature search for relevant previous work and interweave this into their discussion.

Mixed Methods Literature Review Conventions

A third approach entails doing a detailed literature review, collecting and *hearing* the data, going to new literature to help interpret the findings, and then weaving *all of this* literature into the discussion, especially when using mixed methods (Ary, Jacobs, & Sorensen, 2010; Creswell, 2009). They also suggested different approaches to timing the review depending on the particular method being employed. A theoretically oriented study works best with the literature review done early on. Grounded theory, case studies, and phenomenological studies tend to review the literature at later stages of the research process. In these cases, the literature comes into play *after* patterns or constructs are identified, acting as an interpretive aid rather than a guide or a directive for the study. The ultimate caveat is that qualitative researchers should not let the literature review process "constrain and stifle discovery of new constructs, relationships and theories" (Johnson & Christensen, 2012, p. 66).

REVIEW AND ENGAGEMENT

When critically reading a research report, you would

☐ See if the authors clarified *when* they conducted their review of the literature (before the study if quantitative and before, during, and/or after data collection and analysis if qualitative or mixed methods)

☐ In a qualitative paper, check to see that their choice of *when* to conduct and present the literature review made sense for the methodology used in their study (i.e., it did not constrain their discovery of new constructs, relationships, or theories)

CONDUCTING A LITERATURE SEARCH

The author's literature review gives "readers easy access to research on a particular topic by selecting high quality articles and studies that are relevant, meaningful, important and valid and summarizing them into one complete report" (University of Guelph Writing

Services, 2004, p. 1). The key to this process is *selecting* relevant sources from a collection of work generated through a *literature search* (Wiersma & Jurs, 2009). *Search* is Latin *circare*, "to wander, traverse, go about" (Harper, 2016). In plain language, a search means finding materials in the existing and established literature that are relevant to the topic being investigated. Authors wander about and through previous works on the topic, selecting specific pieces to add to their collection for *this* study.

In reality, the process is a bit more complicated and nuanced (Labaree, 2016; University of California, 2011). It entails preparing the research question (see Chapter 6), developing keywords, using search engines, being familiar with an array of sources and types of documents, and making decisions about which ones to keep and which to discard (see the following text for details). The ultimate goal of *the search* is to obtain a "pile of documents" that authors will use to make a case for their research, to help interpret their data, or both (Goodson, 2017, p. 239).

Keywords and Search Engines

Keywords and research questions were discussed earlier in Chapters 4 and 6, respectively. As a reminder, keywords (descriptors) represent the internal structure of the thinking of the author who wrote the document. Authors conducting a literature search should choose a collection of keywords or phrases that they then enter into search engines (information retrieval systems) to identify entries containing those words. Examples of search engines include Google and Google Scholar, Yahoo (which now includes AltaVista), HotBot, MetaCrawler, AOL, and Bing. Keywords (which are usually modified as the search unfolds) help authors search more effectively and efficiently (manually and using technology), especially if they use Boolean logic (i.e., combinations of *and*, *or*, and *not*). Authors can also search by author name, article title, date, or subject (Ary et al., 2010; Boudah, 2011; Gall et al., 2015). This chapter concerns only the possible sources and types of documents and the process of culling a collection of documents from these sources for a specific research question.

Types and Sources of Documents

Table 7.2 provides an overview of the common types and sources of documents that authors can turn to when conducting a literature search (Boudah, 2011; Creswell, 2009; Gall et al., 2015; Suter, 2012; Wiersma & Jurs, 2009).

Primary and secondary sources

Within these sources, authors will find primary and secondary research, both of which are used in a literature review. Primary scholarship is a publication written by the individual(s) who actually conducted the research. When conducting a literature search, authors should rely heavily on primary sources (Randolph, 2009). When citing secondary sources, authors are relying on another person's interpretation of a primary source. These reviews are useful because they can provide new interpretations of previous works, often extending beyond the original work. When authors are interested in ideas from a secondary source, the rule of thumb is to find the original (the primary), read it, and cite it *only* if it fits within the literature review parameters. Relying on someone else's interpretation can be risky (Boudah, 2011; Gall et al., 2015; Kennedy, 2007; Wiersma & Jurs, 2009).

TABLE 7.2 ■ Types and Sources of Documents for a Literature Review

Types of documents:

- Academic journals (paper and online)
- Conference proceedings (papers, abstracts, and poster sessions)
- Books, book chapters, and book reviews
- Encyclopedias and reference books
- Research handbooks and yearbooks (and other compendia)
- Research and policy reports from governments and private institutions
- Technical reports
- Annotated bibliographies
- Dissertations and theses
- Magazines, newspapers, and newsletters
- Monographs and working papers
- Art-based and audiovisual venues
- Patents and copyrights
- Mathematical proofs
- Commercially available tests and manuals
- Statistical documents
- Personal correspondence
- Social media blogs, podcasts, TED Talks, webinars, YouTube, SlideShare

Sources of documents:

- Library holdings (university [academic], school, public, government, specialized)
- Internet
- Professional associations
- Citation indexes and abstracts (e.g., *Psychology Abstracts*, *Social Sciences Citation Index*)
- Databases and computer-assisted searches (e.g., Google Scholar, Web of Science, PsycINFO, WorldCat, PubMed, Scopus, ABI/INFORM, LexisNexis Academic, Gale [now part of Cengage Learning], Communication & Mass Media Complete, JSTOR, Project MUSE, EBSCO, SocINDEX, ProQuest, Ingenta Connect, PhilPapers, POIESIS, Questia, SSRN, Business Source Premier, and more at https://en.wikipedia.org/wiki/List_of_academic_databases_and_search_engines)
- Academic networks like ResearchGate, Academia.edu, LinkedIn, and Mendeley
- Personal holdings and those of colleagues

Steps for Searching and Finding Documents

Authors should engage in a systematic search process, which means performing their literature search according to a plan or system involving careful, perceptive attention to detail (Wiersma & Jurs, 2009). Authors can search the literature by hand or electronically, usually doing both (Boudah, 2011; Wiersma & Jurs, 2009). Table 7.3 summarizes the

TABLE 7.3 ■ Steps in Conducting a Literature Search and Review							
Pick a topic and establish research questions and/or hypotheses	Develop keywords or phrases relevant to the problem	Identify possible sources from which to obtain documents	Use keywords and search terms (modify as necessary) to identify documents from these sources	Keep relevant, delete irrelevant, and critically examine peripheral documents for their inclusion or exclusion (*selection*)	Locate hard copies of or URLs for all documents selected from the search process	*Read* and *summarize* all documents prior to *critically* evaluating each one; delete irrelevant documents and expand the search if necessary	Using the final collection of documents, *organize* them and then *write* the review, which entails a *synthesis* into a case for the research

most common steps involved in the normal search sequence, appreciating that conducting a literature search is not a linear process (Creswell, 2009; Wiersma & Jurs, 2009). The stages are iterative and not necessarily completed in the order presented in Table 7.3 (Imel, 2011; Randolph, 2009). Indeed, depending on what authors find, they may have to limit or broaden their search, a strategy that is aided by accessing the reference lists of papers in the pile of documents found during the search (Goodson, 2017; Wiersma & Jurs, 2009). Randolph (2009) claimed that 90% of relevant articles for a literature review can be found using this search strategy.

Although this entire process is not normally reported in the research paper or report, it is becoming more common for authors to briefly explain their search parameters, identify the search engines, and such (Harris, 2014; Randolph, 2009; Torraco, 2005). As well, although most steps *will* take place during a search, *when* and in what sequence differs with quantitative and qualitative work (see Table 7.1). In the former, the process unfolds before data are collected and analyzed. In the latter, the review of literature can happen in varying degrees before, during, and after data collection and analysis.

Selecting Studies for the Literature Review

Authors should consciously develop a selection system (set of rules) for including and excluding documents found in the search (Kennedy, 2007). *Select* is Latin *selectus*, "to single out one or more of a number of things of the same kind" (Harper, 2016). As the search is unfolding, works that are relevant should be set aside for deeper investigation. Those that are irrelevant should be discarded, and those that are peripheral should be looked at carefully to discern their immediate relevancy (Ary et al., 2010; Fink, 2004; Randolph, 2009).

Randolph (2009) said authors can include both high- and low-quality articles, but they have to report the differences between them, drawing on any and all useful insights for making their case. Others (e.g., Cooper, 1985, 1988) recommended using only high-quality articles. To temper this stance, Gall et al. (2015) advised authors to privilege *authoritative* pieces, defined as those prepared by experts in the field on the research topic. Another measure of authority is the source itself, with journal articles deemed most authoritative because of the peer review process (although there is some argument against this assertion, as discussed in Kennedy, 2007). Also, some journals are considered more authoritative than others because of the makeup, and institutional affiliation, of their editor, editorial board, and reviewers (see Chapter 5).

Wiersma and Jurs (2009) encouraged authors to first focus on the 8 or 10 most recent references because they most likely present state-of-the-art thinking about the topic. Using another tactic, Creswell (2009) suggested authors start with encyclopedia entries (which are concentrated syntheses), move to journal articles, turn to books, move to conference papers, and end with dissertations. Judiciously selecting from each type of source should yield a workable collection, privileging journal articles and authoritative pieces.

Authors are cautioned to be vigilant when selecting documents from the Internet because these are more suspect than juried and peer-reviewed venues (unless the source is a peer-reviewed journal). Five criteria are recommended for judging the quality and relative worth of Internet-based documents: authority (provenance provided), accuracy, objectivity (especially ad-free), currency (entry is regularly updated), and coverage/ease of access (no fees or additional software required for viewing) (Ary et al., 2010; Johnson & Christensen, 2012).

Ending the Search

When is enough, enough? When has an author *selected* enough documents to address the research question? This is an intuitive aspect of conducting a literature search (Wiersma & Jurs, 2009). Wiersma and Jurs (2009) explained that "when the information in the references reviewed seems to stabilize and seems quite complete in the context

REVIEW AND ENGAGEMENT

When critically reading a research report, you would

- ☐ Determine if the authors positioned the literature review in its own stand-alone section

- ☐ See if they, less effectively, positioned the literature review in their Introduction section, with no separate heading

- ☐ In a qualitative paper, determine if they had a separate Literature Review section (likely, they did not; instead, they probably introduced relevant literature in their Discussion section, which is the preferred approach)

- ☐ Assess whether their collection of documents came from sufficiently diverse types and sources (refer to their reference list)

- ☐ Ascertain if they followed the recommended conventions for selecting studies from what they find

- ☐ Judge whether they cited enough references to develop their argument for their study (did not stop searching too soon)

- ☐ Determine if they explained their search parameters and procedures used to find literature, including keywords, and types and sources of documents (seldom done) (see Table 7.3 and Figure 7.1)

of the research problem, the review has reached closure" (p. 65). Patterns will become consistent, additional found studies will reinforce those patterns, methods will become similar, and theories will start to overlap. Creswell (2009) further recommended that authors should map their collection of documents using concept maps, matrices, or flow-charts to expose gaps or excesses in documents and sources. This strategy helps authors to fine-tune the final selection of articles that will comprise their "pile of literature," which must now be critically evaluated before being synthesized into a case for a particular study (Goodson, 2017, p. 239).

CRITICALLY REVIEWING THE COLLECTION OF LITERATURE

Once documents have been systemically found through a literature search, yielding a pile of documents, the authors should read, analyze, and critically evaluate *each* item in their collection before developing relationships among the pieces of literature *and* between the literature and the research question (Fink, 2004). It is the authors' responsibility to convince readers that they are both familiar, and have *critically engaged*, with previous works. In this case, *critical* means careful evaluation and discerning judgment. *Uncritical* means accepting or approving something without analyzing or questioning it (Anderson, 2014; Labaree, 2016) (see Chapter 1). In academic, scholarly writing, critical evaluation constitutes the bulk of the literature review because the literature review "is a discursive essay that critically surveys existing scholarship on a particular topic in a field" (Labaree, 2016). Discursive writing stems from reason and argumentation rather than intuition. Critical reviews involve authors expressing their analysis of the merits of a literary work (Anderson, 2014).

Critical engagement with these selected pieces of literature entails much more than finding fault with a study's research design and execution or with the author's arguments. It encompasses a close examination of the work, seeking to reveal the integrity of the previous researcher's interpretations and knowledge claims. Are there plausible counterexamples? Critical reviews of literature further strive to unveil any unspoken assumptions of the previous researchers. Given their research question, authors will also critically question the appropriateness of the previous work's methods for data collection and analysis. Critical authors will query whether or not previous ideas can be extended to other contexts or be viewed through other perspectives or paradigms. As well, authors engaged in a critical review of the literature will try to discern what might have influenced the previous authors' writing and lines of thought. They will also try to determine if things are missing or overplayed in other scholars' academic conversations (Bak, 2003; Harris, 2014; Taylor & Procter, ca. 2009) (see Chapter 1).

Authors should not be afraid to critique and disagree with earlier scholarship. Indeed, disagreement is better than just presenting an uncritical laundry list or a rehash of others' work (Shon, 2015). In fact, Harris (2014) claimed that "the true strength of research [is the author's] willingness to critically scrutinize, test out, and overturn ideas (rather than accepting them on faith)" (p. 44). Appreciating that authors *do* balk at critiquing others' work, Bak (2003) identified several blocks preventing critical engagement with previous literature. These include cultural conditioning, reliance on opinions, hasty judgment, succumbing to buzzwords and popular labels or memes, resisting change, and not resisting emotive language and logic.

Critical engagement with previous scholarship is the hallmark of a good literature review. A "paragraph-by-paragraph tour of one article after another is mind-numbing to read and not particularly insightful" (Callahan, 2010, p. 303). Gall et al. (2015) confirmed that authors need to do more than provide "a citation or two in parentheses after making a sweeping generalization" about the previous literature (p. 103). This uncritical strategy diminishes readers' trust in the authors' conclusions and interpretations of the cited work. Authors should judiciously tie together insights from previous studies instead of "providing a compendium of references, devoting a paragraph or two to each without connecting the ideas" (Wiersma & Jurs, 2009, p. 69). As well, authors should avoid lumping studies together that deal with the same issue; instead, they should discriminate among them. This strategy is a strong indicator that the author has critically examined the literature (Gall et al., 2015).

In summary, Shon (2015) tendered a four-part formula for a critical review of previous literature on a topic. The first quarter entails correctly understanding, stating, and *summarizing* what others have said on a topic. The next two quarters entail a thematically connected *critique* of the previous literature. The final quarter constitutes a thematic and principled summary and *synthesis* of selected works into an argument for the present study. Following this formula, a good literature review *adds value* to the field; that is, its addition to the field is a valuable contribution. Authors add value to all of the materials they have read by explaining how the salient ideas of others have led up, and help contribute, to a new research problem. And literature reviews are valuable in their *own right* (e.g., helpful, meaningful, worthy) because the authors have judiciously assembled, critiqued, and synthesized prior knowledge, creating something that did not exist in the literature before. Others will now be able to draw on *their* literature review in the future (Greenberg, 2006; Imel, 2011).

REVIEW AND ENGAGEMENT

When critically reading a research report, you would

- ☐ Decide if the authors satisfactorily related their chosen literature back to their research question

- ☐ Ascertain if they *critically engaged* with *each* piece of literature cited in their paper (the many dimensions to this critical process mitigate a paragraph-by-paragraph recitation of each piece)

- ☐ Judge whether they successfully employed Shon's (2015) four-part formula for a critical review of literature

- ☐ Determine if their review of the literature *added value* to the field or discipline

WRITING THE LITERATURE REVIEW SECTION

Writing a literature review is not a linear process; rather, authors move back and forth among the various stages of conducting research (Imel, 2011). But there *is* a process involved, whether it be subliminal or explicit. Once authors have found "the pile of literature" (Goodson, 2017, p. 239) they want to use to prepare a case for their research question and have critically read and synthesized all relevant pieces into a convincing argument, they have to write the Literature Review section of their paper or research report. This process entails many decisions, especially those related to how to organize the material. The entire writing-up process is guided by the principle of synthesis.

Synthesis

Synthesis is Greek *suntithenia*, "placing together," and Latin *synthesis*, "a collection" (Harper, 2016). Synthesis entails combining readings to form something new (Shon, 2015). In this case, that something new is the author's conclusions about what was found in the literature and what this means relative to the research topic being studied. Synthesis is both a by-product and an inherent aspect of the process of scholarly or critical analysis of the sources selected during the search. As authors critically reread and analyze their pile of documents, connections among the different articles begin to form. Through the process of synthesis, patterns emerge that are not evident when each piece is read in isolation. If authors summarize each paper separately, they do not learn how the ideas are related to each other or if some ideas are more significant than others (Taylor, ca. 2006). In contrast, synthesis helps authors construct new knowledge to help address *their* research problem. New knowledge arises from new interpretations of older material and from joining old and new interpretations (Imel, 2011).

Synthesis involves (a) comparing (finding similarities), (b) contrasting (finding differences), (c) finding discrepancies (incompatibilities), (d) critically evaluating, and (e) interpreting the contents of the pieces accumulated for the review (Taylor, ca. 2006). To interpret is to read something and then assign meaning to it or explain its significance relative to the research question. Synthesis also entails identifying how separate works *relate to each other*—that is, placing them in context *to* each other (Suter, 2012). Do they agree, disagree, question, augment, and/or offer alternative perspectives on a research topic or aspects of it? Authors have to acknowledge, and ideally resolve, conflicts and tensions in the literature while recognizing consensus and general agreement (Boote & Beile, 2005; University of California, 2011).

Synthesis results in (a) insights into which sources overlap or share the same ideas or disagree, (b) the identification of commonalities or disparities among readings, (c) an assessment of the strengths and weaknesses of previous research or conclusions, (d) the identification of weak or strong supportive arguments, and (e) fodder for shaping the author's own opinion on the research topic (Taylor, ca. 2006). The ultimate goal of synthesizing the literature is to determine what general conclusions can be reported about a topic, given the entire group of studies related to it and how they relate to each other (Galvan, 2006; Suter, 2012). Integrating previous studies helps shape a more complete picture of the background to the research problem. By neglecting to synthesize, authors risk creating meaningless background information (Ary et al., 2010).

The following examples briefly illustrate unsuccessful and successful synthesis around the integration of five research articles (Taylor, ca. 2006, pp. 2–3).

Example 7.1 Unsuccessful synthesis "Knowles (1978) wrote that meaningful work builds upon life experiences and links new knowledge with previous experiences. Meaningful work contributes to a student's confidence (Bandura, 1997). Meaningful work meets an immediate need (Rogers, 2000). Seifert (2004) claimed that meaningful work contributes to a student's confidence. Finally, Craft (2005) stated that reflective journals can be meaningful tasks for the student" (p. 2).

Example 7.2 Successful synthesis "Given the importance of meaningful learning in increasing student motivation and task persistence (Bandura, 1997; Craft, 2005; Knowles, 1978; Rogers, 2000; Seifert, 2004), it is important to provide relevant and practical clinical teaching to clients" (p. 3).

Synthesis Matrix

Although a synthesis matrix is not usually published in the final paper, it is invaluable for synthesizing the collection of articles found in the literature search. Table 7.4 provides a template for a literature review matrix. This template can be set up as a table in the word processing program, or as a spreadsheet, and completed as the review progresses (Goodson, 2017). As authors find and read each piece they intend to keep, they should enter the relevant details into the matrix. When completed, they can use the patterns evident in the matrix to begin writing their literature review section.

A different approach for synthesis *can* be published with the journal article. Authors can create a table with the rows representing the ideas emergent from the collection of papers and the columns representing the articles that contained the ideas. To begin, authors would enter the name of each article into a column. The document in the far left column is read first. Authors would enter an idea into the first row, then place a tick in that article's column. Each separate row contains one large idea. Authors would continue this process until they have completed reading that article. Upon reading the paper in the second column, they would enter a tick in any row where a similar idea has already been entered. If that idea never appears, they would leave that row blank. They would add any new ideas from the second paper to the bottom of the list, with a tick. This process continues until all documents have been read.

The list in the far left column gets longer upon reading each article, until all are read and a complete list emerges. Tallies of the rows indicate how many times each large idea was mentioned (add up ticks in each row). Tallies of each individual column reveal how many ideas were found in each separate source. By completing the table (matrix), authors create a powerful picture of commonalities, trends, connections, discrepancies, and missing areas in the literature. The resultant table (a synthesis matrix) can be used to begin to write the literature review (Boudah, 2011; Goodson, 2017) and can be published with the paper, if so desired.

Example 7.3 A synthesis matrix McGregor and MacCleave (2007) used this strategy to critically analyze seven artifacts dealing with home economics professional competencies (from Canada, United States, and Australia). They published their synthesis matrix with their paper (with an excerpt below) and used their synthesis to help write their literature review and to inform their seven detailed recommendations.

Figure 7.1 summarizes the main stages of conducting and preparing a literature review. As noted earlier, this process is iterative (not always linear). Authors need to continue the process until they are satisfied with their review of earlier studies pursuant to their topic. Once they have critically engaged with sufficient literature to support their approach to the topic (i.e., identified the gaps and justified their take on the research problem), they have to decide how to organize the material in their literature review section.

FIGURE 7.1 ■ Basic Stages of the Literature Review Process

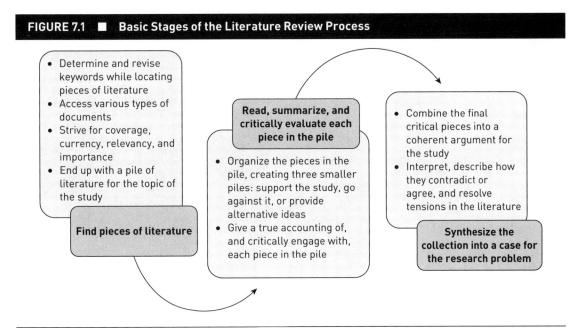

- Determine and revise keywords while locating pieces of literature
- Access various types of documents
- Strive for coverage, currency, relevancy, and importance
- End up with a pile of literature for the topic of the study

Find pieces of literature

Read, summarize, and critically evaluate each piece in the pile

- Organize the pieces in the pile, creating three smaller piles: support the study, go against it, or provide alternative ideas
- Give a true accounting of, and critically engage with, each piece in the pile

- Combine the final critical pieces into a coherent argument for the study
- Interpret, describe how they contradict or agree, and resolve tensions in the literature

Synthesize the collection into a case for the research problem

TABLE 7.4 ■ Template for Literature Review Matrix

Author(s)	Year	Name of source (journal, book, conference paper), with pages, volume, issue	Title	Digital object identifier (DOI)	Points of interest in this article, with page number	Possible quotes to use in paper

Competency Domain	1994 Berry CHEA	1997 Kieren and Badir CHEA	2003 Crown and Gervais for CHEA	1998 Mitstifer for AAFCS Certification Committee	1999 Mitstifer for CAFCS Steering Committee on Higher Education	2002 AAFCS Body of Knowledge	2003 HEIA Australia	Total
	Canada			United States			Australia	Total
Human ecology and family ecosystem	✓	✓	✓	✓	✓	✓		6
Interdisciplinary and integrative	✓	✓	✓	✓	✓	✓		6
Problem solving and decision making	✓		✓	✓			✓	4
Total	3	2	3	3	2	2	1	16

REVIEW AND ENGAGEMENT

When critically reading a research report, you would

☐ Determine if the authors' Literature Review section appears to reflect the three main phases of doing a literature review (found a pile of papers, critiqued each one relative to the others in the pile, and then wrote the synthesized report) (see Tables 7.3 and 7.4 and Figure 7.1)

☐ Determine if they clearly distinguished between their and others' interpretations of a source being cited

☐ Make sure they presented a synergistic *synthesis* of the literature

☐ Per the above, determine if they explained how *each* piece of literature agreed with, disagreed with, questioned, augmented, and/or offered alternatives to *their* approach to the research topic and question

☐ Per the above, ascertain if they adequately resolved conflicts and tensions in the literature vis-à-vis the argument they developed for their research question (instead of presenting meaningless information, totally out of context)

☐ Decide if they convinced you they had read sufficient literature to address their research question and to support their argument justifying their study

Organizational and Presentation Strategies

From an organizational perspective, authors have to decide how to group or arrange their discussion of ideas contained in the studies reviewed (Wiersma & Jurs, 2009). Suter (2012) clarified that, normally, literature reviews are organized by topics, not by the names of the authors of the papers. When preparing to write a literature review, authors have several organizational options. They can do it historically, chronologically, conceptually, theoretically, thematically, methodologically, and by major ideas, arguments, or hypotheses (see Figure 7.2). Cooper (1985) clarified that authors can combine organizational approaches in one literature review, offering as a suggestion "addressing works historically within a given conceptual or methodological framework" (p. 13). Labaree (2016) described such reviews as "hybrid literature reviews."

Historical

A historical perspective is useful if the author wants to showcase the evolution of ideas over time, but only ideas relevant to the research problem (Greenberg, 2006; Labaree, 2016). Authors would arrange their introduction of each piece of literature to reflect their analysis of the development of an idea over time.

Example 7.4 Historical McGregor (2010b) used this approach in her article that traced the home economics profession's historical and contemporary use of the notion of transdisciplinarity. Reporting that transdisciplinarity was coined and initially developed in 1972, she traced its usage in home economics back to only three scholars, C. E. J. Daniels in Wales (in 1980), Marjorie M. Brown in the United States (1993), and herself (Canada), starting in 2004. She used their names as subheadings to organize her literature review.

FIGURE 7.2 ■ Approaches to Organizing and Presenting the Literature Review

- *Historical*: organize the review so it traces the evolution of an idea over time
- *Chronological*: introduce topics in the order they appeared in the literature, using dates as subheadings
- *Conceptual*: organize the review using concepts found in the literature as headings and subheadings
- *Theoretical*: organize using main theories emergent from the literature review
- *Thematic*: use as main headings any themes evident from synthesizing the literature
- *Methods*: arrange studies according to the methods used by others who previously studied the topic
- *Major ideas and trends*: use labels for major ideas or major trends as headings for the literature review
- *Argumentative*: organize the literature presentation so it supports the argument or position underpinning the paper
- *Hypotheses*: present a collection of studies that help develop the rationale for each separate hypothesis

Chronological

Using this approach, authors would introduce topics in the order they appeared in the literature (Labaree, 2016). As an example, Labaree (2016) referred to a literature review that might focus on the "continuing, uninterrupted research about the emergence of German economic power after the fall of the Soviet Union." In this case, the author would read widely on the topic, chronicling the essence of the corpus of research that has explored this phenomenon, organizing the literature by decades or specific years.

Example 7.5 Chronological In her article on the evolution of consumer education curriculum initiatives, McGregor (2015) organized her literature review by decades, and within that, subheadings identified each separate initiative. To illustrate, for the 1980s (main heading), she identified four papers reporting four different consumer education curriculum initiatives and used these as the subheadings: developmental approach (1981), competency-based model (1981), classification of concepts in consumer education model (1982), and a typology of consumers (1982).

Example 7.6 Chronological McGregor (2010c) employed this organizational approach when she described the home economics profession's use of systems thinking. She explained that family systems thinking first appeared in the home economics literature in the 1960s–1970s. This evolved to family ecosystem in the 1970s–1980s, followed by human ecosystem in the 1980s–1990s, evolving to integral (complex emergent systems) in the 1900s–2000s. She used these four terms as headings to organize her literature review.

Conceptual

This approach involves authors reading a collection of articles from which similar *concepts* appear. A concept is a word or phrase that summarizes the essential properties of a phenomenon. For example, "caring" is a concept that evokes certain mental images (The Learning House, 2016). Researchers construct or develop ideas around a phenomenon and give those ideas a name. They become concepts, with other examples including leadership, happiness, well-being, and success (Aswar, 2011) (see Chapter 3). Upon reading the literature, authors would organize their literature review using *concepts* as headings or subheadings and then develop a discussion of each concept drawing from their collection of articles (Cooper, 1985).

> ***Example 7.7 Conceptual*** When developing thoughts of what might constitute *the phenomenon* of a sustainable life path (from a consumption perspective), McGregor (2014) read a broad body of literature on the topic of sustainable consumption and sustainable living and discovered an array of *concepts*, which she used as subheadings in her paper, including the concepts of an examined life, an engaged life, purposeful living, voluntary simplicity, and life acumen and life intentions.

Theoretical

Using this approach, the author would read the literature and then report the most influential theories previously employed to understand a research topic. The literature review section could have subheadings for each theory, or the author could choose to analyze the theories and then present an analysis of their overlap and divergence. This approach can lead to insights about the appropriateness and adequacies of current theories being used to understand a topic (Labaree, 2016; University of Guelph Writing Services, 2004).

> ***Example 7.8 Theoretical*** In her discussion of consumer education philosophies (education philosophical theories), McGregor (2011a) identified 11 such theories and discussed how they are applied to consumer education. Her collection contained a subheading for each theory, including academic rationalism, cognitive, social constructivism, progressivism, self-actualization, and critical philosophies. She argued that the *kind of consumer* prepared for the world is partially dependent upon how educators view the relationship between education (philosophy theories) and consumption because it affects what they will teach, to whom, when, how, and why.

Thematical

Another common approach is for authors to read and analyze the literature they have collected around a research topic, actively looking for patterns or themes to emerge. A *theme* is an idea that recurs or pervades a body of work. Using this approach, authors do not normally delve into the literature with specific themes in mind; rather, they deduce them from iterative readings. Once three or four themes have emerged, they are used as subheadings to organize the literature review. A thematic approach better ensures that authors do not simply summarize each separate piece (Firestone, 2010; Labaree, 2016; University of Guelph Writing Services, 2004). Another twist on the thematic approach is for the authors to ascertain that their topic has undergone thematic reinterpretations over time and then organize their literature review using those insights (Labaree, 2016).

> *Example 7.9 Thematic* If an author pulled together a collection of articles on the topic of hip-hop music and read and reread the literature until patterns emerged, she could organize the literature review using those themes. There might be separate sections on research examining the themes of (a) hip-hop music production, (b) hip-hop music dissemination, (c) hip-hop music interpretation, (d) the political power of hip-hop music, and (e) its use as an empowering voice for an entire generation.

Methodological (meaning methods)

This is a useful approach if authors want to recount studies that employed similar *methods* of sampling, data collection, and data analysis. In this way, authors focus not only on what people *said* but also on *how* they went about obtaining the results or findings that allowed them to say what they did. Another advantage of this approach is that it allows the authors to develop a justification for their research design (Cooper, 1985; Labaree, 2016).

> *Example 7.10 Methods* Labaree (2016) discussed a study focused on the Internet in American presidential politics. He suggested finding literature from American, British, and French scholars and then looking at what *methods* those scholars used to collect, analyze, and interpret data about cultural differences in portraying political leaders on the Internet. Once the literature was reviewed, the authors could organize their literature review by arranging studies together that used the same methods, then commenting on the implications of divergent methods.

Major ideas and trends

Authors can organize their review using major ideas that emerged from the literature. *Ideas* are abstractions (mental impressions) that authors make after reading many papers on a topic. Authors, in effect, distill the essence of the readings into identifiable ideas that are likely somewhat unique to the research problem. Grouping according to these categories can provide a logical organization for presenting the results of the literature review (Greenberg, 2006; Wiersma & Jurs, 2009). Another twist on this is to organize the literature review using the major *trends* that emerged from the literature (Labaree, 2016; University of Guelph Writing Services, 2004). A trend is the general direction in which something is happening, developing, or changing (Anderson, 2014).

> *Example 7.11 Trends* Upon reading an extensive and eclectic body of literature, McGregor (2012) published a book chapter about 10 life-centric megatrends that are countering neoliberal-centric megatrends shaping the world. Each megatrend is a subheading in her chapter, numbered as countertrends—for example, Countertrend 1: No chance to age, Countertrend 2: Localization and globalization (bottom up), Countertrend 4: Redefining prosperity (GPI), and Countertrend 6: Abundance mentality. Using the major trend approach, she made a case for home economists to be aware of both trends and countertrends and to critique both on an ongoing basis.

Argumentative

This approach requires authors to develop an argument or position they want to advocate. After they intentionally choose several topics related to their argument, they then selectively review the literature that helps them develop their argument and make their case (Labaree, 2016). Shank and Brown (2007) recommended three to six important topics that, taken together, can provide sufficient background to justify a study (see Chapter 17 on argumentative essays).

> ***Example 7.12 Argumentative*** McGregor (2011b) published a paper on the role of preprofessional socialization of home economists in higher education and its impact on future-proofing the profession. To make her case that home economics university curricula must socialize a new generation of practitioners if we want to ensure the profession's future, her literature review intentionally comprised three preselected ideas, discussed separately and then woven together to make her argument: (a) the historical discussion of home economics programs in higher education, (b) preprofessional socialization theory and studies, and (c) curriculum design theory.

Hypotheses

Finally, in quantitative work, authors can organize their literature review using their hypotheses. Having decided the former, they would read their accumulated collection of previous works (citations below are example only) and then map out what has been done, leading to a justification for each hypothesis (Ary et al., 2010).

> ***Example 7.13 Hypotheses***
>
> *Hypothesis 1*. This study is interested in how student debt loads have changed over the last 25 years and how this change affects students' solvency (ability to pay bills when they come due). Jones (1989) reported that consumer debt was rampant amongst college students, compromising their solvency for years after graduation. Right (2007) countermanded this assertion, showing instead that college students' debt loads were manageable. More recent scholarship is evidencing a reversion of this trend, with contemporary students bearing an inordinate debt load for years after graduation. Many of these students have declared bankruptcy (Brown, 2016; Marystone, 2017). This study explores the relationship between student debt loads and future solvency, using the following null and alternative hypotheses:
>
> > H_0: There is no relationship between student debt load and solvency after graduation.
> >
> > H_1: There is a direct but negative relationship between student debt load and solvency after graduation (i.e., the higher the debt, the less solvent).

In conclusion, no matter which organizational approach (or combination) the author uses, the ultimate goal is to prepare "a review organized in a way that provides insights into the topic under review" (Imel, 2011, p. 157). A well-organized review provides cues for the reader and gives an indication of what literature was covered, why, and to what extent (Imel, 2011). By making solid organizational choices, authors leave little doubt about the significance of their research topic and their approach to it (Suter, 2012).

REVIEW AND ENGAGEMENT

When critically reading a research report, you would

- ☐ Ascertain which organizational approach the authors used in their literature review

- ☐ Determine if that organizational approach *made sense* for the argument they developed in the Introduction section that supported their research question (see Figure 7.2)

- ☐ Decide if their organizational approach convinced you of the significance of *their* approach to the research problem

CHARACTERISTICS OF A GOOD LITERATURE REVIEW

A good review of the literature will have several prominent characteristics (see Figure 7.3) including being critical, important, relevant, and timely, as well as having sufficient coverage, clarified points of view, and a rigorous, true accounting of previous work.

Critical

There is considerable variety in the quality of research reports and articles in the body of literature for a research topic. The quality of that literature must be critically reviewed. Authors must comment on the strengths and weaknesses of each item in their final collection (Pyrczak, 2008). In addition to the criteria noted previously for critical engagement with the literature, Wiersma and Jurs (2009) recommended that authors assess the *logical validity* to determine if the entire report "fits together and makes sense" (p. 69) (see also Boote & Beile, 2005). In effect, the conclusions should follow from the discussion, which follows from the results and findings, which arise from the methods, which emerge from the literature review and the research questions, all of which are determined by the research methodology (Cooper, 1985; Imel, 2011). Determining this logical fit is "part of the intellectual exercise of critical review" (Imel, 2011, p. 69).

Important

If relevant for making their case, authors should cite *important* works in the field. Called benchmark, classic, landmark, or seminal works, they can bring credibility to the rationale for a study. Knowledgeable readers will look for these types of citations and may query their absence. On the other hand, authors should not cite these works if they bring no meaning to their research argument (Shank & Brown, 2007). Authors are encouraged to avail themselves of the reference lists in other people's papers because they provide a quick synopsis of the topic, validated as important by a variety of scholars (Randolph, 2009). Recurring articles are likely to be key, important papers on the topic (Firestone, 2010; Greenberg,

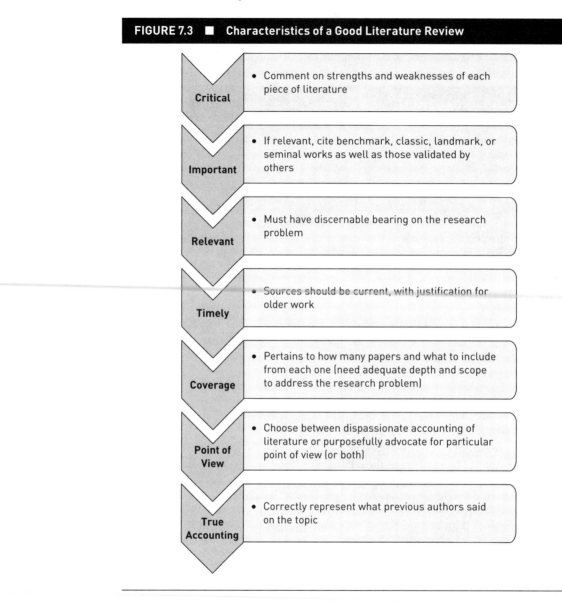

FIGURE 7.3 ■ Characteristics of a Good Literature Review

Critical
- Comment on strengths and weaknesses of each piece of literature

Important
- If relevant, cite benchmark, classic, landmark, or seminal works as well as those validated by others

Relevant
- Must have discernable bearing on the research problem

Timely
- Sources should be current, with justification for older work

Coverage
- Pertains to how many papers and what to include from each one (need adequate depth and scope to address the research problem)

Point of View
- Choose between dispassionate accounting of literature or purposefully advocate for particular point of view (or both)

True Accounting
- Correctly represent what previous authors said on the topic

2006). When a particular author's work is cited by many scholars, it is deemed influential on the thinking around the research topic (Shank & Brown, 2007).

Relevant

Although it may seem like stating the obvious, authors should only cite previous or contemporary work that is *relevant* to their topic. Irrelevant literature only clouds the issue and raises concern about the author's reasoning, logic, and motives. Any literature cited should have a discernable bearing on the research problem (Shank & Brown, 2007). To ensure relevancy, authors should pay special attention to justifying why they included or excluded specific previous research in their review (Boote & Beile, 2005; Gall et al., 2015; Pyrczak, 2008; Wiersma & Jurs, 2009). Criteria for exclusion include lack of topicality, comprehensiveness, breadth, currency, availability, and authority (Boote & Beile, 2005).

Dunkin (1996) urged against both (a) unexplained selectivity, understood to mean excluding a study without justification, and (b) lack of discrimination, which means giving all included studies equal weight or relevance when they are not. "Each reviewer must decide which specific studies to include and exclude from a review and why. And each such decision alters the character of the set as a whole and could also therefore alter the net conclusions drawn from the set" (Kennedy, 2007, p. 139). Harris (2014) further cautioned that drawing the line between relevant and irrelevant literature, vis-à-vis the research question, is an arbitrary act that must be done with full awareness of the consequences: "It shapes how [authors] design their studies and interpret their results. It shapes what they think is known, what they try to find, and what they tell their readers" (p. 40).

Timely

Closely tied to relevancy is *timeliness* or currency of the citations. Authors should not cite too many sources that are old unless that work has a direct bearing on justifying and explaining their approach to the topic, in which case, older pieces are very relevant; that is, relevancy trumps currency (Shank & Brown, 2007). They suggested that if *all* of the works cited are more than five years old, the authors are not current on the topic; research is perpetually changing in most fields and around most topics. Goodson (2017) advised that "the definition of *dated* depends on each academic field's traditions and expectations" (p. 164). An exception to the timeliness rule is theoretical work, which does not expire as quickly as conventional research. That being said, Shank and Brown (2007) applied a 10-year rule to theoretical pieces, asserting that researchers should justify using older and earlier versions of a theory, model, or conceptual framework.

Coverage

A fifth criterion is *coverage*, meaning how much and to what depth previous literature should be cited (Imel, 2011). When reporting on previous studies, authors can examine the literature review, theoretical frameworks, research methods, results or findings, discussion points, conclusions, and practical applications or implications. Their review can include more than one of these foci, in varying degrees of attention and coverage (e.g., depth and breadth) (Cooper, 1985).

Cooper (1985) further explained that authors can approach their *own* literature review with one of four degrees of coverage (and this intended coverage can change as the review of the literature progresses). (a) First, authors can strive to have exhaustive, *comprehensive* coverage of the entire literature, not just a sample of it. When this approach is used, depth (detail) is often sacrificed. (b) The second approach entails *sampling* an entire body of literature, meaning less scope but more depth. (c) A third approach involves referring to only those works cited most frequently in the literature. They are taken as *representative* of many other studies in the field. (d) Finally, authors can cite only those works that have been *pivotal* to the field or the topic. These works likely provided directions for new lines of thinking, investigation, or methods for the topic.

Gall et al. (2015) recognized the challenges inherent in summarizing work from a large number of previous studies. Authors have to find a balance of how much information to include in their literature review (coverage) (e.g., how many papers and what to include from those papers). Actually, Cooper (1985) clarified that authors can choose to combine several of his four coverage strategies in one paper to accommodate specific elements of the topic being examined. For example, an author might provide an exhaustive overview of extant literature on one part of the research topic and representative coverage for more heavily researched aspects of the research question. It may be appropriate to reference one or two pivotal works as well.

Point of View

Authors should also clarify which of two basic points of view they are taking when they review the literature. They can either (a) tender a dispassionate, neutral representation of previous work or (b) choose and then advocate for a particular perspective from the literature. The former approach entails as little interpretation and evaluation of the previous research as possible; instead, the author counts on its prominence in the field to speak for itself. The latter serves to demonstrate the value of a particular point of view, paradigm, theory, method, or practice as it pertains to the research question. Actually, authors may want or need to use both points of view, "first describing dispassionately the contents of an area and then applying a particular perspective to it" (Cooper, 1985, p. 11).

On another note, authors have to justify including or excluding outliers and unconventional thinkers who diverge from mainstream ideas in the literature. Some topics and their interpretation can become politicized, radicalized, and marginalized. Citing such sources can either taint the message or seduce readers (Imel, 2011). When making this inclusion or exclusion decision, authors must make a cautious, judicious choice. Will stirring up the waters interfere with others' reception of their ideas, or will others infer that the author is open-minded and is encouraging controversial discourse?

Rigorous, True Accounting

Finally, when authors prepare their literature review, they need to rigorously and truly account for what previous authors were reporting (Pyrczak, 2008). This applies to them directly citing a primary author and relying on secondary sources; in both instances, authors have to mitigate misrepresenting what the previous work said. Without careful attention to this criterion, authors can inadvertently commit the errors of unwarranted attributions and outright misrepresentation (Dunkin, 1996).

Regarding secondary sources, when referring to another author's citation of a primary source, authors have to make clear whether that person was reporting actual results or expressing an opinion on those results (Pyrczak, 2008). To slip into first person, for example, if I read Smith's (2000) paper, where she contained comments about Brown's (1999) study, I have to discern whether Smith was reporting what Brown found or just expressing her opinion about Brown's work. To ensure a true accounting, I might have to go directly to Brown's paper instead of relying on Smith's interpretation. Authors should be conscious of how they word their comments so readers can discern the original scholar's intent. For example, I could say, "Upon reading Brown's (1999) study, Smith (2000) argued that . . ."

TECHNICAL ELEMENTS OF WRITING EFFECTIVE LITERATURE REVIEW SECTIONS

On a final note, as with other sections of a research paper or report, authors must be cognizant of some basic technical conventions and guidelines when preparing the Literature Review section of a research paper.

Person and Voice

Quantitative literature reviews are normally written in third person and, ideally, in active voice, reflecting this methodology's focus on objectivity and validity. Qualitative literature reviews tend to use first person and active voice because this methodology focuses on personal interpretation and on researchers purposefully positioning themselves in the research process (Zeegers & Barron, 2015).

Tense

The literature review can be written in either past or present tense, but past tense is usually used because the work has already happened. With no overall agreement on this principle, Monash University (2006) provided some general guidelines. When authors are asserting a statement about, or their position on, past scholarship, they can use present tense. When reporting on previous past research, past tense is recommended (but present tense is acceptable). In either case, authors have to be consistent and not slip back and forth between tenses. Present perfect tense is used to indicate that research is ongoing or to generalize about past research.

Example 7.14 Present tense (author's position or statement) Compared to past research on the topic, the authors of this paper *are* investigating the nuances of consumer indebtedness.

Example 7.15 Past tense (referring to previous literature) This particular theory of nuanced consumer indebtedness *was* not popular until the 1970s.

Example 7.16 Present perfect tense (generalize) Several researchers *have studied* the nuances of how consumers become indebted.

Length of Literature Review Section

A literature review "seeks to describe, summarize, evaluate, clarify and/or integrate the content of [previous] primary reports" (Cooper, 1988, p. 107). This task requires a significant amount of space within a research report or journal article; unfortunately, there is no fast and true rule about how long the literature review should be. "In the absence of specific instructions about the length of a literature review, a general rule of thumb is that it should be proportionate to the length of [the] entire paper" (Philadelphia University, n.d.). If the paper is 20 pages long, the literature review should be 3–5 pages in length. If it is 15 pages long, 2–3 pages should suffice. This four-to-one ratio serves as a loose guideline for authors. Sometimes, the length required to make authors' case for their research trumps any magic page number or word count.

Number of References

Firestone (2010) maintained there are also no clear-cut rules for how many references authors should use to complete their literature review. She said it depends on the nature of the research and the size of the existing literature. A controversial topic will require more references than a less debated topic. A relatively obscure topic will yield fewer references than one that has attracted wider attention in the field. If understanding the topic requires examining how knowledge and perspectives have changed over time, a longer reference list may be required to accommodate the historical overview. Conversely, if the nature of the topic dictates only very current information, the reference list may be short (Labaree, 2016). In the end, authors will eventually reach a saturation point and pretty much know they have found and used enough references to make their case (Randolph, 2009; Wiersma & Jurs, 2009).

Journal preferences may be another contributing factor affecting how many references to include. If the word count for an article includes the reference list, the authors will have to prepare a very tightly written review to accommodate space (wordage) for the references or be very selective in what they cite. Suter (2012) recommended a minimum of 6–10 references that provide compelling reasons for the research. Less restrictively, Eaton (2014) proposed a rough, proportional rule for number of references. A 10-page paper would have 10 references in the literature review, a 20-page paper would have 20 references, and so on. This suggestion is tempered by her acknowledgment that the number of references "all depends" on the topic; the nature of the research (e.g., a journal article, thesis, or dissertation); how much literature there *is* to review; and the author's level of scholarship (e.g., novice, experienced, seasoned).

Transitioning From a Summary, Critical Evaluation to a Gap

It is not enough to summarize the previous literature. From a critical perspective, authors must find shortcomings and strengths and present these in a logical and structured manner so that readers can follow their argument. A recommended approach to this transition from summary to critique is to (a) lead with a summary sentence about a point in the article, (b) follow with a critique statement (which pushes against the ideas contained in the previous sentence), and (c) end with an identified gap in the literature. After each or several of these sequences, authors should then (d) state their rationale(s) for doing *their* study

(Shon, 2015). Shon (2015) further advised using specific conjunctions to indicate a transition from the summarizing comment to the critique, including *but, however, while, albeit, although,* and *despite that.*

> ***Example 7.17 Summary-critique-gap-rationale*** Shannon (2006) [SAMPLE CITATION] found that debt is a widespread phenomenon once students graduate from college or university [SUMMARY]. *But* his study was limited to one large college in one large state and to graduates who left the state to obtain employment [CRITIQUE]. Few studies have examined postgraduation debt for students who live in smaller states, graduate from small institutions, and remain in the state to find work [GAP]. This study addresses that gap by including states with smaller populations and students who graduated from very small learning institutions with the intent to stay close to home to work. Their student debt load may differ significantly from those in Shannon's study [RATIONALE].

Boote and Beile (2005) recommended that a high-quality literature review will move from analysis through synthesis to evaluation; it will, respectively, (a) discern the main points of each paper in the pile and (b) weave them together into new understandings, replete with (c) a critical evaluation of the ideas. This movement equates to higher and higher levels of critical engagement with the material found in the literature search (see also Taylor, ca. 2006).

Transitioning From One Major Point to Another

The Literature Review section should contain two to three main ideas, topics, or overall points. Wiersma and Jurs (2009) maintained that authors should use subheadings and transition statements to logically and smoothly move their review from one major point to another. Leading the reader from one topic to another is a recommended heuristic (commonsense rule) when preparing a literature review (University of Guelph Writing Services, 2004). In example 7.12, the researchers organized their review around three main ideas.

> ***Example 7.18 Transitioning statement*** *Considering* that other factors might affect teachers' effectiveness (the dependent variable), the focus of the review *now shifts* to teachers' behaviors (an independent variable).

In this example, the author is referring to two main ideas, literature about teachers' effectiveness and literature about their behaviors.

Minimize Quotations, Responsibly Paraphrase

On a final note, a literature review reflects the author's summary and interpretation of previous works. These thoughts should be recounted in the author's voice and words, meaning direct quotations should be kept to a minimum (Firestone, 2010; Labaree, 2016). Per the usual rules for using quotes, they are appropriate to make or emphasize a point or when it is very difficult to paraphrase the original words (i.e., express the same message using different words) (VandenBos, 2010). Even when paraphrasing, authors still have to provide a citation for the original work (Labaree, 2016), and they must correctly represent the original idea. The ultimate goal is to avoid plagiarism (representing someone else's work as one's own) while giving credit to other scholars' ideas (Firestone, 2010). So the recommended strategy is to minimize quotations while responsibly paraphrasing.

Example 7.19 Paraphrasing and using quotations

Original text from McGregor (2015, p. 35):

"Actually, 'activism is a difficult concept to pin down because it has been used in so many different ways by many different actors' (Angelina, 2010, p. 9). Activism manifests in different content and through different means (Klar and Klaser, 2009). Normally associated with collective actions, 'activism as a concept also includes the ideology, experience, actors, resources and vision that enabled the action to take place' (Angelina, 2010, p. 9). Appreciating that activism has a wide variety of manifestations (Angelina, 2010; Hilton, 2009; Klar and Kasser, 2009), this article focuses on the intellectual actions of individual consumer scholars who drew on their ideologies, experiences, and vision to create new approaches to consumer education."

Paraphrased text, with one quote:

McGregor (2015) asserted that because activism can be conceptualized from so many different perspectives, it is possible to use the term *consumer activist* to refer to individual scholars who design new curricula. Although this approach eschews the conventional notion of activism as "collective actions" (p. 35), it is a valuable contribution to the consumer education literature. It gives researchers a way to frame this consumer-education-related activity as an individual political act, rather than mere curriculum evolution.

REVIEW AND ENGAGEMENT

When critically reading a research report, you would

- ☐ Check to make sure that the authors followed the recommended conventions for tense, voice, person, and length

- ☐ Decide if they employed sufficient references to convince you of their familiarity with the literature germane to their research question (no fast rule for this number)

- ☐ Ascertain if they effectively transitioned from a summary-critique-gap-rationale for each piece of literature contained in the review

- ☐ Check to see that they had two to three main ideas (maybe with subheadings)

- ☐ Determine if they paraphrased instead of using excessive quotations from earlier works

FINAL JUDGMENT ON LITERATURE REVIEW

Taking *all* of the **Review and Engagement** criteria into account, what is your final judgment of the Literature Review section of the paper you are critically reading?

CHAPTER SUMMARY

This chapter focused on the many decisions and processes involved in conducting and reporting a review of the literature pursuant to the research question guiding the study. The chapter started with the purposes of a literature review, moving to methodological conventions around *when* to conduct the review of previous studies. Quantitative studies do the review before collecting the data, and qualitative studies tend to wait and do the review after the data are collected and are being analyzed. Regardless, authors have to *critically engage* with previous work done about the research question, rather than just providing a paper-by-paper summary. The chapter explains in detail the process of *synthesizing* insights gained from this critical engagement. Nine organizational strategies are identified and discussed, showcasing the many choices authors have about how to present their review. The chapter ends with an overview of the seven characteristics of a good literature review and wraps up with a summary of the conventions around length, tense, person, and voice as well as the importance of transition statements and paraphrasing previous work.

REVIEW AND DISCUSSION QUESTIONS

1. What is the main purpose of a literature review in the research design? How does it link with the research question? What does the phrase "gap in the literature" mean?

2. For a quantitative study, explain the role that a literature review plays before data collection compared to during data analysis. How does this differ for a qualitative study? Explain the concept of a *confirmatory* literature review (qualitative study).

3. What do qualitative researchers mean when they say they need "to hear the data" before they conduct their literature review?

4. What do researchers take into consideration when deciding how to select particular documents from the literature for their study?

How do they know when they have enough literature reviewed?

5. Although normally not reported in the research paper, what are the three key phases of conducting a literature review?

6. Explain the process and intent of *critically reviewing* the collected literature (previous scholarship) about a research problem? What would uncritical reading of the literature look like?

7. What was your reaction to the idea that a good literature review actually *adds value* to a field of study? How *does* it add value (what makes its contribution valuable to others)?

8. Explain the crucial role that *synthesis* plays when reporting a literature review. What can be the

result if the authors do not provide a synthesis of previous literature?

9. What is involved in placing each piece of literature in context with the others in the pile? In other words, what is involved in *critically reading and then judging* each piece in the collection?

10. The chapter identified nine different ways authors can organize the presentation of their review of the literature. Explain each one and then identify the approach(es) that resonated

the most with you and why. Which one(s) did you like the least, and why?

11. When reading the Literature Review section of a paper, what criteria should be used to judge if it is a good review? Which of these seven criteria made the most sense to you? Is there any criterion you would not use to judge a literature review? Any you would privilege? Why?

12. Summarize the conventions for length, tense, and using quotations in a literature review.

RESEARCH DESIGN AND RESEARCH METHODS

8 OVERVIEW OF RESEARCH DESIGN AND METHODS

INTRODUCTION

This chapter focuses on the constructs of research design and the Methods section in a research paper. Research design is a larger construct than methods, to be explained shortly. But within a research paper, once the authors have stated the research question, developed an introduction to the study, and presented a review of the literature (and maybe a theoretical framework), their next step is to provide a description of the strategies used to collect and analyze data pursuant to the research question—that is, their methods. This chapter provides a generic discussion of methods, followed with much more detail in Chapter 9 (qualitative methods) and in Chapter 10 (quantitative and mixed methods).

As a caveat, a detailed discussion of how to use specific methods is beyond the scope of this overview chapter, or even this book. There is no attempt to explain how to do a survey, conduct a scientific experiment, prepare a case study, or engage in ethnographic research where researchers immerse themselves in the lives of the participants. That being said, the general discussions in Chapters 9 (qualitative) and 10 (quantitative and mixed methods) will address the basic conventions pursuant to preparing, conducting, and reporting these types of research, which entails identifying common methods.

This generic chapter will begin with a discussion of the larger construct of research design, including the link between research design and research inquiry, research design as logic and logistical, and the most common research designs organized by the three methodologies: qualitative, quantitative, and mixed methods. The conversation then shifts to a general overview of methods (distinguished from methodology). The purposes of the Methods section are identified followed with general introductions to the major differences between qualitative and quantitative inquiries, the major reporting components (subheadings) of each of these research reports, and the topic of rigor and quality in each of the three methodologies.

ETYMOLOGY AND DEFINITION OF METHODS AND RESEARCH DESIGN

Method is Greek *methodus*, "for mode of inquiry or investigation." It stems from *meta*, "after," and *hodos*, "a travelling, a pursuit, a way of teaching or going" (Harper, 2016). In effect, *method* refers to investigating or inquiring into something by going after or pursuing it, especially in accordance with a plan. It involves techniques, procedures, and tasks used in a systematic, logical, and orderly way (Anderson, 2014). Within the context of conducting and reporting research, it is the stage wherein researchers design instruments, apparatus, or procedures or gain site access (if relevant), obtain a sample, and then collect and analyze data from that sample (or entire population) (Johnson & Christensen, 2012). As was discussed in Chapter 2, this book distinguishes between method and methodology, with the latter connoting the philosophical underpinnings of the study.

The other term used in this chapter is *research design*. *Research* is French *recercher*, "to search." In the context of this book, it refers to the accumulation of data that are interpreted, leading to new knowledge. *Design* is Latin *designare*, "to mark out, devise, choose, designate." A design can be defined as a plan used to show the workings of something before it is made or created. It can also mean the underlying purpose of something, in this case, the search for knowledge (Anderson, 2014; Harper, 2016). From a technical stance, the research design refers to the overall strategy that researchers choose to integrate the different components of their study in a coherent and logical way, thereby ensuring they can effectively address the research question using the new knowledge created from the study (Labaree, 2016). Research design also entails logic (Yin, 1984), to be discussed shortly.

RESEARCH DESIGN

Many disciplines mistake research design for methods (de Vaus, 2001). This section explains how this book distinguishes between these terms, respecting the lack of a consensus in the scholarly arena for their usage. *Research design* is a larger construct than method. Per above, methods refer to technical procedures, techniques, or steps taken to obtain information and analyze data for a study. A design is a plan made before something is done (Anderson, 2014). Designing *research* is a process that entails both *logic* (thinking and reasoned judgments) and *logistics* (doing), with logic coming first, inherently shaping logistics (methods) (Yin, 1984).

Research Inquiry and Research Design

The logic and thinking that researchers use to *design their research* is affected both by the (a) methodology (which shapes the research questions and all assumptions underlying the effort), and (b) type of research inquiry they are conducting. In short, (a) *exploratory research* strives to reach a greater understanding of a problem, usually laying the groundwork for future studies; (b) *descriptive research* seeks more information so as to accurately describe something in more detail, creating a fuller picture by mapping the terrain; and (c) *explanatory research* seeks to connect ideas to understand causal inferences (explain relationships) (de Vaus, 2001; Suter, 2012; Yin, 1984). These approaches apply to both quantitative and qualitative research methodologies (except explanatory), with qualitative also seeking to (d) *illuminate meaning and subjective experiences* and (e) *understand processes and structures* (Blaxter, 2013; Shank & Brown, 2007).

Articulating Research Purpose in Research Design

Each of these five types of research inquiry represents the deeper *purpose* of the study (the problem), or the *reasons* for doing it, which is why Yin (1984) said research design is *logical* (i.e., it entails reasoned judgments). Each type of inquiry offers a different *reason* for why the study is needed (e.g., to describe, explore, find meaning, or theorize). Authors must not confuse research purpose (reason for inquiry) with methodology, research design, research question, or methods (see example 8.1). When identifying the nature of their research inquiry, they can use headings in their paper such as *Justification for the Study, Importance of the Study,* or *Objectives of the Study* (Newman, Ridenour, Newman, & DeMarco, 2003). A clearly stated research purpose will help readers formulate a realistic set of expectations about a study and better ensure they evaluate the quality of the study's design within the context of the author's purpose (Knafl & Howard, 1984) (see Chapter 6).

Example 8.1 Research purpose versus question The *problem* is the deeper, more complex *reason* why the researcher is conducting the study (e.g., to explore, describe, explain, or find meaning). Newman et al. (2003) recounted a quantitative study in which the research question was incorrectly presented as the research problem: "What is the effect of making a substantial reduction in class size on student achievement?" The researchers erroneously characterized class size as the problem when in fact students' lack of achievement was the *problem* and the *reason* why this *explanatory* study was needed (i.e., to explain). In this study, reducing class size was but one solution to increasing student achievement. By losing focus on what the real problem was (lack of achievement), the researchers designed an inappropriate study *if* they wanted to *explain* it. An unfortunate consequence of authors neglecting to clearly state their purpose and problem is that some readers may uncritically accept their results and change their practice when they should not.

Research Design as Logical and Logistical

Research designs guide the methods decisions that researchers must make during their studies, and they set the logic by which interpretations are made at the end of studies (Creswell, 2008). To further appreciate the link between research design logic and method, authors can consider this metaphor. Before builders or architects can develop a work plan or order building materials, they must first establish the *type* of building required, its uses, and the needs of the occupants; that is, they must think about their entire build and justify any design decisions they make. Their work plans (methods) to construct the building then flow from this logic (i.e., their reasoned judgments about the build). The same idea holds for a study's research design (de Vaus, 2001).

Research design as logic concerns researchers thinking about what sorts of data are needed to answer the research question, including what methods might be most appropriate to generate those data. The type of research inquiry (i.e., the *purpose* behind the research) shapes the overall structure of the study, especially the methods (Kotler, 2000; Newman et al., 2003). *Research design as logical* equates to a blueprint with specific, sequenced (sometimes iterative) steps that are be completed to bring the plan to closure (i.e., the methods, which are the focus of this chapter). *Research design as logistical* refers to the work plan developed by the researcher to collect evidence and analyze data to answer the research question and respect the type of research inquiry (the logic). *Logistical* means planning and organizing to make sure things are where they need to be so an activity or process can happen effectively (Anderson, 2014). The logic affects the logistics (methods), and the logistics reflect the logic (Yin, 1984) (see Figure 8.1).

Quantitative Research Design Logic

Quantitative research uses a predetermined, fixed research plan based mostly on *reconstructed logic*. This logic of research is based on organizing, standardizing, and codifying research into explicit rules, formal procedures, and techniques so others can follow the same linear plan and *reconstruct* the study. This is the logic of "how to do research" and is highly organized and systematic (Jarrahi & Sawyer, 2009; Neuman, 2000). The type of research inquiry determines the research design created using this logic (see Table 8.1). Should they create a *cross-sectional* design (collect data once from one sample), a *repeated cross-sectional* design (collect data once from different samples), a *longitudinal* design (collect data from one sample over time), a *one-subject* design, an *experimental* design, a *case study,* or some other design (Kotler, 2000)?

FIGURE 8.1 ■ Research Design as Logic and Logistical

Research Design as Logic	**Research Design as Logistical**
Blueprint reflects thinking and reasoning about how best to answer the research question (design decisions, type of inquiry) The **logic** affects the methods (work plan)	*Work plan* and steps required to collect and analyze data from sample to answer the research question (methods to execute the design) The **methods** (work plan) reflect the logic

TABLE 8.1 ■ Three Types of Research Inquiries, With Examples of Quantitative Research Designs		
Exploratory Research Inquiry	**Descriptive Research Inquiry**	**Explanatory Research Inquiry**
Cross-sectional design	Cross-sectional design	Cross-sectional design
Case study design	Longitudinal design	Experimental design
	Case study design	Case study design

Qualitative Research Design Logic

The research designs included in Table 8.1 (based on only reconstructed logic) do not adequately represent "the logic and processes of qualitative research [which] lacks such an elaborate typology into which studies can be pigeonholed" (Maxwell, 2008, p. 214). Maxwell (2008) said "this does not mean that qualitative research lacks design" (p. 215). Instead, qualitative research requires a broader and less restrictive concept of research design, in which researchers use "'logic-in-use' [as well as] 'reconstructed logic' [to accommodate the] 'design in use' [principle]" (p. 216). This is called an *emergent research design* wherein the original plan changes as the research unfolds, meaning it is nonlinear (Creswell, 2009) (discussed in Chapter 9). Regardless, the end result is data that are then analyzed, interpreted, and discussed, leading to conclusions, implications, and recommendations (de Vaus, 2001; Suter, 2012; Yin, 1984).

As a final caveat, de Vaus (2001) explained that researchers should not equate a particular *logistical* method with a particular research design *logic*. It is also erroneous to equate a particular research design with either quantitative, qualitative, or mixed methods approaches. Instead, authors need to bear in mind the link between (a) the purpose of the research (logical inquiry) and (b) their research design (both logic and logistics) (Yin, 1984) and then introduce their Methods section accordingly (see examples 8.2 and 8.3).

> ***Example 8.2 Quantitative research design and method*** This *exploratory, quantitative research inquiry* employed a *cross-sectional research design*. Data were collected from a *purposive sample* using the *survey method*, specifically a piloted *questionnaire* designed for this study. *Descriptive statistics* were used to analyze the data using Minitab software, and the *results* were reported using frequencies, percentages, and means (averages).

> ***Example 8.3 Qualitative research design and method*** This *qualitative research inquiry* employed an *emergent research design*, using the *phenomenological method*. Data were collected from a *snowball sample* of individual participants by way of *interviews*. The data were *thematically analyzed*, and *findings* were reported using quotes and a supportive narrative.

Mixed Methods Research Design Logic

Authors of mixed methods studies should avoid rhetorical logic, meaning they should not assume that one strand of data is only there to embellish their analysis of the other strand and is not really considered to be a necessary part of their analytical interpretation or argument. Mixed methods explanations and interpretations require more challenging logics. Mason (2006) identified five logics, one being *rhetorical*. *Parallel* logic assumes each strand has its own logic (see above), and authors would run these in parallel and report two different sections, one for each strand. A third approach is *corroborative* logic, which concerns itself with data triangulation. Researchers would strive to use data from each strand to corroborate each other (confirm or give support). If researchers use an *integrative* logic, they likely choose this at the beginning of the research design process so they can intentionally link insights from both data streams to get a better picture of the whole phenomenon (see Chapter 10).

Mason (2006) identified *multidimensional* logic as the most challenging type of mixed methods logic. "The argument is that different methods and approaches have distinctive strengths and potential which, if allowed to flourish, can help [researchers] understand multi-dimensionality and social complexity. . . . The logic imagines 'multi-nodal' and 'dialogic' explanations which are based on the dynamic relation of more than one way of seeing and researching. This logic requires that researchers factor into their accounts the different ways of asking questions and of answering them" (pp. 9–10). It differs from the other logics, which assume data integration rather than a data intersection. The latter "involves a *creative tension* between the different methods and approaches, which depends on a dialogue between them" (p. 10). This dialogue cannot occur without everyone involved embracing a logic that respects *multiple dimensions* and points of view (researchers themselves and research methodologies, with attendant assumptions, as discussed in Chapter 2).

REVIEW AND ENGAGEMENT

When critically reading a research report, you would

- ☐ Ascertain whether the authors used the term *research design* when introducing their *methods*, without confusing the two concepts

- ☐ Make sure they shared their thinking and reasoning about how best to answer their research questions (i.e., explained the logic used when creating their research design, especially what type of data were needed to answer their research questions)

- ☐ Per the above, determine if they included a section titled *Justification for* or *Importance of the Study*

- ☐ Determine if they properly referred to *reconstructed* (deductive) logic (quantitative) or *logic-in-use* (qualitative emergent research design) or if they referenced mixed methods logics

- ☐ Determine if they clarified their research design (see Table 8.2)

- ☐ Determine if they explicitly stated the type of *research inquiry* they employed (exploratory, descriptive, explanatory, meaning seeking, or understanding processes and structures)

Most Common Research Designs

Table 8.2 summarizes the most common research designs for each of qualitative, quantitative, and mixed methods studies, discussed in much more detail in Chapters 9 and 10. These approaches to designing research differ because of methodological distinctions, discussed in more detail in the second part of this overview chapter.

TABLE 8.2 ■ Main Types of Qualitative, Quantitative, and Mixed Methods Research Designs		
Qualitative Research Designs (involve changing tactics over the course of the study)	**Quantitative Research Designs (involve adhering to a formal plan with no deviation)**	**Mixed Methods Research Designs (involve some prioritized combination of strategy and tactics)**
• *Interpretive*—insights from interpreting data change the research design • *Investigative*—traces out a phenomenon in its natural field setting • *Participatory*—research design is codeveloped with participants • *Illuminative*—strategically focuses on one aspect of research design • *Instrumentation*—study creates a new data collection instrument • *Sensitization* (descriptive)—sensitizes readers to participants' situation • *Conceptualization* (theory building)	• *Descriptive*—describes what actually exists, as well as its frequency, and then categorizes the information • *Correlational*—examines whether a change in a variable (no manipulation) is related to change in another • *Comparative*—measures variables that occur naturally in existing groups, then compares them to determine their influence on the dependent variable • *Experimental*—manipulates independent variables, measures changes in dependent variable (experiment and control), and infers causal links • *Quasi-experimental*—employs an experimental and control design using existing groups, then cautiously infers causation • *Predictive exploratory*—determines how variables may be used to develop data-based models of a phenomenon • *Survey (nonexperimental)*—examines an already-occurred event in naturally occurring groups	• Use qualitative methods to explain quantitative data (words to explain numbers) • Use quantitative methods to further explain qualitative data (numbers to explain words) • Use both methods to achieve triangulation

METHODS

The discussion now turns from the construct of research design to that of methods, which are understood to include instrument development and apparatus, sampling, data collection, and data analysis, differing for each of the three methodologies used to shape this book: qualitative, quantitative, and mixed methods. This chapter provides a generic discussion of methods, followed with Chapter 9 (qualitative methods) and Chapter 10 (quantitative and mixed methods).

Methodology Versus Methods

Many disciplines use the word *methodology* to refer to *methods* (Schneider, 2014). This section explains how this book uses these terms, respecting the lack of a consensus in the scholarly arena for their usage. This book clearly distinguishes between methodology and methods (see Chapter 2). Methodology (*ology*) is focused on what is involved in creating new *knowledge* and refers to the branch of philosophy that analyzes the principles and axioms of research. The word *method* refers to a system of strategies used to obtain *information* for a study.

Many disciplines' use of the word *methodology* to refer to methods (Schneider, 2014) most likely occurs because the empirical (quantitative) research paradigm is so prevalent. Given its dominance, authors tend to deem it unnecessary to identify it as a method*ology* per se, leaving that term for the data collection and analysis procedures. While respecting this convention, this book assumes that when authors are reporting on instrument development, apparatus, sampling, data collection, and data analysis, they are reporting methods, not methodology (Bryman, 2008). Consequently, this chapter employs the term *methods* for the strategies to obtain *information* for a study, an aspect of research that is deeply informed by methodology (the creation of *knowledge*) (see Chapter 2, Table 2.1 and Figure 2.3).

REVIEW AND ENGAGEMENT

When critically reading a research report, you would

☐ Determine whether the authors used the terms *methodology* and *methods* but did not confuse them

☐ Ascertain if they clarified their methodology before presenting their methods

☐ Check to see if they provided enough information for you to judge the appropriateness of the selected method(s) against the implicitly or explicitly stated methodology

---

Purpose and Importance of the Methods Section

Some scholars feel that the Methods section is the most important part of a research paper (Azevedo et al., 2011; Kallet, 2004). It fulfills several key roles. In this section of their paper, authors have an opportunity to convince readers they have fully documented all of the steps undertaken to collect and analyze data for their study. With sufficient information, readers can rest assured that authors have carefully and systematically thought about their methods, indicating they are clear-thinking and competent researchers who do high-quality work. In particular, in quantitative research, readers need sufficient information to enable them to reproduce the procedures and get similar results (called replicability and reliability). In qualitative work, readers need sufficient information to enable them to determine if the methods and findings are relevant to, and can be adopted in, their context (called dependability) (Dillinger, 2011; Labaree, 2016; Shon, 2015; VandenBos, 2010).

In their Methods section, authors should review previous literature pursuant to the design they will be implementing and openly discuss and debate measurement issues and strategies so they can improve on previous work. Their own Methods section should clearly set out a well-articulated set of procedures that can be consistently reapplied (quantitative) or appropriately adopted in another context (qualitative). By making their measurement choices explicit, authors help readers decide if the study was done well or needs improvement (Harris, 2014).

Following this convention, the Methods section serves the purpose of fostering ongoing debate about how to improve measurement instruments and research procedures, whether qualitative or quantitative. Authors should try to avoid using or perpetuating inconsistent measures and procedures because this creates *discontinuity* in the literature about the particular phenomenon being measured (Choudhuri, Glauser, & Peregoy, 2004; Harris, 2014). As examples, Harris (2014) noted that scholars have developed 200 ways to measure self-esteem, 16 ways to measure aspiration, and hundreds of instruments to measure quality of life, and they have not settled on how to measure gender identity or prejudice. These are examples of discontinuities perpetuated in the literature.

Authors may choose to select from and adapt previous attempts to measure a phenomenon, and if so, they must provide a solid rationale for their method choices. Using this rationale, readers can critically evaluate the study's overall quality (Dillinger, 2011; Labaree, 2016; VandenBos, 2010) (see Chapter 1). As explained in Chapter 2, quantitative and qualitative research embrace different notions of what counts as knowledge, reality, logic, and the role of values. These philosophical differences determine what data are collected and how, and how these data are analyzed and reported.

Major Differences Between Qualitative and Quantitative Intellectual Inquiry

Table 8.3 portrays the main differences between the qualitative and quantitative approaches to scholarship and to academic inquiry (Ary, Jacobs, & Sorensen, 2010; Choudhuri et al., 2004; Creswell, 2009; Driessnack, Sousa, & Mendes, 2007a; Johnson & Christensen, 2012; Patton, 2002; Rolfe, 2006; Suter, 2012). Authors should write their Methods section using language and vocabulary reflective of the approach that informed the inquiry in their study. This narrative would reflect each methodology's respective assumptions about reality, truth, the role of values, the importance of context, the role and voice of the researcher, the applicability of variable manipulation, logics, and so on. Critical readers can use this narrative (its presence or absence) to draw conclusions about the quality of the scholarship. In a mixed methods study, authors would use this information as appropriate when addressing each strand of their research design: qualitative and quantitative.

TABLE 8.3 ■ Main Differences Between Qualitative and Quantitative Intellectual Inquiry	
Qualitative Inquiry	**Quantitative Inquiry**
• Assumes subjective reality is socially constructed and subjective	• Assumes there is an objective reality ready to be discovered
• Appreciates complexity and multiple truths	• Favors parsimony and assumes a single truth
• Research is value bound, and the researcher's values are accounted for	• Research is value neutral, and the researcher's values are muted
• The researcher is the primary instrument (observations, interviews)	• Uses inanimate instruments (scales, questionnaires, checklists, tests)
• Contextualizes findings and applies ideas across contexts	• Generalizes results from a sample to a population
• Portrays natural settings and contexts	• Manipulates and controls variables
• Few participants, many variables	• Few variables, many subjects
• Understands the insider's view	• Presents the objective outsiders' view
• Human behavior is situational	• Human behavior is regular
• Interprets human behavior in context	• Predicts human behavior
• Understands perspectives (empathetic) and exploration	• Provides causal explanations and predictions
• Widely, deeply examines phenomena	• Narrowly tests specific hypotheses
• Focuses on quality, essence, and nature	• Focuses on quantity (how much)
• Presents the world as seen by participants	• Presents social facts devoid of context
• Uses inductive then deductive logic	• Uses deductive then inductive logic
• Searches for patterns and looks for complexity	• Analyzes discrete components looking for the norm
• Uses purposive sampling	• Uses random sampling
• Single cases or small samples	• Large samples with statistical power
• The research design is emergent and evolving	• The research design is predetermined
• Data are words, images, and categories	• Data are numbers (minor use of words)
• Nonlinear, iterative, and creative analysis	• Linear, standardized, and prescribed analysis
• Thematic, patterned analysis of data	• Statistical analysis of data
• Power in rich descriptions and detail	• Statistical power
• Reports are written in expressive, holistic language (thick descriptions)	• Reports are written in precise, conventional, abstract language
• Some studies create theory from the findings	• Use theory to ground the study and interpret results
• Generates understandings from patterns	• Test hypotheses that are born from theory
• Faces conceptual complexity	• Faces statistical complexity
• Strives for trustworthy, credible data	• Strives for reliable and valid data

Major Components (Report Subheadings) of Qualitative and Quantitative Research

Table 8.4 compares the basic stages or major components of both quantitative and qualitative research methods and provides the typical subheadings authors would use to report their respective methods for a study. Purposefully using these headings greatly facilitates others' ability to critically read the Methods section of a research report. If authors fail to explicitly indicate which methodology informed their study, readers can take cues from their subheadings. Absence of these subheadings—or, worse yet, the content relevant to each stage—raises unnecessary flags about the study's integrity and quality. These headings are used in Chapters 9 and 10 to organize the discussion of how to report both qualitative and quantitative research or their strands within a mixed methods study.

TABLE 8.4 ■ Basic Steps (Report Subheadings) of Qualitative and Quantitative Methods	
Qualitative Methods NOTE: These steps are not always linear and sequential	**Quantitative Methods** NOTE: These steps are linear and sequential
• *Site selection and access* (gaining access to the site from which the sample will be drawn) • *Sampling* (people, artifacts from the site[s]) • *Ethical considerations* • *Role of the researcher* (responsible self-accounting, privileges sample's voice) • *Data collection* (from site participants, with the researcher as the key data collection instrument, yielding piles of raw data—words, pictures, graphics) • Thick and deep *(re)presentation of the data* (detailed accounts of the research context and participants' experiences) • *Data analysis* (thematic, patterned examination of the thick data, often done *in concert with* data collection) • Account for *trustworthiness* (along several criteria) • *Data security and management* • *Limitations* of emergent research design	• *Instruments, apparatus, and/or procedures* (tools to collect data) • *Sampling* (people, animals, artifacts from which data are collected) • *Ethical considerations* • *Data collection* (from the sample using the aforementioned tools, yielding a pile of raw data—numbers) • *Data analysis* (statistically examine the pile of raw data to determine its essential features, done *after* data collection) • Account for *validity, reliability,* and *generalizability* • *Data security and management* • *Limitations* of predetermined research design (normally follows the Discussion section)

REVIEW AND ENGAGEMENT

When critically reading a research report, you would

☐ Ascertain whether the authors used language and vocabulary reflective of the research inquiry approach that informed their study (see Table 8.3)

☐ Determine if they used methodology-specific headings to organize their Methods section (see Table 8.4) and fully accounted for and shared their research design logic and logistics

☐ If subheadings are missing, determine if the authors at least included pertinent details for each stage of their respective methodology's research design

TABLE 8.5 ■ Comparison of Criteria to Ensure High-Quality Quantitative and Qualitative Research

Quantitative (Positivistic, Empirical, Deterministic)	Qualitative (Postpositivistic, Naturalistic, Interpretive, Critical)
Striving for **unbiased data** (results are *true* if no bias was introduced, made possible if the researcher's personal preferences, prejudices, and opinions are held at bay during the entire research process).	Striving for **trustworthy data** (data must be truly *transparent* and open to *critical thinking* by reader; trust means acceptance of the *truth* of a statement).
Strategies: judiciously address issues of internal validity to ensure that the study design, implementation, and data analysis are bias free, yielding high levels of evidence of cause and effect (or association); employ representative and random sampling techniques; account for missing and incomplete data; acknowledge funding sources.	*Strategies: triangulation (multiple sources of data); member checks; saturation during data collection; peer review or expert consultations; audit trail (detailed record of researcher's decisions, with reasons); thick descriptions; plausible alternatives; account for negative cases; prolonged engagement in the field.*
Objectivity:	**Confirmability** (subjectivity):
Empirical research is said to be *value free*, meaning the research process should not be influenced by the *researcher's* emotions, preferences, or personal prejudices. Researchers are supposed to dispassionately engage in research from a stance of *value neutrality*, thereby ensuring the truth is found. Judgments about the evidence should not coincide with the researcher's orientation (despite that science is not really neutral; relative value neutrality is more likely than absolute neutrality).	Refers to the *researcher's neutrality* when interpreting data (i.e., self-awareness and control of one's bias); appreciating that values are central to the research process, researchers still have to be sure their findings can be *confirmed* or corroborated by others (i.e., their values did not take over). It is the extent to which findings are shaped by the respondents themselves, rather than the researcher's bias.

Quantitative (Positivistic, Empirical, Deterministic)	Qualitative (Postpositivistic, Naturalistic, Interpretive, Critical)
Strategies: embrace the tenets of the scientific method and empirical inquiry; do not distort research or let one's values intrude by drawing on personal worldviews, motives, self-interest, or customs or by capitulating to external pressures (researchers are especially vulnerable to value intrusion during the interpretation and discussion stage).	*Strategies: reflexivity (involves self-critique and disclosure of what one brings to the research, especially one's predispositions); audit trails; method triangulation; peer review and debriefing.*
Internal validity: This refers to the integrity of the research design. The word *internal* pertains to the inner workings of the research process, designed and conducted to ensure that the researcher measured what was intended to be measured (producing strong, valid data instead of weak, invalid data). Also, the research design should follow the principle of cause and effect. There are seven major threats to internal validity (i.e., measuring something other than what was intended): (a) contamination by an extraneous event (history effect); (b) participants aging or tiring (maturation effect); (c) loss of subjects or attrition between testing (mortality effect); (d) sensitizing subjects with pretest (testing effect); (e) extremely high or low pretest scores (statistical regression effect); (f) subjects are not carefully assigned to test groups (selection bias effect); and (g) unreliability of an assessment instrument (instrumentation effect). *Strategies: take steps necessary to mitigate threats to internal validity (e.g., account for contamination, maturation, attrition, sampling size, group formation and assignment, instrumentation alignment, and testing sensitization).*	**Credibility** (credible to the participants): Did the researchers create a faithful accounting of people's lived experiences (i.e., an *accurate* representation of their reality, from their perspective)? Did the researchers get a full answer to their research question? Also, can others have confidence in the *truth* shared by the researchers (i.e., in their observations, interpretations, and conclusions)? The latter require strong evidence, clear logic, valid data, and ruling out alternative explanations. *Strategies: member checks; detailed, thick descriptions (and lots of quotes); triangulation (methods and data); peer review and debriefing; extended and prolonged fieldwork; researcher reflexivity to mitigate invalidity; cross-case comparisons.*
External validity (asserted by the researcher): Does the truth (conclusions) from the study hold in situations *outside* the study? Researchers have to ask, "How similar is my study to the situation I want to generalize to?" (meaning make a broad statement from a specific case). If too dissimilar, their results and conclusions are not externally valid; that is, they do not *hold true* for other situations (based on statistical assumptions).	**Transferability** (determined by the user): Refers to the degree to which findings can be applied or transferred to other contexts or settings—that is, used more widely by others. It is the researcher's responsibility to provide accurate, detailed, and complete descriptions of the context and the participants so that *users* of the study can determine if the findings and conclusions apply (are transferable) in *their* context (based on similarity of deep descriptors).

(Continued)

TABLE 8.5 ■ (Continued)

Quantitative (Positivistic, Empirical, Deterministic)	Qualitative (Postpositivistic, Naturalistic, Interpretive, Critical)
Strategies: judiciously choose appropriate research design protocol (especially sample size and bias). Then, before asserting that the results are valid in other populations, situations, and conditions, researchers must recognize, consider, and report on factors that mitigate these assertions, notably any interactions (a) among treatment and subjects, settings, and history as well as (b) between subjects and settings. Researchers often temper their assertions by setting out study limitations.	*Strategies: cross-case comparisons; literature comparisons; detailed, thick descriptions; researcher reflexivity to mitigate invalidity; state study limitations (account for selection, setting, and history effects that might make the study unique to only a single group [i.e., not transferable]).*
Reliability (of the instrument and methods):	**Dependability:**
Refers to the extent to which someone else can follow the research design with the same sample and get the same results. Are the methods reproducible and consistent, and is sufficient information provided so others can repeat the approach and procedures? To what extent are variations controlled? The *reliability of the instrument* depends on six types of validity: (a) face validity (subjects think the test is measuring what it is supposed to measure); (b) expert judges think the test is valid; (c) test items actually contain content being measured; (d) compare a new test with a previously validated test (concurrent validity); (e) taking a test is good prediction of a score when the test is taken again in the future (predictive validity); and (f) construct validity (mix of all of the others—did the test measure the intended higher-order construct and nothing else related to it, determined by how the variables are operationalized?). *Strategies: standardized administration of instrument or procedure; internal consistency (i.e., ensure instrument items are actually measuring the underlying construct, reflected in Cronbach's alpha); increase number of test items; use objective scoring; test-retest; ensure that two different forms of one test measure the same thing.*	Related to reliability, researchers have to responsibly provide sufficient information so others can repeat the research design protocol in *their* context but not necessarily get the same results. It refers to the stability of findings over time and in changing research contexts (i.e., others can rely [*depend*] on the study). The latter means the findings, conclusions, and interpretations must be supported by the data. Note that credibility ensures dependability. *Strategies: audit trail; triangulation; rich documentation; intra- and intercoder or observer agreement; approach and procedures are appropriate for the context and can be documented.*

Quantitative (Positivistic, Empirical, Deterministic)	Qualitative (Postpositivistic, Naturalistic, Interpretive, Critical)
Generalizability (breadth of applicability): Researchers want to make broad statements from their specific case (they used a small random sample from a whole population). They want their conclusions to hold for others *not* in their study. Based on statistical assumptions, *generalizability* refers to the extent to which results and conclusions can be applied to people, settings, or conditions *beyond* those represented in the study. *Strategies: account for external validity.*	**Authenticity** (realness for participants): Researchers want to make specific statements about only the people they studied (how the latter see *their* world). So, *authenticity* refers to the extent to which participants' voices and agency are ensured, and it strives for assurances that the researcher has represented all views of all participants (*authentic* means "original, genuine, undisputed"). *Strategies: collaboration with participants; member checking; researcher reflexivity (involves self-critique and disclosure of what one brings to the research).*

INTEGRITY OF RESEARCH DESIGNS

Both quantitative and qualitative researchers have to ensure, respectively, that their data are reliable (can be replicated or adopted) and valid (they measured what was intended to be measured), with results generalizable to those outside the study or adoptable in another setting, respectively. Differences in the philosophical assumptions between quantitative, qualitative, and mixed methods approaches, however, mean researchers tend to employ different terminology for these key aspects of a study's rigor or quality (Ary et al., 2010). And, although very consistent in quantitative research, nomenclature for issues of rigor is not consistent in qualitative research (Suter, 2012) and has a unique twist in mixed methods (Teddlie & Tashakkori, 2006).

Integrity of Qualitative and Quantitative Research Designs

Table 8.5 provides an overview of the most agreed-to approaches and terms used by both types of researchers and of attendant strategies to meet the standard for the specific research methodology (Ary et al., 2010; Creswell & Miller, 2000; Guba, 1981; Johnson & Christensen, 2012; Lincoln, 1995; Nahrin, 2015; Newman, Newman, & Newman, 2011; Shenton, 2004). Table 8.5 addresses issues of unbiased and trustworthy data, objectivity and subjectivity (confirmability), internal validity and credibility, external validity and transferability, reliability and dependability, and generalization and authenticity (representing quantitative and qualitative, respectively). These are discussed in more detail in Chapters 9 and 10.

Integrity of Mixed Methods Research Designs

With more detail in Chapter 10, mixed methods authors have to be concerned with reporting both design rigor and *interpretative* rigor because mixed methods research depends on integration of data from both qualitative and quantitative strands. *Interpretative rigor* evaluates the validity of the conclusions and comprises three standards: (a) *Interpretative consistency* occurs when inferences follow from the findings or results, rather than coming out of the blue. (b) *Theoretical consistency* means inferences are consistent with known theories. (c) *Integrative efficacy* occurs when meta-inferences (integrating initial strand-specific inferences into inferences that apply across the entire data set) adequately incorporate inferences that stem from both the qualitative and quantitative phases of the study; that is, neither is privileged when discussing the outcomes of the study (Teddlie & Tashakkori, 2006).

TECHNICAL ASPECTS OF REPORTING METHODS

In addition to length and organizational logic and approaches, several grammatical conventions inform the preparation of the Methods section of a research paper (e.g., person, tense, and voice) (Lynch, 2014). Each is now discussed.

Length

Suter (2012) suggested that the Methods section is one of the longest sections of a research *proposal* (in the range of five or so pages), but for a *research article*, it is one of the shortest sections. Fox (2013) explained that while the findings of a qualitative paper constitute 30%–40% of the paper, the Methods section is shorter (10%) and requires that authors employ a concise, tight, logical writing style. In a quantitative report, authors should devote about 10%–15% of their paper to their Methods section (Thomas, 2011). The length of this section in a mixed methods study depends on which strand was prioritized, qualitative or quantitative.

Lynch (2014) clarified that the length of a qualitative Methods section is dictated by how much *detail* is required to describe site selection, access, sampling, data collection, and analytical procedures. Authors also have to make available an audit trail (detail) that readers can follow to access researchers' thinking while they implemented and adjusted their emergent research design. The same principle of *detail* holds for a quantitative paper. The quantitative Methods section should be *detailed enough* that (a) it can be repeated by others because its essential characteristics have been recounted (reliability) and (b) readers can judge whether the results and conclusions are valid (i.e., did the study measure what it intended to measure?) (Kallet, 2004). More specifically, detail means those things that could logically be expected to influence the results. "Insufficient detail leaves the reader with questions; too much detail burdens the reader with irrelevant information" (American Psychological Association, 2001, p. 18).

In all three methodologies, authors have to ensure that readers can follow what was done and judge its rigor and quality. Labaree (2016) opined that authors should assume readers possess a basic understanding of the method. This assumption means authors do not have to go into great detail about specific procedures; rather, they should focus on how they *"applied a method*, not on the mechanics of *doing the method.*" The accepted convention is to provide adequate citations to support the choice and application of the methods employed in their study. They need to know their audience and decide how much detail is appropriate (Goodson, 2017; Harris, 2014). If they are reporting a new procedure they developed for their study, more detail is justified, but they should avoid the recipe approach (step-by-step) (The Writing Center, 2014b).

In summary, when deciding on the length of their Methods section, authors have to take "into account the difficult balance between completeness (sufficient details to allow . . . verification [of rigor]) and brevity (the impossibility of describing every technical detail and the need to strictly follow the guidelines/instructions for authors provided by journals and recommendations regarding word count limits)" (Azevedo et al., 2011, p. 232).

Organizational Logic and Approaches

Suter (2012) observed that readers "can easily get lost in a disorganized maze that purports to describe or manage data" (p. 461). Journal editors commonly reject manuscripts due to errors or omissions in the Methods section (Boylorn, 2008; Hesson & Fraias-Hesson, 2010b). To offset this possibility, authors need to choose an organizational framework for their Methods section that "effectively make[s] sense of data and convince[s] the reader that the plan for data management [collection, and analysis] is meaningful, structured, and coherent" (Hesson & Fraias-Hesson, 2010b, p. 461).

"The organization of the method section depends on the author's presentation logic" (Rocco & Plakhotnik, 2011, p. 167). (a) The most common approach is chronological, meaning authors would arrange the discussion of their method in the order that things occurred. (b) Sometimes, in order to describe a complex aspect of their research design, authors may have to shift to a *most-to-least-important* structure within the chronological approach. (c) Another common organizational pattern is *general-to-specific* (Boylorn, 2008; Hesson & Fraias-Hesson, 2010b; Labaree, 2016). (d) Authors can also organize their Methods section using the *major components* of their research design, identified with subheadings, taking direction from Table 8.4 for each of qualitative and quantitative reports (Boylorn, 2008; Hesson & Fraias-Hesson, 2010b; Rocco & Plakhotnik, 2011).

Objective Versus Subjective Writing

When preparing quantitative papers, authors are encouraged to use *descriptive writing* so they can ensure concise, adequate, logical, and detailed descriptions of their methods (Goodson, 2017; Labaree, 2016; Rocco & Plakhotnik, 2011). Goodson (2017) explained that, as ironic as it sounds, when using descriptive writing, authors strive to be objective and avoid subjective judgments of what happened during the sampling or data collection stages. She provided these examples (p. 177):

> ***Example 8.4 Descriptive (objective) writing*** "After examining the pictures, the researcher asked each child to select the picture they [sic] wanted to discuss."

> ***Example 8.5 Nondescriptive (subjective) writing:*** "The **very young** second-graders examined three **interesting pictures** the researcher presented to them. After the children **spent a lot more time than planned** examining the pictures, the researcher

asked each child to select the picture they [sic] wanted to discuss." *(Note* that the words **in bold** represent the writer's subjective judgments of what happened during data collection.)

The use of subjective writing is more allowable in qualitative papers as long as researchers have addressed their inherent biases by (a) engaging in reflexivity (i.e., continuous examination and explanation of how they influenced the research process) and (b) creating an audit trail by which readers can trace the author's cognitive decisions pursuant to putting their research plan into action (Blaxter, 2013). Per example 8.5, if it was a qualitative study, children spending longer than anticipated to examine the pictures may have been a *key moment* that shaped the researcher's understanding of the phenomenon as experienced by those living it.

Person, Tense, and Voice

The different use of language (i.e., person, tense, and voice) in the Methods section of quantitative and qualitative papers reflects the different epistemological and axiological assumptions of these two broad approaches to research (Lynch, 2014).

Person

Authors of quantitative papers conventionally write in third person so as to reflect the objective nature of the scholarship. The Methods section of qualitative papers is often written using a much more subjective tone, employing second, and even first, person because the author (researcher) is the main data collection instrument and is intimately involved in the implementation of the research design plan (Boylorn, 2008; Hesson & Fraias-Hesson, 2010a; Johnson & Christensen, 2012). First person is now acceptable in social sciences but less so in the natural sciences (The Writing Center, 2014b). "This rhetorical choice brings two scientific values into conflict: objectivity versus clarity" (The Writing Center, 2014b, p. 7). The scientific community has yet to reach a consensus about which style should be used, meaning authors should at least consult the journal's preferred style manual or its *Guidelines for Authors* (see Chapter 5).

Tense

Regardless of the research methodology, the Methods section is written in the past tense because the work has already happened (Boylorn, 2008; Hesson & Fraias-Hesson, 2010a; Kallet, 2004; Labaree, 2016). There are a few exceptions. Sentences describing standard procedures commonly used by others are written in present tense (e.g., "This assessment instrument *is* often used in studies focused on student intelligence") (Lynch, 2014). Also, authors should try to avoid using the imperative (e.g., "*Add* 5 grams of the solid to the solution") because it sounds like a recipe approach, which is to be avoided. A narrative structure using past tense is preferred to a step-by-step, recipe model (The Writing Center, 2014b).

Voice

Authors of quantitative papers are encouraged to use passive voice because it places the focus on *what* was done, not who did it. Occasionally, the passive voice is used with a *by phrase*, naming the agent as well as the action (e.g., "The survey was administered *by* the high school principal") (Boylorn, 2008; Hesson & Fraias-Hesson, 2010a). While passive voice should always be used in quantitative papers, authors of qualitative papers can consciously choose what voice they will use (Boylorn, 2008). Normally, authors of qualitative papers employ active voice, which focuses on *who* did the action. This writing strategy makes sense because "qualitative research recognises, and even foregrounds, the role played by individuals—the researcher, the informants and other participants" (Lynch, 2014, p. 33).

Example 8.6 Passive voice Stress was applied to the rubber segments in gradually increasing increments. [focus on what *was* done]

Example 8.7 Active voice Both the researcher and the participants (**we**) examined the graffiti on the walls of the community hall. [focus on *who* did something]

REVIEW AND ENGAGEMENT

When critically reading a research report, you would

- ☐ Judge if the Methods section was long enough to recount what the authors did to sample, collect, and analyze data to answer their research question

- ☐ Ascertain if, overall, they organized their Methods section is such a way that it is meaningfully structured, providing a coherent overview that is understandable (i.e., nothing is missing or inadequately explained)

- ☐ Confirm that quantitative authors used objective writing, avoiding subjective judgments of what happened during the sampling or data collection and analysis stages

- ☐ Determine if they followed the recommended conventions for tense, voice, and person for the methodology

FINAL JUDGMENT ON RESEARCH DESIGN AND METHODS SECTION

Taking *all* of the *Review and Engagement* criteria into account, what is your final, overall judgment of the research design and Methods section of the paper you are critically reading?

CHAPTER SUMMARY

This chapter addressed the very complicated issues of research design and what is involved in reporting the methods employed to sample, collect, and analyze data to answer the research question for a particular study. It began with a discussion of the larger construct of research design, including (a) the link between research design and research inquiry, (b) research design as logic and logistical, and (c) the most common research designs organized by the three methodologies: qualitative, quantitative, and mixed methods (see Table 8.2). The conversation then shifted to a general overview of methods (distinguished from methodology), acknowledging more detailed coverage to follow in Chapters 9 and 10. The purposes of the Methods section were identified, followed with general introductions to (a) the major differences between qualitative and quantitative *inquiry*, (b) the major reporting components (subheadings) of each type of research report, and (c) the topic of rigor and quality in each of the three methodologies. The chapter wrapped up with an overview of the basic grammatical and organizational conventions of reporting and writing up the Methods section of a research paper.

REVIEW AND DISCUSSION QUESTIONS

1. Based on the approach used in this book, how do methods differ from methodologies? How do methods differ from the research design?

2. Distinguish between research design as logical and as logistical (Figure 8.1).

3. How is the research design tied with the type of research inquiry?

4. What are the main differences between qualitative and quantitative *inquiry* and their approach to scholarship (see Table 8.3)? Which of these aspects of scholarly inquiry did you struggle with the most, and why?

5. Compare qualitative research design logic with quantitative research design logic.

6. Identify the basic steps for conducting and reporting both qualitative and quantitative studies, commenting on the issue of linearity and sequentiality. Which method do you feel most comfortable with, and why? How did these differ from approaches to designing mixed methods studies?

7. Explain to someone else in plain language the basic differences in reporting the methods used for qualitative, quantitative, and mixed methods studies.

8. How do qualitative, quantitative, and mixed methods studies differ in how they deal with quality and rigor in their research design (see Table 8.5)?

9. Summarize the conventions for length, tense, person, and voice when preparing the Methods section of a research paper, depending on the methodology.

REPORTING QUALITATIVE RESEARCH METHODS

INTRODUCTION

Chapter 8 discussed the constructs of research design and methods as they relate to each other and to methodology. This chapter focuses on how to conduct and report methods in a qualitative study. Chapter 10 continues the conversation, turning its attention to quantitative and to mixed methods studies.

As a reminder, qualitative studies are concerned with understanding and interpreting participants' lived experiences with a particular phenomenon and the meanings people attach to these experiences. Qualitative data are the participants' words or aspects of other data transformed into words by the researcher, who is the primary data collection instrument, analyst, and interpreter. Unlike quantitative studies (see Chapter 10), there is a nominal consensus around how best to report and organize the Methods section of qualitative studies (Knafl & Howard, 1984).

At a minimum, Knafl and Howard (1984) suggested that authors attend to four reporting requirements, which are included in Figure 9.1 and Table 8.4 (see Chapter 8). They should report on (a) data collection strategies (e.g., site selection, access, sampling, and data collection protocols—steps to organize and process data, as well as data limitations); (b) data analysis (steps to organize, categorize, or summarize data prior to analysis, then analysis protocol); (c) how they managed threats to rigor and quality; and (d) how they derived conclusions from the data. As a caveat, Knafl and Howard suggested that the amount of attention paid to these four key criteria should reflect the *particular* study, space limitations, or both. Also, authors can move beyond these conventions and use topics (subheadings) of their own that are particularly relevant to their study. The rest of this chapter discusses these minimal requirements in standardizing reports of qualitative research, prefaced with an extensive discussion of

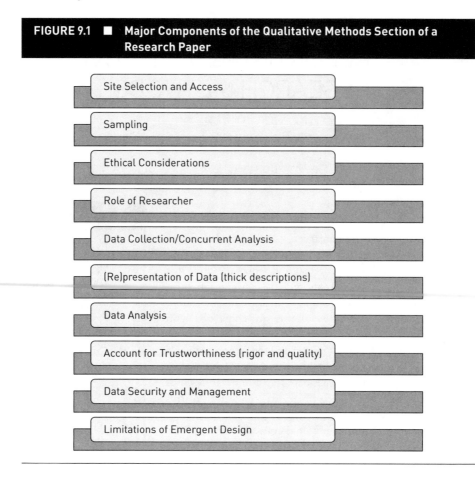

FIGURE 9.1 ■ Major Components of the Qualitative Methods Section of a Research Paper

Site Selection and Access

Sampling

Ethical Considerations

Role of Researcher

Data Collection/Concurrent Analysis

(Re)presentation of Data (thick descriptions)

Data Analysis

Account for Trustworthiness (rigor and quality)

Data Security and Management

Limitations of Emergent Design

what constitutes an emergent research design, the key types of qualitative research designs, and the methods most appropriate for qualitative studies.

QUALITATIVE EMERGENT RESEARCH DESIGNS

Qualitative authors should first orient readers to the big-picture approach they used in their study. Here, they identify the research methodology and the more specific general approach used to sample, collect, and analyze data. Those using the qualitative methodology may introduce their work as qualitative interpretive or qualitative critical (see Chapter 2, Table 2.1). And, although not the approach used in this book, they may also characterize their work as qualitative in conjunction with being narrative, phenomenological, ethnographic, case study, grounded theory, participatory action research, or discourse analysis (Creswell, 2009; Johnson & Christensen, 2012). Chapter 2 argued that these are specific methods used under the postpositivistic qualitative methodology. That being said, all of these perspectives assume that reality is socially constructed, meaning the study has to focus on "those who actually live it and make sense of it (construct its meaning and interpret it personally)" (Johnson & Christensen, 2012, p. 344).

Regardless of the particular methodological or paradigmatic lens, qualitative work usually employs an *emergent research design* (Goodson, 2017). *Emergent* means coming into existence (Anderson, 2014). Instead of a predetermined and fixed research protocol (per quantitative work, as shown in Tables 8.3 and 8.4 in Chapter 8), qualitative authors would report that they were open to adapting their inquiry as their understandings deepened, as situations changed, or both. By avoiding rigid research design plans, qualitative researchers can remain responsive to, and pursue, new paths of discovery as they emerge from the context, participants, and data (Johnson & Christensen, 2012).

Creswell (2009) explained that with an emergent research design, "the initial plan for research cannot be tightly prescribed, and all phases of the process may change or shift after the researcher enters the field and begins to collect data. For example, the questions may change, the forms of data collection may shift, and the individuals studied and the sites visited may be [sic] modified" (pp. 176–177). Smith and Glass (1987) used the term *working design* instead of emergent design, but they meant the same thing. Like the idea of a working title, it is assumed that the final title will be different.

Tullis Owen (2008) explained that "researchers entering the field intent on studying a specific behavior may find another type of interaction worthy of investigation. [Their] observations in the field will influence and promote changes to the study's design" (p. 548). The qualitative researcher's goal is to learn about the problem or issue from the participants, which means shifting directions on the fly to obtain that information (Creswell, 2009; Knafl & Howard, 1984).

Strategic Versus Tactical Research Designs

With this caveat in mind, Shank and Brown (2007) characterized qualitative work as tactical in nature rather than strategic (quantitative) (see Table 9.1). A strategy is an elaborate and systematic plan designed to achieve an important goal. *Being strategic* means doing what is necessary to, or important in, the initiation, conduct, or completion of a plan. A tactic is a particular maneuver or small-scale action, which is made or carried out with only a limited or immediate end in view. *Being tactical* means being skilled at calculating a plan of action to gain a temporary advantage and then changing tactics as the plan (the strategy) unfolds. Quantitative studies are strategic in that the research plan is created in advance and seldom modified once started. The Methods section of a qualitative study recounts the tactical efforts and decisions taken by the researcher to bring about the research so the research question could be addressed (Shank & Brown, 2007). From this tactical standpoint, qualitative researchers have to carefully track all of their procedures and decisions so they can report their final research design in their paper. This report should include their logic-in-use and any decisions taken on the fly (see Chapter 8).

REVIEW AND ENGAGEMENT

When critically reading a research report, you would

☐ Determine if the authors provided a full account of the emergent research design (all logic-in-use decisions taken on the fly); that is, they provided an audit trail

☐ Assess whether the authors were attuned to the nuances of being strategic versus being tactical when creating their research design

TABLE 9.1 ■ Tactical and Strategic Research Designs	
Tactical Designs	**Strategic Designs**
• Short term	• Long term
• Small picture	• Comprehensive big picture
• Kludgy (inelegant, clumsy, lower quality)	• High quality
• *How* (hands-on, buried in detail, busywork)	• *What* and *why* one is doing something (thinking or planning)
• See things from a shorter, narrower perspective	• See things from a longer, wider perspective
• Much easier to develop and to implement (allows things to unfold and develop and can reverse and change tactics quite readily)	• Much harder to develop and to implement (hard to reverse once started)

TYPES OF QUALITATIVE RESEARCH DESIGNS

Beyond the overarching requirement of an emergent research design, there are seven main qualitative research design approaches (Knafl & Howard, 1984; Shank & Brown, 2007) (see Figure 9.2 and Table 9.2). Qualitative research designs involve changing tactics over the course of the study, with each of the seven designs intended to achieve a specific goal. It is incumbent upon authors to clearly articulate which research design informed their qualitative study. Not providing this basic information can create unwarranted confusion for readers, for it inhibits their ability to frame the study through the proper lens. For example, telling readers that it is a participatory research design lets them know right away to expect information about how people in the study *participated in designing the research*.

Goodson (2017) suggested that authors of qualitative studies should use the subheading *Research Design* and then complete four sentences: (a) The research design employed in this study was . . . (b) This design was chosen because . . . (c) The design represents the most appropriate approach for this topic because . . . (d) Employing this research design represents an innovation in the field because . . . Creswell (2009) also recommended that authors discuss how their research design reflected their research questions (see Chapter 2).

Interpretive

To interpret means to assign meaning. In an *interpretive design*, qualitative researchers strive to clarify and elucidate insights from their data and figure out what the data *mean* to the participants. As researchers accumulate more and more data and learn more and more about the topic, their style of gathering data and insights during the study can begin to change. When this happens, the research design becomes both emergent and complex. In the process of interpretation, scholars have to collect and reflect on their own thoughts, impressions, and interpretations as the data collection and analysis process unfolds.

FIGURE 9.2 ■ Emergent and Main Qualitative Research Designs

- Respond to, and pursue, new paths of discovery that emerge from the context, participants, and data (change or shift research design on the fly)

Emergent Research Design

- Interpretive
- Investigative
- Participatory
- Illuminative
- Instrumentation
- Sensitization
- Conceptualization

Types of Qualitative Research Designs

TABLE 9.2 ■ Main Types of Qualitative Research Designs

Qualitative Research Designs (involve changing tactics over the course of the study)	
Interpretive	• The main goal is clarity of focus. The researcher is a puzzle master. In a situation with parts and pieces not yet in a coherent frame, researchers' task is to pull those parts together to make sense of (interpret) the situation. They must find the best way for the puzzle pieces to fit so there is both clarity and the most informative picture possible of the phenomenon as expressed by the participants.
Investigative	• The main goal is to uncover things to gain depth. Choose a puzzling phenomenon, go to the scene, engage with those living the experience, and dig deeper and deeper until pattern(s) start to emerge. Do not go in with preconceived rules or notions. Let things emerge.
Participatory	• The desire is to make things better. Because the research can shift and alter before your very eyes and the boundaries between research and practice can become blurred, researchers have to employ a bottom-up decision-making and empowerment strategy (allowing the community to shape solutions). The research design is codeveloped with the participants.
Illuminative	• The main goal is new insights by shedding light on things. As researchers challenge their own assumptions, they have to set aside any presuppositions and "get out of their box" so they can take a fresh look at the phenomenon (need more or different views) while striving to see things they overlooked or to make new links.
Instrumentation	• The study creates a new data collection instrument that later will be used in quantitative research.
Sensitization	• The study sensitizes readers to the participants' situation (appreciate their feelings), often achieved by letting the participants' strong and heartrending comments speak for themselves.
Conceptualization and Theory Development	• Using inductive logic (moving from particular to general), authors report a new theory, conceptual framework, taxonomy, or typology that emerged from their qualitative data.

When reporting this type of research design in their paper, authors have to recount key (aha) moments that shaped their understandings of the phenomenon as experienced by those living it. While remaining focused on the main research issue, authors have to explain how they *made sense* of the data and kept it within a cohesive framework while it was emerging (Shank & Brown, 2007).

> ***Example 9.1 Interpretive*** James, Bearne, and Alexander (2004) reported a study that focused on research undertaken while the lead author was working full-time as a nursery teacher. The topic was how children construct *meaning* from sociodramatic play, an event where children re-create events or situations they have seen or experienced. In this study, these sociodramatic plays were videotaped. The premise was that watching videos of themselves playing would help children reflect on their learning. Reported in first person, the lead author explored her concerns and the moments of illumination (aha moments) through the research process. She reflected on ways she began to *make sense* of young children's learning, using some *key moments* in the study, especially the moment she realized she could get better insights by analyzing the video clip data without sound. She discovered that by muting the sound, she was able to delve beneath the surface structure of children's sociodramatic play, enabling her to make key findings. She also reported several other discoveries (aha moments) that seemed to lift curtains of understanding to reveal the potential of sociodramatic play in children's learning.

Investigative

An *investigative research design* involves investigating (tracing out) a phenomenon in its natural setting (called field experience). The research process moves from an *initial* investigation, through more established tracings, to a full-fledged accounting of the phenomenon. Authors should wait until the *investigation* has run its full course before they write any articles that report findings, discussion, and conclusions and disclose this strategy in their paper. The investigation entails (a) obtaining background information on the topic (literature review), (b) gaining agreement between the researcher and participants on entry-issue ground rules, (c) letting research participants help define and lead the parameters of the field experience, and (d) careful field watching, documentation, and learning on the part of the researcher (Shank & Brown, 2007).

> ***Example 9.2 Investigative*** Shank and Brown (2007) referred to an investigative study that explored a community-based calculus program in an inner-city housing project. The author was interested in how this math enclave of high-powered instruction came into existence in such an unusual setting. Heeding the *initial* and *evolving* field-based and situation-based rules about how the study should unfold, "the structure and texture and flow of the research project evolved. Once [the researcher] felt that he had a sufficient handle on his main questions, he then moved into the process of gathering his information, organizing it, and reporting his findings" (p. 136). That is, he waited until the research *investigation* had run its full course before he wrote his article that reported findings, discussion, and conclusions.

Participatory

In a *participatory design* (used with action research), qualitative researchers appreciate that there is a constantly shifting focus among the participants involved in the study, their concerns, and the best way to get things going and under way. This research design involves (a) forming community groups at the outset, (b) helping them discover common understandings of the problem being addressed, (c) facilitating an exchange of ideas for change that come from the people at the scene of the problem, and then (d) letting the details for the research plan emerge from the group. Researchers must accept that what might seem to be a finding often plays a role in the emergent research design. Once adjustments in the plan start to wane and the research process (i.e., data collection and concurrent analysis) begins to start working smoothly, researchers can then (e) start looking for findings proper (Shank & Brown, 2007). When writing articles reporting a participatory research design, authors are encouraged to reflect the emergent coprocess that unfolded among the researcher and participants over time.

> *Example 9.3 Participatory* Shank and Brown (2007) discussed an action research study about working with parents on a supplemental character education program for elementary school children. The author's research design accommodated the constantly shifting focus between the people involved, their concerns, and the best way to get things going and under way. Her research report consequently dealt with the dynamics of forming the community and parent groups, finding common problems (and then a research problem and question), and then implementing the coproduced program to effect change.

Illuminative

Shank and Brown (2007) also discussed what they called an *illuminative research design*. To illuminate means to shed more light on a phenomenon, revealing things that are hidden or in the shadows. Despite characterizing qualitative research as mainly tactical (see Table 9.1), they argued that an illuminative approach is actually quite strategic in nature. Being strategic means designing a plan to gain an advantage (Anderson, 2014). Rather than allowing things to unfold naturally without controlling them, as is the norm with qualitative research, an illuminative approach entails focusing a light on the data collection and data analysis process by forming a specific plan to achieve a research goal.

> *Example 9.4 Illuminative* Shank and Brown (2007) recounted a researcher's *strategic* decision (midway through her study) to change tactics and gain access to sealed police records so she could use a computer program to analyze the sealed Internet blogs of five deceased offenders who had killed their classmates. By shining a light on a particular data set (the sealed police records), she was able to shed more light on this phenomenon. She treated the five blogs as one single group and analyzed these data for common themes, threads, and facets of the bloggers' lives that might explain (shed some light on) why they shot their fellow schoolmates.

Instrumentation

Sometimes, a researcher uses qualitative data to develop a structured instrument that will be used later in quantitative research. An *instrumentation design* in a qualitative study entails nonprobability or purposive sampling to obtain participants. The researcher then uses unstructured or semistructured interviews (in-depth and intensive), or participant observation, to collect data from the participants. The qualitative data are then analyzed and categorized, and the findings are used to develop a new data collection instrument for use in quantitative studies (Knafl & Howard, 1984).

> ***Example 9.5 Instrumentation*** In one study, 45 patients were interviewed to identify statements from them about their uncertainty associated with being hospitalized. These data were categorized into types of uncertainty and then transformed into a 54-item Likert scale survey instrument, which was administered to a much larger sample of patients. Although the results were factor analyzed (quantitative research), the author wrote a *qualitative* instrumentation paper reporting on the development of a new *quantitative* instrument (rather than reporting the results of a factor analysis of the data collected using the new instrument) (Knafl & Howard, 1984).

Sensitization

Knafl and Howard (1984) also identified the *sensitization design* (called a descriptive study). To sensitize means to make someone respond to or be affected by something. It involves appreciating the feelings of others (Anderson, 2014). When publishing such a paper, authors would have to provide sufficient descriptions of how participants understand some aspect of their lives such that "the reader is sensitized to the perspective of the group being studied" (Knafl & Howard, 1984, p. 21). The paper would comprise a synthesis of the participants' viewpoints (often using quotes to let the participants' comments speak for themselves). This would be prefaced with the statement that "either few (if any) studies have been done on the topic, or those that have been done have failed to represent this group's point of view" (Knafl & Howard, 1984, p. 20).

> ***Example 9.6 Sensitization*** Knafl and Howard (1984) shared examples of two sensitization studies, one of rape survivors and the other of grieving spouses. They said that the impact of their words, shared by authors in their qualitative research articles, was so powerful that sensitization of their plight was ensured. The respective authors used both direct quotes from interviews and repetition of subjects' similar responses to convey the rape victims' and grieving spouses' common experiences. Authors of both studies presumed that because the impact of the words of the participants was so strong and heartrending at times, the study's significance would become clear by letting the participants' comments speak for themselves. Readers could not help but be sensitized to the participants' emotional and life traumas.

Conceptualization and Theory Development

On a final note, *conceptualization* or *theory development* is the last type of qualitative research design discussed in this section. Using inductive logic (moving from particular to general), authors would report on qualitative research that generated a new theory. When writing the article, authors would immediately notify readers that their intent is to develop a theory or some new conceptualization; that is, the report strives to conceptualize a phenomenon. Through their literature review, they would first convince readers of the conceptual importance of their subject matter. They would then report on the findings generated from employing the grounded theory method, wherein they let a theory emerge from their data. Authors would report that they used theoretical sampling, meaning they changed their research design on the fly for the purpose of obtaining a sample conducive to building their theory. They would report details on how they altered their data-gathering process by changing tactics (i.e., settings, participants, and/or timing of observations) (Knafl & Howard, 1984; Wiersma & Jurs, 2009). Authors would conclude their paper with a "conceptual rendering of the data," including specific new concepts that contributed to their "overall conceptualization of the phenomenon under study" (Knafl & Howard, 1984, p. 22).

Example 9.7 Conceptualization In their discussion of a 1977 study, Knafl and Howard (1984) reported that the study's author used qualitative data about the everyday context of nursing to develop a theory about nursing in an experimental treatment community. This study about nontraditional treatment of people considered to be insane (an acceptable term 40 years ago) provided the data necessary to develop a new theory for nursing practitioners. Drawing on the participants' points of view, she identified *conceptual links within the data* rather than just describing the data. She prefaced her presentation of this new theory with a discussion of why it was necessary, that being society's historical rejection of the insane.

REVIEW AND ENGAGEMENT

When critically reading a research report, you would

- ☐ Ascertain if the authors explicitly identified which of the seven main qualitative research designs was used in their study (see Table 9.2) and why it was the best to answer their research question

- ☐ If this information was missing, determine if they had provided enough information for you to deduce which research design was employed

METHODS APPROPRIATE FOR QUALITATIVE RESEARCH

Beyond the seven common types of qualitative *research designs* just discussed, there are several *methods* that are commonly used in qualitative research, also called qualitative approaches, procedures, or strategies of inquiry. The most common qualitative procedures or strategies of inquiry are set out in Table 9.3 (Ary, Jacobs, & Sorensen, 2010; Creswell,

2009; Johnson & Christensen, 2012). These all hold the basic characteristics of qualitative research set out in Table 8.3 in Chapter 8. Some of these methods (a) seek to understand phenomena and the meanings people attach to them, and others (b) are focused on power relationships in society (Ary et al., 2010). This distinction was used to organize Table 9.3.

TABLE 9.3 ■ Most Common Qualitative Research Methods or Strategies of Inquiry	
Qualitative Method (Strategy, Procedure)	**General Description**
Understand phenomena and the meanings people attach to them	
Case Study (*particular situation*)	Conduct in-depth, intensive exploration of one or more particular situations over a period of time (e.g., individuals, groups, programs, events, activities, processes).
Content Analysis (*meaning in materials*)	Analyze written or visual material to discern its content and meaning; engage in contextualized interpretation of documents (can be quantitative or qualitative).
Grounded Theory (*theory*)	Inductively derive a theory about a phenomenon from the views of the participants in a particular setting (theory emerges from the data).
Ethnography (*culture, social groups*)	Study natural behavior of an intact cultural group in its natural setting over a prolonged period of time (looking for characteristics of people and of cultural scenes).
Narrative (*life stories*)	People's stories of their lives are told to and then *retold* by the researcher. These two stories are combined into a collaborative narrative (an accounting of events).
Phenomenology (*essence of life*)	Identify the essence of human experiences (e.g., family life) as lived and told by the participants (embedded in their conscience). Through prolonged engagement with, and interpretation of, participants' statements, researchers find patterns and relationships that have meaning for the participants—the *essence* of their life experiences.
Historical (*re-create the past*)	Establish facts, interpret them, and arrive at conclusions concerning events in the past so as to better understand the present.
Understand power relationships in society	
Critical (*power*)	Researchers seek to empower social and political change through (a) examining and critiquing assumptions and ideologies that place constraints on people and by (b) focusing on power relationships to foster emancipation.
Feminist (*women's equality*)	Beginning with standpoints and perspectives of women, researchers seek to reveal power imbalances so as to restore (ensure) equity and social equality.
Participatory (*share or take part in*)	Researchers work with communities, emphasizing participation and collective action, inquiry, and reflection so as to ensure empowerment through an action agenda for change.
Discourse (*meaning of words*)	Researchers examine the relationship between words, texts, symbols, and signs and their meanings (also called semiotics); words and signs are powerful sources of meaning (messages, whether intended or not).

As noted in the introduction to this chapter, readers are directed to research methods textbooks for details about the technical nuances of each qualitative research method in Table 9.3 and how it deals with site selection and participant recruitment or document procurement (sampling), primary data collection strategies, and data analysis approaches. Only the basic conventions are described in this chapter so that critical readers can gain a sense of whether authors have responsibly accounted for their research design decisions. To aid in this task, authors should clearly identify which method(s) they employed in their study, with a full explanation of how it was the best method(s) for answering their research question(s) (Choudhuri, Glauser, & Peregoy, 2004).

REVIEW AND ENGAGEMENT

When critically reading a research report, you would

☐ Determine if the authors clearly identified which particular qualitative *method(s)* was employed in their study (e.g., ethnography, narrative), with justification relative to their research question

☐ Ascertain if they explained whether they were seeking understandings, meanings, or power relationships (intent of inquiry)

☐ If yes, determine if their method matched the intent of the inquiry (see Table 9.3)

QUALITATIVE SITE SELECTION AND ACCESS

Figure 9.1 provides an overview of the major components of the qualitative Methods section of a research paper. Each is now discussed in detail, starting with site selection and access. Because qualitative research focuses on the everyday life and real conditions, events, and actions of people, the study has to take place at the site where the phenomenon is happening. And, because researchers often immerse themselves onsite in the participants' real world, authors have to provide detailed descriptions of the site and reasons for its selection. Foremost, authors have to make the case that this site provided the most appropriate setting (locale) for the research question. They have to elaborate on their site-selection strategy by which particular settings, persons, or events were deliberately selected in order to provide information that could not be obtained as well at other sites. Their description of the site(s) should be *so* vivid that readers gain a picture of it, becoming familiar with the unfamiliar (Campbell, 1994; Holloway & Wheeler, 2002).

Authors must also explain their access protocol. Access is defined as "the appropriate ethical and academic practices used to gain entry to a given community for the purposes of conducting formal research" (Given, 2008, p. 2). Authors can choose a site they are familiar with and already have access to, or they can seek out unknown settings where gaining access or entry requires permission from those with authority to grant access (Given, 2008). Normally, one to three sites are chosen for a study, but researchers may need to employ a multisite strategy if they intend to develop a theory (Wiersma & Jurs, 2009).

In their paper, authors should report any and all of these four main access strategies: (a) obtained institutional review board (IRB) or research ethics board (REB) approval of their research protocol (which deals with ethics, confidentiality, no harm, recruitment, consent, and withdrawal); (b) gained access through community, organizational, or government lines of authority; (c) used gatekeepers and key informants as entry points; and (d) ethically gained access to Internet and virtual communities (e.g., listservs, chat rooms, course discussion postings, blogs, mailing lists, and newsgroups) (Creswell, 2009; Given, 2008).

One of the most significant criteria for selecting a site for a qualitative study is cultural representativity (Babor, Stenius, Savva, & O'Reilly, 2004). Cultural theorists define this as the process by which meaning is produced and exchanged among members of a culture through the use of language, signs, and images that stand for or represent things (Hall, 1997). Authors must satisfy readers that the site they chose best meets this criterion, especially since qualitative research seeks understandings and meanings (Shank & Brown, 2007).

QUALITATIVE SAMPLING

Once the sites are selected and access is approved, researchers have to draw a sample (subset) of people or artifacts that can best represent, and be used to re-present, the phenomenon in question. Using nonprobability sampling, researchers may include one or a combination of people, events, institutions, and written or visual material and documents (*Social Science & Medicine*, 2010) (see Figure 9.3 for the most common qualitative sampling strategies).

Wilson (2000) explained that *hierarchical sampling* is often used, meaning qualitative researchers start with large units (villages or schools), then smaller units within those sites (households), and, finally, individuals within those units (parents and children). As well, qualitative research normally employs *purposive sampling*, defined as selecting participants on purpose because they can best provide information required to answer the research question. Purposive sampling is also useful when developing theory, wherein researchers would strive for *theoretical saturation*, meaning new data no longer bring new insights, the concept being developed is dense, and its relationship to other concepts is well established and validated (Boudah, 2011; Mack, Woodsong, Macqueen, Guest, & Namey, 2005; Patton, 2002).

Other appropriate sampling techniques for qualitative research include quota and snowball sampling. Regarding *quota sampling*, rather than using a list of particular people purposively chosen for the study, researchers would decide ahead of time what characteristics people must have to be part of the sample and how many people are needed and then recruit until they have met the quota (a prescribed or fixed number). With *snowball sampling*, people are selected because others in the sample frame used their social network and recommended them as a good fit with the research question. These sampling strategies allow researchers to focus on the people most likely to experience, know about, or have insights into the research topic (Mack et al., 2005).

Critical case sampling involves selecting one single unit that provides a critical test of a program or a theory (e.g., the researcher chooses a school that has implemented a recommended program and observes for a year). With *comprehensive sampling*, used when the number of units is very small, researchers include every unit in their sample. For example, a study of Indigenous students in a Caucasian-dominated school would include all

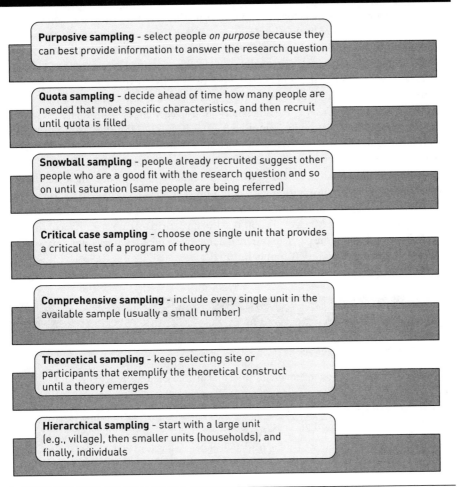

FIGURE 9.3 ■ Qualitative Sampling Strategies

Purposive sampling - select people *on purpose* because they can best provide information to answer the research question

Quota sampling - decide ahead of time how many people are needed that meet specific characteristics, and then recruit until quota is filled

Snowball sampling - people already recruited suggest other people who are a good fit with the research question and so on until saturation (same people are being referred)

Critical case sampling - choose one single unit that provides a critical test of a program of theory

Comprehensive sampling - include every single unit in the available sample (usually a small number)

Theoretical sampling - keep selecting site or participants that exemplify the theoretical construct until a theory emerges

Hierarchical sampling - start with a large unit (e.g., village), then smaller units (households), and finally, individuals

Indigenous students. When using *theoretical sampling*, researchers would select a site or a case that exemplifies the theoretical construct and then continue to select participants from the site as the research unfolds and the theory emerges (Ary et al., 2010).

Sample Size

How large should the sample frame be for a qualitative study? "Determining adequate sample size in qualitative research is ultimately a matter of judgment and experience in evaluating the quality of the information collected against the uses to which it will be put, the particular research method and purposeful sampling strategy employed, and the research product intended" (Sandelowski, 1995, p. 179). From a practical stance, the ultimate sample size depends on the research question, the research objectives, resources, time available, and availability of participants (Ary et al., 2010; Mack et al., 2005).

Aside from practical matters, the main criterion is redundancy of information (*saturation*) (Ary et al., 2010). Researchers have to ensure that their sample size is (a) large enough to support claims of having achieved either informational redundancy or theoretical saturation but (b) not too small, thereby limiting the deep, case- or site-oriented analysis that is the raison-d'être of qualitative inquiry (Sandelowski, 1995). Typical sample sizes vary from a few up to 30 participants. A smaller sample size is justified because power in qualitative research comes from thick and dense descriptions of lived experiences, social processes, cultures, and narrative accounts. In contrast, quantitative studies are guided by statistical power necessitating larger samples (Driessnack, Sousa, & Mendes, 2007a) (see Chapter 10).

Authors have to clarify which sampling approach they used in their study and provide a solid justification for this research design decision (Babor et al., 2004). Also, they have to clarify the recruitment strategy they used to screen potential participants, the number to be recruited, location(s) or sites, and any ethical guidelines and protocols. These decisions are normally developed in consultation with community leaders or local experts. It is permissible to change the recruitment strategy for participants as long as the proper approvals are obtained (Labaree, 2016; Mack et al., 2005). Also, if participants are coauthors of the paper, authors have to clarify if the participants' real names were noted or if pseudonyms were used to protect their confidentiality (Campbell, 1994).

REVIEW AND ENGAGEMENT

When critically reading a research report, you would

☐ Ascertain if the authors clearly explained their site selection process and the procedures taken to gain access

☐ Determine if they clarified their sampling protocol, including which type of sampling was used, recruitment strategies, and any justifications for their sample size (mention of saturation) (see Figure 9.4)

☐ Check to see if they explained how (if) the people from the site were involved in the access and sampling process

RESEARCHER'S ROLE

One of the defining features of qualitative research is that researchers are the primary data collection instrument. They can assume one of three main roles (observer, interviewer, or researcher) along a continuum: (a) complete participant (people do not know the researcher is in the group); (b) participant-observer (either active participant, privileged observer, or limited observer); (c) complete observer (nonparticipant outside the group, whose members do not know they are being observed); (d) clinical interviewer; or (e) action researcher. Authors have to justify this role, satisfying readers that it fit with the research question and the theoretical framework (if there is one) (Campbell, 1994; Choudhuri et al., 2004; Johnson & Christensen, 2012; Leckie, 2008; Shank & Brown, 2007; Wolcott, 1988).

Usually, researchers immerse themselves in the site and the context, and they work with participants before, during, and after the study. For this reason, when reporting a qualitative study, authors have to acknowledge their roles as researchers in the study. This is especially important if they collected data using participant observations. In these instances, authors have to clarify the nature and the extent of their participation with those observed. They also have to explain how their roles developed and changed over the course of the study (Knafl & Howard, 1984). Leckie (2008) identified several recurring roles, starting with being a researcher (insider or outsider). Participants may view the researcher in several confounding roles, including a friend, mentor, negative agent (causes participants to reflect on their lives), parent, professional, social activist, and therapist. Through reflexivity, researchers can glean which, if any, of these roles came into play during the study, and authors must recount how they dealt with any attendant issues, which could affect the trustworthiness of the data.

Authors also need to address personal and professional connections between themselves and participants, the sites or settings, and the research topic. Previous and ongoing relationships can create difficult ethical issues and power imbalances. The research design can easily become compromised and overly biased. To offset issues of qualitative validity, researchers have to identify reflexively, and account for, any personal biases, values, and personal background that could influence the study (especially their interpretation of the data) (Creswell, 2009; Leckie, 2008) (to be discussed shortly). This reflexivity is required because of the *interactionist nature* of the relationship between the researcher and the participants and because of the emergent, unfolding nature of the research design. Authors need to recount both how they interacted with study participants and their reflections on those interactions, likely recorded in their field notes or journal (Leckie, 2008). The ultimate objective is to provide evidence that the participants' voices were privileged rather than the researcher's.

QUALITATIVE ETHICAL CONSIDERATIONS

Research with humans is rife with ethical issues, meaning ethical norms play a powerful role in the research design process. Without conscientious decisions, researchers can exhibit ethical lapses, which can harm participants or expose them to risk of harm (Gall, Gall, & Borg, 2015; Shamoo & Resnik, 2015). "The complexities of researching private lives and placing accounts in the public arena raise multiple ethical issues for the researcher" (Dence, Iphofen, & Huws, 2004, p. 10).

Authors of qualitative research papers have to include a statement affirming that their research design was approved by an IRB or REB at their institution, funding agency, or overall site organization (e.g., school board). These ethical reviews normally address issues of (a) respect for human dignity, which entails formal consent and full awareness of the harm and benefits of the research; (b) balancing harms and benefits; and (c) justice, meaning risks or benefits should not fall disproportionally on any particular group in the study (Given, 2008).

Johnson and Christensen (2012) and Preissle (2008) discussed ethics in qualitative research, explaining that all research serves some moral intent. Qualitative scholars have identified major principles that should be respected in qualitative research designs (Dence et al., 2004; Mack et al., 2005; Preissle, 2008) (see Table 9.4). Preissle (2008) clarified that "the ethical conduct of qualitative research is complex, evolving, and contingent across the course of a study and is a matter of continuing debate in the qualitative research community of practice" (p. 277). Authors do not need to report these issues in their paper because the IRB or similar statement suffices (Johnson & Christensen, 2012). But authors and critical readers of qualitative papers can benefit from a general sense of what is involved in obtaining ethical approval for a qualitative research design.

TABLE 9.4 ■ Major Ethical Considerations in Qualitative Research Designs
• *Honesty*—do not fabricate, falsify, suppress, or misrepresent data. Do not deceive participants (withhold or mislead, unless justified to answer the research question)
• *Subjectivity*—researchers have to reflexively account for their own biases, opinions, values, and personal background that might influence their interpretation of data
• *Integrity*—researchers have to be transparent, open, and candid (moral soundness)
• *Informed consent, respect for human dignity*—tell participants about the study (purpose, procedures, risks, and benefits) and give them the opportunity to voluntarily participate or decline; ensure they can withdraw with no penalty
• *Humane* consideration of participants (civilized, compassionate, moral, and intellectual concern); ensure participants are protected from undue intrusion, distress, indignity, physical discomfort, personal embarrassment, or other harm
• *Protection* from mental (emotional) and physical harm or pain, or risk thereof
• *Ethics of care and justice* while *not exploiting* participants; underrepresented groups should not become further marginalized or excluded
• *Confidentiality, anonymity, privacy, and the ethics of consequences*—protect the identity of participants in the study and also alleviate any disadvantages to participating in the study
• *Member checking and access*—ensure that participants have the opportunity to see how their perspective is being interpreted and that they have access to what is published about them
• *Respect and address the interests and concerns* of relevant stakeholders and participants
• *Responsible reporting and dissemination* of findings, conclusions, and recommendations—show concern for consequences of what is reported and how

QUALITATIVE DATA COLLECTION

Once the site(s) is chosen, access is gained, and the participants are recruited and enrolled in the study, researchers have to collect data from them, nonhuman sources, or both. Authors have to report the qualitative data collection method(s) they employed in their study. The most common types are (a) observation, (b) individual interviews, (c) focus groups, and (d) document or artifact analysis (see Figure 9.4). Many qualitative research designs employ multiple data collection methods, a strategy intended to strengthen *data triangulation*. This is defined as verifying and validating the data collected about a phenomenon so as to confirm or resolve discrepant findings (Gall et al., 2015). For example, a researcher may analyze documents, observe three participants, interview each participant individually, and then conduct a focus group of these three people.

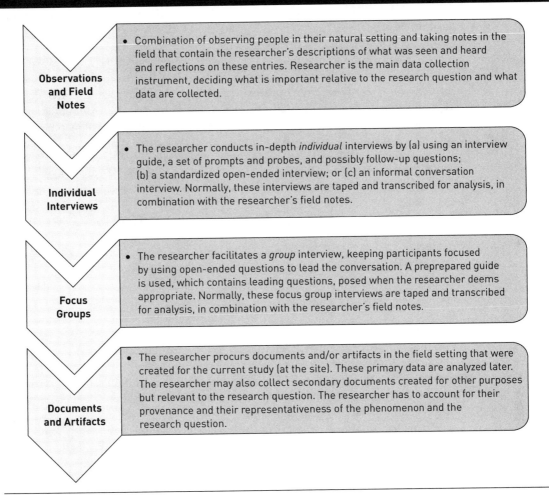

FIGURE 9.4 ■ Qualitative Data Collection Strategies

Observations and Field Notes
- Combination of observing people in their natural setting and taking notes in the field that contain the researcher's descriptions of what was seen and heard and reflections on these entries. Researcher is the main data collection instrument, deciding what is important relative to the research question and what data are collected.

Individual Interviews
- The researcher conducts in-depth *individual* interviews by (a) using an interview guide, a set of prompts and probes, and possibly follow-up questions; (b) a standardized open-ended interview; or (c) an informal conversation interview. Normally, these interviews are taped and transcribed for analysis, in combination with the researcher's field notes.

Focus Groups
- The researcher facilitates a *group* interview, keeping participants focused by using open-ended questions to lead the conversation. A preprepared guide is used, which contains leading questions, posed when the researcher deems appropriate. Normally, these focus group interviews are taped and transcribed for analysis, in combination with the researcher's field notes.

Documents and Artifacts
- The researcher procurs documents and/or artifacts in the field setting that were created for the current study (at the site). These primary data are analyzed later. The researcher may also collect secondary documents created for other purposes but relevant to the research question. The researcher has to account for their provenance and their representativeness of the phenomenon and the research question.

As a caveat, researchers can stop collecting data when they have reached the point of *data saturation*, defined as when new cases or observations no longer disclose or reveal new information. To justify that saturation has occurred, authors have to affirm both the sufficiency of data and that the data are sufficiently varied (Babor et al., 2004; Suter, 2012). Babor et al. (2004) recommended that researchers "analyze a small data batch carefully first and only then determine what additional data will be needed" (p. 86). This advice acknowledges the aforementioned emergent nature of the qualitative research design. Finally, authors must account for the strategies they employed to ensure the validity of the data they collected (see upcoming section "Integrity of Qualitative Research Designs"). Each of the four main qualitative data collection methods is now discussed.

Observations and Field Notes

Ary et al. (2010) explained that qualitative observation is "more than just 'hanging out'" (p. 431). Because the goal is to provide a complete description of the behavior in a specific, natural setting, researchers have to observe for an extended period of time so they can collect the narrative and words articulated by the participants about their lived experiences. Researchers are striving to understand complex interactions in natural settings. They usually use *field notes* to *record* their observations, which constitute what is written down or captured by the observer during and after making observations. Notes made in the field can take the form of handwritten notations or entries into a computer program, photographs, drawings, graphics, scribbles, sketches, and audio and video recordings.

Because these field notes are analyzed to provide insights to help answer the research question, researchers have to make their notes as soon as possible following their observations in the field, to ensure nothing is lost or misconstrued (i.e., within minutes or hours) (Ary et al., 2010; Johnson & Christensen, 2012). Ideally, when interacting directly with participants, handwritten field notes should not be made until after leaving the field (Gall et al., 2015).

Field notes contain two components: (a) descriptions of what the researchers saw and heard and (b) their reflections on these entries. Descriptions focus on the setting, people, events, interactions, and reactions. Reflections concern the researchers' personal feelings and impressions of the notes and what they contain, as well as any observations about the research design, how well it is working, and whether adjustments have to be made in order to answer the research question (Ary et al., 2010). Authors have to truthfully recount how their reaction with their field notes affected their emergent research design. This is very important because as noted before, the researcher is the main data collection instrument in qualitative research. Researchers decide what is important and what data are actually recorded (Johnson & Christensen, 2012). Authors should include the aforementioned information about the researcher's role during fieldwork (see previous section) before or with the Data Collection section of their article. In review, data collection is informed by the researcher's (a) level of involvement (amount of participation, ranging from complete observer to nonobserver); (b) extent of revealment (full disclosure to full secrecy); (c) amount and duration of time spent in the setting (intensive or extensive); and (d) the study's focus (specific and well-developed questions, or exploratory) (Ary et al., 2010).

Individual Interviews

Researchers can use *in-depth individual interviews* with participants so as to gain insights into their inner world. The basic research protocol (procedure) is to enter the interview with (a) a set of open-ended questions (called an interview guide) and (b) a set of prompts or probes in case the conversation stalls or participants need clarification. After the interview, the researcher may want to pose follow-up questions about issues that emerged during the data collection process. A variation to this approach is the *standardized open-ended interview* during which a guide is used, but the interviewer does not change the wording or sequence of the questions with subsequent participants. Researchers can also opt for an *informal conversation interview*, which involves discussing topics of interest with the participant and following all leads that emerge from the interview; nothing is predetermined. If this data collection format is truly spontaneous (and cannot be taped), the researcher has to immediately take field notes (Gall et al., 2015; Johnson & Christensen, 2012).

Focus Group Interviews

These are a form of *group interview* wherein participants collectively take part in a discussion facilitated by a skilled interviewer. They are called focus groups because the interviewer keeps participants *focused* on the topic by using open-ended questions to lead the conversation (Ary et al., 2010). Interviewers use a prepared *interview guide* comprising one sheet of approximately 10 leading questions. They choose when questions should be posed, depending on the flow of the conversation. The in-depth conversations are normally taped, transcribed, and analyzed (Johnson & Christensen, 2012). Focus groups provide opportunities for the researcher to elicit feelings and opinions from participants that might not have emerged through individual interviews (Gall et al., 2015).

Document and Artifact Analysis

Sometimes, the research question cannot be answered unless the research design includes the procurement of documents and other artifacts found in the field setting (created or naturally occurring). Examples include (a) public records and other official documents (curricula, minutes, annual reports, student records); (b) archived research data (census, opinion research, longitudinal data); (c) media artifacts (newspapers, newscasts, podcasts, social media); (d) personal documents (letters, diaries, journals, correspondence, pictures, videos, audio recordings); and (e) physical data or traces left by people (footprints, wear on floor tiles or books, trash). (f) Artifacts or relics are physical objects found or created in the field.

Documents generated in the field during the data collection process are called primary data. Sometimes documents or artifacts already exist in the field and were not created for the current research purpose. These are called secondary data (Ary et al., 2010; Johnson & Christensen, 2012). Authors should identify which of these types of secondary documents were collected to be analyzed, accounting as best as possible for their origins, authenticity, and representativeness. And they should explain how they were used as part of the data triangulation protocol (Ary et al., 2010).

QUALITATIVE DATA MANAGEMENT, SECURITY, AND STORAGE

Some journals ask authors to explain their data management strategies, appended to the Data Collection or Data Analysis section. These strategies include how data were stored, how they were backed up and/or converted to other formats (if relevant), where they were secured and how, access protocols, if audio- or videotaped interviews were transcribed and by whom (their expertise for this task), and how data were handled after the study ended (security, archived, destroyed) (Babor et al., 2004; Corti, 2008; Rocco & Plakhotnik, 2011). "Data management is important because it ensures safekeeping or future proofing of data during the research process. Good data management reduces the risk of data loss, increases accuracy and verifiability, and reduces the loss of productivity if core staff members leave before the end of the project. It also offers greater potential for longer term data preservation and increases the ability to reanalyze older data sets" (Corti, 2008, p. 193).

REVIEW AND ENGAGEMENT

When critically reading a research report, you would

- ☐ Check to see if the authors clearly articulated the researchers' role in the research design
- ☐ Determine if they adequately addressed ethical considerations (see Table 9.4)
- ☐ Ascertain if they clearly explained their data collection approach (some combination of four possible strategies)
- ☐ Determine if they set out a well-articulated and sufficiently discussed set of procedures for data collection from their sample
- ☐ Check to see if they accounted for data triangulation and for data saturation
- ☐ Confirm that they reported their data management strategy

INTEGRITY OF QUALITATIVE RESEARCH DESIGNS

Authors of qualitative research papers have to acknowledge the standards they set to achieve high quality and maintain integrity in their research design. They must also clearly spell out the steps they took to meet each standard, appreciating that sometimes one strategy can address several standards (Ary et al., 2010; Patton, 2002; Rocco & Plakhotnik, 2011). For clarification, this book assumed that qualitative research is naturalistic and postpositivistic, meaning it is concerned with trustworthiness, authenticity, confirmability, dependability, and other criteria. In contrast, quantitative scholarship (deterministic, empirical, positivistic methodology) is concerned with validity, reliability, and generalizability, discussed in Table 8.5 in Chapter 8 (see also Chapter 10).

Like quantitative scholars, qualitative researchers still have to ensure that their data are reliable (they can be adopted in other contexts) and valid (they measured what was intended to be measured). However, although very consistent in quantitative research, nomenclature for issues of quality in qualitative research is not consistent across fields (Suter, 2012). Table 9.5 provides an overview of the most agreed-to approaches and terms used by qualitative researchers, with attendant strategies to meet the standards for this research methodology (Ary et al., 2010; Creswell & Miller, 2000; Guba, 1981; Johnson & Christensen, 2012; Lincoln, 1995; Nahrin, 2015; Newman, Newman, & Newman, 2011; Shenton, 2004). This table speaks to issues of trustworthy data, subjectivity (confirmability), credibility, transferability, dependability, and authenticity.

TABLE 9.5 ■ Criteria to Ensure High-Quality Qualitative Research

Qualitative (Postpositivistic, Naturalistic, Interpretive, Critical)	
Striving for **trustworthy data** (data must be truly *transparent* and open to *critical thinking* by the reader; trust means acceptance of the *truth* of a statement).	*Strategies:* triangulation (multiple sources of data); member checks; saturation during data collection; peer review or expert consultations; audit trail (detailed record of researcher's decisions, with reasons); thick descriptions; plausible alternatives; account for negative cases; prolonged engagement in the field.
Confirmability (subjectivity): Refers to the *researcher's neutrality* when interpreting data (i.e., self-awareness and control of one's bias); appreciating that values are central to the research process, researchers still have to be sure their findings can be *confirmed* or corroborated by others (i.e., their values did not take over). It is the extent to which findings are shaped by the respondents themselves, rather than the researcher's bias.	*Strategies:* reflexivity (involves self-critique and disclosure of what one brings to the research, especially one's predispositions); audit trails; method triangulation; peer review and debriefing.
Credibility (credible to the participants): Did the researchers create a faithful accounting of people's lived experiences (i.e., an *accurate* representation of their reality, from their perspective)? Did the researchers get a full answer to their research question? Also, can others have confidence in the *truth* shared by the researchers (i.e., in their observations, interpretations, and conclusions)? The latter require strong evidence, clear logic, valid data, and ruling out alternative explanations.	*Strategies:* member checks; detailed, thick descriptions (and lots of quotes); triangulation (methods and data); peer review and debriefing; extended and prolonged fieldwork; researcher reflexivity to mitigate invalidity; cross-case comparisons.
Transferability (determined by the user): Refers to the degree to which findings can be applied or transferred to other contexts or settings—that is, used more widely by others. It is the researcher's responsibility to provide accurate, detailed, and complete descriptions of the context and the participants so that *users* of the study can determine if the findings and conclusions apply (are transferable) in *their* context (based on similarity of deep descriptors).	*Strategies:* cross-case comparisons; literature comparisons; detailed, thick descriptions; researcher reflexivity to mitigate invalidity; state study limitations (account for selection, setting, and history effects that might make the study unique to only a single group [i.e., not transferable]).

(Continued)

TABLE 9.5 ■ (Continued)

Qualitative (Postpositivistic, Naturalistic, Interpretive, Critical)	
Dependability: Related to reliability, researchers have to responsibly provide sufficient information so others can repeat the research design protocol in *their* context but not necessarily get the same results. Dependability refers to the stability of findings over time and in changing research contexts (i.e., others can rely [*depend*] on the study). The latter means the findings, conclusions, and interpretations must be supported by the data. Note that credibility ensures dependability.	**Strategies:** *audit trail; triangulation; rich documentation; intra- and intercoder or observer agreement; approach and procedures are appropriate for the context and can be documented.*
Authenticity (realness for participants): Researchers want to make specific statements about only the people they studied (how the latter see *their* world). So authenticity refers to the extent to which participants' voices and agency are ensured, and it strives for assurances that the researcher has represented all views of all participants (*authentic* means original, genuine, undisputed).	**Strategies:** *collaboration with participants; member checking; researcher reflexivity (involves self-critique and disclosure of what one brings to the research).*

REVIEW AND ENGAGEMENT

When critically reading a research report, you would

- ☐ Determine if the authors explicitly and thoroughly accounted for steps taken to ensure qualitative scholarship of a high standard and integrity (see Table 9.5)
- ☐ Judge whether they correctly differentiated between criteria for a qualitative versus quantitative study (i.e., they applied the correct criteria for the type of study)

QUALITATIVE DATA ANALYSIS

Most qualitative data are in the form of words or text. To illustrate, researchers convert verbal, recorded interviews into transcripts (words, sentences, paragraphs). Documents and records consist of words. The researcher's field notes are handwritten or typed words (van den Hoonaard & van den Hoonaard, 2008). The exceptions are photographs, drawings, artwork, videos, and audio recordings, which are still considered data. In these cases, researchers interpret what these data mean relative to the research question and then report their interpretation using their own words. The result is a huge pile of raw data, colorfully described by Merriam (2009): "In the pile to your left are a hundred or so pages of transcripts of interviews. In the middle of the table is a stack of field notes from your on-site observations, and to the right of that is a box of documents you collected, thinking they might be relevant for your study" (p. 170).

All of this text (data) has to be analyzed. Regardless of the particular data collection method (see Table 9.3), qualitative data analysis has a number of common features. "These include simultaneous data collection and analysis, the practice of writing memos during and after data collection, the use of some sort of coding, the use of writing as a tool for analysis, and the development of concepts and connections of one's analysis to the literature in one's field" (van den Hoonaard & van den Hoonaard, 2008, p. 186).

In the spirit of this chapter, this section does not provide a detailed discussion of each of these phases because authors do not normally report this information in their research article. However, it behooves critical readers to gain some nuanced understanding of this iterative process so they can critically assess if the authors reported enough to enable others to judge the rigor of the scholarship and to determine what was actually done to analyze the massive amount of data yielded with qualitative research. To that end, a truncated overview of this process is provided in the following text.

Data Interim Analysis

As noted already, a qualitative research design is emergent, meaning data collection and analysis occur simultaneously. Insights gained from this process are used to make necessary adjustments to the working plan (research design) for the study so the research question can be addressed. Researchers use a process called *interim analysis. Interim* means temporary until something more permanent and complete is established (Anderson, 2014). In this process, researchers gain deeper and deeper understandings of their research topic with each round of data collection. As this concurrent process unfolds, fewer data are collected, and more analysis is produced. The large pile of raw data is eventually *reduced* to the data the authors choose to analyze and report in their paper (Johnson & Christensen, 2012; Wiersma & Jurs, 2009). Authors should acknowledge when they have used interim analysis.

Data Analysis Spiral

During data analysis per se, researchers, through a process of multiple readings of the massive body of text, become intimately familiar with their data. During this iterative, recursive, and dynamic process, researchers move through three key stages: (a) familiarization with and organization and management of the data; (b) deeper engagement with the data through reading, reflecting, coding, and reduction; and (c) interpreting, writing, and representing (re-presenting or displaying) the data for others to read (Ary et al., 2010). Creswell (2009) called this the data analysis spiral. So as not to get caught up in a never-ending spiral, authors should wrap up analysis of the data when (a) the data sources have been fully mined and exhausted, (b) categories are saturated, and (c) regularities have emerged in conjunction with a sense of integration (Lincoln & Guba, 1985). Authors should acknowledge when they have used the data analysis spiral strategy.

Coding and Patterns

Although authors have to succinctly and responsibly report their data analysis process, *most* of their discussion will be focused on (a) their coding approach and (b) how they found patterns and then themes in their data (Rocco & Plakhotnik, 2011). Coding involves sorting and reducing the data (sort from large to very specific categories) so the researcher can find things that "appear regularly and seem important" relative to the research question (Ary et al., 2010, p. 483). Researchers will repeatedly read the mountain of text and code some combination of words, phrases, sentences, and paragraphs (called coding units). Authors have to report on interrater reliability if several people coded and analyzed the data or on intrarater reliability if one person analyzed it once or more (Goodson, 2017).

The three most common coding strategies reported in qualitative studies are open, axial, and selective coding, with analysts moving progressively through them. Open coding entails reading the whole data set, flagging quotations, pulling them out of the text, and *aggregating* them into a collection of categories or themes, which are assigned a name. A large number of codes emerge during this process, upwards of 100. Axial coding involves *clustering* these open codes into even tighter groups around a central point, reducing them down to 20 or 30 clusters, with labels. Selective coding involves *integrating* or *connecting* the axial codes into even tighter clusters, creating concepts or dimensions of a theory, usually 10 or fewer (Boudah, 2011). In short, when coding, researchers move from aggregation, through clustering, to integration and connections. Authors should report this in their paper.

> *Example 9.8* Birochi and Pozzebon (2016) reported this approach, which they used to augment a grounded theory on financial education. Their two final theoretical concepts were the informational dimension and the communicative dimension of transformative financial education, gleaned from open, axial, and then selective coding of semistructured interviews, the researchers' field notes, and documents.

Themes in Qualitative Data

Moving from specific to general, through multiple and repeated levels of analysis, qualitative researchers often use inductive logic to create themes (Creswell, 2009). A theme represents components or fragments of ideas or experiences (in this case, the words in the text) that may be meaningless when viewed alone but have meaning when brought together (Aronson, 1994). When a thematic analysis is employed, a research paper normally reports five to seven themes (Creswell, 2009).

When writing their data analysis section, authors have to provide enough evidence in their paper to support their assertion that they actually did find a particular theme. This thematic evidence takes the form of direct quotes from the texts (along with the author's interpretation). Others may read the same database and come up with different themes, so authors have to explain how *their* categories, themes, and assertions were developed. A theme can be said to exist if (a) a recurring idea threads its way through the data (albeit using different words); (b) the same words, phrases, or even sentences are repeated across the data; (c) a few incidences occurred very forcefully; (d) a topic was raised or discussed frequently; or (e) a large number of people expressed the same idea (extensiveness) (Krueger, 1998; Morgan, 1998; Owen, 1984).

Authors can use other techniques to represent their data, guided by which method they used (see Table 9.3). Examples of representation or display strategies, other than themes (which use direct quotes), include concept maps, graphs, pictures, diagrams, sketches, figures, tables, frameworks, models, propositions, and stories or cases (which involve the extensive use of descriptive, narrative text) (Ary et al., 2010).

Computer Qualitative Software Programs

Many researchers prefer to hand-code their data, using color-coded highlighters, colored pencils, numbering systems, index cards, sticky notes for memos, and literally cutting paper with scissors and pasting (glue or scotch tape) to rearrange coded text into themes. They prefer to eyeball and frequently reexamine the data rather than depend on computer-assisted qualitative data analysis software (CAQDAS) (Ary et al., 2010; Suter, 2012; van den Hoonaard & van den Hoonaard, 2008). But, as qualitative software evolves, efforts to simulate all tasks done off screen continue to increase (Maietta, 2008). If authors opted to use a computer software program to analyze their data, they need to identify the program in their paper (Ary et al., 2010; Creswell, 2009; Suter, 2012).

There is always a concern that researchers will rely too heavily on the software, distracting them from *thinking about* their data and what it means. So, for transparency's sake, authors have to let readers know that they used technology as an analytical tool (Ary et al., 2010). In brief, CAQDAS "help[s] users to organize and record their thoughts about and reactions to data as well as access and review the material they have organized and recorded" (Maietta, 2008, p. 103). CAQDAS contains some combination of (a) document systems that allow users to store all documents in their original format (including Word files and multimedia files such as audio, video, and photos); (b) memo systems (like sticky notes) that can also be edited and coded; (c) coding and category systems (e.g., gender, age, religion); (d) filtering systems for data searching and retrieval; (e) diagramming tools (e.g., mind maps, concept maps, models, networks, trees, and other graphic representations of codes, relationships between codes, themes, and theoretical concepts and constructs); and (f) data storage and management systems (Ary et al., 2010; Maietta, 2008).

The four most common examples of CAQDAS are ATLAS.ti, QSR NVivo, MAXQDA, and HyperRESEARCH. Other software programs are gaining popularity, including HyperQual 2, Ethnograph 6.0, HyperTRANSCRIBE, C-I-SAID, Qualrus, WordStat, Leximancer, TextAnalyst, TextQuest, AnnoTape, DICTION, Framework, and Transana (Ary et al., 2010; Maietta, 2008). Software packages are useful when (a) the data comprise various forms of media (e.g., field notes, videos, transcripts, and audio recordings); (b) there is a large amount of data; or (c) complex forms of analysis are desired (Gall et al., 2015).

QUALITATIVE STUDY LIMITATIONS

Authors of qualitative research papers have to acknowledge any limitations to their research design, especially sampling, data collection, and data analysis. Chapter 14 provides more details about limitations in general. Qualitative limitations restrict and constrain (a) how confidently the findings can be adopted in another setting, (b) how well the researcher was able to measure what was intended, (c) how well participants' voices were authenticated, and (d) the neutrality of the researcher's interpretations of the data (Boudah, 2011; Labaree, 2016). Most important, limitations can compromise getting a full answer to the research question (Babor et al., 2004).

"Honesty, openness, and candid revelation of a [qualitative] study's strengths and limitations according to commonly held standards of practice are typical indicators of the integrity of the scholarship" (Preissle, 2008, p. 276). Labaree (2016) explained that there can be limitations with the method and with the researcher. The former includes sample size, measures or strategies to collect data, and sufficiency of data to analyze them and find trends or themes. Issues pertaining to the researcher can include site access, longitudinal effects, cultural and other types of bias, and even language fluency.

Depending on the nature of the limitations, authors can choose to place the limitations at either (a) the beginning of the Discussion section so readers know about them before reading the findings or (b) the end of the Discussion section, framing them as issues that need further study and modifications. Either way, authors should identify each limitation, concisely explain why it exists, provide reasons why it could not be overcome, assess its impact on findings and conclusions, and, if appropriate, suggest how others can avoid the limitation in the future (Labaree, 2016). As a form of summary, Figure 9.1 identifies the major components to be covered when reporting the methods employed in a qualitative study.

REVIEW AND ENGAGEMENT

When critically reading a research report, you would

- ☐ Determine if the authors thoroughly reported their data analysis protocols, acknowledging if they used an emergent research design and if computer software was employed

- ☐ Check to see that they followed accepted methodological conventions for reporting their data analysis strategies

- ☐ Ascertain if they adequately focused on their coding strategies, if relevant

- ☐ Determine if they reported themes, explained the evidence they accepted, and confined their themes to seven or less

- ☐ Check to see if they noted whether their analytical approach was iterative and if they employed the data analysis spiral principle

- ☐ Determine if they chose to report study limitations at the end of the Methods section instead of at the end of the Discussion section and if this approach made sense

FINAL JUDGMENT ON
QUALITATIVE METHODS SECTION

Taking *all* of the *Review and Engagement* criteria into account, what is your final judgment of the Methods section of the qualitative paper you are critically reading?

CHAPTER SUMMARY

The chapter began by explaining what constitutes an emergent research design, along with strategic versus tactical research designs (see Table 9.1). The discussion turned to the identification and explanation of seven qualitative research designs (see Table 9.2 and Figure 9.2), with examples. The conversation turned to the methods most appropriate for qualitative studies organized by those that help researchers (a) seek to understand phenomena and the meanings people attach to them and (b) focus on power relationships in society (see Table 9.3). The basic steps involved in a qualitative research design (see Figure 9.1) were then used to organize an extensive, wide-ranging, comprehensive profile of qualitative methods. Topics included site selection and access, ethical considerations, the researcher's role, and the iterative and emergent process of data collection and analysis. Table 9.5 identified the criteria used for qualitative research to ensure a high-quality study characterized by rigorous standards and integrity: trustworthy data, subjectivity (confirmability), credibility, transferability, dependability, and authenticity.

REVIEW AND DISCUSSION QUESTIONS

1. Examine the basic steps for conducting and reporting qualitative studies, commenting on the issues of linearity and sequentiality (see Figure 9.1).

2. What was your gut reaction to the idea of an *emergent* research design, compared to a predetermined research design? Had you ever thought of research as both tactical and strategic (see Table 9.1)? Do you agree with attributing these research designs to different scholarly approaches?

3. The chapter reported on seven different qualitative research designs (see Table 9.2 and accompanying text). After carefully reading this material, comment on which approach(es) made the most sense to you, and why.

4. There are many different methods for data collection and analysis that can be employed with the qualitative research methodology (see Table 9.3). How do those focused on understanding phenomena and the meanings people attach to them differ from those focused on power relationships?

5. Why does a qualitative researcher have to include a section on the researcher's role but a quantitative researcher does not?

6. Comment on the ethical considerations of qualitative studies (see Table 9.4).

7. Would it be wrong for authors of qualitative papers to report strategies they used to ensure reliability and validity in their research design? Fully explain your answer (see Table 9.5).

8. What criteria are qualitative researchers supposed to use to ensure a high-quality study? Were you familiar with these before reading this chapter? Were you comfortable with them as sufficient to ensure a high standard of scholarship? Explain your answers.

INTRODUCTION

Chapter 9 addressed the research conventions that authors should follow when conducting and reporting a qualitative study. This chapter continues the conversation about methods with an overview of both quantitative and mixed methods studies. The latter involves a research design that includes both qualitative and quantitative strands. Chapter 8 provides a more general discussion about each of the research designs and methods as part of any research protocol.

QUANTITATIVE RESEARCH DESIGN

Although qualitative research is naturalistic and occurs in the real life of the participants (see Chapter 9), quantitative research designs depend mainly on the *scientific method*, which in turn depends on objective and unbiased *empirical* observations of the world. *Empirical* is Greek *empeiria*, "experience" (Harper, 2016). Quantitative research is referred to as empirical, which means being derived from experiments and observations rather than from theory. In a scientific experiment, researchers manipulate variables and normally employ the principles of randomization and control. Within the quantitative research methodology, *observation* refers to researchers observing natural variations in existing situations.

Scientific Method

The scientific method includes both confirmatory and exploratory science (see Figure 10.1). The *confirmatory scientific method* involves posing and testing hypotheses and models that allow people to describe, explain, and modify the real world. Using estimation and inferential statistics (see Chapter 12), scholars posit causal relations between independent

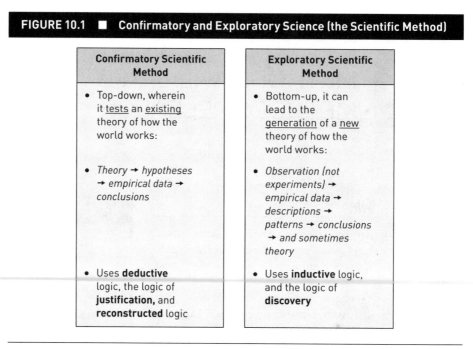

FIGURE 10.1 ■ Confirmatory and Exploratory Science (the Scientific Method)

Confirmatory Scientific Method	Exploratory Scientific Method
• Top-down, wherein it <u>tests</u> an <u>existing</u> theory of how the world works:	• Bottom-up, it can lead to the <u>generation</u> of a <u>new</u> theory of how the world works:
• *Theory → hypotheses → empirical data → conclusions*	• *Observation (not experiments) → empirical data → descriptions → patterns → conclusions → and sometimes theory*
• Uses **deductive** logic, the logic of **justification,** and **reconstructed** logic	• Uses **inductive** logic, and the logic of **discovery**

and dependent variables. When estimating parameters or assessing causal relationships, both random and systematic errors must be minimized. Random errors concern sampling and measurement issues. Systematic errors or biases affect validity (i.e., did the study actually measure what it intended to measure or estimate?). These errors can occur due to (a) bias when sampling, (b) controlling or not controlling for confounding variables, and (c) flawed measurement instruments. Internal validity refers to the integrity of the study (how it *was* conducted), and external validity refers to being able to apply the results *after* the study to a larger population (Azevedo et al., 2011) (see Table 8.5 in Chapter 8).

The *confirmatory approach* to the scientific method is top-down, wherein it tests an existing theory of how the world works (using deductive logic and the *logic of justification*—theory, hypotheses, data, and conclusions). In contrast, the *exploratory scientific method* involves making observations (not experiments), searching for patterns, and then making tentative conclusions or generalizations about how some aspect of the world operates. This bottom-up approach to science is inductive and often leads to theory generation. It follows the *logic of discovery*—observation, empirical data, descriptions, patterns, conclusions, and sometimes theory. Taken together, these two approaches constitute what is known as *the scientific method* (Johnson & Christensen, 2012) (see Figure 10.1).

Deductive Reasoning

When employing the scientific method, scholars use mostly deductive reasoning as they strive for generalization (but they can also employ inductive and abductive [best guess] reasoning) (Ary, Jacobs, & Sorensen, 2010; Azevedo et al., 2011; Kallet, 2004). "Deductive reasoning is the process in which the researcher begins with an established theory or framework, where concepts have already been reduced into variables, and then gathers evidence to assess, or test, whether the theory or framework is supported. Generalization is the extent to which conclusions developed from evidence collected from a sample can be extended to the larger population" (Sousa, Driessnack, & Mendes, 2007, p. 503) (see also Chapter 17 for more information about deductive reasoning).

Types of Quantitative Research Designs

Authors have to clearly and succinctly describe the specific quantitative research design they used in their study. In review, there are two overarching research designs for quantitative studies. *Descriptive studies* (nonexperimental) use a large sample frame, measure subjects once, and strive to establish naturally occurring "associations" between variables. *Experimental studies* include a smaller, random sample, which is measured before and after a treatment, striving to establish "causal" relationships (Labaree, 2016) (see Chapter 12).

In more detail, the seven common quantitative research designs fall into these two camps, experimental and nonexperimental, and are described in detail below (see Figure 10.2 and Table 8.2 in Chapter 8). *Experimental designs* focus on direct, causal relationships while nonexperimental designs focus on associations (Creswell, 2009; Shank & Brown, 2007; Sousa et al., 2007). Experimental designs also vary on how much control the researchers have to manipulate independent variables and on their ability to employ random sampling. *Nonexperimental* quantitative research designs differ among each other on *when* data are collected (one point in time or over time) and the timing of the event being studied (retrospective/past or prospective/future). In a retrospective research design, the researcher studies the current phenomenon by seeking information from the past. In a prospective research design, the opposite occurs. The researcher relates the present to the future by observing a present phenomenon from cause to future effect (Azevedo et al., 2011; Sousa et al., 2007).

Note that Chapter 12 contains a more detailed discussion of the statistical nuances of quantitative research designs, with a more general discussion presented in the following

FIGURE 10.2 ■ Quantitative Research Designs

- Researcher adheres to a formal plan with no deviation

Predetermined Research Design

- Descriptive
- Correlational
- Comparative
- Experimental
- Quasi-experimental
- Predictive exploratory
- Survey (nonexperimental)

Types of Quantitative Research Designs

section, organized from the most to least control over variables and the use of random sampling. This material is prefaced with the following succinct description, using a continuum (from Baltimore County Public Schools, 2015):

> If the researcher views quantitative design as a continuum, one end of the range represents a design where the variables are not controlled at all and only observed [as they naturally occur]. Connections amongst variables are only described [also includes exploratory predictive]. At the other end of the spectrum, however, are designs which include a very close control of variables, and relationships amongst those variables are clearly established [experimental]. In the middle, with experiment design moving from one type to the other, is a range which blends those two extremes together [correlational and comparative].

Descriptive

Descriptive research designs do what the name suggests: They describe what actually exists, determine the frequency with which it occurs, and categorize the information. Usually, little is known about the phenomenon, necessitating a systematic examination. Researchers do not manipulate variables, nor do they search for cause and effect. Instead, they identify characteristics of a group at one point in time or changes over time without exploring the cause and effect of these characteristics. Data derived from a descriptive research design reveal the prevalence of problems, opinions, and other phenomena across an entire population. Examples include the Gallup Poll (public opinions), government census, household expenditure data, and crime statistics. When analyzing descriptive data, analysts determine the central tendency and variability of scores (Gall, Gall, & Borg, 2015) (see Chapter 12). They normally do not begin with a hypothesis, but their results may provide the basis for potential hypotheses that direct subsequent correlational, experimental, or quasi-experimental designs (Baltimore County Public Schools, 2015; de Vaus, 2001; Gall et al., 2015; Sousa et al., 2007).

> ***Example 10.1 Descriptive*** Examples of descriptive studies include a description of the tobacco habits of teenagers, the attitudes of scientists toward climate change, or the kinds of physical activities in nursing homes and how often they occur (Baltimore County Public Schools, 2015). Shank and Brown (2007) provided an example of a study that examined children's views on global warming and what social and situational factors might influence those views. The researchers used a survey, and children were queried on issues concerning awareness, concern, perceived responsibility, and self-efficacy (these factors formed the dependent variable). The results *described* the children along these four psychological dimensions and tendered recommendations for curricular changes.

Correlational

Unlike an experimental design, which seeks causal links, a nonexperimental, *correlational design* seeks *associations*—hence, the name *correlated*. To cause means to produce an effect. To relate means to be connected, but not in a causal manner (Anderson, 2014); when a correlation has been established, researchers have to *infer* cause (de Vaus, 2001).

"Simply because one event follows another, or two factors co-vary, does not mean that one causes the other" (de Vaus, 2001, p. 3). Instead of determining whether a change in one or more variables *causes* a change in another, a correlational design examines whether a change in one or more variables is *related* to changes in another (Sousa et al., 2007). Correlational research does not look at *differences between* groups or what causes them; rather, it looks for *relationships within* a single group. Also, researchers test the null hypothesis, but independent variables are not manipulated; rather, they are identified and studied as they occur naturally in a setting (Baltimore County Public Schools, 2015; Gall et al., 2015).

The whole purpose of using correlations in research is to figure out which variables are connected or interact with each other—that is, naturally associated. When people see one variable changing, they can have an idea of how the other will change. Correlational research often entails the researchers using variables they cannot control, meaning they are naturally occurring.

> ***Example 10.2 Correlational*** A researcher could be studying how grade level and age affect students' predispositions to like or dislike the science curriculum. Both grade level and age are naturally occurring, meaning students are the age they are and in the grade they are in. These independent variables cannot be manipulated. Researchers cannot make students older or younger, and they cannot switch them to higher or lower grade levels.

These nonexperimental correlational designs (employing statistical procedures and continuous data) are used in situations where it is either impossible (see example 10.2) or unethical to manipulate the independent variables (e.g., a study on addictive drug use). For this reason, most correlational statistical procedures are not statistically powerful enough to justify causal interpretations. This leaves only associations (i.e., descriptions of the extent of the relationship between variables). However, associations are often used to generate hypotheses for experimental and quasi-experimental studies. Correlational designs often generate scattergrams and coefficients gleaned from the Pearson product-moment correlation, the Spearman rank-order correlation, or linear regressions (Gall et al., 2015; Raulin & Graziano, 1994; Sousa et al., 2007) (see Chapter 12).

Comparative

Comparative designs *are* experiments, but there is no random assignment to the groups; instead, researchers use already formed groups (e.g., classrooms, organizations, or family units). Also, comparative designs are variable oriented, but researchers cannot manipulate the independent variables; rather, they can only measure variables that occur naturally and then *compare* them to determine their influence on the dependent variable. They rely on naturally occurring variations rather than on intentional manipulations that cause variation. For example, researchers might obtain their sample from preexisting rural and urban settings rather than creating rural and urban settings. A comparative design uses discrete data (fixed values determined by *counting*), unlike correlational designs, which use continuous data (different values between two points determined by *measuring*) (Gall et al., 2015; Suter, 2012).

As with experimental designs (see next), when using a comparative design, researchers pose hypotheses (or research questions) about the differences in variables and then *compare* different groups or variables to explain *presumed causes* for the differences—that is, *possible* cause-and-effect relationships. Common statistical tests include the *t* test, the chi-square test, the Mann-Whitney *U* test, the Wilcoxon signed-rank test, and the Kruskal-Wallis test (Gall et al., 2015; Shank & Brown, 2007; Sousa et al., 2007; Suter, 2012).

Example 10.3 Comparative Shank and Brown (2007) recounted a study where researchers *compared* students' performance when taking multiple-choice exams in five different course units on their own ratings of factors that might affect their test performance (including student effort to prepare for exams, student ability to perform well on exams, and teacher input). Researchers could not control any of these variables; they could just measure and compare them. They found that while student ability and teacher input correlated most strongly with exam performance, students rated their own effort to prepare for exams as the most important factor. Appreciating this incongruence, the researchers concluded that students' perception of teacher input must be included in any assessment of what shapes their exam performance. Even though students did not see it as important, it was *presumably causing* them to fail or pass the tests.

Experimental

The word *experiment* stems from Latin *experri*, "to try" (Harper, 2016). These studies are called experiments because a scientific procedure (method) is undertaken *to try* to make a discovery, test a hypothesis, or demonstrate a known fact (Anderson, 2014). *Experimental designs* strive to confirm or disconfirm a researcher's predictions (in the form of hypotheses) of the effects of treatments or interventions. A *true experiment* involves (a) obtaining a sample, (b) randomly assigning people to a control group (does not receive the treatment) and a treatment group, and (c) determining if the variation in treatment (independent variables) had an effect on the dependent variable. In an experimental design, researchers control extraneous variables, manipulate independent variables, measure any changes in the dependent variable, and infer causal links (Creswell, 2009; Shank & Brown, 2007) (see Chapter 11).

Generally speaking, when using experimental designs, researchers can (a) compare two or more groups (*between-subject design*), often using *factorial designs*; (b) study only one group (*within-group design*) using a common approach called *repeated measures* (people in the group are assigned to different treatments during the experiment); or (c) study one person (*single-subject design*) over time, whereby the treatment is administered and then withheld to determine its impact. These strategies often include some sort of *pretest-posttest design* (Creswell, 2009) (see Chapter 12). Researchers usually predict, in advance (via hypotheses), the impact they expect from the treatment or the intervention and then determine if their results either confirm or deny their predictions (Shank & Brown, 2007).

Example 10.4 Experimental Dr. Sandy Brown hypothesized that Drug X will cause a decrease in anxiety. She collected a random sample of 600 individuals who completed a baseline assessment and were found to have high levels of anxiety. She divided them into three groups. The first was the control group, which received a sugar pill every day (no drug). The second group was given a low dose of Drug X each day (100 mg), and the third group received a 250-mg dose each day (these two are the experimental groups). After recording results for two months, Dr. Brown analyzed her data and determined that those who were in the experimental groups had a *statistically significant* decrease in anxiety. She also found that the anxiety level of those receiving the higher dose decreased much faster than that of those in the low dose group and the control group. She concluded that Drug X *causes* a reduction in anxiety, as she had hypothesized (Williams, 2016).

Quasi-experimental

When researchers have to use *existing* groups (e.g., classroom, organization, or family unit), they cannot randomly assign people because they already belong to the group. So, the researcher uses convenience sampling, and the research design is called a *quasi-experiment* (*quasi* meaning almost). Like the true experiment (see example 10.4), this study design still employs an experimental and control group, in that one experiences the condition and one does not (Creswell, 2009).

> *Example 10.5 Quasi-experimental* Imagine a researcher who wants to study the effects of a natural disaster on people's health. The former (the national disaster) cannot be manipulated, but researchers can compare the health status of those who experienced a disaster with those who did not. But a word of caution. Because of nonrandom sampling, authors have to be cautious with their causal inferences (Raulin & Graziano, 1994).

Examples of quasi-experimental research designs include (a) *nonequivalent control groups* (naturally occurring groups), (b) *differential research* designs (classify existing groups and then look for differences between them), (c) *interrupted time-series* designs (measure a single natural group several times before and after an intervention), and (d) *single-subject* designs (expose one person to all interventions at different points in time) (Raulin & Graziano, 1994).

Predictive exploratory

Shank and Brown (2007) identified a fifth option, which they called an *exploratory design* (they also referred to this as a *quantitative predictive design*). Authors would identify, measure, and then compare important variables in attempts to *explore* how they may be used to eventually develop data-based models of a particular phenomenon. The primary focus of predictive exploratory research is to predict some variable of interest using information from other variables (called predictors). The development of the proper set of predictors for a given variable is often the focus of such studies (Belli, 2009).

> *Example 10.6 Predictive exploratory* In one such study, the researcher used an *exploratory process* to collect a series of data relevant to the academic performance of male juvenile offenders to see if she could build an effective predictive model based on these data (peer support ratings, missed homework, victim awareness survey, part-time employment, positive drug testing, and grade point average [GPA]). From five predictor variables, she identified, via factor analysis, two *main predictive factors*: (a) responsible student behavior and (b) social awareness. She concluded that the ability to use these data to create a model of both assessment and intervention remains to be *explored* (discussed by Shank & Brown, 2007).

Survey design (nonexperimental)

Finally, *surveys* are an important quantitative research design, but they are not experiments in the true sense because they do not have comparison groups, random assignment to those groups, or manipulation of variables. Instead, there is a natural assignment to groups being studied, and the intervention or condition being examined has already happened naturally rather than being imposed or manipulated (Sousa et al., 2007). Surveys or questionnaires provide numeric *descriptions* of attributes of a population by studying a random sample of that population (convenience sampling is acceptable but less desirable than random). The survey design strategy includes cross-sectional data collected at one point in time or longitudinal data collected over time, both using questionnaires and/or structured interview instruments (accounting for validity and reliability; see Table 8.5 in Chapter 8). The data are analyzed using descriptive and/or inferential statistics (see Chapter 12), with the intent to generalize from a sample to a population (Creswell, 2009).

Example 10.7 Survey design In their 1980 study, Bean and Creswell used a survey instrument to study the factors affecting student attrition in a small liberal arts college. After obtaining a sample of 169 women students, they reported their characteristics (descriptive sample information). They used a survey instrument (called a questionnaire) that had been developed and tested three times at other institutions (accounting for its validity and the reliability of the research design at other sites). The 116-item Likert-like survey instrument (with questions also designed to capture factual information pertaining to GPA, ACT scores, and such) was administered to the sample frame. The Likert items were based on scale from "a very small extent" to "a very great extent." The data were exposed to a factor analysis (inferential statistics) to determine concurrent and convergent validity. Multiple regression and path analysis were then used to analyze the data, leading to a causal model about factors affecting female student attrition from a small liberal arts college.

REVIEW AND ENGAGEMENT

When critically reading a research report, you would

☐ Determine if the authors clearly identified which of the seven main research designs was employed in the study (see Figure 10.2 and Table 8.2 in Chapter 8)

☐ Judge whether what they did actually reflected the research design that they specified (e.g., did not use a survey instrument and call it an experiment)

☐ Ascertain if they seemed aware of the difference between how experimental and nonexperimental research designs handle randomization and variable manipulation

☐ Per the above, glean if they appreciated the difference between naturally occurring (already formed or existing) variables and experimental variables

☐ Ascertain if they seemed aware of the difference between how experimental and nonexperimental research designs handle association versus causal relations (see also Chapter 12)

☐ Confirm if they justified the research design they used relative to their research question

Integrity (Rigor) of Quantitative Research Designs

Quantitative researchers have to ensure that their data are reliable (they can be replicated in another study) and valid (the study measured what was intended to be measured), with results generalizable to those outside the study (Ary et al., 2010). Terminology or nomenclature for issues of rigor in quantitative research is very consistent (Suter, 2012). Table 10.1 provides an overview of the most agreed-to approaches and terms used by quantitative researchers, with attendant strategies to meet the standards for this research methodology (Ary et al., 2010; Creswell & Miller, 2000; Guba, 1981; Johnson & Christensen, 2012; Lincoln, 1995; Nahrin, 2015; Newman, Newman, & Newman, 2011; Shenton, 2004). This table addresses issues of unbiased data, objectivity, internal validity, external validity, reliability, and generalization.

TABLE 10.1 ■ Criteria to Ensure High-Quality Quantitative Research

Quantitative (Positivistic, Empirical, Deterministic)	
Striving for **unbiased data** (results are *true* if no bias was introduced, made possible if the researcher's personal preferences, prejudices, and opinions are held at bay during the entire research process).	*Strategies:* judiciously address issues of internal validity to ensure that the study design, implementation, and data analysis is bias free, yielding high levels of evidence of cause and effect (or association); employ representative and random sampling techniques; account for missing and incomplete data; acknowledge funding sources.
Objectivity: Empirical research is said to be *value free*, meaning the research process should not be influenced by the *researcher's* emotions, preferences, or personal prejudices. Researchers are supposed to dispassionately engage in research from a stance of *value neutrality*, thereby ensuring the truth is found. Judgments about the evidence should not coincide with the researcher's orientation (despite that science is not really neutral; relative value neutrality is more likely than absolute neutrality).	*Strategies:* embrace the tenets of the scientific method and empirical inquiry; do not distort research or let one's values intrude by drawing on personal worldviews, motives, self-interest, or customs or by capitulating to external pressures (researchers are especially vulnerable to value intrusion during the interpretation and discussion stage).
Internal validity: This refers to the integrity of the research design. The word *internal* pertains to the inner workings of the research process, designed and conducted to ensure that the researcher measured what was intended to be measured (producing strong, valid data instead of weak, invalid data). Also, the research design should follow the principle of cause and effect. There are seven major threats to internal validity (i.e., measuring something other than what was intended): (a) contamination by an extraneous event (history effect); (b) participants aging or tiring (maturation	*Strategies:* take steps necessary to mitigate threats to internal validity (e.g., account for contamination, maturation, attrition, sampling size, group formation and assignment, instrumentation alignment, and testing sensitization).

(Continued)

TABLE 10.1 ■ (Continued)

Quantitative (Positivistic, Empirical, Deterministic)	
effect); (c) loss of subjects or attrition between testing (mortality effect); (d) sensitizing subjects with a pretest (testing effect); (e) extremely high or low pretest scores (statistical regression effect); (f) subjects are not carefully assigned to test groups (selection bias effect); and (g) unreliability of an assessment instrument (instrumentation effect).	
External validity (asserted by the researcher): Does the truth (conclusions) from the study hold in situations *outside* the study? Researchers have to ask, "How similar is my study to the situation I want to generalize to?" (meaning make a broad statement from a specific case). If too dissimilar, their results and conclusions are not externally valid; that is, they do not *hold true* for other situations (based on statistical assumptions).	***Strategies:*** *Judiciously choose an appropriate research design protocol (especially sample size and bias). Then, before asserting that the results are valid in other populations, situations, and conditions, researchers must recognize, consider, and report on factors that mitigate these assertions, notably any interactions (a) among treatment and subjects, settings, and history as well as (b) between subjects and settings. Researchers often temper their assertions by setting out study limitations.*
Reliability (of the instrument and methods): Refers to the extent to which someone else can follow the research design with the same sample and get the same results. Are the methods reproducible and consistent, and is sufficient information provided so others can repeat the approach and procedures? To what extent are variations controlled? The *reliability of the instrument* depends on six types of validity: (a) face validity (subjects think the test is measuring what it is supposed to measure); (b) expert judges think the test is valid; (c) test items actually contain content being measured; (d) compare a new test with a previously validated test (concurrent validity); (e) taking a test is good prediction of a score when the test is taken again in the future (predictive validity); and (f) construct validity (a mix of all of the others—did the test measure the intended higher-order construct and nothing else related to it, determined by how the variables are operationalized?).	***Strategies:*** *standardized administration of instrument or procedure; internal consistency (i.e., ensure instrument items are actually measuring the underlying construct, reflected in Cronbach's alpha); increase number of test items; use objective scoring; test-retest; ensure that two different forms of one test measure the same thing.*
Generalizability (breadth of applicability): Researchers want to make broad statements from their specific case (they used a small random sample from a whole population). They want their conclusions to hold for others *not* in their study. Based on statistical assumptions, generalizability refers to the extent to which results and conclusions can be applied to people, settings, or conditions *beyond* those represented in the study.	***Strategies:*** *account for external validity.*

Quantitative Instrument, Procedures, and Apparatus

Figure 10.3 provides an overview of the major components of the quantitative Methods section of a research paper. The conversation begins here with instrument, procedures, and apparatus.

Authors of quantitative research papers have to identify and describe any instruments, procedures, or apparatus they used to collect data from their sample. These may involve survey instruments, questionnaires, tests, experiments, intervention protocols, predeveloped and validated assessment tools, or any materials or special devices (mechanical or electronic) designed for the study. Examples of the latter include software, drugs, machines, mechanical models, or visual stimuli. Authors have to provide sufficient details so that readers can evaluate the relevance of and/or duplicate the procedures. At a minimum, authors have to make a statement saying the procedural details are available upon request. If the research involved a complicated protocol, authors may want to include a diagram, table, or flowchart. They also need to convince readers that their instruments and such were validated to ensure they are measuring what they intended to measure (see Table 10.1). And authors should provide their rationale and assumptions for any experimental procedures used in the study. The Methods section may make reference to appendices that contain key aspects of the research design protocol (Azevedo et al., 2011; Dillinger, 2011; Kallet, 2004; Newman & Newman, 2011).

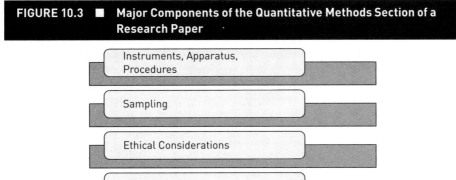

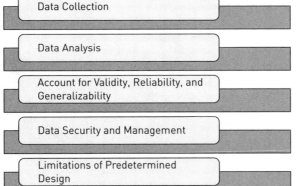

FIGURE 10.3 ■ Major Components of the Quantitative Methods Section of a Research Paper

Instruments, Apparatus, Procedures

Sampling

Ethical Considerations

Data Collection

Data Analysis

Account for Validity, Reliability, and Generalizability

Data Security and Management

Limitations of Predetermined Design

Quantitative Variables

Authors need to identify the variables they measured, manipulated, and controlled for in their study. Respectively, these are the dependent, independent, extraneous, and modifier variables. These variables are discussed in much more detail in Chapter 11. Authors especially need to account for independent variables and any other variable of particular importance to the study. They should provide both *conceptual* and *operational definitions* of all variables. While the former definition type is considered fairly standard for the phenomenon in question, the latter includes steps taken by the researchers to manipulate a specific variable in *their* study. Operational definitions tell the reader exactly what was done to manipulate a variable. For example, saying the room was made really dark is too vague. If people want to replicate the study, they need to know exactly how dark and how the illumination was changed (e.g., dimming the lights, closing the blinds) (Ary et al., 2010; Azevedo et al., 2011).

> *Example 10.8 Conceptual and operational definitions* Imagine a study focused on how happiness is affected by stress. The dependent variable, happiness, is *conceptually defined* as a state of well-being characterized by emotions ranging from contentment to intense joy. In one study, the researcher *operationalized* stress (the independent variable that is manipulated) as exposing subjects to extended blasts of loud music. Another researcher operationalized stress as placing subjects in a traffic jam, making them late for an important appointment. Both measured how stress affects happiness, but they differed on how they exposed subjects to stress (i.e., how they put it into operation).

Operational definitions also ensure that all readers interpret the study from a similar frame and use common definitions. Authors should make sure *their* hypothesis states there is a relationship between happiness and stress as measured by such and such (Newman & Newman, 2011). Finally, because no single operational definition of an abstract concept can encompass that concept completely, authors also have to discuss how their operationalization of an independent variable yielded a *valid* measure of the phenomenon (Ary et al., 2010; Azevedo et al., 2011) (see Table 10.1).

> *Example 10.9 Operational validity* In their study on whether people enjoyed a movie, researchers decided to operationalize this concept by standing outside a movie theater and counting the number of people smiling as they exited the movie. Although this may indeed be a measure of whether people enjoyed the movie, they could be smiling for so many other reasons. This is not a strong operationalization of this variable because validity is likely not ensured. The researchers may actually be measuring something else entirely—that is, some other construct. Maybe someone inside the theater told each departing person that they were going to receive a free ticket because they attended the movie. In this case, the researcher may actually be measuring people's gratitude and surprise at the theater's marketing strategy, rather than if they liked the movie.

REVIEW AND ENGAGEMENT

When critically reading a research report, you would

☐ Ascertain if the authors used methodology-specific headings to organize their quantitative Methods section (see Figure 10.3) and fully accounted for and shared their research design

☐ Determine if they set out a well-articulated and sufficiently discussed set of procedures, tasks, and instruments that can be consistently replicated and reapplied in other studies

☐ Confirm that they accounted for the key variables in their study, providing both conceptual and operational definitions

☐ See if they clearly distinguished between conceptual and operational definitions of their variables, citing relevant research when necessary

☐ Determine if they discussed the operational validity of the variables used in their study (i.e., confirm what they did to manipulate the variables to ensure they measured what they intended to measure) (see Table 10.1)

Quantitative Sampling

In their Methods section, authors have to explain how they obtained their sample from the full population. They have two options once they have chosen their *target population*. They can employ *probability sampling* (using chance procedures, meaning everyone in the population has a chance of being chosen) and *nonprobability sampling* (not chosen using chance procedures). If they employed probability sampling, authors have to explain whether they used *random*, *stratified*, *cluster*, or *systematic* sampling or some combination. If they employed nonprobability sampling, they have to justify their use of either *convenience*, *purposive*, or *quota* sampling (described previously under sampling for qualitative research) (Ary et al., 2010) (see Figure 10.4).

Probability sampling

Random sampling is the best known and most ideal, preferred sampling procedure for quantitative research. Statistically, random means equal chances for each item (Anderson, 2014). When opting for random sampling, researchers are trying to select their subjects in a way that the researcher's biases are not permitted to operate. "They are pledging to avoid a deliberate selection of subjects who will confirm the hypothesis" (Ary et al., 2010, p. 151). With random sampling, chance alone dictates who is included in the study. Chance is defined as the occurrence of an event in the absence of an obvious design; that is, the study is not subjected to the biases of the researcher (remember, quantitative research is intended to be bias free and objective, as shown in Table 10.1). Subjects or participants can be randomly selected by the roll of a die, the flip of a coin, drawing names, drawing or assigning numbers, or via a random number generator (Creswell, 2009; Johnson & Christensen, 2012; Wiersma & Jurs, 2009). An example of the

FIGURE 10.4 ■ Quantitative Sampling Strategies

Probability Sampling

- **Random sampling** means equal chances for each item or subject to be selected (chance mitigates researcher's bias)
- **Stratified sampling** involves identifying several strata (subgroups) and randomly drawing from each one
- **Cluster sampling** involves breaking the population into clusters or groups that are outwardly similar (they are from same population) but are inwardly different
- **Systematic sampling** entails taking every *k*th case from the entire list of the population

NonProbability Sampling

- **Convenience sampling** means subjects are selected because of their convenient accessibility and proximity to the researcher
- **Purposive sampling** means selecting people *on purpose* because they can best provide information to answer the research question
- **Quota sampling** involves deciding ahead of time how many people are needed that meet specific characteristics, and then recruiting until quota is filled

latter is *Research Randomizer*, www.randomizer.org (Urbaniak & Plous, 2013). Sometimes researchers enumerate all the individuals in a population and then employ a table of random numbers to draw their sample (Ary et al., 2010).

When simple random sampling is not feasible or appropriate for the research question, there are three common alternative approaches. *Stratified sampling* involves identifying several strata (subgroups) within a population and then randomly drawing a sample from each stratum. For example, researchers may divide an adolescent population into three groups based on the size of the towns in which they live (small, medium, and large) and then draw randomly from each sized town. Researchers can use *cluster sampling* when they want to use random sampling but the population is too large to enumerate. Instead, they would choose a group of people clustered naturally together. For example, instead of sampling all high school students in the United States, researchers could get a list of all of the schools, randomly select a few schools from this list, and then use all students in those schools. Finally, *systematic sampling* involves taking every *k*th case from the entire list of the population. If the list is randomized, the sample can statistically be considered a reasonable substitute for a random sample. But if the list is not in random order, the resultant sample would not be representative of the population (Ary et al., 2010).

Random assignment

If the study being reported is an experiment, and the authors intend to generalize to the wider population, they have to explain how they randomly assigned people to groups before they were exposed to the treatment or intervention. Random assignment requires a chance procedure as well. It usually involves using a table of random numbers to divide subjects into groups, and then another chance procedure (e.g., a coin toss) is used to decide who gets the treatment and who is in the control group (no treatment). This procedure ensures the groups are statistically equivalent *before* the experiment or intervention begins (Ary et al., 2010).

Sample size and representativeness

Authors have to report and justify the size of their sample. They should use an uppercase N for the whole sample and a lowercase n when referring to parts of the sample. For example, "One third ($n = 15$) of the entire sample ($N = 45$) was insolvent." Actually, the *representativeness* of the sample is more important than its size. "A random sample of 200 is better than a random sample of 100, but a random sample of 100 is better than a biased sample of 2.5 million" (Ary et al., 2010, p. 157). They go on to explain that *statistical power calculations* are the best way to determine how big a sample needs to be to be representative of the population. Without going into statistical details in this chapter, suffice it to say that determining the number needed in a sample "is really a function of how precise you want to be—that is, how large or small an effect size you want to be statistically significant, how much chance of a Type I error you are willing to live with, and how much probability of rejecting a false null hypothesis you want" (Ary et al., 2010, p. 169) (see Chapter 12).

Type I and II errors are discussed in Chapter 12 on statistics, as is the topic of what constitutes rejecting a null hypothesis. To clarify, *effect size* is a number that indicates the difference between two groups on a particular variable. For example, it could be the degree to which participants in the experimental group show superior performance compared to the control group. If the effect size is large (i.e., if the magnitude of the difference is large), the test of statistical significance will have the power to reject the null (Gall et al., 2015). Finally, "Cohen's 1988 book is the standard reference for determining the minimum sample size for the different statistical tests" (Gall et al., 2015, p. 169). Researchers determine ahead of time their desired effect size, consult Cohen's book to determine minimum sample size, and then proceed to obtain their sample. More details are provided in Chapter 12.

Quantitative Ethical Considerations

Harris (2014) observed that in empirical research reports, ethics is often "given short shrift" (p. 85). This lack of attention to ethics in an article is unfortunate because, as a general rule, when human participants are involved, researchers have to follow the rules and procedures of their institution, and these are usually in keeping with federal regulations (Wiersma & Jurs, 2009). To offset readers' doubts about the research ethics of a particular study, if humans are involved in quantitative research, authors should at least include a statement asserting that their research design was approved by an institutional review board (IRB) or a research ethics board (REB) at their institution, funding agency, or other organization (e.g., school board). Authors should also comment on how they dealt with any ethical issues that arose and were not addressed in their approved research design protocol (Labaree, 2016).

Shamoo and Resnik (2015) discussed ethical considerations when conducting empirical, quantitative research (see Table 10.2). Collectively, these principles ensure the well-being of human participants and guarantee their rights before, during, and after the study (Creswell, 2009; Suter, 2012). As with qualitative studies, authors do not need to report these issues in their paper because the IRB or similar statement suffices (Johnson & Christensen, 2012). What matters is that "with consideration to participants, research sites, and potential readers [and users], studies can be designed that contain ethical practices" (Creswell, 2009, p. 93), and that design intent should be reported in the paper.

TABLE 10.2 ■ Ethical Considerations for Quantitative Research

Honesty—do not fabricate, falsify, suppress, or misrepresent data. Do not deceive participants (withhold or mislead, unless justified to answer the research question).

Data integrity—alert potential users of the limits of the data's reliability and applicability; researchers should not exaggerate the accuracy or statistical explanatory power of their data.

Objectivity—interpret and present results objectively (bias free).

Fairness and truthfulness—be fair and truthful when applying the scientific method.

Informed consent, respect for human dignity—tell participants about the study (purpose, procedures, risks, and benefits) and give them the opportunity to voluntarily participate or decline (avoid coercion); ensure they can withdraw with no penalty.

Humane consideration of participants—be civilized, compassionate, and moral and show intellectual concern.

Protect participants from undue intrusion, distress, indignity, physical discomfort, personal embarrassment, or other forms of harm and risk.

Confidentiality, anonymity, privacy—protect the identity of participants in the study (unless they give permission otherwise).

Properly train all research personnel (especially for clinical trials and experiments).

REVIEW AND ENGAGEMENT

When critically reading a research report, you would

☐ Ascertain which of the common quantitative sampling approaches the authors used

☐ Determine if they clearly articulated the steps they took to minimize both bias and randomization errors (especially when sampling [representativeness] and assigning to groups)

☐ Confirm that they discussed the issues of Type I or Type II errors and explained how they dealt with these by focusing on sample size and effect size to ensure statistical power (see also Chapter 12)

☐ Check that they adequately addressed ethical considerations (see Table 10.2), with a minimum IRB statement

Quantitative Data Collection

Quantitative data are numbers. Once the sample is secured, researchers have to collect data (numbers) from the sample frame, using any instruments, procedures, and apparatus designed or procured for their study. Typical data collection strategies for quantitative studies include experiments; clinical trials; computer simulations; observing, counting, and recording well-defined events; obtaining data from information management systems; and administering surveys with closed-ended and/or open-ended questions (via paper-based, face-to-face, telephone, Web-based, or wireless devices). Other data collection methods include positivistic case studies and content analyses (see Newman & Newman, 2011).

Data collected by the researchers in order to address their research question are called primary data. Some empirical studies also entail secondary data, which were collected previously by someone else and not for this particular research question. Good examples are census data and national longitudinal survey and panel data like the *Labour Force Survey*, the *Survey of Family, Income, and Employment*, or *Americans' Changing Lives*. Researchers manipulate these preexisting statistical data using computational techniques (using computers for something otherwise tedious or unsolvable by hand calculations). Regardless of the form of data but especially for primary data, authors should provide information about when the data were collected, where, and by whom (e.g., themselves, coresearchers, or trained assistants) and indicate if their instrument was pilot tested before its final implementation. A pilot test is a small-scale trial that helps identify issues with instructions, unclear items, formatting issues, typographical errors, and/or other issues (Labaree, 2016; Newman & Newman, 2011).

> ***Example 10.10 Quantitative data collection*** For this study, five equally trained research assistants observed four classrooms each, dispersed throughout four schools in the Smith Falls School Division (i.e., 20 classrooms in total, 5 in each school). Data were collected during school hours in the spring of 2015, during the months of March to May. Each of the 20 observation sessions lasted one hour. The research assistants used a predeveloped, standardized, and pilot-tested observation checklist that had been validated by a panel of experts.

Quantitative Validity and Reliability

Authors of quantitative, empirical studies must report on the validity of their study design (internal and external) and the reliability of their procedures and instruments. People need to be able to trust that researchers measured what they intended to measure, that there is sufficient information for them to replicate the study, and that the results can be generalized beyond the study. Authors have to identify which type of validity and reliability they built into their research design and which strategies they took to ensure their study met conventional standards of rigor for the quantitative, positivistic research approach (see Table 10.1 for extensive details on this very important part of a quantitative paper). Because judging the strength of an empirical research design requires identifying threats to validity and reliability, authors have to convince readers that the steps they took to address these were the most preferable design choice given their circumstances

(Newman & Newman, 2011). Any limitations created by these research design decisions must be addressed in the Limitations section, which follows the Discussion section.

Quantitative Data Analysis

Because quantitative data are numbers, they are analyzed using descriptive statistics, inferential statistics, or both. Chapter 12 discusses this topic in extensive detail. At a minimum, when writing their Analysis section for a quantitative paper, authors need to identify which statistical procedure(s) was used to analyze their data, whether regression analyses, analyses of variance (ANOVAs), multivariate analyses of variance (MANOVAs), structural equation modeling, hierarchical linear modeling, multiple discriminant analysis, multidimensional scaling, or some combination. If employed, they must identify which statistical software program was used (e.g., SPSS, SAS, LISREL, Minitab, Excel) (Johnson & Christensen, 2012; Newman & Newman, 2011; Shank & Brown, 2007).

As appropriate, authors should report the p value (level of significance), degrees of freedom (df), F value, t value, mean squares (MS), sum of squares (SS), confidence intervals, and correlations (r). These stats are often indicated in tables or as footnotes to tables, as particular results are reported. Ideally, authors would provide a power analysis that justified the effect size used for the study, if appropriate (see previous section on sample size and representativeness) (Johnson & Christensen, 2012; Newman & Newman, 2011; Shank & Brown, 2007).

If descriptive statistics were used, authors should report such things as sample size, frequencies, percentages, means, medium, mode, range, standard deviations (SD), z scores, chi-square (χ^2) test, and simple correlations (r) (Johnson & Christensen, 2012; Newman & Newman, 2011; Shank & Brown, 2007). If relevant, authors should explain how they handled *missing data* and why the absence of these data did not undermine the validity of their analysis (see Chapter 13). They should also explain how they *cleaned* their data set, which involves detecting and correcting (or removing) corrupt, incomplete, irrelevant, or inaccurate parts of the data set (Labaree, 2016). Overall, authors must provide a solid rationale for their statistical design choices and cite supportive literature for their data analysis decisions (Newman & Newman, 2011). They also need to know their reading audience and decide whether statistically sophisticated detail is appropriate or if they need to simplify things and educate their readers (Goodson, 2017; Harris, 2014).

Quantitative Study Limitations

Discussed in more detail in Chapters 6 and 14, limitations are those aspects of a study that are beyond the researcher's control but impact validity (internal and external) and reliability. Things such as sampling, measurement and instrument errors, inadequate statistical power, group selection or assignment bias, and experimental and treatment effects have to be reported in the study. These research design issues can affect generalizability to subjects beyond the current study. To facilitate reporting them in the Discussion section, authors need to identify each limitation, concisely explain why it exists, provide reasons why it could not be overcome, assess its impact on results and conclusions, and, if appropriate, suggest how others can avoid the limitation in future studies (Labaree, 2016).

REVIEW AND ENGAGEMENT

When critically reading a research report, you would

- ☐ Determine if the authors clearly explained their data collection procedures (e.g., experiment, survey, or clinical trial)

- ☐ Check to see if they clearly distinguished between primary and secondary data, with rationales

- ☐ Determine whether they provided a solid rationale for their statistical design choices and cited supportive literature for their data collection and data analysis decisions

- ☐ Confirm that they identified which statistical procedure(s) was used to analyze their data (e.g., ANOVA) and any statistical software programs

- ☐ Determine that, for inferential statistics, the authors reported the basic conventions related to explaining the statistical significance of their data (especially p values and df)

- ☐ Determine that, for descriptive statistics, the authors reported the basic conventions related to explaining the statistical significance of their data (e.g., means, chi-square, or coefficients)

- ☐ Judge whether they used a reporting style that respected the statistical prowess of their likely audience

FINAL JUDGMENT ON QUANTITATIVE METHODS SECTION

Taking *all* of the ***Review and Engagement*** criteria into account, what is your final judgment of the quantitative Methods section of the paper you are critically reading?

MIXED METHODS RESEARCH DESIGN

In some instances, the research question is best answered with data collected from a combination of quantitative and qualitative *methods*. Most research methods textbooks now contain either a separate chapter or an integrated discussion of the advisedness and nuances of employing mixed methods. It is "recognized as the third major research approach or *research paradigm*, along with qualitative research and quantitative research" (Johnson, Onwuegbuzie, & Turner, 2007, p. 112). Mixed methods research has become a desirable approach in its own right (Bryman, 2008), despite the challenge of keeping in mind all of the conflicting philosophical underpinnings and assumptions (Newman et al., 2011) (see Chapter 2).

Philosophical Quandary

Indeed, Chapter 2 addressed the nomenclature of this research approach, examining whether it should be called *mixed methodologies* (mixing axioms) or *mixed methods* (mixing data collection and analysis strategies). This is a philosophical quandary because any research question mirrors a philosophy (methodology), which in turn dictates appropriate methods. For example, asking people what meaning they attach to being insolvent is not the same research question as asking how many people are insolvent, what type of debt they hold, and how much. The former question is postpositivistic, interpretive, and qualitative, best answered by using participants' words. The latter question is positivistic, empirical, and quantitative, best answered by using numbers and statistics.

Despite this philosophical quandary, "there is increasing awareness that both methodologies can be used in a single study to address the same research question . . . or related research questions" (Gall et al., 2015, p. 475). One thing is certain: "The term *mixed methods* applies only to studies that employ both quantitative and qualitative methods" (Gall et al., 2015, p. 479). And the term refers only to instances when qualitative and quantitative methods are used within a *single* research project or study (Driessnack, Sousa, & Mendes, 2007b).

For clarification, a study that employs two quantitative methods (e.g., survey and experiment) or two qualitative methods (e.g., case study and grounded theory) cannot be called mixed methods because the study falls within only one research methodology. Also, if the findings from a qualitative study (e.g., thematic analysis) are required to develop a different quantitative study (e.g., a survey), this cannot be reported as a mixed methods design. They have to be part of the *same* phased study, addressing one research question. Authors need to be cognizant of these distinctions so they do not mislabel their research design. "Being able to identify the characteristics of the study that make it mixed methods and giving the design a specific name conveys to readers the rigors of their study" (Creswell, Plano Clark, Gutmann, & Hanson, 2003, p. 162).

Mixed Methods Main Research Designs

"If abstract patterns of numbers [statistics] can tell us one thing about a phenomenon, what will a set of verbal descriptions tell us that we could not get from abstractions? If a compelling narrative illustrates an important [subjective] point, what happens when we try to nail down the particulars of that point using objective methods?" (Shank & Brown, 2007, p. 190). To address this issue, three major mixed methods research designs have evolved over time. Researchers can use (a) qualitative methods to explain quantitative data (words to explain numbers) or (b) quantitative methods to further explain qualitative data (numbers to explain words). In effect, "words can add meaning to numbers and numbers can add precision to words" (Suter, 2012, p. 370). Researchers can also use (c) both methods to achieve triangulation (Creswell et al., 2003; Driessnack et al., 2007b; Shank & Brown, 2007). Triangulation entails using multiple data sources in an investigation to produce understanding. The idea is that researchers can be more confident with a result or finding if different methods lead to the same result or finding.

Example 10.11 Main mixed methods research designs

- Qualitative data could be used to create a theoretical framework (via the grounded theory method). Researchers could then conduct a quantitative study to test or extend the new theory and report both methods in one paper.

- Using quantitative methods, researchers could statistically analyze their survey data and then use qualitative methods to explain the existence of unexpected (unhypothesized) patterns or uncover mechanisms that might have created the pattern (i.e., by gathering data from those experiencing the pattern) (Shah & Corley, 2006).

- Researchers could collect data using both methods (e.g., a survey and interviews) and then determine points of agreement or contradictions in the data, leading to triangulation (Creswell et al., 2003; Driessnack et al., 2007b).

REVIEW AND ENGAGEMENT

When critically reading a research report, you would

- ☐ Ascertain if the authors engaged with the philosophical issue of mixing philosophies versus mixing methods

- ☐ Determine if they provided a full rationale for why a mixed methods study best addressed their research question

- ☐ Check to see if they ensured that their mixed methods study used *both* quantitative and qualitative strands, which addressed the same research question, albeit perhaps privileging one over the other (i.e., they did not mislabel this section)

Mixed Methods Degree of Data Integration

As discussed in Chapter 13, the crux of the mixed methods approach is *data integration* (including strand-specific inferences and meta-inferences across strands). *Integrate* is Latin *integrare*, "making whole" (Harper, 2016). Integration involves mixing things that were previously separate (Anderson, 2014). The assumption is that both types of data (numbers and words) are needed to answer the research question, so the study design has to involve some degree of integration. Creswell et al. (2003) provided a complex typology of mixed methods research designs to ensure some degree of integration, which authors and critical readers are encouraged to consult.

In brief, the two strands can be integrated (a) during the data collection stage, (b) during analysis or the interpretation stage, or (c) across the whole study (data collection and data analysis). The latter ensures the highest degree of integration. In some studies, the data are not integrated at all; rather, they are reported in two separate papers (Bryman, 2008; Creswell et al., 2003; Driessnack et al., 2007b) (see Chapter 13).

The most common ways of mixing the data are discussed in detail in Chapter 13 because the Results and Findings section is where authors report the inferences they gained from mixing the strands. In brief, these research design approaches include (a) merging them, (b) connecting them (by using the data from analyzing one strand to inform how to collect data in the other strand), and (c) embedding data from the lower-priority stand into the primary strand so as to provide additional information (see Figure 10.5). Authors must explain and justify how they dealt with data integration in their study, and to what degree, to best answer their research question.

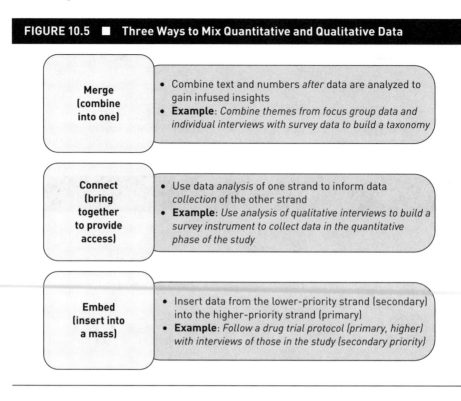

FIGURE 10.5 ■ Three Ways to Mix Quantitative and Qualitative Data

Merge (combine into one)
- Combine text and numbers *after* data are analyzed to gain infused insights
- **Example**: *Combine themes from focus group data and individual interviews with survey data to build a taxonomy*

Connect (bring together to provide access)
- Use data *analysis* of one strand to inform data *collection* of the other strand
- **Example**: *Use analysis of qualitative interviews to build a survey instrument to collect data in the quantitative phase of the study*

Embed (insert into a mass)
- Insert data from the lower-priority strand (secondary) into the higher-priority strand (primary)
- **Example**: *Follow a drug trial protocol (primary, higher) with interviews of those in the study (secondary priority)*

Order of Mixing Methods to Ensure Data Integration

Authors must also report the particular approach they used to sequence their use of the two different methods or *strands* (qualitative and quantitative). Regardless of which approach was used (see Figure 10.6), authors have to explain their design choice relative to its ability to answer their research question.

First, the mixed methods research design can entail one method following the other (*sequential*). Second, both methods can occur at the same time (*concurrent* or *parallel*). Respectively, with *concurrent* designs, inferences from both data sets are made during analysis in an integrated manner, while *parallel* designs entail each data set leading to its own inferences. Third, a *fully mixed* or *fully integrated* design involves mixing both approaches throughout the entire study (the two data sets are merged) (Ary et al., 2010; Creswell, 2009).

Fourth, with an *embedded* design, one form of data supports the other. A fifth approach, *conversion* design, involves converting one form of data to another form (e.g., numbers to words), which are then analyzed. A final approach, *transformative* design, involves using a theoretical lens to guide the study in combination with mixing methods (Ary et al., 2010; Creswell, 2009) (see Figure 10.6). There are many computations and alternative strategies pursuant to these approaches, but their discussion is beyond the scope of this chapter (see Creswell, 2009; Creswell et al., 2003; Teddlie & Tashakkori, 2006). What matters is that authors clearly explain and justify the approach used in their study.

FIGURE 10.6 ■ Ways of Organizing or Sequencing the Order of Mixed Methods in a Study

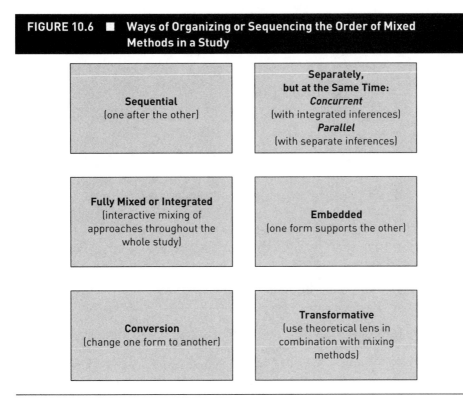

Priority of Qualitative and Quantitative Methods

In some mixed methods designs, the quantitative or the qualitative strand may be given more emphasis than the other, and in other studies, both might have priority. Authors should indicate this in their paper, relative to how best to answer their research question. They may want to use Morse's (1991) notation system when reporting their mixed methods. Uppercase letters are used to indicate prominence, and lowercase letters indicate less-dominant or lower-priority methods for the particular research question. A plus (+) sign means the methods occurred at the same time, and an arrow (⇨) indicates sequence.

Example 10.12 Morse's shorthand for strands (priority and occurrence)

- QUAL+ QUAN: both are equally important and occurred at the same time

- QUAL Quan: qualitative was privileged, followed with quantitative

- QUAN Qual: quantitative was privileged, followed with qualitative

Rigor in Mixed Methods Studies

Authors should report on two types of rigor in mixed methods studies, *design* and *interpretative* (see Figure 10.7). *Design rigor* refers to steps taken to meet the standards for each of quantitative validity and reliability and qualitative trustworthiness (see Table 10.1). *Interpretative rigor* evaluates the validity of the conclusions and comprises three standards: (a) *Interpretative consistency* occurs when inferences follow from the findings or results, rather than coming out of the blue. (b) *Theoretical consistency* means inferences are consistent with known theories. (c) *Integrative efficacy* occurs when meta-inferences (integrating initial strand-specific inferences into inferences that apply across the entire data set) adequately incorporate inferences that stem from both the qualitative and quantitative phases of the study; that is, neither is privileged when discussing the outcomes of the study (Teddlie & Tashakkori, 2006).

Rationale for Mixing Methods

Although now an accepted approach to research design, authors still have to justify *why* a combination of quantitative and qualitative methodologies was the best way to address *their* research question (Bryman, 2008; Newman et al., 2011; Johnson & Christensen, 2012). Bryman (2008) found that the majority of authors (73%) do provide rationales for using mixed methods, and of those who do, 85% provided up to three reasons for mixing them. Authors should use the aforementioned protocols when reporting the respective components of their research design (i.e., the qualitative strand and the quantitative strand) (Newman et al., 2011). The ultimate recommendation is that authors need to clearly explain their mixed methods research design protocol in sufficient detail that they convey the complexity of, and justification for, the plan, often accompanied with a flowchart or path diagram (Suter, 2012).

FIGURE 10.7 ■ Rigor in Mixed Methods Studies

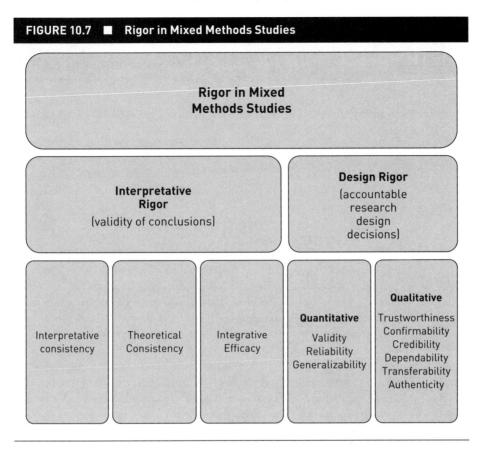

FINAL JUDGMENT OF MIXED METHODS METHODS SECTION

Taking *all* of the ***Review and Engagement*** criteria into account, what is your final judgment of the mixed methods Methods section of the paper you are critically reading?

CHAPTER SUMMARY

The chapter began by clarifying that quantitative studies are grounded in the empirical scientific method, which includes confirmatory and exploratory science (see Figure 10.1). The chapter then identified and explained seven quantitative research designs (see Figure 10.2 and Table 8.2 in Chapter 8), with examples. The basic steps involved in a quantitative research design (see Figure 10.3) were used to organize an extensive, wide-ranging, comprehensive profile of quantitative methods, including but not limited to sampling, ethical considerations, data collection, and data analysis. Table 10.1 identified the criteria used to ensure a quantitative research study characterized by high standards, integrity, rigor (reliability and validity), and generalizability. The chapter concluded with a discussion of the mixed methods approach, which involves using both methodological strands, informed by the principle of data integration. The three main research designs were explained. Researchers can use (a) qualitative methods to explain quantitative data, (b) quantitative methods to further explain qualitative data, or (c) both methods to achieve triangulation. The three most common ways to mix both strands were introduced (merge, connect, and embed; see Figure 10.5), as were the six ways to sequence doing each strand in a study (see Figure 10.6). Finally, in addition to design rigor (see Table 10.1), mixed methods design also has an additional criterion of interpretative rigor, concerned with the validity of the conclusions (strand-specific and meta-inferences) (see Figure 10.7).

REVIEW AND DISCUSSION QUESTIONS

1. Explain the difference between confirmatory and exploratory science as they relate to the scientific method.

2. Would it be correct for researchers reporting a quantitative study to comment on how they ensured trustworthy data and the credibility of the research design? Explain your answer.

3. Comment on the role of *probability* in quantitative sampling protocols.

4. Compare and contrast the ethical considerations of quantitative and qualitative studies (see Table 10.2 and Table 9.4 in Chapter 9).

5. How do quantitative and mixed methods studies differ in data collection and data analysis procedures and protocols?

6. How do qualitative and mixed methods studies differ in how they deal with quality and rigor in their research design (see Table 10.1 and Figure 10.7)?

7. Comment on the ethical considerations pursuant to quantitative studies (see Table 10.2).

8. Researchers conducting mixed methods research face a philosophical quandary. Explain their dilemma.

9. This chapter identified several ways to design a mixed methods study so that *integrated* inferences can be generated from the data arising from two strands of research (qualitative and quantitative). Identify these six approaches, and explain when integration actually happens in each approach (see Figure 10.6).

10. Describe the research convention shorthand that has been developed to help researchers clarify which of the two strands was prioritized in their study, and when they occurred.

11. In addition to *research design* rigor for both the qualitative and quantitative research strands, what other type of rigor has to be accounted for when reporting mixed methods outcomes? What are its three main components? (See Figure 10.7.)

RESULTS AND FINDINGS

11 STATISTICAL LITERACY AND CONVENTIONS

INTRODUCTION

This chapter addresses statistical literacy and statistical conventions. The content will not lead to any level of statistical expertise (formal training is required for that); rather, the intent is to help people recognize basic statistical approaches, traditions, and conventions when they encounter them in a research article or report. It begins with a brief history and definition of statistics as a field of study and practice, followed with a discussion of what it means to be statistically literate. It ends with general information about three basic statistical conventions: (a) measurement scales (four types of data), (b) statistical variables, and (c) experimental and nonexperimental research. As a caveat, the voice of this chapter deviates from the rest of the book. Rather than speaking to what an author needs to know (and, by association, what a critical reader needs to know to be able to critique scholarly work), it provides a plain-language discussion of statistical concepts and conventions. The same caveat holds for the companion chapter on descriptive and inferential statistics (Chapter 12).

HISTORY OF STATISTICS

In the 1600s, governments in England and France began to collect numbers they thought reflected the "health of the *state*" (e.g., births, deaths, marriages, and age). These numbers became known as *statists* and, when first collected, were called "political arithmetic." They are now known as *statistics* (Bracey, 2006, p. 6). The *ics* is Latin *ikos*, "matters relevant to" (Harper, 2016). So *statistics* literally means matters relevant to the state. Today, the term *statistics* is used in two ways: (a) With a capital *S*, it refers to the name of a branch of mathematics. (b) With a small *s*, it refers to numbers and probabilities

LEARNING OBJECTIVES

- Appreciate the brief history of statistics and understand the laws of predictability and their central role in statistics

- Explain the concept of statistical literacy (interpret, evaluate, and communicate statistical information)

- Identify and differentiate between four types of data (nominal, ordinal, interval, and ratio) and explain how they are used to create measurement scales in quantitative studies

- Compare and contrast the basic statistical variables (11) used in quantitative research

- Compare and contrast experimental and nonexperimental research along an array of criteria, especially randomization and variable manipulation

- Identify, with examples, four basic experimental research designs and four basic nonexperimental research designs

derived from calculations on raw numerical data, the focus of this chapter (Schmidt & Brown, 2012).

LAWS OF PROBABILITY AND CHANCE

The crux of modern-day statistics is the *laws of probability*, a measure of how likely it is that some event will occur (Gal, 2002). *Probability* is Latin *probabilitatem*, "credibility" (Harper, 2016). "In light of the data, what is the probability that the obtained results are due to chance?" (Nestor & Schutt, 2015, p. 11). How credible (capable of being believed) are the results? What role did chance play?

Chance is Latin *cadentia*, "that which falls out," a term used in dice (a game where dice are tossed and then *fall out* of a person's hands) (Harper, 2016). In alternate usages, *chance* is defined as a possibility of something happening (e.g., "There is a chance it will rain"). But, of relevance to this chapter on statistics, it can also mean something randomly occurring in the absence of an obvious design or discernable cause. If chance is involved, events cannot be foreseen or controlled (Anderson, 2014; Gal, 2002). Because empirical science is deeply concerned with certainty, predictions, and control, quantitative researchers use statistics to mitigate chance (Johnson & Christensen, 2012) (see Figure 11.1).

STATISTICAL LITERACY

Statistical literacy is central to people's lives, but the focus of this chapter is the realm of creating, publishing, reporting, and critiquing research (Gal, 2002). Anyone who encounters, and tries to evaluate, numerical information needs to be statically literate (Aliaga et al., 2010). Simply stated, "statistical literacy is the ability to understand and critically evaluate statistical results that permeate daily life, coupled with the ability to appreciate the contributions that statistical thinking can make in public and private, professional and personal decisions" (Gal, 2002, p. 2). When applied to research,

> the term "statistical literacy" refers broadly to two interrelated components, primarily (a) people's ability to *interpret and critically evaluate* statistical information, data-related arguments, or stochastic phenomena [both chance and predictable], which they may encounter in diverse contexts, and when relevant (b) their ability to *discuss or communicate* their reactions to such statistical information, such as their understanding of the meaning of the information, their opinions about the implications of this information, or their concerns regarding the acceptability of given conclusions. (Gal, 2002, pp. 2–3)

If people are statistically literate, they have the ability to evaluate number-based truth claims. They can critically understand numbers that are used as evidence in arguments (see Chapter 17). Using their ability to read and interpret statistics, they can accept or take issue with a researcher's conclusions and claims (Gal, 2002; Schield, 2010) (see Figure 11.2). This literacy entails "understanding the basic language of statistics (e.g., knowing what statistical terms and symbols mean and being able to read statistical graphs), and understanding

FIGURE 11.1 ■ Laws of Probability and Chance

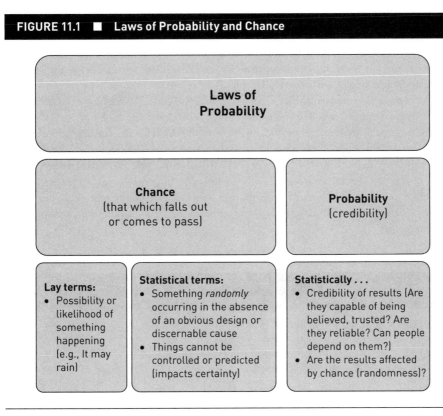

Laws of Probability

Chance
(that which falls out or comes to pass)

Probability
(credibility)

Lay terms:
- Possibility or likelihood of something happening (e.g., It may rain)

Statistical terms:
- Something *randomly* occurring in the absence of an obvious design or discernable cause
- Things cannot be controlled or predicted (impacts certainty)

Statistically . . .
- Credibility of results (Are they capable of being believed, trusted? Are they reliable? Can people depend on them?)
- Are the results affected by chance (randomness)?

FIGURE 11.2 ■ Statistical Literacy

Understand, interpret, and then critically evaluate any number-based truth claims and data-related arguments in a research report

Discuss or communicate one's reactions to conclusions and truth claims, which are based on statistical numbers (express one's understandings, opinions, concerns)

some fundamental ideas of statistics" (Aliaga et al., 2010, p. 14), the focus of the rest of this chapter and of Chapter 12. If people are statistically illiterate, they will not be able to understand, critique, or comment upon the credibility of the numbers or how authors used them to create truth claims, draw conclusions, and formulate arguments pertaining to a particular data set in a quantitative study.

Laypersons may view statistics as an accumulation of facts and figures (e.g., a baseball player's batting averages), but researchers see statistics as methods for analyzing and making sense of numerical data (Wiersma & Jurs, 2009). This intellectual task requires fundamental knowledge about statistical conventions (Ary, Jacobs, & Sorensen, 2010). This chapter explains some fundamental statistical concepts: (a) measurement scales (types of data), (b) statistical variables, and (c) experimental versus nonexperimental research. Chapter 12 follows with information about the two basic approaches to statistics: descriptive and inferential, with the latter prefaced with a discussion of association and causation.

REVIEW AND ENGAGEMENT

When critically reading a research report, you would

☐ Ascertain if the authors seemed conversant with the laws of probability and the role of chance in quantitative research (see Figure 11.1)

☐ Judge whether they conveyed the impression that they are statistically literate

TYPES OF STATISTICAL DATA

In statistics, variables are expressed as numbers. There are four types of statistical data: nominal, ordinal, interval, and ratio (see Figure 11.3). These numbers represent, respectively, names, order, distance, and magnitude of relations. These data types vary on the arithmetic operations to which they can be exposed: adding, subtracting, dividing, multiplying, ranking, and averaging. The type of data is thus interlocked with the type of statistical test that can be used to analyze the data (Michell, 1986) (see the upcoming section and Chapter 12).

Nominal Data

Some variables are expressed as 1 and 2 (e.g., 1 = male and 2 = female), with no concern for their order. These are called *nominal* or categorical scales, with nominal meaning *name* (Anderson, 2014). Common nominal variables include socioeconomic demographics and other characteristics of a population or sample. The nominal scale allows researchers to categorize, label, classify, name, or identify kinds of things that cannot be quantified (i.e., only their existence, not their amount, can be measured). These numbers cannot be meaningfully averaged, added, subtracted, or ranked. They are usually reported with frequency counts (*n* =) and percentage points (e.g., 65% [*n* = 1,000] of the sample were high school dropouts) (Gall, Gall, & Borg, 2015; Johnson & Christensen, 2012; Suter, 2012).

FIGURE 11.3 ■ Measurement Scales: Nominal, Ordinal, Interval, and Ratio

NOMINAL
- Name a category, then assign a number to it (boy = 1, girl = 2)
- Cannot measure the amount, only the existence
- Cannot be meaningfully averaged, added, subtracted, or ranked (can indicate frequency and percentage)

ORDINAL
- Their order matters
- Can rank or place them on a continuum (e.g., first to last)
- Can indicate fastest, but not *how* fast compared to the rest (cannot measure differences)

INTERVAL
- Distance between data points is equal (consistent)
- Can be averaged to gain meaningful results (but cannot multiply or divide because zero is meaningless)
- Can report differences (e.g., temperature differences)

RATIO
- The zero is meaningful (it means the complete absence of the characteristic being measured, e.g., currency or money)
- If you want to talk about something missing, need ratio data
- Can say "something is twice as . . . than something else" (can measure magnitude of relations)

Example 11.1 Nominal data In a study focused on age and gender (masculinity and femininity), age could be represented as 1 = ages 10–15, 2 = ages 16–20, 3 = ages 21–30, and 4 = age 31 and higher. Gender could be represented as 1 = female, 2 = male, 3 = transgender, 4 = agender, and 5 = other.

Ordinal Data

Data that represent rankings or placement on a continuum are called *ordinal* data (meaning their order matters). These data tend to rank things from most to least (called a rank-order scale), including winners in a race, scores on a test, or credentials to qualify for graduate school. Examples are 1 = fastest, 2 = next fastest, 3 = slowest (Gall et al., 2015; Johnson & Christensen, 2012; Suter, 2012). They are often found in questionnaires, using Likert scales. "When responding to a Likert item, respondents specify their level of agreement or disagreement on a symmetric agree-disagree scale for a series of statements. The range captures the intensity of their feelings for a given item" (Burns & Burns, 2008, p. 245).

Example 11.2 Ordinal data In the survey question "Is your general health poor, reasonable, good, or excellent?" researchers may have those answers coded on a Likert scale, respectively, as 1, 2, 3, and 4. In this example, the variable health is rated or ranked from the worst state of health (*poor*) to the best state of health (*excellent*).

Of note is that although these data indicate which data point is highest, they do not reveal how much higher it is than the other data points. If a student is ranked in high need of more instruction, this scale does not help educators judge how *much more* help this person needs than the second-highest person. This scale only lets people rank something. It is useful in some instances, like awarding scholarships, selecting a job candidate for hire, or choosing whom to admit to a graduate program (Gall et al., 2015; Johnson & Christensen, 2012; Suter, 2012).

Interval Data

When there is an equal distance or interval between each data point, the data are called *interval*; that is, the difference between data points is consistent. *Interval* means "space in between" (Anderson, 2014). In interval data, the 0 (zero) is meaningless, which limits the type of statistical manipulation possible. Interval numbers are often averaged to get meaningful results, for example IQ scores, personality traits, aptitude tests, and reading achievement. Ary et al. (2010) urged "caution when interpreting statistics derived from such data. The statistics imply interval-level information when the information is actually often somewhere between ordinal and interval" (p. 103). Researchers can report differences between positions on the scale (e.g., temperature differences) or add the numbers on an interval scale to get an average (e.g., scores on students' test), but they cannot multiply or divide the numbers (Ary et al., 2010).

Example 11.3 Interval data Common examples are the numbers on a Fahrenheit or Celsius thermometer, a ruler, a speedometer, or a clock. For the thermometer, the distance (interval) between 10° and 20° is the same as that between 80° and 110° (10 units). A temperature of 0° does not *mean* that there is no heat.

Ratio Data

The ratio scale uses *ratio* data, so named because, unlike interval data, the "existence of the zero makes it meaningful to take ratios. . . . Hence, we can say that person A is twice as tall as person B" (Zuse & Bollman-Sdorra, 1992, p. 214). Having a true zero point is the distinguishing feature of this scale, the most well-known scientific measure. For ratio data, a zero means a complete absence of the characteristic being measured. Having an absolute zero allows for a wide range of descriptive and inferential statistics (Ary et al., 2010). Also, if people want to talk about something not existing, they need ratio data (Gall et al., 2015; Johnson & Christensen, 2012; Suter, 2012).

Example 11.4 Ratio data An example of ratio data is currencies, where someone can have zero dollars or zero euros. In another example, someone may have absolutely zero knowledge of a language or an academic discipline, including statistics. Aside from money, other common variables for ratio data include distance, duration, length, height, and weight.

To understand the idea of ratio data, consider the following scenario. "You've been waiting in line at the store for what seems like a while now, and you check your watch for the time. You got in line at 11:15am and it's now 11:30. Time of day falls into the class of data called interval data. . . . Seeing that the time is 11:30, you think to yourself, 'I've been in line for fifteen minutes already . . . ???' When you start thinking about the time this way, it's considered ratio data. [You have been in line *much longer* than intended]" (Castello, 2014, p. 23).

This time example reflects the magnitude of relations, which is the key feature of ratio data. With ratio data, it makes sense (is meaningful) to say something is *twice as* long as, farther away from, hotter than, or heavier than something else. Some people can be *three times as* good at statistics as the rest of the class. Also, while ordinal data cannot measure *how much* of a difference, ratio data can. These numbers can be meaningfully added, subtracted, multiplied, or divided (ratios) (Ary et al., 2010; Zuse & Bollman-Sdorra, 1992).

Measurement Scales

In statistics, variables (numbers) can be organized into *scales* so as to measure something. *Scale* is Latin *scala*, "ladder" (Harper, 2016). A scale is a graduated range of values forming a *system* for measuring something. The word *scale* is used to name a measurement instrument based on that system (i.e., a statistical measurement scale) (Anderson, 2014). A measurement scale is a set of numbers that represents the range of values for *a particular* variable in a *particular* study (Gall et al., 2015).

Example 11.5 Measurement scales

- If the variable is sex, the scale could be 1 (*male*) and 2 (*female*) for one study, and it could be 1 (*female*), 2 (*male*), and 3 (*transgender*) for another study (nominal data, names).

- If the speed of a skater is the variable, the scale could be 1 (*fastest*), 2 (*next fastest*), and 3 (*slowest*) (ordinal data, in this case ordered most to least).

- If the variable is temperature, the scale is the numbers on the thermometer (interval data, distance).

- If the variable is currency, the scale could be Canadian dollar, euro, and rand amounts for one study and U.S. dollar, pound, and baht amounts for another study, with each study able to have zero currency (ratio data).

Motulsky (2009) cautioned that the measurement scale approach to classifying data types is not as comprehensive as it appears because the categories are not as clear-cut as they sound. Context matters. For example, in a psychology study about color perception, color *names* are nominal variables. But in physics, color becomes a *ratio* variable because its wavelength can be measured. Michell (1986) concurred that there are issues with this approach.

TABLE 11.1   ■   Relating Measurement Scales to Statistical Tests

Type of Statistic	Measurement Scale			
	Nominal	Ordinal	Interval	Ratio
Frequency distribution	yes	yes	yes	yes
Mode (number that occurs most often)	yes	yes	yes	yes
Percentiles and median (50% of the numbers are above and below it)	no	yes	yes	yes
Mean and standard deviation	no	no	yes	yes
Ratios and coefficients	no	*depends on the context* (e.g., Pearson product-moment correlation needs interval data, but Spearman rank-order correlation needs ordinal data)		yes

Nonetheless, measurement scales now play a key role in research design, again because each type of scale yields data that are suitable to *different kinds* of statistical analysis (see Table 11.1 for a basic overview). Simply put, the type of data (measurement scale) determines the type of statistical analysis that can be used to analyze the data. A cardinal rule is to *not* make interval and ratio claims about ordinal or nominal data (see Chapter 12 for more details).

REVIEW AND ENGAGEMENT

When critically reading a research report, you would

☐ Ensure that the authors demonstrated familiarity with the types of data and associated measurement scales and used their selected ones correctly (nominal, ordinal, interval, and ratio) (see Figure 11.3 and example 11.5)

☐ Determine if they applied the correct arithmetic operations on their selected data scales

☐ Confirm they did not overreach what can be concluded from their measurement scale (e.g., did not make interval or ratio claims about ordinal or nominal data)

☐ Determine if they ran the correct statistical procedure on their type of data (see Table 11.1)

STATISTICAL VARIABLES

Variable is Latin *variabilis*, "changeable" (Harper, 2016). Discussions about variables are usually organized around two key ideas: (a) dependent and independent (and related) variables (see Table 11.2) and (b) experimental and nonexperimental statistical research (Lund & Lund, 2013). These two topics are very intertwined, making it difficult to decide which one to discuss first. That being said, the discussion herein begins with an overview

TABLE 11.2 ■ Basic Nine Statistical Variables	
Type of Variable	**Explanation**
Dependent and Independent	The dependent variable is determined, influenced, or controlled by the independent variable; these terms are most applicable for experimental researchers' *hypothesized* cause-and-effect claims.
Criterion and Predictor	The criterion variable refers to *presumed* outcome (akin to the dependent variable), and the predictor variable refers to *presumed* effect (similar to the independent variable). These terms are best suited for nonexperimental *association* claims.
Constants	A constant does not *vary* and has only one value, so it cannot be called a variable, which changes and has different values. If a variable is intentionally part of the research design but does not change, it is called a *constant* for that study.
Controls	To control means to limit, restrict, or regulate. Researchers intentionally measure just one aspect of a variable that normally has more than one value (e.g., just including women in the study is called "controlling for sex").
Moderator	These visible and measurable variables influence the direction or strength of the relationship between the independent and dependent variables.
Intervening	The independent (and sometimes moderating) variables indirectly influence the dependent *through* the invisible and hard-to-measure intervening variable (to intervene means to come between so as to alter things).
Extraneous and Confounding	*Extraneous* means irrelevant or unrelated. These variables can influence the dependent variable but are beyond the researchers' control, and sometimes even their awareness. They make it difficult to determine the actual impact of the independent (intentionally manipulated) variable. Extraneous variables can *confound* the results.
Spurious	The independent and dependent variables appear to be related *but* are not because some third, spurious variable is influencing *both* of them. *Spurious* means false. It is hard to detect or determine the spurious influence, but if identified, it can be controlled for in a study.

of the basic statistical variables, followed with a separate section on the two overarching approaches to empirical research: experimental and nonexperimental (with more details in Chapter 12).

Dependent and Independent Variables

In an experiment, the *dependent* variable (DV) is studied and expected to change. The researcher determines how (if) and to what degree *independent* variables (IVs) actually change or influence the dependent variable (Ary et al., 2010; Creswell, 2009; Johnson & Christensen, 2012). Independent variables are not normally dependent on or conditioned by anything else (for the exceptions, see the discussion below about moderating and intervening variables). Instead, they are used in a scientific study to see how (if) *they* affect something *else*, which is dependent on them. Gall et al. (2015) referred to the dependent variable in a scientific study as the "hypothesized effect" and the independent variable as the "hypothesized cause" (p. 159).

Example 11.6 Dependent and independent If researchers were interested in how rainfall affects plant growth, they would use the term *variable* for each of rainfall and plant growth. In this example, plant growth is the dependent variable, so called because plant growth is suspected of being *dependent* on rainfall, the independent variable.

Criterion and Predictor Variables

Belli (2009) clarified that, strictly speaking, the terms *dependent* and *independent variable* are not applicable to nonexperimental research (which does not employ experiments). The more appropriate terms are, respectively, *criterion* and *predictor* variables (Suter, 2012). The word *criterion* means a standard, rule, or test on which a judgement or decision is made (Anderson, 2014). So, in effect, nonexperimental researchers use statistical *tests* to judge whether there is a *relationship* between the predictor and criterion variables (i.e., an association). Criterion values are being predicted or understood (i.e., decisions are being made about them) on the basis of information about related variables (called predictor variables) (Lund & Lund, 2013). Actually, the word *predictor* loosely equates to *independent*, and *criterion* to *dependent*. *Predictor* means the "presumed effect," and *criterion* means the "presumed outcome" (rather than hypothesized cause and effect) (Gall et al., 2015; Lund & Lund, 2013; Simmons & Michael, 2002). They differ in that independent variables allow causation statements and predictor variables do not, allowing association claims instead (Ridner & Wilson, 2016).

It is still acceptable to use the terms *dependent* and *independent* in nonexperimental studies, but researchers must be careful to avoid causal language. Causal claims are much weaker in nonexperimental studies, which are better suited to association claims (Belli, 2009). A change in the predictor variable may correlate with a change in the criterion variable, *but* it does not mean the change *caused* anything. All it means is that there is some sort of relationship or association between the two variables, which could be positive or negative, weak or strong (determined using correlational statistics, discussed in Chapter 12).

Example 11.7 Criterion and predictor In one study, the researcher used college applicants' SAT score as the predictor variable and their college grade point average (GPA) as a criterion variable. She found through regression analysis that there seems to be a strong correlation (association) between SAT scores and college GPA. However, because this was a correlational research design, she could not conclude that strong SAT scores caused high college GPAs. She concluded that this association more likely has something to do with a number of factors including hours spent studying, time spent working off campus, or socioeconomic status.

Constants

Researchers can use both *constants* and *variables* in their research. In a study, variables can change and have different values, but *constants* have only *one* value (Suter, 2012). If a variable is an intentional part of the research design but does not vary, it should be called a *constant*. Wiersma and Jurs (2009) clarified that the practice of using constants has some drawbacks, including logistical problems (if some people are eliminated from the study), reduced data, and reduced external validity (because results are generalized to only the restricted group in the constant).

Example 11.8 Constants If all of the subjects in a study are in Grade 11, then grade level is a *constant* because only one grade is studied. If the study included Grades 8 and 11, grade level would become a *variable*. In another example, if a researcher compared the effectiveness of teaching methods A and B on community college students, the education level of the students is a *constant* because no other education level is included in the research design except for community college. If the experiment compared the effectiveness of the two teaching methods on high school, university, *and* community college students, educational level would then become a *variable* (Ary et al., 2010; Gall et al., 2015; Johnson & Christensen, 2012).

Controls

Researchers can also use constants to *control* unwanted sources of influence in a study. By purposefully "controlling for" variables that normally have more than one value, researchers can better discern the true influence of the independent variable on the dependent variable. They would build the *control* variable into their research design and plan for it (Wiersma & Jurs, 2009). In effect, researchers would intentionally measure just one aspect of a variable that normally has more than one value.

Example 11.9 Controls An example is including only females in a study. Instead of the *variable* sex (male and female), the constant is *one* sex, female; that is, the study "controlled for sex." In another example, if researchers want to measure how much water flow increases when different types of faucets are opened, they must make sure the water pressure is held constant in all treatments (the controlled variable) because it too affects water flow (Creswell, 2009; Suter, 2012).

Moderator Variables

A moderator variable is a third variable that is believed to have a significant contributory or contingency effect on the dependent-independent relationship. Moderating variables (M) are visible and can be measured or manipulated (Johnson & Christensen, 2012). Their actions change the strength or direction of an effect between the independent and dependent variables for cause-and-effect relations (or the predictor and criterion variables for associations). The moderator variable can be qualitative (nonnumerical such as class or sex) as well as quantitative (numerical such as weight or age) (Deviant, 2010).

Example 11.10 Moderator A study might determine that there is little to no difference between teaching style (lecture versus cooperative) and students' test performance scores. However, if further analysis revealed that lecturing works best with introverts and cooperative learning with extroverts, it could be said that the relationship between teaching style and student test performance is influenced by the student's personality type (i.e., the moderator variable).

Intervening Variables

To intervene means to come between something in order to alter the course of events (Anderson, 2014). In some instances, when independent and moderating variables cannot provide adequate explanations of what is being observed, researchers may have to turn to a third type of variable, called an intervening variable (IVV). The first two variables (independent and moderator) indirectly influence the dependent *through* the intervening variable. Examples of intervening variables include learning, motivation, attitude, intelligence, memory, intentions, and expectations. Unlike moderating variables, which are visible, intervening variables are *internal* to the participants of the study and cannot be seen, measured, or manipulated. The researcher has to deduce, presume, or judge their presence (Johnson & Christensen, 2012). Intervening variables "stand between the independent and dependent variables, and they mediate the effects of the independent variable on the dependent variable" (Creswell, 2009, p. 50).

> ***Example 11.11 Intervening*** Imagine researchers did not find a *direct* relationship between students asking questions during class (dependent) and their perception of how supportive the teacher is of questioning during class (independent). However, the students' perceptions of their teachers' support of questioning (independent) indirectly affected them asking questions (dependent) by way of the students' inhibition to ask questions in the first place (intervening variable) (Johnson & Christensen, 2012). In another example, if consumers succeed in remaining solvent (dependent variable), it may be due to their financial knowledge (independent variable), their *attitude* toward debt (intervening variable), or both. The participants' internal attitude *stands between* solvency and financial knowledge. They may be very knowledgeable about finances but have no problem with being in debt (attitude).

Extraneous Variables

Extraneous means irrelevant, unrelated, unconnected, not pertinent, and off the point (Anderson, 2014). An extraneous variable *might* influence the dependent variable, but extraneous variables tend to lie beyond the researchers' control, their awareness, or both. Extraneous variables are interesting but not relevant to the research question. However, they can confuse the issue because they make it difficult, if not impossible, to determine the actual impact of the independent variable. Their presence lowers internal validity (whether the study measured what it intended) because their effects on other variables cannot be separated (Suter, 2012; Wiersma & Jurs, 2009). Examples of extraneous variables include participants' age, their maturity, their test-wiseness, historical events, changes in experimental procedures, and attrition (Gall et al., 2015).

> ***Example 11.12 Extraneous*** A researcher who wants to know the impact of coffee intake on memory recall for a word list should measure the participants' age (an extraneous variable) and then "control for age" during the statistical analysis. This approach is recommended because age and memory are known to be related to each other, so "controlling for age" helps rule out its influence on a study examining caffeine and memory. This particular study is not about age and memory; the research question is about caffeine and memory.

Confounding Variables

When extraneous variables are not sufficiently dealt with during the research design process, external readers of the study report will be able to come up with alternative explanations for the research results. Researchers can control for extraneous variables by randomization or by holding them constant (Johnson & Christensen, 2012). "Failure to recognize and control for extraneous variables may result in a form of contamination known as confounding [which in research means] 'mixed-up' results" (Suter, 2012, p. 137). When an extraneous variable and the independent variable change together, things get mixed up.

> *Example 11.13 Confounding* "If two methods of teaching are studied by comparing one method taught in the fall with the other method taught in the spring, then the teaching method (independent variable) is confounded with the time of year (extraneous variable)" (Suter, 2012, p. 137). It is hard to know if the teaching method or the time of year is affecting the dependent variable.

Spurious Variables

Finally, *spurious* means apparent but actually false (Anderson, 2014). A spurious relationship between variables means the independent variable really has no effect on the dependent, but they appear related because some other variable influences *both* of them (Ary et al., 2010). A spurious finding can be explained away by a hidden factor that was not actually measured or observed in the study. It exists, but its influence cannot be readily detected (Creswell, 2009). If the relationship is totally spurious, it will completely disappear when controlling for the third variable (Johnson & Christensen, 2012).

> *Example 11.14 Spurious* If a study about men and heart attacks showed that short men were more likely to have heart attacks than tall men, it would be spurious to claim that height per se causes heart attacks. A third variable, perhaps nutrition or genetics, is more likely the cause because it could lead to *both* a lack of growth (height) and a weaker cardiovascular system (heart attack) (Suter, 2012). If the relationship is totally spurious, it will completely disappear when controlling for the third variable, nutrition or genetics.

REVIEW AND ENGAGEMENT

When critically reading a research report, you would

- ☐ Determine if the authors provided sufficient descriptions of their dependent and independent variables when making causation claims

- ☐ Ascertain if they provided sufficient descriptions of their criterion and predictor variables when making association claims

- ☐ Check to see that they clearly accounted for other variables in their research design (e.g., constants, moderators, intervening, extraneous) (see Table 11.2 and related text)

EXPERIMENTAL AND NONEXPERIMENTAL RESEARCH

There are two basic approaches to conducting statistically oriented research, an experiment and a nonexperiment. In an experiment, researchers purposefully determine how the independent variable will vary and then observe the effect of that manipulation on the dependent variable (Suter, 2012). To that end, they can *manipulate* the independent variable in one of three ways. They can (a) *implement or withhold* a technique (called presence or absence of technique), (b) vary the *amount* of a technique received by study participants, and (c) vary the *type* of technique or conditions presented to participants. Random assignment and active manipulation are only used in experimental research where scholars want to determine a *cause-and-effect relationship* (Johnson & Christensen, 2012).

In nonexperimental research, the focus is still on variables, but they are *not* manipulated; instead, these variables exist in natural situations and are observed. An example would be observing and comparing the behavior of drug users and non–drug users (control group). The researcher cannot randomize the sample, and no independent variable is being manipulated, normally because it is impractical or unethical (Shuttleworth, 2015). These nonexperimental observational studies allow researchers to compare subjects against a control group, but researchers have no control over the "experiment" or the composition of the control group (Wiersma & Jurs, 2009).

This so-called *naturalistic nonparticipant observation* does not involve the quantitative researcher's intervention. It is simply the researcher studying behavior that occurs naturally in natural contexts (unlike a controlled laboratory or an artificial setting) (see Table 11.3). To avoid confusion, readers need to understand that qualitative *participant observation* refers to when the researcher *does* intervene in the environment while watching people's behavior that is otherwise not accessible, for example an ethnographic study (Wiersma & Jurs, 2009).

Experimental Research

Despite being an incredibly involved topic, there is some fundamental information people should know about *experimental research*. In a nutshell, researchers change (i.e., manipulate) some parts of a situation either by themselves or through collaborators, like specially trained research assistants. They introduce an intervention into the situation and measure its effect on the dependent variable (Gall et al., 2015). In an experiment, researchers systematically change (manipulate) one or more independent variables to determine if there is a *causal* relationship, controlling for as many extraneous variables as possible (Johnson & Christensen, 2012).

Types of settings

Experimental research can occur (a) in a field experiment (a real-life setting), (b) in a laboratory (or other artificial setting), and (c) over the Internet (Johnson & Christensen, 2012). These experiments all involve experimental and control groups, randomized assignment to the experimental groups, manipulation of independent variables, and control of extraneous variables. Only the experimental group receives the treatment or intervention (caused by manipulating the independent variable) (Creswell, 2009; Johnson & Christensen, 2012).

TABLE 11.3 ■ Comparison of Experimental and Nonexperimental Quantitative Research Designs		
Criteria	**Experimental Research Design**	**Nonexperimental Research Design**
Variables	✓ Independent and dependent (plus other types of) variables	✓ But more appropriate to call them predictor and criterion variables
Manipulate variables	✓	No, researchers observe in natural setting and interpret to form conclusions
Randomize samples	✓	No, subjects already belong naturally
Experimental group	✓ Receives the intervention	No, but have two or more groups that are compared
Control group	✓ Does not receive intervention	✓ Does not receive intervention but cannot randomly assign participants to control group
Type of claim	Cause and effect (causal claims)	Association claims
Location of research	• Lab setting • Field setting • Artificial setting • Internet	Where participants are located (their natural setting)
Type of research design	• True experiment • Factorial true experiment • Quasi-experiment • Single case intervention over time	• Group comparison (causal-comparative) • Correlational • Survey (questionnaires, polls, interviews) • Case studies

Randomization

In addition to the importance of manipulation and control in experimental research, *randomization* is a procedure that ensures each participant has the same chance of being in a group. More important, it is the best technique for ensuring groups are as similar as possible on all variables at the start of the experiment; that is, they are *equated*. This strategy ensures the researcher has more confidence that the independent variable is not confounded. Random assignment can happen by throwing a die, drawing names, drawing or assigning numbers, or using a random number generator (Creswell, 2009; Johnson & Christensen, 2012; Wiersma & Jurs, 2009). An example of the latter is *Research*

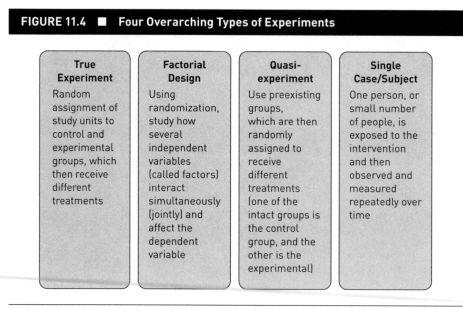

FIGURE 11.4 ■ Four Overarching Types of Experiments

True Experiment	Factorial Design	Quasi-experiment	Single Case/Subject
Random assignment of study units to control and experimental groups, which then receive different treatments	Using randomization, study how several independent variables (called factors) interact simultaneously (jointly) and affect the dependent variable	Use preexisting groups, which are then randomly assigned to receive different treatments (one of the intact groups is the control group, and the other is the experimental)	One person, or small number of people, is exposed to the intervention and then observed and measured repeatedly over time

Randomizer, www.randomizer.org (Urbaniak & Plous, 2013). Sometimes researchers enumerate all the individuals in a population and then employ a table of random numbers to draw their sample (Ary et al., 2010).

Types of experiments: true, factorial, quasi, and single case

There are four overarching types of experiments (true, factorial, quasi, and single case) (see Figure 11.4), with many permutations that are not discussed in this chapter.

True experiment. First, a *true experiment* involves random assignment to groups, the creation of experimental and control groups, *and* the manipulation of independent variables (Ary et al., 2010; Gall et al., 2015; Johnson & Christensen, 2012; Suter, 2012). It is truly an experiment (when other approaches are considered not to be) because of these criteria: randomness and the purposeful application of different things to different groups to determine the effect. Actually, Salkind (2010) noted that the exact meaning of the adjective *true* in this instance has been debated, but the defining distinction is that units of a study are randomly assigned to different treatment conditions.

Example 11.15 True experiment

Dr. Sandy Brown hypothesized that Drug X will cause a decrease in anxiety. She collected a random sample of 600 individuals who completed a baseline assessment and were found to have high levels of anxiety. She divided them into three groups. The first was the control group, which received a sugar pill every day (no drug). The second group was given a low dose of Drug X each day (100 mg), and the third group received a 250-mg dose each day (these two are the experimental groups). After recording results for two months, Dr. Brown analyzed her data and determined that those who were in the experimental groups had a *statistically significant* decrease in anxiety. She also found that the anxiety level of those receiving the higher dose decreased much faster than that of those in the low dose and control groups. She concluded that Drug X *causes* a reduction in anxiety, as she had hypothesized (Williams, 2016).

Factorial. Second, a *factorial designed true experiment* is required for complex social phenomena. This design studies how several independent variables interact *simultaneously* to influence the dependent variable (how they all *factor in* to understanding the phenomenon). The researcher manipulates more than one variable at the same time in order to study their *joint effect* (via their interaction) on the dependent variable as well as their individual effect. In these instances, the independent variable is called a *factor* (i.e., something that contributes to or factors into a result). In these studies, the independent variables are factors in the research design. An *interaction effect* means that a factor has an effect on the dependent variable but only under certain manipulated conditions in the experiment. Ideally, the study is randomized, but this can be a real operational challenge for some studies (Ary et al., 2010; Gall et al., 2015; Johnson & Christensen, 2012; Suter, 2012).

Example 11.16 Factorial design

An example would be a research design for an educational program where researchers want to look at a variety of program variations to see which works best. They can vary the amount of time that students receive instruction, with one group getting one hour of instruction per week and another group getting four hours per week. And they can vary the setting, with one group getting the instruction in class (probably pulled off into a corner of the classroom) and the other group being pulled out of the classroom for instruction in another room. This is an example of a 2 × 2 factorial design, so named because there are two factors (time in instruction and setting) and each factor has two levels (one and four hours, and in and out of the classroom).

Quasi-experimental. Third, a *quasi-experimental* research design involves manipulation of independent variables but does *not* involve random assignment of participants to comparison groups, meaning researchers have less control of extraneous variables. Instead, quasi-experiments use preexisting, intact groups, which are randomly assigned to treatment conditions (Belli, 2009). *Quasi* means somewhat or almost experimental (Anderson, 2014). Matching is a common control technique used in instances when random assignment into groups is not possible. In the matching process, once researchers have identified two or three independent variables that are closely related to the dependent variable, they find a group that *matches* these independent variables and use it as the control group (i.e., *quasi*, "almost the same"). Another approach is to match participants on certain traits and then make sure one of these individuals is assigned to each group (Creswell, 2009; Suter, 2012).

Example 11.17 Quasi-experimental

In a study about school dropout rates, researchers could use two *intact, similar groups* (schools), with one the control group and the other the treatment (intervention) group. They could implement the treatment at the intervention group and compare the results to the other school that did not receive it, to see if it had any effect on dropout rates.

When interpreting quasi-experimental results, researchers must be critically aware of, and consider threats to, both internal and external validity (Ary et al., 2010; Belli, 2009; Suter, 2012). If inadequate steps are taken to control the experiment (internal validity), efforts to generalize outside of the experiment are jeopardized (external validity). Also, if extraneous variables have not been adequately controlled (due to lack of randomization), it is difficult to reach truly *valid* causal conclusions in quasi-experimental research (Johnson & Christensen, 2012). Quasi-experimental research "permits researchers to reach *reasonable* [emphasis added] conclusions even though full control is not possible" (Ary et al., 2010, p. 316).

Single-case/subject. Finally, a *single-case or single-subject* design involves multiple observations of the effects of an intervention (manipulation of an independent variable) over time. Once baseline information is obtained, the person or small number of individuals is exposed to the intervention and observed repeatedly over time. Time series research can be experimental if groups are formed or individuals are chosen randomly and there is a control group (Ary et al., 2010; Creswell, 2009; Johnson & Christensen, 2012; Wiersma & Jurs, 2009).

Example 11.18 Single-case design

Over the period of a semester, researchers repeatedly exposed students to a documentary film designed to change their attitudes about sustainability, in concert with repeated measurements of their attitudes to determine the effect produced by repeated exposure to the film.

REVIEW AND ENGAGEMENT

When critically reading a research report, you would

- ☐ Determine if the authors properly identified their research as experimental or nonexperimental

- ☐ Ascertain if they appreciated that experimental research is for causal claims and nonexperimental research is for association claims

- ☐ Check to see that they demonstrated knowledge that experimental research uses the principles of randomization and manipulation while nonexperimental research does not (see Table 11.3)

- ☐ Confirm they identified their research setting (contrived versus natural)

- ☐ Determine if they clarified which of the four types of experiments were used in their research design (true, factorial, quasi, or single case) and any permutation used for their study (see Figure 11.4 and Table 11.3)

- ☐ Ascertain if they justified their research design as the best way to answer their research question or address their hypotheses

Nonexperimental Research

In nonexperimental research, manipulation of the independent variable cannot happen because it is either unethical or impractical to do so (or the group already exists, meaning people already belong). This is a key feature of nonexperimental research. For example, researchers cannot ask people to take illegal drugs to study their effect on behavior. Instead, they can ask drug and non–drug users to complete a questionnaire or agree to be interviewed (Belli, 2009; Lund & Lund, 2013; Shuttleworth, 2015). In nonexperimental quantitative research, variables are studied as they exist naturally in intact groups. Johnson and Christensen (2012) explained that in these circumstances, researchers "do the best we can, and sometimes this means that we must use weaker research methods" (pp. 42–43). This means that researchers can conduct quantitative research to determine relationships between variables without using experiments (Gall et al., 2015).

Rather than manipulating, controlling, or altering independent variables in an experiment, they rely instead on the interpretation, observation, or interactions of existing settings to come to their conclusions. In these instances, they have several research design options for conducting nonexperimental studies, with the acknowledgment that there is little agreement about how to classify these approaches (Belli, 2009). Researchers can (a) use the *group comparisons* research design (also called *causal-comparative research*) to see if a relationship is present; (b) opt for *correlational research*, where they seek evidence of association (not cause and effect); and (c) administrate surveys or (d) prepare case studies (Ary et al., 2010; Gall et al., 2015) (see Figure 11.5). Longitudinal studies examine variables exhibited by a group or groups over time (Ary et al., 2010; Johnson & Christensen, 2012). All of these approaches are too weak to make a cause-and-effect statement, but these studies are useful if they show an association or offer interpretations and insights not possible with experiments (Belli, 2009; Hill, 1965; Johnson & Christensen, 2012). Each is now discussed.

Group comparisons

When conducting group comparisons (also called *ex post facto*, from a thing done afterwards), the study design incorporates a single *categorical* (nominal, name) independent variable and a single *quantitative* dependent variable. The latter (dependent) can be measured across a scale, its numeric value has meaning, and it can be subjected to arithmetic operations (e.g., multiply and divide). Examples of dependent variables include height, weight, and GPA (Belli, 2009). The categorical (independent) variable is a preexisting, naturally occurring variable that cannot be manipulated (e.g., age, sex, eye color, and grade level). These variables differ in kind but not in amounts, which is one reason they cannot be manipulated, nor can people be randomly assigned to them because they already belong (Ary et al., 2010; Johnson & Christensen, 2012).

Example 11.19 Group comparison

Imagine the independent variable is student retention (with two *categories*, held back or not held back in the first grade) and the dependent variable is students' level of academic achievement, for example test scores that can be *quantified*. The level of

FIGURE 11.5 ■ Four Types of Nonexperimental Research			
Group Comparisons	**Correlational**	**Surveys**	**Case Studies**
Use already existing groups who manifest *one* variable (no randomization and no manipulation) and then measure them on another variable; examine how two previously existing groups vary on one variable	Choose preexisting groups and then *measure* them on at least two continuous variables; obtain scores on two or more variables for each preexisting group or subject to determine if there is an association between the independent and dependent variables (no randomization and no manipulation of variables)	Select a *sample* of respondents and (a) administer a questionnaire, (b) conduct interviews, or (c) poll them to gather data, which are then used to describe the *population* (no randomization and no manipulation of variables)	In-depth investigation of a phenomenon in its natural setting; the *case* is the situation, and the study reports an *analysis* of the situation (no randomization and no manipulation of variables)

academic achievement in Group 1 (*held back*) and Group 2 (*not held back*) would be compared. Which group of Grade 1 students had the higher academic achievement, those who were held back a year or those who were not?

Correlational

This type of research involves correlational equations and correlational coefficients (a number between –1 and +1), to be addressed in Chapter 12. Basically, researchers would be looking for a relationship between two *quantitative* variables in a natural setting. If they find a positive correlation (i.e., the independent is associated with an *increase* in the dependent), they can conclude there *is* a relationship (i.e., the variables are *associated*), but they cannot claim one variable caused the other (Johnson & Christensen, 2012). They could say that "the higher a student's self-esteem (independent), the better their class performance (dependent)," but they could *not* say that self-esteem was the direct cause of the improvement in class performance. This causal claim is impossible for three reasons: (a) The independent variable was not manipulated. (b) It is very difficult to know which variable occurred first (called temporal order). And (c) there are usually too many other reasons why the relationship was observed—that is, too many *extraneous* variables that are not explained, which could offer alternative explanations (Hill, 1965; Johnson & Christensen, 2012).

For clarification, the major distinction between group comparison and correlational research is that with group comparison, the researcher "categorizes the participants into at least *two* groups on *one* variable and then compares them on the other variable.

In correlational research, a researcher deals with *one* [emphasis added] group of individuals measured on at least *two* [emphasis added] continuous variables" (Ary et al., 2015, p. 27). Note that a *continuous* variable can have different values between two points and is determined by *measuring*. People can be 65 inches tall or 66 inches tall but also 65.5 inches tall. In comparison, a discrete variable has fixed values, determined by *counting*. A family can have 2 children or 3 children but not 2.4 children (Gall et al., 2015).

Example 11.20 Correlational study

A researcher is interested in the effect of maternal infection during pregnancy on fetal development and pregnancy outcome. The researcher cannot manipulate an infection, but she can document if the mother has any infections. So, the researcher starts the study by collecting data from pregnant women regarding their history of infection during their current pregnancy. Next, the researcher observes fetal development and pregnancy outcomes for each woman. Finally, the researcher analyzes the relationship (association) between maternal infection and fetal development and the outcome of the pregnancy (Patidar, 2013).

Surveys

Survey research is a third approach to nonexperimental, statistically oriented research. Using instruments such as questionnaires, opinion polls, and interviews, researchers collect and then summarize data that (a) contain descriptions of the characteristics of different groups or (b) measure their behaviors or attitudes, beliefs, or opinions toward an issue. Surveys help researchers investigate how variables change together, but there is no random assignment to groups, nor are any variables manipulated (Ary et al., 2010; Wiersma & Jurs, 2009).

Example 11.21 Surveys

A researcher could interview students, asking them what kind of menu they want in the school cafeteria. Consumers could be surveyed to determine their perceptions of online shopping. Citizens could be polled to reveal their preferences for, or positions on, an environmental tax.

Case studies

In nonexperimental research, the researcher does not have complete control over conditions and aspects of the study. The researcher does not manipulate the participant's experience or circumstances or the situation. There is no random assignment to groups, nor is there any manipulation of variables (Belli, 2009). Reflecting these features, a final type of nonexperimental research is the case study. Case studies involve an "in depth study of instances of a phenomenon in its natural setting context while conveying both the researcher's and the participants' perspectives and using procedures that test the validity and applicability of its findings" (Gall et al., 2015, p. 343). They often address multiple variables that are measured at several points in time. Cases are useful in their own right, and they can also serve as sources of testable hypotheses for future research.

Example 11.22 Case study

McGregor (1993) *studied* the development and evolution of a policy network for banking machines in Canada (during a 20-year time frame) and then wrote up a *case* (an overview of a particular situation or set of circumstances) that contained details about who was involved, when, for how long, their main points of concern, their relationships and interactions with other stakeholders, and the end policy result of the network actors' interactions.

REVIEW AND ENGAGEMENT

When critically reading a research report, you would

☐ Determine if the authors properly identified their research as experimental or nonexperimental

☐ Check to see that they clarified which of the four types of nonexperiments they used in their research design and any permutation used for their study (see Figure 11.5 and Table 11.3)

☐ Ascertain if they justified their research design as the best way to answer their research question or to address their hypotheses

FINAL JUDGMENT ON THE STATISTICAL DISCUSSION

Taking *all* of the **Review and Engagement** criteria into account, what is your final judgment of the statistical discussion in the paper you are critically reading?

CHAPTER SUMMARY

As a preamble to Chapter 12 on descriptive and inferential statistics, this chapter focused on a brief history of the idea of statistics and what it means for authors and critical readers to be statistically literate (see Figure 11.2). A brief discussion of the laws of probability and chance was provided (see Figure 11.1) because statistics is predicated on probability. The four main types of data were discussed in some detail (nominal, ordinal, interval, and ratio) (see Figure 11.3), as was how they are employed in a study as measurement scales (see example 11.5). The notion of a scale was explained, followed with which type of scale can be used for particular statistical procedures (see Table 11.1). The concept of a variable was defined, in conjunction with an overview of the most commonly used statistical variables (see Table 11.2). The chapter ended with the distinctions between experimental research designs (four types, Figure 11.4) and nonexperimental research (four types, Figure 11.5). The criteria of randomization, variable manipulation, experimental and control groups, types of claims (causal and association), and types of research settings were used to differentiate between these two basic quantitative research designs (see Table 11.3). The chapter will conclude with a transition statement moving readers from a discussion of statistical conventions to the ins and outs of descriptive and inferential statistics (Chapter 12) (see Table 11.4).

TABLE 11.4 ■ Overview of Chapter 11 ("Statistical Literacy and Conventions") and Chapter 12 ("Descriptive and Inferential Statistics")		
Chapter 11	**Chapter 12**	
Statistical Literacy and Conventions	**Descriptive Statistics**	**Inferential Statistics**
History of Statistics	Measures of Central Tendency (mean, mode, and median)	Association and Causation
Laws of Probability and Chance		
Statistical Literacy	Measures of Variation (range, variance, and standard deviation and bell curve)	Hypotheses (null and research)
Statistical Data Types (nominal, ordinal, interval, and ratio) and Measurement Scales		Estimates (point and interval)
Statistical Variables (11)	Measures of Relative Standing (percentile rank and z scores)	p value and Level of Significance
Experimental Research (true, factorial, quasi, and single case)	Measures of Relation - Contingency tables (chi-square) - Regression analysis (correlational coefficient and scatter graphs)	Type I and Type II Errors
Nonexperimental Research (group comparisons, correlational, surveys, case studies)	Reporting Descriptive Statistics	
		Statistical Power and Statistical Significance
		Sample Size and Effect Size
		Common Inferential Statistical Tests - parametric (r, p, t, F) - nonparametric (x^2, z) Reporting Inferential Statistics

Transitioning to Chapter 12

Chapter 12 extends this basic conversation about statistical conventions by focusing on the two main approaches to statistics, descriptive and inferential, the latter prefaced with a section on association and causation. Chapter 12 explores (a) the four types of measurements for descriptive statistics (i.e., central, variable, relative, relationships) and then shifts to inferential statistics, with a focus on (b) hypotheses and estimates, (c) *p* value and level of significance, (d) Type I and II errors, (e) statistical power (sample size and effect size), and (f) the most common inferential statistical tests. Together, Chapters 11 and 12 provide a very basic primer on statistics (see Table 11.4).

REVIEW AND DISCUSSION QUESTIONS

1. Explain the *laws of probability* and how they factor into statistics. In this process, use the terms *chance* and *random*.

2. What are people able to do if they are *statistically literate*? Explain how this skill connects with being a critical reader of quantitative papers.

3. Compare and contrast the four types of statistical data. When are they used in a study, and why are they called a *measurement scale*? What is the scale measuring?

4. Each statistical procedure needs a particular type of statistical data. Explain why this is so.

5. There are at least 10 types of statistical variables. Why are they called *variables*? Identify these variables, explaining each one to someone else using plain language.

6. Why do the experimental and nonexperimental approaches to research use different terms for dependent and independent variables?

7. Compare and contrast a causal claim versus an association claim. What are the names of the variables used for each claim?

8. Which was easier for you to understand and why, a moderator or an intervening variable?

9. Explain the differences between experimental research and nonexperimental research designs, as simply as possible. When is an experiment not an experiment?

10. In a nutshell, explain how each of the four types of experimental research designs differ from each other (see Figure 11.4). What do they all have in common?

11. In a nutshell, explain how each of the four types of nonexperimental research designs differ from each other (see Figure 11.5). What do they all have in common?

12

DESCRIPTIVE AND INFERENTIAL STATISTICS

INTRODUCTION

Chapter 11 provided an overview of basic statistical conventions: (a) types of statistical data and associated measurement scales, (b) the most common types of statistical variables, and (c) experimental and nonexperimental research designs. This chapter continues this statistical conversation, focusing on the two main approaches to statistics, descriptive and inferential, the latter prefaced with a section on association and causation. As with the previous chapter, this chapter provides a plain-language discussion of descriptive and inferential statistics. The content will not lead to any level of statistical expertise (formal training is required for that); rather, the intent is to help readers recognize basic statistical approaches, traditions, and conventions when they encounter them in a research article or report. Together, Chapters 11 and 12 provide a very basic primer on statistics.

BASIC DIFFERENCES BETWEEN DESCRIPTIVE AND INFERENTIAL STATISTICS

Scholars often combine both descriptive and inferential approaches in their study design. Succinctly, descriptive statistics pertain to a *particular* data set (i.e., *describe* just those data), while inferential statistics enable researchers to extrapolate the meaning of their results beyond the data set, to the *general* public, or the specific population from which the sample was drawn, called generalizability (Wiersma & Jurs, 2009).

Unlike descriptive statistics, inference also involves the *laws of probability*, with *probability* meaning the measure of how *likely* it is that something will happen (Anderson, 2014). These laws enable researchers to use the term *likelihood* when

(Continued)

Learning Objectives (Continued)

- Compare and contrast the nuances of parameter testing (hypothesis) and parameter estimation for inferential statistics, and distinguish between the purpose of null and research hypotheses and parameter single-point and interval estimates

- Explain the concept of the *p* value and how it is related to level of statistical significance

- Distinguish between Type I and Type II inferential errors

- Define *statistical power* and explain how it is related to sample size and to effect size

- Compare and contrast the concepts of parametric and nonparametric inferential statistical tests

- Identify and explain the differences among the four most common inferential statistical procedures (tests) (hint: appreciating their history helps you achieve this objective), and explain what has to be included when reporting inferential statistics in a research report

referring to *statistical significance*. Probability in statistical science helps researchers determine if "the relationship discovered by statistical methods is 'real' (or not due to chance)" (Suter, 2012, p. 48). The famous statistical expression *p* < .05 (*p* is less than point oh five) means *statistically significant*, or a 95% *likelihood* that the result is not a fluke caused by chance (Suter, 2012) (see Chapter 11). A cursory overview of the two basic approaches to statistics is provided in Table 12.1, followed with more detailed discussions.

REVIEW AND ENGAGEMENT

When critically reading a research report, you would

☐ See if the authors refrained from generalizing *descriptive* data to the wider population (i.e., confined their conclusions to that data set only)

☐ Determine if they purposefully *generalized* inferential data beyond the study's data set

DESCRIPTIVE STATISTICS

Descriptive statistics allow the researcher to draw conclusions about the current data but do *not* allow conclusions about any population outside of the current data set (the latter require inferential statistics). When using descriptive statistics, researchers would be interested in some combination of four types of measurement (see Figure 12.1): (a) measures of central tendencies (i.e., mean, mode, and median); (b) measures of variability or dispersion (spread out or clustered); (c) measures of relative position or standing (one variable relative to another); and (d) measures of relationships or correlations (between two or more variables) (Ary, Jacobs, & Sorensen, 2010; Johnson & Christensen, 2012; Mackey & Gass, 2005; Wiersma & Jurs, 2009). Statisticians have designed different statistical tests for each of these four measures (see Table 12.1).

Measures of Central Tendencies

When using measures of central tendencies, researchers try to get a sense of what is typical or characteristic of their data set. They can measure (a) the mean (average score), (b) the mode (the value that occurs most often), and (c) the median (the middle number in a set of numbers arranged in either ascending or descending order; 50% of the numbers are above it, and 50% are below it). A simple rule is to use the *mean* when the data are evenly distributed and the *median* when the data are skewed (meaning there is an outlier, an extremely high

TABLE 12.1 ■ Overview of Descriptive and Inferential Statistical Approaches

Descriptive Statistics	Inferential Statistics	
Confined to a particular set of data (cannot generalize beyond this study)	Can generalize beyond this data set Laws of Probability	

Four types of measurements	Two main approaches	

• **Average** (typical)
• **Variation** (spread out or clustered)
• **Relative position or standing** (compared to another)
• **Relationship** (between two things, called correlation)
	Estimation
	
	(calculate roughly or approximately)
	
	Study whole *population* by estimating from a random sample
	
	Estimate parameter (characteristics) of a population
	
	   • Point estimation (one number)
	   • Interval estimation (point is between two numbers)
	   • Confidence intervals (*belief* that the estimated point is within this range—it may not be)
	   • Confidence levels (*chance* [%] that estimated point is within this range)
	   • Margin of error (value of estimated point, ±Y)
		Hypothesis testing
		
		(supposition based on limited evidence)
		
		Use *sample* data to generalize to population
		
		Get a statistic (fact)
		
		from a sample
		
		   • Causation and association
		   • Levels of significance (*p* value)
		   • Null and research hypotheses
		   • Type I and II errors
		   • Statistical power
		   • Sample size and effect size

Statistical Tests		

• *Frequency distribution* (*n =*)
• *Mode, mean, and median* (for averages)
• *Range* and *standard deviation* (for variability)
• *Percentile rank* (%), and *z* scores (for relative standing)
• *Correlation* (single number, *r* value for relationships, an association)
	t *test* independent (comparing two means) (*t* value)
	
	Analysis of variance (ANOVA)
	
	   • One-way ANOVA (*F* test)
	   • Two-way multifactorial
	   • Repeated measures
	   • Analysis of covariance (ANCOVA)
	   • Multivariate (MANOVA) (e.g., factor analysis, cluster analysis, multidimensional scaling)
	
	Correlation, linear regression analysis (*r* value, causal)
	
	   • Simple regression (one independent variable)
	   • Multiple regression (impact of numerous simultaneous influences [independent] upon one dependent variable)
	   • Nonlinear regression (one or more independent and dependent variables; the line through the data is *curved,* indicating an optimal best fit, e.g., a Lorenz curve)
	
	Nonparametric analysis
	
	   • Chi-square for contingency tables (χ^2 test)	

FIGURE 12.1 ■ Four Types of Measurements for Descriptive Statistics			
Central Tendencies	**Variation**	**Relative Standing**	**Relationships (correlations)**
Give a sense of what is typical or characteristic of a data set (indicates average, most often, or the middle)	Gives a sense of how similar (clustered) or different (dispersed) people are with respect to a particular variable (range, variance, and standard deviation)	Gives a sense of how one person or thing compares to others on a variable (i.e., where it/she/he stands compared to others) (percentile ranks, and z scores)	Gives a sense of the existence, strength, and direction of a relationship between variables (associations, not causation) (frequencies, percentages, or coefficient between −1 and +1)

or low number) (Ary et al., 2010; Johnson & Christensen, 2012). The following example illustrates why it matters *which* of the three values (numbers) is reported (from Jill, 2003).

Example 12.1 Mean, mode, and median

These are the salaries for seven people who graduated from university with a biology degree (listed in ascending order):

$27,000

$29,000

$33,000

$34,000

$39,000

$39,000

$5,000,000

The last person in the list ($5 million) got a job playing basketball for the NBA (the outlier). The median salary is $34,000, the mode salary is $39,000 (it occurs twice), and the mean is about $750,000. The number reported by the author truly affects the impression created about the import of the study. Claiming that a university student with a biology degree will earn on average $750,000 is very misleading (although correct for *this* data set). A more meaningful statistic would acknowledge removal of the outlier, leaving the average salary at $33,500.

Measures of Variation

Measures of variation tell how similar or different people are with respect to a particular variable. If all of the numbers for a variable are the same, there would be no variation. A little bit of variation means people are similar, and the mean, mode, and median are indeed typical of the population. When there is a lot of variation, people are different (Johnson & Christensen, 2012). Variation measures are calculated using *range*, *variance*, and *standard deviation*. Range is a crude measure based on only two values, the two most extreme values—that is, the highest and lowest. In addition to crudeness, range is severely affected by outliers. Because standard deviation is based on *the distance* from the mean, a rogue number that is far away from the mean can really affect this statistic.

Example 12.2 Range variation

In example 12.1, salaries ranged from $27,000 to $5,000,000. If the outlier was not in the data set, the more *meaningful* salary range would be $27,000–$39,000.

Bell curve

The image of a *bell* is used to represent the distance of the group's scores from the average score (i.e., the variation). A bell's curve contains a hump, two downward curves, and two tails. If the data are evenly distributed around the mean, it is called a *normal* distribution *bell curve*. If the distribution is not normal, it is said to be *skewed* toward one tail or the other, with the downward curve being very steep (in close to the mean) or long (stretching away from the mean). As an example, a long curve to the left might indicate that most of the class failed a midterm test. If the long curve was to the right, too many passed the test (Johnson & Christensen, 2012; Suter, 2012) (see Figure 12.2).

The two most common statistics for measures of variation are *variance* and *standard deviation* (SD). Both include all of the data values, not just the highest and the lowest (which is called the range). Once the mean is known (the average), the variance and SD measures gauge how far the data are from the mean (distance)—that is, the difference between a person's raw score and the group's mean. Variance captures the *average* deviation, and standard deviation captures *how far* (distance) the numbers tend to vary from the mean (or how concentrated they are around the mean). Standard deviation is the most frequently used measure of variability (Ary et al., 2010) and is the focus of the next section. The bell curve comes into play in this discussion.

Standard deviation

An SD of 0 (zero) would mean that every single number in the data set is exactly the same; that is, there is *no variation*. One score above and below the mean is an SD of 1. If there is a normal distribution curve, roughly 68% of the raw scores will *always* fall within 1 SD (under the hump in the bell), 95% within 2 SD (along the curve), and 99.7% within 3 SD (ends of the tails). This is called the *68–95–99.7 rule*. An SD of 1 means the raw scores "belong to the mean." If the scores are not too far from the mean (which is desired), the SD will be low. As the scores move away from the mean, 1 SD at a time, patterns of change emerge that did not cause the mean. If there is a lot of fluctuation in the scores from the mean, there will be a higher SD, and one will want to look further to explain what is going on (Johnson & Christensen, 2012; Suter, 2012).

FIGURE 12.2 ■ Bell Curves

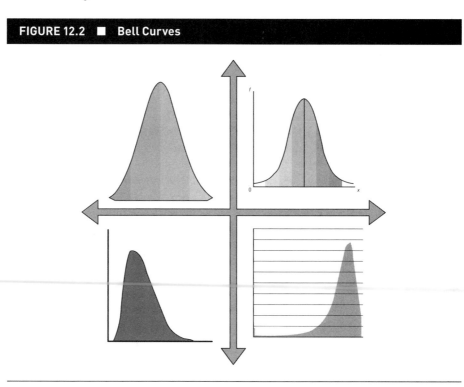

Source: Adapted from Microsoft clip art.

Some situations require a small SD, examples being parts manufacturing or quality control. Too much deviation from the required measurement could mean the parts will not fit together. In other situations, a large SD is not necessarily a bad thing. It just means there is a lot of variation in the particular group being studied. An example would be salaries.

Example 12.3 Standard deviation

If a descriptive data set is large enough and there are no sampling errors, it will look like a normal bell curve. Applying the *68–95–99.7* rule, the researcher can expect that if the average test score for a final exam is 75, then 68% of the raw scores will fall between 64 and 86, and 95% will fall between 53 and 97. This class reflects average performance, with a few excelling and a few failing.

Example 12.4 Standard deviation

Sometimes researchers form boundaries (i.e., set the SD ahead of time) and then make judgments (Suter, 2012). A nutrition researcher determined ahead of time that 20 pounds would be a reasonable weight for people to vary from a desired (mean) weight of 135 pounds (effect size). Anything else would be unhealthy. In this study, if the data have a normal distribution (i.e., a large enough sample with no errors), more than two thirds (68%) of participants would weigh between 115 and 155 pounds. And 95% would weigh between 95 and 175 pounds. A standard deviation of 2 pounds would be too small to suggest health implications, but an SD of 40 pounds would be too high (unhealthy).

In summary, using just the mean (average) and the SD, researchers can determine how similar or different people are in a data set. If there is a normal curve with an SD of 2 and most scores are close to the mean, people can safely use the mean to *describe* the whole sample. But a normal curve and a larger SD of 12 could imply that people are more different than they are alike in this data set, meaning the average (mean) cannot be used to describe the whole (Gall, Gall, & Borg, 2015). Matters change when the curve is not normal but is skewed (slanted, or heavy on one end).

Example 12.5 Skewed bell curve

Consider the example of teachers' salaries across states. With a normal distribution, one would expect to see an approximately equal number of states above and below the average salary of $52,000. But if only five states have the average, the curve is said to be skewed, meaning "a majority of the scores [are] bunched on one side of the mean and the other scores tail off on the other side of the mean" (Gall et al., 2015, p. 156). This result prompts researchers to wonder why salaries are so different in these five states.

Measures of Relative Standing

Sometimes researchers want to know how one person compares to others on a variable (for example, scores on a midterm exam). Knowing that a student obtained 73% on a test is more meaningful if one knows other students' scores on the same test. This is called a measure of relative standing and is calculated using percentile rank and *z* scores. Percentile rank tells where a person stands relative to a *reference group*. It is the percentage of scores that fall below a particular raw score. The *z* score positions people against *the mean* because it tells how far their score deviates from the average score. The number representing a *z* score is represented as ±1.00, or some other standard deviation (Johnson & Christensen, 2012).

Example 12.6 Percentile rank

Jenny scored 680 (raw score) on a verbal reasoning test. In this data set, her score corresponds to a percentile rank of 96%, which means that 96% of others taking the test scored lower than she did (only 4% scored higher). She did not score 96% on the test; rather, 96% of the rest scored lower than her score of 680.

Example 12.7 z score

Jenny's raw score of 680 on the verbal reasoning test equates to a *z* score of +2.00 SD. This score means she did better than the average person (i.e., scored higher than the mean). John's *z* score was −2.00, meaning he scored below the mean. Alice's *z* score was +3.50, which is far above average for this particular test group, even better than Jenny's.

Example 12.8 z score on two different tests for same person

Jenny got a *z* score of +2.00 on a verbal reasoning test and a *z* score of +5.00 on a written reasoning test. This tells us that she did better on the written test than on the verbal test.

REVIEW AND ENGAGEMENT

When critically reading a research report, you would

☐ Ascertain if the authors correctly used measures of central tendencies to get a sense of *typical characteristics* of a data set (reported using mean, mode, and median) (see Figure 12.1)

☐ Per the above, determine if they conscientiously reported central tendency measurements so as to not misrepresent their data, accounting for skewed outliers

☐ Determine if they correctly used measures of variation to study how *similar or different* people are on a variable (reported using range, variance, and standard deviation)

☐ Check to see that the authors correctly used measures of relative standing to gain a sense of how one person *compares* to others on a variable (reported as percentile rank and *z* scores)

☐ If they shared a bell curve diagram, confirm that they correctly interpreted it

Measures of Relationships

Finally, when using descriptive statistics, researchers can examine relationships among variables using either contingency tables (cross tabulations) or linear regression analysis. A *contingent* is a group of people with a common feature, forming part of a larger group (Anderson, 2014). These are called contingency tables because they represent a group of people with common features. They are also called cross tabulations because the statistical procedure presents the results in a table (i.e., tabulates results), comparing across groups. Contingency tables use nominal data (give the category [the common feature] a name and then assign that name a number [e.g., male sex = 1, female sex = 2, other sex = 3]). Using these tables, researchers can compare the relationship between two categorical (nominal) variables.

The lay notion of *regress* means to resort to an original state (Anderson, 2014). In statistics, it is an irregular use of the term (an anomaly) and means measuring the extent to which one variable is related to another (Swinscow, 1997). Also, statistically, regression is considered to be a transitive verb, meaning it needs a direct object to complete its meaning; in this case, regression *analysis* (Anderson, 2014). Regression analysis not only tells researchers if there is a relationship between variables. It also provides information about the strength and direction of the relationship. Regression analysis uses either ordinal or interval data. Both contingency tables and regression analysis identify associations (*not* causation) (Gall et al., 2015; Johnson & Christensen, 2012). Contingency tables and regression analysis are now discussed in more detail.

Contingency tables

Using contingency tables, researchers can interpret and then report the existence of relationships between two nominal (categorical) variables (e.g., gender and political party identification). A contingency table comprises four cells, with the rows representing one nominal variable and the columns representing the other nominal variable. Called a cross tabulation, the cells can contain percentages (%) or frequencies (*n* = 12) (Johnson & Christensen, 2012). The column totals are called *marginal totals* or *frequencies*, and the bottom right corner cell is the *grand total*, *N* or 120%. The significance of the results is often determined using the chi-square test, which helps researchers accept or reject the null hypothesis when the data are on nominal scales (Gall et al., 2015) (to be discussed shortly).

Example 12.9 Contingency table using percentages

Table 12.2 profiles U.S. political party identification by sex. Analysis shows that more than three quarters of the sample identified with the Democratic Party (77.2%). It also shows that males have the highest *rate* of membership (proportion) for the Democratic Party (85.2%) compared to females (69.8%). Depending on what point the author wants to make, this could be restated as less than one quarter of the sample identified with the Republican Party (22.5%), with females indicating a higher rate of Republican Party membership (30.2%) than males (14.8%). If campaigning for the Republican Party, people would have to intensify their efforts considerably (given the propensity of the sample to align with the Democratic Party), paying slightly more attention to men than women.

Example 12.10 Contingency table using frequency counts

Using survey data of 600 people (300 males and 300 females), researchers determined the number of males and females who said sex education in school is and is not important. This information (frequency counts) was used to create a contingency table, which displays the frequency data for each of these two nominal variables (see Table 12.3). Analyzing the table reveals that most people in the study felt that sex education in school is important (*n* = 482, 80%). But there was a difference between males and females (sex). Virtually all males believed sex education in school is important (*n* = 292, 97%). And, while most females also said it was important

TABLE 12.2 ■ Political Party Identification by Sex Contingency Table (Percentages)

Political Party Identification	Sex		Total
	Males	Females	
Democrat	85.2%	69.8%	77.5%
Republican	14.8%	30.2%	22.5%
Total	120%	120%	120%

TABLE 12.3 ■ Sex and Importance of Sex Education in School Contingency Table (Frequency Counts)

	Males	Females	Total
Receiving sex education in school is *not* important	8	112	$n = 118$
Receiving sex education in school *is* important	292	190	$n = 482$
Totals	$n = 300$	$n = 300$	$N = 600$

($n = 190$, 63%), more than a third of them did not think so ($n = 112$, 37%). One conclusion is that females have more varied opinions on this topic than males. Females were much more inclined to say sex education in school is not important.

Chi-square test of statistical significance. The chi-square *test of significance* needs some explanation. Chi-square results are reported in contingency tables. When testing for significance (*inferential* statistics, described in the next section), researchers calculate the chi-squared statistic value [$(O - E)^2/E$] with O meaning observed frequency and E meaning expected *by chance*. The *expected* frequency for each cell is calculated using the data set for the contingency table. It is the *row total times the column total divided by the total* N *for the table*. In the contingency table, the cells contain both the expected value (frequency) and what was observed in the data. If the value that was observed in the data is *less* than expected, the data in the cell are *not* statistically significant; that is, no effects were discovered. An interpretation of that particular cell's frequencies is not warranted because the data were obtained by chance. But if the observed value is greater than expected, the data in that cell are statistically significant (95% sure it is not due to chance) (Trochim & Donnelly, 2007).

Example 12.11 Chi-squared statistic

An example is provided in Table 12.4 (Stockburger, 1998). This study examined the incidence of men getting AIDS depending on their sexual orientation (homosexual, heterosexual, or bisexual). Homosexual men had a greater incidence of AIDS than would be expected by chance (Observed 4, Expected 2.1). This result means the data in the cell are statistically significant (i.e., there is something going on aside from chance). The same thing holds for men who were bisexual (Observed 3, Expected 1.5). Also, men who were heterosexual tended to *not* have AIDS (Observed 16, Expected 12.6). Note as well that, when the computed χ^2 statistic exceeds the critical value in the table for a $p < .05$ probability level, researchers can reject the null hypothesis; that is, the result is statistically significant (95% sure it is not due to chance).

TABLE 12.4 ■ Contingency Table With Observed and Expected Chi-square Values					
Incidence of AIDS		**Man's Sexual Orientation**			**Total**
		Prefer men (homosexual)	**Prefer women (heterosexual)**	**Prefer both (bisexual)**	
Have AIDS	Observed	4	2	3	$n = 9$
	Expected	2.1	5.4	1.5	
	Difference	1.9	−3.4	−1.5	
Do not have AIDS	Observed	3	16	2	$n = 21$
	Expected	4.9	12.6	3.5	
	Difference	−1.9	3.4	1.5	
Totals		$n = 7$	$n = 18$	$n = 5$	$N = 30$

REVIEW AND ENGAGEMENT

When critically reading a research report, you would

☐ Determine if the authors correctly used nominal data to create their contingency table

☐ Check to see if their choice of frequency counts or percentages best explained their results in their contingency table

☐ Check to see if their choice of frequency counts or percentages best explained their results in their contingency table

☐ Ascertain if they took the extra step to determine if their results were statistically significant (using the chi-square test of significance)

☐ Judge if they sufficiently massaged the cell data in their contingency table to get the best insights into what their descriptive results mean

Regression analysis

Using linear regression analysis computer software, researchers can determine (a) if there *is a relationship* between a dependent variable and one or more independent variables, and its *strength* (a number between −1 and +1); (b) the *effect* on the dependent variable of any changes in the independent variables (direct or inverse); and (c) the *direction* of the effect (increase or decrease) (Gall et al., 2015; Johnson & Christensen, 2012; Sykes, 1992). More details follow.

Example 12.12 Correlation regression

When exploring the relationship between the starting salary of new university graduates and their grade point averages (GPAs), researchers found an *r* value of +.89. There *is* a relationship between GPA and starting salary, and it is strong, positive, and direct. As GPA goes up, starting salaries are higher, and vice versa, as GPA goes down, starting salaries are lower. This result can be used to encourage students to get a high GPA because it means they will get paid more when they are initially hired. If there had been no relationship, people's starting salary would not change, no matter what happened to their GPA; that is, there would be no link at all between GPA and starting salary.

Interpreting the coefficient number r *value.* A computer software program (e.g., SPSS, SAS, or Excel) generates a regression coefficient (a single number) from the data set, a number ranging from –1 to +1, with a 0 in the middle. The software then pictorially plots this in a scattergram or scatterplot (to be discussed shortly). This coefficient is expressed as the *r* value (*r* for relationship). An *r* value of 0 means there is no relationship; that is, no matter what is done with the independent variable, the dependent variable is not affected. The higher the number (*r*), the more evidence there is of a relationship (i.e., an association). To illustrate, an *r* value of 1.0 means there is a perfect relationship. The number 92 ($r = .92$) is very close to 120, indicating a very strong relationship. An *r* value between .25 and .75 means a moderately strong relationship. Any number below 25 ($r = .25$) is getting closer to 0 and represents a weaker relationship (Trochim & Donnelly, 2007) (see Figure 12.3).

Interpreting regression scattergrams. Computer programs (e.g., SPSS, SAS, or Excel) are used to obtain a regression equation, and the results are shown in a scattergram or scatterplot. These graphs (which plot the data set) contain a horizontal x-axis (independent variable) and a vertical y-axis (dependent variable). The data are represented using a cluster of dots, and a real or imaginary *straight line* is drawn through the cluster of data; hence, the name *linear* regression (Graybill & Iyer, 1994). A *nonlinear* regression refers to scatter graphs with *curved* lines through the data cluster, representing, for example, situations where the dependent variable increases (decreases) with the independent variable but the *magnitude* of the rate of change becomes smaller and smaller (necessitating a curved line) (Graybill & Iyer, 1994).

The straight line can be horizontal or varying degrees of vertical (slope), leaning to the left or right (see below). While a simple linear regression has only one independent variable, multiple regressions have two or more independent variables that need to be plotted (Sykes, 1992). The shape of the cluster of data in the scatterplot indicates the strength of the relationship (see Figure 12.3).

In more detail, an *r* value of 1.0 means there is a perfect relationship, with a very compressed (flat) circle. The number 92 ($r = .92$) is very close to 120 but with a less flat circle. An *r* value between .25 and .75 means moderately strong, with a fuller circle. Any number below 25 ($r = .25$) represents a weak relationship with the circle being very full, remembering that no relationship ($r = 0$) is a full circle. In summary, if a circle were drawn around the cluster of data in the graph, its shape would vary from a perfect circle (no relationship) to a collapsed or compressed oval (a relationship). The flatter the circle (the more tightly clustered the data), the stronger the relationship (Trochim & Donnelly, 2007) (see Figure 12.3).

FIGURE 12.3 ■ Strength of Relationship and Shape of Scattergram/Scatterplot		
r value	Strength of relationship	Shape of scattergram/plot
$r = 1.0$	perfect	
$r = .76$ to $r = .99$	very strong	
$r = .75$ to $r = .25$	moderately strong	
$r = .24$ to $r = .01$	weak	
$r = 0$	no relationship	

Interpreting the plus and negative signs. The same scattergram interpretation principles hold for a negative r value as for a positive r value. *Negative* means the dependent variable decreases when the independent variable is changed. In more detail, a plus sign (direction) attached to the coefficient number ($r = +.72$) indicates there is a *positive* relationship, meaning the effect of any change in the independent variable is to *increase* the dependent. A negative sign ($r = -.72$) means a *negative* relationship, indicating that any change in the independent variable will *decrease* the dependent variable (Gall et al., 2015). For example, the more people drink, the more their balance and coherence decline.

Interpreting the slope of a data cluster. To be more specific, researchers need to know if the relationship is direct or inverse (indirect), regardless of whether it is positive or negative. If there is a *direct* relationship, both move in the same direction; that is, when one goes up, so does the other (and vice versa). If *indirect* or inverse, they move in opposite directions; that is, when one goes up, the other goes down (and vice versa). This aspect of the regression is represented by the *slope* of the data cluster—that is, whether the line or cluster leans to the right or left. When there is no relationship ($r = 0$), there is no slope, represented by a straight line parallel to the horizontal x-axis. When there is a *direct* relationship, the line (slope) steeples upward to the right. When there is an inverse relationship, the line (slope) steeples upward to the left (Trochim & Donnelly, 2007).

Figure 12.4 shows various scattergrams (also called scatterplots) for different *r* values (strength), directions (increase or decrease), negative or positive relationships, and slopes (direct or inverse effects) (Trochim & Donnelly, 2007).

Regression analysis and statistical significance. Readers must heed one additional point about regression analysis. When used for *descriptive* statistics, researchers input their data into a computer program, which generates an *r* value indicating the existence and strength of a relationship between independent and dependent variables (i.e., they are *associated*, but we cannot say one caused the other). An *r* = .73 indicates a moderately strong relationship or *association* (Trochim & Donnelly, 2007).

FIGURE 12.4 ■ Examples of Scattergrams

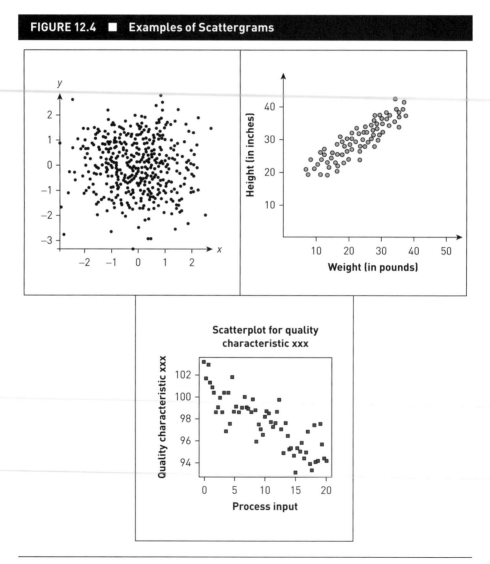

Source: Adapted from Microsoft clip art.

To be able to *infer* statistical significance (i.e., *cause and effect*), researchers need to set a predetermined *p* value (e.g., *p* < 0.5) for their null hypothesis. They now take the computer-generated *r* value from their data set (along with standard deviation and degrees of freedom) and consult a table of critical *r* values at the back of any statistics textbook. To complete the example from the previous paragraph, imagine the critical *r* value from the table is .4438. Because the critical *r* .4438 is less than the *p* < 0.5 set by the researchers, it can be concluded that this is not a chance occurrence, meaning the correlation (*r* = .73) is statistically significant and warrants further examination. In other words, it is *more than* an association (Trochim & Donnelly, 2007).

Common correlation coefficients. Regressions are concerned with how much the dependent variable changes with each one unit of change in the independent variable(s) (Johnson & Christensen, 2012). The most common correlation coefficients for descriptive statistics are the *Pearson product-moment correlation* (parametric) and the *Spearman rank-order correlation* (nonparametric). They differ on which type of measurement scale is used, with Pearson being interval and Spearman being ordinal—hence, its name rank-order (Wiersma & Jurs, 2009). They also differ, respectively, on whether they are calculated using the sample values from the population (parametric) or not (nonparametric) (Jones, 1996).

Reporting Descriptive Data

When reporting descriptive data in their research paper, authors can represent it numerically, graphically, and by commentary (often in combination). The previous discussion addressed the numerical representation of descriptive statistics (raw data, standard deviation, variance, *r* value, mean, mode, median, range, frequency counts, percentages, percentile ranks, and *z* scores). Graphical (visual) representations include tables (especially contingency tables, scatterplots, histograms, bar graphs, and pie graphs [see Chapter 13]). Finally, data can be represented by commentary, entailing text that explains the meaning and the import of the data contained in the numerical and graphical representations (usually in the Discussion section; see Chapter 14) (Gall et al., 2015; Johnson & Christensen, 2012; Mackey & Gass, 2005).

REVIEW AND ENGAGEMENT

When critically reading a research report, you would

- ☐ Determine if the authors provided and correctly interpreted regression coefficients and scattergrams/plots when reporting descriptive results (see Figure 12.3)

- ☐ Ascertain if they applied the correct statistical correlation relative to the measurement scale (e.g., Pearson for interval data, Spearman for ordinal data)

- ☐ Judge if they used an effective combination of numbers, graphics, and commentary when reporting *descriptive statistics*

- ☐ Determine if they took the extra step to see if their descriptive result was statistically significant (inferential) using their predetermined *p* value, the computer-generated *r* value, and a table of critical *r* values

ASSOCIATION AND CAUSATION

Anyone dealing with inferential statistics must be cognizant of the difference between causation and association, respectively, *causal* inference or inference of *association* (Pearl, 2009). A *causal* relationship means *x* caused *y* (i.e., made it happen). Correlation refers to *x* being *associated* with *y* but not necessarily causing *y* to happen (Bracey, 2006). Before discussing inferential statistics, this section addresses causation and association and what is involved in researchers determining if a perceived association is actually a causal relationship.

Example 12.13 Association

During World War II, it was observed that Allied bombers were less accurate when the weather was more clear (the opposite of what one would expect). But their inaccuracy had nothing to do with the weather, per se (i.e., was not caused by it). It was more likely because the enemy was also more active in the good weather (and were shooting at the Allied bombers). The increased enemy opposition meant the Allies were distracted by avoiding their bullets, accounting for their reduced accuracy when firing on the enemies in clear weather (Dallal, 2001).

Causal Inference and Inference of Association

Causal inference entails inferring the presence and the magnitude of cause-and-effect relationships from data. Many scholars privilege causation, asserting that focusing on only associations is misdirected research and can lead to misinformed practice, irrelevant or damaging policy, and ineffective programs (Daniel & De Stavola, 2012). But *inference of association* can be a very valuable research tool. It means observing things and concluding they *appear* to be related to each other, opening the door for further research. However, it is important to note that "the slogan 'correlation does not imply causation' can be translated into a useful principle: one cannot substantiate causal claims from associations alone. . . . Behind every causal conclusion there must lie some causal assumption that is not testable in observational studies" (Pearl, 2009, p. 99). In order for researchers to make a claim of causality, they have to find a mechanism causing the effect (Pearl, 2009).

Example 12.14 Causal mechanisms

- Dallal (2001) explained that, despite all of the statistical evidence, the causal relationship between smoking and cancer and heart disease could not be nailed down until researchers identified the substance in tobacco that triggered (caused) the disease (i.e., find the mechanism).

- It was observed that, as the amount of lemons imported from Mexico increased, the U.S. traffic fatality rate decreased. The lack of a plausible mechanism (how could a lemon cause a traffic fatality?), and the small effect size (only a 6% drop in fatality), invites alternate explanations. There is likely not a causal relationship between importing lemons and dying in a car accident.

- As the time to defibrillation after a heart attack increased, the survival rate decreased. The presence of a plausible mechanism (lack of oxygenated blood causes death), and the large effect size (a 62% reduction in survival rates after timely defibrillation), wards off alternate explanations. There is likely a causal relationship. The sooner the heart is shocked, the higher the chances of living.

Moving From Association to Causation

"The process of causal inference is complex, and arriving at a tentative inference of a causal or non-causal nature of an association is a subjective process" (Kumar, 2011). Hill (1965) developed a seminal set of criteria for determining if an association is in fact a causation. Prefacing his collection of criteria, he commented thus: "Our observations reveal an association between two variables, perfectly clear-cut and beyond what we would care to attribute to the play of chance. What aspects of that association should we especially consider before deciding that the most likely interpretation of it is causation?" (p. 295). The criteria most commonly applied to all research are set out in Table 12.5 (Hill, 1965). The mental exercise involved in moving from an association claim to a causal claim is set out in Figure 12.5.

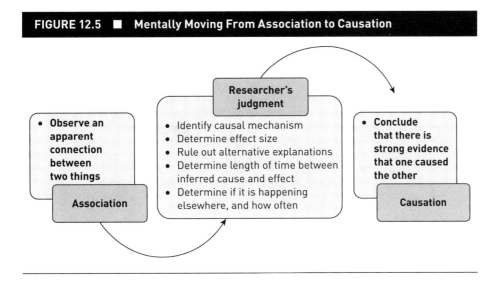

FIGURE 12.5 ■ Mentally Moving From Association to Causation

Researcher's judgment

- Observe an apparent connection between two things

Association

- Identify causal mechanism
- Determine effect size
- Rule out alternative explanations
- Determine length of time between inferred cause and effect
- Determine if it is happening elsewhere, and how often

- Conclude that there is strong evidence that one caused the other

Causation

Recommended Causation and Association Vocabulary

For clarification, certain words are considered appropriate for reporting cause-and-effect results, including *causes, is to blame for, from, changes, because of, leads to, due to, makes, accounted for, influences, effects, affects, promotes,* and *impacts.* When reporting associative results, researchers can say *attributed to, associated with, tied to, is related to, connected with, affiliated with,* and *linked to* (Cofield, Corona, & Allison, 2010; Miller, 2015).

TABLE 12.5 ■ Hill's (1965) Criteria for Causation (Passing From Association to Causation)	
Criterion	Explained
Strength	A strong effect (outcome) (determined using statistical tests) from the cause is more likely to be *causal* than a weak effect.
Consistency	The criterion is more likely to be causal if the association occurs repeatedly at other times and places and is observed by several researchers (replication).
Specificity	The more specific the criterion (the cause) to the effect, the more likely the association to be causal (if the cause is *specific* to the effect, meaning something else is not causing it).
Plausibility	The more the association agrees with accepted practice and is consistent with other knowledge, the more likely it is causal.
Temporality	What is attributed as the cause *must* precede the effect; the length of time between the cause and the effect matters as well (the closer, the better).
Coherence	The association must be in unity with known facts thought to be related (i.e., compatible with existing theory and knowledge). Note that some claims of causality may cause paradigm shifts because people have to reject current knowledge.
Alternate explanations	The more the researcher has taken into account and ruled out alternate explanations, the more likely the association is causal.

Example 12.15 Causation and association vocabulary (Miller, 2015, pp. 43–44)

Poor wording 1: "The effect of white hair on mortality was substantial, with five times the risk of any other hair color."

Why: The phrase "the effect of *x* (white hair) on *y* (mortality)" implies causality, when in fact other things could explain the hair color/mortality pattern (i.e., alternative explanations).

Poor wording 2: "White hair increased the risk of dying by 400%."

Why: The active verb (*increased*) suggests that white hair brought about the higher mortality rate. Unless there is good reason to suspect this (i.e., coherence), authors should avoid causal language.

Slightly better wording: "The whiter the hair, the higher the mortality rate" or "As hair gets whiter, mortality increases."

Why: These versions are written in neutral, purely descriptive language, failing to provide guidance about whether these patterns are thought to be causal or just an association.

Better wording: "People with white hair had considerably higher mortality rates than people with a different hair color. However, most people with white hair were over age 60—a high-mortality age group—so the *association* between white hair and high mortality is probably due to their mutual association with older age."

Why: Using the more neutral verb (*had*) and linking both white hair and high mortality with old age helps readers grasp that white hair is not likely to be the cause of higher mortality; instead, there is likely just an association, confounded by other factors. For, with this wording, the focus shifted from the attribute (white hair) to other possible differences between people who do and do not have the attribute, differences that could explain (confound) the hair color/mortality pattern (e.g., age).

REVIEW AND ENGAGEMENT

When critically reading a research report, you would

☐ Determine if the authors met most of Hill's (1965) seven criteria for making an *inferential* causation claim (moving from association to causal) (see Figure 12.5)

☐ Ascertain if they used statistically appropriate vocabulary when communicating causation and association claims (i.e., did not infer causation for an association by choosing the wrong words)

INFERENTIAL STATISTICS

To *infer* means to draw from specific cases to more general cases (Anderson, 2014). In this scenario, the *specifics* of a woman holding a baby diaper, wearing a spit-up-stained shirt, and warming a baby bottle on the stove lead one to infer that the woman is a mother (a *general* position based on observed *specifics*). In the field of statistics, *inferential* statistics allow researchers to draw a relationship found in a specific *sample* (a specific case) to the larger, *general* population (called *general*ization). They can also examine relationships or differences between groups within a sample that did not happen by chance (Wiersma & Jurs, 2009).

To explain inference, consider that any given population comprises a set of *parameters* (characteristics or factors) that define it and determine its scope (its boundaries and limits). *Parameter* is Greek *para*, "issuing from," and *metron*, "measure" (Harper, 2016). A parameter is a measurable factor of a population. Because it is usually impossible to measure a whole population, researchers draw a sample from it and collect statistics about the sample. A statistic is any number calculated from a sample (not the whole population) (Thomas, 2008). To help remember this, both *parameter* and *population* start with the letter *p*, and *sample* and *statistic* start with *s*. "Inferences are made and conclusions are drawn about parameters from the statistics of the sample—hence, the name inferential statistics" (Wiersma & Jurs, 2009, p. 405).

There are two main approaches to inferential statistics: (a) hypotheses testing and (b) parameter estimations. To *test* is to validate (as strong), and to *estimate* is to judge something to be probable (Anderson, 2014). Being strong (valid) is more forceful than being probable (estimated). Put simply, when *estimating*, researchers normally use research questions to deal with approximate calculations. They use hypothesis testing when they are interested in validity, a different perspective. Estimation would ask, "*By how much* does this new drug delay relapse?" while hypothesis testing would ask, "*Does* the new drug delay relapse?" (Thomas, 2008). The following section describes the differences between these two approaches (see Figure 12.6).

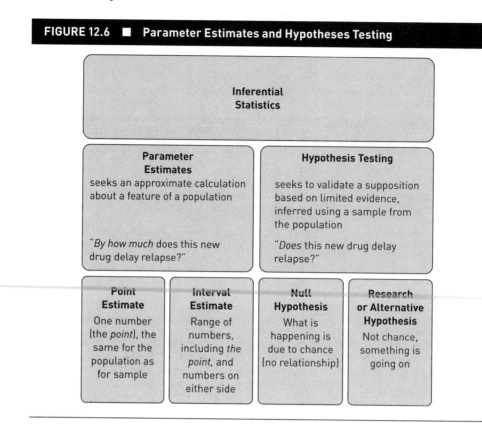

FIGURE 12.6 ■ Parameter Estimates and Hypotheses Testing

Inferential Statistics

Parameter Estimates
seeks an approximate calculation about a feature of a population

"By how much does this new drug delay relapse?"

Hypothesis Testing
seeks to validate a supposition based on limited evidence, inferred using a sample from the population

"Does this new drug delay relapse?"

Point Estimate
One number (the *point*), the same for the population as for sample

Interval Estimate
Range of numbers, including *the point*, and numbers on either side

Null Hypothesis
What is happening is due to chance (no relationship)

Research or Alternative Hypothesis
Not chance, something is going on

Hypothesizing Parameters (Hypotheses Testing)

A parameter is a characteristic that can help identify or classify something. Typical *statistical* parameters are mean, mode, medium, and variance (discussed earlier). The most common approach to *inferring* parameters from samples (which are chosen from an entire population) is to test hypotheses. Researchers make conjectures about one or more characteristics about a population (parameters). These conjectures (best guesses based on incomplete information) are posited in a statement called a hypothesis (rather than a research question, discussed in Chapter 6). Researchers test the hypothesis by collecting a sample from the whole population and running statistical procedures on the sample. If the hypothesis is consistent with the sample, it is retained as a tenable value for the parameter, the entire population (Wiersma & Jurs, 2009).

Example 12.16 Hypothesizing parameters (testing hypotheses)

A researcher hypothesizes that both males and females (whole population) have *equal* "attitudes toward independent reading." If the *sample* means between males and females are close, the researcher can conclude that the hypothesis is plausible; that is, the population means are equal (males and females have *equal* "attitudes toward independent reading"). If the mean scores are very different, the hypothesis is rejected, meaning the samples differ significantly according to this statistical test. Said another way, the population means are not equal (i.e., males and females have *different* "attitudes toward independent reading") (Wiersma & Jurs, 2009).

Hypothesis testing

In more detail, when hypothesis testing, researchers develop hypotheses about a population and then *test* them on the basis of observations of a sample drawn *from* that population (Ary et al., 2010). A hypothesis is a supposition made by using limited evidence and is the starting point for further investigation (Anderson, 2014). People assume something (propose it) and then use the hypothesis as a premise from which conclusions are inferred. The term *hypothesis testing* is used because researchers have to determine if their supposition is acceptable or if it has to be rejected. The basic tool for this process is the *null hypothesis*. *Null* means none or no (Harper, 2016). A null hypothesis says there will be *no* relationship between the dependent and independent variable(s). The null *assumes* that any observed relationship is simply by chance (Ary et al., 2010).

Actually, many researchers intentionally state the null (i.e., what happens will be due to chance), *hoping* they can reject this assumption when their results show that something *is* going on that warrants further investigation (Suter, 2012). In a simple analogy, researchers are similar to a prosecuting attorney in that they bring the null hypothesis "to trial" believing there will be strong evidence against it. Researchers usually believe the null is *not* true, but they approach scholarship as if it *is* true, seeking evidence to refute it (Boudah, 2011; Johnson, 2006). If they refute it (reject the null), they can then move forward with the alternative or research hypotheses, which say there *is* a relationship between the variables. More details about hypotheses are provided in Chapter 14.

Example 12.17 Null hypothesis

"There is no significant relationship between solvency (dependent variable) and debt load (independent variable)." Whatever happens is due to chance. If this null statement cannot be retained (i.e., it turns out that more than chance is involved), it means that solvency may actually *be* affected by debt load, a result that warrants further research. An appropriate research question would be "How does debt load (owing money) affect people's ability to remain solvent (have sufficient money to pay debts owed)?" An alternative (research) hypothesis might be "There is a direct, inverse relationship between solvency (dependent variable) and debt load (independent variable)."

REVIEW AND ENGAGEMENT

When critically reading a research report, you would

☐ Ascertain if the authors clearly listed their null and/or research hypotheses, numbering them for ease of reference

☐ Determine if they clearly reported whether the hypotheses were supported or refuted; did they accept or reject the null?

Parameter Estimations

Rather than hypothesizing about parameters, researchers can estimate them. Estimating a parameter entails collecting data about a phenomenon from a sample and then *estimating* the characteristics of the phenomenon *from* the sample (rather than *testing* a supposition [hypothesis] about the population using a sample) (Wiersma & Jurs, 2009). An estimate is an approximate calculation. It is someone's judgment or appraisal, like an estimate for car repairs (rather than a firm quote) (Anderson, 2014).

For clarification, "statistics" are *calculated*, but the corresponding "parameters" are *estimated*; that is, the "sample statistic is calculated from the sample data and the population parameter is inferred (or estimated) from this sample statistic" (Jones, 1996). Using statistical inference, people "estimate **parameters** (characteristics of populations) from **statistics** (characteristics of samples). Such *estimations* are based on the laws of probability and are *best estimates* rather than absolute facts" (Ary et al., 2010, p. 148, bold in original, italics added). The accuracy of the estimation increases as the sample size increases, meaning researchers have to carefully decide how big their sample should be (Jones, 1996) (to be discussed shortly).

Single-point and interval estimates

Also, there are two types of estimates, a *single-point* estimate and an *interval estimate* (a range of numbers with a confidence interval—the chance that the estimate [point] falls within this range). Put simply, the single point for the population is the same value number as the sample statistic. On the other hand, the interval contains estimates (plural) expressed as plus or minus (e.g., 50 lb ± 5, meaning the value for the population could range from 45 to 55 pounds) (Brown, 2009; Wiersma & Jurs, 2009).

The calculated confidence interval is only an *approximation* to the exact one, which is *why* it is called an estimate. In practice, confidence intervals are typically stated at the *95% confidence level* and are set by the researcher, not by the data. This means the researcher is 95% confident that the estimate will fall within the range of numbers, while appreciating that the interval computed from the sample may in fact not include the true value of the population. That is why it is called an estimate, an approximation. Because the sample is random, so is the confidence interval that is obtained (Field, 2013).

Indeed, both point estimates and interval estimates are made from random sample data (not the whole population) (Brown, 2009; Wiersma & Jurs, 2009). A good estimator must satisfy three conditions (i.e., unbiased, consistent, and efficient). Respectively, it must be equal to the mean of the population (parameter), meaning it is *unbiased*. As the sample size increases, the estimator value must get closer to the value of the population parameter (be *consistent* with the population). And it has to have the smallest variance of all estimators that *could* be used (relatively *efficient*, so the estimation is the best approximation possible) (Jones, 1996). The larger the sample, the stronger the estimate (Field, 2013).

Example 12.18 Point and interval estimation

In order to estimate the average weight of the population of fourth graders in the state of Utah, the researcher took a random sample from this population and then inferred (estimated) the average weight. She did this and found that the mean of her random sample was 70 pounds. The best *point estimate* (one number) for the whole state is that fourth graders weigh on average 70 pounds each. But inferential statistics also calculated a confidence *interval estimate* of 70 ± 8. This estimate provides more information than just the single point estimate. Their weight would be "70 pounds give or take 8 pounds" or range from 62 to 78 pounds (Wiersma & Jurs, 2009).

Example 12.19 Point estimation

"Decision theory provides powerful motivation for point estimators. If I'm a hot dog vendor then I might be interested in an *estimate* of how many hot dogs people will buy so that I know how many to stock. I can't stock a fuzzy number of hot dogs; I need to pick one number and go with it. So the idea is to introduce a loss function and try to make a decision that makes the expected loss small. If the loss is some sort of measure of distance between our decision (the number of hot dogs we decide to stock) and a *parameter* (the actual number of hot dogs that people want to buy), then, in this setup, the problem is essentially one of point estimation" (Guy, 2012).

REVIEW AND ENGAGEMENT

When critically reading a research report, you would

☐ Ascertain if the authors clearly stated what parameters were being estimated and how (point estimate or interval estimate) (see Figure 12.6), with justification

☐ Determine if they reported a confidence level for their estimates (approximations)

☐ Confirm that they addressed the issue of sample size and the power of their estimations

☐ Check to see if they discussed whether their estimator met the criteria for a good estimation

---

In addition to parameter estimation and hypothesis testing, several key concepts come into play when using inferential statistics, including (a) *p* value and the level of significance, (b) Type I and II errors, and (c) statistical power (including sample size and effect size).

p Value and the Level of Significance

Before conducting their study, researchers have to decide how strong the evidence has to be before they will reject the null and accept that something is actually going on. This predetermination is called the *level of significance.* In statistics, a result is significant if it did not arise from chance. This idea is expressed as a *p* value. Different academic referencing styles use different italic, case, and hyphen conventions to report *p* value, with this chapter using the American Psychological Association (APA) citation style (VandenBos, 2010)—that is, an italicized, lowercase *p* with no hyphen between it and the word *value* (*p* value).

Per the basic tenet of statistics, the letter *p* stands for probability: the *probability value*. The *p* value is a number between 0 and 1. A *p* of 0 means no chance at all. A *p* of 1 means all chance. The *p* number represents the probability that the null hypothesis is true (i.e., nothing is going on except by chance). *P* is a cutoff level beyond which things are not happening due to chance. The two most common *p* values are .05 and .01, read respectively as 5% and 1%. A *p* value of .0414 is read as 4.14%. A *p* value of .0001 means the chance of making an error in rejecting or accepting the null is 1 in 12,000 or less (Ary et al., 2010). A very low *p* value corresponds with the very high probability of correctly concluding there is a difference; that is, the null can be rejected, and the research hypothesis can be explored (Miller, 2015).

The *rule of thumb* is to set the risk level of not encountering chance at 5%, *p* < .05. This means there is less than a 5% likelihood that the phenomenon being tested occurred by chance alone. This is also referred to as the *95% criterion*. If the computer-calculated *p* value (see the next paragraph) is greater than the researcher's chosen value of .05 (for example *p* < .058), the result "tends toward significance," meaning more research must be done before conclusions can be made. With *p* < .01, researchers are accepting even less incidence of chance (1%, 1 in 120), and *p* < .001 is as close to certain as a result can be (1 in 1,200 or less) (Johnson & Christensen, 2012). A *p* of 90% or higher is generally acceptable for most disciplines (Pirk et al., 2013).

In a study, researchers first set a *p* value that they will accept for *their* study. The computer program analyzes the data set, and then it generates a *p* value for the *data set*. Researchers must compare their predetermined level of significance to this computer-generated number. A computer-generated *p* value of .06 (tip, read 60) is larger than the researcher-determined *p* value of .05 (read 50), meaning the null is accepted (i.e., the result is due to chance). A computer-generated *p* value of .03 (read 30) is less than the researcher-determined *p* value of .05 (read 50), meaning the null is rejected. When the null hypothesis (which says there is no relationship) is rejected, the result is said to be *statistically significant*, meaning something is going on that is more than coincidence or mere chance (Johnson & Christensen, 2012; Suter, 2012) (see Figure 12.7).

As a caveat, *p* values are often misunderstood and misreported, even in the best journals and by the foremost scientists and researchers. Despite its conventional usage, some statisticians view the previous explanation of what a *p* value means as incorrect. They would suggest that if the *p* value is .03, it is tempting to conclude that there is a 97% chance that the observed difference reflects a *real* difference between populations and a 3% chance that the difference is due to chance. However, this would be an incorrect conclusion (Frost, 2015).

Frost (2015) explained: "If you think a P value of 0.05 equates to a 5% chance of a mistake, boy, are you in for a big surprise—because it's often around 26%! . . . [Y]ou'll need a P value around 0.0027 to achieve an error rate of about 5%." In plain language, he asserted that the *p* value is how likely people are to *observe what they observe* in their sample, not whether the null hypothesis is actually correct. He explained that what *can* be said about the *p* value of .03 is that random sampling from identical populations would lead to a difference smaller than that observed in 97% of experiments and larger than that observed in 3% of experiments. Despite this interesting interpretation, quantitative scholars use the *p* value as explained in this chapter.

FIGURE 12.7 ■ Relating Researchers' Preset *p* Value to a Computer-Generated *p* Value

Researchers set a *p* value for *their study*		The computer generates a *p* value for *the data set*	Researchers compare their preset *p* value with the computer's *p* value	Researchers accept or reject the null hypothesis
0	No chance at all		If the computer number is *larger* than the researchers' number, the null is accepted.	*Accepting (retaining) the null* means nothing is going on (just a chance result); the result is not *statistically significant*.
< .0001	1 in 12,000 it is chance		If the computer number is *less* than the researchers' number, the null is rejected.	*Rejecting the null* means something is going on (other than chance); the result is *statistically significant*.
< .001	Less than .01% it is chance 1 in 1,200			
< .01	Less than 1% it is chance 1 in 120			
< .05 the 95% criterion	Less than 5% it is chance 1 in 20			
1	All chance			

REVIEW AND ENGAGEMENT

When critically reading a research report, you would

☐ Ascertain if the authors clearly stated what parameters were being estimated and how (point estimate or interval estimate) (see Figure 12.6), with justification

☐ Determine if they reported a confidence level for their estimates (approximations)

☐ Confirm that they addressed the issue of sample size and the power of their estimations

☐ Check to see if they discussed whether their estimator met the criteria for a good estimation

Type I and II Errors

In *inferential* statistics, *error* does not mean blame; rather, it refers to a fluke in sampling or to a chance occurrence. Researchers must accept that *erroneous* inferences are very possible (Gall et al., 2015). Retaining the null means there really *is no* relationship (just a chance result), and rejecting it means there *is* a relationship between the dependent and independent variables. The *p* value cannot fix blunders when researchers make mistakes or *errors* when interpreting their results. Because hypotheses are suppositions based on *limited* evidence, it *is* possible to make a mistake when deciding to keep or reject the null. There are two types of errors the researchers can make (mistakes of judgment), called Type I and Type II errors (Ary et al., 2010; Suter, 2012).

A *Type I error* occurs when researchers mistakenly reject a true null (when they should have retained it). This is a *false alarm*, wherein the researchers think there is something when there is not (they wrongly believe it). Conversely, if the null is not true, but the researchers mistakenly retain it, a *Type II error* has been committed (they should have rejected it). This is a *miss*, meaning there *is* something going on, and they missed it. The consequences of a Type I error are normally more serious than for Type II because people using the results may make unwarranted changes (when they should have left things alone). On the other hand, a Type II error means people using the results may keep the status quo when a change is actually warranted (Ary et al., 2010; Gall et al., 2015; Jones, 1996; Suter, 2012) (see Figure 12.8).

Researchers can minimize these errors by picking a very small *p* value for their study (*p* < .05, or better yet *p* < .01) and by using a large sample (Jones, 1996). Although everyone might not agree, Gall et al. (2015) proposed that "it is better to make the error of concluding [that] an ineffective new practice is effective than the error of concluding that an effective new practice is ineffective" (p. 174).

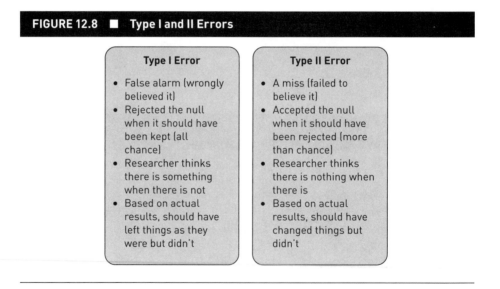

FIGURE 12.8 ■ Type I and II Errors

Type I Error

- False alarm (wrongly believed it)
- Rejected the null when it should have been kept (all chance)
- Researcher thinks there is something when there is not
- Based on actual results, should have left things as they were but didn't

Type II Error

- A miss (failed to believe it)
- Accepted the null when it should have been rejected (more than chance)
- Researcher thinks there is nothing when there is
- Based on actual results, should have changed things but didn't

Example 12.20 Type I and II errors

Type 1 Error—Researchers in a drug trial concluded (in error) that the new drug is more effective than the conventional drug, when in fact it is not. Based on this erroneous inference, they pursued testing the new drug when this strategy was unwarranted because it is not more effective than what already exists. They should have considered abandoning it.

Type II Error—Researchers in a drug trial concluded (in error) that the new drug is *not* more effective than the conventional drug, when in fact it is. Based on this erroneous inference, they stopped testing the new drug because they thought it was a blind alley. Abandoning the drug was unwarranted because it *is* more effective than what existed already (Gall et al., 2015).

Statistical Power (and Statistical Significance)

In empirical, quantitative research, *power* refers to "the number of subjects needed to give the investigator the desired power to reject the null hypothesis for specified effect size and level of significance" (Ary et al., 2010, p. 169). It is the ability of a statistical procedure to detect an effect, *if* the effect actually exists. Statistical power refers to avoiding a Type II error (i.e., retaining the null when it should have been rejected). "Statistical power is directly related to sample size. The larger the sample, the greater the statistical power. In practical terms, this means that we are more likely to find statistical significance with large samples than with small samples" (Wiersma & Jurs, 2009, p. 339). If a research design (especially sample size) has statistical power, the statistical procedure can detect group differences or relationships (Johnson & Christensen, 2012) (see Figure 12.9).

Researchers can deal with statistical power before or after the study. The a priori (before) approach tries to make sure the sample size is large enough even before collecting the data

---

FIGURE 12.9 ■ Statistical Power

Statistical power
- The smaller the sample size, the easier it is to commit a Type II error (think there is nothing when there is)
- Harder to detect group differences or relationships with smaller sample
- Less likely to find *statistically significant* results (cause and effect)

STATISTICAL POWER
- The larger the sample size, the easier it is to avoid a Type II error (accept a false negative)
- Easier to detect group differences or relationships with a larger sample
- Easier to discover weaker relationships with a larger sample
- More likely to find *statistically significant* results (cause and effect)

(see the next section on effect size). A post hoc statistical power analysis is conducted after the data have been analyzed and the decision has been made to retain the null hypothesis (likelihood of committing a Type II error) (Garbin, 2016). In both instances, researchers consult Cohen's (1988) book *Statistical Power Analysis for the Behavioral Sciences* to determine minimum sample size.

Statistical significance

Statistical power is also related to *statistical significance*, which simply means the statistical results are not due to sample fluctuations or chance. In inferential statistics, the term *significant* does not imply *importance*, and the term *statistical significance* is not the same as research, theoretical, or practical significance or importance (Wiersma & Jurs, 2009); see example 12.21. In plain language, a statistic is significant if it was not caused by chance. If it was caused by chance, it is considered to be an insignificant result in a particular study, meaning it has little to no value to the researcher when addressing the research problem.

Example 12.21 Statistical power and statistical significance

A researcher who was studying childhood obesity had a sample mean of 77 pounds, and the hypothesized value of the population mean was 75 pounds. This very small difference in weight was found to be statistically significant (not chance), but a 2-pound difference probably has no practical importance, meaning programs would not have to change (Wiersma & Jurs, 2009).

In another study that used an ANOVA statistical procedure, students who were eligible for free lunches had a mean on the science section of the Pre-Admission Content Test (PACT) that was roughly 20 points higher than the mean of students who were not eligible for free or reduced-price lunch. This difference is statistically significant and most likely is of practical significance (importance) as well. It implies that students who are hungry perform less well on science tests than those students who are not hungry. To address this result, the school could consider providing a free lunch for everyone if it wanted to improve science scores (Wiersma & Jurs, 2009).

Sample Size and Effect Size

When using inferential statistics, the larger the sample size, the greater the statistical power. And, if researchers can determine ahead of time what effect they want to see, they can better determine the size of the sample needed to best ensure statistical precision and power, called *effect size*.

Example 12.22 Sample and effect size Researchers believe that a particular intervention must change scores on a measure by 15 points in order to improve academic performance. If they know the effect size (15), as well as their predetermined significance level ($p < .05$) and the desired level of statistical power (possibly .80), they can determine the necessary sample size *before* they start their study (Wiersma & Jurs, 2009).

Example 12.22 also exemplifies situations where researchers want to know if their intervention will have *practical* significance (let alone statistical significance) (Gall et al., 2015). In another example, the effect size for a study about an educational program might be "a number that indicates the degree to which participants in the experimental group show superior performance compared to the comparison group, called the control group; that is, no educational program or [participants] are in an alternative program" (Gall et al., 2015, p. 61).

If the effect size from the statistical analysis is large (i.e., if the magnitude of the difference between group means is large), the test of statistical significance will have the power to reject the null (there is more going on than chance) (Gall et al., 2015). In other words, the *size* of the difference between the means *affects* the researchers' ability to assume something is going on not caused by chance. Also, if researchers are interested in uncovering weak relationships between variables, they will need a larger sample size. And, with the proper effect size, strong relationships can be uncovered with fewer participants (Suter, 2012), remembering the Golden Rule that "the larger the sample size, the greater the statistical power."

For a final clarification, in experimental research designs (see Chapter 11), effect size refers to the magnitude of difference in outcomes among experimental groups or experimental conditions. For nonexperimental research designs, effect size is the degree of difference between intact groups and conditions as observed in natural settings (Boudah, 2011).

REVIEW AND ENGAGEMENT

When critically reading a research report, you would

☐ Accepting that erroneous inferences *are* possible, determine if the authors addressed any issues of *Type I* and *Type II errors* (possible misjudgments when deciding to keep or reject the null). This includes justifying the *p* value chosen and the sample size (see Figure 12.8)

☐ Check to see if they commented on *statistical significance* (ruled out chance) and the *power* of their statistical procedures, affected by sample size and by effect size (they should have commented on these, too) (see Figure 12.9)

☐ Judge whether the authors appreciated the differences between *statistical significance* (ruled out chance) and any practical, theoretical, or research significance or the importance of the result (i.e., did not confuse them)

Most Common Inferential Statistical Tests

On a final note, as briefly noted in Table 12.1, statistical inferential tests can be organized into four broad categories, according to whether they are parametric or nonparametric (see Table 12.6 for even more details). Regarding the four categories, researchers could be interested in whether (a) two groups are different, (b) three or more groups are different, (c) there is a relationship between variables, and (d) what they observed is what they expected. This deceptively simple summary cannot do justice to the richness of statistical theory and procedures. Such knowledge requires a solid grounding in introductory, intermediate, and advanced statistics courses, beyond the scope of this book.

TABLE 12.6 ■ Fundamental Inferential Statistical Tests		
Statistical Test	History	Typical Tests and Their Purpose
PARAMETRIC		
t test	Often called *Student's test statistic*. William Sealy Gosset was a university chemist and professional statistician working at the Guinness brewery (and he also took university courses). He developed a way (a test) to monitor the quality of the company's stout beer. *Student* was his pen name when he published the article about the new statistical test (1908), and *t* is short for test.	Compare two groups to see if they are different • Treatment-control research designs • Pretest and posttest research designs Statistical tests: • *One-tailed (one-sided)* t *test* detects an effect in one direction • *Two-tailed (two-sided)* t *test* detects an effect in both directions • z *test* uses actual population mean rather than a sample mean • *One-sample* t *test* (also *paired-difference* t *test*) (Wilcoxon signed-rank test and Welch's *t* test [not good if there are outliers]) • *Independent two-sample* t *test* (two groups' means distilled to one value)
F test	*F* stands for Ronald Fisher, whose name was used by George Snedecor to honor Fisher's earlier work (1920s) by naming this test after him.	Compare three or more groups to see if they are different. Look at differences *within* groups (due to natural circumstances) and *between* groups (due to a treatment or an intervention). In experiments, variables are manipulated by researchers. In nonexperiments, no variables are manipulated; the phenomenon is naturally occurring and is observed and interpreted. The statistical test is called ANOVA (analysis of variance), with popular research designs: • *One-way ANOVA* (two or more independent *groups*) • *Factorial* ANOVA (interactions among the treatments)

Statistical Test	History	Typical Tests and Their Purpose
PARAMETRIC		
		• *Repeated measures ANOVA* (the same subjects are used for each treatment, especially in longitudinal studies) • *Multivariate analysis of variance* (MANOVA), used when there is more than one dependent variable
r value	*r* stands for relationship and for regression, a term first coined in the 1800s by Francis Galton to describe when something regresses down toward the average (returns to a former state).	Determine relationships between and among variables (strength, direction, and slope). • *Simple linear regression* (one independent variable) • *Multiple linear regression* (impact of numerous simultaneous influences [independent] upon one dependent variable) • *Nonlinear regressions* (one or more independent and dependent variables; the line through the data is *curved*, not straight, indicating an optimal best fit, e.g., a Lorenz curve)
NONPARAMETRIC		
X^2 test	The test and its name are credited to Karl Pearson (1900). It is named after the 22nd Greek alphabet letter *chi* (χ, pronounced *ki*, like *high*). It is called the *chi-square distribution test* or *Pearson's chi-squared test*. It is also called the *goodness of fit test* (i.e., how well what is observed *fits* with what was expected).	Compare what is observed with what was expected. Frequency counts of categorical data between two independent groups are displayed in contingency tables or cross tabulations (matrices). If what is *observed* is higher than what was *expected*, the data in a cell are statistically significant (more than chance) and warrant interpretation. Uses descriptive statistics (not inferential) because data are categorical (e.g., 1 = *male*). Data cannot be manipulated; they are what they are (e.g., age, eye color, sex). Statistical tests: • *One-tailed (one-sided)* t *test* (in a normal distribution, deviations from the mean are possible in only one direction) • *Two-tailed (two-sided)* t *test* (in a normal distribution, deviations from the mean are possible in both directions)

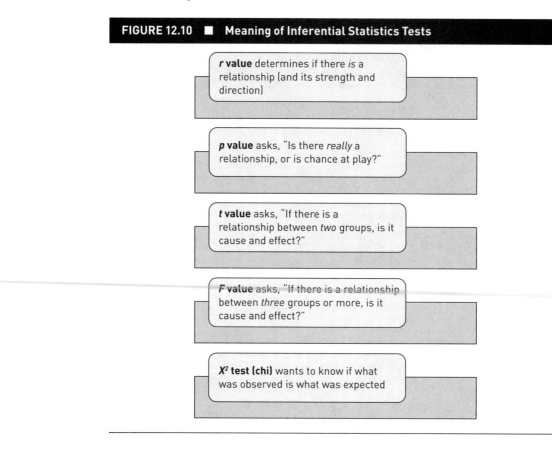

FIGURE 12.10 ■ Meaning of Inferential Statistics Tests

r **value** determines if there *is* a relationship (and its strength and direction)

p **value** asks, "Is there *really* a relationship, or is chance at play?"

t **value** asks, "If there is a relationship between *two* groups, is it cause and effect?"

F **value** asks, "If there is a relationship between *three* groups or more, is it cause and effect?"

X² **test (chi)** wants to know if what was observed is what was expected

In summary, when using inferential statistics, the *r* value determines *if* there is a relationship (and its strength and direction); this means there is an association. The *p* value asks, "Is there *really* a relationship, or is chance at play?" The *t* value asks, "If there is a relationship between *two* groups, is it cause and effect?" The *F* value asks, "If there is a relationship between *three* groups or more, is it cause and effect?" For the latter two, researchers have to satisfy that their results match enough of Hill's (1965) criteria so that an association can progress to a causation (see Table 12.5 and Figure 12.5). The χ² (chi-square) test wants to know if what was observed is what was expected (see Figure 12.10).

REVIEW AND ENGAGEMENT

When critically reading a research report, you would

☐ Look to see if the authors clearly indicated whether they were conducting parametric or nonparametric statistical tests (see Table 12.6) (did they use these terms?)

☐ If a parametric test, determine if they clarified whether it was some combination of *t* test (compare two groups), *F* test (compare three or more groups), or *r* value (determine relationships) (see Figure 12.10)

☐ Per the above, ascertain if the authors clearly stipulated which statistical tests were conducted (e.g., one-tailed *t* test, one-way ANOVA, simple linear regression) (see Table 12.6), with justification relative to their research questions or hypotheses

☐ If a nonparametric test (nominal data), ascertain if the authors reported a chi-square test (ruled out chance) to determine if their results were *statistically significant* (did they observe what they expected, or was it chance?) (see Table 12.6)

Reporting Inferential Statistics

When authors are reporting inferential statistics (estimates or hypotheses), they must indicate which of these statistical values were employed: r, p, t, F, χ^2, and z (see Figure 12.10), and they must discuss levels of significance and the statistical power of their tests (linked to sample size and effect size). Another important point of discussion is how much chance of a Type I error they were willing to live with. If researchers set their p value above .05 (which is uncommon but happens) (see Figure 12.7), they have to account for a Type I error (i.e., thinking there is something when there is not). A p value of $< .05$ means they are 95% confident that the results are not due to chance. A p value of $< .10$ or $< .20$ means they are 90% and 80% confident, respectively, with 90% or higher generally acceptable for most disciplines (Pirk et al., 2013).

FINAL JUDGMENT ON THE DESCRIPTIVE OR INFERENTIAL STATISTICAL DISCUSSION

Taking *all* of the **Review and Engagement** criteria into account, what is your final judgment of the descriptive and/or inferential statistical discussion in the paper you are critically reading?

CONCLUSION

Together, Chapters 11 and 12 provide a primer on statistics (see Table 12.7). Novice researchers and critical readers of research are encouraged to consult statisticians and data managers who are trained to work with large data sets and to conduct and help others interpret tests of statistical significance and association. Seeking help lessens the need to "plead ignorance" and eschew critically analyzing the research report (Gall et al., 2015, p. 181).

TABLE 12.7 ■ Overview of Chapter 11 ("Statistical Literacy and Conventions") and Chapter 12 ("Descriptive and Inferential Statistics")		
Chapter 11 **Statistical Literacy and Conventions**	**Chapter 12**	
	Descriptive Statistics	**Inferential Statistics**
History of Statistics	Measures of Central Tendencies (mean, mode, and median)	Association and Causation
Laws of Probability and Chance		
Statistical Literacy	Measures of Variation (range, variance, and standard deviation and bell curve)	Hypotheses (null and research)
Statistical Data Types (nominal, ordinal, interval, and ratio) and Measurement Scales		Estimates (point and interval)
Statistical Variables (11)	Measures of Relative Standing (percentile rank and z scores)	p value and Level of Significance
Experimental Research (true, factorial, quasi-, and single-case) Nonexperimental Research (group comparisons, correlational, surveys, case studies)	Measures of Relations: – Contingency tables (chi-square) – Regression analysis (correlational coefficient and scattergrams)	Type I and Type II Errors
	Reporting Descriptive Statistics	
		Statistical Power and Statistical Significance
		Sample Size and Effect Size
		Common Inferential Statistical Tests: – Parametric (r, p, t, F) – Nonparametric (χ^2, z)
		Reporting Inferential Statistics

CHAPTER SUMMARY

Chapter 11 discussed the basic statistical conventions of the difference between experimental and nonexperimental research designs, the four main types of statistical data and associated measurement scales, and the basic statistical variables. Chapter 12 extended that conversation by discussing (a) the four types of measurements for *descriptive* statistics (i.e., central, variable, relative, and relationships), which included a detailed overview of such basic conventions as standard deviation, the bell curve, contingency tables, chi-square, regression correlational coefficients, and scattergrams. A discussion of causal inference and inference of association prefaced a fuller discussion of inferential statistics. An overview of Hill's (1965) seminal criteria for moving from an association claim to a causal claim introduced the final section on *inferential* statistics. The latter focused on (b) hypotheses (null and research) and estimates (point and interval), (c) *p* value and the level of significance, (d) Type I and II errors, (e) statistical power (sample size and effect size), and (f) the most common inferential statistical tests (see Table 12.6 and Figure 12.10). The chapter ended with some comments about how to report descriptive and inferential results in a research paper.

REVIEW AND DISCUSSION QUESTIONS

1. What is the fundamental difference between descriptive and inferential statistics?

2. What are the four types of measurements common to *descriptive* statistics, and what is the intent of each one (i.e., "gives a sense of _____")?

3. For *measures of central tendencies*, why does it matter which of three different statistics is reported?

4. Explain the principle illustrated by the *normal bell curve*. What about a *skewed bell curve*? Explain this in plain language.

5. Why would researchers or practitioners be interested in *measures of relative standing*?

6. Compare and contrast the insights gained from contingency tables versus regression analysis (coefficients) (two *measures of relationships*).

7. Explain to someone else how to interpret a scatterplot or a scattergram.

8. Authors have three strategies for reporting descriptive statistic results in their paper. Identify and elaborate on each one.

9. What is the difference between "an *association* between two variables" and "a *causation* effect between two variables"? Why is there such a slippery slope when reporting these statistical claims? People often dismiss association claims as not important. Why is this shortsighted?

10. Explain Hill's (1965) criteria for moving with confidence from an association to a cause-and-effect claim. Why is the onus on the researchers/authors to get this right (to not overstate their claim)? What strategy can they use so as to not miscommunicate their statistical result?

11. Descriptive statistics pertain to just the data in a particular study. To what do inferential statistics apply? Why do researchers have to make *inferences* from their data?

12. Compare and contrast the process of *hypothesizing* parameters (testing a hypothesis) versus *estimating* parameters.

13. Explain the difference between a *null* hypothesis and the *research* (alternative) hypothesis, in plain language, so someone else can understand it.

14. Explain what the concept of *statistical significance* means when using inferential statistics. How is this different from *practical significance*?

15. Inferential statistics involves two *p* values (*p* stands for probability), one created by the researcher before data collection and one generated by computer software from the data. Explain how these two *p* values are used to determine if a result is *statistically significant*.

16. Researchers draw inferences from their results when analyzing numbers. Explain the two types of *errors* they can make during this process and why avoiding them matters.

17. Inferential statistics is concerned with *statistical power*. Explain this concept. What can researchers do to make sure the statistical procedures they run on their numerical data are powerful enough to detect a cause-and-effect claim?

18. Table 12.6 explains the four most common inferential *statistical tests*. Identify them, explaining the intent of each one. Compare and contrast inferential statistical tests with descriptive statistical tests.

19. A set of *statistical shorthand conventions* has been developed to help report inferential statistics. Identify five of the most common conventions and explain each one (e.g., *p*, *F*).

13 RESULTS AND FINDINGS

INTRODUCTION

In the Results or Findings section, authors bring readers to a point of convergence, where all of the previous threads finally connect (i.e., introduction, research problem, literature review, theory, and methods) (Goodson, 2017). Goodson (2017) went so far as to propose that the "results or findings section in your journal article constitutes the heart and soul of your research report" (p. 192). For some readers, this part of the paper contains "the bottom line, the take-home message from [the] study" (p. 193). Readers often flip to this section first and read nothing else in the paper (Chua, ca. 2003; Locke, Silverman, & Spirduso, 2010). They just want to know *what was found*, expecting authors to be skilled at weaving and integrating things together in a coherent, stand-alone manner. After distinguishing between the two terms *results* and *findings* and explaining the purpose of this section of a research report, this chapter discusses the basic conventions of reporting qualitative findings, quantitative results, and mixed methods findings and results.

DISTINGUISHING BETWEEN RESULTS AND FINDINGS

Whether or not authors use the term *findings* or *results* varies by academic discipline, type of study, and personal style (Goodson, 2017). Although not set in stone, a familiar convention is to use the term *results* to report quantitative studies and *findings* to report qualitative studies (Goodson, 2017; Lincoln & Guba, 1985; Shank & Brown, 2007). This actually makes sense. *Findings* is Old English *findan*, "to come upon, meet with, discover; to obtain by search or study." As qualitative researchers strive to find something unusual or overlooked that might shed light on a problem, they literally find and discover things. On the other hand, *result* is

(Continued)

Learning Objectives (Continued)

(relative to the research question), missing data, and negative results; and the protocols for reporting numerical results (text, tables, figures)

- Gain a deep understanding of the reporting conventions for mixed methods research; describe why the principle of integration is the crux of reporting mixed methods data, and explain the many strategies available to researchers to ensure that integration happens; compare and contrast strand-specific inferences and meta-inferences

- Demonstrate an appreciation for the challenges unique to reporting each of qualitative, quantitative, and mixed methods studies

Middle English *resulten*, "to arise as a consequence" (Harper, 2016). Quantitative researchers try to cause results to happen by manipulating (or observing natural) variables; that is, they seek consequences (cause-and-effect revelations) or possible associations. Results are products of numerical calculations (Goodson, 2017; Shank & Brown, 2007) (see Figure 13.1).

Not everyone agrees with this distinction. For example, when discussing how to report quantitative results, Labaree (2016) assumed the terms are synonymous, referring to them as "results [a.k.a., "findings"]." Shuttleworth (2015) referred to authors "writing the results section, announcing your findings to the world" (p. 100). Some scholars call this section *Results* and then use the term *findings* in the accompanying text. Others do the opposite. This chapter (indeed the whole book) uses the term *findings* for qualitative work and *results* for quantitative work. Authors are advised to consult with disciplinary conventions, journal requirements, and the like as they decide which approach to use in their paper.

PURPOSE OF RESULTS OR FINDINGS SECTION

Very simply, the purpose of this section of a research paper is to present to readers the *key* results or findings from the study (Bem, 2004; Kretchmer, 2008b; Shuttleworth, 2015). If something is key, it provides access to or understandings of something, in this case, the outcomes of the methods used to collect and analyze data to answer the research question(s). Primary

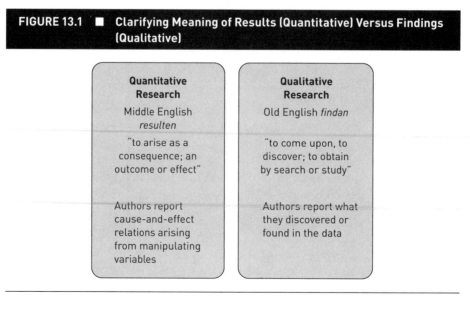

FIGURE 13.1 ■ Clarifying Meaning of Results (Quantitative) Versus Findings (Qualitative)

Quantitative Research	Qualitative Research
Middle English *resulten*	Old English *findan*
"to arise as a consequence; an outcome or effect"	"to come upon, to discover; to obtain by search or study"
Authors report cause-and-effect relations arising from manipulating variables	Authors report what they discovered or found in the data

findings or results are deemed significant relative to (a) their ability to address the research questions or hypotheses, (b) the author's summary and critique of the literature, and (c) any theories used to underpin the study (Shon, 2015). They "are the golden nuggets of journal articles; they are what the article is 'about' [and] contain the central claims of the authors—the citable points" (Shon, 2015, p. 60).

With or Without Interpretation

Authors can choose from two common reporting approaches. First, they can present just the results or findings with no interpretation, leaving the latter for the Discussion section. If they opt for this approach, they should title this section *Results* (for quantitative research), *Findings* (for qualitative research), and *Findings and Results* for a mixed methods study. Second, authors can combine the presentation of their results or findings with their interpretation (especially for qualitative work). In this case, the heading in the paper should be *Results and Discussion* (quantitative) or *Findings and Discussion* (qualitative) (Bem, 2004). Whether results and findings are separate from their discussion "depends on the most effective and understandable method for presentation" (Wiersma & Jurs, 2009, p. 89).

Qualitative papers

Given the interpretive nature of qualitative work, it makes less sense to separate the findings from their interpretation, unlike quantitative work, which is objective in nature, without bias. Qualitative papers often interweave the findings with the author's immediate interpretation, supported with raw data in the form of quotations (to be discussed shortly). This approach entails stating a finding and immediately interjecting comments about why it emerged and what it means. Authors achieve this by weaving prose text (their interpretive narrative) into the participants' words (quotes) so as to interpret any manifest and latent ideas embedded in the data (Creswell, 2009; Hancock, 2002; Locke et al., 2010). *Manifest* means participants actually used specific words, and *latent* means the researchers inferred something from the data set (their words).

It is also acceptable to present just the data in the Findings section (e.g., just the themes, with their supportive quotes), leaving the interpretation to the Discussion section (Ary, Jacobs, & Sorensen, 2010; Shank & Brown, 2007; Wiersma & Jurs, 2009). It is also common for authors to report a case study or a narrative as a separate finding, followed with the discussion in a separate section (Wiersma & Jurs, 2009). Both approaches are totally acceptable. The former would be labeled *Findings and Discussion*, and the latter would have the heading *Findings*.

Actually, qualitative authors can opt for a third approach, wherein they have a section called *Findings and Interpretation*, followed with a separate Discussion section. In this instance, they would interpret what they think a finding means as they report it, and leave any larger examination of its import to the Discussion section (see Chapter 14). The Discussion section queries, "*So what?*" (Geletkanycz & Tepper, 2012). Why should people care about what the data say? What is known now that was not known before this study? Why are these findings significant? What is their value? Why do they matter? How might others capitalize on these findings (Anderson, 2015; Annesley, 2010; Geletkanycz & Tepper, 2012; Hess, 2004; Matthews & Matthews, 2008)?

Quantitative papers

In a quantitative paper, readers normally do not expect to see comments from authors about *why* they think a certain result occurred, *unless* the author has intentionally integrated results with discussion and used the appropriate label for the section. Otherwise, readers anticipate the Results section in a quantitative, empirical study to be a clear, logical, bias-free accounting of the key, major results (Goodson, 2017; Labaree, 2016). Authors should present only clean results so that readers can bring their own lens to bear with nothing clouding their thoughts. Also, if authors just point out what the empirical data show, readers cannot debate these facts. "Nothing readers can dispute should appear in the Results section" (The Writing Center, 2014b, p. 8). Finally, authors must mention (un)expected correlations between variables but not speculate about or postulate what is going on, leaving this interpretation for the Discussion section.

> **Example 13.1 Clean presentation of a result** Solubility increased as the temperature of the solution increased.

> **Disputable result:** Solubility increased as the temperature of the solution increased. *This might be* the result of excessive stirring during the heating process or *because* the heating element was larger than specifications required.

> **Example 13.2 Clean presentation of a result** In this sample, participants who had sexual relationships with multiple partners also had sexually permissive attitudes. This association was statistically significant at the .01 level of probability.

> **Disputable result:** In this sample, *it was obvious* that participants with *promiscuous* sexual behavior also had sexually promiscuous attitudes. (Note that both *obvious* and *promiscuous* are judgmental and condemning, with the author overreaching the data) (from Goodson, 2017).

Jewel and Story Metaphors

When reporting results or findings, authors can gain inspiration from two metaphors. First, Bem (2004) tendered the *jewel metaphor*: "Your overriding purpose is to tell the world what you have learned from your study. If your results suggest a compelling framework for their presentation, adopt it and make the most instructive findings [sic] your centerpiece. Think of your data set as a jewel. Your task is to cut and polish it, to select the facets to highlight, and to craft the best setting for it" (p. 106).

Second, authors can *tell a story* that focuses on answering the research questions (Bem, 2004). In effect, authors need to "tell the story the data tell" (Ary et al., 2010, p. 493). They should use English prose (i.e., straightforward, everyday communication), supported with nontext tools like tables, figures, and charts and perhaps quotes from the participants. This story line approach permits readers to decide how much detail they personally want to pursue at each juncture of the author's story, enabling them to skip ahead in the story line to the next main point (i.e., the next key finding or result) (Bem, 2004; Fox, 2013; Ryan, 2006).

For a qualitative paper, *a good story* offers both clarity and vivid descriptions of the story the research data tell, replete with full (lightly edited) quotes and a "red thread" narrative and interpretation (Choudhuri, Glauser, & Peregoy, 2004). A red thread is a weaver's reference to a critical thread that holds the entire fabric together (Munker, 2012). It is the authors' line of reasoning by which they assert their interpretations of the data (Johnson & Christensen, 2012).

For a quantitative paper, *a good story* provides a balance between statistical conventions and plain language prose. Authors should not state numbers without writing a good story about them. As illustrated by Bem (2004), "Do not tell us that the three-way interaction with sex, parent condition, and self-esteem was significant at the .05 level unless you *tell us immediately and in English* [emphasis added] that men are less expressive than women in the negative conditions if the father watches—but only for men with low self-esteem" (p. 135). He posited that authors and their prose are the masters and the statistics are the slaves.

REVIEW AND ENGAGEMENT

When critically reading a research report, you would

- ☐ Check to see if the authors consistently employed the convention *findings* for qualitative and *results* for quantitative (see Figure 13.1)

- ☐ Determine that if they did not use this convention, they at least were consistent in their use of one or the other (did not use both terms)

- ☐ Judge if they properly labeled this section (If Results or if Findings, there was no interpretation. If Results and Discussion or Findings and Discussion, data were interpreted as they were presented.)

- ☐ Determine if they presented an objective accounting of quantitative results (just the facts, with no personal biases or opinions)

- ☐ Ascertain if they identified *unexpected* quantitative results but left speculation about what they mean to the Discussion section

- ☐ Determine if the authors successfully wove a red thread narrative, blended with quotations, throughout the Findings section of a qualitative paper

- ☐ Confirm they successfully balanced statistics with plain language prose in a quantitative paper

REPORTING QUALITATIVE FINDINGS

As previously indicated, this book uses the term *findings* when referring to qualitative research. Compared to quantitative research, qualitative studies are more diverse, less standardized, and more complicated forms of inquiry (see Chapter 9). Qualitative papers do not all follow the same format, because there are no templates for the design, execution, or reporting of qualitative studies (Locke et al., 2010) as there are for quantitative studies. Yet, readers of qualitative papers *will* expect authors to report on the basic aspects of conducting research, including their findings.

Despite the "absence of a standard format for reporting qualitative research" (Knafl & Howard, 1984, p. 17), an array of conventions has evolved over time to guide authors in reporting their findings in a research paper. This section provides an overview of those protocols, ranging from the more pressing issues of what to include and exclude, how to organize the presentation of findings, how to ensure comprehensiveness, and how to re-present the participants' words in quotes while simultaneously interpreting their meaning through a story line, to the more mundane issues of length, tense, and person.

Qualitative data are words. When *presenting* their findings, authors have to actually *re-present* the participants' words as evidence of answering the research question. The researcher has to describe how participants understood what was happening in their setting (i.e., their internal, personal, subjective understanding) (Locke et al., 2010). Authors need to demonstrate these findings with *thick, descriptive details* (using quotes, short vignettes [brief, evocative descriptions], field note excerpts, and authors' prose), as well as figures, tables, graphs, charts, pictures, diagrams, sketches, and frameworks or visual models (Ary et al., 2010; Johnson & Christensen, 2012). These data displays (a) highlight salient features of the data; (b) give vivid and rich color to the setting, participants, context, cultural scenes, and events of the study; and (c) allow readers to consider some of the same evidence encountered by the researcher (Johnson & Christensen, 2012; Locke et al., 2010). Key aspects of this reporting protocol are now discussed.

As a caveat, this chapter does not recount the nuances of the *writing-up process* for a qualitative study, referring to how authors move iteratively among *data–write–analyze–write–data–analyze–write* so they end up with findings *to* report (see Goodson, 2017, and Ryan, 2006, for more details). Instead, it focuses on what is involved in reporting any selected findings in an article. Realistically, when writing a journal article, authors cannot exhaustively report everything they found in their study; instead, their selection of what to report depends on what evidence they need to satisfy discerning readers that they have answered their research question(s) and, in the process, also told a good, convincing story (Ary et al., 2010; Goodson, 2017; Johnson & Christensen, 2012; Kretchmer, 2008b; Ryan, 2006).

REVIEW AND ENGAGEMENT

When critically reading a research report, you would

- ☐ Determine if the authors chose sufficient evidence to convince readers they had answered the research question (or addressed the hypotheses if applicable)
- ☐ Judge if they appeared conversant with the basic conventions of reporting qualitative findings

Organizing the Presentation of Findings

Ary et al. (2010) noted that "a qualitative report may not follow a conventional [scientific] organizational format" (p. 493). Indeed, the most efficient and effective organizational format for qualitative papers has "to be discovered by the researcher" (Shank & Brown, 2007, p. 147). Nonetheless, authors have several options for organizing their Findings section. They can use their research questions or the study's objectives, themes, topics, or categories. They can also use a taxonomy that emerged from their data or that previously existed (Marradi, 1990). Some authors may want to use a typology they developed from their data analysis or that already existed (Johnson & Christensen, 2012) (see Chapter 3).

Authors can organize their findings using an a priori (earlier) literature-based conceptual scheme (created by someone else). Conversely, if relevant, authors can organize their Findings section using a conceptual scheme based on a grounded theory that emerged from *their* data (Johnson & Christensen, 2012). Silverman (2000) clarified that a qualitative paper rarely flows from the chronological order of when things happened or were found. Regardless of the approach, authors should use subheadings, which constitute their specific sense-making system employed to organize the presentation of their selected findings (Shank & Brown, 2007). The Findings section in a qualitative paper often includes more subheadings than does a quantitative Results section (Johnson & Christensen, 2012).

Descriptions Versus Interpretations

When reporting their findings, it is imperative that authors present a mix of descriptions and interpretations of the data (Choudhuri et al., 2004). At the same time, readers have to be able to distinguish between data and the author's interpretation (Blaxter, 2013; Öhman & Löfgren, ca. 2010). To describe is to give a detailed account in words, while to interpret means to explain the meaning or significance of something (Anderson, 2014) (see Figure 13.2). Authors should combine reporting what they actually saw (via verbatim quotes) with what they personally inferred. When offering interpretations of data, they must clearly indicate they are inferring something from the data rather than describing the data (Wolcott, 1990).

On a related issue, authors must avoid presenting too much detail with too little interpretation. They must also avoid providing so much interpretation that there is too little detail to support their assertions (Johnson & Christensen, 2012). Finding this balance comes with time and practice and is also dictated by a journal's word limitations

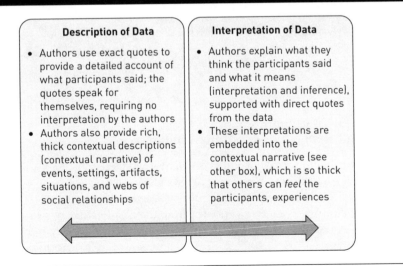

FIGURE 13.2 ■ Difference Between Data Descriptions and Data Interpretations

Description of Data

- Authors use exact quotes to provide a detailed account of what participants said; the quotes speak for themselves, requiring no interpretation by the authors
- Authors also provide rich, thick contextual descriptions (contextual narrative) of events, settings, artifacts, situations, and webs of social relationships

Interpretation of Data

- Authors explain what they think the participants said and what it means (interpretation and inference), supported with direct quotes from the data
- These interpretations are embedded into the contextual narrative (see other box), which is so thick that others can *feel* the participants, experiences

(Johnson & Christensen, 2012). When interpreting qualitative data, authors must acknowledge their role in the research design, thereby accounting for any personal biases, opinions, values, or prejudices that might influence the interpretation process (Creswell, 2009). In these instances, authors may need to include a special section on reflection and synthesis at the end of a particular finding, the Findings section, the manuscript itself, or some combination (Shank & Brown, 2007) (see Chapter 9).

> ***Example 13.3 Description and interpretation when reporting findings*** Fear of community leadership was a strong theme in the data. Jane expressed deep concern around this, saying [DESCRIPTION] she "felt scared and threatened when she attended public meetings." Robert claimed he "wanted to run and hide every time the leader came into the room." Anna Marie actually shuddered and frantically looked from side to side when the community leader walked up to the podium to speak. These comments and actions imply that members of this community did not trust their leadership [INFERENCE]. I also observed tension during community meetings and noted these moments in my field notes. Upon further reflection, I acknowledge that I was looking for these types of reactions when analyzing the data. But I am confident that these selected quotes illustrate the theme of "fear of community leadership."

REVIEW AND ENGAGEMENT

When critically reading a research report, you would

☐ Determine if the authors chose subheadings that clearly revealed the sense-making system they used to organize their qualitative findings (e.g., themes, research questions, topics, categories, taxonomies, typologies, theory constructs or concepts)

☐ Ascertain if they clearly distinguished between a description of qualitative data (participant articulated) and their own interpretation of it (author's inference) (see Figure 13.2)

☐ Confirm they balanced data descriptions and data interpretations

☐ Determine if they avoided presenting too much detail with too little interpretation, or vice versa

☐ Determine if they acknowledged their role in a qualitative research design, ideally with reflective statements

Formats for Reporting Qualitative Findings

Qualitative findings can be reported in diverse ways. Depending on the approach used to conduct the study, authors may choose to "provide a chronological narrative [story] of an individual's life (narrative research), a detailed description of [the essence of] their experiences (phenomenology), a theory generated from the data (grounded theory), a detailed portrait of a culture-sharing group (ethnography), or an in-depth analysis of one or more cases (case study)" (Creswell, 2009, p. 193). Conventions exist for each of these reporting protocols, the details of which are beyond the scope of this chapter.

Research purpose and reporting findings

How findings are reported can depend on the research purpose (Knafl & Howard, 1984), as shown in Table 13.1. If the purpose of the qualitative study was to gather data that will be used to develop a quantitative instrument, authors should not report the qualitative part of the study (i.e., no quotations, no themes, no categories). Instead, they should report the instrument. If the intent was to illustrate quantitative findings, authors should sparingly scatter brief excerpts (direct quotes) from interviews throughout the numbers and statistics in the quantitative Results section (Knafl & Howard, 1984; Lofland, 1976).

If the intent was to sensitize readers to the depth of emotions people felt about something, authors should use verbatim quotes that express the strength of the participants' understandings. Finally, if reporting a new theory that emerged from the grounded theory method, the author has to include both a discussion of the new theory along with the raw data (quotes) used to develop the theory. The basic formula is to devote 60% of the Findings section to conceptualizing the theory and 40% to restating supportive quotes (Knafl & Howard, 1984; Lofland, 1976).

TABLE 13.1 ■ Formats for Reporting Qualitative Findings	
Purpose of Research	**Recommended Reporting Format**
Develop a quantitative instrument	Report the instrument (not using quotes, themes, or narratives)
Illustrate quantitative findings	Scatter quotes selectively throughout the quantitative (numerical) Results section
Convey participants' depth of emotions	Use verbatim quotes interspersed with the author's interpretive narrative
Report a new theory (from grounded theory method)	Devote 60% to a discussion of the new theory and 40% to supportive quotes
Narrative research	Provide a chronological account of a participant's life story by describing him or her, individuals, conditions, relationships, events, and life episodes (i.e., tell a good story)
Phenomenological research	Provide detailed descriptions of the essence of participants' experiences (concrete and evocative text) by providing illustrative examples and quotations, bringing readers into a closer relationship with the phenomenon
Ethnography	Develop a detailed portrait of a culture or group of people such that their reality feels true, the portrait has impact, and authors have confirmed being reflexive
Case study (the *case* is the real-life situation, and the *study* is the analysis of it)	Prepare an in-depth account sufficient to convince readers that either a real-life situation has been analyzed or a real-life problem has been solved

Findings can also be reported using other approaches. Authors may wish to present their findings by their data collection methods. For example, they may want to present the findings from their interview data, focus group, and then document analysis. They may choose to present their data by reconstructing them into cases. For example, if they developed a case for each of three public policy organizations, they could present each organization's case in turn. It is incumbent upon the authors to clarify their approach to reporting their findings (Ary et al., 2010; Johnson & Christensen, 2012; Rocco & Plakhotnik, 2011).

REVIEW AND ENGAGEMENT

When critically reading a research report, you would

☐ Determine if the authors' reporting format matched their research purpose (see Table 13.1)

☐ Ascertain if the authors explicitly commented on any link between research purpose and reporting format

Themes

Using themes or topics is a very common procedure for reporting qualitative findings (Ary et al., 2010; Johnson & Christensen, 2012). To be fair, some argue that distinguishing between a theme and a topic is splitting hairs, because the terms are synonymous (even used to define each other). But technically, they are different. A theme is a recurring thread or pattern that the author finds *in* the data, while a topic is a specific subject, situation, or event that is thought about by the author outside of the data (Anderson, 2014). Themes can be imposed on the data or emerge from the analysis (Choudhuri et al., 2004). Either way, they are not causal in nature; rather, they are common threads that seem to warrant deeper investigation (Shank & Brown, 2007).

Authors need to appreciate what constitutes a theme. Discussed in Chapter 9, a theme represents components or fragments of ideas or experiences (in this case, the words in the text) that may be meaningless when viewed alone but have meaning when brought together (Aronson, 1994). Other words for themes are *categories*, *codes*, *labels*, *units*, and *concepts* (Ryan & Bernard, 2003). A theme can be said to exist if (a) a *recurring* idea threads its way through the data (albeit using different, nuanced words); (b) the same words, phrases, and even entire sentences are *repeated* across the data; (c) a few incidences occurred very *forcefully*; (d) a topic was raised or discussed *frequently*; or (e) a large number of people expressed the same idea, not necessarily using the same words (*extensiveness*). Because people may read the same data set and come up with different themes, authors have to explain how *their* themes and assertions were developed (Owen, 1984; Krueger, 1998; Morgan, 1998).

Most qualitative research papers report five to seven themes, which are often used as subheadings when organizing the Findings section (Creswell, 2009). The usual strategy is to identify a theme and then provide a collection of quotes (raw data) as evidence that the theme was found (Corden & Sainsbury, 2006). "The quotes should support and enrich the researcher's summary of the patterns identified by systematic analysis" (Öhman & Löfgren, ca. 2010, p. 2).

Example 13.4 A theme with supportive quotes A thematic analysis of the interview data revealed three themes. Children were (a) angry at their parents and (b) sad with the state of their parent–child relationship yet (c) hopeful that things could get better. Regarding the anger expressed by the children, the following quotes were chosen because they represent a recurring idea that threaded its way through the data, albeit using different words. Joan (pseudonym) said, "Each night I go to bed with my stomach roiling because of a fight I had with my mother about what I can wear to school the next day. She makes me so angry I could scream." Along a similar vein of thought, Fred commented that "He is always yelling at me. I get so mad at him because nothing I do is right. My head hurts sometimes I get so mad at him."

Authors must provide sufficient and convincing evidence of their theme. Otherwise, they expose their research to skepticism (Johnson & Christensen, 2012). Especially, the quotes they choose must actually illustrate the theme they claim emerged from the data (Creswell, 2009). In example 13.5, the quotes chosen as evidence do not support the theme of anger. They are more appropriate for the second theme of sadness.

Example 13.5 A theme with irrelevant, unsupportive quotes A thematic analysis revealed three themes. Children were (a) angry at their parents and (b) sad with the state of their parent–child relationship yet (c) hopeful that things could get better. Regarding the anger expressed by the children, Joan (pseudonym) said, "I wish she would cook me breakfast in the morning. It is lonely to get up alone and not see anyone." Along a similar vein of thought, Fred commented that "My Dad is always watching TV. He never even says hi when I come home from school. It's like I don't exist."

These examples represent sadness rather than anger.

Major topics

Instead of themes, authors may choose to report their findings as *major topics* (Ary et al., 2010; Johnson & Christensen, 2012). While a theme is a central idea revealed through repeated readings of text (discerned by the researcher), a topic is a subject chosen by the authors to help present *their* thoughts upon reading the text. A topic explains and states what something is about, while a theme *infers* what the text is about. Despite reading the same text, people may come away with different topics to discuss. To showcase their unique interpretation of the data, authors can select a topic around which to gather their thoughts pursuant to a central point in the data (admin, 2015b). For example, authors may choose education as their topic, and then speak to that topic while drawing insights from their content analysis of the data. This would be different from identifying a theme and then presenting quotes as evidence for the theme.

Example 13.6 Reporting a major topic Dr. Rand conducted a content analysis of 10 provincial curricula documents pertaining to having computers in every classroom. To organize her report, she let her thinking gel around one major takeaway from the data—there was simply no agreement on the merits of this pedagogical innovation. Some sources loved the idea, others hated it, and others were sitting on the fence. Her report focused on the major topic of "Why was there such ambivalence?"

This reporting format is not the same thing as reporting themes that threaded through the data. Instead, she was relying on *her* thoughts, stating them, and then trying to explain what she found upon reading the data. She can use data she coded in her content analysis (excerpts from the documents) to support her assertions.

Using Quotations

Quotations are one of the most common approaches to re-presenting participants' words as supportive evidence of a finding. A quote is a short passage taken from one source and repeated in another (Anderson, 2014)—in this case, from data transcripts or field notes to a journal article or research report. Authors can use quotations as (a) evidence for interpretations of the data (the same way tables are used for statistical data); (b) evidence to illustrate themes; (c) a means to help readers understand the complex processes by which participants make sense of their lives; (d) evidence of the strength of participants' views or the depth of their feelings (which cannot be provided in the author's prose); (e) a way to enhance the readability of the report (providing color, vividness, and richness); and (f) a way to give participants a voice (Corden & Sainsbury, 2006).

How many quotes?

Many ideas exist around how many quotations to use and their length. Authors can vary the length of the quotes from short to long embedded passages (Creswell, 2009). In some instances (e.g., narratives, life stories), authors may need to use a fairly long excerpt from their data (sometimes several pages) upon which they attempt to unpick the meaning of the participants' words about their life story (Corden & Sainsbury, 2006). Fox (2013) suggested that in a journal article, one strong quotation is usually enough to illustrate a finding. Indeed, he felt that not all findings in a journal article need a quotation; still, quotes are recommended to allay skepticism and doubt about the trustworthiness and defensibility of the findings (see Chapter 9). In contrast, Hancock (2002) recommended that authors select a range of quotations "to illustrate such features as: the strength of opinion or belief; similarities between respondents; differences between respondents; [and] the breadth of ideas" (p. 23) (see also Creswell, 2009).

"There are no standard rules for how many data to use but enough should be included to provide evidence for readers that the [claim] is sound" (Rocco & Plakhotnik, 2011, p. 173). Somehow, authors have to find a balance between too many and too few quotations (Babor, Stenius, Savva, & O'Reilly, 2004). One suggestion is to use both quotes and thematic tables or grids, without overlap. Also, as authors gain more experience analyzing qualitative data, their analytical and interpretive skills tend to improve. They depend less on multiple quotations, becoming more selective as a way to account for comprehensiveness (Corden & Sainsbury, 2006).

Authors also have to balance selectivity (cannot use all quotes) with inclusiveness (do not exclude anyone) at the same time they avoid using too many quotes from a few participants (who either were very articulate or had a lot to say). Authors can judge how many quotations to use by examining best practices of colleagues, journals, funders, and publishers (Corden & Sainsbury, 2006). They would do well to remember that it "is better to work very well with a limited number of extracts from your data . . . than to do a poor job with too much data" (Ryan, 2006, p. 103).

Presenting quotes

When presenting quotations, authors may want to use indents or special formatting (perhaps *italics* or a different font) to call attention to them in the manuscript. To respect ethical considerations, confidentiality, and privacy, authors must use pseudonyms instead of real names when attributing quotes to participants (Blaxter, 2013; Creswell, 2009). Corden and Sainsbury (2006, pp. 19–22) provided a very detailed account of strategies and conventions for presenting quotes, including editing, formatting, and attributions.

On a final note, some argue that quotes should never be allowed to speak for themselves. They have to be accompanied with some degree of interpretation, which authors can accomplish by summarizing the major finding in their own words and then illustrating it with quotations (Fox, 2013). Others disagree, suggesting that "many quotations will 'speak for themselves' as they are examples of the manifest level of analysis—what people actually said" (Hancock, 2002, p. 23). When authors are reporting a latent analysis (inference), they need to preface their selection of quotations with their interpretation of the data. Using this approach, authors extract the meaning of what participants said, and use approximations to support their inferences through careful selections of quotes.

> ***Example 13.7 Manifest analysis with a quote that speaks for itself*** Every participant in the study said these words: "I do not want to go to school anymore."

> ***Example 13.8 Latent analysis, where quotes cannot speak for themselves*** In his paper, Dr. Almond observed that many participants expressed some sense of not wanting to attend school anymore. He used the following quotes as evidence of his assertion. Mary said she "cried every morning when she got up because she had to face bullies again." Mark felt fear when he got on the bus, noting that he "felt sick to my stomach at the thought of going to school each day." Margaret's eyes widened when going to school was mentioned, and she said, "Please don't tell my mom that I said I skip school every day." Note that others may read these quotes and conclude that the real theme is not fear of going to school but fear of being bullied. When making inferences via latent analysis, it is up to the authors to convince readers that the quotes are sufficient evidence of the claim being made.

Thick Descriptions

To help readers judge the integrity and rigor of the findings, authors must present *rich* and *thick descriptions* of the settings, participants, context, and events. These descriptions have to be *so rich* that readers can vicariously experience the research setting and better understand the conclusions posited by the author (Ary et al., 2010). A thin description would have little flesh or evidence to support the author's assertion that a finding was found. If something is thin, it lacks substance and is weak and inadequate. In contrast, if something is thick, it is made up of a lot of things, close together, making it strong (Anderson, 2014). Thick descriptions involve "detailed portrayals of the participants' experiences, going beyond a report of surface phenomena to their interpretations, uncovering feelings and meanings of their actions" (Holloway & Wheeler, 2002, p. 13). By using thick descriptions, authors can communicate a holistic picture of the participants' experiences and the meanings the participants attached to them (Creswell, 2009).

Authors can create thickness by giving thorough, vivid, detailed accounts of situations, contexts, emotions, and webs of social relationships. Through clear descriptions of the setting, the people, and the research process, authors help readers follow the researchers' pathway and how they accounted for the participants' notion of their own reality. If the descriptions are thick enough, they show readers "what they would experience were they in the same situation as the participants" (Holloway & Wheeler, 2002, p. 14) (see Figure 13.2).

REVIEW AND ENGAGEMENT

When critically reading a research report, you would

- ☐ Determine if the authors explained what they accepted as evidence of a theme
- ☐ Ascertain if they followed the protocols for using quotations as evidence of thematic findings (number of quotes, presentation protocols)
- ☐ Confirm that the quotes they used supported the proposed thematic finding
- ☐ Determine if they balanced selectivity with inclusiveness when presenting quotes
- ☐ Check to see if they ensured that their qualitative narrative contained rich and thick descriptions of settings, participants, contexts, and events

---

Relating Qualitative Findings to the Literature Review

As discussed in Chapter 7, authors often eschew conducting a formal literature review *before* their qualitative study; instead, they collect data, analyze them, and then find pertinent literature, which they weave into their presentation of their findings (Ary et al., 2010). They adopt this strategy because they think a preliminary review of the literature may place constraints on their interpretation of the data. The problem they are investigating is likely not well developed in the literature, so they prefer *listening* to their own data first, then reading what others might have said about a similar phenomenon (Ramalho, Adams, Huggard, & Hoare, 2015). Qualitative researchers should not let the literature review process "constrain and stifle discovery of new constructs, relationships and theories [in their data]" (Johnson & Christensen, 2012, p. 66).

Using Numbers to Report Qualitative Findings

Because qualitative data are words, often taken from very small sample frames, "the application of numbers to qualitative data should be done with caution, and the process for doing this should be clearly articulated" (Öhman & Löfgren, ca. 2010, p. 2). Authors may want to avoid saying how many people said something, using instead such language as "most people said" or "a few people felt." Descriptive statistics can be quite meaningless if authors report "20% said" when that 20% means one person out of five. A better strategy is to say "Only one of five participants said . . ." (National Foundation for Educational Research, 2016) and then use a powerful quote to illustrate the import of this finding.

Length

The Findings section is often the longest part of a qualitative paper. The discursive data (study specific and ungeneralizable) comprise participants' words (usually in quotes), accompanied with the researcher's interpretive, contextual red thread (Blaxter, 2013). Fox (2013) suggested that the Findings section should constitute 30%–40% of the paper, with the Discussion comprising 10%–20%. Although discursive data require more space to report than numerical data, authors of qualitative papers have to be as concise as possible (i.e., express a lot in a limited space) (Blaxter, 2013). They have to be selective with what they report while convincing readers their evidence addresses the research questions (Ary et al., 2010).

Tense, Person, and Voice

This section about reporting qualitative findings ends with some technical comments about tense, person, and voice. Generally, authors of qualitative papers should use a combination of past and present tense. When *presenting* a finding from their own study, they should use the past tense (e.g., "The study show*ed* . . ."; Considerable agreement *was* noted") (McAnsh, 2002), although using present tense sometimes better captures the immediacy and reality of the topic and its importance (Corden & Sainsbury, 2006). When *commenting* on a finding or comparing it to other studies, authors should use present tense (e.g., This finding *is* in agreement with earlier studies) (McAnsh, 2002).

The Findings section of qualitative papers is often written using a subjective tone, employing second and first person (Creswell, 2009). This approach is acceptable because researchers (usually the authors) are the main data collection instrument, and are intimately involved in implementing the research design plan (Boylorn, 2008; Hesson & Fraias-Hesson, 2010a; The Writing Center, 2014b). Using first person also enables authors to distinguish their voice, ideas, and opinions from those of the participants (Ary et al., 2010).

Authors of qualitative papers can consciously choose what voice they will use (Boylorn, 2008). They are not obligated to use passive voice like quantitative authors (reporting on what was done, rather than who did it). That being said, qualitative authors normally employ active voice, which focuses on *who* did the action or said something (Silverman, 2000). This writing strategy makes sense because "qualitative research recognises, and even *foregrounds*, the role played by individuals—the researcher, the informants and other participants" (Lynch, 2014, p. 33). When reporting findings, authors need to clearly identify who is saying what, indicating if it is the participants' words, the author's interpretation of their words, or comments from the author's field notes or other documents (Wolcott, 1990). The guiding principle is that any evidence used to back up a finding has to be attributed to the correct party (Lynch, 2014).

> ***Example 13.9 First person, active voice when reporting a finding*** Anne (pseudonym) said "*I was* very frightened when the community center was broken into and quit going so often." She was not alone in this reaction. *When I* consulted *my* field notes, *I recalled* that the manager of the community center remembered a decline in people visiting the center after the break-in. The *local media reported* gripping fear in the community, which affected the normally heavy use of the center for socializing and of solidarity.

REPORTING QUANTITATIVE RESULTS

As previously indicated, this book uses the term *results* when referring to quantitative research. Compared to qualitative research, quantitative studies yield numbers that need to be creatively and clearly re-presented using well-established scientific and academic conventions and protocols. The writing in the Results section has to be very precise, even somewhat rote, as dictated by these conventions. Authors should provide "information sufficient (a) to describe and otherwise characterize the properties of all raw data collected, (b) to warrant the use of particular analytic techniques and adjustments, (c) to display adequately the output of all analyses computed, (d) to facilitate accurate and meaningful interpretation of [results], and (e) to enable meta-analytic and other secondary analyses of data from the study" (Norris, Plonsky, Ross, & Schoonen, 2015, p. 473). Also, authors should use conventional scientific and mathematical symbols (see Figure 13.3) and define or explain any unique symbols (Gillett, 2015; Wiersma & Jurs, 2009).

Interpretation or Noninterpretation

The most basic reporting convention in a quantitative paper is that authors should not interpret results as they identify and present them. Interpretation is supposed to happen in the Discussion section (see Chapter 14). Results should not be combined with the discussion *unless* the journal or discipline traditionally combines them into one section (Kretchmer, 2008b). On the other hand, Labaree (2016) suggested that blending the two is acceptable and is actually a sign of a more skilled academic, scientific writer. Whether results are separate from their discussion "depends on the most effective and understandable method for presentation" (Wiersma & Jurs, 2009, p. 89).

Minimal interpretation or evaluation of results prevents authors from moving beyond the basic patterns in the data (Chua, ca. 2003; Shuttleworth, 2015). By not immediately interpreting results, authors respect the tenet of scientific objectivity, allowing others to bring their own interpretative lens to the results. Authors should not contaminate the results with their subjective interpretations; instead, this section should be a clear, logical, bias-free accounting of the key, major results. Authors should also avoid opinion-type or value-laden words such as *obviously*, *expected*, *not surprising*, *interesting*, *undeniable*, *exciting*, and *provocative* (Chua, ca. 2003; Goodson, 2017; Labaree, 2016).

FIGURE 13.3 ■ Examples of Mathematical and Scientific Symbols

+ plus/positive

− minus/negative

± plus or minus

÷ divide

× multiply

← is less than

→ is more than

≡ is identical with

∵ because

∴ therefore

∞ infinity

∩ intersection of two sets

∪ union of two sets

⊂ included in/is a subset of

Σ sum

∈ is an element of

∫ integral

% percent

! factorial

√ square root

≈ approximately

■ end of mathematical proof

Whichever approach is chosen, authors must be consistent; that is, either they do not interpret any results, or they interpret every result. If adhering to the no-interpretation principle, authors need to be aware that trying to present a result without interpreting it is a slippery slope. It is very tempting, and sometimes almost unavoidable, to resist trying to explain why a result was found at the point of reporting the result (see Anderson, 2015, who provided the following examples). To catch themselves on this slope, authors should edit for opinion-type or value-laden words (as noted earlier).

Example 13.10 Result with no interpretation The duration of exposure to running water had a pronounced effect on cumulative seed germination percentages (Fig. 2). Seeds exposed to the 2-day treatment had the highest cumulative germination (84%), 1.25 times that of the 12-hr or 5-day groups, and four times that of controls.

Example 13.11 Result with slippery slope toward interpretation The results of the germination experiment (Fig. 2) *suggest that the optimal time* for running-water treatment is two days. This group showed the highest cumulative generation (84%), with longer (5-day) or shorter (12-hr) exposures producing smaller gains in germination when compared to the control group. *NOTE*: [T]his statement strays subtly into interpretation by referring to *optimality*, and then tying the observed result to this idea. Other readers may have a totally different interpretation of this major result, which was that "seeds exposed to the 2-day treatment had the highest cumulative germination (84%)."

Comprehensiveness

Because of the large amount of numerical data generated in a quantitative study, authors cannot report everything. They have to be selective in choosing which results to report, leaving out the least important and irrelevant (Goodson, 2017). The basic rule is to report only those results needed to answer the research question(s), support or refute the hypotheses, or both. Following this rule better ensures that the results contained in the paper are *comprehensive*, meaning they are complete and sufficient to achieve the task of answering the research question(s) or addressing the hypotheses. Authors also have to resist including irrelevant data or results, just because they found them (Shuttleworth, 2015; The Writing Center, 2014b). The general rule is to avoid overwhelming readers, who often just want the bottom line, the take-home message (Goodson, 2017).

Negative Results

In the process of ensuring comprehensiveness (i.e., completeness), authors need to report *negative* results (Shuttleworth, 2015) (meaning something is absent, in disagreement, or undesirable) (Anderson, 2014). If the result was not anticipated or wanted, it may mean the hypothesis was incorrect and needs to be reformulated, or perhaps the author unexpectedly stumbled onto something that warrants further study. Moreover, the *absence* of an effect may be very telling. In any case, the result may be of importance to others despite it not supporting the hypothesis in the current study. Results that are contrary to what were expected or desired have, for years, been considered *bad data*. However, if the study was well executed, they are simply *the* results and need to be highlighted and interpreted in the Discussion section. Shuttleworth (2015) believed that writing a Results section without negative results invalidates the paper and is extremely bad science.

Many important discoveries, innovations, and new hypotheses can be traced to negative results (Anderson, 2015; Labaree, 2016; Shuttleworth, 2015). Actually, valuing negative results is a relatively new trend in science (Granqvist, 2015). Granqvist (2015) made a strong case for publishing negative or controversial results, arguing that authors should resist their *positive bias*, which leads them to dismiss results that were not wanted or expected. In fact, a new journal was launched in 2014 called *New Negatives in Plant Science*. The first of its kind, other disciplines are expected to follow suit. Authors can take inspiration from this recent trend and consider reporting their negative results, augmented with a rich discussion and possible recommendations for future research.

Example 13.12 Negative findings leading to new research (Anderson, 2012)

A classic example of negative results being recognized by researchers as scientific and ushering in a paradigm shift in science took place in the 17th century. Albert Michelson and Edward Morley conducted sequential experiments in the late 1880s seeking to enhance the accuracy of the prevalent aether theory [a medium that was one supposed to fill all space and support the propagation of electromagnetic waves]. All of their efforts to advance the theory led to a continual rejection of their research hypotheses. A few years later, these null results were published in the *American Journal of Science* and played an important role in inspiring new experiments, including a well-known one that confirmed a major physical theory proposed by Albert Einstein in 1905: the special theory of relativity.

Missing Data

If relevant, authors have to account for any missing data as well as any analytical or statistical methods employed to address them (including replacing them or understanding the impact of their absence) (Drotar, 2009; Johnson & Christensen, 2012). Data can become missing (not present when expected or supposed to be) for several reasons: (a) nonresponse (either to individual items or to the entire data collection instrument); (b) response error (incorrect or untrue answers); (c) loss of participants in a longitudinal study (due to death, attrition, or dropout); (d) partial loss of information due to coarsened data (i.e., rounded, grouped, or truncated); and (e) a skipped pattern in a survey (mistakenly did not answer a question, which said, "If no, skip to #15") (Schafer & Graham, 2002).

Furthermore, authors have to confirm if the data were *missing at random* (MAR, an ignorable nonresponse) or *missing not at random* (MNAR, a nonignorable nonresponse); that is, the author cannot ignore the fact that people did not respond. It is very possible that nonresponders were very different from those who responded, and this needs to be acknowledged and discussed. Authors have to handle these missing data or values in a transparent and principled manner so as to mitigate or minimize conceptual difficulties and any statistical, computational challenges (Schafer & Graham, 2002).

Example 13.13 Missing data due to nonresponse to certain items, with explanation of how this was handled In this study, those with higher incomes were less likely to report income, but the research design included variables for years of education and for number of investments, which were used as proxies for income.

Example 13.14 Nonignorable nonresponse In this study, those with the highest incomes tended to not answer most of the questions about investing. This is troublesome because one would assume they do invest, providing them with the higher income. This result implies they may have very different investment patterns than those with medium incomes. But because of the missing data, the authors can only speculate as to why people did not respond to these questions. Future studies need to address this phenomenon.

Organizing Quantitative Results

To be meaningful for and accessible by readers, quantitative results have to be logically organized. To that end, authors should begin their Results section with a statement about the order in which their results will be presented, identifying pertinent subheadings (see Table 13.2).

The most common convention for organizing quantitative results is using the hypotheses in the same order in which they were proposed. This approach entails using a subheading such as *Hypothesis 1*; restating the hypothesis in full form; stating if it was supported, partially supported, or refuted; and then succinctly presenting the data used to support this assertion (Drotar, 2009; Locke et al., 2010). This approach usually entails restating the statistical procedures used to analyze the data, with the level of detail depending on whether this information was previously presented in the Methods section of the paper. In the Results section itself, the "full output of all inferential tests should be reported, including at minimum the magnitude and direction of the statistic itself (e.g., the t or F value), the degrees of freedom used in the calculation, and the exact p value (all reported regardless of 'significance')" (Norris et al., 2015, p. 475). After the hypothesis-driven results are

TABLE 13.2 ■ Strategies for Organizing Quantitative Results

- Present *hypotheses* in the order in which they were proposed in the paper, restating them, confirming support or refutation, with statistics
- Restate each *research question* or *objective*, in the order in which it was proposed, reporting pertinent results
- Present *major results*, with appropriate subheadings, beginning with the easiest to understand and moving to the more complex
- Use *different data collection methods* as subheadings, presenting results for each method according to the order in the Methods section (e.g., survey, interviews, then diaries)
- Present results from the *most to least important*, with justification for this order, using relevant subheadings

reported, secondary results can be identified (Drotar, 2009; Jones, 2016; Locke et al., 2010) (see Chapters 11 and 12).

A second approach is to organize the results using the research questions or the study's objectives, in the same order they were proposed. As with the hypotheses, authors should fully restate the particular research question or objective so readers are reminded of what is being studied (Goodson, 2017). Once restated, authors should report pertinent results, using the same format for the remaining questions or objectives.

Third, authors can organize the quantitative Results section using their major results (Wiersma & Jurs, 2009). A result is major *if* it is significant (worthy of consideration) or important relative to answering the research question(s) or hypotheses. If this organizational approach is used, authors should begin with the easiest-to-understand results and then move to the more complex and involved major results (Goodson, 2017). Fourth, authors can organize their results in chronological order, according to the methods upon which the results are based. If a method was reported, authors would present attendant results. Finally, they can order the results from what they deem to be most to least important, with justification and relevant subheadings (Drotar, 2009; Jones, 2016; Kretchmer, 2008b) (see Table 13.2).

REVIEW AND ENGAGEMENT

When critically reading a research report, you would

☐ Determine if the authors logically organized the presentation of their results, with appropriate subheadings and a clarifying statement (see Table 13.2)

☐ Ascertain which approach they used, and judge if it made sense for presenting their results (would you recommend a different tactic?)

Presenting Numerical Results

Quantitative data are numbers. Authors can use one or both of two tools to present their numerical results: (a) written text and (b) nontextual elements, particularly numbers arranged in tables and symbolic representations (e.g., figures). The general rule is to use the combination that best and most clearly shares the results with readers (Anderson, 2015; Locke et al., 2010; The Writing Center, 2014b). As a general rule, authors should strive for three to four nontextual visuals that represent the most important results, appreciating that some papers do not require them (Goodson, 2017; Johnson & Christensen, 2012; Locke et al., 2010). The following information describes each of text, tables, and figures, and the role they play when presenting quantitative results.

Per long established conventions, when using nontextual elements, authors must sequentially number and label each table or figure (called a *table title* and *figure caption*, respectively) and refer to it in their text (e.g., "see Table X"). If appropriate, the figure should include a *legend*, which explains any symbols or colors (Johnson & Christensen, 2012). All nontextual elements should be able "to stand alone as an intelligible presentation" of key results (Locke et al., 2010, p. 172). People should be able to discern what the table or figure means without any accompanying text or interpretation from the author

(Johnson & Christensen, 2012; Kretchmer, 2008b; Locke et al., 2010). If they found it lying on the floor, they would know what it meant.

Text

The Results section always begins with narrative text (sentences or paragraphs), the key purpose being to logically guide readers to the most important study results. Text in the Results section should be short (just a few lines or a short paragraph for each result) and should describe but not interpret or evaluate the result (see earlier discussion) (Anderson, 2015; The Writing Center, 2014b; Vanderbilt University, 2010). Authors should prepare one to two paragraphs for each table or figure (Newman & Newman, 2011). They should tell readers exactly what *key* result(s) is (are) contained in *each* table or figure (Anderson, 2015; Drotar, 2009; Kretchmer, 2008b; The Writing Center, 2014b; Vanderbilt University, 2010).

Text is also necessary for describing the import of a statistic. As noted earlier, authors should not state numbers without writing a good story about them. Each statistically nuanced presentation of a result should be re-presented in plain-language prose (Bem, 2004). Also, when describing their results in words, authors are encouraged to describe the patterns in the data, not in the statistics (Chua, ca. 2003). The statistics are just numbers waiting to be interpreted. It is the author who can intellectually see and then report on the patterns.

> *Example 13.15 Reporting results with lay language* A paired-samples *t* test was conducted to evaluate the potential impact of belonging to a student organization on the student's grade point average (GPA). There was a statistically significant increase in GPA from prior to entering the student organization (M = 2.78, SD = .64) to their GPA after a semester in the student organization (M = 2.85, SD = .63), $t(66)$ = 2.45, p < .05 (two-tailed). The mean increase in GPA was .07 with a 95% confidence interval ranging from –.14 to –.01. The eta-squared statistic (.08) indicated a moderate to large effect size. *In other words, students who joined a student organization benefited from an increase in their GPA at the end of the semester. The medium to large effect size intimates a strong relationship between membership in a student organization and improved student GPA.*

If they use tables and figures along with text, authors should not repeat information (i.e., avoid redundancy). One way to avoid repetition is to be less specific in the text and more specific in the table. To illustrate, if the result in the table shows 23.9%, authors could write "Results indicated that almost one quarter of . . . (see Table X)" (Shuttleworth, 2015). Authors should use their text to highlight major results or trends that are evident in the table or figures. They should save the "juiciest bits of data" for their text and not hide them in the table (Chua, ca. 2003).

Tables

In addition to text and prose, authors should use tables (comprising rows and columns) to present their primary (most important) results. Tables are supplemental to the text in that they complete the narrative portrayal of the results. They (a) show the most important results in compact and economical formats, (b) condense large volumes of raw data while preserving the basic characteristics of those data, and (c) efficiently show variation in data (although tables are not as useful for unchanging measurements). In these latter instances, authors should use text to state that nothing happened until a certain data point and then report the latter in a smaller, more effective table. In fact, authors may not need any tables at all if they do not have a great deal of data or if the data do not vary a lot (Johnson & Christensen, 2012; Locke et al., 2010; Vanderbilt University, 2010).

Types of tables. To present precise, specific numeric values, two types of tables may be needed. First, *descriptive* tables profile the sample and demographics, as well as any descriptive statistics (e.g., percentages, frequencies, or means). Second, *inferential* tables show the results of inferential statistical procedures applied to the data (e.g., ANOVA, regression analysis, MANOVA) (Ary et al., 2010; Newman & Newman, 2011) (see Chapter 12). Regarding inferential statistics, authors should construct a table for each hypothesis and report key information about, but not limited to, "tests of significance, effect size [strength of the relationship], significance or nonsignificance, *p* value, degrees of freedom, corrections for multiple comparisons, sample size, power estimates, replicability estimates if possible, and partial regression weights or beta weights" (Newman & Newman, 2011, p. 188).

Formatting tables. Authors should try to limit any table to a single page, and position it as close as possible to its first reference in the text, tactics affected by journal formatting. Most scientific journals require authors to include statistical information in their tables, sometimes as a footnote in a smaller font (e.g., standard deviation, *p* values, *t* values) (Locke et al., 2010; Vanderbilt University, 2010; Wiersma & Jurs, 2009). When decimal numbers are used in a table, one point past the decimal point is usually sufficient. In the table itself, authors should line the numbers up by decimal point. Readers should be able to read the table vertically instead of horizontally; that is, like information should be arranged in the columns (up and down) instead of the rows (across). To accommodate journal formatting, authors are encouraged to avoid vertical lines in the body of the table (Vanderbilt University, 2010), as shown in examples 13.16 and 13.17. Authors are strongly advised to examine the journals' *Guidelines for Authors* for information on how to prepare tables and figures (Newman & Newman, 2011).

Example 13.16 *Information results presented horizontally, lines within table, decimals out of line*

Trial	1	2	3	4
Length of rope sample (inches)	132.899	117.5	109.3	103.8
Height difference (inches)	51.0	95.567	139.6	200.133

Example 13.17 *Information results presented vertically, no lines in table, decimals lined up*

Trial	Length of rope sample (mm)	Height difference (mm)
1	132.9	51.0
2	117.5	95.6
3	109.3	139.6
4	103.8	200.1

On a final note, they should not include a table just to show they have the data; rather, if the table does not warrant discussion in the text, relative to answering the research question or hypothesis, it should not be used in the paper (Johnson & Christensen, 2012; Locke et al., 2010; Vanderbilt University, 2010).

Symbolic, visual representations

If authors feel that readers will not get the full impact of a result by just reading the text or looking at numbers in tabular form, a figure might be appropriate (The Writing Center, 2014b). But figures must provide assistance to readers in ways that are superior to what could be accomplished through text or tables, along one of three dimensions: economy of expression, emphasis of primary result, or dramatic visual impact (Locke et al., 2010).

Whereas tables contain exact values in numerical form, symbolic representations offer a more artistic, emotive, creative, and memorable display of results. They are called symbolic because they involve the use of *symbols* (visual images) to stand in for and convey numerical ideas. Figures can take many forms: pie charts, bar graphs, line graphs, polygons, scatterplots, pictures, diagrams, maps, and flowcharts (The Writing Center, 2014b). Also, while tables are usually used to present primary quantitative results, figures are good for presenting general comparisons, trends, linkages, relationships, processes, and relative proportions (Creswell, 2009; Locke et al., 2010; Wiersma & Jurs, 2009).

Regardless of their form, figures should be used sparingly and effectively. A "'picture is worth a thousand words,' but a poorly designed figure can cost more than a thousand words to explain it" (Wiersma & Jurs, 2009, p. 90). Table 13.3 profiles the three most common types of figures and when it is appropriate to use them: pie charts, bar graphs, and line graphs (The Writing Center, 2014b; University of Leicester, 2012; Vanderbilt University, 2010). The type of figure depends on the type of data (e.g., interval, ordinal, categorical, discrete) (see Chapter 11), and what authors want to show (e.g., patterns, trends, proportions, frequencies) (Ary et al., 2010).

No matter what form, figures are especially useful for perceiving and presenting patterns in the data. The pattern jumps out and becomes evident (Goodson, 2017; Newman & Newman, 2011). They are also very appropriate for reporting the results of complex statistics, such as structural equation modeling and path analysis, which describe interrelationships between multiple variables and constructs (Drotar, 2009). They can also be used to represent a complex theoretical formulation or the empirical results of a complex interaction. Regardless, all figures should reflect simplicity, clarity, and continuity in formatting and be informative (Johnson & Christensen, 2012).

REVIEW AND ENGAGEMENT

When critically reading a research report, you would

☐ Determine if the authors followed the conventions for reporting numerical results (text, tables, and figures) (see Figure 13.3 and Table 13.3)

☐ Judge if their approaches to text, figures, and tables compromised or ensured readers' ability to understand their results

TABLE 13.3 ■ Common Types of Figures and Their Usage	
Type of Figure	**Basic Usage and Conventions**
Pie charts	• Compare proportions or relative amounts between various categories (proportional or frequency distributions) • Show parts of a whole (if the whole totals 100%) • Represent categorical data with relatively small number values • Should not include more than five or six slices • 3D pie charts are discouraged because they are hard to read
Bar graphs (horizontal, vertical, stacked, histograms)	• Show direct comparison of data • Compare the number, frequency, or other measure (e.g., mean) for different discrete categories or groups • Show time-series data when the number of intervals is small • Use vertical bars for presenting categories • Use horizontal bars when comparing proportions or relative amounts • Histograms are good for number ranges or for showing how two groups compare on the same dimension (continuous data) • Stacked bar graphs are hard to read and, hence, less effective
Line graphs	• Show patterns and trends over time • Used to show time series—that is, how variables change over a continuous period of time • Best for showing five or more data points • When plotting data, use symbols along well-spaced lines (more effective than just line styles: dashes, colors, or thickness)

Source: Figures adapted from Microsoft clip art.

Transitioning From Results to Discussion

Authors have two options when wrapping up their Results section, before moving onto the Discussion section (if the noninterpretive approach was used). First, they can present results one at a time with a summary statement for each one, often done with longer papers. Second, they can present a thorough overview of all of the results, wrapping up the entire section with a summary statement (frequently used for shorter papers). The summary statement (often included in the abstract) should tie the separate results together, providing a narrative bridge to the Discussion section (Labaree, 2016; Shuttleworth, 2015; Wiersma & Jurs, 2009).

Length of Results Section

The Results section is the shortest element of a quantitative research paper, mainly because the more lengthy discussion is in a separate section of the paper (Chua, ca. 2003). The length (word, paragraph, pages) should be guided by the amount and type of data being reported (Labaree, 2016). Authors are encouraged to canvas various journals in their discipline to gain a sense of the average length of the Results section.

Part of the length equation is figuring out how much data to include. If authors feel very compelled to include additional aspects of their results, they can place them in an appendix (providing the journal is willing to do so) (see Chapter 4). Some journals now provide supplemental results for authors' papers at their website (Drotar, 2009; Leech, 2012; Stange, Crabtree, & Miller, 2006). Authors can also reduce length by assuming people know how to perform most statistical tests, negating the need to show their work so others can follow their calculations. They must, however, specify the statistical software program and the version they used to analyze their data (Drotar, 2009; Shuttleworth, 2015).

Person, Voice, and Tense

On a final note, the basic language conventions for reporting empirical, quantitative results are third person, past tense, and passive voice, although active voice is appropriate and even preferred by some scholars. Authors should use present tense when referring to some aspect of a table or figure (e.g., "Table X *shows* means and standard deviations"). These conventions reflect the objective nature of quantitative research. Scientific papers are intended to convey new information and knowledge, not be a creative writing venue. Writing should be concise and specific. Authors should avoid such nonspecific or vague phrases such as "appeared to be greater than" or "demonstrates promising trends that" (Anderson, 2015; Ary et al., 2010; Boudah, 2011; Creswell, 2009; Labaree, 2016).

> **Example 13.18 Less concise (22 words), second person, present tense** In *our* study, the sample *is* made up of 31 students. The 31 students *are* divided into 20 boys and 11 girls.

> **Example 13.19 Concise (13 words), third person, past tense** *The* sample of 31 students included 20 boys and 11 girls.

REVIEW AND ENGAGEMENT

When critically reading a research report, you would

- ☐ Ascertain whether the authors transitioned to the Discussion section with a summary of key results
- ☐ Determine if they followed the conventions for length, person, voice, and tense

---

REPORTING MIXED METHODS RESULTS AND FINDINGS

The final section of this chapter focuses on how to report results and findings from mixed methods studies. As a reminder, mixed methods studies involve instances when qualitative and quantitative methods are used within a *single* research project or study (Driessnack, Sousa, & Mendes, 2007b) (see Chapter 10). The following section discusses integration as an overarching principle of reporting mixed methods, including barriers to integration, the role of meta-inferences, and achieving integration via connecting, merging, or embedding data. After discussing the fit of data integration and organizational approaches to the mixed methods Results and Findings section, the chapter concludes with some thoughts on how many papers to publish from a mixed methods study and where. As a caveat, the conventions for person, tense, and voice still apply for reporting both qualitative findings and quantitative results.

Principle of Integration

Some *degree of integration* is the key feature of mixed methods results (Creswell, 2008). *Integrate* is Latin *integrare*, "to make whole" (Harper, 2016). Integration involves intermixing things that were previously separated (Anderson, 2014). When applied to mixed methods papers, integration refers to mixing quantitative results and qualitative findings, normally at (but not restricted to) the interpretive stage of a study (Ivankova, Creswell, & Stick, 2006; Onwuegbuzie & Teddlie, 2003). It is "an intentional process" resulting in both types of data becoming interdependent, referring to the mutual benefit gained from connecting the two strands of research (Guetterman, Fetters, & Creswell, 2015, p. 554). Data integration results in a coherent "whole . . . that is greater than the sum of the individual qualitative and quantitative parts" (Guetterman et al., 2015, p. 555).

Barriers to Integration

Integration of data interpretations can be very difficult (Ary et al., 2010). "Integration is . . . not well developed or practiced" (Guetterman et al., 2015, p. 555). In fact, Bryman (2008) found that only 18% of researchers genuinely integrated their mixed methods findings and results in their articles. Nearly half presented the results and findings separately, in a parallel fashion. O'Cathain, Murphy, and Nicholl (2008) also found that researchers mainly ignored the integration imperative and described only the separate strands. They concluded that "judgements about integration could rarely be made due to the absence of an attempt at integration of data and findings from different components within a [mixed methods] study" (p. 92).

Presenting the results and findings of a mixed methods study *is* a challenge. Authors should be guided by the *degrees of integration* principle (Creswell, 2008; Morse & Maddox, 2014), appreciating the barriers that hinder integration (see Figure 13.4). Bryman (2008) identified the challenges of (a) teamwork, where authors do not reference each other's work; (b) timelines, wherein one part of the study is done (and published) before the other; and (c) journal prejudices against mixed methods research. Additional challenges to integration include resource limitations, sampling issues, page and word limitations, and analytic and interpretive issues. The latter refer to (a) conflicting findings and results, (b) concerns about the point of interface (i.e., what result should be used to springboard to the next research phase), (c) unbalanced emphasis on QUAN and QUAL strands, (d) the validity of the data sets, and (e) whether respective authors think the two methodologies (assumptions) should be combined (Creswell, 2008; Creswell, Klassen, Plano Clark, & Smith, 2011) (see Chapter 2).

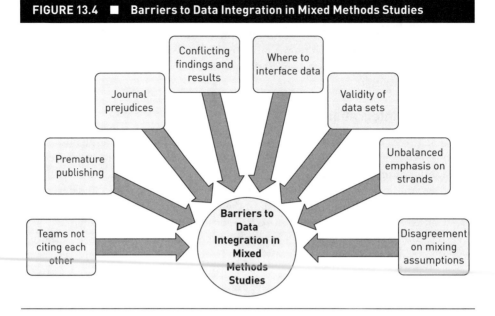

FIGURE 13.4 ■ Barriers to Data Integration in Mixed Methods Studies

Regardless of these difficulties, it "is important for integration to be provided in all mixed research reports [whether it is] throughout the manuscript [or in a] separate section near the end that provides meta-inferences and focuses specifically on integration" (Leech, 2012, p. 877). As a caveat, authors must attend to reporting validation procedures for each strand (e.g., triangulation, member checking, threats to validity and reliability) (Creswell et al., 2013; Creswell & Tashakkori, 2007; Fetters, Curry, & Creswell, 2013). Also, authors have to acknowledge the priority they gave to the two strands (QUAL and QUAN): equal weight or differential (Creswell, 2010; Morse, 1991) (see Chapter 10).

Meta-inferences

Integration requires authors to pay special attention to reporting *meta-inferences* (see Chapter 10). As authors interpret each strand (qualitative and quantitative) of the study, they will draw initial, strand-specific inferences (a conclusion based on evidence and reasoning). When these separate, initial inferences from numbers and text are creatively woven together, meta-inferences arise (*meta* means across). Integrative efficacy occurs when meta-inferences (formed from integrating initial inferences) adequately incorporate inferences that stem from both the qualitative and quantitative phases or strands of the study (Teddlie & Tashakkori, 2006).

Example 13.20 Initial and meta-inferences When statistically analyzing survey results, researchers noticed that subjects indicated they often failed to report credit card debt when claiming bankruptcy. From this result, the researchers *inferred* that the subjects were breaking the law. When reading the interview transcripts from selected subjects, a theme emerged that the subjects did not know they had to report credit card debt when claiming bankruptcy. In fact, they were very unknowledgeable about the legality of the entire process. The researchers thus *inferred* that they were irresponsible consumers for not availing themselves of this information. However, upon reading a white paper report to the Senate, researchers learned that bankruptcy trustees often offered truncated and short explanations of the bankruptcy process, if any at all. Trustees justified this approach by citing a hole in the legislation. When taking all data sources into account and examining their initial reactions to the data, the researchers revised their initial inferences and reached a *meta-inference* instead, concluding that the bankruptcy system and law were flawed, rather than consumers being irresponsible. They would not have come to this *meta-insight* (across all data sets) if they had just relied on the survey, the interview data, or the document analysis.

REVIEW AND ENGAGEMENT

When critically reading a research report, you would

☐ Determine if the authors respected the principle of integration in a mixed methods study, at least to some degree (see Figures 13.4, 13.5, and 13.6 and Table 13.4)

☐ Ascertain if they reported their validation procedures for both strands (e.g., reliability, validity, trustworthiness, and triangulation) (see Chapter 8, Table 8.5) while attempting data integration

☐ Check to see if they adequately dealt with meta-inferences (i.e., their overarching inferences balanced insights from both the qualitative and quantitative strands of the study, not privileging or ignoring either one)

Integration via Connecting, Merging, or Embedding

When authors *do* report integrated findings and results, they have to provide evidence of connecting, merging, or embedding one type of data in the other. The more successful they are in these three strategies, the more convincing their research report (Creswell, 2010) (see Figure 13.5).

Connecting

Connecting is defined as bringing things together to better communicate (Anderson, 2014). Integration through connecting involves analyzing one data set (e.g., a quantitative survey) and then using that information to inform subsequent data collection (e.g., qualitative interview questions or identifying participants for interviews). The reverse is also true. Insights from analyzing qualitative interviews can help create a quantitative survey instrument. In effect, the data *analysis* of the first strand or phase of research provides information that informs the data *collection* step of the second strand or phase. They build on each other, help explain each other, or both (Creswell, 2008; Creswell et al., 2011).

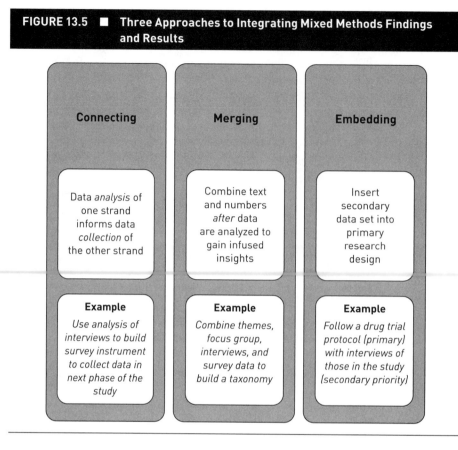

FIGURE 13.5 ■ Three Approaches to Integrating Mixed Methods Findings and Results

Connecting	Merging	Embedding
Data *analysis* of one strand informs data *collection* of the other strand	Combine text and numbers *after* data are analyzed to gain infused insights	Insert secondary data set into primary research design
Example	**Example**	**Example**
Use analysis of interviews to build survey instrument to collect data in next phase of the study	*Combine themes, focus group, interviews, and survey data to build a taxonomy*	*Follow a drug trial protocol (primary) with interviews of those in the study (secondary priority)*

Merging

Merging is defined as combining things to create a new whole (Anderson, 2014). In mixed methods studies, merging involves combining texts and numbers so as to obtain a more holistic and inclusive interpretation of the data. This merging is best facilitated if authors purposefully design their study so they generate types of data that will be conducive to later merging of the databases. The two databases and sets of findings and results are brought together for analysis and comparison. Merging typically occurs *after* the data are analyzed (e.g., statistically and thematically) (Creswell et al., 2011; Fetters et al., 2013).

Example 13.21 Merging In a study focused on depression among patients aged 65 and over, researchers collected (a) quantitative data from a survey of physicians, (b) quantitative survey data from patients via self-reported ratings of depression (on a five-point Likert scale), (c) qualitative data from semistructured interviews with selected patients, and (d) qualitative data from a small focus group of physicians. Upon analyzing and then merging these data, it became evident from comparing (a) qualitative themes present in patient interviews and physician focus groups with (b) quantitative demographic and survey ratings that a typology of differing emotions and feelings of depressed patients toward their physicians could be created from the merged data. This new typology can then inform practice and future research.

Embedding

To embed means to introduce or implant something into an existing mass (Anderson, 2014), much like inserting a journalistic reporter into a war zone. Military metaphor aside, integration of data through embedding happens when data collection and data analysis are linked at multiple points during the research process. Embedding is most often used in experimental intervention research designs, with integration happening at the pretrial, trial, and/or posttrial phases. Authors have to be cognizant of not threatening the validity of the experimental trial design as they embed a secondary data source into the larger, more primary data source (Creswell, 2008; Creswell et al., 2011; Fetters et al., 2013).

Example 13.22 Embedding In effect, "a data set of secondary priority is embedded within a larger, primary [research] design. An example is the collection of supplemental qualitative data about how participants are experiencing an intervention during an experimental [drug] trial. Alternatively, a qualitative data collection may precede an experimental trial to inform the development of procedures [pretrial] or to follow an experimental trial to help explain the results of the trial [posttrial]" (Creswell et al., 2011, p. 6). Normally, an experimental trial is focused on cause and effect, not how this mechanism works. In this example, the large mass is the experimental trial (did the drug work or not?), and the voices of the participants were embedded into this primary mass. In this particular study, the participants' opinions were secondary to whether the drug was effective or not, the primary focus of the research.

REVIEW AND ENGAGEMENT

When critically reading a research report, you would

☐ Ascertain if the authors convincingly employed some combination of the approaches to data integration (connecting, merging, embedding) (see Figures 13.5 and 13.6)

☐ Judge whether you think their data integration approach created a convincing account of their research

In addition to achieving integration by connecting, merging, and embedding data, authors can combine data by comparing or contrasting results through narratives, data transformation, and joint data displays (Creswell et al., 2011). Data can also be integrated through triangulation (Aarons, Fettes, Sommerfeld, & Palinkas, 2012). Each is now discussed.

Narratives

Once the data are analyzed, authors can use narratives to illustrate integration, using one of three approaches. First, they can *weave* both qualitative findings and quantitative results together on a theme-by theme or concept-by-concept basis. Each theme or concept is developed using both words and numbers. Second, they can use the *contiguous* narrative approach, which involves presenting qualitative findings and quantitative results in separate sections of the same paper. Third, authors can use a *staged* narrative approach wherein they separately publish the different stages of the mixed design in different papers (Creswell et al., 2011) (see the last section of this chapter).

Data transformation

Quite simply, researchers would turn their numbers into text, their text into numbers, or both. Once this transformation is complete, they can then integrate the data to obtain richer insights into the phenomenon. A common approach is to code the qualitative data and then count the frequency of the codes identified (i.e., content analysis). Authors can then integrate the quantitative numeric data with the transformed qualitative text, which is now expressed in numbers (Creswell et al., 2011).

> ***Example 13.23 Data transformation*** McGregor (1993, 2004) used this approach in her study about the formation of a Canadian policy network for the electronic fund transfer system (EFTS) (banking machines and debit cards). She analyzed more than 1,000 documents using content analysis, converted this qualitative data to numbers and frequencies, and then merged these data with 17 qualitative case studies to create relational data, which were used to conduct a sociometric network analysis. This data transformation and subsequent integration helped her create a new model for policy network emergence, evolution, and resolution, something that would not have been possible without these layers of integration.

Joint data displays

Joint displays of data are an especially promising strategy to establish and then report integration. As the name implies, they involve presenting both numeric and text data in a table, figure, matrix, or graph that simultaneously portrays both words and numbers (Guetterman et al., 2015). They are a way to "integrate data by bringing the data together through a visual means to draw out new insights beyond the information gained from separate quantitative and qualitative results" (Fetters et al., 2013, p. 2143).

Authors have several options. They can (a) choose a side-by-side comparison of numbers and text. They can (b) use an approach called statistics by themes or themes by statistics. Other options include (c) path diagrams, (d) a side-by-side comparison with a theoretical lens, and (e) instrument development displays where authors show how they used data from a qualitative study to help create a quantitative instrument. Guetterman et al. (2015) provided excellent pictorial examples of each of these approaches. Joint displays are powerful tools for illustrating the interdependency between numbers and text when integrating findings and results into meta-inferences and meta-insights. They show how numbers and text can interface and inspire deeper understandings of the phenomenon (see example 13.24).

Example 13.24 Joint data display

Table Comparison of Information From Interview Data and Survey Data

	Qualitative Findings	Quantitative Results
	Face-to-Face Interview	**Telephone Survey**
Theme 1 How and why people become indebted	Five factors affecting how people became indebted	50% said they did not know how they became so indebted
Theme 2 People's feelings about being in debt	Four dimensions of what it *means* to be in debt	60% refused to answer survey questions about how they felt about being in debt (missing data)
Theme 3 Perceptions of how to remedy the situation	Overall, five valid "get out of debt" strategies were discovered in the qualitative data	90% said they had no idea how to get out of debt

This joint display is powerful in that it shows how the voices of the participants as expressed in the interviews provide context for the percentages obtained from the survey. To illustrate, despite that 50% said they did not know how they became indebted, the interviews provided insights from those who did express comments pursuant to this theme. Also, although the majority refused to answer survey questions about how they felt about being in debt (missing empirical data), a thematic analysis of the interview data revealed four insights into this emotive aspect of this phenomenon, as expressed by those living it.

Triangulation

In regards to integration of results and findings, triangulation is a process whereby researchers strategically use multiple methods together so they can examine convergence, expansion, and complementarity of the data sets (see Table 13.4). Regarding *convergence*, authors want to know if the findings and results from the two strands provide the "same answers to the same questions." For example, did interview data concur with a factor analysis? Did the concurrent use of qualitative data validate the results obtained from quantitative analysis? *Complementarity* is achieved when different methods provide "related answers to related questions." By integrating the two strands, authors can gain depth as well as breadth of understanding of the phenomenon; that is, they can find more *complete* insights than when data are analyzed and interpreted separately. Finally, authors can report *expansion* of their inferences if one method provides "answers to questions raised by the use of another method." For example, by sequentially examining the qualitative data (e.g., focus groups), researchers can further elucidate and explain unanticipated findings from quantitative analysis (e.g., survey results) (Aarons et al., 2012; Swartout, 2014), as shown in example 13.24.

TABLE 13.4 ■ Three Approaches to Triangulating Mixed Methods Data Sets	
Approach	**The two strands provide**
Convergence (affirmation)	"The same answers to the same questions"
Complementarity (more complete insights when interpreted together)	"Related answers to related questions"
Expansion (further elucidation)	"Answers to questions raised by the use of another method"

In summary, authors can choose from an array of approaches to integrate their data and its interpretation (see Figure 13.6). Each approach yields different degrees of and nuances into strand-specific and meta-inferences required to answer the research question, the hypothesis, or both.

Fit of Data Integration (Coherence)

After clarifying which integration approach(es) they employed in their study and reported in their paper, authors should report on the *fit of their data integration* efforts; that is, they have to affirm if combining the strands helped them better answer their research question (Fetters et al., 2013). To do this, they need to acknowledge the issue of inferential *coherence*, defined as clearly and logically holding together to form a whole (Anderson, 2014). A *good fit* of data integration leads to an overall sense of understandability and agreement because the data *fit together* (i.e., they complement [complete], expand, or affirm each other). If the exercise of integrating data from the two strands yields incoherent insights (i.e., instead of fitting well together, they push against each other), authors have to address these concerns as well.

FIGURE 13.6 ■ Approaches to Integrating Data and Interpretations

Integrate

- **Connect** one strand with another (build on each other)
- **Merge** text with numbers
- **Embed** secondary data into primary
- **Narratives**
- **Data transformation** (change numbers to words and vice versa)
- **Joint data displays** (simultaneously display words and numbers)
- **Triangulation**

Inferential coherence can be verified in one of three ways (see Figure 13.7). First, coherence is *confirmed* when the findings and results of both strands validate (confirm) each other. When the two data sources provide similar conclusions, the researchers' inferences have greater credibility. Second, integration of qualitative and quantitative data may result in *expansion*, wherein the data diverge (differ), leading to new insights. In these cases, researchers' insights expand or get larger because the data address different aspects of the phenomenon, or they complement central aspects.

Finally, data integration may lead to *discordance*, which happens when the findings and results from the two strands are inconsistent, incongruous, contradictory, conflicting, or in disagreement. Authors have to report how they dealt with any discord within their integrated data. They can report on potential sources of bias, examine methodological assumptions, question methods procedures, or some combination of these three. They can gather additional data, reanalyze existing databases to resolve differences, seek explanations from theory, or challenge the validity of the constructs. They can also pursue further analysis of their separate and integrated databases and report in follow-up studies (Fetters et al., 2013).

FIGURE 13.7 ■ Three Dimensions of Coherence (Fit of Data Integration)

Confirmation	Expansion	Discordance
• Similar conclusions from both data sets validate the author's inferences and increase validity and credibility	• Divergent data (addressing different aspects of the phenomenon) can actually lead to new and expanded insights	• Integration may lead to discord, which must be acknowledged (inconsistencies, contradictions, incongruencies)

REVIEW AND ENGAGEMENT

When critically reading a research report, you would

☐ Ascertain if the authors convincingly employed some combination of alternative approaches to integration, especially joint displays and data transformations, and made this research design choice evident (see Figures 13.5 and 13.6)

☐ Judge whether the authors successfully employed data triangulation (see Table 13.3)

☐ Determine if they provided a discussion of coherence (i.e., whether data integration helped or hindered them—created confirmation, expansion, or contradictions) (see Figure 13.7)

Organizing Mixed Methods Results and Findings Section

A review of the nascent literature about writing up the Results and Findings section of mixed methods papers showed that authors can avail themselves of several organizational strategies (Leech, 2012), not unlike those for separately reporting the strands (see previous sections of this chapter). That is, they can organize the presentation of their (non)integrated results and findings by research question, theoretical framework, themes, topics of interest, or a results narrative (Leech, 2012; Morse & Maddox, 2014).

Authors can also use (a) the standard linear-analytic approach to organize an entire article (e.g., from research question through to conclusion), (b) the narrative approach (discussed earlier), or (c) the order and/or event approach. The latter includes but is not limited to chronological; critical event; comparative illustration (present results two or three times in different ways); theory building; and dialectical logic (each component/strand [QUAL and QUAN] is presented, then critiqued by the other, with mixed (meta) perspectives presented at the end) (Johnson & Christensen, 2012; Leech, 2012).

When writing mixed methods papers, authors are encouraged to creatively and responsibly organize and "present the material in the way that best conveys the information from the study to the reader" (Leech, 2012, p. 878), while sufficiently warranting any assertions with data and evidence (Johnson & Christensen, 2012) (see Table 13.5). Authors may want to use an organizational heading called *Integration of Results and Findings* (Morse & Maddox, 2014).

TABLE 13.5 ■ Organizational Approaches for Mixed Methods Results and Findings	
Organizational Approach	**Explained**
Standard linear-analytic approach	Use conventional approaches for reporting findings or results (e.g., research questions, hypotheses, particular methods, themes, major results), likely with no to little integration
Narrative (written account of connected events or points)	• Use separate reports for qualitative findings and quantitative reports with no integration • Use separate reports for qualitative findings and quantitative reports with an integration section • Use fully integrated synthesis (no separate reports)
Order and/or event approach	• Chronological order • Critical events • Comparative illustration (present results and findings two or three times, in different ways)
Theory building	Identify the new concepts and constructs emergent from the data and present them as a new coherent theory, taxonomy, or typology
Dialectical logic (logical discussion of opinions)	Each component/strand (QUAL and QUAN) is presented, then critiqued by the other, with mixed perspectives presented at the end

When critically reading a research report, you would

☐ Determine which approach the authors used to organize and report their mixed methods outcomes (see Table 13.5)

☐ Judge if they chose an appropriate approach for organizing and reporting their mixed outcomes so they creatively and responsibly reported their study and addressed their research questions

Number and Nature of Papers to Publish and Where

A final concern is where and how authors should publish or report their study. In addition to how to organize the Results or Findings section *within* a paper, authors have several options for *when* and *where* to publish different parts or strands of the entire study, decisions that reflect the *degree of integration* in the study (Stange et al., 2006), as shown in Table 13.6.

First, authors can publish a quantitative and a qualitative paper in *separate* journals, ideally with clear reference or links to the other article(s). This approach does not involve any integration. Second, they can publish concurrent or sequential papers on each of the quantitative and qualitative strands in the *same* journal, again without integration (i.e., two separate papers in the same journal). This approach depends on the journal editor's cooperation (Stange et al., 2006). These are often called *companion* papers because they are intended to complement each other.

Third, authors can publish separate quantitative and qualitative papers and then a third article that draws insights from the analyses across the two methods. This involves writing three different subreports (i.e., *three articles*) about how each addressed the research question(s) or hypotheses: the qualitative findings part, the quantitative results part, and

TABLE 13.6 ■ Different Approaches to Publishing Mixed Methods Results and Findings		
Degree of Integration	**Number of Papers**	**Number of Journals**
No integration	Two papers, one each on qualitative results and quantitative findings	Two different journals
No integration	Two papers, one each on qualitative results and quantitative findings, publishing one after the other in different issues or volumes	The same journal
Separate integration	Three papers, one each on qualitative results and quantitative findings, with a third paper providing the integrative synopsis	All three in same journal or spread out over different journals
Total integration	One paper that describes findings and results from both strands with overarching insights as they emerged during the analysis and writing-up process	One journal

then a part that synthesizes the two. These papers may be published in the same or different journals (Stange et al., 2006). They can also be called *companion* papers.

Finally, authors can publish *one integrated article* in one journal that describes both strands and their respective findings and results, concurrently drawing overarching insights (Stange et al., 2006). This approach involves merging data from all methods so patterns and trends can emerge (Ary et al., 2010; Johnson & Christensen, 2012). Conclusions gleaned from the two strands are integrated to provide fuller understandings of the phenomenon (Creswell & Tashakkori, 2007).

> ***Example 13.25 One integrated paper*** Christ (2007) collected data in three phases, using different methods over a period of time. Data from a quantitative survey, cross-site qualitative case analyses (three sites), and a single critical qualitative case analysis were reported separately, and then integrated. Christ determined that leadership characteristics and staff cohesion had a direct effect on the provision of disability support services for university students. This insight would not have emerged if the study had been limited to just one of the three methods, or if the findings and results had not been examined collectively, enabling meta-inferences to emerge and be reported.

REVIEW AND ENGAGEMENT

When critically reading a research report, you would

☐ Determine if the authors clarified whether there are companion pieces to this paper (containing other interpretations of the data) (see Table 13.5)

☐ Judge if splitting the reports compromised your ability to gain the most from their study

CONCLUSIONS: UNIQUE CHALLENGES OF THREE APPROACHES

In conclusion, this chapter focused on how to report the findings of a qualitative study, the results of a quantitative study, and a mixed methods study. Each approach has its unique challenges that must be adequately addressed so as to respect the contributions it can make to a discipline's knowledge base and its body of knowledge (see Figure 13.8).

FIGURE 13.8 ■ Challenges Unique to Reporting Qualitative Findings, Quantitative Results, and Mixed Methods

Qualitative Study

- Central role of researchers and their self-reflexivity
- Balance description and interpretation of data (with enough data to convince readers an assertion is supported)
- Ensure thick, rich descriptions of participants' words and world (privilege their voice)
- Central role of themes and quotations when (re)presenting findings
- Timing of literature review relative to data collection and analysis
- Longest section of the paper

Quantitative Study

- Present statistical results with no interpretation (happens in Discussion)
- Balance usage of text, tables, and figures to present key numerical results (respecting statistical conventions and the need for plain language explanations)
- Acknowledge negative results and missing data
- Literature review completed before data collected
- Shortest section of the paper

Mixed Methods Study

- Principle of integration (both data and interpretation)
- Central role of meta-inferences in addition to strand-specific inferences
- Decisions of when and where to publish different strands of the study (QUAL, QUAN, or combined)
- Timing of literature review, before, during, and after data collection/analysis
- Length varies with which strand is given most prominence

REVIEW AND ENGAGEMENT

When critically reading a research report, you would

☐ Determine if the authors demonstrated an appreciation for the challenges unique to reporting each of qualitative, quantitative, and mixed methods studies (see Figure 13.8)

FINAL JUDGMENT ON FINDINGS AND RESULTS

Taking *all* of the ***Review and Engagement*** criteria into account, what is your final judgment of the Findings and/or Results section in the paper you are critically reading?

CHAPTER SUMMARY

After explaining the methodological and etymological distinctions between the terms *findings* and *results*, the chapter discussed the purpose of results and findings and the challenges of achieving that purpose for each of qualitative and quantitative research. At the crux of this is the best way to present results and findings while interpreting them (now or later). The rest of the chapter was divided into how to report qualitative findings, quantitative results, and mixed methods findings and results. Some challenges for qualitative research are balancing both the process of describing and interpreting the data, providing supportive evidence for the existence of a theme, learning the protocols around using participants' quotations, and providing thick and rich descriptions (so as to ensure high-quality findings that can be trusted).

The section on quantitative results dealt with issues of comprehensiveness (have to answer the research question or hypothesis), missing data and negative results, organizational strategies for presenting results, and conventions for reporting numbers (text, tables, and figures). The chapter ended with an overview of reporting protocols and conventions for mixed methods studies, especially the principle of data integration and the steps/strategies researchers can take to ensure integration before data collection, during analysis, or both. The importance of moving from strand-specific inferences to meta-inferences was discussed as were barriers to integration in mixed methods studies. The importance of addressing the fit of data integration was followed with various organizational approaches, and a discussion of how and where to publish the study to reflect the degree of data integration.

REVIEW AND DISCUSSION QUESTIONS

1. How did this book distinguish between results and findings, relative to the quantitative and qualitative research methodologies?

2. How did you feel about the lack of agreement around which term should be used to report outcomes from a study?

3. The chapter discussed the issue of whether or not results and findings should be reported cleanly with no interpretation or if it is all right to interpret as outcomes are presented. What is your opinion on this issue? If you have

had the chance to read articles that separated rather than combined results/findings with interpretations, which approach did you prefer, and why?

4. In a qualitative study, authors have to balance data description with data interpretation. Explain why this is an issue.

5. Qualitative data are words. What challenges arise for researchers when reporting their findings? Quantitative data are numbers. What challenges arise for researchers when reporting

their results? Mixed methods data are both numbers and words. What challenges arise for researchers when reporting their results and findings, which ideally are integrated?

6. What does the phrase *thick, rich descriptions* mean, relative to reporting qualitative findings?

7. Reporting formats for qualitative studies differ according to the purpose of the research (see Table 13.1). Compare and contrast the different reporting formats.

8. Themes are a common approach for reporting qualitative findings. Identify six criteria that researchers can use as proof they actually found a theme in their data. Which combination of these criteria do you recommend? Why? Explain some of the issues researchers have to work through when using quotes as evidence for themes.

9. Recalling the assumptions of the empirical, quantitative research methodology (Chapter 2), why is it important that results be presented in a bias-free, objective manner?

10. What is an author concerned with when focused on *comprehensively* reporting quantitative results?   What is involved in reporting negative results and missing data? Had you ever considered it appropriate to address these two aspects of quantitative data?

11. Which of the five approaches to organizing a quantitative Results section did you prefer, and why? Explain why you did not like some approaches, relative to ease of grasping the results being reported.

12. How surprised were you at the complicated conventions of presenting numerical results in a paper (e.g., tables, figures, and text)? Explain your answer.

13. *Integration* is the cornerstone of presenting mixed methods findings and results. Define integration, and discuss some of the many barriers to data integration that researchers face. Use plain language to explain the notion of *meta-inferences* compared to initial, strand-specific inferences.

14. Compare and contrast connecting, merging, and embedding as approaches to mixed methods data integration. Compare and contrast the idea of joint data display versus data triangulation (two approaches to integration that can be used in mixed methods studies).

15. What strategies can authors use to report whether integrating their data was useful or whether it created unexpected issues for them (called "fit of data integration" or coherence)?

16. Data integration in a mixed methods study can happen in degrees, which affects how authors report their study. Turing to Table 13.5 and related text, do you believe that some degree of integration should be mandatory, or is it all right to publish the strands separately?

17. Which of the five recommended organizational approaches for the Results/Findings section of a mixed methods paper did you prefer, and why?

18. Summarize the conventions for length, tense, person, and voice when preparing the Findings and Results sections of each of qualitative, quantitative, and mixed methods research papers.

DISCUSSION, CONCLUSIONS, AND RECOMMENDATIONS

DISCUSSION

INTRODUCTION

The Discussion section is the heart of the paper, the most original part (Kretchmer, 2008a). Authors directly and personally create their discussion points, reflecting *their* original thoughts, independent of others' thoughts. Their discussion points reflect new insights that emerged from relating their findings or results back to the literature review of previous studies and to any theory used in the study; that is, evidence-based interpretations are presented rather than objective reporting (Anderson, 2014; Ellinger & Yang, 2011; Labaree, 2016; Ramakantan, 2007; Skelton & Edwards, 2000). In the process of creating original discussion points, authors must relate their work back to the original research question, with the proviso that the research question itself *was* original (Geletkanycz & Tepper, 2012; Jammal, 2010; Kastens et al., 2014).

DISCUSSION DEFINED

Discuss is Latin *discutere*, "to dash to pieces, and to agitate" (Harper, 2016). As authors discuss their results and/or findings, they are "stirring things up" so as to stimulate readers' interest in their study and its significance. Dictionary meanings of the word *discuss* include (a) consider by talking over, (b) have a conversation about, (c) present in detail for examination, and (d) talk about in order to convince others or to reach conclusions (Anderson, 2014).

Discussion Versus Conclusion

In research and in academic inquiry, discussion refers to the mental process involved in examining, investigating, and debating an idea (Harper, 2016). For clarification, discussions and conclusions are closely tied together, with some papers including them in one section (Brown, 2014). This book separates them into two chapters because they serve different roles in research. A conclusion (see Chapter 15) is a position, opinion, or judgment reached after careful consideration of the significance and implications of findings or results (i.e., the discussion). To discuss means to talk about, while to conclude means to wrap up (Harper, 2016).

There is little agreement on whether the conclusions should be included in the Discussion section, with this chapter asserting that they serve different functions in reporting research, thereby warranting different criteria to judge them. A paper can have a section called *Discussion and Conclusions*, which is acceptable as long as both tasks are effectively attended to using relevant conventions. In reality, many authors of research papers have a section called Conclusions, but it actually contains discussion points (interpretation), not wrap-up points. In some disciplines, this is an acceptable convention. In other disciplines, there is no separate Discussion section, only a short Conclusion section (Brown, 2014).

DISCUSSION RELATIVE TO RESULTS AND FINDINGS

The Results or Findings section highlights "What was found?", answering the question "What do the data say?" (Azar, 2006). The Discussion section queries "*So what?*" (Geletkanycz & Tepper, 2012). Why should people care about what the data say? What is known now that was not known before this study? Why are these results or findings significant? What is their value? Why do they matter? What do the results or findings mean relative to what was discussed in the literature review? How might others capitalize on the results or findings? (Anderson, 2015; Annesley, 2010; Geletkanycz & Tepper, 2012; Hess, 2004; Matthews & Matthews, 2008).

The Discussion section is normally separate from and follows the results or findings, but it is acceptable to combine them into one section. In empirical work, this section would be called *Results and Discussion* (Ellinger & Yang, 2011; VandenBos, 2010; Wiersma & Jurs, 2009). Because of the discursive nature of qualitative data and the iterative nature of qualitative research, with research stages occurring concurrently, it is hard to separate the findings from their interpretation (Blaxter, 2013; Plakhotnik & Rocco, 2009; Wiersma & Jurs, 2009). Consequently, qualitative work often has just one section, which is called *Findings and Discussions*. But it is also common to report themes, a case study, or narratives as separate findings, followed with their discussion (i.e., two different sections) (Wiersma & Jurs, 2009).

The Discussion section is challenging in a mixed methods study because it entails integrating both the quantitative and qualitative strands, and it is hard to explain how meta-inferences were developed. Authors can have a section for *Findings* (qualitative strand), a section for *Results* (quantitative strand), and a section for *Integrated Results and Findings*, followed with a *Discussion* section. They can have one *Results and Findings* section with relevant subheadings (results, findings, integrated), followed with a *Discussion* section. They also can have one large section called *Integrated Results, Findings, and Discussion*, with appropriate subheadings.

Whether results and findings are separate from their discussion "depends on the most effective and understandable method for presentation" (Wiersma & Jurs, 2009, p. 89).

Regardless, authors need to follow the appropriate conventions and apply the appropriate criteria when reporting results, findings, and discussions because they each serve different functions (see the next section). Succinctly, results and findings are descriptive and deal with facts or insights (depending on the research methodology), while discussions are interpretive, explaining and dealing with points emergent from data and their analysis (Bunton, 2005; Goodson, 2017; Shuttleworth, 2015).

PURPOSE OF DISCUSSION

Discussion sections serve three key functions or purposes. They can summarize, explain, and examine the data, often used in some combination (Day & Gastel, 2006; Ellinger & Yang, 2011; Shank & Brown, 2007) (see Figure 14.1). Combining these functions in one paper is an indication of a seasoned scholar who is familiar with the important role that discussions play when reporting a study. Their use together provides readers with more insightful "takeaways" from the study.

FIGURE 14.1 ■ Three Key Functions of the Discussion Section

Summarize Salient Results or Findings

- Flag or recap salient points (deemed significant, leading to new insights)
- The intent is to set the reader up for explanations and an examination of the import of particular results or findings (which involves going beyond the evidence)

Explain Results or Findings

- Help readers understand *why* the author thinks a point is salient
- Link salient point back to literature, theory, and research question (bolster the *why*)
- Temper urge to speculate (hedge), favoring instead evidence-based explanations of why a point is salient

Examine Implications

- Convince readers they can use the author's analytical and synergistic insights (discussion points); help them mentally connect with the salient points
- Describe how findings or results will impact some combination of future research, theory development, policy, and practice

Summarize Salient Results and Findings

First, authors have the option of summarizing their research by recapping the most important findings or results in the first paragraph of the Discussion section, choosing the most salient points from which to embark on a narrative of why *these* results or findings matter (Azar, 2006; Day & Gastel, 2006). "It should be a direct, declarative, and succinct proclamation of the study results [with no] reference to data or study design" (Hess, 2004, p. 1439). Also, rather than repeating the results or findings, authors should "'go beyond the evidence'" (Skelton & Edwards, 2000, p. 1469). Moving beyond the evidence (but not repeating or inflating the results or attributing unwarranted importance) helps put the results or findings in context, transcending the facts or insights emergent from analyzing the data (Azar, 2006; Bem, 2004; Hess, 2004; Kastens et al., 2014). Transcending means taking people to new places and new states of understanding and insights (Harper, 2016).

> ***Example 14.1 Result summary leading into discussion*** Burr, Hubler, and Kuns (2017) recently conducted a study about time constraints and financial cost as the two main barriers to people attending relationship education (RE). The first paragraph of their Discussion section was a summary of the key results for one of these two variables, time constraints. "Overall, the results show that the preference for many would be to spend 1 to 3 hours in RE, maximum. The *t*-test result showed that men reported a preference for an even less amount of time to spend in RE" (p. 30). After these results were discussed in three paragraphs, the results for the second variable, financial cost, were summarized and then discussed. "Many reported a willingness to spend around $50 (almost one-quarter of the respondents chose $50) on RE. . . . The cost differences did not significantly differ by gender, but more male respondents also reported a significantly higher financial incentive preference to attend RE than did female respondents" (p. 30).

Explain Results and Findings

Second, beyond summarizing, authors can *explain* these salient results or findings (Shank & Brown, 2007), meaning they make plain or understandable what is not immediately obvious (Anderson, 2014). Authors should not rely on readers to intuitively appreciate the import of their work. The discussion narrative helps readers understand *why the author* thinks the results or findings matter (Azar, 2006). In order to explain the results or findings, authors have to carefully read and reread their Results or Findings section while concurrently referring to the research questions, the literature reviewed for this study, and any theories underpinning the study (Brown, 2014; Day & Gastel, 2006; Shank & Brown, 2007).

"The interaction between the presentation of the data and the existing literature provides new insights, raises unexplored issues, and clarifies further research needs" (Plakhotnik & Rocco, 2009, p. 110). This back-and-forth process yields insights that emerge from assigning meaning to the connections (i.e., interpreting the results or findings). *Interpret* is Latin *interpretari*, "understanding something, and making sense of it." It refers to a person's perception or judgment of something (Anderson, 2014; Harper, 2016).

> ***Example 14.2 Explaining results and findings*** Per example 14.1, Burr et al. (2017) went beyond just summarizing their results. They systematically teased out what they

thought each one meant, tying it back to previously cited literature. As an example, this is part of their discussion of the financial cost result. "Many reported a willingness to spend around $50 (almost one-quarter of the respondents chose $50) on RE. This finding [sic] is somewhat similar to that of Morris et al. (1999) who found that participants who paid $30 for a marriage workshop believed this is a reasonable cost (inflation adjustments suggest that $30 in 1999 would be about $43 in 2016)" (p. 30).

Speculation and hedging

Shank and Brown (2007) acknowledged that when interpreting their results or findings so as to explain them, authors may have to speculate about what they mean. To speculate means to form an opinion or come to a conclusion based on incomplete information (i.e., insufficient facts or insights) (Anderson, 2014). Azar (2006) called this "productive speculation [or] suppositional reasoning."

Authors should acknowledge when they are speculating by prefacing the sentence with "In speculation" or "In conjecture." Iyer and Muncy (2016) used this strategy in their paper about how people's subjective well-being is affected by their attitude toward consumption. "This focus on a world that is too big for the person to substantially impact would likely lead to negative feelings and evaluations of life. It is important to note here that we did not measure the feeling of autonomy or self-determination and so this is simply a conjecture and other possible reasons for the result obtained could exist. For example, . . ." (p. 62).

Authors should minimize speculation in their discussion and not stray too far from their data (i.e., not overreach it) (Azar, 2006; Bitchener & Basturkmen, 2006; Hess, 2004). Excessive speculation will not stand scrutiny and risks even credible parts of the research coming into question and being discredited (Ramakantan, 2007). It is not wrong for authors to speculate, because the *maybe* and *perhaps* statements often lead to future hypotheses or research questions. But speculation should not be allowed to "run amok" (Skelton & Edwards, 2000, p. 1470).

The use of hedge words is a clear indication that authors are speculating. These words include *maybe, perhaps, appear, postulate, seem to be, might be, apparently, presumably, probably, possibly, seemingly,* and *likely.* Hedging lets authors avoid any overprecise commitment to an idea. Hedge words intimate that authors are sidestepping an issue or, worse yet, are overstating a situation (Anderson, 2014). The excessive use of hedge words and speculation can also convey the impression that authors are presenting their discussion points without conviction (Hyland, 1996). The strength of their claims about what the study means can become questionable (see Figure 14.2).

When explaining their results or findings, authors can include both evidence-based and speculation-based discussion points but should judiciously use the latter (Azar, 2006; Boudah, 2011; Skelton & Edwards, 2000). The general rule in academic writing is one hedge word per sentence (Matthews & Matthews, 2008).

> **Example 14.3 Hedging (too many hedge words)** "The cause of consumer insolvency is unknown, but one *possible* cause *might* be using credit from sources *presumed* to be credible."

> **Example 14.4 Hedging (using one word)** "The cause of consumer insolvency is unknown, but one *possible* cause is using too much credit from questionable sources."

Examine Implications of Results and Findings

Third, authors can use the Discussion section to *examine* the implications of their findings or results, although implications can also be included in the Conclusions section (Day & Gastel, 2006; Shank & Brown, 2007). Implicate is Latin *implicare*, "to associate with" (Harper, 2016). The intent is to help readers make mental connections with the discussion points. Implications tell others how they can use the results and findings and the author's attendant analytical and synergistic insights (Wiersma & Jurs, 2009). In brief, implications can pertain to the impact of the results and findings on some combination of (a) future research (both research design and research directions), (b) theory development, (c) practice, and (d) policy (Bunton, 2005; Ellinger & Yang, 2011; Evans, Gruba, & Zobel, 2011; Geletkanycz & Tepper, 2012; Hess, 2004; Labaree, 2016; Shank & Brown, 2007).

> ***Example 14.5 Examining results and findings*** Per example 14.3, Burr et al. (2017) also examined what they thought each result meant. As an example, they found that "Many reported a willingness to spend around $50 (almost one-quarter of the respondents chose $50) on RE." They then posited that "this finding *suggests* [emphasis added] that some financial investment may not be completely unreasonable for many potential attendees" (p. 30). This implication tells people how they can use this result in their RE practice. Part of Burr et al.'s literature review focused on whether or not RE programs should provide financial incentives for people to attend or if they should just charge for the program outright and assume that people are willing to pay.

In this book, the topic of implications is further covered in the chapter about conclusions (Chapter 15), but that information is still relevant for judging implications presented in the Discussion section. If it makes sense to introduce an implication while interpreting the salient point, authors should do so. In the Discussion section, the implication would be offered as part of the expanding conversation. In the Conclusions section, it would be a wrap-up point, drawing the conversation to a close. The author's approach to examining implications "depends upon the most effective and understandable method for presentation" (Wiersma & Jurs, 2009, p. 89).

REVIEW AND ENGAGEMENT

When critically reading a research report, you would

☐ Ascertain if the authors provided more than just a summary or recap of their salient results or findings

☐ Check to see that they used some combination of *summarize*, *explain*, and *examine* when preparing their discussion

☐ Determine if they used the Discussion section to expand the conversation about the issue or phenomenon

☐ Confirm that they based their discussion points on evidence from the study instead of their personal opinions and feelings

☐ Determine if they minimized hedging and speculation, favoring instead evidence-based explanations (see Figure 14.2)

☐ Affirm they properly labeled the Discussion section, as just either a discussion or an integration of results/findings and discussion, perhaps with conclusions

DISCUSSION AND THE CONCEPT OF SIGNIFICANCE

Achieving these three purposes (i.e., summarize, explain, and examine) (see Figure 14.1) requires convincing others of the *significance* and the relevance of the results or findings from a particular study (Skelton & Edwards, 2000). Without this persuasive element in a research paper or report, readers are less likely to engage with the study. If something is significant, it is important, meaningful, noteworthy, momentous, weighty, and of consequence (Anderson, 2014). If it is insignificant, it is not worthy of notice or attention relative to the research question and has little value or worth for anyone.

Dimensions of Research Significance

Research scholarship can be significant along many dimensions (see Figure 14.2). For example, Drotar (2008) identified four dimensions: (a) empirical (data and their interpretation contribute to new knowledge), (b) method (employed more valid methods than previously used in the field), (c) theoretical, and (d) practical. Authors can frame the significance of their study around some combination of these four factors: new knowledge, new methods, new theory, or new applications.

Sternberg and Gordeeva (1996) identified similar and then additional features of research that can make it significant (they used the terms *influential* and *impactful*). In short, a research article is significant if it (a) contributes to theory development and advancement, especially by explaining the phenomenon better than previous work; (b) makes an obvious contribution to the knowledge base; (c) adds something new and substantial (including

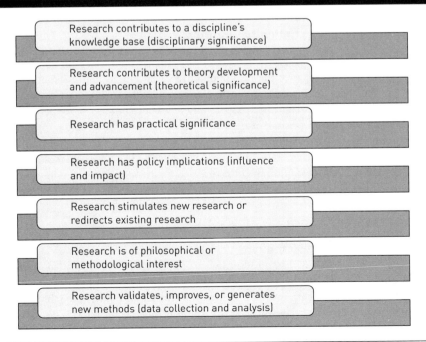

FIGURE 14.2 ■ Dimensions of Research Significance, Influence, and Impact

Research contributes to a discipline's knowledge base (disciplinary significance)

Research contributes to theory development and advancement (theoretical significance)

Research has practical significance

Research has policy implications (influence and impact)

Research stimulates new research or redirects existing research

Research is of philosophical or methodological interest

Research validates, improves, or generates new methods (data collection and analysis)

integrating previously unintegrated ideas, as in conceptual papers); (d) has practical significance; (e) is of methodological interest; or (f) generates research by providing new and exciting ideas. They clarified that not all articles will show all of these characteristics; however, taken together, these factors explained half of the variance in their data set—that is, what makes research significant.

Interestingly, several of the attributes of influential research that Sternberg and Gordeeva (1996) identified as "relatively unimportant" are considered significant by others, including (a) providing evidence that supports an existing theory (theory confirmation), (b) presenting a general theory that does not fit with existing theories, and (c) highlighting implications and providing concrete practice examples. To illustrate, while Sternberg and Gordeeva said that theory contributions were only relatively important, Geletkanycz and Tepper (2012) asserted that "impactful studies are ones which explore larger questions of theoretical significance" (p. 256). Authors should use these six attributes (see Figure 14.3) to argue the significance of their research (i.e., why people should pay attention to it), making a strong case and citing relevant literature in their Discussion section.

Significance Versus Novelty

As a point of clarification, Drotar (2008) asserted that "scientific significance is not the same as novelty" (p. 2). *Novel* means interesting or unusual (Anderson, 2014) but not necessarily meaningful or of value for the research question. To be significant, research results and findings must make an impact, some combination of scientific (in the general sense), theoretical, and practical, *relative to the research question*. Furthermore, significant results and findings will exceed any thresholds or benchmarks already set in the field (i.e., what is already known or not known). It is incumbent upon authors to position their work in the context of existing benchmarks and clearly explain how their work exceeds them, thereby making their work significant (Geletkanycz & Tepper, 2012).

Significant Versus Statistically Significant

Also, in empirical work, results that are not *statistically* significant can still be significant, especially if they advance the field and address other important questions (Drotar, 2008). "No statistical significance" is not the same as "no difference" (Shuttleworth, 2015). If interpreted "in a balanced and circumspect way" (Drotar, 2008, p. 3), results of this sort (including unexpected, surprising, or negative results, described in Chapter 13) can play a role in advancing a field's knowledge base (Ary, Jacobs, & Sorensen, 2010). Geletkanycz and Tepper (2012) agreed, calling them "nonfindings," described as "prominent and unanticipated insights" (p. 258). Nonfindings constitute rich fodder for discussion points, provided the study was well executed (Drotar, 2008).

Theoretical Significance

Even studies that disconfirm a theory can have research and disciplinary significance. Any theories that cannot withstand scrutiny eventually need to be discarded, paving the way for alternative explanations of reality (Drotar, 2008). "The failure to find rigorous support for key theoretical arguments is in itself informative and rather thought-provoking, and such findings are certainly helpful in continued theoretical development"

(Geletkanycz & Tepper, 2012, p. 258). Nonfindings and unsupported hypotheses "constitute a rich, yet commonly foregone, way to inform theoretical understandings" (Geletkanycz & Tepper, 2012, p. 258). Authors should not shy away from acknowledging these nonfindings. Rather than a sign of weakness or of flawed scholarship, they are a validation of authors' insights into the significance of their scholarship as it pertains to theory development.

Bottom line, authors "need to promote if not champion their work in no uncertain terms" if they intend to convince others of its significance (Drotar, 2008, p. 2). Their arguments for significance must be meaty and persuasive but clearly accessible, compelling, and credible (Geletkanycz & Tepper, 2012).

REVIEW AND ENGAGEMENT

When critically reading a research report, you would

- ☐ Determine if the authors convinced you that their analytical points and synergistic insights will be useful in the discipline (knowledge base) and in your practice and/or research

- ☐ Ascertain if they clearly explained how *what* they found in their study moves things forward in the field

- ☐ Check to see if the authors made a point of explaining the significance of their study, preferably along several dimensions (see Figure 14.3)

- ☐ Determine if they referred to issues of nonfindings and their significance (even if they were not statistically significant, if quantitative research)

FUNDAMENTAL QUESTIONS TO ADDRESS IN THE DISCUSSION

Depending on what their data analysis reveals, authors can choose to include several lines of thought in their discussion, all pertaining to how their data relate to what has already been found in the field. It is critical that authors build "a bridge between a study's findings and the larger literature. It is only through a connection to broader understanding that the . . . 'value added' of a given study can be interpreted and, indeed, appreciated" (Geletkanycz & Tepper, 2012, p. 257). In the literature review, authors explain what *is* already known about their research problem. This convention holds whether the review was prepared in advance (quantitative), or during qualitative analysis, when it is called confirmatory literature. In the discussion, authors tell readers how their study moved things *forward from* what is already known (Anderson, 2015; Drotar, 2009; Labaree, 2016).

There is a collection of fundamental questions to address in the Discussion section (Ellinger & Yang, 2011). First, authors can *discuss* whether their results and findings (a) confirm, (b) change, (c) contradict, (d) challenge, or (e) otherwise advance (extend and expand) existing understandings. Second, (f) did their study provide totally new insights or information that can advance the field's knowledge base about the phenomenon in question? (g) Did they find an unexpected or surprising outcome not previously documented in the literature? (h) Did their results or findings resolve an existing controversy in the literature or raise another one? Third, (i) did their results or findings connect to an entirely different body of literature, thereby opening the field up to a more holistic understanding of the phenomenon? (j) Did their data analysis reveal gaps in the literature that had not been previously exposed or adequately described? (k) Did their results or findings help them interpret others' results or findings so that, when combined, better understandings emerge?

Authors will not have to address all of these questions—that is, the three main areas of existing understandings, new understandings, or new connections (see Figure 14.3). Seldom does one study yield data that reflect all of these fundamental questions (e.g., confirms, changes, challenges, and contradicts). But authors do need to relate their results and findings to similar studies (Hess, 2004). Drawing on this roster of questions aids in this central role of a discussion (Figure 14.3 was extrapolated from Anderson, 2015; Annesley, 2010; Azar, 2006; Drotar, 2009; Ellinger & Yang, 2011; Geletkanycz & Tepper, 2012; Hess, 2004; Jones, 2016; Kastens et al., 2014; Kretchmer, 2008a; Labaree, 2016; Lerner, ca. 2003; Shank & Brown, 2007; Swales, 1990).

Table 14.1 shares examples of these fundamental questions, taken from the Discussion section of an article about students' perceptions of the RateMyProfessors.com website (Bleske-Rechek & Fritsch, 2011). Information in this table illustrates how their findings (a) fit with what is known; (b) challenge, contradict, and extend existing knowledge; and (c) reveal new insights around the topic of students rating their professors on a public website. It is a good example of authors placing their results in the context of previous research that was set out in the literature review and of explaining new things they uncovered and learned from their study (Johnson & Christensen, 2012; Jones, 2016; Shuttleworth, 2015). Note that although this was a quantitative study, Bleske-Rechek and Fritsch (2011) used the word *finding* instead of *result* when preparing their discussion points.

FIGURE 14.3 ■ Fundamental Questions for Discussion Section

Existing Understandings	New Understandings	New Connections
• Confirmed • Changed • Contradicted • Challenged • Resolved a controversy	• New insights, meanings, and understandings • New knowledge • New theories or conceptualizations • Introduced a new controversy • Surprising or unexpected outcome not previously in the literature • Revealed previously unknown gaps in the literature	• Connected to an entirely different body of literature • Opportunity to reinterpret others' work, creating synergy and more holistic understandings of the phenomenon

TABLE 14.1 ■ Examples of Fundamental Questions in a Discussion Section (extrapolated from Bleske-Rechek & Fritsch, 2011)	
Fundamental questions in Discussion section	**Examples from Bleske-Rechek and Fritsch's (2011) Discussion section, with relevant wording in *bold italics***
Introductory statement for their Discussion section, recapping salient results	"In this study we ***documented a number of findings that could be used to inform faculty and researchers' judgments*** about online rating sites such as RateMyProfessors.com. ***First***, . . ." (p. 8)
Reference to previous study that their results support	"***As documented in previous investigations*** of online rating sites (Silva, Silva, Quinn, Draper, Cover, & Munoff, 2008), ***we also found that*** instructors received more favorable than unfavorable ratings, and tended to be rated as higher in quality than in easiness" (p. 8).
Noting how their results coincided with a study noted in the literature review	"Second, some instructors were rated more favorably than other instructors were, ***a finding that coincides with Riniolo et al.'s (2006) observation*** that 'ratings are widely dispersed and not just clustered at the extremes on the 5-point student evaluation scale . . .'" (p. 8).
Explaining how their study contradicted an earlier study	"The finding of more favorable ratings overall is ***especially important in light of past research*** showing that students tend to give more negative ratings when they are anonymous (Feldman, 1979)" (p. 8).
Their result expanded on one from the study they replicated	"Moreover, ***while we replicated previous research*** with student evaluations of teaching that has shown instructors in math and natural sciences are rated as more difficult, ***we also showed that*** students (a) did not rate math and natural sciences instructors as any lower in quality than other instructors" (p. 9).
New insights from their study	"***Another finding of the current study*** was a consistent degree of consensus among students about a given instructor's quality, regardless of how many students had provided the ratings. In other words, degree of consensus about an instructor, on average, was the same if that instructor had 10 ratings as if the instructor had 50 ratings. . . . ***[I]t seems that students and instructors should be cautious*** in interpreting a small number of posts or any individual post taken on its own" (p. 9).

"***The current study also documented*** that students agree about low quality instructors and, in particular, high quality instructors. In fact, differences in mean quality ratings accounted for 70% of the variance in degree of consensus about instructor quality" (p. 9). |

(Continued)

TABLE 14.1 ■ (Continued)

Fundamental questions in Discussion section	Examples from Bleske-Rechek and Fritsch's (2011) Discussion section, with relevant wording in *bold italics*
Speculating about what a result might mean	"Yet, only a minority of students post on RateMyProfessors (Bleske-Rechek & Michels, 2010; Davison & Price, 2009), *which implies* that students who post must be different somehow from students who do not. *Are they more conscientious, or do they feel a stronger sense of obligation to inform their fellow students? If so, why?"* (p. 9).
Limitations of their study	The findings of the current study are *potentially limited by several factors. First*, we chose to analyze all instructors (with 10 or more ratings) from one institution rather than a few instructors from many institutions. . . . *Other concerns about our data stem from* the nature of the RateMyProfessors.com website. . . . It is likely that these related concerns are relatively minor. . . . *However, we recognize that if we knew* which students were rating which instructors, *we could have* computed interrater reliability coefficients as measures of student consensus" (pp. 9–10).
Discussion ends with a strong conclusion	"[P]ublic display of the chili pepper and students' comments about instructors' personality and appearance will probably *continue to cause skepticism that will outweigh any statistical evidence of the site's utility. Our study has added to that statistical evidence. We demonstrated* strong student consensus about instructor quality, which did not hinge on instructor easiness. Trends in student ratings on RateMyProfessors mirror those found on traditional student evaluations of teaching (Coladarci & Kornfield, 2007; Sanders et al., 2011). *In the aggregate, RateMyProfessors.com is providing useful feedback about instructor quality"* (p. 10).

REVIEW AND ENGAGEMENT

When critically reading a research report, you would

☐ Determine if the authors presented a mix of how their study confirmed, challenged, changed, contradicted, or extended previous work (see Figure 14.3)

☐ If not a mix, check to see which fundamental question(s) they did address, and judge whether they seemed appropriate relative to their results or findings and their research question

☐ Ascertain if they addressed some combination of relating results or findings to existing understandings, adding new understandings, or making new connections (Figure 14.3)

☐ If a theory was used, check to see that the authors referred back to any theory, conceptual framework, or model to help discuss their results or findings

LIMITATIONS

The limitations of a study are a key part of the Discussion section; yet many scholars ignore or underplay them (Geletkanycz & Tepper, 2012; VandenBos, 2010). Limitations are defined as those characteristics of the research design (especially methods) that impact or influence any interpretations of the results or findings (Bem, 2004; Labaree, 2016) (see Chapters 9 and 10). These research design characteristics include failings, defects, or restrictions that limit or place boundaries on what can be deduced (implied or inferred) from the results and findings (Anderson, 2014).

Put another way, limitations determine what authors *cannot* say about their study results or findings (Fritz, 2008). "Every study has limitations" (Drotar, 2009, p. 341). For that reason, virtually all papers include study limitations at the end of the Discussion section, usually with its own subheading *Limitations*, placed just before the Conclusions section (Azar, 2006; Labaree, 2016; Lai, 2013; Ellinger & Yang, 2011). In the Limitations section, authors are saying "'we have thought about the limitations but we think it [sic] would not affect [sic] our study' or 'our results are meaningful despite these limitations'" (Lai, 2013).

Threats to Validity

Foremost regarding limitations, it is incumbent upon authors to clearly explain any threats to validity for an empirical study and any threats to trustworthiness if a qualitative methodology was employed (Boudah, 2011; Drotar, 2009; Kretchmer, 2008b) (see Chapter 8, Table 8.5). Validity concerns whether the study measured what it was intended to measure. Internal validity refers to how well the study *was* conducted, and external validity pertains to the use of the findings or results *after* the study is completed (i.e., applied to people not included in the study [quantitative] or in another context [qualitative]).

Internal validity

Internal validity can be threatened in both research methodologies. In empirical studies, researchers often try to establish a causal relationship. The most common threats to internal validity in empirical research include study design mistakes, measurement and instrument errors, and inadequate statistical power (e.g., the sample was too small) (Drotar, 2009; Johnson & Christensen, 2012). Threats to internal validity in quantitative research also include history, maturation, mortality, attrition, pretesting, compensatory rivalry, and resentful demoralization (Michael, 2004). In qualitative research, authors need to be wary of internal threats to credibility, plausibility, applicability, confirmability, and consistency (Boudah, 2011; Labaree, 2016) (see Chapter 8, Table 8.5).

External validity

External validity threats include sampling size and bias and any characteristics of the sample that compromise generalizing the results (quantitative) or transferring the findings to other contexts (qualitative) (Boudah, 2011; Drotar, 2009; Johnson & Christensen, 2012; Miles & Huberman, 1994). Threats to external validity in quantitative research include group selection or assignment bias, the Hawthorne effect, and treatment as well as experimental effects (Michael, 2004).

Authors conducting qualitative research must also be concerned with sample and data collection issues that might restrict the possibility of getting a full answer to their research question. External threats to trustworthiness can include researcher bias and credibility, participant self-reporting bias, methods chosen for the research design, and issues with access to the site and the participants (Blaxter, 2013; Boudah, 2011; Creswell, 2009; Labaree, 2016; Newton, 2013).

Authors of mixed methods studies have to report the aforementioned strand-specific design validity concerns as well as interpretative validity, which concerns the validity of the conclusions when integrating data from two strands to gain richer insights (Teddlie & Tashakkori, 2006) (see Chapter 10, Figure 10.7).

Temper Limitations

It is important that authors avoid an apologetic tone when identifying their study limitations. After all, these limitations stem from justified research design choices (delimitations, discussed in Chapter 6) (Jones, 2016; Kastens et al., 2014; Kretchmer, 2008a; Labaree, 2016). As well, when framing their limitations, authors should avoid discrediting their method or the significance of their study (Lai, 2013). Labaree (2016) urged authors to not apologize for issues that they never intended to investigate; that is, authors should limit the limitations to the research problem and research design in question.

Nonetheless, by being honest and identifying key limitations or weaknesses, authors acknowledge that their study can be improved. Authors should judiciously choose one or two salient limitations, those that pose the greatest threat to validity-related issues. Too many limitations raise questions about the integrity of the study (Annesley, 2010; Azar, 2006; Brown, 2014; Christopher, Marker, & Zabel, 2015; Drotar, 2009; Hess, 2004; Hindle, 2015; Shuttleworth, 2015). Authors "should answer the question: do these problems with errors, methods, validity, etc. eventually matter and, if so, to what extent?" (Labaree, 2016).

Authors are further encouraged to present counterarguments that temper any threats to the validity or trustworthiness of their study (Annesley, 2010; Azar, 2006; Bitchener & Basturkmen, 2006; Christopher et al., 2015; Drotar, 2009). They need to "explain why the limitations are not a huge issue, or how the merits of the [results or] findings outweigh the limitations of the particular study [because the limitations] are nominal at best" (Christopher et al., 2015, p. 761). Authors have to convince readers that their conclusions are not negatively affected by their study limitations; that is, readers can have confidence in the data and any pursuant conclusions (Annesley, 2010; Labaree, 2016; Lai, 2013). These examples illustrate efforts to temper perceived threats to research design and interpretative rigor.

Examples 14.6 Tempering limitations with counterpoints

Sample size (quantitative): Authors can acknowledge that although their empirical study had a small sample, they were able to demonstrate statistically significant results with a robust effect size.

Sample size (qualitative): Authors can say they believe the informants were representative of other indebted students (in the colloquial sense of the word), but they are not (nor need they be) representative in a statistical sense. The findings were never intended to be generalized beyond the research site, so sample size was not an issue. Steps were taken to ensure transferability of the findings (see Fritz, 2008).

Generalization (quantitative): An empirical study that looked at the efficacy of a new diabetes treatment in First Nations patients had very positive results, but they may not apply to other ethnicities. This statement could be made, followed by a comment about how the results might still be widely applicable as they will help with patient-specific treatment in all parts of the world.

Particularity and transferability (qualitative): Authors can say that future studies need to address the extent to which trends revealed in their single-school-board case study can be extrapolated to other geographical areas or school boards. In the meantime, their findings shed valuable insights into the dynamics of the research site for *their* study, insights that did not exist before.

Self-reported data: In qualitative research, people's narratives and life stories are prone to bias (e.g., selective memory, telescoping, attribution, and exaggeration). Authors can convince readers that their findings are rigorous by explaining the effectiveness of any measures taken to deal with these biases (see Labaree, 2016).

Theory bias: Authors can admit that their approach to theorizing about their research problem was indeed shaped by their own cultural background and experiences. They can then mitigate this by stating that any and all attempts at identifying and categorizing narratives are bound by culture, so their study is not compromised (see Fritz, 2008).

Humility and Limitations

When acknowledging their limitations, authors need to avoid "appearing arrogant, condescending, or patronizing" (Kallestinova, 2011, p. 187). Some scholars call limitations the *humility section* of the paper (Cone & Foster, 2006; Hess, 2004). Humility (modesty and reservedness about one's importance) "goes a long way in advancing the acceptability of your manuscript to readers. . . . Because any particular study is often inherently flawed by limitations, be humble in your [discussion]" (Christopher et al., 2015, p. 761).

When using a humble voice, authors would write their limitations using conservative language that does not overstate the study outcomes while providing strong evidence for each discussion point. They would provide clear and concise explanations of the results or findings by letting "the findings themselves do the talking" (Christopher et al., 2015, p. 761). Cabrita, Mealha, and Queiroz de Barros (2014) explained that this tone can be achieved by using epistemic reporting verbs (e.g., *cause* and *suggest*), intransitive verbs (e.g., *seem* and *tend*), and nonassertive epistemic adverbs (e.g., *presumably, certainly,* and *maybe*), combined with modal verbs (e.g., *may* and *could*) and passive voice. As noted before, authors have to be conscious of not hedging too much while trying to convey a conservative tone.

Example 14.7 Humble, conservative language

"It *may* be *claimed by* those embracing the results of this study that students who leave university with large debt loads *tend* to become insolvent more often."

Upon encountering conservative language, readers should be more inclined to infer the excellent quality of the study, provided the author has minimized speculative hedging. Grounded in humility, the overall objectives of identifying limitations in the Discussion section are to respectfully (a) alert others to possible issues with sampling, data collection and analysis, and generalization or transferability, as well as (b) help others consider ways to further research, theories, practice, or policy (Ellinger & Yang, 2011).

REVIEW AND ENGAGEMENT

When critically reading a research report, you would

☐ Determine if the authors specified any *limitations* to their interpretation of the data and its use beyond the study

☐ Check to see if they alerted readers to possible issues with sampling, data collection and analysis, and generalization or transferability, as well as helped others consider ways to further research, theories, practice, or policy

☐ If they did not have a Limitations section, judge whether you think one was warranted

☐ Ascertain if they effectively addressed, to your satisfaction, any concerns about study validity (did they measure what they intended to measure?)

☐ Using the grammatical mechanics for conservative language, ascertain if their tone was humble and conservative (and, if not, whether it bothered you)

ORGANIZING THE DISCUSSION SECTION

Approaches to organizing the Discussion section can differ depending on which research methodology was used: quantitative, qualitative (including critical or interpretive), or mixed methods. Because it is the longest section of a research paper or report, authors need to break it into manageable and logically coherent sections, with subheadings (Jones, 2016; Kastens et al., 2014; Labaree, 2016). The particular subheadings depend on the organizational approach the author chooses, of which there are several, possibly used in some combination (see Table 14.2). Each approach is discussed in more detail in the following text.

Summarize Key Outcomes, Then Systematically Discuss

First, authors can transition from the results/findings to their interpretation by judiciously summarizing them in the first few paragraphs of the Discussion section (Geletkanycz & Tepper, 2012). This suggestion is often tempered with a cautionary note. Instead of rehashing them, authors should briefly recap the key results or findings (no more than three or four) and then focus on what they mean (African Virtual University, ca. 2015; Annesley, 2010; Bem, 2004; Drotar, 2009). Authors can use the study's "key findings as the departure point for explaining how the results bring resolution to the puzzle that motivated the research to begin with" (Geletkanycz & Tepper, 2012, p. 258). Annesley (2010) further recommended that authors consider restating their research question or the purpose of the

TABLE 14.2 ■ Approaches for Organizing the Discussion Section	
Organizational Approaches	**Explanation**
Summarize, then discuss	• Restate the research question(s) • Summarize (recap) three or four major findings or results, in the order they were presented in the Results or Findings section • Using appropriate subheadings, systematically discuss each key result or finding by using extensive critical and creative interpretation; this involves (re)connecting with the literature review and/or theory and anchoring the discussion to the research question
Specific to general	• Restate the research question • In an interpretive narrative, using appropriate subheadings, move from specific to general by first connecting key findings or results back to the literature review (or consult confirmatory literature for the first time, if qualitative) • Then, connect any pertinent findings or results to relevant theory introduced earlier in the paper • Finally, connect relevant findings or results to general practice, if appropriate • This progressive approach moves from significance of outcomes to specific previous works to big-picture significance
Hypotheses	• Restate a hypothesis • Indicate if it was confirmed, refuted, or not • Discuss what this result means, reconnecting with the literature review and/or theory • Use statistically correct language to indicate causation or association (see Chapter 11) • Repeat for each hypothesis
Research questions	• Restate the research question (with appropriate subheading) • Relate relevant findings or results back to previously introduced literature and/or theory, using evidence from the study to answer the research question • Relate qualitative findings, for the first time, to confirmatory literature and use that literature to develop discussion points • Repeat for each research question
Themes	• Use major themes as subheadings to organize the discussion of findings • Use a blend of authors' prose (narrative interpretation of the data) and quotations from the data set to convince readers that the theme is legitimate • Draw on any previously noted literature, as well as new literature gathered as analysis unfolds, and discuss what finding this theme means for others

study in the first sentence of these transitional paragraphs, *before* summarizing the major results or findings.

Once the results or findings are briefly restated, authors can engage in extensive critical and creative interpretation, which can lead to a compelling discussion narrative because the results or findings are infused with meaning (African Virtual University, ca. 2015; Hess, 2004). Drotar (2009) suggested that authors "discuss the most important or significant findings first followed by secondary findings" (p. 341). This organizational approach will require creative subheadings (Jones, 2016; Kastens et al., 2014), which act as part of the red thread that pulls readers through the paper to its end (Munker, 2012).

Once briefly introduced in the transitional paragraphs, Labaree (2016) recommended that authors discuss the major results or findings in the same order they were described in the Results or Findings section. He suggested that authors briefly recap their key results or findings (no more than three or four) and then systemically review each one. Ellinger and Yang (2011) concurred, recommending that authors introduce a finding or result and then "logically consider [it] in relation to the literature previously reviewed" (p. 143). In this process, they would address the aforementioned fundamental questions for a Discussion section. For each finding or result, they would ponder whether it confirmed, challenged, contradicted, et cetera (see Figure 14.3) previous work done on the topic. This mental exercise yields the narrative shared in the discussion.

Organize From Specific to General

A second organizational strategy is to arrange the discussion so it flows from specific findings or results related to the literature, to findings or results related to the theory, and finally to practice, if appropriate (Kretchmer, 2008a; Labaree, 2016). Annesley (2010) concurred, using the metaphor of an inverted cone or funnel to explain this strategy. He envisioned the discussion as starting from a very narrow perspective, unfolding to the broader overview of the significance of the results or findings. After restating the research question or purpose of the research, authors should broaden the discussion so it relates findings to the literature and then move to an even broader perspective of the "big picture significance" (Annesley, 2010). How does this study advance future research, the knowledge base of the field, attendant theory, or related practice and policy (see Figure 14.3)?

Mixed methods studies

A unique challenge arises with mixed methods studies because authors have to deal with meta-inferences and data integration. In addition to summarizing the results and findings, explaining them, stating limitations, and addressing implications (i.e., moving from general to specific), authors have to especially (a) address the novelty of the "mixed methods" approach, in that it requires data integration. (b) They are urged to present their integrated findings and results using visual representations (such as joint data displays). This approach facilitates their discussion of meta-inferences from integrated findings. And (c) authors have to consciously identify and further explain the meta-inferences emergent from their integrated analysis (Hashemi & Gohari Moghaddam, 2016).

The general caveat, as they move from general to specific, is that authors should use summative and explanatory *move statements* to help readers make connections between the strands. These linguistic moves provide more complete understandings of integrated insights (see Chapter 6, Table 6.9). Readers may come to the same assessment as the authors about what the integrated data mean, or they may not. The effective use of move statements helps to "assist readers in maximizing their understandings of the interplay of different types of data, especially when [mixed methods] findings are complicated and/or contradictory" (Bronstein & Kovacs, 2013, p. 359).

> **Example 14.8 Move statements in mixed methods studies** In terms of the homeless respite program, both the qualitative and quantitative strands found the same contradictory outcome. Receiving care at a homeless respite facility predicted lower odds of attaining housing, but (in contradiction) staying at the facility for over 30 days predicted better access to housing. *This conflicting result was supported by* [MOVE STATEMENT] interviews with respite care providers and high-risk cohort members (homeless people) who explained that moving into housing directly from homeless respite care happened only when people stayed longer than the normal length of stay at the respite program (Meschede, 2010).

Organize and Discuss by Hypotheses

Third, authors of a quantitative study can use subheadings that reflect each hypothesis. This entails restating each hypothesis, confirming if it was supported or not, and noting relevant statistical procedures (Drotar, 2009; Johnson & Christensen, 2012; Kretchmer, 2008a). This is a very clean and transparent approach to presenting and discussing key empirical results. There are some considerations to bear in mind when interpreting a hypothesis for discussion, to be addressed next.

> **Example 14.9 Results reported using hypotheses**
>
> *Results of hypotheses testing*
>
> Correlation analysis was used to analyse the relationships among expectations, perceptions, satisfaction, behavioural intentions, and service quality. The confidence level was 95 per cent for all hypotheses. All but two of the hypotheses were supported (H4c–H4d).
>
> *H1.* Perceived service quality is positively correlated to satisfaction (supported).
>
> A Pearson product-moment correlation analysis was conducted to test H1. This analysis revealed a significant positive correlation between perceived service quality and student satisfaction ($r = .64$, $p < .05$). H1 was supported. If students perceived service quality level as high, their satisfaction tended to be high. . . .
>
> Perceived service quality has significant positive correlations with favourable behavioural intentions (see Table III). H3 was supported. Students who perceived high levels of service quality were more likely to have favourable behavioural intentions rather than unfavourable behavioural intentions (Khoo, Ha, & McGregor, 2017, pp. 8–9).

Research and null hypotheses

Empirical studies are grounded in hypotheses (predictions about relationships between variables) (Shuttleworth, 2015). When interpreting and discussing the import of their results, authors have to deal with both hypothesized results (research and null) and unhypothesized results (Ary et al., 2010; Suter, 2012). Regarding the former, research hypotheses predict outright what will happen. Null hypotheses assume that whatever someone is trying to prove will *not* happen. Alternative hypotheses pertain to "the something else" that may have influenced the results (Lund & Lund, 2013). For the null, there will be no effect, and for the research hypothesis, there will be an effect (with the direction often specified) (Johnson & Christensen, 2012).

Example 14.10 Hypotheses, null and research

Null hypothesis H_0: Obtaining medical training has no effect on a doctor's performance.

Research hypothesis H_1: Obtaining medical training has a direct, positive effect on a doctor's performance.

If the research hypothesis H_1 is supported, the authors need to state this (see example 14.9). In their Discussion section, they would comment on what it means relative to the previous literature or to related theory cited in the paper. Normally, researchers "set up the null hypothesis in order to knock it down," paving the way for a rich discussion of what their results might mean (Suter, 2012, p. 391). They use the phrase "reject the null hypothesis" to reflect that the relationship they found was not by chance; it was statistically significant, warranting further *discussion* (Suter, 2012, p. 391). If the null H_0 is rejected (e.g., obtaining medical training *did* affect doctors' performance), authors need to discuss what this means (Lund & Lund, 2013; Suter, 2012). The process of discussing what these results mean is usually more complex than expected, rarely clear-cut, and challenging to complete. But this is the main role of the Discussion section (Shuttleworth, 2015).

Retaining the null hypothesis

An even more challenging discussion issue emerges if the null H_0 hypothesis is retained (what happened in this study was due to chance). Authors face more cognitive obstacles when interpreting and discussing what this result means, *unless* the intent of the study was to retain the null (Bitchener & Basturkmen, 2006; Lund & Lund, 2013; Suter, 2012). This discussion-related challenge arises because, as tempting as it is to do so, "it is incorrect to present a retained null hypothesis as evidence of *no* relationship between variables. A retained null must be interpreted as *a lack of evidence* [emphasis added] [from this study] for either the truth or falsity of the hypothesis" (Ary et al., 2010, p. 611). Authors "cannot *accept* [emphasis added] the null hypothesis, but only find *evidence against it* [emphasis added]" (Lund & Lund, 2013). This nuance can pose intriguing intellectual challenges to authors who are striving to explain what their results mean without resorting to excessive speculation and hedging. Indeed, the Discussion section is not always about what was found; sometimes it is about what was *not* found and how to deal with that (Shuttleworth, 2015).

Discussing unhypothesized results

Sometimes, when analyzing and interpreting their empirical results, researchers will observe an unexpected and unhypothesized relationship between their variables (Ary et al., 2010). Brown (2014) explained that the writing and analysis process can bring out subtle new discoveries. Ary et al. (2010) called these results "serendipitous discoveries" (p. 614) and offered two-pronged advice. Authors should record and analyze them with the same rigor they used when discussing their predicted relationships but be cautious of the potential spurious nature of the discovery. *Spurious* means a result appears to be true while actually being false (Anderson, 2014); after all, these results were not predicted, and the study did not review any literature or theory to support their prediction. It is recommended that authors view these results with caution. If they wish to pursue them, they can acknowledge the discovery in their Conclusions section and recommend it as the subject of future studies. That way, authors can recognize the potential value of any serendipitous discovery but not overstate its meaning (Ary et al., 2010; Shuttleworth, 2015).

Statistically correct language

A final issue is the use of statistically correct language when discussing results stemming from hypotheses. Empirical studies require authors to report statistical results. It is important that they do not use causal language to report and discuss correlational and associative relationships, and vice versa (Azar, 2006; Cone & Foster, 2006). For clarification, a causal relationship means *x* caused *y*. *Correlation correlated* refers to things being associated with each other but not necessarily causing each other to happen (Bracey, 2006) (see Chapter 12).

Research conventions have developed such that clear vocabulary choices now exist for reporting causal versus correlational results. To report a cause-and-effect result, authors can use *causes, is to blame for, from, because of, due to, accounted for, influences, effects,* and *impacts.* When reporting associative results, authors can say *attributed to, associated with, tied to, is related to, connected with, affiliated with,* and *linked to* (see Chapter 12, Example 12.15). Using inappropriate language easily misleads both scientifically trained and novice readers (Cofield, Corona, & Allison, 2010; Miller, 2015).

> ***Example 14.11 Statistically correct language*** Professor Smith recently conducted a study where she used correlational statistics, striving to see if there was a relationship between student dropout rates and student consumption of energy drinks. The regression statistics she ran showed there was an association between the two variables, but one did not cause the other. However, when reporting her results, she said, "The results showed that student dropout rates can be *partially accounted for* by students' consumption of energy drinks." What she should have said to indicate an association between the variables was "Student dropout rates are *associated with* student consumption of energy drinks." The former leads unwary readers to think one *causes* the other when in fact the researcher's results did not support this assertion.

Organize by Research Questions or Themes

Finally, authors can organize their discussion by their research questions, while concurrently relating the results or findings back to the literature review and any theoretical frameworks used to scaffold the study (Labaree, 2016) or consulted while analyzing qualitative data. Or, they can use the themes emergent from their analysis. "When presenting data thematically, the literature should be integrated into the discussion of the theme. If cases or stories are presented intact [in the Findings section], they should be followed by an examination of the case or story in terms of the conceptual framework of the study" (Plakhotnik & Rocco, 2009, p. 110). Regardless, the balance between presenting data and discussing their meaning has to be carefully considered when reporting qualitative research (Plakhotnik & Rocco, 2009) (see Chapter 13). Authors can also use realistic examples to explain these sorts of findings or to convince readers of their import and significance (Choudhuri, Glauser, & Peregoy, 2004; Swales, 1990).

REVIEW AND ENGAGEMENT

When critically reading a research report, you would

☐ Ascertain which organizational approach the authors used

☐ Determine if they chose an appropriate organizational approach to best showcase their study (see Table 14.2)

☐ If they reported by hypotheses, determine if they properly dealt with the null and research hypotheses

STAYING FOCUSED AND ON TOPIC

The Discussion section is related to how selected results and findings relate back to the research question. Some of the authors' comments can be considered to be off topic if they are not within the bounds of the current discussion (and attendant research question). Authors can avail themselves of several research conventions pursuant to keeping their Discussion section focused and on topic. These pertain to adding new literature, inserting new results or findings, dealing with emergent patterns in the data, and containing tangential issues.

Adding New Literature in the Discussion

The Discussion section should be rich with references to similar work and background material needed to interpret the results or findings (Annesley, 2010; Kastens et al., 2014). Conventions and strategies for adding new literature differ for each of quantitative, qualitative, and mixed methods papers.

Quantitative research

Quantitative researchers can be guided by a deeply entrenched research convention— only references from the literature review can be cited in the Discussion section. Those particular references were judiciously and carefully chosen because they served to clarify what has been done or not relative to the research problem and the research question (Ellinger & Yang, 2011). So, when interpreting their results, authors of quantitative papers should anchor their deliberations only in the literature they reviewed, and do so by drawing out those studies that are most relevant for explaining the results when writing their discussion points (Annesley, 2010; Ellinger & Yang, 2011; Jammal, 2010; Jones, 2016).

The African Virtual University (ca. 2015) tempered this convention with its suggestion that, when writing their Discussion section, authors of quantitative papers should "avoid introducing new information [from the literature], theories or citations *unless absolutely necessary* [emphasis added]" (p. 13). Labaree (2016) was the rare exception to the idea of not using new literature in a quantitative discussion. He asserted that "besides the literature review section, the preponderance of references . . . is usually found in the discussion section." He said that when authors are writing their discussion, they can revisit key sources already cited in the literature review, or they can "save them to cite later in the discussion if they are more important to compare with your results than being part of the general research you used to provide context and background information."

Qualitative research

For a qualitative study, "the literature search—when and how—is of a more ambiguous character" (Hallberg, 2010, p.1). In general, quantitative scholars always conduct the literature review before conducting the study and then draw on only *that* literature to discuss the results. However, there is disagreement among qualitative researchers about the role of the literature review and when it should happen (Gay, Mills, & Airasian, 2006). The existing literature serves as contextual and theoretical background in quantitative work; however, many qualitative scholars view literature reviews as a "constraining exercise rather than a guiding one" (Ramalho, Adams, Huggard, & Hoare, 2015, p. 1).

The preferred approach in qualitative work is to "hear the data" and then go to the literature to find work that helps discuss what it means. Hallberg (2010) described this as "listen and look with an open mind" (p. 1). He further explained that "when a hypothesis, model or theory can be discerned in [qualitative] data, a relevant literature search should [then] be conducted and interwoven into the [discussion]" (p. 1). The final discussion may well incorporate previously noted and new literature to help interpret the findings. The new material is called *confirmatory* literature (Betts Adams, 2016). The general consensus seems to be that qualitative authors should do some preliminary reading (reported as a truncated literature review) before the study begins, and then return to that as well as turn to new, confirmatory literature to interpret and discuss their findings (Hallberg, 2010; Ramalho et al., 2015).

Grounded theory, case studies, and phenomenological studies tend to review the literature at later stages of the research process. In these cases, the literature comes into play *after* patterns or constructs are identified, acting as an interpretive aid rather than a guide or a directive for the study (Johnson & Christensen, 2012). A theoretically oriented study works best with the literature review done early on. The ultimate caveat is that qualitative researchers should not let the literature review process "constrain and stifle discovery of new constructs, relationships and theories" (Johnson & Christensen, 2012, p. 66).

Mixed methods research

In mixed methods studies, authors should report on a detailed literature review that they conducted *before* the study began. Then, they need to collect and "hear" their data. Next, they need to go to *different* (confirmatory) literature and then *weave* that together with the first detailed review to inform their discussion (Ary et al., 2010; Creswell, 2009). This approach respects the research conventions for both quantitative and qualitative methodologies, respectively.

Adding New Results or Findings

The Discussion section serves to interpret the results or findings, not present them for the first time. For this reason, authors cannot present any results or findings in the Discussion section that were not already presented in the Results or Findings section. As explained previously, a well-developed discussion will identify the most salient results or findings, which then become the main *discussion points*. Based on this research convention, there is no need to introduce new or different results or findings. Authors may choose to use graphs or charts to summarize results and findings for their discussion, but these should not contain new data either.

If the results or findings and their discussion are presented as one unit (with a heading like *Results and Discussion*), authors should present a result or finding and then discuss it immediately. This approach lessens the chance of introducing a "new" result or finding into the discussion (see Chapter 13). Finally, authors need to be wary of mistaking the reiteration of a result or finding for its interpretation; repeating it is not the same thing as explaining what it means (Anderson, 2015; Azar, 2006; Day & Gastel, 2006; Drotar, 2009; Kastens et al., 2014; Labaree, 2016; Wiersma & Jurs, 2009).

Patterns in the Data

When interpreting their results or findings, authors may wish to comment on any major patterns that emerged from their analysis. Did things change over time or differ across spatial dimensions (e.g., geography, locations, or groups)? Were there any patterns that the researcher expected to emerge but did not? The presence or absence of these major patterns could become powerful discussion points (Kastens et al., 2014). It can be very easy to go off topic if authors use this approach to developing a discussion point. To stay focused, they have to use their research question as their anchor.

Labaree (2016) suggested that, in quantitative papers, authors should describe the pattern and any evident principles and then place the pattern in perspective by relating it to literature previously reviewed in the paper. Qualitative researchers would identify interesting or compelling patterns in their data and then seek confirmatory literature to help explain them. Goodson (2017) recommended using graphs or other visual depictions to help illustrate patterns, as long as no new data are introduced.

Example 14.14 New major pattern Professor Smith had been studying school dropout rates for a number of years and was very familiar with the literature on this topic. She had previously completed comparative analyses across many countries. In her most recent quantitative study, she expected to see previously observed dropout rates but was surprised when a new pattern emerged. Instead of a different rate for each country, now students were dropping out at the same rate in all countries. She had not predicted this, yet there it was. As a first step, she now turns to her previously cited literature, drawing on it to discuss possible causes for this change in pattern, all the while using her research question as her anchor.

Stay on Point, Tangential Issues

When discussing their results or findings, authors need to avoid injecting tangential issues. *Tangential* means irrelevant or only slightly relevant (Anderson, 2014) to the research problem or research questions. Because they can dilute the discussion point and confound (surprise or bewilder) readers, they tend to cause distraction and confusion. Side issues (as they are often called) tend to obscure the discussion point because there is no clear link to the study's research question(s) (Hess, 2004; Kastens et al., 2014; Kretchmer, 2008a).

Ironically, in their desire to be comprehensive, authors can fall prey to the temptation of adding depth when in fact tangential issues create a superficial and shallow commentary (Azar, 2006). Going off on a tangent ignores the basic tenet of a Discussion section, which is to follow a logical and coherent stream of thought (Labaree, 2016; Plakhotnik & Rocco, 2009). If the author really does not want to lose a possible connection to the research problem or question, Brown (2014) recommended relegating tangential issues to end notes.

> *Example 14.13 Off on a tangent* Professor Smith was so intrigued with the new major pattern she found in her research that she immediately started to discuss this result. But instead of tying it back to her well-established literature review and knowledge base that she had developed over years, she began going off on tangents. Rather than drawing on the conventional reasons for explaining student dropout rates, she proposed that the media were playing a key role in preventing students from studying. Media are too distracting. She then referred to how the diminutive size of students' dorm bedrooms affected how claustrophobic they felt, which affected their inclination to meet in groups for homework. Without peer study support, students just dropped out. On and on she went, until these side topics became so irrelevant to her research problem that her discussion became incoherent. Her research question related to a cross-country comparative analysis of student dropout rates, but her tangents were not country or context specific.

REVIEW AND ENGAGEMENT

When critically reading a research report, you would

- ☐ Make sure the authors did not introduce unreported results and findings

- ☐ Ascertain if they explicitly related discussion points back to the research question(s), objectives, or hypotheses

- ☐ For a quantitative paper, determine if they referred back to the literature review to help discuss their results and that no new literature was introduced

- ☐ For a qualitative study, check to see if that new, confirmatory literature used to interpret the findings was relevant to the research question

- ☐ If they chose data patterns as discussion points, determine if they kept the discussion focused on the research questions

- ☐ Determine if they stayed on point and avoided tangential issues

ENSURING STRONG AND RESPONSIBLE DISCUSSIONS

A strong Discussion section will reflect alternative interpretations of the data and the application of both creative and critical thinking (Sternberg & Gordeeva, 1996). Uninspired interpretation of the results or findings will not lead readers to see the significance of the study. Truncated interpretations can be frustrating to read, with readers wanting more. Unexplored explanations aside from the obvious can also mitigate people's future engagement with the study, meaning less of a chance to change practice, research, or policy. Authors have a responsibility to present a strong and responsible discussion of the import of their study, and that includes alternative interpretations and the use of both critical and creative thinking.

Employ Alternative Interpretations

Authors should heed the principle of applying alternative explanations to interpret their results and findings instead of falling back on their assumed, biased, predicted, preferred, or favorite explanations (Labaree, 2016). By giving even treatment to each possible explanation for what was found, authors can create ideas for "future research that may lead to their discrimination" (Kastens et al., 2014). Sternberg and Gordeeva (1996) recognized alternative interpretations as a key criterion for an influential paper. This entails approaching a result or finding from several different perspectives, culminating in an unambiguous interpretation of its meaning. Attending to the plausibility of various accounts or alternative explanations respects both the obvious and the latent merit of findings and results (Geletkanycz & Tepper, 2012). Authors should offer alternative views, with a discussion of why the final one they chose is most consistent with *their* data (Choudhuri et al., 2004).

> *Example 14.14 Multiple explanations of a result* Professor Smith found that student dropout rates were *associated with* their consumption of energy drinks. An association means that things are related to each other but they do not cause each other. What might explain the connection between consuming energy drinks and dropping out of school? (1) Overstimulation makes it difficult to concentrate, leading to lower grades and dropping out of school. (2) Spending time with friends and peers offsite consuming these drinks draws students away from school, leading to declining attendance and academic achievements, and eventually dropping out. (3) Teachers frustrated with amped-up students decide to punish them by lowering their marks, assuming they would reduce consumption so their grades would improve. This procedure backfired, however, causing grades to fall and students to fail—hence, drop out. Which, if any, of these alternate explanations best addresses this result, relative to the research question? Dr. Smith concluded that teacher frustration was the most consistent with her study's data.

Bring Alternative Interpretations to Unexpected Findings or Results

Instead of ignoring unexpected results or findings, authors should report them and then offer alternative interpretations of what they might mean relative to the research question and the problem statement (Annesley, 2010; Kretchmer, 2008b; Labaree, 2016). Although a particular result or finding may not provide evidence in favor of a hypothesis or not support the claims the author wants to make, not addressing unexpected findings or results means the author might reach inappropriate conclusions (African Virtual University, ca. 2015; Jammal, 2010; Kallestinova, 2011; Kastens et al., 2014). And, if the unexpected result or finding is profound, it can serve as a powerful new direction for future research (Labaree, 2016). When discussing an unexpected result or finding, authors should begin the paragraph with that outcome and then discuss it from several perspectives (Kretchmer, 2008b). As discussed in the final segment of this chapter, this process of employing alternative explanations entails creative thinking (Sternberg & Gordeeva, 1996), while avoiding excessive speculation and hedging.

Critical and Creative Perspectives

Stating that results or findings are inconclusive is the easy way out (Shuttleworth, 2015). Instead, authors are tasked with critically and creatively "convincing the reader of the merits of the study results" (Hess, 2004, p. 1439). Indeed, the development of discussion points poses unique "cognitive demands," which are very dependent on "critical perspectives" (Bitchener & Basturkmen, 2006, p. 7). Others concurred (Goodson, 2017; Jones, 2016), with Labaree (2016) noting that writing a Discussion section requires both critical *and* creative thinking. Both of these mental exercises help authors "formulate deeper, more profound understandings of the research problem under investigation" (Labaree, 2016), leading to critical and creative insights into the data. Sternberg and Gordeeva (1996) found that creative interpretation of data in the Discussion section was rated in the top 10 for what constitutes an influential article.

When thinking critically, authors would challenge the *validity* of an idea while thinking creatively would challenge the *uniqueness* of the idea. Thinking critically means authors would use their ideas as judgment and justification points. But from a creative perspective, their ideas would become stepping-stones to lateral, outside-the-box perspectives. Critical thinking strives to find the correct answer using analysis while creative thinking knows there is no correct or best answer; instead, there is a legitimate place for hunches and intuitive thinking. Authors thinking critically would concentrate on what they know about their results and findings and draw on relevant sources to support this knowing. But when thinking creatively, they would scan for answers and explanations in unexpected places. Rather than looking for constancy and consistency (critical thinking), creative thinkers would tolerate contradictions and inconsistencies (Paul, 1993; Suter, 2012; Whetten & Cameron, 1995; Winsor, 1986) (see Figure 14.4).

When writing up discussion points, authors need a mix of critical thinking (logic and reasoning) and creative thinking (generative, unconventional, spontaneous, breakaway insights) (Labaree, 2016). Both poles of thinking are inseparable aspects of excellent thought (Paul, 1993), and both are required if authors intend to rigorously interpret their results and findings. Criticality and creativity have an intimate relationship in purposeful thinking. The interpretive, intellectual work undertaken to create a powerful Discussion section involves "creativity and [is] criticality interwoven in one seamless fabric" (Paul, 1993, p. 18).

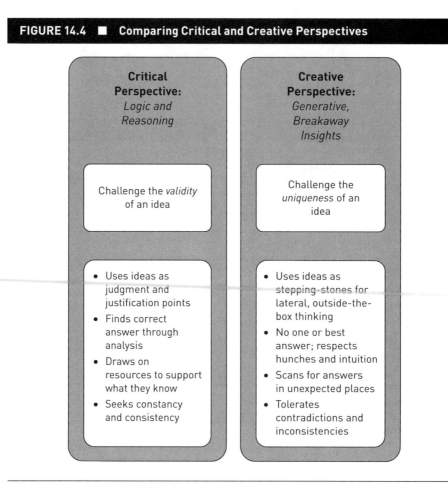

FIGURE 14.4 ■ Comparing Critical and Creative Perspectives

Critical Perspective:
Logic and Reasoning

Challenge the *validity* of an idea

- Uses ideas as judgment and justification points
- Finds correct answer through analysis
- Draws on resources to support what they know
- Seeks constancy and consistency

Creative Perspective:
Generative, Breakaway Insights

Challenge the *uniqueness* of an idea

- Uses ideas as stepping-stones for lateral, outside-the-box thinking
- No one or best answer; respects hunches and intuition
- Scans for answers in unexpected places
- Tolerates contradictions and inconsistencies

Example 14.15 Critical and creative interpretation in Discussion section
Dr. Jones is writing the Discussion section of her research paper on the findings from her study on the homeless population and their ability to eventually regain housing. She found that people struggled with this because they could not make the transition from having a home, to losing it, to finding another. Previous studies supported the principle of her finding, that people who are homeless struggle with regaining housing (Brown, 2010; Smith, 2014; Wainwright, 2017 [sample citations]). But these were quantitative studies focused on the economics of obtaining shelter. Dr. Jones's study was concerned with what people went through as they transitioned from the homeless state to being housed. Insights from previous scholars might not be appropriate to interpret her findings. She asked herself, "What else might explain this finding?" Putting on her creative thinking cap, she wondered. Maybe people resist this transition because of their lack of resiliency and their fear of losing their home again. Maybe they just do not have it in them to lose another home, so it is just easier to stay on the street. Or maybe homeless people now find themselves in a

familiar, albeit rather unconventional, community of like-minded people, and transitioning to formal housing means they risk losing this solidarity. She draws on these creative interpretations as well as critical thinking logics to develop her discussion points, remaining aware of the pitfalls of hedging and speculating.

REVIEW AND ENGAGEMENT

When critically reading a research report, you would

☐ Determine if the authors approached their findings or results from several perspectives, tendering alternative interpretations of what their study meant, culminating in a clear interpretation of its meaning

☐ Ascertain if they addressed unexpected findings or results, suggesting their import while minimizing hedging and speculation

☐ Confirm that they used a combination of critical and creative perspectives when writing their discussion points (see Figure 14.4)

TECHNICAL STRATEGIES FOR DISCUSSION SECTIONS

On a final note, as with other sections of a research paper or report, authors must be cognizant of some basic technical conventions and guidelines when preparing the Discussion section (i.e., length, tense, voice, and person).

Length of Discussion Section

"Since every paper has its unique results and findings, the Discussion section differs in length, shape and structure" (Kallestinova, 2011, p. 187). Generally, the Discussion section is one of the longest sections of the paper (Jones, 2016). Some actually call it "a brief essay in itself" (Jammal, 2010, p. 6). Some recommend that the Discussion section be as long as the Results or Findings section, if separate. Others advise against a lengthy discussion, suggesting it be "as short as possible, while clearly and fully stating, supporting, explaining, and defending [and] discussing important and directly relevant issues" (Kretchmer, 2008a, p. 1). Bem (2004) claimed that in quantitative work, "there is a $-.73$ correlation between the clarity of an investigator's results and the length of his or her discussion section" (p. 16). In other words, the longer it is, the harder it is for readers to glean the meaning or import of the results.

Ultimately, the Discussion section may be brief or extensive provided it is tightly reasoned, self-contained, and not overstated (Johnson & Christensen, 2012; VandenBos, 2010). It should be long enough to discuss the results or findings against previous work cited in the literature review section but short enough to not appear rambling or unfocused, which runs the risk of detracting from the true merits of the paper (African Virtual University, ca. 2015).

Shortening the length

Several strategies exist for shortening and focusing the discussion. Authors should discuss their most important results or findings in more detail than their secondary results or findings (Bem, 2004). Primary results and findings are actively sought by researchers, while secondary ones are less important yet still pertinent to the research question(s) (University of Waterloo, 2014). Authors should avoid repeating, reiterating, or restating results or findings already presented without interpreting them (this shortens the length) (Drotar, 2009; Kastens et al., 2014). Labaree (2016) cautioned, "Don't write two results sections!" This is an unnecessary step that adds length and distracts readers from the true purpose of the discussion (African Virtual University, ca. 2015).

If authors feel the need to remind readers of a result or finding before they discuss it, they can use a bridging sentence to link a brief statement of the result or finding to its interpretation. For example, "In the case of 'restate finding' . . . [bridging statement], the finding suggests that [interpretation]" (Labaree, 2016). Finally, authors are cautioned against meandering in the Discussion section because it can create a superficial (shallow) discussion as well as a lengthy one (Geletkanycz & Tepper, 2012; Lerner, ca. 2003). To offset this possibility, authors should be concise, brief, and specific (Kretchmer, 2008a).

Tense, Voice, and Person

When writing the Discussion section, authors are encouraged to use active voice (see more details in Chapter 16). Active voice is more authoritative and convincing than passive voice. Authors should use present tense when referring to their work (specific facts and/or insights) but past tense when referring to previous studies (Anderson, 2015; Kallestinova, 2011; Kretchmer, 2008a; Labaree, 2016; Lerner, ca. 2003; Ramakantan, 2007). Quantitative research Discussion sections use third person, with Labaree (2016) acknowledging that first person is acceptable if it is not used too much. The critical and interpretive research methodologies (qualitative) are more inclined to employ first and second person in the Discussion section than are authors of quantitative papers (Wheeler, 2005). It goes without saying that authors should not denigrate, insult, attack, or bully authors of other studies (Hess, 2004; Ramakantan, 2007).

> *Example 14.16 Tense* This study *shows* that the pattern of student dropout rates across countries *is* becoming aligned, a result that *contradicts* previous research. Smith (2010) and others *found* that these rates *were* different across nations.

> *Example 14.17 Qualitative first person and tense My* results *are* surprising relative to previous research. Whereas others *have determined* that children tend to hate school and drop out early (King, 2015; Queen, 2010), *my* work *shows* that they *are* staying in school longer. *I think* this finding has profound implications.

> *Example 14.18 Quantitative third person and tense The* results of this study *are* surprising relative to previous research. While others *have determined* that children tend to hate school and drop out early (King, 2015; Queen, 2010), *these results* show that they *are* staying in school longer. *The implications* of this result are profound.

REVIEW AND ENGAGEMENT

When critically reading a research report, you would

- ☐ Determine if the authors followed the recommended conventions for length, tense, voice, and person when preparing their Discussion section

- ☐ Ascertain if the tenor of their Discussion section reflects tight writing that respected the tenets of staying focused while constraining length

FINAL JUDGMENT ON DISCUSSION SECTION

Taking *all* of the *Review and Engagement* criteria into account, what is your final judgment of the Discussion section in the paper you are critically reading?

CHAPTER SUMMARY

The Discussion section is the heart of the paper. It should contain the author's original thoughts about what the study means for others. To that end, this chapter began by distinguishing between discussion points and concluding remarks, followed with an overview of the different conventions for relating results and findings to the discussion of their import. Then, the three main functions of a Discussion section were addressed (summarize, explain, and examine), as were the topics of hedging and speculation. The chapter then focused on how the development of discussion points is linked with the many dimensions of research significance and with other aspects of significance (novelty, practical, theoretical).

Discussion sections should address three basic questions, dealing with how the study (a) relates to existing understandings in the literature, (b) brings new understandings, and (c) makes new connections. After these were discussed in some detail, the conversation turned to study limitations and how authors need to explain how threats to validity affect their conclusions and implications. The discussion then focused on five major approaches to organizing a Discussion section, shifting to an overview of strategies to keep the Discussion section on track and focused. After explaining the importance of employing alternative interpretations of the results and findings and the role of critical and creative thinking, the chapter ended with basic grammatical conventions for writing Discussion sections.

REVIEW AND DISCUSSION QUESTIONS

1. Why is the Discussion section considered to be the most original part of a research paper?

2. Compare and contrast a discussion and a conclusion. What principles have to be followed if they are combined in one section in a research paper? What principles have to be followed if the results or findings are combined with the discussion?

3. Describe the three key functions of a discussion.

4. Why might hedging or speculation become an issue in a Discussion section?

5. Relate the notion of *significance* to the process of preparing and presenting a discussion of the study's findings or results. Research can have significance along many dimensions. Describe each one, and then comment on the two or three dimensions that you think must be included in a discussion, with reasons.

6. Referring to Figure 14.4, identify what you think are the most compelling lines of thought that authors should include in their discussion so they can effectively place their outcomes in context.

7. What are some of the challenges researchers face when reporting the *limitations* of their study (i.e., things that were out of their control yet impact their implications)? What role does *humility* play in this process?

8. Table 14.2 summarizes the five recommended approaches to organizing a Discussion section. Which of these approaches do you prefer,

and why? In particular, explain some of the challenges authors face when reporting their results using their hypotheses. What are the consequences of authors not using statistically correct language when reporting quantitative results?

9. The chapter identified four strategies for keeping a discussion focused, on track, and on topic. Identify these and comment on which one (if any) gave you pause for thought. Especially comment on the issue of whether or not new literature should be introduced, given the intended purpose of a discussion.

10. Why do you think authors are advised to bring *multiple* perspectives to bear when interpreting their results or findings as they discuss them?

11. Compare and contrast a critical and a creative perspective to interpreting study findings or results in a discussion. In your experience, which approach do you think is used most often, and why?

12. Summarize the conventions for length, tense, person, and voice when preparing the Discussion section.

15 CONCLUSIONS

INTRODUCTION

To conclude means to sum up an argument or a text (Anderson, 2014). The Discussion section of a research paper addresses the questions of "What do we know now that we did not know before, and why do we care?" Authors will have developed a "red thread" argument telling people why they think their study is important. The conclusions emphasize what the authors have been arguing for in their Discussion section. Concluding comments serve to wrap up the discussion and forcefully bring it to a close (Evans, Gruba, & Zobel, 2011). They address the questions of "Now what? What should people think about now? What implications and inferences can be drawn from the data and their analysis? What does this all mean? What challenges were raised? What new meanings emerged?" (Holewa, 2004; Labaree, 2016).

As a caveat, not all readers of research articles approach the conclusions the same way. Many skip everything, not reading the paper at all, and go right to the end; what did the authors conclude from their study? They trust that the author knows how to effectively prepare a Conclusions section for a research report (Chubbuck, 2009; Ramakantan, 2007). A more critical reader would read the entire article or report and then discern whether the conclusions reflected the main arguments and insights gleaned from the paper. The authors' conclusions cannot be left to trust because, in most cases, "authors give minimal attention to [conclusions]" (Ellinger & Yang, 2011, p. 123).

LEARNING OBJECTIVES

- Distinguish between discussion points (stimulate conversation) and concluding thoughts (wrap up conversation)

- Compare and contrast concluding thoughts and summarizing the paper

- Explain the four main purposes of the Conclusions section

- Describe the array of closing strategies available for writing concluding comments

- Explain the three levels along which authors can direct their conclusions

- Gain awareness of things to avoid in the Conclusions section

- Appreciate the technical and grammatical conventions for preparing concluding comments

CONCLUSION DEFINED

As a reminder, to discuss means to (a) consider by talking over, (b) have a conversation about, (c) present in detail for examination, and (d) talk about in order to convince others or to reach conclusions (Anderson, 2014). To state it bluntly, to discuss means to talk about. To conclude means to shut up. With more finesse, *conclude* is Latin *concludere*, for *con*, "together," and *cludere*, "to shut or enclose" (Harper, 2016). Concluding is defined as the act of ending something, of bringing it to a close (Anderson, 2014), in this case, the line of thought in a research paper.

Every study is motivated by a research problem (see Chapter 6). In the conclusions, the authors relate the findings or results back to this problem (Bunton, 2005). A conclusion is a position, opinion, or judgment reached after careful consideration (i.e., discussion). It is also the last main section of a discourse, usually containing a summing of points and a statement of opinions or decisions reached by the authors (Anderson, 2014). The conclusion "should close the discussion without closing it off" (Bellanca, 1998, p. 1). It should "bring momentary closure and reflection . . . but in the process opens up new directions" (Shank & Brown, 2007, p. 187).

RELATING CONCLUSIONS TO DISCUSSION AND SUMMARIES

Authors have to face several key intellectual and interpretive choices when preparing their Conclusions section. They have to decide whether it will be a stand-alone section or be combined with the discussion. They also have to decide if their conclusions should contain a summary of their study or if the summary should be a stand-alone section, following the Discussion section. There is little agreement in the literature on either of these issues.

Stand-Alone Conclusion or Combined With Discussion

There are varied opinions about whether the conclusion should be a stand-alone section or be part of the discussion. The conclusions can be either (a) a paragraph at the end of the *Discussion* section (with no heading) or (b) a stand-alone section with its own heading, *Conclusions*. A research paper can also have a section called *Discussion and Conclusions*, which is acceptable as long as both tasks are effectively attended to using relevant conventions (Brown, 2014). In reality, for many papers, the section titled Conclusions actually contains discussion points (interpretation), not wrap-up points. In some disciplines, this is an acceptable convention.

The preferred convention in a research article is for a separate Conclusions section because it serves a different function than a discussion. If there is a separate Conclusions section, the Discussion section should not draw any conclusions (Brown, 2014; Evans et al., 2011; Fritz, 2008; Hess, 2004; Labaree, 2016). To discuss means to talk about, while to conclude means to wrap up (Harper, 2016). Conclusions serve to bring closure to the argument or red thread pulling the reader through the entire article (Munker, 2012). This book assumed there are qualitative differences between what is contained in a Discussion section and a separate Conclusions section (Bunton, 2005); hence, there is a chapter on each one.

Summaries Versus Conclusions

Before describing the purposes of conclusions and identifying closing strategies for crafting effective conclusions, the connection between a summary and a conclusion has to be addressed. There is little agreement in the literature about whether or not the Conclusions section should contain a summary of the paper. Many feel the summary should be a stand-alone section at the end of the Discussion section, rather than part of the Conclusion, mainly because they serve different functions, necessitating different criteria to judge their quality (Bellanca, 1998; Labaree, 2016; Shuttleworth, 2015; University of Richmond, 2010). As Evans et al. (2011) noted, "[s]ummaries are not conclusions" (p. 176). Others are comfortable with the Conclusions section being prefaced with a summary of the research design and the main findings or results (Annesley, 2010; Bunton, 2005, Parish, 2013; Shank & Brown, 2007; WikiHow, ca. 2016).

Labaree (2016) acknowledged the appropriateness of summarizing *the argument* for the reader and restating the research problem, but he did not advise summarizing the methods or results and findings. Others suggested that if authors must summarize the entire paper in the Conclusions section, they should do so with fresh language (Freedman & Plotnick, 2008). "Synthesize, don't summarize: Include a brief summary of the paper's main points, but don't simply repeat things that were in [the] paper" (The Writing Center, 2010, p. 2). Synthesizing instead of summarizing convinces readers that the paper is "a 'complete thought' rather than a collection of random and vaguely related ideas" (WikiHow, ca. 2016, p. 2).

Summary conventions

If authors choose to include a summary of the paper in the Conclusions section, it will make the conclusion longer, ranging from one to two pages in length. The elements of a summary should mirror the same order as in the paper. Using one to two paragraphs (about 10 sentences), the summary restates the research question (and hypotheses if appropriate). The methods and research design are briefly described, followed with one to three sentences about the key results or findings and the key discussion points. Authors should eliminate wordiness (especially avoid adverbs, like "This is an *especially* interesting result"), be concise, avoid quotes, and use scientifically accurate language (Psychology Writing Center, 2010). With this approach to writing a summary, readers should be able to gain 70%–80% of the data or main points presented in the paper before reading the ultimate conclusions (Parish, 2013).

Example 15.1 Summary prefacing conclusions In summary, this study was guided by one research question, "How do people *feel* about being in debt?" This qualitative study was conducted in the spring of 2016 in an eastern Canadian province. Data were gathered using a focus group comprising 10 people who self-identified as being in debt (snowball sampling). There was an even split between males and females, ranging in age from 20 to 65 years. A trained facilitator conducted the two-hour-long, taped focus group using a standardized, predetermined interview guide. The researcher also attended and took field notes, during and after data collection. The transcribed data and field notes were thematically analyzed, yielding three major themes: (a) different notions of what "being in-debt" means, (b) intensity of feelings about indebtedness, (c) and age cohort differences. Based on the discussion of the import of these findings, *several conclusions can be drawn* as they pertain to financial and credit counselors.

Example 15.2 Recapping results throughout the conclusions Otto and Webley (2016, pp. 366–367) provided a good example of recapping results through concluding comments, shared in the following multiparagraph quote. The study added to knowledge on financial decision making by investigating the importance of saving during adolescence and exploring differences between adolescent savers and adolescent non-savers. With the above-mentioned limitations in mind, a *number of conclusions* [emphasis added] can be drawn from the results obtained.

First, we found that for adolescents, saving is a meaningful option for getting larger sums of money. . . . For policymakers, this *could imply* [emphasis added] that when saving becomes more salient as an option for dealing with an income constraint situation, adolescents may be particularly interested to learn about saving and saving products that are suitable for them.

Second, our attempt to describe the characteristics of adolescent savers and non-savers generated valuable information about the importance of money management skills and self-control for financial decisions made when young. . . . [This finding *suggests that*] [emphasis added] saving accounts designed for children should have features that facilitate the development of a saving habit early in life.

. . . In addition, results suggest that the investigation of impatience and temptation-handling strategies in childhood will contribute to a better understanding of the development of saving behavior. . . . [T]his knowledge *should be used* [emphasis added] to develop appropriate (and more targeted) curriculum materials for financial education programs that address children early in life.

. . . [In a fourth result], the strategy "negotiate, borrow, dis-save" was associated with money from parents received irregularly for certain activities, possibly subject to negotiation. . . . *Future research should* [emphasis added] investigate the saving behavior of children and their parents over time to find out how (low, medium, and high income) parents can, for example, improve parent–child money-related conversations. (Otto & Webley, 2016, pp. 366–367)

REVIEW AND ENGAGEMENT

When critically reading a research report, you would

☐ Determine if the authors used the full weight of their paper to speak with conviction

☐ Ascertain if they related their concluding points back to the research question(s)

☐ Check to see if they either prefaced their concluding comments with a brief summary (using fresh language) or provided a separate Summary section after the Discussion section

☐ Ascertain if they summarized the argument threaded throughout the paper before presenting their conclusions

☐ Determine if they prepared a separate Conclusions section with its own heading *or* if they integrated conclusions into the Discussion section in such a way that interpretation was clearly distinguishable from the wrap-up

PURPOSE OF CONCLUSIONS

Samuels (2004) offered an interesting simile, likening the Conclusions section of a research paper to the last chord in a song. A chord is a group of musical notes sounded together in harmony. Upon hearing the chord (i.e., reading the conclusion), the reader should feel the piece is complete and done. The echoes of the chord, the possibilities stemming from the research and its implications, should linger with the reader. In effect, the conclusion is the authors' last chance to make their pitch, to persuade readers of their point of view. At this point of the paper, authors have the full weight of the paper behind them and should be able to state their final points succinctly, with conviction. It is their chance to tie up their argument and bring closure to a complex discussion (Edelson, 2015; Labaree, 2016). The lasting impression they create should resonate with readers long after they have finished reading the paper, like the chord in the song (Bellanca, 1998; Chubbuck, 2009; Labaree, 2016; Samuels, 2004) (see Figure 15.1).

Chubbuck (2009) tendered a more aggressive simile, recommending that authors end their argument "with a bang." She said the conclusion should "have snap" (p. 111), making readers snap to attention rather than getting bored or frustrated with an inadequate wrap-up to the whole paper. Instead of repeatedly belaboring the same point or engaging in platitudes or generalizations, authors should consider the conclusions as "one of the set pieces of their argument" (p. 111). A set piece is something that has been carefully or elaborately planned or composed. It is a self-contained message or section of a paper arranged for maximum effect (Anderson, 2014). "Going out with a bang" means finishing something in a spectacular manner, by creating a lasting impression.

Whether creating a resonating note or a resounding bang, authors must appreciate the main purposes of a Conclusions section. It allows authors to "consider broader issues, make new connections, and elaborate on the significance of the findings [for other researchers and for practitioners]" (The Writing Center, 2010, p. 1). What does the author think the key points might *mean* for others in the field? What are the likely consequences of any new insights for the field or for practitioners? Why is it important that others pay attention to these results or findings and their analysis?

FIGURE 15.1 ■ Conclusion as Last Chord of a Song Simile

**Conclusion is like the
last chord of a song:**

- Makes piece seem complete and done
- Echoes of the research should linger with readers
- Using the full weight of the paper (song), authors speak with conviction about their research
- Tie up the argument and bring it to a close, so it resonates with readers long after they read the paper (like the echoes of a song)

Example 15.3 Conclusion Overall, the study revealed significant positive relationships among perceived service quality, satisfaction, and favourable behavioural intentions in PTEIs in Singapore. The results showed that perceived service quality influences consumer/students' satisfaction which, in turn, has an impact on consumers' intentions to remain loyal to the institution, and even pay a higher fee to remain with the institution. Specifically, the effects of perceived service quality on favourable behavioural intentions were mediated by satisfaction. Hence, when a consumer/student is satisfied, favourable behavioural intentions towards the institution are strengthened. This result implies that raising student satisfaction could improve an institution's competitive positioning in a new world where the student/university relationship is viewed as a market exchange. The reality of conceiving university students as consumers is not going away any time soon, i.e., all will benefit from richer understandings of this conceptualisation and phenomenon. (Khoo, Ha, & McGregor, 2017, p. 15)

REVIEW AND ENGAGEMENT

When critically reading a research report, you would

- ☐ Determine if the authors developed conclusions that reflect the main arguments developed and insights drawn in the paper

- ☐ Check to see that they confined their conclusions to one to two paragraphs

- ☐ Ascertain if they wrote a conclusion that stayed with you after stepping away from the paper (see Figure 15.1)

Conclusions have four main purposes, often addressed in combination. Authors can use the Conclusions section to (a) explore the broader implications of a key finding or result, especially for particular audiences; (b) tender suggestions for future research (topics, methods, theories, or literature); (c) place their results or findings in the context of research in the field, thereby positioning others to take up the cause; and (d) speculate about how the results or findings may affect practice or policy (Bunton, 2005; Ellinger & Yang, 2011; Evans et al., 2011; Hess, 2004; Labaree, 2016; Shank & Brown, 2007) (see Figure 15.2).

Explore Broader Implications

Implicate is Latin *implicare*, "to associate with" (Harper, 2016). The intent of writing conclusions is to help readers make mental connections (associate) with the key points. Authors are encouraged to explore the *broader* implications of their research outcomes (including what it means beyond the confines of this sample or population). Especially, this entails two things, pointing out the obvious as well as the not-so-obvious implications of the study. Broader implications are not directly evident. They are secondary or indirect effects of a finding or result. Authors are well positioned to reveal and expand on these less obvious implications by highlighting key points that are novel or refreshing, especially unexpected insights or understandings (Ellinger & Yang, 2011).

FIGURE 15.2 ■ Four Purposes of Conclusions Section

Explore Broader Implications
- Explain how a key finding/result affects a particular audience
- Tease out real-world implications of particular outcomes
- Highlight import of novel or refreshing results/findings
- Bring attention to unexpected outcomes or analytical insights

Suggest New Research
- Recommend new research agendas
- Suggest how current research can be reframed
- Recommend broaching different theory, methods, literature, research contexts
- Identify negative results as new research opportunities

Relate Main Contributions to Existing Literature
- Place insights from the study in the larger field of inquiry, enticing others to take up the cause and engage with the issues
- Use summary of main outcomes to help others make connections with the study and its implications

Identify Practice or Policy Implications
- Practice innovations or interventions (public, private, civil)
- Technical advancements (especially within industry)
- Policy initiatives (government, organizations, enterprises)
- Curricular innovations

Exploring broader implications depends on deduction as well as inference, defined as the reasoning involved in making a logical judgment without full evidence or direct observation (Anderson, 2014). When stating implications to others, authors actually do not know if the key point in question will have this meaning for others; they are inferring it from *their* discussion of the results or findings. In all fairness, someone else may analyze the same result or finding and come to a different set of conclusions and implications. By forming opinions and expressing implications, authors are telling others what *they* think the results and findings mean for others, despite that the data did not expressly state these meanings. As a caveat, Labaree (2016) cautioned authors against "delv[ing] into idle speculation. Being introspective means looking within yourself as an author to try and understand an issue more deeply, not to guess at possible outcomes [or implications]" (p. 3). Forming implications also requires critical thinking (Freedman & Plotnick, 2008) (see Chapter 14).

Example 15.4 Exploring broader implications Participants expressed real anger when they learned their community center was being closed down. An obvious conclusion from this finding is that the community should find some way to reopen the center. But a deeper, broader issue is what is the implication that participants expressed the emotion of anger rather than fear? Other findings in the study pointed to repressed fear among participants, who relied on the community center for support and sanctuary. Combined, these findings prompt the conclusion that more is going on under the surface in this community, which needs to be investigated at greater depth.

Chubbuck (2009) further advised authors to consider the scope of their topic and ask if it has "real-world implications" (p. 1). Does it make sense to draw broader and greater implications from the study, or should the scope be confined? Authors should avoid applying the results or findings to people or settings that are very dissimilar to their study (Boudah, 2011).

Suggest New Research

Regarding the second purpose of conclusions, developing suggestions for new research could entail the formation of new research agendas, which enables other scholars to continue the stream of research on the phenomenon in question. New research could lead to the development of new knowledge because "deeper and more illuminating insights can be generated" (Ellinger & Yang, 2011, p. 122). Research-related insights can also extend to how to enrich theory and theory building on the phenomenon. And, they can include innovations in research design such as different or alternate theories, literatures, samples, research contexts or settings, and methods for data collection and analysis (Drotar, 2009; Ellinger & Yang, 2011). Labaree (2016) recommended that authors consider addressing any negative aspects of their research design (e.g., drawbacks, problems, or challenges) or negative results as opportunities to explain how they might justify future research (see Chapter 13).

> *Example 15.5 Suggesting new research* From Conitzer (2006, p. 291), the hierarchy introduced in this dissertation provides a natural guide to future research. . . . Natural directions for future research include pushing existing domains deeper down the hierarchy, as well as introducing new domains or formalizing domains that already exist in the real world—and (presumably) studying them at the shallowest levels first. Additionally, in the context of mechanism design for bounded agents (and especially automated mechanism design for bounded agents), it is not yet completely clear how mechanisms should be evaluated. Thus, future research at these nodes will also involve developing a general theory for such evaluation. Domain-specific studies, such as the ones we did on voting, may help in doing so. Much research also remains to be done on topics orthogonal to the hierarchy, such as preference elicitation and distributed computation of outcomes (see Section 1.4). These topics can be studied at each node in the hierarchy, for any domain.

Place Research in Disciplinary Context

Third, something as simple as summarizing the contributions of the study to the existing literature can position the results or findings and analytical insights within the larger field of disciplinary inquiry. This purpose is achieved by connecting the paper's major results or findings, plus any provocative analytical insights, with the wider conversation about an issue as it is presented in other published writings. This process helps readers glean how to benefit from the work accomplished in the research and reported in the paper.

Placing the research in a larger context can entice others to become engaged with the topic. Well-articulated conclusions help other researchers *find* themselves connected to the study (Chubbuck, 2009). Chubbuck (2009) suggested that when developing their conclusions, authors should ask themselves, "How does your analysis matter in the context of history, politics, science, literature, or other disciplines in which the [paper] is written?" (p. 1).

> ***Example 15.6 Placing the study in disciplinary context*** "[The data and insights from this study] expand the body of knowledge relating to behavior changes that promote healthier lifestyles and have the potential to promote wellness especially in the at-risk populations. [It does so by] addressing subsystem issues such as the physical environment, education, transportation, healthcare and social services, and mechanisms available in the community to provide care for coping with and solving problems" (Pattypie, 2017).

Identify Practice and Policy Innovations

Finally, practice and policy innovations encompass recommending courses of action that, if adopted, would address specific problems experienced by practitioners. These could be specific practice interventions, technical advancements (especially for industry), policy initiatives, or curricular innovations (Bunton, 2005; Ellinger & Yang, 2011; Labaree, 2016).

> ***Example 15.7 Policy innovations*** The policy challenge lies in making the opportunities extant in much of the nonfarm economy accessible to the majority of rural Africans who haven't the education, skills, or financial or social capital to get into the many lucrative niches available across the continent. We argue for (i) creating clear institutional ownership over rural nonfarm matters within government and research institutions, (ii) investing in sustainable rural financial systems that can reach previously excluded sub-populations, (iii) redoubling efforts in education and health to stem the serious threats posed by HIV/AIDS and violence in rural areas already deficient in skills and education, and (iv) increased investment in the physical and institutional infrastructure necessary to make markets accessible to all, including the need for post-crisis reconstruction. (Barrett, Reardon, & Webb, 2001, p. 329)

REVIEW AND ENGAGEMENT

When critically reading a research report, you would

- ☐ Determine if the authors wrapped things up but did not close off the conversation
- ☐ Confirm they explored the broader implications of their study (explained the import of *key* outcomes)
- ☐ Check to see if they suggested new research agendas and perhaps different research contexts
- ☐ Ascertain if the authors identified recommended changes to methods, theoretical perspectives, and/or literature to review
- ☐ Determine if they made connections to existing literature, enticing others to take up the cause
- ☐ Ascertain if they identified practice and/or policy innovations or interventions (see Figure 15.2)

CLOSING STRATEGIES FOR EFFECTIVE CONCLUSIONS

When crafting conclusions, authors can focus their conclusion at the higher level, by answering the research questions; the middle level, by dealing with aspects of their argument or with broad claims; or the lower level, which entails reflecting on specific results or findings (Bunton, 2005; Labaree, 2016; Peng, 1987) (see Figure 15.3). Bunton (2005) found disciplinary variation in the Conclusions sections for science and technology disciplines and in the humanities and social sciences. Science and technology scholars tended to focus on the higher level of research questions and broader claims, while humanities and social sciences authors tended to draw conclusions around the lower level of specific findings or results. Also, science and technology scholars focused on conclusions for future research, while humanities and social sciences scholars developed conclusions around practical implications for immediate use in their fields. Authors should remain aware of, but not be constrained by, these disciplinary profiles.

Regardless of their focus (high, mid, or low level), authors can choose from many interesting closing strategies, depending on their purpose in the conclusion (see Figure 15.2) as well as their writing style, audience, and intended tone and the actual results and insights they want to highlight. Authors should think about what they want to leave with their readers, the takeaway, and then pick the strategy or strategies that best suit their research questions. As a caveat, regardless of which closing strategy they choose, authors cannot introduce new *information* in the Conclusions section (Edelson, 2015; Holewa, 2004; Labaree, 2016; WikiHow, ca. 2016). The eight most common closing strategies to use when crafting effective conclusions are set out below (see Figure 15.4).

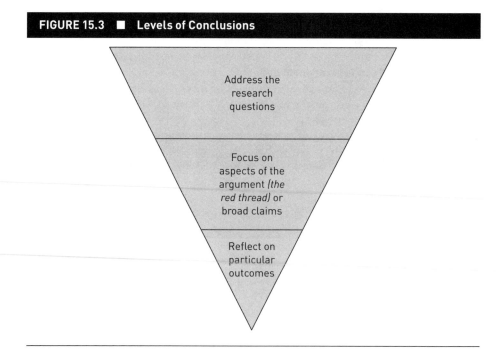

FIGURE 15.3   ■   Levels of Conclusions

Address the research questions

Focus on aspects of the argument *(the red thread)* or broad claims

Reflect on particular outcomes

Provocative Question

Authors can choose to conclude their paper with a provocative question. Such questions encourage readers to engage in lateral thinking about the concluding point. Provocative questions challenge readers' preconceptions about an issue (or a proposed solution). They encourage readers to uncover perceived constraints and barriers that may be holding back forward action on the issue (Reed, 2010). By using this strategy, authors anticipate that others will enter into debate, dialogue, and/or creative discourse around the main point of the paper. This mental exercise helps people gain new perspectives on the topic, moving the research agenda forward (Holewa, 2004). Provocative questions are especially relevant when the author uses a *projective conclusion*. This approach involves projecting a future outcome of the circumstances being discussed or the solutions proposed (Jonker, 2015).

Example 15.8 Provocative questions

- If there were no constraints, what would the ideal solution or outcome look like?

- Imagine nothing changes. What would happen then, and where would people be in a year's time?

- Imagine fast-forwarding two years after the implementation of this recommendation. What will things look like?

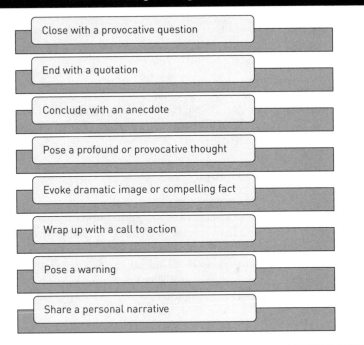

FIGURE 15.4 ■ Common Closing Strategies for Conclusions Section

- Close with a provocative question
- End with a quotation
- Conclude with an anecdote
- Pose a profound or provocative thought
- Evoke dramatic image or compelling fact
- Wrap up with a call to action
- Pose a warning
- Share a personal narrative

Quotations

It may be appropriate to use a quotation that was introduced in the Introduction section of the paper, only this time the authors add further insights derived from the paper. The authors would reframe the essence of the quotation by using their interpretations of their results or findings. Quotations are effective because words from recognized experts or instigators lend authority to the authors' concluding point, helping to confirm, amplify, or complicate it (add a new spin or perspective) (Bellanca, 1998; Edelson, 2015; Freedman & Plotnick, 2008; Labaree, 2016). Chubbuck (2009) advised judicious caution when using quotes. The impact of the authors' concluding point may be lost if someone else's words are used to close the paper.

> ***Example 15.9 Ending conclusion with quotation*** The focus of this paper was the impact of living in a consumer culture. Educators are urged to embrace the idea of *alternative* perspectives to a consumer culture. "The alternative to the free market consumer culture is a set of covenants that supports neighborly disciplines, rather than market disciplines, as a producer of culture. These non-market disciplines have to do with the common good and abundance as opposed to self-interest and scarcity" (Block, Brueggemann, & McKnight, 2016, pp. 6–7).

Anecdotes

Anecdotes (short accounts of relevant incidences) add reality, texture, and poignancy to a concluding point. Chubbuck (2009) recommended revisiting an anecdote raised earlier in the paper, but from a different angle in the conclusion. The chosen anecdote needs to be short, to the point, and relevant to the conclusion being drawn and presented for the readers' consideration. Authors should briefly explain the source, purpose, and meaning of an anecdote before or after using it. The anecdote should, for the most part, be self-explanatory (Jewell, 2016).

> ***Example 15.10 Anecdote*** The findings imply that people need to give the issue of raising children more thought. People in the local community recently started a salon where citizens can gather and engage with this idea. The account of this incidence emerged during the focus groups.

Profound or Provocative Thought

Authors can also pose a profound or a provocative thought in their concluding comments. If a thought is profound, it shows knowledge and insight, usually with intensity. Often, the simplicity of the truth in the comment is enough to change people's perspectives; it makes them stop and think. Provocative comments deliberately stir up emotions to stimulate interest and discussion (Bellanca, 1998; Chubbuck, 2009; Edelson, 2015; Freedman & Plotnick, 2008; Labaree, 2016). The examples below follow from example 15.10 and address the issue of people's preparedness to raise children.

> ***Example 15.11 Profound thought*** Children having children. What a *profound* societal dilemma.

Example 15.12 Provocative thought Perhaps the time has come for everyone to obtain a license to have children, just like they have to get a license to drive a car.

Drama

For dramatic and lasting effect, authors can evoke a vivid image or state a startling statistic or fact. This is a good option when the author wants to drive home the main, ultimate point of the paper and make it stick (Freedman & Plotnick, 2008; Labaree, 2016). Drama excites people. It makes them connect with the ideas in the concluding comments. Dramatic gestures or overtures are arresting and usually highly emotional (Anderson, 2014). Vivid images or startling facts will resonate with readers and are even more effective if substantiated and supported with references to credible and reputable sources (Freedman & Plotnick, 2008). Example 15.15 offers a startling statistic that serves to illustrate this strategy.

Example 15.15 Dramatic, compelling fact Thirty years ago, the average Canadian owed 25 cents of every dollar earned. Today, this number stands at $1.65 (Statistics Canada as cited in Evans, 2016). The income-to-debt ratio of most Canadian households has become *untenable*. Household debt continues to *soar*.

Call for Action

As noted previously, authors can use the Conclusions section as a call for action, namely to undertake more or different research, implement intervention strategies (practice), or change policy. Authors of papers about public or scientific issues may especially want to make a call for action, versus a paper on educational philosophy, for example (WikiHow, ca. 2016). Authors may call for a specific course of action (Freedman & Plotnick, 2008; Labaree, 2016), or they can end with a general comment that "someone needs to do something." The latter is less likely to encourage action or be viewed as a clarion call for that important first step toward changing future research or practice. A call for action often involves issuing a challenge to readers by redirecting them to information in the paper that they can consider applying in their own context (Holewa, 2004).

Example 15.14 Call for action This paper profiled the political skills of lobbying and advocacy and of writing internal position papers and external briefs. Local, provincial, and national associations, as well as individual practitioners and professionals, *are challenged to improve* their political confidence by learning, practicing, and honing these political skills.

Warning

In some instances, it might be prudent for authors to end their paper with a warning, a statement that indicates a possible or impending danger or problem (University of Richmond, 2010). This strategy will definitely leave a lasting impression because it evokes anxiety, fear, and concern. The author of a paper about pollution could end with an estimate of the harmful, irreversible effects of continued pollution in the coming years. In all honesty, this strategy could also backfire if the warning is so dire that readers become immobilized. Although a paper that "deals with a contemporary problem should warn readers of the possible consequences of not attending to the problem" (Labaree, 2016, p. 3), authors have to balance this with not ending on a negative note (Auman, n.d.). The conclusion is meant to inspire and leave readers with a sense of hope and a desire to become engaged, not to discourage or daunt them. Consider this example of a warning-based conclusion.

> ***Example 15.15 Warning*** Without immediate changes to educational practice, vulnerable students run the dire risk of continuing to fall through the cracks, setting up a dynamic of lifelong failure. Kids *are doomed* without our help.

Relevant Narrative

Finally, if the authors' discipline or field of study encourages personal reflection, it might be effective to share a narrative (story) from their personal life as it relates to the concluding point (Freedman & Plotnick, 2008; Labaree, 2016). This strategy entails wrapping up the argumentation in the paper by communicating directly to the reader, in first person. This is actually a powerful ending to a paper because of its shock value. Most academic journals are published in third person. A first-person narrative conclusion stands out because it flaunts convention.

> ***Example 15.16 Personal narrative*** This paper explored the stages of transformative learning, which are triggered by a disorienting dilemma. *My life* fell apart when my department closed down. I wish I had been familiar with this theory. It would have helped me navigate and anticipate the range of emotions and personal growth that I actually experienced.

REVIEW AND ENGAGEMENT

When critically reading a research report, you would

- ☐ See if the authors' conclusions targeted different levels: high level (research question), middle level (red thread argument, or main claims), and low level (specific result or finding) (see Figure 15.3)

- ☐ Determine if the authors used effective closing strategies (see Figure 15.4)

THINGS TO AVOID IN THE CONCLUSIONS SECTION

Authors should avoid apologizing for their research. They should judiciously use emotional appeals, and they cannot introduce any new information into their concluding comments. Doing so threatens or undermines their authority, and it can create unwarranted confusion and skepticism. As noted earlier, authors have the full weight of the paper behind them now and should be able to state their final points succinctly, with conviction.

Do Not Apologize

The Golden Rule when drawing conclusions from research is *Do not apologize*. Apologetic statements downplay the author's authority and discoveries. Apologizing also conveys the impression that the author has doubts about what is being concluded, which readers could interpret as an untrustworthy discussion of the results or findings. This is unfortunate because immersion in the research for an extended period of time presumably leads to expertise on this particular approach to the topic (Bellanca, 1998; Chubbuck, 2009; Labaree, 2016; WikiHow, ca. 2016). Authors should repress the urge to apologize for the paper or their claims, and avoid statements that undercut all of the authority they have built up in the paper.

> ### Example 15.17 Apologizing
>
> - This is just one approach to examining this problem; there may be other and better approaches.
>
> - *I* may not be an expert, and it is only *my* opinion, but the results seem to support this conclusion.

Actually, by noticing if they are writing in first person, authors can more readily recognize and avoid apologizing for their claims (Edelson, 2015) (see second sentence in example 15.17).

Avoid Emotional Appeals

Edelson (2015) further cautioned against making personal, sentimental, and emotional appeals that are out of character with the tone of the paper. In a research climate deeply entrenched in third-person, objective writing, this tone can undermine the author's authority. Although the sentimentality may be heartfelt, it is normally considered out of character for academic research (The Writing Center, 2010). Furthermore, an emotional appeal can be construed as the author losing objectivity, which is especially frowned upon in positivistic, empirical scholarship. The latter demands a causal connection to support the claim rather than an emotive appeal to support the claim.

> ### Example 15.18 Emotional appeal
> It is recommended that high schools provide day care for teenagers who have children but still want to finish school. Think of their plight and the stress they will endure if they do not have sufficient care for their child. *Imagine how horrible* their life will be if they cannot finish school.

No New Information

Regardless of which closing strategy they choose, authors cannot introduce new *information* in the Conclusions section; instead, it is a chance to introduce new *meanings* and new or *expanded ways of thinking* about the topic. This entails new insights and new, creative approaches for how to reframe or reconceptualize the research problem (Edelson, 2015; Holewa, 2004; Labaree, 2016; Wikihow, ca. 2016). On a related issue, authors should never make a claim in the conclusion that is not substantiated by the paper. A hint that this is happening is when the author seems to be introducing new information or a new idea (Labaree, 2016). The reader's perplexed reaction is "Where did *this* come from?" Example 15.19 illustrates the confusion caused when new information or a new idea is introduced into the conclusion.

> ***Example 15.19 Introducing new information (not recommended)*** A paper explored the issue of consumer protection policy governance for Internet shopping. The role of many stakeholders was discussed but not the role of media. However, in the conclusion, the author recommended that the consumer policy governance network for Internet shopping *must* include the media because they have such influence on consumer shopping. It was the first time the word *media* was even used in the paper. This claim is simply not substantiated by the paper.

Strategically posing a provocative question is an alternate strategy to directly introducing a new idea, topic, or piece of information. If carefully executed, this backdoor strategy serves to attract readers' attention to the *new* information without breaching the principle of no new information in the conclusion (University of Richmond, 2010). Example 15.20 is intended to illustrate a provocative question, grounded in the larger conversation from which it arose. This alternative strategy should not set off warning bells, as did example 15.19.

> ***Example 15.20 Alternative strategy to refer to new information*** This paper considered the role of many stakeholders who might be involved with governing Internet consumer transactions. Although media were not one identified as a key stakeholder in this paper, what might the network dynamics look like if their contributions were taken into account? Media have a profound impact on consumers, which intimates media might also have a role in governing Internet marketplace transactions. For the sake of ensuring representative network dynamics, future research could explore this relationship.

REVIEW AND ENGAGEMENT

When critically reading a research report, you would

☐ Determine if the authors avoided apologies, made no emotional appeals, and did not add new information or data

☐ Judge whether the quality of their research was called into question if they employed these strategies

TECHNICAL STRATEGIES FOR WRITING EFFECTIVE CONCLUSIONS

On a final note, as with other sections of a research paper or report, authors must be cognizant of some basic technical conventions and guidelines when preparing the Conclusions section. Aside from length, authors can rely on several conventions grounded in grammar, vocabulary, and syntax (the way words are arranged in a sentence) (Bellanca, 1998).

Length of Conclusions

Conclusions must be well developed and well crafted, which is a deep challenge, given their recommended length (Freedman & Plotnick, 2008; Labaree, 2016). Basic convention holds that the Conclusions section should be one or two paragraphs at most. Any longer and it becomes too difficult for authors to wrap things up (Jonker, 2015). The intent of the conclusion is to focus on implications, evaluations, and insights in a tight, crisp, and concise manner (Evans et al., 2011; Labaree, 2016). As a general rule, the length of the Conclusions section should reflect the length and complexity of the paper or the research report (Freedman & Plotnick, 2008).

Bunton (2005) clarified that theses and dissertations tend to have longer conclusions, even chapters on their own, averaging nine pages. The information in this book on how to write and critically evaluate conclusions pertains to research *articles*, appreciating that the general principles still apply to larger research reports. Despite comprising the shortest section of a research paper, the conclusions play a crucial role. In concert with the Introduction, they frame the body of the paper by reflecting the authors' thoughts and by bridging their ideas so as to bring closure to the argument shaping the paper (The Writing Center, 2010). If done well, readers gain access to the authors' thoughts on *why* their research matters, all within one to two paragraphs (Labaree, 2016).

Tense, Person, and Voice

The Conclusions section is written in present tense because the author's opinions exist now and are in the present. However, authors will likely have to use some combination of past, present perfect, and future tense as well, depending on their message. Past tense and perfect present will be required to restate a finding or result or to refer to the study's research questions, and future tense will be required to refer to the need for additional research (Swales & Feak, 2004).

> ***Example 15.21 Tense usage in conclusions*** This study **has examined** a specific geographic area to determine if residents lived in poverty and, if so, why. Although the study **found** evidence of poverty within the geographic area, it **was not** possible, from the data collected, to determine if the effects of technology integration **cause** (or **caused**) such high levels of poverty. This result **supports** the conclusion that further studies **will be** necessary to determine the effects of technology integration on the poverty levels of this geographic area.

Quantitative scholars tend to use third person and avoid first and second person. Qualitative researchers are more inclined to use first and second person when framing their conclusions (Swales & Feak, 2004). For vigorous, clear writing, authors should opt for the active voice when writing their conclusions. Active voice identifies who will be taking the action. Authors can use passive voice if they do not want to attribute their recommended conclusion to particular agents. Passive voice (the subject is acted upon, evident with the use of *by the*) appears to convey information that is not limited or biased by individual perspectives or personal interests (Toadvine, Brizee, & Angeli, 2017).

Example 15.22 Third person, passive voice Results from this study support **the** conclusion that more insights can be garnered **by** scholars conducting future research around the issue of poverty and technology integration.

Example 15.23 First person, active voice Findings from this study lead **me** to conclude that **community planners** should conduct more research to gain deeper understandings around the link between technology, integration, and poverty.

Vocabulary (Move Statements)

When preparing conclusion statements, authors can rely on several conventions grounded in appropriate vocabulary (Bellanca, 1998). Authors can use one of several words to indicate they are concluding a line of thought (i.e., moving from discussion to conclusions): *for these reasons, in effect, altogether, overall, ultimately, all in all,* and *consequently.* Other examples include *in conclusion, in summary, to conclude, in closing,* and *as shown in this study.* Bunton (2005) called these *move statements,* which enable authors to transition from the discussion to the Conclusions section.

Some scholars approve of this vocabulary strategy because it is such a visible transitioning tool (The Writing Center, 2010) while others believe these phrases are redundant, characterized as overused, unnatural, wooden, and trite (Edelson, 2015; WikiHow, ca. 2016). To soften this possibility, Auman (n.d.) recommended using these words in the middle of the sentence instead of at the beginning. Ultimately, prefacing move statements with conclusion-related vocabulary is a stylistic choice, which may affect the impact of the message for some readers (Samuels, 2004).

Example 15.24 Move statements Our qualitative study found that participants held an array of feelings about what it means to be in debt. Some participants said it was just a part of life that had to be managed. Others did all they could to avoid owing money because being in debt meant they had failed as a person. Still others expressed anger and frustration that they had to borrow at all, intimating they had lost control of their life. *In effect,* there was no one set of feelings about what it means to be in debt. *For this reason,* credit counselors and consumer educators have to prepare their educational materials accordingly, appreciating that a one-size curriculum does not fit all.

Monosyllabic Words

When framing their concluding thoughts, authors should use simple language, including mainly one-syllable words (Chubbuck, 2009). Short, monosyllabic words and short sentences are strong. They are "compact and give language the strength of dense wood having short fibres" (Cockerill, 2005). Although "short sentences have punch, long sentences belabour the point, dragging and trailing as they . . . gasp their way to the finale" (Chubbuck, 2009, p. 109). Authors should avoid this technique because it conveys the impression they are not sure of what to say.

Example 15.25 Long sentence and multisyllable words Results from this experiment seemed to suggest that future researchers might want to consider examining this phenomenon, given that those involved with counseling grief-stricken students seemed to require extended training and orientation to be successful.

Example 15.26 Short sentence and monosyllable words Future studies should focus on teachers who work with grief-stricken students. The teachers' counseling success depends on the right training.

Syntax

Syntax refers to the way words are arranged in a sentence. When writing conclusions, authors should use parallel sentence structure because this technique establishes balance and order, which may be needed at the end of a complex discussion (Bellanca, 1998; Chubbuck, 2009). Parallel structure entails using the same pattern of words when two or more ideas are connected, creating the impression that all ideas are of equal importance. In example 15.27, reflection comes across as more important, whether intended or not, because it is prefaced with *to* while the other two ideas are not, and it lacks a suffix (does not have *ing*):

Example 15.27 Incorrect, unparallel sentence Fred likes reading, writing, and to reflect.

Example 15.28 Correct parallel sentence Fred likes reading, writing, and reflecting.

Finally, authors can also use compound sentences, especially as a last sentence. These sentences contain two independent clauses of equal rank, which are joined by a coordinating conjunction (and sometimes a comma or a semicolon). The conjunctions include *for, and, nor, but, or, yet,* and *so.* Again, this strategy balances the complexity of the discussion (Bellanca, 1998).

Example 15.29 Compound sentences

- Canada is a rich country, *but* it still has many poor people.

- Future researchers could explore this line of thinking, *or* they could dismiss it as irrelevant.

REVIEW AND ENGAGEMENT

When critically reading a research report, you would

☐ Determine if the authors followed the recommended conventions for length, tense, voice, and person when preparing their conclusions

☐ Check to see if they made good use of *move statements* to transition from a discussion point to a concluding comment

FINAL JUDGMENT ON CONCLUSIONS SECTION

Taking *all* of the *Review and Engagement* criteria into account, what is your final judgment of the Conclusions section in the paper you are critically reading?

CHAPTER SUMMARY

This chapter reinforced the importance of the short but influential Conclusions section of a research report. It began with the warning that many people read just this part of a paper, counting on the authors' finesse with preparing their concluding thoughts. Faced with this responsibility, authors have to appreciate how concluding comments differ from, but are related to, discussion points and how conclusions relate to summaries of the paper. The discussion then turns to the four main purposes of a Conclusions section: explore broader implications; suggest new research; relate study to existing literature; and identify policy, practice, and theoretical implications.

Next, the chapter profiles eight closing strategies, ranging from provocative questions to warnings and personal narratives. Things to avoid when creating concluding remarks are also discussed, especially no apologies and no new information. The chapter ends with an overview of technical and grammatical concerns when framing concluding remarks. If done well, the concluding thoughts make the paper resonate with readers, increasing the likelihood they will engage with the study in the future.

REVIEW AND DISCUSSION QUESTIONS

1. Why do you think the Conclusions section is limited to one or two paragraphs?

2. Compare and contrast a discussion and a conclusion. What principles have to be followed if they are combined in one section in a research paper?

3. Compare and contrast a conclusion and a summary. What principles have to be followed if they are combined in one section in a research paper? Which approach do you prefer, separate or combined, and why?

4. Conclusions serve four key purposes or functions. Identify and explain each one. Which combination of them do you think would be most effective, and why?

5. Figure 15.3 sets out the three levels that authors can target when forming their conclusions. Why do you think different disciplines have favored particular levels? Had you ever thought of this notion before?

6. Authors can choose from an array of closing strategies when forming their conclusions. Consider these individually, and then suggest which two to three are likely to be the most compelling for critical readers. Explain your answer.

7. There are also some strategies to be avoided when framing conclusions. Identify and explain these, and then comment on the strategy you think should always be avoided, and why.

8. Summarize the conventions for length, tense, person, and voice when preparing the Conclusions section.

9. Why do you think special focus should be paid to move statements and syntax when wrapping up a paper?

INTRODUCTION

In review, the Results or Findings section profiles "What was found?" The Discussion section focuses on "So what does this mean, and why do we care?" The Conclusions section deals with "What are the implications?" (Labaree, 2016). These elements of a research report inform the development of recommendations, which deal with "Where to next? What are the next steps people should consider taking, given what was found and what the results and findings seem to mean?" Recommendations "tell the reader what to do; what decisions to make, what course of action to take, what alternative solution is superior or what further work needs to be undertaken" (Blicq, 1992, p. 152).

RECOMMEND DEFINED

Recommend is Latin *recommendare*, "praise, present as worthy." Latin *re* means "with reference to," and *commendare* means "commit to one's care, to commend" (Harper, 2016). In effect, if authors of a research paper recommend something, they are presenting the idea as worthy of future consideration and placing its implementation in the care of others. Recommending includes (a) putting forward as something suitable for a purpose; (b) advising as a best choice (to commend); (c) presenting as worthy of confidence, acceptance, and use; (d) suggesting a course of action; and (e) representing an idea as expedient and advisable (Anderson, 2014).

LOGICAL CONNECTIONS INFORMING RECOMMENDATIONS

Writing the recommendations brings the entire research project to a close, which unfolded through the mental exercises of discussions and conclusions (see Figure 16.1). To reflect the argument's internal consistency, recommendations *must* be self-evident upon reading the paper or the research report, which contains the basis (arguments) for the author's recommendations. Recommendations must be logical extensions of the conclusions, which are logical extensions of the discussion, which are logical extensions of the literature review, all of which is informed by the research questions (Aswar, 2011; Blicq, 1992; Edinburgh Napier University, 2012; Saga, 2011; UniLearning, 2000; Weaver & Weaver, 1977) (see Figure 16.2).

Above all else, recommendations cannot "come out of the blue." This is an English language idiom meaning something appears unexpectedly, without warning, and without preparation (Sullivan & Tseng, 2002). Recommendations "call people to action" based on the information, arguments, and evidence in the paper (i.e., the case built up in the paper). If an idea does not stem from the paper, it cannot be a recommendation (Bentley, 2011; Saga, 2011; Weaver & Weaver, 1977). Per example 16.1, the author cannot recommend that future research examine the impact of media on consumer policy governance if the paper did not discuss media and governance.

> *Example 16.1 Recommendation coming out of the blue* A recent paper explored the issue of consumer protection policy governance for Internet shopping. The role of many stakeholders was discussed but not the role of the media. However, the author strongly recommended that the consumer policy governance network for Internet shopping *must* include the media because they have such influence on consumer shopping. It was the first time the word *media* was used in the paper. This recommendation is simply not substantiated by the paper; it came out of the blue.

FIGURE 16.1 ■ Comparing *Discuss*, *Conclude*, and *Recommend*

Discuss	Conclude	Recommend
• Consider by talking over • Have a conversation about • Present in detail for examination • Talk about in order to convince others or to reach conclusions	• End something • Bring something to a close (but do not close it off) • Reach a position, opinion, or judgment after careful consideration • Present the last main section of a discourse, usually containing a summary and a statement of opinions or decisions	• Put forward as something suitable for a purpose • Advise as a best choice (to commend) • Present as worthy of confidence, acceptance, and use • Suggest as a course of action • Represent an idea as expedient and advisable

FIGURE 16.2 ■ Logical Connections Informing Recommendations

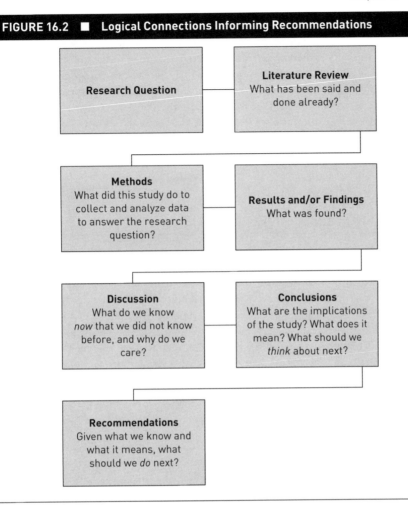

REVIEW AND ENGAGEMENT

When critically reading a research report, you would

☐ Determine that the authors did not confuse the roles of *discuss*, *conclude*, and *recommend* (see Figure 16.1)

☐ Ascertain if they ensured that all of their recommendations stem from the paper (did not come out of the blue) (see Figure 16.2)

Relating Recommendations to Conclusions

Academic research articles sometimes have a Recommendations section at the very end, after the Conclusions section, but recommendations are more often presented as part of the discussion or the conclusions (Jones, 2016; Weaver & Weaver, 1977; Wiersma & Jurs, 2009). This book has a separate chapter on each of these research conventions because they serve different functions, thereby warranting different criteria to judge them. So, even if authors opt to weave their recommendations into their one- to two-paragraph Conclusions section, they still need to make sure the conclusions served their purpose and the recommendations served their purpose. Respectively, the conclusions wrap up the paper-long argument developed around a research question, and the recommendations advise those who are interested in what they should do next, now that they have finished reading the paper.

RESEARCH VERSUS NONRESEARCH RECOMMENDATIONS

This chapter provides information about writing and judging *research* recommendations. But people can also include recommendations in government, industry, or civil organization reports, ideas that are not necessarily based on academic, scholarly research. Recommendations proposed in academic papers tend to be more tentative in nature than those proposed in technical reports, in business reports, or to policy makers (Centre for Independent Language Learning, 2008b; Saga, 2011). *Tentative* means provisional, cautious, and uncertain (Anderson, 2014). But if an academic piece *does* include recommendations, there are basic conventions and principles that the authors can follow so they can achieve the purposes of recommendations in a research paper.

Purpose of Recommendations

Recommendations serve several purposes (see Figure 16.3). The overall intent is to identify potential actions to be taken in response to research findings or results and any discussion of their import (Bentley, 2011). Recommendations can (a) provide solutions to problems, solutions that emerged from, or were inspired by, the discussion and any concluding thoughts. They can (b) be used to suggest possible courses of action for the future, ideas that arose from the conclusions (especially changes to, or new directions for, research, practice, theory, and policy). Recommendations can also (c) be used to suggest how things can be improved or progressed, whether it be research, practice, theory, or policy (Edinburgh Napier University, 2012; Royal Melbourne Institute of Technology, 2008). Some recommendations (d) are intended to identify preferred alternatives to the status quo. These alternatives should be justified, meaning they are the ones best supported by the results or findings and the discussion points and claims (Aswar, 2011; Ellinger & Yang, 2011; Sonnenberg, ca. 2002).

Recommendations for future actions and future research can take several additional forms. Authors can recommend follow-up work that remains to be done, such as replicating or extending the study or challenging the choice of theory used in the study. They can recommend that others carry out new research that was not feasible in the current study. Authors can also offer suggestions for how to design future studies, especially changes to methods and the overall research design (including logics and logistics, described in Chapter 8). They can also urge readers to consider the study's implications (Blicq, 1992; Bruce, 2001b).

Example 16.2 Recommendations for changes to research design and methods
In a recent study about consumers' understandings of nutrition marketing terms, Haroldson and Yen (2016) tendered three strong recommendations about how the research design and methods should change in future studies. "Future studies should explore these differences and make necessary modifications to ensure that validity and reliability are still well established. Future studies should consider alternative

FIGURE 16.3 ■ Purpose of Recommendations

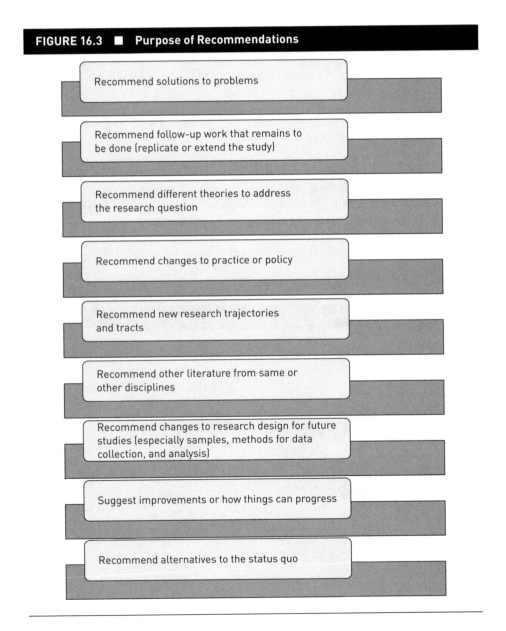

Recommend solutions to problems

Recommend follow-up work that remains to be done (replicate or extend the study)

Recommend different theories to address the research question

Recommend changes to practice or policy

Recommend new research trajectories and tracts

Recommend other literature from same or other disciplines

Recommend changes to research design for future studies (especially samples, methods for data collection, and analysis)

Suggest improvements or how things can progress

Recommend alternatives to the status quo

data collection methods to validate the measurement items and yield relevant information about consumer behaviours and knowledge. Instead of using a convenience sample, researchers should consider using market research panels, online forums, and listservs to reach a broader audience" (p. 31).

AUDIENCES FOR RECOMMENDATIONS

Recommendations can target different audiences. Authors can encourage academics to engage in more or different research, literature, or theorizing. They can advise policy makers to effect policy changes (e.g., deregulate, regulate, analyze, evaluate). Recommendations can target practitioners and professionals so they can examine and change their practice, with this including the industry sector, civil society, and the media. And recommendations can pertain to educators and administrators vis-à-vis curriculum, pedagogy, instruction, and training initiatives (Northam, 2011) (see Figure 16.4). In example 16.11, the author targeted three audiences: researchers, educators and curriculum organizers, and the field or discipline.

Regardless of the intended audience, the tone and directions within the recommendations must be suitable to the culture of the discipline, profession, sector, or organization unless the intent is to shake things up on purpose, in which case going against the culture might be warranted (Centre for Independent Language Learning, 2008b). Discerning readers of authors' recommendations would be able to judge whether the authors targeted the most relevant audience(s) for their ideas. Authors should avoid applying insights from their study to people or settings that are dissimilar to their study (Boudah, 2011).

FIGURE 16.4 ■ Audiences for Recommendations

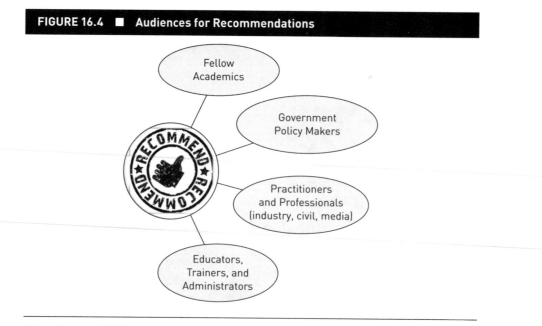

Source: Image used with permission of Microsoft.

Example 16.3 Recommend to appropriate audience In one study, researchers studied student enrollment in small liberal arts colleges, with a focus on why students were dropping out. They determined that enrollment depended on the academic program, the students' age and maturity, their part-time employment, and their marital status. Rather than target their recommendations to university administrators so they could use the information to mitigate declining enrollments, the authors unfathomably wrote their recommendations for local retailers (where students worked) and the students' spouses or partners. It would have made more sense for them to prepare recommendations about the academic programs and the university policy about working students and direct those to university administrators.

CHARACTERISTICS OF EFFECTIVE RECOMMENDATIONS

Good, effective recommendations will meet several key criteria, noted here in no particular order (see Table 16.1). They will be concise, meaning a lot is expressed in a few words. Recommendations will be clear and unambiguous; that is, they will be easy to understand and interpret without multiple meanings. What is expected should be readily evident. A good recommendation will be specific in that it provides precise details. It will be concrete and easy to envision, not abstract. Vague, imprecise recommendations can reveal insufficient analysis and/or discussion of the results and findings (Bentley, 2011; Lee, 2013; Morel, 2012; Saga; 2011; Weaver & Weaver, 1977).

A good recommendation will be realistic. The person making the recommendation must have a practical and sensible sense of what can be achieved or expected by those tasked with taking action. It will be actionable and workable. Pragmatically, the cost of implementing the recommendation must also be realistic, whether it is financially, fiscally, personally,

TABLE 16.1 ■ Criteria for Effective Recommendations	
Criteria for Effective Recommendations	**Explanation**
Concise	Say a lot with few words
Clear and unambiguous	Easy to understand and interpret without multiple meanings
Specific	Provide precise, exact details
Concrete	Readily evident (not abstract or hard to envision)
Realistic	Actionable, workable, and affordable
Logical	Flow readily and directly from discussion and conclusions
Feasible	Possible and practical for people to achieve or accomplish
Ethical	Just, fair, honest, not improper, and appropriate
Legal	Within the law

technically, or politically (Edinburgh Napier University, 2012; Lee, 2013; Morel, 2012; Northam, 2011; Saga, 2011; Weaver & Weaver, 1977).

Good recommendations have other features. They will flow logically and directly from the conclusions so the reader can see the basis for the author's suggestions; otherwise, a discerning reader may be skeptical about the legitimacy of the recommendation. Concurrently, effective recommendations will be relevant to the topic at hand, as set out in the problem statement, introduction, and research questions. They should make sense as a solution to the problems addressed in the research (Edinburgh Napier University, 2012; Northam, 2011; Saga, 2011).

Good recommendations will be feasible and achievable, meaning it is possible and practical for someone to accomplish the recommended action. Meeting this criterion may involve clarifying both strategies for actuation and measures for successful achievement, as well as suggesting time frames. Effective recommendations will be ethical in that they do not recommend anything unjust, dishonest, improper, or inappropriate for the situation. Hand in hand, they will be legal. Unlawful recommendations will either be implemented or not and, if so, can come back to haunt the researcher who made the suggestion (Centre for Independent Language Learning, 2008b; Saga, 2011; Weaver & Weaver, 1977). For clarification, recommendations that do not fit this collection of criteria are not wrong; they are simply not sufficient to ensure implementation; that is, they will not be as effective (Northam, 2011).

REVIEW AND ENGAGEMENT

When critically reading a research report, you would

☐ Check to see that the authors recommended some combination of problem solutions; follow-up or future research actions; changes to policy, theory, or practice; method modifications; and new research questions or trajectories (see Figure 16.3)

☐ Confirm that they identified their intended audiences deemed most appropriate for their ideas (see Figure 16.4)

☐ Ascertain if they matched the tone of their recommendations with the intended audience

☐ Determine if they met most of the criteria for an effective recommendation (see Table 16.1)

LANGUAGE FOR COMMUNICATING RECOMMENDATIONS

All writing is persuasive, and savvy writers can strategically use language to persuade readers to act on their recommendations (Taylor, 2007). Because recommendations are about action, verbs play a key role. In grammar, verbs are words that describe action, defined as the process of doing something to achieve an aim (Anderson, 2014). Main verbs suitable for recommendations include *recommend, suggest, advocate, propose, advise, urge, is imperative,* and *is indicative.* Of special importance to recommendations are actionable verbs, modal verbs, and, less so, imperative verbs (Centre for Independent Language Learning, 2008b; Saga, 2011; UniLearning, 2000) (see Figure 16.5).

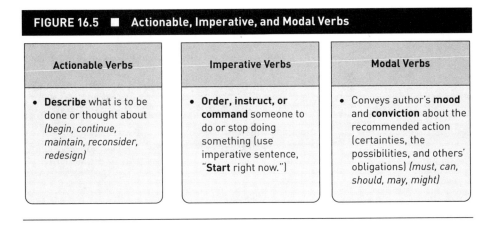

FIGURE 16.5 ■ Actionable, Imperative, and Modal Verbs

Actionable Verbs	Imperative Verbs	Modal Verbs
• **Describe** what is to be done or thought about *(begin, continue, maintain, reconsider, redesign)*	• **Order, instruct, or command** someone to do or stop doing something (use imperative sentence, "**Start** right now.")	• Conveys author's **mood** and **conviction** about the recommended action (certainties, the possibilities, and others' obligations) *(must, can, should, may, might)*

Actionable Verbs

If authors want readers to take action, they can preface their recommendation with actionable verbs (Saga, 2011). Action verbs describe what people can do or think rather than describe their state or condition at a point in time (like a linking verb). Instead of saying, "Practitioners could consider *starting* a new intervention program" (linking verb), the author could say, "Practitioners should *start* a new intervention program." Actionable verbs help authors tell readers exactly what they want done or thought (either physical or mental action). Several actionable verbs appropriate for research recommendations include *continue, begin, stop, start, reconsider, redesign, reevaluate, rethink,* and *maintain* (see more action verbs at Wake Forest University, 2011). Action verbs can have a past, present, or future tense. Past-tense action verbs end with *d, ed,* and *ied.* Present-tense action verbs end with *s, es,* and *ies.* Future-tense action verbs are special words like *will, is going to,* and *shall* (Grammarly, 2017; Jefferson County Schools, Tennessee: Project LA, 2002; K12 Reader, 2015).

Imperative Verbs

With caution, authors who are writing recommendations can also elect to use imperative verbs (UniLearning, 2000). Known as *bossy words,* they tell someone what to do (or not). These verbs help authors create an imperative sentence, whereby the sentence gives an order, a command, or an instruction (e.g., *Don't* touch that. *Stop* right now. *Answer* my question!). *Imperative* means that some action or nonaction is of vital importance, essential, and urgent (Anderson, 2014). The root form of the verb is used to create the imperative, which means nothing is in front of it and there are no suffixes, like *ing, ed, ion,* or *s* (Grammarly, 2017). The imperative sentence can end with a period or an exclamation mark, which is actually not an accepted convention in academic writing. Just as recommendations can have various audiences, imperative verbs require an audience too because that audience is being asked to do or not do something (Yule, 2006).

Example 16.4 Imperative verb These results truly compel researchers to reconsider their current approach to this issue. *Stop* right now and change research directions!

TABLE 16.2 ■ Modal Auxiliary Verbs Organized by Modal Force					
Certainty (*will, would, shall, must*)		**Possibility, Ability, and Permission** (*may, might, can, could*)		**Obligation and Necessity (presumes freedom to act)** (*have to, need to, must, should, ought to*)	
Will	What is believed to be true about the present (making deductions)	May	Something will happen or is already happening (about 50% sure)	Have to	Expresses a general obligation based on a rule or the authority of another
		May	Refers to things happening in certain situations		
Would	Confidently speaks to an unrealized future	Might	Conveys the possibility of something happening, but is tentative, doubtful (about 30% sure)	Need/need to	Indicates an obligation or necessity for someone else to do something
Shall	Indicates personal intention	Can	Something is possible and can actually happen; indicative of ability	Need/need to	Can imply that an external source is required to act, rather than the speaker acting
Must	What can be inferred or concluded to be a logical interpretation of a situation (do not have all of the facts)	Can	Speaks to choice and opportunities	Must	Expresses a strong obligation of what must happen (often perceived as prescriptive and preachy)
		Can	Expresses contingencies		
Should	Expresses what may reasonably be expected to happen if everything goes according to plan (making a deduction)	Could	Theoretically, something might be possible or might happen, but not for sure	Should/ought to	Refers to obligations where people have a choice
		Could	Hypothetical or conditional		

REVIEW AND ENGAGEMENT

When critically reading a research report, you would

☐ Determine if the authors seemed to distinguish between actionable, imperative, and modal verbs (see Figure 16.5)

☐ Judge if you think they were cognizant of the powerful role of verbs when making recommendations

Modal Verbs

Consider this recommendation, "High school principals *must* undertake research about alcoholism in school." The main verb *undertake* is prefaced with the modal verb *must*. How would a reader's sense of the author's conviction behind this recommendation shift if the modal verb were changed to *might*? "High school principals *might* undertake research about alcoholism in school." Most people can recall reading a bracing, convincing, and well-argued paper and then finding themselves shaking their heads at the end when the authors prefaced their conclusions and recommendations with the modal verbs *might* or *could*. If the author was so convincing in the arguments in the Discussion section, why not use stronger modal verbs to entice readers to take action—*must, should, have to, need to*? The humble modal verb has a lot of power and conveys intense messages at the end of a research report or paper.

Modal verbs play a crucial role when framing recommendations (Centre for Independent Language Learning, 2008b). They convey the speakers' *mood*, how they feel about what is being proposed and recommended. They reflect the authors' opinions, attitudes, beliefs, and assertions, intentionally or not, ideally the former. There are 10 single-word modal verbs: *should* (*ought*), *may* (*might*), *can* (*could*), *would* (*will* and *shall*), and *must* (Huddleston & Pullum, 2005) (see Table 16.2, from Dury, ca. 2000; Foster, 2015; Gould, 2011; Kosur, 2012; Landry, 1982; University of York, 2007). Often called modal *auxiliary verbs*, they help, support, and supplement the main verb by conveying the mood and state of mind of the speaker or writer (Gould, 2011; Gregori, 2011; Huddleston & Pullum, 2005; von Fintel, 2006).

Example 16.5 Modal verbs and their messages

- "I *propose* that all home economics educators *should* become philosophically savvy." The tone (mood) shifts when the modal verb is changed. "I *propose* that all home economics educators *might* become philosophically savvy." *Should* conveys obligation, and *might* conveys possibilities, something to ponder.

- "Many recommend that the profession of home economics *ought to* change its name." "Many recommend that the home economics profession *could* change its name." While the main verb *recommend* conveys the notion that a course of action is being proposed, the modal verb conveys the emotion and the conviction of the person making the recommendation. In this example, *ought to* conveys a moral obligation, and *could* conveys a possibility.

Modal Force

Modal verbs express *modal force*, which is the mental energy, sentiment, emotion, and mood behind the authors' ideas—that is, their level of commitment, resolve, detachment, or conviction to what they are proposing (Kosur, 2012). As a caveat, this chapter focuses on modal force rather than modal flavor. Modal force expresses the strength of the authors' belief about an idea while modal flavor underpins what is shaping their belief. Flavors include what authors know and desire, a particular goal, specific rules or regulations, the circumstances, authors' sense of the world, their own propensity to act, or their disposition (inclinations) (Hacquard, 2011; Kratzer, 1991; von Fintel, 2006). It is impossible to discern modal flavor when critically reading a research report because readers do not have access to the author's mind. McGregor (2016) provided a detailed discussion of modal flavor.

Authors can express one of three main modal forces (their state of mind or mood when they formed the recommendation) (see Figure 16.6). The author (a) is *certain* about the recommendation (likelihood and predictability); (b) thinks it is *possible* for others to engage in the action being recommended (degree of possibility, ability, permission); or (c) thinks it is necessary for others to take on the recommendation; that is, they have an *obligation* to do something (Gould, 2011; Hacquard, 2011; Palmer, 2001). In addition, authors can use modal verbs to convey intent, promise, willingness, and ability (Foster, 2015). And modal verbs can express contingencies, conditionality, commands, and preferences (Kosur, 2012).

Whether authors recognize it or not, modal verbs have a lot of power. The perceived force of an argument or the author's articulated recommendation will affect the readers' receptiveness to the recommendation. Table 16.3 profiles the principal modal verbs and their force when attached to a recommendation. Note that some modal verbs cross over between certainty and obligation (especially *must* and *should*) (Simon, 2013). The authors' intended meaning can be discerned by checking paraphrases preceding the modal verb (e.g., *it is possible that, if all goes as planned, given what we know*) (Dury, ca. 2000). Each modal force is now explained in sufficient detail that authors can be fully cognizant of their verb choices and critical readers can discern, or at least infer, authors' mood when preparing their recommendations (i.e., certainty, possibility, or obligation).

FIGURE 16.6 ■ Modal Forces

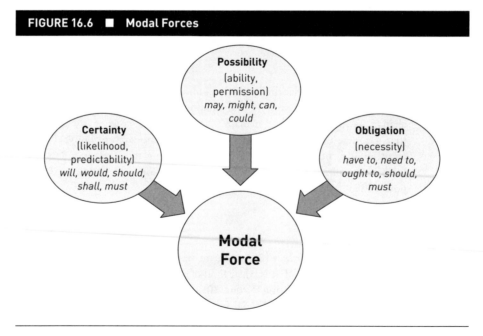

TABLE 16.3 ■ The Force Indicated by Specific Modal Verbs			
Modal Force	**Essence of the Force**	**Explanation of the Force**	**Strength of Modal Verb Force**
Certainty	– Knowledge is free of error – Mental state of being free of doubt	*Verifiable certainty*—beyond question, dispute, or doubt *Credible certainty*—believable argument underpinning the recommendation *Belief-based certainty*—conviction that judgment supporting the recommendation is true	*Will*—the most certain
			Must—very certain, but some doubt
			Would—confident it *can* happen sometime in the future
			Should—confident will happen *if* things go as planned
Possibility	Capable of happening, existing, or being achieved	Recommendation reflects a blending of both the authors' *ignorance* and their *knowledge*, leading to affirmation of a possibility (able to happen but not certain it will)	*May*—strong possibility (not as strong as *will*)
			Might—tentative (weaker than *may*)
			Can—capable of happening (weaker than *may* and *might*)
			Could—hypothetically could happen but weaker conviction than *can*
Obligation	*Recommend* things that are necessary and important to do *Give advice* about things deemed to be a good idea	*Necessary*—essential and indispensable *Necessary*—unavoidable and requisite *Should*—moral overtones *Should*—indicates expected behavior	*Must*—strong moral overtones
			Must—strong conviction of future obligation
			Should—weaker than *must* and *have to*
			Have to—bound by external authority
			Need to happen for completion or achievement
			Ought to—people have a choice

Certainty

Certainty refers to either (a) knowledge that is free of error or (b) the mental state of being without doubt (DeRose, 2009; Westphal, 1995). If people are certain, they express their ideas with assurance, conviction, and confidence. Certainty has several forms: verifiable, credible, and belief-based (Firth, 1967; Reed, 2010). First, in its simplest form, *certainty* means beyond question, dispute, or doubt. Once something has been *verified*, it cannot be doubted. Second, something is certain when it has the highest degree of *credibility*, either intrinsically or as a result of an argument. If something is credible, it is believable or trustworthy (Anderson, 2014). Third, certainty can mean the *belief* that the judgment supporting a recommendation is true. This refers to subjective belief (one's personal perspectives and experiences are informing the recommendation) and objective belief (the recommendation is not influenced by personal factors).

Three modal verbs are used to express certainty: *will*, *must*, and *would* (and sometimes *should*). *Will* expresses the most certainty and is used to convey the belief that a future state or event is certain to occur. *Must* is appropriate when the speaker has deduced that a future state or event is the most logical or rational outcome. *Must* also conveys a strong feeling of certainty; nevertheless, there is still some doubt in the speaker's mind. *Must* can also be used when the speaker feels sure that something is real because she or he sees strong evidence of it. *Would* is used when the author wants to speak confidently to an unrealized future; it is not true in the present, and it may or may not happen in the future. *Should* can be used when expressing certainty if the author has deduced that something may reasonably be expected to happen if everything goes according to plan (Simon, 2013).

Example 16.6 Certainty modal verbs

- Educators *will* change the future if they embrace this radical idea (conveys author's certainty that this change will occur)

- The future *must* change if educators embrace this radical idea (conveys author's belief that this is the most logical outcome)

- By embracing this radical idea, educators *would* change the future (conveys author's confidence that this can happen, sometime, eventually)

- If things go as planned and teachers embrace this radical idea, the future *should* change (conveys author's realization that contingency comes into play)

Possibility

Possibility is a fundamental modal concept (Chappell, 2006). If the event or state of affairs is not being thought about, it becomes impossible to actualize. If something is possible, it is capable of happening, existing, or being achieved, meaning it has not happened yet. In fact, most possibilities never actualize but remain "condemned to an existence in the twilight of being" (Butchvarov, 1960, p. 337). Yet people still envision things that might be capable of happening, existing, or being achieved. Statements of possibility reflect a "blending of ignorance and assurance concerning facts" (Ewer, 1905, p. 8). Authors forming recommendations with this modal force would proceed from what they know and do not know from their research results and findings and attendant discussion, leading to a recommendation for others to take action—that is, the affirmation of a possibility (Ewer, 1905).

Four modal verbs are used to express sentiments of possibility: *can*, *could*, *may*, and *might*. *Can* means the same thing as "it is possible to." Because *can* is associated with ability (*may* with permission), it is often used to convey the possibility of an action due to some skill or capability. *Can* also refers to choice and opportunities, and it expresses contingencies (If X *can* . . . , then . . .). *Could* is used to express possibility in hypothetical or theoretical situations.

It is weaker and more tentative than *can*, with a sense that something is less than likely to manifest. The negative forms *cannot* and *could not* mean inability, impermissibility, or impossibility (Department of Justice, 2015; Foster, 2015; Gould, 2011; Simon, 2013).

May expresses a strong possibility that something is already happening or will happen (but not as strongly as *will* [certainty]). *Might* is weaker than *may*, connoting a tentative, doubtful, and less certain sense of the possibility of something happening (Foster, 2015; Gould, 2011; Simon, 2013). Relative to *may*, the modal verbs *can*, *could*, and *might* are weak, indicating a lack of commitment or confidence (Celce-Murcia & Larsen-Freeman, 1999).

Example 16.7 Possibility modal verbs

- Educators *can* change the future if they embrace this radical idea (conveys author's belief that educators have the skills; hence, change is possible)

- Educators *could* change the future if they embraced this radical idea (conveys author's weaker assertion that change is possible)

- Educators *may* change the future if they embrace this radical idea (conveys author's strong belief that change will happen or is already happening)

- Educators *might* change the future if they embraced this radical idea (conveys author's doubtfulness [lack of confidence] that change will actually happen)

- Educators *might* want to consider embracing this radical idea, if they want to change the future (conveys author's suggestion to ponder this possible action)

Obligation

Authors use obligation force when they want to (a) recommend things that are necessary and important to do or (b) give advice about things deemed to be a good idea. Five modal verbs can be used to express obligation: *should*, *must*, *ought to*, *need to*, and *have to*. The latter two are called phrasal modal verbs and are linked to an infinitive (or verb used with *to*) (Himma, 2013, 2015). *Should*, *must*, and *ought to* indicate that the authority for the stated obligation comes from the person articulating it. *Have to* is used to reflect being bound by rules and regulations set and overseen by some external authority (not the speaker, and the speaker cannot change the rules) (Simon, 2013). *Need to* indicates an obligation or the necessity to do something (Landry, 1982).

Should and *must* are used when the author is offering a subjective, personal opinion. *Should* is used to (a) describe an expected or recommended behavior or a future circumstance, (b) offer advice, or (c) prescribe normative behavior (without the stronger force of *must* and *have to*). Regarding *should*, even if the author feels morally entitled to put forth the case for a recommendation, the reader is not obligated to comply (i.e., is not morally bound) (Himma, 2015). There must be some conditions affecting readers or listeners that make it desirable for them to carry out the recommended action (Leiss & Abraham, 2014).

Ought to is used in the more general sense and has a more objective meaning than *should* (Simon, 2013). It can also convey the idea that readers have a choice. In its deontic use (moral overtones), *must* expresses the author's conviction that others have a strong sense of obligation or necessity to do something. *Must* refers to a future obligation. In short, while *should* (internal) is milder, *have to* (external) and *must* (internal) represent strong obligations (Simon, 2013; Wikipedia Encyclopedia, 2016b).

Obligation can also refer to what is *necessary*, which means essential and indispensable (pressingly needed). *Necessary* can also mean unavoidable or requisite (needed for the achievement or completion of something). In those instances, speakers should use *need* or *need to* (Huddleston, ca. 2010; Simon, 2013). *Need* indicates an obligation or necessity to do something (Landry, 1982). One caution should be noted. *Need* can allow speakers to distance themselves from the recommended act. It can imply that an external source is required to act, rather than the speaker acting (Vine, 2004).

Example 16.8 Obligation verbs

- Educators *should* embrace this radical idea so they can change the future (conveys author's personal opinion that this behavior is expected)

- Educators *must* embrace this radical idea if they ever want to change the future (conveys author's conviction that educators are obligated to do this)

- Educators *ought to* embrace this radical idea if they want to change the future (conveys author's acceptance that educators have a choice to do this or not)

- In order to change the future, educators *have to* embrace this radical idea (educators are bound by an external authority to do so)

REVIEW AND ENGAGEMENT

When critically reading a research report, you would

☐ Determine if the authors chose modal verbs that reflect the actual mood (certainty, possibility, obligation) threaded throughout their discussion and their conclusions; that is, did their modal verb choice resonate with you given what you had just read? (See Tables 16.2 and 16.3 and Figure 16.6.)

☐ Ascertain if the authors' mix of the three modal forces seemed appropriate for the message they appeared to be conveying.

CRAFTING AND ORGANIZING EFFECTIVE RECOMMENDATIONS

This section focuses on how to craft, present, and organize recommendations at the end of a research paper or report. Topics include the scope of recommendations, using prose versus a list (numbered or bulleted), various organizational categories when presenting in a list, and the choice between stand-alone and supportive statements.

Scope of Recommendations

Concerning scope, regardless of how many recommendations are proffered, each recommendation would ideally include *who* will act, *what* is to be done (prefaced with a modal verb), *when* and *how*, and to *what standard* (Royal Melbourne Institute of Technology, 2008). In reality, authors tend not to reflect this full scope for a recommendation, but obviously, the more detailed the suggestion, the easier it is for others to take action and implement it.

At a minimum, recommendations should include *what* is to be done and by *whom*, with an expression of *modal force* (i.e., the author's sense of certainty, possibility, or obligation). The additional criteria of *how*, *when*, and to *what standard* are more likely to appear in business reports, technical reports, or policy recommendations, per Saga's (2011) observation that academic papers tend to present more tentative recommendations relative to other sectors.

Example 16.9 Minimum scope in a recommendation

Medical doctors *must* refrain from giving nutrition advice to patients. [*who*, modal verb, *what*]

Example 16.10 Maximum scope in a recommendation

By the end of 2016, all medical doctors *must* refrain from giving nutrition advice to patients and do so by redirecting them to the nutritionists on staff. [*when*, *who*, modal verb, *what*, *how*]

Prose Versus List (Numbered or Bulleted)

Authors have several options for organizing the recommendations tendered in a research paper or report. Critical readers can discern a lot from this aspect of reporting research. In most instances, recommendations are listed rather than set out in prose. With the latter approach, key ideas can remain hidden in paragraph form and not be highlighted (see example 16.2). The style of presentation matters because it affects readers' accessibility to the recommendations. Lists are cleaner than prose (paragraphs) because each recommendation is more visible.

Example 16.11 Recommendations using combination of prose and numbered list, with modal verb italicized

Clucas (1997, pp. 162–163) tendered the following recommendations for research in the field of technology education.

1. Given the changing nature of technology, a series of longitudinal studies, based on this model, *would* [emphasis added] document trends and thereby increase the potential that decisions regarding the composition of the technology education curriculum would be relatively current and less exposed to personal bias.

2. While the current spheres of human/technology interaction model considers [*sic*] the technology education curriculum from a global viewpoint, it

may [emphasis added] be advantageous to conduct research which considers the distribution of the curriculum organizers across this model in the context of the age-related or developmentally-related [*sic*] needs of the learner.

3. Given that this study provides a basis for concluding that construction is a curriculum organizer which contributes to technological literacy and general education, defining the attributes that constitute technological literacy in the area of construction *would* [emphasis added] prove to be of value to the discipline. Such an effort *would* [emphasis added] enable technology educators to derive construction related [*sic*] course content from a research base.

4. Research related to other technology education organizers that provides a means of defining their contribution to the discipline and to the goals of general education and technological literacy *would* [emphasis added] be of value to the field of technology education.

Another concern is whether the list of recommendations is numbered or bulleted. Bullets are more generic, with numbers intimating importance. Authors should clarify why they are using a numbering or a lettering scheme (Saga, 2011). Also, numbering may be preferred because it is easier for others to refer to a number than a bullet (Morel, 2012).

Example 16.12 Numbered list I would like everyone to refer to Recommendation 2.1.

Example 16.13 Bulleted list I would like everyone to turn to page 15, and find the 10th bullet down from the top (or 5th up from the bottom).

REVIEW AND ENGAGEMENT

When critically reading a research report, you would

- ☐ Ascertain if the authors used at least a minimum scope for each recommendation (i.e., *what*, *who*, and a modal verb)
- ☐ Determine if they listed their recommendations (with or without a stem statement)
- ☐ Check to see if they decided to number or letter the recommendations for ease of reference

Options for Presenting Lists of Recommendations

If authors choose to use a list to present their recommendations, they can organize it from several different perspectives (see Figure 16.7). (a) If different things in the future demand different solutions, the recommendations can be presented as a bulleted or a numbered list for these contingencies, with appropriate headings. (b) If recommended actions are imperative, they should be listed in order of priority and described as such. (c) If one action depends on the previous one (contingent), the list should be organized to reflect this sequence and explained as such. (d) If the recommendations have equal weight, they can be listed in the order they emerged from the discussion and/or the conclusions (perhaps using similar headings) (Edinburgh Napier University, 2012; Saga, 2011; UniLearning, 2000; Weaver & Weaver, 1977).

(e) Recommendations are often organized into categories according to the intended audience, including educators, administrators, policy makers, parents, industry, students, community leaders, or media (see example 16.11, where the author targeted three audiences: researchers, educators and curriculum organizers, and the field or discipline). (f) If authors wish to identify ideas for future research, they can organize their recommendations so they address various research elements, including different problems, literature to review, methods to consider, theories to consult, or methodologies (research paradigms) to employ (Saga, 2011) (see Example 16.2).

Example 16.14 Recommendations focused on changes to research design

In the future, other scholars interested in this topic *can*

(1) extend the focus of specific components of the macro-relational consumer policy framework (beyond that of this study),

(2) extend research methods and analyses (beyond network analysis), and

(3) align with complementary bodies of literature or conceptual frameworks so as to broaden the application of the macro-relational consumer policy framework (McGregor, 1993).

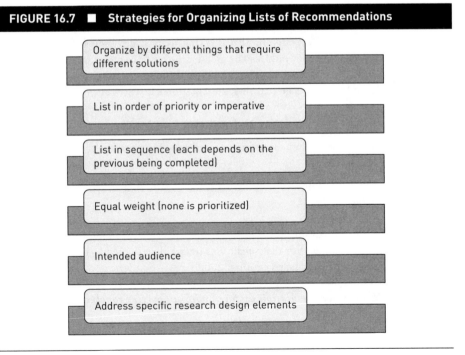

FIGURE 16.7 ■ Strategies for Organizing Lists of Recommendations

Organize by different things that require different solutions

List in order of priority or imperative

List in sequence (each depends on the previous being completed)

Equal weight (none is prioritized)

Intended audience

Address specific research design elements

Even in this example, one automatically wonders if the numbered order has significance. Should people pay more attention to the first recommendation, or does it have equal weight with the others? Authors are encouraged to clarify their organizational assumptions and principles when listing recommendations, appreciating that this is seldom done in practice, leaving readers to their own devices.

Stand-Alone and Supportive Statements

Authors can choose to write the recommendations as separate, stand-alone statements (see example 16.11), or they can preface a list of recommendations with a stem statement. The latter approach would be appropriate when listing recommendations according to the target audience (Morel, 2012; Saga, 2011). Example 16.15 illustrates this idea along with the principle that recommendations can be one statement followed with bullets (Morel, 2012).

Example 16.15 Recommendations prefaced with stem statement for specific audience

It is recommended that school principals [*stem statement*]

- provide professional development for teachers,
- include parents and guardians in the curriculum process, and
- exclude retailers and business owners from the school's business.

Saga (2011) recommended stating the recommendation without any introductory statement or rationale. He believed the "body of the report itself has already done that work. It is more important to cut through the verbiage and give the audience clear, easy to understand actions." Others recommended either prefacing the recommendation with a rationale or placing the rationale afterward, arguing that this strategy provides context for the idea (see example 16.11). This approach would also be useful if the paper or report is lengthy and multidimensional (i.e., a lot of different themes and ideas, each warranting recommendations) (Centre for Independent Language Learning, 2008b; Morel, 2012; Weaver & Weaver, 1977).

Example 16.16 Recommendation prefaced with a supportive result

Results showed that children's learning in Grades 1–3 improves if they have a nap during the day.

Recommendation 6: Educators *should* schedule a daily nap into the elementary school timetable.

Authors can also use an introductory sentence or paragraph linking the recommendation back to the discussion and/or the conclusions (rather than the results or findings, per se) (Centre for Independent Language Learning, 2008b).

Example 16.17 Recommendation prefaced with supportive conclusion

The results of this study about students grieving the suicide of a fellow student lead us to conclude that students are harmed when schools lack guidelines preventing untrained staff from offering grief counseling. In light of this conclusion, the following recommendations are made concerning training for educational staff pursuant to student grief counseling:

Recommendation A Teachers should be given intense grief-counseling training.

Recommendation B School boards should pay for this training.

Recommendation C Students and parents need to be advised that this training is taking place so they can feel more confident in the school's services for this pressing issue.

In lieu of a full statement prefacing the recommendation, authors can refer back to the aspect of the problem that the *particular* recommendation addresses (Centre for Independent Language Learning, 2008b; Saga, 2011) (see example 16.11, items 1 and 3 in the list).

***Example 16.18 Recommendation linked back to aspects of research problem* (modal verb *italicized*)**

> *Given that* [state aspect of problem], someone *should* [indicate action].
>
> *In light of* [state aspect of problem], someone *could* [indicate action].
>
> *In view of* [state aspect of problem], someone *might* [indicate action].
>
> *Because* [state aspect of problem], someone *must* [indicate action].

REVIEW AND ENGAGEMENT

When critically reading a research report, you would

- ☐ Determine if the authors explained their organizational approach (e.g., prioritization, chronological, equal weight) (see Figure 16.7)
- ☐ Determine if they opted to provide supportive statements/results/findings to justify their recommendations
- ☐ Check to see if they linked each recommendation back to some aspect of the research problem

TECHNICAL STRATEGIES FOR PRESENTING RECOMMENDATIONS

On a final note, as with other sections of a research paper or report, authors must be cognizant of some basic technical conventions and grammatical guidelines when preparing the Recommendations section (i.e., length, tense, voice, and person).

Length

If there is a separate Recommendations section, it is usually longer than the Conclusions section (which is one to two paragraphs in length). While a research paper normally has one single-spaced page or less for recommendations, a thesis, dissertation, technical report, or policy paper might have two to three pages of recommendations. The length of the

Recommendations section depends on which organizational categories and principles are being applied (see Figure 16.7). There is no hard-and-fast rule for length (Royal Melbourne Institute of Technology, 2008).

In fact, many research papers do not have a separate section for recommendations. Instead, authors may choose to weave their recommendations throughout their Discussion or Conclusions section. This is where they can judiciously use actionable, imperative, and modal verbs to their best advantage. They will also need to consciously use *main verbs* pursuant to the idea of recommendations: *recommend, suggest, advocate for, propose, advise, urge, is imperative that, is indicative of.*

> ***Example 16.19 No separate Recommendations section*** In a recent study about consumers' understandings of nutrition marketing terms, Haroldson and Yen (2016) tendered three strong recommendations in the last paragraph of their Discussion section, using the modal verb *should*, which indicates an obligation force. "Future studies *should explore* [emphasis added] these differences and make necessary modifications to ensure that validity and reliability are still well established. Future studies *should consider alternative* [emphasis added] data collection methods to validate the measurement items and yield relevant information about consumer behaviours and knowledge. Instead of using a convenience sample, researchers *should consider using* [emphasis added] market research panels, online forums, and listservs to reach a broader audience" (p. 31).

Active and Passive Voice

Although it is not wrong to use passive voice, Saga (2011) and others recommended that researchers should use active voice when preparing their recommendations. Active voice is more authoritative and assertive, better ensuring someone takes up the suggested action. Writing in an active voice uses direct action verbs rather than weaker, passive ones. When writing in passive voice, any version of the verb *to be* (*being, been*), conjugated (i.e., prefaced with *was, were, am, has, have, is, are*) and followed with the proposition *by*, is a sure indication of passive voice (Gammarly, 2017).

> ***Example 16.20 Simple example of passive and active voice***
>
> **Passive:** The leftovers *were eaten by* hungry children.
>
> **Active:** Hungry children *ate* the leftovers.

> ***Example 16.21 Research-focused passive and active voice***
>
> **Passive:** Future research about alcoholism in school *must be undertaken by* someone in the school system.
>
> **Active:** High school principals *must undertake* research about alcoholism in school.

The passive voice is used to show an interest in the person or object that *experiences* an action rather than the person or object that *performs* the action, which is active voice. Active voice is more likely to be noticed by readers because it makes the text sound more authoritative. Because it is more assertive, active voice is especially relevant in an argumentative essay (like a position paper) (Gammarly, 2017). The active voice version of example 16.21 is authoritative, assertive, and direct, while the passive voice is less convincing at first glance. It lacks punch and any motivation to act because no one is targeted for action.

Authors should also use the passive form if they think that the thing receiving the action is more important or should receive the most emphasis. They can also use the passive form if they do not know who is doing the action or if they do not want to mention who should be doing the action. In example 16.20, the passive voice focuses on the leftovers, and the active voice focuses on the children. The active voice makes the identity of who is taking action very clear, enabling the author to direct attention to this person. In example 16.21, the passive voice focuses on the research (which is to be acted upon), and the active voice focuses on the principals (who are supposed to take action). On a final note, if the author wants to specifically identify who should take or avoid action, passive voice would be more appropriate ([not] done *by* whom) (Saga, 2011).

Example 16.22 Recommendation identifying actor (passive)

Passive: Results from this study support the recommendation that university assignments *should* not be graded *by* professors using red ink [focus on who should *not* be acting].

Active: Results from this study support the recommendation that university assignments *should* not be *graded* with red ink [focus on the action].

Grammar

On a more technical note, recommendations should be grammatically parallel. Parallel structure entails using the same pattern of words when two or more ideas are connected, creating the impression that all ideas are of equal importance. In a parallel sentence structure, authors do not mix up suffixes in a string of clauses (e.g., *ing*, *ed*, *s*, *ion*). They choose one suffix and use it consistently (Bellanca, 1998; Bentley, 2011; Morel, 2012; Centre for Independent Language Learning, 2008b).

Example 16.23 Parallel sentence structure

Incorrect: The author provided several reasons for why it is important to be research literate. She listed "build*ing* confidence, gain*ed* integrity, and ensure*s* a reputation.

Corrected (with *ing*): The author provided several reasons for why it is important to be research literate. She listed "build*ing* confidence, gain*ing* integrity, and ensur*ing* a reputation."

REVIEW AND ENGAGEMENT

When critically reading a research report, you would

- ☐ Determine if the authors followed the recommended conventions for length, tense, voice, person, and grammar

- ☐ Decide whether any inadequate appreciation for these conventions affected your judgment of the rigor of the research.

FINAL JUDGMENT ON RECOMMENDATIONS

Taking *all* of the **Review and Engagement** criteria into account, what is your final judgment of the Recommendations section in the paper you are critically reading?

CHAPTER SUMMARY

This chapter focused on the importance of recommendations and how best to frame and present them. The conversation started with the caveat that recommendations cannot come out of the blue. They have to "follow from" the argument threaded through the paper (see Figure 16.1). After distinguishing between conclusions and recommendations (and the different roles they play) (see Figure 16.2), the discussion turned to the nine purposes that recommendations can serve, followed with an overview of the eight characteristics of effective recommendations. The chapter then turned to the topic of verbs when writing recommendations, with a special focus on modal verbs and on modal force (the writer's conviction when posing the recommendation). There are three modal forces (certainty, possibility, and obligation), and each is recognizable through the use of particular modal verbs. An extensive overview of strategies for crafting, presenting, and organizing a Recommendations section was provided (see Figure 16.7). The chapter ended with some basic grammatical conventions, especially the use of passive and active voice.

REVIEW AND DISCUSSION QUESTIONS

1. Compare and contrast the role of conclusions and recommendations. Do you think it would cause confusion if they were combined in the same few paragraphs? Why?

2. What does the term *self-evident* mean in relation to forming recommendations (hint: use Figure 16.1)?

3. By posing recommendations, authors try to tell others what actions the latter should take in the future. What sorts of actions can authors choose from when framing their recommendations (see Figure 16.3)? Do you think any of these actions are more important than others? Why?

4. If authors do choose to present recommendations for future actions, what criteria should be used to judge if they have developed a good and an effective recommendation?

5. Recommendations are concerned with future actions; hence, verb choice is an important decision made by authors. Compare and contrast the three types of verbs that come into play when writing recommendations.

6. Why do modal verbs play such an important role when framing recommendations? What conclusions can a critical reader draw from the author's choice of modal verb?

7. Why is the mood of the author (as conveyed by the modal verb) so important for a critical reader of a set of recommendations? What three moods (modal forces) can be conveyed by verb choice? Which of these forces do you think is most compelling (i.e., likely to make you take action)?

8. What conclusions might a critical reader draw if there is a disconnect between the argument and the evidence presented in the Discussion section and the choice of modal verb in the recommendation?

9. What risk do authors take if they do not *consciously* select their modal verbs when writing their recommendations?

10. Why is active versus passive voice so important when writing recommendations?

11. What does the phrase "scope of the recommendation" mean? What should be the minimum scope of a recommendation, and why?

12. Authors have to make a lot of decisions when deciding how to present their recommendations relative to their supportive argument and evidence. Identify and explain each of six such organizational approaches. Why does it matter if the author presents recommendations in a list or in paragraphs (prose form)?

13. What are the implications regarding the impact of the study, if the author chooses to not provide recommendations?

ARGUMENTATIVE ESSAYS AND THEORETICAL PAPERS

ARGUMENTATIVE ESSAYS: POSITION, DISCUSSION, AND THINK-PIECE PAPERS

INTRODUCTION

This book has addressed how to implement and to critique the components of a basic research paper: research methodology, research question and introduction, literature review, theory/conceptual framework, methods, results/findings, discussion, conclusions, and recommendations. But not all research or its presentation conforms to the principles of this approach (McLean, 2011). Authors choosing to write position, discussion, or think-piece papers have to conform to the principles of sound reasoning and effective argumentation. Argumentative essays are "a legitimate and important form of [scholarly] discourse" (Kennedy, 2007, p. 139). Weaknesses in the argumentative logic and reasoning of these papers threaten the rigor of the scholarship (Wiersma & Jurs, 2009).

Despite there being subtle differences among position, discussion, and think-piece papers, to be explained, their similarities as a genre of writing justify the focus of this chapter. They all depend on a solid argument; hence, authors must use the proper criteria for developing an argument grounded in persuasive writing and rhetoric, and solid logic and argumentation (McLean, 2011; Morrow & Weston, 2016).

ARGUMENTATIVE ESSAYS

The process of argumentation involves a higher level of reasoning than that associated with conventional research papers. Indeed, the entire paper is based on a proposition or a premise about some topic—that is, a proposal offered for acceptance or rejection. Anticipating objections, authors use their scholarly paper to present their reasoned attempt to sway others to accept their logic and evidence in support of this proposition. They often use a particular format to organize their paper:

LEARNING OBJECTIVES

- Appreciate that argumentative essays are judged on the principles of sound reasoning and argumentation

- Explain the essence of what is involved in getting people to accept a proposition or premise about a topic or issue

- Compare and contrast the purpose of position (opinion), discussion, and think-piece papers

- Elaborate upon the format for argumentative essays (thesis, antithesis, synthesis)

- Appreciate the role of persuasive writing and rhetorical appeals in argumentative essays

- Explain Aristotle's three forms of rhetoric (ethos, pathos, logos), and describe the intent of the rhetorical triangle

- Compare and contrast deductive and inductive argumentation

- Appreciate the power of logical fallacies

thesis (introduction), antithesis (body of the paper), and synthesis (conclusion). Their persuasive rhetoric (appeals to logic, emotion, and character) requires the accumulation, judgment, and use of evidence; the use of deductive and inductive logic; and the avoidance of fallacious reasoning (Morrow & Weston, 2016; Scott, 1998).

Succinctly, the argumentative essay is a genre of writing that requires authors to (a) investigate a topic; (b) collect, generate, and evaluate evidence; (c) establish a position on the topic; and then (d) present a clear thesis, expanded upon with sound reasoning, logic, and argumentation. Through extensive research of the literature and previously published material, authors learn about the topic and understand different points of view regarding the topic so they can choose their *own* position and then support it with the evidence collected during their research (antithesis and synthesis) (Baker, Brizee, & Angeli, 2013).

Western Logic

As a caveat, this chapter about argumentation is grounded in Western notions of philosophy, logic, and rationality, appreciating there are alternative approaches. For example, Western logic, based on Greek thought, is dualistic (either/or) and sequential and linear. It cannot handle contradictions and randomness very well, approaching these using deductive and inductive logic. Eastern logic is pluralistic (and/also) and can support contradictory and conflicting patterns of thought. It is both sequential and able to see patterns and cycles (Rohmann, 1999; Smith, 2011).

COMPARING POSITION, DISCUSSION, AND THINK-PIECE PAPERS

Position papers (sometimes called opinion or white papers), discussion papers, and think pieces are legitimate tools for contributing to the cumulative improvement of theoretical knowledge and to help ideas grow (Max Planck Institute of Economics, 2006; McLean, 2011).

They are vehicles for sharing potentially profound perspectives, which can stimulate wider discussion, debate, dialogue, and discourse (Bamber, 2014; European Health Psychology Society, 2014). Authors who want to persuade and influence others to accept their opinions and perspectives can opt for this type of academic research paper (McLean, 2011; Morrow & Weston, 2016; Sanders, Tingloo, & Verhulst, 2005; Tucker, Derelian, & Rouner, 1997). The differences between these three legitimate forms of an argumentative essay will now be explained (see Figure 17.1).

Position (Opinion) and Discussion Papers

Position is Latin *positionem*, "affirmation," a statement asserting the existence or truth of something. Discussion is Latin *discussionem*, "examination or investigation." Distinctly different, *position* means *a* point of view on a topic, and *discussion* means an *exchange of* views on a topic (Anderson, 2014; Harper, 2016). The main difference between these two types of papers is that position papers entail an explicit expression of *a* position on an issue while discussion papers share balanced information on a topic (several perspectives) without necessarily espousing any particular position (American Academy of Family Physicians, 2016).

FIGURE 17.1   ■   Comparing Position, Discussion, and Think-Piece Papers

Position Paper	Discussion Paper	Think-Piece Paper
• Author asserts a *personal* statement about a topic or issue based on a well-reasoned argument • Author takes a position on an issue • Author anticipates the opinion has merit and is worthy of others' consideration and adoption	• Author locates, analyzes, and synthesizes \ others' *exchanges* on a topic or issue • Author shares a balanced coverage *(investigation)* of others' positions on, and knowledge of, an issue or a topic (their perspectives) • Author anticipates that the soundly argued discussion will become part of the larger conversation	• Author shares conceptually advanced, yet evolving, views on a topic • Through reasoned arguments, author raises questions and challenges current thinking • Author anticipates feedback and hopes to stimulate thinking and provoke academic dialogue, debate, or discourse

In a position paper, the authors' role is to choose, defend, explain, and document the reasoning behind *their* point of view or position. *Opinion* is Latin *opinari*, "to think, believe" (Harper, 2016). It is a view or judgment ideally, but not necessarily, based on facts or knowledge (Anderson, 2014). After researching the topic, authors should form their *own* opinion, which is why these are sometimes called *opinion papers*. Conversely, in a discussion paper, the author has to find and present various perspectives on an issue, ideas that might become part of a larger, discipline-wide or practice-focused discussion on the topic (Anderson, 2014; Maimon, Peritz, & Yancey, 2005; McLean, 2011; Murray, 2003). In a discussion paper, authors do not necessarily articulate any preferred position, but they can (American Academy of Family Physicians, 2016).

Both papers are the same in that they present arguable positions intended to convince readers that the authors' ideas are valid, defensible, and worth heeding. They both contain background information in the form of data, a literature review, or both, integrated with the authors' opinions and their reasoned arguments. Both papers follow the conventions of an argumentative essay, to be discussed shortly (McLean, 2011; Murray, 2003).

Example 17.1 Position (opinion) paper (explicit position on an issue)

Recently, the *Animal* journal published an opinion piece (position paper) on the role of livestock in a sustainable diet from a land-use perspective (van Zanten, Meerburg, Bikker, Herrero, & de Boer, 2016). The authors *took the position* that optimal use of human food waste leftover streams enables the livestock sector to produce protein (meat for human consumption) by feeding the human food leftovers to animals so as to avoid competition for arable land to both feed animals and feed humans. They *developed their position* by integrating background information (from a literature review) with their own ideas to tender a *succession of opinions* (arguments) in support of their final position. They prefaced each opinion with their assumptions, and they addressed self-posed questions to help develop their position (e.g., "We asked ourselves," "Should we shift to," "What does this mean"). *In their reasoned opinion*, we can create a diet that sustains the world population (achieve food security) while mitigating competition for scarce, arable land to feed livestock and to feed humans. *It was their opinion* that arable land should not be used to feed animals so humans can eat their protein. Their paper shared their arguments for this position, asserting that it makes an important contribution to future sustainable diets.

Example 17.2 Discussion paper (collection of views on an issue)

The *International Journal of Nursing Studies* published a discussion paper about the link between physical health problems and serious mental illness (SMI) (Robson & Gray, 2007). They immediately clarified that their "paper *summarises and synthesises* [emphasis added] the current literature on the physical health of people with serious mental illness and *adds to the debate* [emphasis added]" (Robson & Gray, 2007, p. 457). Per the tenets of a discussion paper, they drew on a *variety of perspectives* to share an exchange of ideas found in the literature about this issue. Their argumentative logic first involved addressing the epidemiology of the morbidity and mortality of people with SMI, to make the point that they die due to physical health problems that can be responsibly monitored and treated. This argumentative strategy served to anchor the next part of their logic, which was a discussion of why people with SMI have such poor physical health. The purpose of this protracted, wide-ranging discussion was to prepare readers for their closing point that routine monitoring of people with SMI is required to best ensure their optimal care. In particular, they anticipated their discussion would *add to the debate* about the role of the mental health nurse in monitoring people with SMI. *They argued that* it is a life-and-death issue.

Length, person, tense, and tone

Position (opinion) and discussion papers tend to average three to five single-spaced pages in length. Complex issues will require longer papers. The Introduction section should comprise several paragraphs. The Conclusions section should be one to two paragraphs, with the bulk of the paper treating the arguments.

These types of papers should be written in active voice, present tense, and third person (American Institute for Conservation of Historic and Artistic Works [AIC], 2013; Dowden, 2004; Landsberger, ca. 1996; McLean, 2011; Wheeling Jesuit University, n.d.). Authors should minimize use of first person, reserving it for personal anecdotes if these strengthen their argument. Second person (e.g., *you, yours*) should be avoided because it implies the reader is either the target or the accomplice of the writer, which should not be the case. The argumentative paper is intended to communicate the author's defendable opinion, which was reasoned and developed independently of others (Wheeling Jesuit University, n.d.).

As well, authors should remain conscious of the tone of the document, striving for diplomacy mixed with authority rather than superiority or condescension (see Chapter 14 for a discussion of humble, conservative writing). This tone can be achieved by avoiding words like *obviously, of course, surely*, and *without doubt*. Resorting to use of these words conveys the impression that rationality and reason have taken a back seat to a cogent and valid argument (Wheeling Jesuit University, n.d.). Finally, authors should not get too personal nor should they attack others when developing arguments for their position or perspective (McLean, 2011).

Transition words

Authors need to prepare clear transition statements so readers can follow the argument and appreciate when a new claim is being made. Transition statements reflect the author's approach to developing a logically coherent argument and contribute to the flow of the argument (AIC, 2013; Dowden, 2004; Guilford, 2015; Landsberger, ca. 1996; McLean, 2011; Murray, 2003; Wheeling Jesuit University, n.d.).

In more detail, transition phrases and words "help the reader progress from one idea (expressed by the author) to the next idea. Thus, they help to build up coherent relationships within the text. . . . [T]hey not only connect ideas, but can also introduce a certain shift, contrast, or opposition, emphasis or agreement, purpose, result or conclusion, etc. in the line of argument" (Possel, 2013). Examples of transition words and phrases are presented in Table 17.1 (Possel, 2013). They are considered to be cohesive devices that help hold the argument together. They are the glue of the red thread that helps authors weave their argument into a convincing, cohesive whole.

TABLE 17.1 ■ Examples of Transition Phrases and Words		
Type of Transition	**Sample Transition Phrases**	**Sample Transition Words**
Agreement, addition, similarity	• *in light of* • *equally important* • *not to mention* • *to say nothing of* • *in the first place* • *as a matter of fact* • *not only . . . but also*	• *moreover* • *as well as* • *together with* • *correspondingly* • *furthermore* • *comparatively* • *similarly*
Support, emphasis, or examples	• *in other words* • *said another way* • *that is to say* • *important to realize* • *with attention to* • *for this reason* • *another key point*	• *notably* • *especially* • *to demonstrate* • *for instance* • *certainly* • *surely* • *to be sure*

(Continued)

TABLE 17.1 ■ (Continued)

Type of Transition	Sample Transition Phrases	Sample Transition Words
Effect, consequence, result	• *as a result* • *under those circumstances* • *in that case* • *for this reason*	• because • then • hence • therefore • consequently • accordingly • thus
Opposition, contradiction, limitation	• *in contrast* • *of course . . . , but* • *at the same time* • *on the other hand* • *then again* • *after all* • *in spite of*	• but • or • while/although • instead • nonetheless • regardless • however
Purpose, condition, cause	• *granted (that)* • *to that end* • *in order to* • *seeing/being that* • *on the condition that* • *for the purpose of* • *in view of*	• in case • when • if • because • as • since • inasmuch as
Conclusion, summary, restatement	• *in the final analysis* • *all things considered* • *for the most part* • *generally speaking* • *as can be seen* • *in any event* • *in either case*	• usually • in summary • in conclusion • in brief • on balance • altogether • overall

Think-Piece Papers

Sometimes authors use think pieces to share their unpublished and evolving views on a topic. They are often used to test ideas and arguments as a precursor to research to be published at a later date. Think pieces are also useful for stimulating other people's thinking about the author's large ideas, which are at an advanced stage of conception. These papers constitute very valuable research because academic think pieces entail rigorous scholarship, argumentation, and intellectual contributions (Max Planck Institute of Economics, 2006). Like position papers, they reflect an amalgamation of literature and the authors' intellectual insights. The authors' argument can lose credibility if their literature review omits essential citations and contrasting perspectives (Kline & Farrell, 2005) and if their argument is not cogent and/or valid (Lindsay, 2012).

Think pieces deeply reflect an author's professional and personal engagement with an idea of importance and substance. Through a think piece, authors can raise questions and challenge crucial concepts in the field, often leading to innovations. Think pieces are intellectually stimulating (Cohen, 2014; Lindsay, 2012). They serve to facilitate academic discussion of emerging topics and key ideas without the benefit of empirical evidence (i.e., primary experimentation or study). Instead, authors anticipate future validation of the ideas if or when other scholars or practitioners judge they have merit (Lindsay, 2012; Max Planck Institute of Economics, 2006) (see Figure 17.1).

Example 17.3 Think pieces (provoking people to think about an issue)

- Before it held a full conference on the topic, the United Nations Research Institute for Social Development (UNRISD) arranged for a think-piece series about the social and solidarity economy (see www.unrisd.org/ ssethinkpieces). These ideas were used before, during, and after the conference (see an example at Utting, 2013).

- UNRISD's recent *Young Scholars Think Piece Series* is intended to offer alternative perspectives about social development, highlight marginalized viewpoints, and bring to the fore neglected issues as viewed by younger scholars. Four papers were published in the first edition of these think pieces (see an example at Tengler, 2014).

- The Washington-based *Transparency and Accountability Initiative* (www .transparency-initiative.org) published three think pieces in a 2015 series on citizens' movements and state accountability (for an example, see Halloran & Flores, 2015).

- In the spirit of achieving the United Nations' sustainable development goals (SDGs), the Seoul-based United Nations Development Programme (UNDP) announced a new *Development Solutions Think Piece Series*, with one paper posted (see Messick, 2015).

Because think pieces are intended to provoke thought, the authors' ideas should be conceptually rich. These papers should contain judiciously selected background material (e.g., data and literature) that reflects the authors' personal opinion and their analysis of an idea (Cohen, 2014; "Think Piece," 2016). Beyond engagement with data and literature, the author must also "make intellectually sound, and academically appropriate, judgments [and arguments]" (Cohen, 2014, p. 1). The resultant think piece is judged for "the quality, depth, and complexity of the argument; the use of evidence to support the thesis; [and] the clarity and elegance of the prose" (Cohen, 2014, p. 1). The latter is enriched with the creative use of transition phrases and words (see Table 17.1).

Length and format

There is no one standard or uniform format for a think piece. They vary in length and the extent of idea elaboration (Cohen, 2014; Piantanida, 2001). But because they too depend on the development of a sound argument, *academic think pieces* should be considered argumentative essays and prepared and judged accordingly (see the next section).

REVIEW AND ENGAGEMENT

When critically reading a research report, you would

☐ Ascertain if the authors clearly identified their paper as a position, discussion, or think piece (see Figure 17.1)

☐ Per the above, determine if they articulated *their* position in a position paper, shared an integration of *other* people's perspectives in a discussion paper, and tendered *their* developing conceptual and theoretical ideas in a think piece (see Figure 17.1); that is, they adhered to the purpose of each type of essay

☐ Check to see if they followed the recommended conventions for length, tense, voice, person, and the use of transition phrases and words

FORMAT FOR ARGUMENTATIVE PAPERS

The discussion now turns to a fairly detailed overview of the format employed when writing argumentative essays. *Argument* is Latin *arguere*, "to prove, demonstrate, make clear" (Harper, 2016). Argument can mean both (a) a heated exchange and (b) a set of reasons given in support of something (Anderson, 2014). In the context of argumentative essays, an argument does not mean a fight or a disagreement. Instead, an argument is an attempt to persuade others by giving reasons or evidence (premises) for a particular position (claim) (to be discussed shortly) (Bennett, 2015; Guilford, 2015; Morrow & Weston, 2016; The Writing Center, 2014a; Wallace & Wray, 2011).

Arguments are an important concept in academic writing and research. To develop these persuasive messages, an argumentative, academic essay comprises three parts: (a) the introduction (thesis), (b) the body or antithesis (the author's arguments with their supportive evidence contrasted with counterarguments), and (c) the conclusions (synthesis) (Guilford, 2015; Johnson, 2000; Kashatus, 2002; Morrow & Weston, 2016; Sanders et al., 2005) (see Figure 17.2 and Table 17.2).

Introduction/Thesis

In the Introduction section, authors should introduce the topic and related issues along with pertinent background information, followed with a thesis statement (one sentence, not framed as a question). The thesis equates to the authors' basic premise from which subsequent statements can be inferred (Anderson, 2014; Murray, 2003). The thesis is the authors' point of view on the topic—that is, the position they are going to endorse. Authors base their entire argument on this premise, proposition, or thesis

FIGURE 17.2 ■ Thesis, Antithesis, and Synthesis

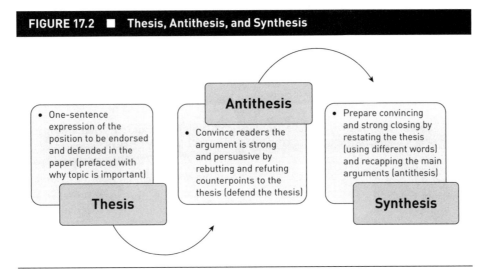

- **Thesis**
  - One-sentence expression of the position to be endorsed and defended in the paper (prefaced with why topic is important)

- **Antithesis**
  - Convince readers the argument is strong and persuasive by rebutting and refuting counterpoints to the thesis (defend the thesis)

- **Synthesis**
  - Prepare convincing and strong closing by restating the thesis (using different words) and recapping the main arguments (antithesis)

TABLE 17.2 ■ Elements of an Academic Argumentative Essay

Elements of Argumentative Essay	Parallel Research Paper Element	Explained
Thesis (Greek *thesis*, "a proposition")	Introduction	Anticipating others will not agree, authors follow an explication of background information on a topic with a one-sentence expression of the position they are going to endorse and defend in their paper.
Antithesis (Greek *antitithenai*, "set against")	Body of the Paper	This section of the paper contains the authors' three or more main arguments (claims) in favor of their thesis with supportive evidence (cited facts and opinions) contrasted with counterarguments. The authors try to convince readers that their argument is strong and persuasive by rebutting and refuting counterpoints to their thesis. They can either reject another point, say it is irrelevant to their thesis, or say their point is stronger than another valid one.
Synthesis (Greek *sunthesis*, "place together")	Conclusions	In order to close strongly and convince readers to believe them, the authors have to restate why their topic is important, restate their thesis (using different words), recap their three main arguments, and create a wrap-up statement that reflects their complex argument.

(Dowden, 2004; Kashatus, 2002; University of Hawaii, 1998). For this reason, the thesis must be *arguable*, meaning a reasonable person could disagree with it. An obvious and indisputable truth will not work as a thesis. A good thesis statement inherently demands proof because the authors' goal in an academic argument is to gain acceptance of their ideas in an arena where others, for their own reasons, may not agree (Guilford, 2015; Morrow & Weston, 2016; Murray, 2003; Sanders et al., 2005).

> ***Example 17.4 Thesis statement*** The thesis "all children should be given a proper diet" is weak because no reasonable person would disagree. The thesis statement "all schools should provide students with breakfast so they can be more assured of a proper diet" is more controversial. Not everyone holds the same view of the role of schools relative to parents or guardians. Upon stating this thesis, the author now has to make the case that many parents cannot adequately feed their own children, meaning the school has a responsibility to assume this role.

Body/Antithesis

Antithesis means being in opposition to something. Preparing an antithesis is a rhetorical device (see next section) whereby authors pull together contrasting ideas, with the intent to argue for their *own* points (Anderson, 2014). In the body of the paper, authors should clearly set out the points they want to make in defense or support of their main thesis. Authors should have no fewer than three serious arguments (claims) to support their thesis, and they must be discussed in depth, with evidence (Landsberger, ca. 1996; Murray, 2003; Scott, 1998; The Writing Center, 2014a). These should be informed and educated points, with documentation to back them up (Landsberger, ca. 1996; Murray, 2003).

When developing their counterpoints to opposing arguments, authors can either (a) acknowledge that someone else *has* a good point, and then try to convince readers of the merit of their *own* argument; (b) maintain the other argument is irrelevant; or (c) reject the other point and explain why it is mistaken (Murray, 2003; Ozagac, 2006; Sanders et al., 2005; The Writing Center, 2014a). Their intent is to convince others that opposing points of view are not convincing enough to dismiss the thesis they are arguing and the position being discussed (Guilford, 2015).

The main reasons for rebutting or refuting counterpoints (i.e., opposing views to the authors' ideas) are insufficient, partially correct, or completely wrong claims by others (Ozagac, 2006). The author's intent is to convince readers that *their* argument is stronger and more convincing than the counterarguments for their position (thesis) (Guilford, 2015; Morrow & Weston, 2016; Murray, 2003). The following examples illustrate refutations to counterpoints of an argument about the merits of using Reiki (a healing technique based on channeling energy) (Ozagac, 2006, p. 3).

> ***Example 17.5 Counterargument*** People should trust Western medicine instead of traditional medicine because the former is effective and scientifically proven.
>
> ***Refuting insufficient claim*** Reiki is also scientifically proven to be effective and does not have side effects.

Example 17.6 Counterargument Serious illnesses and cancer cannot be treated with traditional medicine. They require modern medicine.

Refuting partially correct claim But modern medicine cannot treat serious illnesses if they are not diagnosed in time.

Example 17.7 Counterargument Reiki, like all alternative healing methods, requires a lot of time.

Refuting completely wrong claim If done regularly, Reiki requires less time for healing than modern treatments.

Evidence

Authors must provide evidence to support their arguments (i.e., both their pushback against counteropinions and their assertion of their own claim). This evidence normally comprises some combination of facts and opinions (Claremont College, 2011; Kashatus, 2002; Landsberger, ca. 1996; Morrow & Weston, 2016; Scott, 1998; University of Hawaii, 1998; Wallace & Wray, 2011; Wheeling Jesuit University, n.d.). Examples of facts include scientific measurements, eyewitness testimony, statistics, and verifiable factual knowledge. Authors can also draw on expert opinions and testimony expressed by an established authority in the field—that is, informed opinions developed through research or competence (e.g., a child psychologist or a lawyer). Authors may judiciously draw on anecdotal evidence (Baker et al., 2013; Wheeling Jesuit University, n.d.), being careful not to introduce fallacies (i.e., a failure in their reasoning) (see the last section of this chapter).

When presenting their evidence, authors have to ensure that it is strong, convincing, and from a variety of sources (Baker et al., 2013; Claremont College, 2011; Wallace & Wray, 2011). Each argument should be supported by at least three sources of evidence (Murray, 2003). These references add to the credibility of the position being argued or to the points of discussion (AIC, 2013; Kashatus, 2002; Landsberger, ca. 1996; Murray, 2003; University of Hawaii, 1998; Wheeling Jesuit University, n.d.).

Conclusion/Synthesis

To wrap up an argumentative essay, authors should (a) restate why their topic is important, (b) forcefully reiterate their thesis (using different words than in the introduction), (c) recap their main arguments with supportive evidence, and (d) synthesize the discussion into an effective and logical wrap-up statement (Baker et al., 2013; Landsberger, ca. 1996; Morrow & Weston, 2016; Murray, 2003; Sanders et al., 2005). The authors' objective at the end of a position or discussion paper is to "close strongly" and make readers believe them (Scott, 1998, p. 4). This is possible if authors can convincingly illustrate that (a) they have a sophisticated understanding of issues and opposing positions and (b) their arguments are complex and well reasoned, with substantial evidence (Claremont College, 2011).

Box 17.1 illustrates the progression from thesis through antithesis to synthesis. In preparation for the 2014 *Higher Education Close Up* conference in Lancaster, England, keynote speakers were asked to prepare a think piece as a preamble to their formal keynote. Bamber (2014) used the argumentative essay format for her think piece.

BOX 17.1

Progression From Thesis Through Antithesis to Synthesis in an Argumentative Essay (quotations from Bamber, 2014, emphasis added)

Introduction

"*I am especially interested in* how we make a difference by involving university staff in the scholarship of teaching and learning (SOTL), and, specifically, how we can use scholarship to help them change practices."

Thesis Statement

"How [can] we engage staff in SOTL who might not otherwise be inclined to do so? At what level, and in what ways? *I will argue* that the 'think global, act local' notion is useful here. *My suggested approach is* for staff to use high level, global data in combination with local data to generate meaningful evidence for their own context."

Body (antithesis)

"In [this] section I will *lay out my terrain of interest—* postgraduate taught provision—and *some of the evidence* available to us globally." After saying "I *will consider* how we can tackle the lack of helpful evidence around PGT [postgraduate-taught students], especially at the local level," Bamber presented three arguments (claims) with supportive evidence:

Claim (argument) 1: "Further investigation is required . . . *I would suggest* that this further investigation has to take place at the local level, as close as possible to the programmes in question, *because* the complexity of PG provision means that each site will throw up its own idiosyncrasies."

Claim (argument) 2: "How can we gather evidence to learn from our students, inform our teaching, and increase our own scholarship? . . . *I suggest* an evidence-informed approach, using multiple data sources, with a different mix in each context. These multiple data sources are then triangulated, cross-validated by looking at the situation from several angles. Three different sources of data are in the mix: Research, Evaluation and Practice Wisdom."

Claim (argument) 3: "How, then, to take this mix of data, and move from gathering evidence on the PG student experience to scholarship? And how to involve colleagues (and students) in that scholarship? *I would contend* that scholarship has certain key elements [which can be managed by] . . . taking a systematic approach to investigating what students are experiencing, with the aim of advancing practice *beyond* our own classrooms, not just *in* them."

Conclusion (synthesis)

"*At the beginning of this piece*, I asked how we engage staff in SOTL who might not otherwise be inclined to do so? At what level, and in what ways? *I have suggested* that an evidence-informed 'think global, act local' approach, using global data such as surveys in conjunction with our own local data, is *most helpful* in encouraging scholarship in the PGT student experience."

REVIEW AND ENGAGEMENT

When critically reading a research report, you would

☐ For any of these types of argumentative essays, determine if the authors presented a well-reasoned and strongly articulated argument, convincing you of their ideas, with substantive evidence

☐ Determine if they demonstrated the ability to correctly present their thesis, antithesis, and synthesis by following the tenets of a sound argumentative essay (see Figure 17.2 and Table 17.2)

☐ Per the above, check to see if they especially showed they know how to deal with counterarguments to their basic premise (an arguable, one-sentence thesis)

☐ Per the above, determine if they were able to address all sides to an issue, take a side, and then persuade others of their particular argument (antithesis)

PERSUASIVE WRITING AND RHETORICAL APPEALS

Because position, discussion, and think-piece papers strive to *persuade* readers toward an argument, they demand persuasive writing (AIC, 2013; Maimon et al., 2005; McLean, 2011; Scott, 1998). To persuade means to induce someone to something (to lead someone) through reasoning or argument (AIC, 2013; Anderson, 2014; Axelrod & Cooper, 1993). In a position paper, authors have to address all sides of an issue, then take one side and persuade readers to accept their arguments. In order to persuade readers that their argument is valid and sound (deductive argument) or cogent and strong (inductive argument), authors have to know their audience and have insights into how they think and will react to the arguments presented in the paper (Murray, 2003; Scott, 1998).

Actually, authors "need to be *persuasive*, not *loud*. The point is not to beat an idea to death, but to invite the reader to look squarely at opposing points of view and conclude that the side you've chosen to argue is, after all, the most reasonable argument" (Wheeling Jesuit University, n.d.). The more compelling the collection of facts and opinions (evidence), the more persuasive the argument (Claremont College, 2011; Landsberger, ca. 1996). Persuasive writing hinges on Aristotle's three forms of rhetoric (ethos, pathos, and logos), which are discussed next. This topic is followed with a section on deductive and inductive argumentation, with the chapter ending on a discussion of logical fallacies.

Aristotle's Three Forms of Rhetoric

Rhetor means orator, speaker, or communicator (Harper, 2016). *Rhetoric* refers to authors using language in a persuasive or effective manner so as to convince readers or audiences of their views regarding a topic or an issue (Hanson, 2011). Aristotle identified three forms of rhetoric: ethos, pathos, and logos. *Ethos* (Greek for *character* and *ethical*) refers to the author's credibility and reputation, *pathos* (Greek for *experience*) to the readers' emotions, and *logos* (Greek for *word*) to a well-reasoned argument (Callaway, 2007; Fahnestock, 2002; Guilford, 2015; Hanson, 2011; Perkins, 2007) (see Table 17.3 and Figure 17.3).

Rhetorical Triangle

Guilford (2015) suggested that authors should combine these three appeals to create balanced arguments. Fahnestock (2002) recommended starting with ethos (the author's character and credibility), then moving to pathos (emotionally reaching the audience), and ending with logos (the actual, reasoned arguments). The intent is to "weave the various appeals into a single convincing argument" (Guilford, 2015, p. 7). Indeed, the three rhetorical elements are interconnected, often represented in the rhetorical triangle (see Figure 17.4). To best address ethos, authors have to find their *own* attitude about the topic and work out how they understand it. This insight better helps them express their persona, or voice. Authors also need to consider their audience's expectations, knowledge level, and dispositions regarding the topic (pathos). With these understandings in hand (themselves and the audience), authors can better develop persuasive and convincing arguments (logos) (Hanson, 2011).

FIGURE 17.3 ■ Three Forms of Rhetorical Appeal

ETHOS
- Greek, *character* and *ethics*
- Author's credibility and reputation (appeal to readers' need for trustworthy sources)

PATHOS
- Greek, *experience*
- Author needs to anticipate and appeal to readers' emotions, values, beliefs, experiences

LOGOS
- Greek, *words*
- Author's well-reasoned argument (appeal to readers' rationality, and ability to reach conclusions)

FIGURE 17.4 ■ Rhetorical Triangle

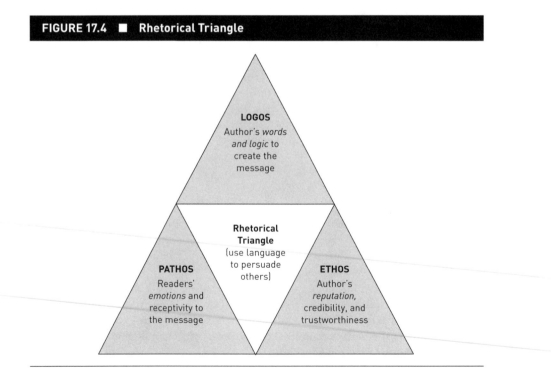

TABLE 17.3 ■ Aristotle's Three Forms of Rhetorical Appeal		
Ethos **Evoke Trust**	**Pathos** **Evoke Emotions**	**Logos** **Evoke Reason**
• Persuade readers by appealing to their need for a trustworthy source • The credibility of the argument is based on the author's reputation • The argument is trustworthy if the author is trustworthy and seen to have authority and respect regarding the topic • Also, claims are more credible if the document is free of internal errors in syntax, grammar, and mechanics	• Persuade readers by appealing to their emotions • By respecting the readers' anticipated feelings about the issue, authors can place them in a better mood to receive the arguments • This appeal reaches their emotions, values, beliefs, experiences, dispositions, attitudes, and knowledge about the issue or topic • This appeal also touches readers' sense of identity and their self-interest	• Persuade readers by appealing to their rationality and by using logical reasoning (deductive and inductive) • By providing true and tangible evidence (i.e., by giving reasons), authors can appeal to readers' logical mental powers to form conclusions, judgments, and inferences (through the clarity of their claims) • This appeal is strengthened by the use of quotations, citations from experts and related literature, statistics, and factual data

Ethos

Regarding *ethos*, authors are trying to demonstrate respect for readers' ideas and values, evoking their trust in the argument (Callaway, 2007). Authors have to avoid alienating readers with their arguments (Guilford, 2015). Readers may not accept an author's argument if evidence is misrepresented, implications have been misunderstood, or individuals or groups are maligned (Guilford, 2015). To offset this possibility, Hanson (2011) recommended that authors respect multiple viewpoints when developing their arguments, reference their sources used for evidence, and be conscious of the tone of the paper. She also advised authors to step back and make sure they actually have the appropriate background for the topic. Are they knowledgeable enough to develop valid and/or cogent arguments for this topic? A well-written document and clear prose also improve people's opinions of the worthiness of an author's ideas (i.e., no syntax, mechanical, or grammatical errors). As simple as it sounds, good writing and prose improve the credibility of any claim.

Pathos

When it comes to *pathos*, authors are trying to get readers to identify with the topic by evoking an emotional response from them (Callaway, 2007). However, authors have to avoid creating the impression that emotions are subverting reason. They can do this by being conscious of "the overall texture of the argument," which is shaped by their choice of words, whose "force is cumulative" (Guilford, 2015, p. 11). Hanson (2011) cautioned authors to ask themselves if they are manipulating readers or if their own emotions are in conflict with the logic they are trying to exercise. Readers may also reject arguments if they feel insulted or that their self-interest or identity is being challenged (Fahnestock, 2002).

Logos

Regarding *logos*, authors are trying to evoke a cognitive, rational response from readers or their audience (Callaway, 2007). Readers will be less alienated if the authors' arguments are free of faulty reasoning and logical fallacies and if their premises are true and arguments are valid and sound or cogent and strong (Guilford, 2015) (to be discussed in the final two sections of this chapter). To offset this possibility, authors must support their arguments with strong reasons and credible evidence (i.e., be well documented) and ensure that their logical argument is arranged in well-reasoned order (Hanson, 2011). Readers will be less inclined to reject an argument if the authors' facts and values resonate with them; that is, they can agree upon them. These facts and opinions are contained in the premises and assumptions of the argument, justifying and supporting the ultimate claim the authors are trying to make (Fahnestock, 2002).

REVIEW AND ENGAGEMENT

When critically reading a research report, you would

- ☐ Determine if the authors demonstrated an appreciation for the importance of *persuasive* writing, without which they were not able to convince you of the merit of their argument

- ☐ Confirm that they effectively melded a combination of the three forms of *rhetoric* or judiciously chose one of them to make their point (ethos, pathos, logos) (see Figure 17.3 and Table 17.3)

- ☐ Ascertain if they wrote in such a way that you could readily discern which rhetorical form they privileged (i.e., appealed to readers' emotions or rationality or depended on their own reputation and character) (see Figures 17.3 and 17.4)

DEDUCTIVE AND INDUCTIVE ARGUMENTATION

In the body (antithesis) of an argumentative essay, authors are developing and supporting arguments in favor of their position. Basically, they are attempting to intentionally show a relationship between their premises (assumptions) and their claim (conclusion) (Bennett, 2015; Mahon, 2010a). Authors can let readers know when they are introducing an argument by using particular words or phrases, called premise indicators and claim indicators. Table 17.4 presents the most common indicators used in argumentative essays (Bowser, 2009; Matarrese, 2006; Morrow & Weston, 2016).

Example 17.18 Premise and claim indicators

- *Given that* (*premise*) she is not breathing, we *can conclude* (*claim*) she has died.

- *Assuming that* (*premise*) the sun will be shining, *it follows that* (*claim*) it will not be raining.

- *Seeing that* (*premise*) everyone is here, *it must be* (*claim*) the case that no one is missing.

- *Inasmuch* (*premise*) as we want to tell the truth, *this implies that* (*claim*) we are always honest.

TABLE 17.4 ■ Examples of Words Indicative of Premise and Claim	
Premise indicators	**Claim indicators**
• since	• therefore
• as/as indicated by	• wherefore
• because	• accordingly
• for	• we may conclude
• in that	• entails that
• may be inferred from	• hence
• as	• thus
• given that	• consequently
• seeing that	• we may infer that
• for the reason that	• whence
• for one thing	• so
• inasmuch as	• it follows that
• owing to	• which implies that
• insofar as	• as a result
• to the extent that	• ergo
• in view of	• demonstrates that
• follows from	• which proves that
• considering that	• which means that
• assuming that	• necessarily
	• it must be that

In the body of an argumentative essay, authors can employ one or both of two basic arguments, deductive and inductive. *Deduce* is Latin *deducere*, "to lead down." It refers to drawing a conclusion from something already known (Harper, 2016). Deductive reasoning moves from the general to the specific. As an example, Jim knows business is slow at the golf course when it rains. He looks out the window and observes that the weather is cold and rainy. These two general points lead Jim to the more specific deduction that business at the golf course will be slow today (Guilford, 2015). For a deductive argument, if the premises (assumptions) are *true*, the claims *must* be true, with 100% certainty (Smith, 2010).

Induce is Latin *inducere*, "to lead into by persuasion or influence" (Harper, 2016). Inductive reasoning moves in the opposite direction of deduction, from specific to general. Jim, from the previous example, tastes several hard green apples from the trees on the golf course and then draws the general conclusion that *all* hard green apples are sour (paving the way for him to be proven wrong if someone can find one that is sweet). For inductive arguments, if the premises (assumptions) are *believable* or *conceivable*, the claim is *probably* true (51% or better) (Bowser, 2009; Smith, 2010) (see Figure 17.5). When expressing their arguments, authors can avail themselves of a vocabulary of deductive and inductive indicator words (Bowser, 2009) (see Table 17.5).

Premises, assumptions, and claims can be true or false. Appreciating this, authors and readers will benefit from knowledge of five key terms relevant to assessing the rigor of arguments: *true*, *valid*, *sound*, *strong*, and *cogent*. Deductive arguments exhibit validity and soundness. Inductive arguments reflect strength and cogency (Bennett, 2015; Bowser, 2009; Mahon,

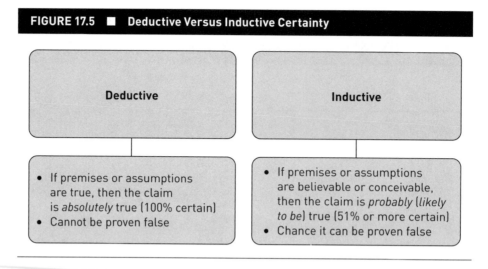

FIGURE 17.5 ■ **Deductive Versus Inductive Certainty**

Deductive

- If premises or assumptions are true, then the claim is *absolutely* true (100% certain)
- Cannot be proven false

Inductive

- If premises or assumptions are believable or conceivable, then the claim is *probably* (*likely to be*) true (51% or more certain)
- Chance it can be proven false

2010b; Morrow & Weston, 2016) (see Table 17.6 for a reasoning decision tree). The following discussion of deductive then inductive arguments clarifies these terms in more detail.

Deductive Argument

In a deductive argument, if the premises are true, the conclusion *must* be true (Morrow & Weston, 2016; Muehlhauser, 2009). "The premises are intended to provide *such strong support* [emphasis added] for the conclusion that, if the premises *are* [emphasis added] true,

TABLE 17.5 ■ **Examples of Words Indicative of Deductive and Inductive Arguments**

Deductive indicator words (100% certainty)	Inductive indicator words (51% or higher certainty)
• probable	• certainly
• improbable	• absolutely
• plausible	• definitely
• implausible	• unequivocally
• likely	• indisputably
• unlikely	• unmistakably
• reasonable	• undeniably
• unreasonable	• incontrovertibly
• possible	• irrefutably
• impossible	• unquestionably
	• incontestably
	• conclusively

TABLE 17.6 ■ Deductive and Inductive Decision Tree

DEDUCTIVE			INDUCTIVE		
Valid (true, well founded)	OR	Invalid (untrue because it is based on incorrect assumptions)	Strong (firmly established)	OR	Weak (gives way under pressure)
Sound (based on facts)	OR	Unsound (not based on facts)	Cogent (persuasive, convincing, conceivable)	OR	Uncogent (unconvincing, inconceivable)
A sound argument 1. Must be a valid argument and 2. Must have true premises and a true conclusion		All invalid arguments are unsound. Because of erroneous information and assumptions, the conclusions must be false.	A cogent argument 1. Must be a strong argument and 2. Must have true premises and a true conclusion		All weak arguments are uncogent. Because the assumptions are questionable, the conclusion is unconvincing.

then it would be *impossible* [emphasis added] for the conclusion to be false. . . . [T]he truth of the conclusion is thought to be completely guaranteed" (IEP Staff, n.d., p. 1). Deductive reasoning is based on absolutism; that is, once proven true, the conclusions are always, absolutely, true or correct. If the premises are accepted as true (*sound*) and there are no flaws in the reasoning (*valid*), authors cannot assert their premises and then deny their conclusion (Cline, 2012). More important, readers have no choice but to accept the authors' conclusion with complete (absolute) certainty, no matter how counterintuitive or emotionally dissatisfying this acceptance may be (Smith, 2010) (see Table 17.6).

> **Example 17.9 Deductive argument** *Given that* all bachelors are unmarried males, and *given that* this person is a bachelor (A), it can be *deduced* with certainty that this person is an unmarried male (B).

Per example 17.9, deductive reasoning allows deriving B from A but *only* where B is a formal consequence of A. Put simply, true assumptions or premises always lead to true conclusions or claims (Morrow & Weston, 2016).

Regarding validity and soundness, a deductive argument is *valid* if the claim follows from the premises (even if the premises are false). In logic, if something *follows*, it must be true because of something else that is true (Rundell, 2007). Example 17.10 is a *valid argument* despite that one of the premises is false (dogs are not immortal). It is valid because the claim is about the content of the premises (dogs) (its soundness will be addressed in a moment). Example 17.11 is an *invalid argument* because the conclusion does not follow from the premises, despite both *assumptions being true*. The claim is about Socrates *the cat* while the first premise is about *dogs* (Mahon, 2010a).

Example 17.10	Example 17.11
Valid argument (because the claim follows from premises, even though one is false)	**Invalid argument (because the claim does not follow from the premises, despite both being true)**
1. All dogs are immortal. (premise, albeit incorrect) 2. Socrates is a dog. (premise) → Socrates is immortal. (claim)	1. All *dogs* are mortal. (premise) 2. Socrates is a cat. (premise) → Socrates is mortal. (claim)

The most common problem authors will encounter when developing a deductive argument is that at least one of their assumptions (premises) is false, making their argument unsound (Guilford, 2015; Mahon, 2010a). "If the argument is sound, there is nothing in the world that can alter the truth [of the claim]" (Mahon, 2010a, p. 6). A *sound* argument puts an end to all discussion and debate. In example 17.12, the argument is valid but not sound because dogs are not immortal (a false assumption). Example 17.13 is both valid and sound, meaning that both of the assumptions (about dogs) are true, as is the claim that follows them (it is about dogs). As a further caveat, while *valid* and *invalid* apply to an argument, *sound* and *unsound* apply only to a *valid* argument (see Mahon, 2010b).

Example 17.12	Example 17.13
A valid but unsound argument due to a false premise	**Sound and valid argument because all assumptions are true and the claim follows from them**
1. All dogs are immortal. (premise, albeit false) 2. Socrates is a dog. (premise) → Socrates is immortal. (claim)	1. All dogs are mortal. (premise) 2. Socrates is a dog. (premise) → Socrates is mortal. (claim)

Examples 17.14 and 17.15 further illustrate a deductive argument. Both examples deal with rain and the wetness of the ground but differ in their *minor* premise, with the *major* premise being consistent: "If it is raining, then the ground is wet" (Cline, 2012). These examples profile good and bad reasoning.

Example 17.14	Example 17.15
A valid deductive argument (good reasoning)	**An invalid deductive argument (bad reasoning)**
1. **If** it is raining, **then** the ground is wet. 2. **It is raining.** 3. **Therefore,** the ground is wet (*because it is raining, the ground is wet*).	1. **If** it is raining, **then** the ground is wet. 2. **The ground is wet.** 3. **Therefore,** it is raining (*because the ground is wet, it is raining*).

The first premise specifies a *conditional relationship*. This is denoted by the **if/then** structure of the sentence. If A happens, then B happens too. This is called the **major** premise of the argument (#1).

The **minor premise** of the argument (#2) tells us that the **"if"** part of the major premise does take place; it is raining.

The third statement, the **conclusion**, then asserts that the **"then"** part of the first statement took place as well.

- This is a *valid* argument because the truth of the **minor premise** gives us grounds to accept the **conclusion** as 100% true.

At first glance, it is tempting to believe that this argument shows good reasoning as well.

- The **minor premise** of the argument (#2) tells us that the **"then"** part of the major premise does take place; the ground is wet.

However, this argument is *invalid* because the truth of the **minor premise** (#2) does not give us grounds to accept the **conclusion** as 100% true.

- Aside from rain, there are *other reasons* the ground could be wet: The sprinkler system could be on, the water hose could be broken, there could have been a flood, or the swimming pool could have overflowed.

Inductive Argument

In an inductive argument, if the premises are true, the conclusion (claim) is *probably* true (Muehlhauser, 2009). "The premises are intended only to be *so strong* [emphasis added] that, if they *were* true, then it would be *unlikely* [emphasis added] that the conclusion is false. . . . [T]he premises provide *good enough* [emphasis added] reasons to believe the conclusion is true" (IEP Staff, n.d., p. 1). Because inductive arguments are settled only in degrees of certainty, they are open to the possibility of being proven wrong one day (Smith, 2010).

> ***Example 17.16 Inductive argument*** *If* all of the swans that we have observed so far are white (A), we may reasonably *induce (infer)* the possibility that all swans are white (B). We have *good reason to believe* this conclusion from the premise, but the truth of the conclusion is not guaranteed. Indeed, it was discovered that some swans are black.

Per example 17.16, inductive reasoning allows *inferring* B from A despite that B does not necessarily follow from A. A might provide a very good reason to accept B, but it does not ensure B with 100% certainty. If any of the premises (assumptions) turn out to be false, then their argument would be *less convincing* and more open to be proven wrong (Smith, 2010).

Whereas deductive arguments exhibit validity and soundness, inductive arguments exhibit strength and cogency. Strength is expressed as a weak or strong argument. An inductive argument cannot be valid or invalid. It can only have degrees of certainty, rather than 100% certainty. A *strong* argument is one where the claims are *likely* to happen (51% change or greater) but are not guaranteed. In a *weak* inductive argument, the claim probably does not follow from the premises. In an inductive argument, what matters is that the premises support the argument, not whether they are true or false (Bowser, 2009; Cline, 2012; Smith, 2010).

Cogent means persuasive, convincing, conceivable, and believable (Anderson, 2014). A cogent (believable) argument is strong, and all premises are true. Even one false premise makes an inductive argument weak. All weak arguments are *uncogent* (less believable).

As a caveat, authors cannot conveniently ignore premises or assumptions that would weaken their argument (Smith, 2010).

In summary, "inductive arguments are strong if the conclusion follows probably from the premises and weak if it follows only improbably from the premises" (Cline, 2012) (see Table 17.6). When preparing inductive arguments, authors would assume that if their assumptions are true, their claim is *probably* true, with the chance that someone may eventually prove them wrong. To ensure cogency (a convincing argument), authors can either (a) provide very strong evidence to support their assumptions or (b) draw a weak conclusion by explicitly using words such as *probably*, *possibly*, or *maybe*. If they want readers to accept their inductive argument, authors should avoid absolute statements because only deductive arguments are based on absolutism, the tenet of 100% certainty (Bowser, 2009; Smith, 2010). Inductive arguments are more *provisional* in nature, meaning they can possibly change in the future (Ellis, 2015). Example 17.17 illustrates cogency and strength in inductive reasoning (Cline, 2012).

Example 17.17 Cogency and strength in inductive reasoning

Strolling through the woods is usually fun. The sun is out, the temperature is cool, there is no rain in the forecast, the flowers are in bloom, and the birds are singing. Therefore, it should be fun to take a walk through the woods now.

- Assuming that you care about those premises, then the argument is *strong*.

- If you didn't care about the factors mentioned (perhaps you suffer from allergies and don't like it when the flowers are in bloom), it would be a *weak* argument for you.

- Assuming that the premises are all true, then this is also a *cogent* argument (i.e., believable, conceivable).

- If any of the premises turned out to be false (for example, if it *is* actually raining), then the argument would be *uncogent* (less convincing).

- If additional premises turned up, like reports of bears in the area, then those premises would *weaken* the argument, making it *uncogent* (unconvincing).

In summary, when developing an argument for a thesis, the truth of the assumptions and the validity of the facts are the crux of good reasoning and of any attendant claims or conclusions:

- A deductive argument is *sound* when all of the *assumptions are true*.
- A deductive argument is *valid* when the assumptions *actually do* guarantee the conclusion with 100% certainty.
- An inductive argument is *cogent* (convincing) when all of the *assumptions are true*.
- An inductive argument is *strong* (firmly established) when the assumptions *actually do* support the conclusion with a 50% degree of probability or higher (Hollenberg, 2017).

REVIEW AND ENGAGEMENT

When critically reading a research report, you would

☐ Determine if the authors effectively used *deductive* and/or *inductive* logic when writing their antithesis (i.e., developed arguments and claims to support their thesis, their position) (see Figure 17.5 and Table 17.5)

☐ Ascertain if they effectively employed words indicative of *premise* and *claim* (see Table 17.4)

☐ Check to see if they effectively employed words indicative of deductive and inductive arguments (see Table 17.5)

☐ Confirm they did not overreach their line of reasoning by mistakenly claiming a deductive argument was valid and sound when it was not (see Table 17.6)

☐ Determine that they did not overreach their line of reasoning by mistakenly claiming an inductive argument was cogent and strong when it was not (see Table 17.6)

☐ Per the above, judge whether they appeared to be able to follow the deductive and inductive logic decision tree (see Table 17.6)

LOGICAL FALLACIES

The exercise of expressing arguments and counterarguments in an argumentative essay is predicated on four assumptions. First, arguments require no less than two competing agents, with different sides presenting different opinions and positions on an issue. This is called the *convention of bilaterality*. Second, authors who are posing arguments must accept the risk that they may be proven wrong and convinced otherwise. Third, authors must ensure that as many viewpoints as possible are aired, considered, and defended, called the *fairness doctrine*. Finally, when authors prepare arguments for argumentative essays, they are committing to the *logic of rationality* (Scott, 1998). Regarding the latter, this final section provides an admittedly overly brief but focused introduction to logical fallacies in argumentative essays (see Figure 17.6).

Fallacies

Fallacy is Latin *fallacia*, "deception or artifice" (Harper, 2016). A fallacy is a misleading or false belief caused by a person's error in reasoning when making an argument; that is, the person failed to make a valid or convincing argument by purposely or inadvertently creating a deceptive message (Anderson, 2014; Bennett, 2015). Unfortunately, logical fallacies are an inherent part of argumentative work (Wallace & Wray, 2011). Worse, they are dangerous because "arguments become persuasive for all the wrong reasons—sort of like optical illusions for the mind" (Bennett, 2015, p. 8).

It is not easy to recognize or challenge logical fallacies and flaws in reasoning (Bennett, 2015). But they must be found and contested because "fallacies threaten the value" of scholarly contributions (Suter, 2012, p. 10). Bennett (2015) identified over 300 logical fallacies. Table 17.7 provides examples of the most common fallacies found in academic writing (in no particular order) (Bruce, 2001a; Richardson, Smith, & Meaden, 2012; Weber & Brizee, 2013).

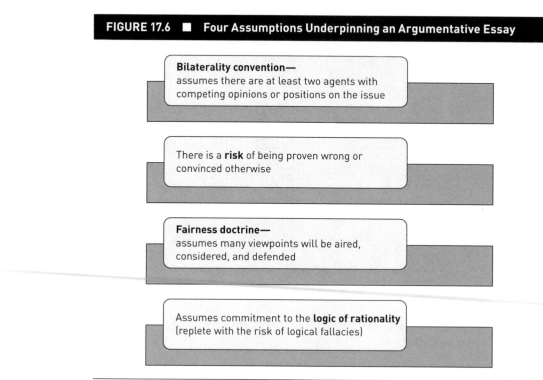

FIGURE 17.6 ■ Four Assumptions Underpinning an Argumentative Essay

Bilaterality convention—
assumes there are at least two agents with competing opinions or positions on the issue

There is a **risk** of being proven wrong or convinced otherwise

Fairness doctrine—
assumes many viewpoints will be aired, considered, and defended

Assumes commitment to the **logic of rationality** (replete with the risk of logical fallacies)

TABLE 17.7 ■ Common Logical Fallacies Found in Academic Argumentative Essays (extrapolated from Bennett, 2015)

Fallacy	Explanation
Strawman	Misrepresenting someone else's argument to make it weaker and easier to dismiss
Slippery slope	Asserting that if A happens, B will happen so A *cannot* be allowed to happen
Bandwagon	Validating an idea by saying it is popular, it is a fact, or everyone is doing it
Black or white (either/or)	Present only two alternatives as possibilities when more exist
Ad hominem	Latin for "to the person." This involves undermining people's arguments by attacking their character or personal traits rather than their position on an issue
False cause	Presuming that a real or perceived relationship between things means one causes the other
Loaded question	Posing a real or rhetorical question that cannot be answered without appearing guilty
Circular argument	Restating the argument (saying same thing, using different words) rather than proving it
Begging the question (claim)	Asking people to accept the conclusion *before* they can accept the premises; authors begin with what you are trying to end up with

Fallacy	Explanation
False analogy	Using a very small degree of similarity between things to create an impression they are almost identical
Anecdotal	Using personal experience or an isolated example instead of a valid argument (especially to dismiss statistics that weaken one's argument)
Appeal to emotions	Using emotional appeal instead of a compelling argument
Tu quoque	Latin for "you also"; involves answering a criticism with another criticism so as to avoid dealing with the initial criticism
Ambiguity	Using double meanings to mislead or misrepresent the truth
Texas sharpshooter	Cherry-picking evidence to suit an argument
Argument from silence	Basing the conclusion on the absence of evidence rather than the existence of evidence
Personal incredulity	Saying "I cannot believe that this is true, so it must be false" (disbelief, skepticism, mental rejection)
Raising the bar	Dismissing someone's evidence presented for a claim, and then demanding that even greater or different evidence be presented
Red herring	Distracting readers from the topic at hand by introducing a separate argument that is easier to speak to (ends up misleading readers)
Relative privation	Dismissing an argument by claiming there are more important problems to address, regardless of whether these bear relevance to the initial argument

Any author's concerted effort to sway readers to a particular point of view may be inadvertently thwarted if this basic convention of rational argumentation goes unheeded. The appearance of fallacies in the argumentative essay undermines the logic of the entire argument. Their presence can lead readers to conclude that the author did not respect others' perspectives on the issue and did not refute others' points of view (Weber & Brizee, 2013). Conveying mistaken beliefs or falsities weakens the essay to the point of rejection or, at the minimum, skepticism on the readers' part. It is incumbent upon authors to be vigilant when preparing argumentative essays vis-à-vis logical fallacies.

Example 17.18 Research fallacies A *fallacy* is an error in reasoning, usually based on mistaken assumptions. Two examples follow (taken from Trochim & Donnelly, 2007).

An *ecological fallacy* occurs when authors draw conclusions about individuals based only on their analysis of group data. For instance, researchers of a study measured the math scores of a particular classroom. They found that students in this classroom had the highest average score in the district. The researchers concluded that all students from that class "must be a math whiz." Aha! Fallacy! To avoid this fallacy, the authors need to empirically determine how individuals perform (not just rely on group averages). Just because a student comes from the class with the highest average does not mean she or he is automatically a high scorer in math. She or he could be the lowest math scorer in a class that otherwise consists of math geniuses.

An *exception fallacy* is the reverse of the ecological fallacy. It occurs when authors reach a group conclusion on the basis of exceptional cases. This kind of fallacious reasoning is commonly at the core of sexism and racism. In one study, male researchers observed one woman make driving errors and concluded that "all women are terrible drivers." Wrong! Fallacy! To avoid this fallacy, authors need to look at (research and investigate) whether there are correlations between certain behaviors and certain groups, such as the relationship between abilities and sex and gender, rather than relying on one datum point to make gross, and potentially damning, overgeneralizations.

REVIEW AND ENGAGEMENT

When critically reading a research report, you would

☐ Determine if the authors refrained from introducing any *logical fallacies* (flaws in their reasoning) in their argumentative essay, meaning they did not undermine the logic of their argument with errors and mistakes in their reasoning (see Table 17.7) (very difficult for you to discern)

☐ Per the above, check to see that they avoided these particular fallacies: bandwagon, ad hominem, circular argument, false analogy, ambiguity, Texas sharpshooter, and red herring (see Table 17.7)

FINAL JUDGMENT ON ARGUMENTATIVE ESSAY

Taking *all* of the *Review and Engagement* criteria into account, what is your final judgment of the argumentative essay that you are critically reading?

CHAPTER SUMMARY

This chapter purposefully focused on argumentative essays because they do not comprise the regular elements of a research paper. This means they cannot be judged using the criteria for a good literature review, a thorough Methods section, or a set of conclusions. Instead, they have to conform to the principles of a good argument and to valid and/or sound logical reasoning. To that end, the chapter began by comparing and contrasting the three most basic forms of argumentative essays: position (opinion) papers,

discussion papers, and think pieces. This clarification was followed with a detailed overview of the format for writing an argumentative essay: thesis, antithesis, and synthesis. The discussion then turned to the concept of persuasive writing and the key role played by Aristotle's rhetorical appeals: ethos (character), pathos (emotions), and logos (logic). The chapter then presented a very detailed discussion of both deductive and inductive argumentation, ending with a brief introduction to logical fallacies in argumentative essays.

REVIEW AND DISCUSSION QUESTIONS

1. What key factor differentiates argumentative essays from conventional research papers?

2. Compare and contrast the intent of a position, discussion, and think-piece paper. What do they all have in common?

3. Identify and describe the three parts of any argumentative essay. Were you familiar with these concepts before reading this chapter?

4. Compare and contrast the purpose of a *thesis*, an *antithesis*, and a *synthesis*. Can an author write an argumentative essay and leave any of these out? Explain your answer.

5. What is the author's goal when preparing an academic argument?

6. Explain the concept of *persuasive writing*. What would make an argument nonpersuasive?

7. Compare and contrast Aristotle's three *rhetorical* appeals. In your opinion, which of these appeals would be most persuasive in an academic argumentative essay, and why?

8. Recount a speech or paper you have heard or read recently that was convincing and suggest why this was so, using Aristotle's three rhetorical appeals. Had you ever thought these types of appeals might be why some communications resonated with you and others did not?

9. Compare and contrast inductive and deductive argumentation, in some detail.

10. Which of these two types of arguments do you tend to find most convincing, and why?

11. How is a valid and sound argument different from a strong and cogent argument?

12. How is an invalid and unsound argument different from a weak and uncogent argument?

13. What is a logical fallacy? Why is it important that these be avoided in argumentative essays, relative to the persuasive nature of these academic papers?

18 CONCEPTUAL AND THEORETICAL PAPERS

INTRODUCTION

Chapter 3 provided a detailed discussion of the role of conceptual frameworks, theories, and models when conducting research. This chapter is about how to write a paper that reports a new theory or a conceptual framework, which may or may not have been used in a study. Both types of manuscripts are considered to be important forms of scholarly work, contributing significantly to a discipline's intellectual renewal and evolution (Smithey Fulmer, 2012). These papers are nonempirical in nature and do not report on primary research (quantitative, qualitative, or mixed methods); therefore, a different set of criteria is needed to judge their quality (Cropanzano, 2009). Because each type of paper represents a different intellectual process, each should be constructed and labeled appropriately and judged critically using relevant criteria (Cropanzano, 2009; Plakhotnik & Rocco, 2009; Rindova, 2011; Salomone, 1993; Watts, 2011; Whetten, 1989; Yadav, 2010).

CHAPTER CAVEATS

Three caveats inform the content of this chapter, which focuses "on the craft of constructing a theory [or conceptual] paper" that reports a new theory or conceptual framework developed by the author (Smithey Fulmer, 2012, p. 327). First, this chapter does not address how to (a) develop a theory, (b) judge a theory, or (c) develop a conceptual framework. For that information, readers are directed to other source documents (e.g., Bacharach, 1989; Corley & Gioia, 2011; Cramer, 2013; Dubin, 1978; Jabareen, 2009; Patterson, 1983; Rindova, 2011; Torraco, 2005; Weick, 1995; Whetten, 1989; Yadav, 2010).

LEARNING OBJECTIVES

- Appreciate the double meaning of *conceptual framework*

- Compare and contrast the purpose of conceptual versus theoretical papers

- Identify the structural elements of both conceptual and theoretical papers

- Explain the special role played by the literature review in both types of papers

- Describe the idea of writing a theory paper based on how far it has been conceptualized, operationalized, tested, and applied

- Explain the four criteria appropriate for judging argumentative rigor in conceptual and theoretical papers (especially analytical and generative reasoning)

Steps in Developing a Theory

That being said, the generic steps involved in theory development are briefly discussed here because they subtly inform the content of a theory paper. On a side note, although readers of a theory paper will not be able to discern the author's intellectual dynamics involved during the theory development process, it helps to know that these include "intuition, experience, observations, reasoning, and the concepts that emerge from the literature" (McLean, 2011, p. 213).

Generically speaking, researchers cannot develop a new theory until they find and then critique existing theories (called *source theory*) or determine that no theory exists for the phenomenon in question (Steiner, 1988). Based on this premise, Steiner maintained that theory development entails three overall stages (see Table 18.1). (a) Researchers have to be able to first *recognize* a theory when they see one and then *determine* what kind of theory it is (i.e., describe and interpret it). She called these *source theories*. These steps are necessary because the stages involved in developing the *wanted* theory depend on the type of source theory, whether it is scientific, philosophical, logical, mathematical, or praxiological (study of human conduct). Also, regarding theory type, *analytic theory* does not add to the content of knowledge, but *synthetic theory* does because its truth is ascertained by experience. The subsequent steps to building the *wanted theory* are (b) criticism of existing source theories (*explication* and *evaluation*) and then (c) construction of the wanted theory (*emendation* and *extension*). This chapter focuses on writing the paper that reports the new theory or the new version of an existing theory.

TABLE 18.1 ■ Fundamental Steps in Building a Theory		
Stages of Theory Building	**Substeps**	**Explained**
1. **Locate** *source theories*	Recognize	Identify, describe, and interpret extant theories that are still in existence (and ideally in use).
	Determine	Ascertain the type of source theory so it can be critiqued using the appropriate criteria. The type of source theory affects the general structure and function of the wanted theory stemming from it (see next).
2. **Critique** *source theories*	Explicate	Critique and then give a full account of the source theory, both its content (concepts and their definitions) and its form (assumptions, generalizations, propositions).
	Evaluate	Judge the theory to determine its worth (i.e., its goodness, beauty, or utility but especially its epistemic truth); determine what needs to be done to address the theory's content, form, or both.
3. **Construct** *wanted theory*	Emend	Correct and revise the existing theory to address issues with its content, form, or both (may lead to a new theory).
	Extend	Build on the existing theory to address issues with its content, form, or both; that is, make it more complete, make it more comprehensive, or broaden it (enlarge its scope, influence, or meaning) (may lead to a new theory).

Choosing a Theory for a Study

As a second caveat, this chapter does not discuss how to *choose* a particular theory or conceptual framework to anchor a study, often referred to as conceptually and theoretically *framing* scholarly work. Nor does this chapter address the researchers' ability to then *employ* the theory chosen for their study. This information is covered in Chapter 3.

Double Meaning of Conceptual Framework

As a third caveat, there are two meanings for *conceptual framework*, only one of which is the focus of this chapter (see Figure 18.1). Scholars have recently started using the term *conceptual framework* to refer to the blueprint for a *particular* study (e.g., Ravitch & Riggan, 2016; Rocco & Plakhotnik, 2009). Used this way, the term reflects the process and components of introducing the problem, covering the relevant literature, proposing methods, and perhaps explicating a particular theory to scaffold the study (already discussed in Chapters 3, 6, 7, and 8). From this perspective, the conceptual framework serves to logically link the various components of the research design (Sitko, 2013). Taken together, they equate to the *proposal* for a thesis, a dissertation, or a funding request.

With this usage of the term, a conceptual framework becomes the researchers' mental picture of a phenomenon and how best to approach it in a *particular* study (i.e., their framing of one research project) (Casanave & Li, 2015; Imenda, 2014; Maxwell, 2013). Indeed, Shields and Rangarajan (2013) described a conceptual framework as "the way ideas are organized to achieve a research project's purpose" (p. 24). From this perspective, a conceptual framework is valid only for *one* study. Imenda (2014) explained that a carefully put-together conceptual framework is immediately and narrowly applicable to *a particular*

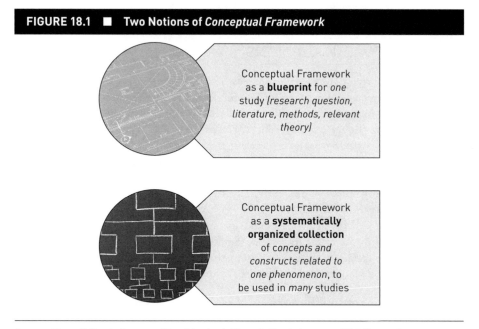

FIGURE 18.1 ■ Two Notions of *Conceptual Framework*

Conceptual Framework as a **blueprint** for *one* study *(research question, literature, methods, relevant theory)*

Conceptual Framework as a **systematically organized collection** of *concepts and constructs related to one phenomenon*, to be used in *many* studies

Sources: Photo © iStockphoto.com/Branislav (top); Photo © iStockphoto.com/Hiob (bottom).

study, and a specific research problem (see Chapters 6 and 8, respectively, for more details about research questions and research design and methods for a particular study).

Rather than the blueprint for *one* study, this chapter takes a broader perspective of the term, assuming that a conceptual framework is a group of concepts and/or constructs that are broadly defined and systematically organized to provide a focus, a rationale, and/or a tool for the integration and interpretation of information, leading to new knowledge. These conceptual frameworks can be used to help create the blueprint for (framing of) any *number* of studies (see Figure 18.1).

On a final note of clarity, conceptual frameworks are usually expressed abstractly through word models or pictorial models (O'Toole, 2013; Smyth, 2004). A *word model* is a clear statement and description of each element (concept or construct) in the framework and any processes that link it to the research phenomenon (Kimmins, Blanco, Seely, Welham, & Scoullar, 2010). Formalized conceptual frameworks are often viewed as precursors to a formal theory. The latter is more advanced because it also contains propositions and assumptions about reality (Callahan, 2010; Castro-Palaganas, 2011; Robey & Baskerville, 2012) (see Chapter 3).

REVIEW AND ENGAGEMENT

When critically reading a research report, you would

☐ Determine that the authors clearly identified their paper as a theory paper or a conceptual paper

☐ Check to see that they demonstrated they could distinguish between a theory and a conceptual framework (see Figure 18.2); that is, they did not mislabel the paper

PURPOSE OF CONCEPTUAL VERSUS THEORETICAL PAPERS

"Current usage of the terms *conceptual framework* and *theoretical framework* are vague and imprecise" (Jabareen, 2009, p. 51). But it *is* possible to distinguish between them, appreciating that both frameworks are built on well-founded, rigorous, coherent, and convincing argumentation (Robey & Baskerville, 2012; Whetten, 1989) (see Chapters 6 and 17). Succinctly, a theory paper reports on a specific theory (or work related to theory development) while a conceptual paper reports on a specific conceptual framework (or work related to it) (Rocco & Plakhotnik, 2009).

Just as a "theory proper" is different from a conceptual framework (see Chapter 3), the papers that report these initiatives differ as well (Albers, 2014). Effectively and properly structuring either a theory or a conceptual paper is just as important as the conceptualization of the actual theory or the framework (Smithey Fulmer, 2012). Because theories and conceptual frameworks are not the same thing, they require different styles of papers, with attendant criteria for judging their quality (see Figure 18.2).

Purpose of Conceptual Papers

A conceptual paper relates concepts to specific issues or research problems so as to advance and systematize knowledge. They can serve to (a) define a concept, (b) map the

FIGURE 18.2 ■ Main Purpose of Conceptual Versus Theoretical Papers	
Conceptual Paper	**Theoretical Paper**
• Maps the conceptual terrain of a phenomenon (takes conceptual stock) by identifying disparate concepts, defining them, and connecting them to the phenomenon • Presents a sound argument for *integrating* the disparate concepts into a new, conceptually robust framework, which can then be used to generate ideas for new theories	• Presents a collection of defined concepts connected through a network of propositions undergirded by particular assumptions of reality • Presents a sound, discursive argument for the new theory being advanced, which represents a *system* of ideas and suppositions pursuant to a phenomenon

research terrain or conceptual scope of a research problem, or (c) systematize relations among concepts and between the concepts and the phenomenon in question (Rocco & Plakhotnik, 2009). Conceptual papers do not normally include empirical data; rather, they address questions that cannot be answered with more facts, requiring instead a sound argument. They reflect theoretical thoughts and speculations about a topic. The researchers make a case for a specific argument by raising a point and then expanding on that thought through opinion or debate. The researchers provide supporting thoughts to substantiate their conceptual contributions (Dauber, 2014; Gilson & Goldberg, 2015; Golash, 2005), despite that the conceptualization is abstract and has not yet been proven (McLean, 2011).

In more detail, a conceptual paper identifies and defines concepts, constructs, and their relationship to a specific topic or phenomenon, compared to a theory paper, which connects stand-alone concepts into a network of propositions (Gilson & Goldberg, 2015; Rindova, 2011). Conceptual papers tend to be discursive, meaning they involve reasoning and argumentation. They depend on the author's well-informed opinions and arguments (McLean, 2011). By nature, they require the author to have a very deep understanding of the topic or issue being addressed (BCS Information Retrieval Specialist Group, 2006). "[F]amiliarity with a broad base of literature give[s] an author fertile ground from which new ideas may emerge and grow to fruition" (Watts, 2011, p. 309).

If effective, highly conceptual papers can change the way that disciplinary scholars think (Whetten, 1989). This is because they report the results of research focused on integration and on proposing new relationships and associations among concepts and constructs relative to a particular phenomenon (Gilson & Goldberg, 2015). Examples of conceptual papers include those that (a) integrate existing perspectives into a more holistic view, (b) share a collection of insights into current professional issues, or (c) provide a well-reasoned reaction or response to previously published articles on a particular disciplinary or professional issue (Watts, 2011). Conceptual papers can report on (d) research that explored the conceptual foundations of a field as well as (e) scholarship that made connections among multiple bodies of literature and knowledge bases to make knowledge claims about a phenomenon (Callahan, 2010). They may present (f) synthesis (e.g., reviews or integrative frameworks); (g) completely new ideas; or (h) discussions of substantive domains that have not received adequate conceptual attention (Yadav, 2010).

Yadav (2010) confirmed that a conceptual paper does not present data and/or their analysis. Because they are "unfettered by data-related limitations" (p. 5), conceptual papers are especially useful for idea generation that can eventually initiate theory development. He explained that conceptual papers "take stock of emerging empirical evidence, concepts, and explanations—including the underlying ontological, axiological, and epistemological assumptions" (p. 5).

Purpose of Theoretical Papers

Theoretical papers can both advance a particular theoretical perspective and report on a systematic evaluation of alternative theories in a given domain. This chapter tends to focus on the former. All theories are based on axioms and assumptions, which inform the propositions explicating the links among the theory's concepts (see Chapter 3). A paper that reports on a new theory or revisions to an existing theory presents a "supposition or system of ideas intended to explain some phenomena" and usually contains "a set of principles on which the practice of an activity is based (i.e., a theory of information seeking behaviour)" (BCS Information Retrieval Specialist Group, 2006, p. 4).

Theory papers can (a) refine and expand existing theoretical constructs, (b) analyze and evaluate an existing theory, (c) critique and point out flaws in a theory that includes alternative research propositions, or (d) demonstrate the advantage of one theory over another (Watts, 2011) (see again Table 18.1). In addition to a new theory, theory papers can present (e) theoretical synthesis (integrative frameworks), (f) propositional inventories, or (g) new analytical modes (Yadav, 2010). They can (h) report on scholarship that develops the foundation for eventual theory development (Rocco & Plakhotnik, 2009), and they may include (i) syntheses of existing bodies of theory, (j) treatises in formal theory construction, (k) the history of theory, or (l) a metatheory (a theory devised to systematically examine and analyze other theories) (Callahan, 2010).

Regardless, like conceptual papers, theory papers are discursive, relying on the author's ability to frame and execute a sound argument (see Chapters 6 and 17). Papers reporting theories that are grounded in mathematics or some other formalism are less discursive in nature (BCS Information Retrieval Specialist Group, 2006; Whetten, 1989) (see Chapter 3).

REVIEW AND ENGAGEMENT

When critically reading a research report, you would

☐ Determine if the authors appreciated the different purposes of a theory and a conceptual framework paper (see Figure 18.3 and accompanying text)

☐ If they did not appreciate the differences, decide if this affected your judgment of the quality of the paper

STRUCTURAL ELEMENTS OF CONCEPTUAL AND THEORETICAL PAPERS

Neither type of paper (theoretical or conceptual) has a rigid or suggested format; that is, there is no one correct approach to writing these sorts of papers (McLean, 2011; Salomone, 1993). After the unique role of the literature review in both a conceptual and a theory paper is described, an overview is provided for how to organize the different structural elements of each one (providing two different models for a theory paper) (see Table 18.2).

Special Role of the Literature Review

In a conventional quantitative paper, the literature review serves to identify what has been done already on a topic, justifying the need for research with a different focus, and

TABLE 18.2 ■ Structural Elements in Conceptual and Theoretical Papers		
Structural Element of the Paper	**Conceptual Paper**	**Theoretical Paper**
Title	Same rules as conventional paper	Two-phrase, longish title, which specifies main idea of the theory
Abstract	Select a structure that makes the content immediately accessible to readers (balance succinctness and completeness)	Should reflect the argumentative structure of the paper (why a new theory, why *this* new theory)
Introduction	Clarify what issue is being conceptualized in what new way (what is the new contribution), doing so with a directive purpose statement, not a thesis statement	Identify phenomenon in question, provide context/background justifying need for new theory, and give brief overview of how *this* new theory (or revision) will address it (no supportive arguments and no presentation of the theory in this section)
Role of Literature Review	Reflects researcher's ability to pull disparate pieces from the literature into a new whole—a synergetic, conceptual integration	Place new theory in context by setting out relationships between older and existing theories, justifying the proposed theory (or revision)
There is no Methods section and no Results or Findings section.		
Presentation of New Contribution	The bulk of the paper recounts the framework, its concepts/constructs, and their definitions, with special attention to conceptual integration (how disparate building blocks from literature were woven together) and conceptual robustness. May also include a diagram or model.	The bulk of the paper is a recounting of the theory, its assumptions, its concepts, and their definitions, all propositions (with rationales). May also include a diagram or model.

(Continued)

TABLE 18.2 ■ (Continued)

Discussion	• How will the new conceptual framework help explain the phenomenon (how does it add value to the field)? • How will it affect practice or research designs? • Provide arguments supporting the new framework, using a balanced discussion of its merits relative to other approaches	• Testability of the theory • Tractability of the theory (ease of use) • Explain significance of any extension, modification, or refinement of existing theory • Provide arguments supporting the theory, using a balanced discussion of its merits relative to other approaches
Implications	• Relate new conceptual framework (especially specific concepts) to pertinent research problems • Address its heuristic power (potential commonsense usefulness) • How might it affect future initiatives to develop theory	• Identify potential users and provide solid reasons that should convince them to engage with the theory (infer why the new theory matters for them) • Convince readers of timeliness, uniqueness, and originality of theory
Conclusions	Wrap up by convincing readers of the merit of the new conceptualization: • Redirect readers to the foundational and conceptual premises of the framework • Recapture the line of reasoning to convince readers of the soundness and robustness of the conceptual framework	Wrap up by articulating specific, logically deduced benefits of the theoretical argument and the theoretical contribution for future research

it provides an anchor for interpreting results or findings. Qualitative papers turn to the literature after the data are analyzed to find earlier studies to help explain the findings (see Chapter 8). Conceptual and theory papers normally do not include a problem statement or Methods section, but they both heavily rely on literature reviews (Callahan, 2010); however, "how that literature is used may be very different from the ways in which it is used in other articles" (McLean, 2011, p. 209). In fact, the literature review plays a different role in each of a theory paper and a conceptual paper (see Figure 18.3).

Theory paper literature review

In a theory paper, the purpose of the literature review is to draw lessons from the literature—that is, to learn from past scholars and apply those lessons to the theory being proposed and reported in the paper. McLean (2011) argued that only by gaining a broad-scope understanding from multiple sources of what has been written *theoretically* about the phenomenon can the author of a theory paper bring together and report on all elements of

FIGURE 18.3 ■ Role of Literature In a Theory Versus Conceptual Paper

Literature Review in Theory Paper	Literature Review in Conceptual Paper
• Learn lessons from previous *theoretical* writings about a phenomenon, and then strive for a large theoretical step that brings new headway to tractably theorizing about a problem • Use current and related literature to isolate a new feature of a family of problems that changes the way people theorize about it	• Synthesize and integrate formerly *disparate* (isolated) bodies of literature into a new conceptualization of a phenomenon • Employ integrative thinking to create provocative new conceptual perspectives by generating big ideas pulled together into a new conceptual whole

the theory. The author should examine literature focused on different aspects of the research problem, aiming for a large theoretical step that promises to bring new headway to tractably address the problem (Board & Meyer-ter-Vehn, 2014).

Making headway means making progress or moving closer to achieving something (Anderson, 2014). Toward that end, the "researcher-theorist is compelled to rely on thorough and scholarly exploration and study of current and related literature and research, as well as on her or his own observed experiences of the phenomenon in the real world" (Lynham, 2000a, p. 245). From this array of literature, authors should strive to theorize in such a way that they manage to "isolate a new feature of a family of problems that changes the way we think" (Board & Meyer-ter-Vehn, 2014, p. 2).

Conceptual paper literature review (role of integration)

The literature review also holds a prominent place in a conceptual paper (Balkin, 2009). Authors should extend what others have established about a concept and build on those conceptual contributions (McLean, 2011). Also, the literature must be critically analyzed and then synthesized into a new whole; conceptual integration is the hallmark of conceptual papers. "A paragraph-by-paragraph tour of one article after another is mind-numbing to read and not particularly insightful" (Callahan, 2010, p. 303). The literature review in a conceptual paper "should never slip into a series of summaries. Instead, it should be structured around the original argument. All references to the literature should refer directly to that structure" (Parncutt, 2015, p. 8). Otherwise, the paper runs the risk of becoming a hodgepodge of confusing ideas rather than a clean, elegant, integrative piece (Cropanzano, 2009).

"Conceptual articles perform an invaluable function by critiquing and integrating extant . . . perspectives" (Yadav, 2010, p. 2). A useful literature review depends on *synthesis* (see Chapter 7), which is the key to a well-written conceptual paper because it entails the examination of different parts, culminating in a new whole (Balkin, 2009). *Integration* is imperative as well because, without it, researchers cannot create "provocative new perspectives on key issues in the field" (Torraco, 2005, p. 356). Martin (2007) defined integrative thinking as "the ability to face constructively the tension of opposing ideas and instead of choosing one at the expense of the other, generate a creative resolution of the tension in the form of a new idea that contains elements of the opposing ideas but is superior to each" (p. 15).

Reviewing past research and then integrating that research with attendant insights can create new conceptualizations of a phenomenon; that is, it can generate big ideas (Yadav, 2010). A good conceptual paper underscores commonalities in the literature that build coherence, achieved by systematizing research that, up to this point in time, was in isolated bodies of literature. A conceptual paper reflects the researcher's success at pulling disparate pieces into a coherent new whole (Cropanzano, 2009).

REVIEW AND ENGAGEMENT

When critically reading a research report, you would

☐ Determine that the authors used subheadings appropriate for reporting a theory or a conceptual framework (see Table 18.2)

☐ Ascertain if they used the literature as expected for the type of paper they wrote (see Figure 18.3)

ELEMENTS OF A CONCEPTUAL PAPER

Salomone (1993) shared an interesting discussion of the creative process involved in creating new conceptualizations of a phenomenon. This mental process entails *speculative* thinking, by which he meant the "creative leap beyond the mere association of similar ideas" (p. 73), whereby the researcher's creative mind generates new ideas. These ideas emerge through the process of synthesis and integrative thinking, by which the researcher creates a comprehensive conceptual perspective that "transcends and then links divergent" concepts into a new whole (p. 73), elements that would otherwise not be united. This whole speculative process depends on a combination of "rational reasoning skills and artistic, intuitive talents" (p. 76).

Creativity during the development of the actual conceptual framework aside, this chapter strives to help authors prepare, and people to critically read, the final product, the actual paper that reports the new conceptual contribution. "The scope and structure of conceptual papers varies [sic]" (Watts, 2011, p. 309). After acknowledging this variation, Watts (2011) tendered a five-part model for a conceptual paper: introduction, review of literature, presentation of new concept (procedures or positions), discussion and implications, and conclusions (see Table 18.2). While all structural elements (subheadings in a paper) will be addressed below, the cornerstones of conceptual papers are the literature review and the presentation of the new concept.

Introduction

Although the introduction to a conceptual paper serves the same purpose as for a regular research paper (see Chapter 6), it is important in a conceptual paper that the authors include early on their position and do so in a purpose statement. This clearly identifies the sole focus of the paper and clarifies what issue is being conceptualized in a new way. While a thesis statement makes an assertion about a topic, a purpose statement clarifies the purpose, scope, and direction of a paper (Watts, 2011).

The introductory purpose statement for a conceptual paper should be (a) specific and precise (not broad and obscure); (b) concise (a lot of information in a few words); (c) clear and easy to understand (rather than vague, confusing, or ambiguous); and (d) stated in terms of intended outcomes (what the reader will learn or gain from the paper) (Zent, 2001). A conceptual paper is, after all, based mainly on theoretical thoughts and speculations about a topic, argued by researchers who are experts in the area and believe they have something new to contribute (Salomone, 1993). So, it is very important that the author of a conceptual paper clearly state what that new contribution is, in a clear and comprehensive manner.

> ***Example 18.1 Conceptual paper introductory purpose statement*** The purpose of this paper is to present a new conceptual framework about a sustainable life path for conscientious consumers. Readers will appreciate how related literature has been integrated into a new perspective of sustainable consumption, based on the notion of consumers embarking on a lifelong journey of engaged consumption (see Box 18.1, McGregor 2014).

Literature Review

The literature review has to convince readers that the new conceptualization has merit, best achieved by relating the concept to the existing literature. Balkin (2009) added that conceptual manuscripts "provide a thorough review of the literature and integrate previous research and data into the new concept, problem, theory, or phenomenon not previously examined in [the] literature" (p. 1). But, he cautioned that conceptual papers "move beyond a mere literature review [by providing] a strong theoretical [or conceptual] foundation or a synthesis of ideas" (p. 1). Authors of conceptual papers may choose to either separate the literature review from the presentation of the conceptual framework or integrate the two sections (Watts, 2011) (see Box 18.1).

Presentation of the New Conceptualization

Regardless, a conceptual paper must include a detailed accounting of the new conceptual framework (i.e., the presentation of the new conceptualization). The description of the new approach should be easy to understand and set out with exacting specificity (Watts, 2011). The paper should formally and precisely define all concepts, explicate how they relate to or interact with each other, and explain how they inform the phenomenon in question. As the concepts are defined, the architect of the conceptual framework should try to maintain a consistent level of abstraction while making sure that all relevant dimensions are clearly explained (BCS Information Retrieval Specialist Group, 2006; Yadav, 2010). Once the concepts are defined, the authors have to provide evidence of effective integration or combination of these concepts to develop the proposed new conceptual framework. They have to show how they used these concepts and their relationships as building blocks for a new framework, providing support from some combination of the literature and the logic they used to weave the concepts into a new whole (Yadav, 2010).

Also, when presenting the conceptual framework, authors should identify any underlying assumptions about why this collection of concepts makes sense in specific conditions. In addition to justifying this particular conceptual development, the author must position it against competing approaches, explaining how the new approach adds value (i.e., improves existing conceptualizations or fills a conceptual gap) (BCS Information Retrieval Specialist Group, 2006; Robey & Baskerville, 2012; Yadav, 2010).

Calling this *internal consistency*, Yadav (2010) confirmed that the arguments supporting the inclusion of concepts must be coherent and not contain logical contradictions or tautologies (saying the same thing twice using different words). The concepts and/or constructs comprising the new framework must be *theoretically meaningful* rather than conceptually ad hoc (a hodgepodge of ideas). Finally, when competing arguments for this new idea are considered and eliminated (or accommodated), the conceptual framework is said to be *conceptually robust* (Robey & Baskerville, 2012; Yadav, 2010). Box 18.1 profiles McGregor's (2014) paper that presented a new, life-path-oriented conceptual framework for sustainable, engaged consumption.

BOX 18.1

McGregor (2014) argued that a conceptual framework was needed to help people view consumption as a journey—a complex, lifelong process rather than a series of discrete, separate, cumulative events (shopping trips). To achieve this, she read a broad body of literature on the topics of sustainable consumption and sustainable living and discovered an array of never-before-integrated concepts and constructs. The sustainable life path conceptual framework was developed through the *conceptual integration* of the sister concepts of voluntary simplicity, living simply, life intentions, and life acumen, grounded in the idea of an examined, engaged, and purposeful life. Each concept or construct was prefaced with its own focused literature review, and the paper was held together with a red thread leading readers through the conceptual argument. McGregor culminated with a model of the conceptual framework (see next page) reflecting how each concept relates to the phenomenon, indicating *internal consistency* and affirming the framework is *theoretically meaningful*. The new conceptual framework adds value because it conceives a *sustainable life path* as involving a pathfinder's lifelong, engaged journey such that life's examined decisions sustain all life, especially when purposefully consuming with acumen in a complex world and when fulfilling the role of life-way innovator and leader for the good of humanity and the earth, now and in the future. The new framework is *conceptually robust* because competing ideas were considered and dismissed.

BOX 18.1

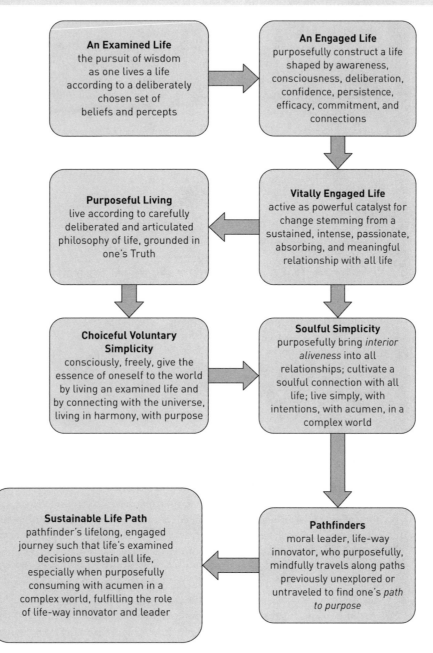

An Examined Life
the pursuit of wisdom
as one lives a life
according to a deliberately
chosen set of
beliefs and percepts

An Engaged Life
purposefully construct a life
shaped by awareness,
consciousness, deliberation,
confidence, persistence,
efficacy, commitment, and
connections

Purposeful Living
live according to carefully
deliberated and articulated
philosophy of life, grounded in
one's Truth

Vitally Engaged Life
active as powerful catalyst for
change stemming from a
sustained, intense, passionate,
absorbing, and meaningful
relationship with all life

**Choiceful Voluntary
Simplicity**
consciously, freely, give the
essence of oneself to the world
by living an examined life and
by connecting with the universe,
living in harmony, with purpose

Soulful Simplicity
purposefully bring *interior
aliveness* into all
relationships; cultivate a
soulful connection with all
life; live simply, with
intentions, with acumen, in a
complex world

Sustainable Life Path
pathfinder's lifelong, engaged
journey such that life's examined
decisions sustain all life,
especially when purposefully
consuming with acumen in a
complex world, fulfilling the role
of life-way innovator and leader

Pathfinders
moral leader, life-way
innovator, who purposefully,
mindfully travels along paths
previously unexplored or
untraveled to find one's *path
to purpose*

Discussion and Implications

The Discussion section of a conceptual paper takes on a different role than it does in a conventional research paper. In the latter, the discussion serves to link the results or findings back to the literature review and to any stated theory so as to interpret the results or findings of the study. In a conceptual paper, which has no theory, methods, results, or findings, the discussion still serves an interpretation role, but now it provides an understanding of how the new framework helps explain the phenomenon and/or how it affects practice. The Discussion section may also provide suggestions for future dialogue and research and, if appropriate, potential theoretical trajectories (Balkin, 2009; Watts, 2011).

In effect, the Discussion section can explore the concepts comprising the framework in terms of opportunities for research and implications of theory and practice (Rocco & Plakhotnik, 2009). The authors should spend a considerable effort spelling out the implications of pulling these concepts into a new framework. Authors must "relate the proposed conceptual development to the problems being addressed" (BCS Information Retrieval Specialist Group, 2006, p. 12). Yadav (2010) added that authors can address the innovativeness of the new framework by explaining its "heuristic power" (p. 15), or its potential usefulness for future researchers when designing their studies.

> ***Example 18.2 Conceptual paper discussion*** McGregor (2014) summarized the main conceptual contributions of her new conceptual framework and their import. "Reframing consumption as unfolding along a sustainable life path as defined in this paper is a conceptual innovation. Perceiving consumers as pathfinders is also a new way to envision consumer behaviour, as is framing consumption as a lifelong journey, a way to 'live life on purpose,' with intention, passion, conviction and simplicity—an engaged path to purpose. . . . With this concept, researchers and practitioners can now suggest that people acting in their consumer role could choose to become pathfinders, engaged leaders and life innovators committed to a sustainable life path that moves them along their journey toward a more examined life" (p. 18).

Conclusions

In the Conclusions section of a conceptual framework paper, authors should (a) briefly summarize the content of the paper and (b) reemphasize the foundational, conceptual point they were trying to make, either by reiterating the key premises or by creating a closing argument. The latter seeks to guide the readers' attention to the key foundational premise, which is grounded in supportive arguments (Watts, 2011). Closing arguments do not contain new information; rather, they remind readers of the logic used to develop the conceptual framework, and recapture the line of reasoning and intuitive thought that led to the new framework being proposed in the paper (Salomone, 1993). A good closing argument should convince readers that the framework is conceptually sound and that the author's faith in its potential contributions to new knowledge, theoretical innovations, and practice has merit.

> ***Example 18.3 Conceptual paper conclusion*** McGregor (2014) wrapped up her conceptual paper by referring to her logic and to the new contribution. "Figure 1

recaptures the line of thinking and the logic used to develop the concept of sustainable life path shared in this paper. The integration of this collection of constructs lead to a more considered and more comprehensive definition of sustainable life path, an innovative way to conceive consumer decisions as a complex, nuanced, lifelong journey and process rather than a collection of one-at-a-time decisions made during cumulative transactions" (p. 18).

REVIEW AND ENGAGEMENT

When critically reading a research report, you would

- ☐ Determine if the authors used subheadings appropriate for reporting a conceptual framework (see Table 18.2)

- ☐ Ascertain if they organized their paper so their conceptual framework is clearly accessible (This means they presented an integrated collection of disparate, defined, concepts into a new, synthesized whole, with a solid rationale. They clearly stated what issue was being conceptualized.)

- ☐ Check to see if they respected the specific role the literature review plays (see Figure 18.3 and Table 18.2)

- ☐ Determine if they presented a deeply integrated synthesis of the literature, which led to the new framework (see Figure 18.3)

- ☐ Judge whether they met the criteria recommended for judging the quality of a conceptual paper

ELEMENTS OF A THEORETICAL PAPER

The purpose of a theory paper is to ultimately alter research practice (Kilduff, 2006; Whetten, 1989). Despite this important role, Parncutt (2015) asserted that "there is not much out there about writing a theoretical paper [regarding] how to approach it or evaluate it" (p. 2). Because there is no single, most-preferred way to write or organize a theory paper, it is important that authors direct conscious attention to a variety of structural elements. When successful, they will have "leverage[d] the structure of the manuscript to aid in effectively communicating their theoretical contribution" (Smithey Fulmer, 2012, p. 330).

Said another way, the author uses the basic elements of any research paper to highlight the paper's theoretical nature and its contribution (picking and choosing from elements and weights given to each) (see Table 18.2). Foremost, a good theory paper encompasses a seamless flow of ideas reflecting both (a) a sequence of ideas and organizational elements and (b) the logical argument and its relationship to existing ideas in the field (Kilduff, 2006).

Title and Abstract

"Although these elements of a theory paper are the smallest, they do a lot of work" (Smithey Fulmer, 2012, p. 328). The title of a theory paper tends to be longer than that for a conventional research paper. The length is needed to express the specificity of the theory for experts in the field (Parncutt, 2015; Smithey Fulmer, 2012). It often comprises two phrases, separated with a colon. The first phrase in the title (before the colon) can succinctly state the topic (e.g., "Consumer Moral Leadership") or use an image or metaphor (e.g., "Spider Plant's Revenge") (Smithey Fulmer, 2012). Smithey Fulmer (2012) explained that a good theory paper title will refer to the core idea of the theory, in the simplest language possible.

Example 18.4 Theory paper titles

- *An Alternative Approach: The Unfolding Model of Voluntary Employee Turnover.* In this title, Lee and Mitchell (1994) indicated that their theory about voluntary employee turnover provides an alternative approach for predicting this phenomenon, with its new focus on unfolding decisions.

- *Integrated Theory of Health Behavior Change: Background and Intervention Development.* With this title, Ryan (2009) tells readers that her paper presents a new theory of health behavior change. The core idea in her theory is that an integrated perspective is needed. The title also indicates that the paper provides supportive background justifying the need for a new theory and that she used the theory to develop an intervention for use in practice.

The abstract of a theoretical paper should reflect the argumentative structure of the paper (Parncutt, 2015). To that end, it would introduce the controversy or rationale for why it is important to develop a new theory. Then, the abstract would briefly describe the key elements in the *supportive argument* justifying the new theory and identify key *contributions* of the theory. It would end with the main conclusions supporting the need for a new theory and this *particular* version of the theory (University of Sydney, 2016). Smithey Fulmer (2012) suggested another intent for the abstract, which is to state the core constructs and aims of the theory and the article reporting the theory.

Example 18.5 Theoretical paper abstract At the moment, the research on voluntary employee turnover seems to be dominated by two general but contrasting orientations. We argue that our third orientation will produce additional debate, hypothesizing, and empirical research that, ultimately, will complement the current body of knowledge. Our new theory of employee turnover applies constructs and concepts from decision making, statistics, and social psychology. As a new theoretical contribution, the process of employee turnover is modeled by four distinctive decision paths, each involving distinctive foci, psychological processes, and external events. We identify five ways this new theory contributes to the management literature, and we recommend that it be empirically tested in the future (adapted from Lee & Mitchell, 1994).

Introduction

In the Introduction section of a theory paper, the author should explain the nature or the context necessitating a new theory, giving some indication of how the theory will address an issue. No arguments are presented in the introduction, and the details of the new theory are not discussed. More appropriate is a statement explaining how a new theory will address the phenomenon in question. The author should not state conclusions in this section because the arguments supporting the new theory have not yet been presented to the readers (University of Sydney, 2016), and conclusions follow from the arguments (Parncutt, 2015).

The introduction to a theory paper should clearly identify the essence of the new theoretical contribution, whether it is an applied theory or a highbrow theory (Board & Meyer-ter-Vehn, 2014). *Essence* means the choicest, most essential or vital part of an idea (Anderson, 2014). Board and Meyer-ter-Vehn (2014) recommended a *canonical introduction*, one that reflects the simplest and most significant form possible of the theory without losing generality. Their formula includes (a) the broad motivation for a new theory and (b) a one- to two-paragraph description of the new contribution, as self-explanatory as possible at this point in time, since the new theory has not yet been explained.

> **Example 18.6 *Theoretical paper introduction*** This article has several major goals. The first goal is to argue that massacres and genocides are among the most important problems psychologists can study, given that they have traditionally theorized about love. The second goal is to review various theories of the forces behind massacres and genocides and to argue for one such theory emphasizing the often-contributing role of hate translated into action. Goals 1 and 2 provide the motivation for a new theory. The third goal is to present a theory of hate and its development and to discuss how hate can become one cause of massacres and genocides. The theory does not account for all aspects of hate, but it does account for at least some of the salient ones, specifically types of hate and the stories that underlie them (adapted from Sternberg, 2003).

Context for the New Theory

Smithey Fulmer (2012) observed that some authors of theory papers eschew the "solely generic section headings [employing instead] descriptive headings that introduce concepts or mirror the structure and flow of the theoretical model" (p. 328). That being said, the bulk of a comprehensive theory paper will set out in detail any relationship between older and existing theories of the phenomenon, thereby providing a context for the theory (Steiner, 1988). As well, the paper will relate the new theory (or its revised version) to current practice in the discipline or profession, providing a different sort of theoretical context. This strategy confirms the relevancy of the proposed new theory (BCS Information Retrieval Specialist Group, 2006; Board & Meyer-ter-Vehn, 2014).

Note that this aspect of presenting the theory does not require empirical proof that the theory holds. Instead, the paper depends on the clear presentation of arguments supporting the *need* for this new theory, arguments that must be presented clearly, with justification (BCS Information Retrieval Specialist Group, 2006; Robey & Baskerville, 2012). Without empirical support for the theory, the paper depends on the robustness of key arguments that have carefully compared and contrasted alternative theories (Yadav, 2010). The authors should clarify their underlying logic, assumptions, and views, which should be believable and justifiable. This "foundation of convincing argumentation" paves the way for less resistance to, and easier acceptance of, the proposed theory (Whetten, 1989, p. 494) (see Chapter 17) (see Box 18.2).

Presentation of the New Theory

A key part of a theory paper (its heart) is the section that contains the assumptions, the concepts and constructs (with their definitions), and any propositions stating relationships among the concepts (BCS Information Retrieval Specialist Group, 2006; Board & Meyer-ter-Vehn, 2014). These elements should be identified early in the paper (Smithey Fulmer, 2012). The assumptions underpinning the theory should be clearly articulated because they indicate what is being *assumed* about reality—that is, what is being accepted without proof (Arena, 2012). Assumptions specify the boundaries of the phenomenon as set out by *this* theory (Balucanag-Bitonio, 2014). The assumptions can be articulated in varying degrees in the paper, from explicit (preferred) to tacit (implied but not stated) (Nkwake, 2013) (see Chapter 3, Box 3.1, for an example of economic theory).

Each concept used in a theory must be specifically defined for *that* theory. A theoretical definition states what the concept means in a particular theory, compared to an operational definition, which is made up by any researcher measuring the concept in a study (The Learning House, 2016). In fact, concepts are the vocabulary (words) that people use when applying a theory, so it is very important that a theory paper defines these words in the context of the theory (Aswar, 2011) (see Chapter 3).

Not all authors choose to include the propositions for their theory in the paper, nor do they have to (Kilduff, 2006), but those who do can follow some basic conventions. In these cases, the propositions are "an organic part of the article and have a logical and coherent flow" (Smithey Fulmer, 2012, p. 329). Instead of a lengthy discourse followed with a long list of propositions at the end of the paper, authors should preface each proposition with a logical argument. The propositions then appear to emerge from the argument (i.e., they are organic). As well, they should all be worded in a way that is consistent with the terminology used in their supportive argument (Smithey Fulmer, 2012). And the paper should provide a rationale for each proposition, explaining if it stems from previous empirical findings, a related theory, or personal practice and experience (Board & Meyer-ter-Vehn, 2014; Webster & Watson, 2002).

This section of a theory paper often contains figures or diagrams, which are not the theory but do serve as "powerful tools for clarifying and enhancing the theoretical ideas in a paper" (Smithey Fulmer, 2012, p. 330). These graphs and figures tend to constitute boxes and arrows, used to illustrate the theoretical constructs and their relationships (Cropanzano, 2009; Smithey Fulmer, 2012) (see Chapter 3). Kilduff (2006) cautioned against using them in a theory paper if they can potentially distract from the message being conveyed. He called them extraneous elements of the paper and advised omitting them if they do not add value when articulating the theory. If the theory falls outside the "logical positivistic framework," the theory paper could instead "add value to existing ideas, push forward hitherto unexplored questions, or challenge conventional thinking" (Kilduff, 2006, pp. 253–254). Box 18.2 illustrates the basic tenets of what is involved in presenting a new theory.

Discussion

The Discussion section of a theory paper should address such issues as the testability of the theory in practice and its tractability (how easy it will be to use). In the event that the proposed theory is an extension, modification, or refinement of an existing one, the

BOX 18.2

George P. Moschis (1986) published a book reporting a new theory about the then relatively new idea of consumer socialization from a life cycle perspective. His theory reflects an integration of several perspectives into a unified theoretical framework (p. xii). The Introduction section provides the context for the need for such a theory, with one chapter focused on contemporary theories that contributed to his new theory (e.g., developmental, social learning, and social systems theory). Grounded in both explicit and implicit assumptions, his theory comprises nine overarching constructs or concepts that he theorized affect consumer socialization (see right column). Each of these concepts has its own chapter, which includes definitions. He then presents 197 propositions, averaging 22 propositions per concept. Each numbered proposition is prefaced with a several-paragraph-long supportive argument, citing relevant literature/sources (e.g., Proposition 8.1 stands for the first proposition in Chapter 8). There is no stand-alone list of propositions; rather, their presentation is organic, emerging after a contextual positioning in supportive, theoretically related literature. In the final chapter, he notes that little alternative theory was available at the time but that his theory was supported with considerable, available, empirical evidence. He further explained that the propositions are not as specific as he would like because of lack of knowledge in particular areas. He believed his new theory about consumer socialization could be applied in many different settings like research, marketing, education, and immigrant acculturation.

Chapter 5

Family Influence 14 propositions

Chapter 6

Peer Influences 19 propositions

Chapter 7

Mass Media 37 propositions

Chapter 8

Other Agents 14 propositions

Chapter 9

Age and Life Cycle 38 propositions

Chapter 10

Gender and Birth Order 21 propositions

Chapter 11

Socio-economics 19 propositions

Chapter 12

Racial Influences 18 propositions

Chapter 13

Cultural/Subcultural 17 propositions

197 Total

Examples:

After citing and explaining the contributory relevance of 18 different sources, Moschis (p. 164) offered

Proposition 8.1: Consumer education courses at school are more effective when they teach skills relevant to present and immediate consumption needs than when they teach skills relevant to needs in the distant future.

After citing and explaining the contributory relevance of 14 different sources, Moschis (p. 191) offered

Proposition 9.18: Anticipatory orientations determine how a person behaves as a consumer at a given stage in the life cycle.

After citing and explaining the contributory relevance of one source, Moschis (p. 110) offered

Proposition 6.9: Peer influences on the young consumer are carried into the youth's family, influencing adult consumer socialization and consumer behavior.

discussion should include reference to any experimental work that shows the proposed extension is significant and useful and has been successfully applied (BCS Information Retrieval Specialist Group, 2006; Lynham, 2002b). Modifications of existing theories should significantly alter scholars' views about how much the field is impacted (i.e., the scope of the theory) and how different the theory is from current thinking (i.e., degree of radicalness) (Whetten, 1989).

Still in the Discussion section, the theory paper should clarify linkages to research on the phenomenon, going beyond token statements of the value of using the theory. Arguments supporting the theory should reflect broad, current understandings of the subject while at the same time offer theoretical innovations (Parncutt, 2015; Whetten, 1989; Yadav, 2010). The theory is most convincing if it is supported by several sources, using multiple supportive arguments, what Parncutt (2015) called "convergent evidence" (p. 9). The tone of a theory paper should be one of "seasoned thinking, conveying completeness and thoroughness" (Whetten, 1989, p. 494).

> ***Example 18.7 Theoretical paper discussion (arguments supporting the theory)***
> "For basic researchers, a central issue has been to understand the concepts that prompt employees to leave an organization voluntarily [i.e., quit]. On the one hand, concepts external to the employee, a pull theory, have been studied primarily by market-oriented researchers, in which work was focused on job alternatives and how such alternatives surface. . . . On the other hand, constructs internal to the employee, a push theory, have been studied primarily by psychologically oriented [sic] researchers, who focused on job-related perceptions and attitudes. . . . The purposes of this article are (a) to present a general theory of voluntary employee turnover based on some earlier ideas suggested by Lee and Mitchell (1991). . . . A detailed theory, named the *unfolding model* of voluntary employee turnover, is presented. According to this theory, concepts and constructs from both market-pull and psychological-push approaches contribute to the decisions and behavior of people who voluntarily leave an organization. In addition, the theory describes certain conditions when neither a push nor pull approach is applicable as an explanation for employee turnover" (Lee & Mitchell, 1994, pp. 51–52).

Conclusions

Any conclusions in a theory paper must stem from the evidence presented in the arguments supporting the new theory, and no new arguments can be introduced in the Conclusions section (Parncutt & Painsi, 2006; University of Sydney, 2016). The implications (what using the theory means) depend on the claim that a new theory is needed (the main thesis of the theory paper, set out in the Introduction). Some readers may not like the conclusions of a theory paper because of what it means for them (either implied or inferred) (Parncutt, 2015). Consequently, the Conclusions section (and any implications) of a theory paper must address the issue of "Who cares about this theory?" The author has to identify who will be interested in the theory and *convince* them to engage with it relative to further theorization, research, and practice (Whetten, 1989).

To that end, the theory paper must present a balanced discussion of the merits of the theory relative to other approaches, rather than just espouse this one new approach (BCS

Information Retrieval Specialist Group, 2006; Watts, 2011). The authors must clearly articulate how their theoretical innovation has key implications for future scholarship in the discipline, for practice, or both. What does it really mean for others if the theory *is* valid or at least a promising idea? Authors must convince readers of the theory's timeliness, uniqueness, and originality, and they must entice them to explore its relevancy in their scholarship and knowledge advancement (Parncutt, 2015) (see Table 18.3). In the final conclusion, the author of a theory paper has to "specify the logically deduced implications for research of a theoretical argument" (Whetten, 1989, p. 492).

TABLE 18.3 ■ Convincing Rhetoric About Theory's Importance	
Elements of a Convincing Rhetoric	**Explained as they relate to the import of the theory**
Parsimonious	Accounts for observed data with a relatively simple explanation
Scope	How much and how the discipline or field will be impacted by the theory
Radicalness	Innovative, novel, and progressive, departure from current thinking
Relevancy	Closely appropriate to the matter at hand, the phenomenon of interest
Timeliness	Presented at a favorable time in the theoretical evolution of the discipline
Uniqueness	One of a kind (unlike other theories of the phenomenon)
Original	Others can confidently pattern their theoretical work on this theory
Tractability	How easy it is to use in research and practice
Utility	Usefulness and beneficialness when conducting research or practice
Testability	Affirm theory can be tested so it can be judged (be supported or falsified by the data of actual experience)

Example 18.8 Theoretical paper conclusions (merits of the new theory). "The duplex theory [of hate] has advantages over alternative theories both of hate and of the development of terrorism, massacres, and genocide. First, the theory accounts both for the structure of hate and its development and for the interaction of feelings and actions (through feelings and action triangles). All of these elements are needed in a complete theory. . . . The duplex theory accounts for both structure and development [of hate]. Second, the theory is relatively comprehensive in accounting for the structure of hate, [positing that] the seven different kinds of hate have different manifestations and are likely to have different consequences. . . . Sixth, the theory may provide a more compelling account of how terrorism, massacres, and genocides develop than do alternative theories. . . . Seventh, and finally, the duplex theory may be more nearly complete as well as systematic in its account of the causes of hate—and subsequently of terrorism, massacres, and genocide—than are competing theories. It points out the

many ways in which hate can be fomented and manifested and in which it may lead to terrorism, massacres, and genocides through stories stressing the need to eliminate certain groups of people" (Sternberg, 2003, pp. 322–323).

Example 18.9 Convincing rhetoric about import of a theory Sharma, Knowlden, and Nahar (2017) developed a new theory called the Multitheory Model (MTM) of Health Behaviour Change. They wanted people to use this theory to develop intervention programs to mitigate binge drinking in college students. At the end of their article, they spoke positively and strongly about the importance of their theory, referring to several criteria in Table 18.3, placed in brackets within the following quote [emphasis added]. "Since the [six] constructs of the theory have proven track records, it is likely that this theory would be useful in modifying this health behaviour [UTILITY]. The theory is parsimonious, as there are only 3 constructs for initiation and only 3 constructs for sustenance [PARSIMONIOUS], so it should be appealing to students, practitioners, and researchers [UTILITY] who should apply it either independently or in association with brief motivational interventions to modify binge drinking behavior in college students [TRACTABILITY]. To test the efficacy of such an intervention, one can [employ one of five possible research designs, whose empirical results] can be used to discern changes over time in constructs of the theory and behaviors that can be indicative of the efficacy of this theory [SCOPE]" (Sharma et al., 2017, p. 54).

REVIEW AND ENGAGEMENT

When critically reading a research report, you would

- ☐ Determine if the authors used subheadings appropriate for reporting a theory (see Table 18.2), appreciating there is no one way to do this
- ☐ Ascertain whether they organized their paper so their theory is clearly accessible (meaning assumptions, concepts, definitions, a network of propositions, and perhaps hypotheses) (see Box 18.2)
- ☐ Check to see if they respected the specific role the literature review plays in a theory paper (see Figure 18.3 and Table 18.2)
- ☐ Confirm whether they convinced you of the import of their theory (see Table 18.3)
- ☐ Judge if they met the criteria recommended for judging the quality of a theory paper

STAGE OF THEORY BEING PUBLISHED IN A THEORETICAL PAPER

The two previous sections profiled the major building blocks that can be used (and how) when writing theory or conceptual framework papers (see Table 18.2). This section takes a broader perspective about theoretical papers, explaining the scope of the paper as it relates to *how much* of the theory to publish. Lynham (2002b) suggested that anyone developing a theory (that has not been published yet) moves iteratively among five components, with each always occurring but not always in the same sequence: conceptual development, operationalization, confirmation or disconfirmation of the theory, application in practice, and continuous refinement and development of the theory (see Figure 18.4). Authors should clarify how much of their theory they are publishing in a particular paper, ranging from presenting it (a) without having been tested, (b) with evidence of empirical validation, (c) with examples of its application in practice, or (d) with refinements or further development of an earlier version.

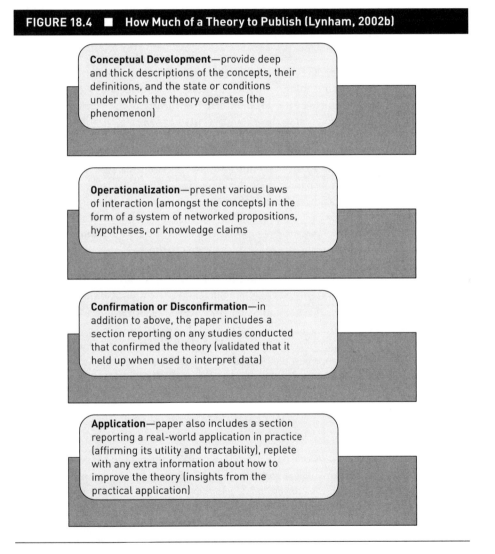

FIGURE 18.4 ■ How Much of a Theory to Publish (Lynham, 2002b)

Conceptual Development—provide deep and thick descriptions of the concepts, their definitions, and the state or conditions under which the theory operates (the phenomenon)

Operationalization—present various laws of interaction (amongst the concepts) in the form of a system of networked propositions, hypotheses, or knowledge claims

Confirmation or Disconfirmation—in addition to above, the paper includes a section reporting on any studies conducted that confirmed the theory (validated that it held up when used to interpret data)

Application—paper also includes a section reporting a real-world application in practice (affirming its utility and tractability), replete with any extra information about how to improve the theory (insights from the practical application)

Conceptual Development

In more detail, the author could start the paper with a section on conceptual development (note that this may in fact comprise the entire paper, if the theory has not yet been operationalized). This aspect of reporting a theory (a) describes the key elements or concepts of the theory with their definitions, (b) sets out an initial explanation of their interdependence, and (c) explains the general limitations and conditions under which the theoretical framework can be expected to operate (Lynham, 2002b). A stable and bounded theory is better ensured with deep and thick descriptions of the constructs and concepts and how they are related (McLean, 2011). The concepts (called units of the theory) are the variables whose interactions constitute the subject matter of the theory (Lynham, 2002a). At this stage of the theory's life, a network of propositions or hypotheses has not been developed.

Example 18.10 Conceptual development

Lee and Mitchell (1994) developed a model (theory) to help understand the thought processes involved when employees voluntarily leave an organization (i.e., were not fired), creating the problem of turnover. In their 40-page paper, they explained that they used concepts from another theory to develop their conceptualization, Beach's (1990) image theory. They provided an overview of that theory's main *assumptions* and then its main *constructs*. Their theory used image theory's concepts to understand voluntary employee turnover, informed by general processes, which they *conceptualized* as decision paths. Their theory comprised four decision paths that employees can follow as they interpret their work environments, identify options, and enact responses (one of which is to leave voluntarily—that is, to quit). Each path unfolds over time. The authors *pictorially represented* their model in a matrix, which they called a "heuristic summary of the unfolding model" (p. 70). There are two main theoretical *concepts*. The first is "shock," which employees experience, jarring them toward deliberate judgments about their position and the possibility of leaving voluntarily. The second is "mental deliberations" (employees' thought processes in light of the shock). Lee and Mitchell identified five contributions of their new model, including that it was a "much needed theoretical change." However, they did not provide a set of propositions or hypotheses, and they did not test their theory. Instead, they reported that "[t]urnover research badly needs some new theory. Our ideas on turnover are well grounded in existing theory as well as personal experience. As such, we believe that these new ideas merit empirical testing" (p. 85).

Operationalization

If advanced enough, the second part of a theory paper could translate or convert the theory into observable, confirmable components. Again, this may in fact comprise the entire paper, in combination with the conceptual development process. The components include propositions, empirical indicators, possible hypotheses, and/or knowledge claims (i.e., operationalization). These components contribute to people's trust and confidence in the new theory. Stating these laws of interaction about how the concepts influence each other is a theory's major contribution to knowledge (Lynham, 2002a, 2002b). Lynham (2002a) clarified that hypotheses can be developed by both the theorist and subsequent researchers applying the theory. Rigorous operationalization of the theory helps potential users trust its readiness for testing and for evidence-based verification through research inquiries and studies (McLean, 2011). Operationalization also involves explaining the boundaries or limitations of the theory, meaning the small part of the world that the theory strives to model or explain. As well, it specifies both the level of complexity the theory addresses and the different conditions under which the theory operates (called the system states of the theory) (Lynham, 2002a).

> ***Example 18.11 Theory conceptualization and operationalization*** In a 30-page article, Sternberg (2003) began his theoretical paper by explaining that the field of psychology has not generated many theories of hate, with those developed focused on either individuals or groups but not both. With this well-developed rationale, he introduced his new theory called the *Duplex Theory of Hate*. He articulated five *assumptions* (claims) about "hate reality" that underpin his theory. This was followed with a pictorial *model* of his triangular structure of hate, comprising three components (*concepts*). He explained that "[n]o claim is made in regard to statistical independence [of the three theoretical concepts]. Rather, the claim is made that they can be and at times are separated in feelings of hatred people have toward individuals or groups" (p. 306). Each of these components (concepts) and their *subconcepts* were theoretically *defined*, with supportive literature. Using these concepts and subconcepts, Sternberg created a typology of seven types of hate. Although not using the term *proposition*, he then proposed that these components of hate *are related to* terrorism, massacres, and genocides along four degrees of danger. This notion was supported with a table listing 18 *hypotheses* of how these are related. Each hypothesis was *conceptually developed*, with supportive literature. Sternberg explained seven *benefits* of his new theory (akin to the system states of the theory). He concluded by acknowledging and explaining four *limitations* to his new theory of hate.

Confirmation or Disconfirmation (Testing)

The author could stop at the operationalization stage and publish a paper that sets out the phenomenon the theory is intended to address, the theory's concepts and their definitions, and how they are related to each other via a network of propositions or hypotheses (i.e., conceptual development and operationalization). It is important to note that "'proof' that a theory holds is not a necessary requirement for a theoretical paper to be acceptable" (BCS Information Retrieval Specialist Group, 2006, p. 4). *But*, if the architect of the theory wants it to be used by the rest of the field and by practitioners, the paper should go further. If available, the author could include sections in the paper on confirmation and/or application of the theory.

Consequently, in addition to developing the theory, the author would report on a study designed to confirm the theory. This inquiry would entail using the theory to interpret data and results, thereby attesting to the strength of the conceptualizations and operationalizations. The author would discuss whether or not the theory held up. Was it able to help explain, predict, control, describe, or interpret reality (Lynham, 2002b; Watts, 2011; Yadav, 2010)? Including this information is especially relevant when the new theory is an extension of a previously tested theory (BCS Information Retrieval Specialist Group, 2006).

Colquitt and Zapata-Phelan (2007) tendered a comprehensive discussion of theory building and theory testing. They asserted that proper empirical testing can "temper enthusiasm for appealing but invalid" (p. 1281) theories. "Early tests of a theory are typically concentrated on establishing the validity of the theory's core propositions. In subsequent tests, researchers begin exploring the mediators that explain those core relationships or the moderators that reflect the theory's boundary conditions. Eventually, in yet further tests they begin expanding the theory by incorporating antecedents or consequences that were not part of the original formulation" (p. 1282).

> ***Example 18.12 Theory confirmation (testing)*** Per example 18.10, the creators of the unfolding model of voluntary turnover tested their theory and published that paper in 1996 (Lee, Mitchell, Wise, & Fireman, 1996). As explained in their abstract, they "reported on a test of Lee and Mitchell's model of voluntary employee departure from an organization. Data gathered from interviews with nurses who had recently quit their jobs and a mailed survey were analyzed qualitatively via pattern matching and quantitatively through correlations, analysis of medians, log linear modeling, and contingency tables. Although the data *generally supported the theory* [emphasis added], several *nonconforming* [emphasis added] cases revealed ambiguities in the model and therefore opportunities for improvement [which were addressed in some detail]" (p. 5). They further explained that "although *not all theory-based predictions were confirmed in the present study* [emphasis added], some meaningful points should be highlighted" (p. 32). First, their study provided preliminary *empirical support* for the concept of shock. Second, their model explained, *as predicted*, the unfolding process of voluntarily leaving a position (i.e., quitting and terminating employment).

Application

Some authors may be able to go even further and add a section in their paper on the application of their theory in practice. A real-world application of the theory is not the same thing as the former stage of confirmation of the theory in a purposefully designed study. Practitioners using the theory to inform their interactions with clients is a real test of how practical the theory is in the world of practice. This application provides invaluable insights into ongoing development of the theory. A paper of this nature could include refinements of the conceptualization and operationalization of the theory (Lynham, 2002b). Also, using an existing theory in new applications should improve the theory rather than just reaffirm its utility. And these improvements should focus on several elements of the theory, with compelling evidence. The evidence can pertain to the logic underpinning the theory (the internal consistency), the consistency of its predictions (empirical evidence), or its assumptions (epistemology) (Whetten, 1989).

Sharma et al.'s (2017) theoretical paper reported the use of the Multitheory Model (MTM) of Health Behaviour Change to develop an intervention focused on altering binge drinking behavior among college students. In this particular paper, they provided a framework for an intervention based on the theory, along with suggestions for how others could apply the intervention in practice. But they did not report on the actual intervention, although they have reported such applications in other papers (Vinayak Nahar, personal communication, April 2017). Ryan (2009), on the other hand, wrote a paper that reported on her application of her theory-based intervention in practice, thereby validating the real-world utility and tractability of her theory of health behavior change (see example 18.4).

Example 18.13 Theory application

In her theoretical article, Ryan (2009) presented a new midrange descriptive theory, the Integrated Theory of Health Behavior Change (ITHBC), and demonstrated the application of the theory in the development of an intervention. After introducing the theory, including concepts, definitions, and relationships among concepts (with a pictorial model), she explained that it was foundational to the development of an intervention by clinical nurse specialists targeting the prevention or attenuation of osteoporosis. Ryan clarified that the intervention contained the required theoretical constructs of knowledge and beliefs, self-regulation skills and abilities, and social facilitation. The intervention began with assessing each woman in terms of these dimensions of health behavior change. This particular intervention focused on the self-management behaviors of calcium and vitamin D intake, weight-bearing exercise, and balance enhancement, which are associated with long-term bone health. Ryan asserted that the participants' achievement of these outcomes provided a measure of the effectiveness of the intervention and, by association, the validity and tractability of the theory in application and in clinical practice (see Table 18.3).

In summary, a theory paper could include all four components (Lynham, 2002b) (see Figure 18.4), which is possible if the author has tested the theory and applied it in practice. Without the latter, the author can report on the essence of the theory and any studies undertaken to validate it. To the lesser extent, the author can report on the new theory but with no reference to its validation in research or its application in practice, leaving that to future work. The purpose of some theory papers is to build a case in support of a new theoretical framework (Cropanzano, 2009). To that end, McLean (2009) suggested using Lynham's (2002b) *four* stages as a way to determine how much of a theory to report in a theory paper.

REVIEW AND ENGAGEMENT

When critically reading a research report, you would

- ☐ Determine if the authors made judicious decisions about what to include in their theory paper (especially, that they did not say they had confirmed their theory if they had not conducted a study to test it) (see Figure 18.4)

- ☐ Decide whether their lack of attention to this detail affected your judgment of the quality of the paper

RIGOR IN CONCEPTUAL AND THEORETICAL PAPERS

Robey and Baskerville (2012) argued that a perfect argument is not the only parameter by which to judge a conceptual or theoretical paper. They identified four additional criteria specific to judging the rigor of conceptual and theoretical articles (see Figure 18.5). (a) *Logical consistency* involves taking care and paying close attention when structuring the arguments in the paper. If there are inconsistencies, contradictions will arise. (b) A convincing, effective *rhetorical strategy* respects the mood and likely receptivity of the audience. Authors should exert creativity when selecting and constructing their arguments. (c) *Completeness of argument* refers to there being a sufficient set of arguments to compel readers to embrace the author's ideas. If necessary, one argument leads to another, culminating in a convincing set of reasons that support an idea (see Chapter 6). (d) Finally, a conceptual or theoretical paper is rigorous if readers accept it as a *meaningful contribution* to knowledge. The conceptual or theoretical contribution adds value to the field.

Robey and Baskerville (2012) maintained that these four criteria (Figure 18.5) are "equal in value to [research methodological] rigor" (p. 4). To make this point, they presented their approach along two axes (two aspects of rigor). The vertical y-axis represents the *mode of reasoning aspect* (generative and analytical). The horizontal x-axis represents moving through the process of developing supportive arguments, comprising process and product (the *means-end, red thread aspect*) (see Figure 18.6).

Modes of Reasoning y-Axis

Robey and Baskerville's (2012) model includes two modes of reasoning, analytical and generative reasoning (vertical y-axis). They maintained that the authors of a rigorous conceptual paper will develop their concepts using both modes of reasoning. When engaged in *analytical reasoning*, people focus on, and constrain their attention to, the topic of analysis. They confine their judgments to what they know of and can deduce from the topic. However, when people want to generate novel ideas using integrative thinking, *generative reasoning* is invaluable. It requires letting one's attention drift toward concepts not previously associated with the topic (Howard-Jones, 2008) (see Chapter 14 for a discussion of critical and creative perspectives).

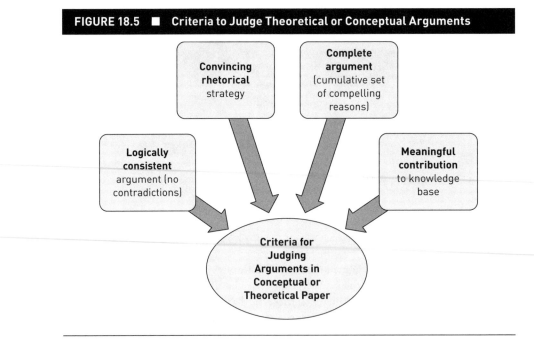

FIGURE 18.5 ■ Criteria to Judge Theoretical or Conceptual Arguments

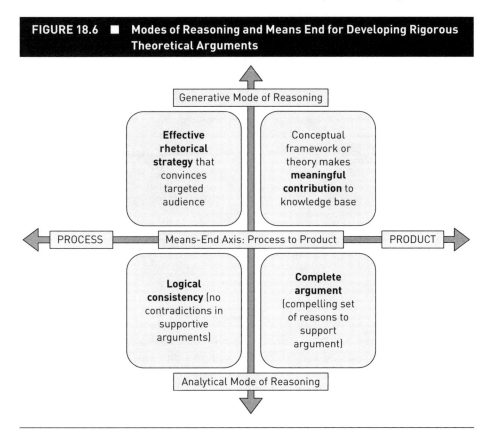

FIGURE 18.6 ■ Modes of Reasoning and Means End for Developing Rigorous Theoretical Arguments

Generative reasoning is a process of strategic thinking oriented toward creating and inventing ideas (rather than calculating and finding them) (de Wit & Meyer, 2010). Given that both theories, and especially conceptual frameworks, depend heavily on synthesis and integration (Balkin, 2009; Yadav, 2010), generative reasoning is extremely apropos for these types of papers. Note that a red thread (the horizontal x-axis) pulls both the writer and readers through the paper, taking people from one crucial point to the next, from the start to the end (Munker, 2012) (see Figure 18.7).

Judging Reasoning and Argumentation

Regarding the vertical y-axis, *analytical reasoning* is judged using logical consistency (no contradictions) and argumentative completeness. *Generative reasoning* is judged using effective rhetoric and meaningful contributions. If *analytical reasoning* is evident in the paper—that is, the discussion is focused on just one topic—the argument has to be logically consistent (no contradictions), and the argument must be complete (run its full course). When strategically thinking about creating and inventing ideas (*generative reasoning*), the author's arguments must be persuasive (effective rhetoric), and the final conceptual framework or theory must make a valuable and meaningful contribution to the field, in part because the supportive arguments are *so* convincing (Robey & Baskerville, 2012).

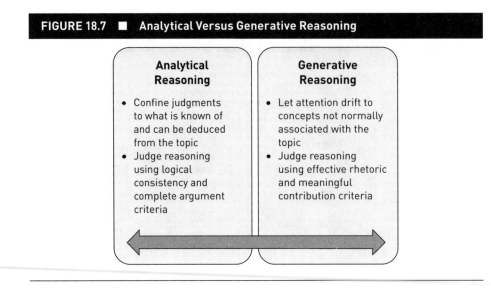

FIGURE 18.7 ■ Analytical Versus Generative Reasoning

Analytical Reasoning

- Confine judgments to what is known of and can be deduced from the topic
- Judge reasoning using logical consistency and complete argument criteria

Generative Reasoning

- Let attention drift to concepts not normally associated with the topic
- Judge reasoning using effective rhetoric and meaningful contribution criteria

The horizontal x-axis (the red thread) concerns both the process and the product of developing an argument. The authors must develop their theoretical or conceptual argument in a *pragmatic* way (process), using the most effective rhetoric possible to create a significant theoretical contribution in a *complete* way (product). The *process* is judged using two criteria: a convincing, effective rhetoric and logical consistency (no contradictions). The final *product* (the argument scaffolding the theory paper and the actual theory) is judged using the other two criteria: completeness of argument (run its full course) and the meaningful contribution of the theoretical or conceptual framework.

REVIEW AND ENGAGEMENT

When critically reading a research report, you would

☐ Determine if the authors presented a sound argument for the acceptance of their theory or conceptual framework and that this argument met the criteria for a rigorous argument (see Figure 18.5)

☐ Ascertain if they, ideally, employed both generative and analytical reasoning to develop their supportive argument (see Figures 18.6 and 18.7)

☐ If they used analytical reasoning, check to see if they focused on one topic using a logically consistent argument (no contradictions)

☐ If they used generative reasoning, ascertain if they used lateral thinking combined with an effective rhetoric, persuading you that they made a meaningful contribution to the discipline (see Table 18.3)

☐ Per the above, determine if they developed a strong red thread that pulled you through their paper (used effective rhetoric and brought their argument to a close)

FINAL JUDGMENT ON CONCEPTUAL OR THEORETICAL PAPER

Taking *all* of the **Review and Engagement** criteria into account, what is your final judgment of the conceptual or theoretical paper that you are critically reading?

CHAPTER SUMMARY

This chapter focused on a particular form of academic scholarship, conceptual and theoretical papers. After clarifying the different purposes served by each type of paper (see Figure 18.2), the discussion shifted to the format authors should use to organize their paper. After acknowledging that there is not set format for either type of paper, the special role that the literature review plays in each paper was addressed. It is an integrative instrument in a conceptual paper and a theoretical-step instrument in a theory paper. Table 18.2, and extensive supportive narrative text, profiled the key structural elements in both papers, distinguishing between each one. These elements constitute the organizational subheadings in the published paper. The section on organizing theoretical papers concluded with information about how authors can convince readers that their new theory is important (see Table 18.3). The conversation turned to Lynham's idea of what to include in a theory paper, determined by how well developed it is (ranging from only the conceptual stage, through to being successfully applied in practice (see Figure 18.4). The chapter concluded with a detailed discussion of what criteria to use to judge the rigor of a conceptual or theoretical paper, mainly its supportive, red thread argument (see Figures 18.5, 18.6) and the author's mode of reasoning (analytical and generative) (see Figure 18.7).

REVIEW AND DISCUSSION QUESTIONS

1. How is a conceptual framework for a *particular* study different from a conceptual framework for a number of studies?

2. Theory papers and conceptual papers involve different intellectual processes on the part of the author. Explain how they differ.

3. How do theoretical and conceptual papers differ in their purpose?

4. Explain how the principle of argumentation is key to writing theory papers and conceptual papers, given that both papers are discursive in nature.

5. Using Table 18.2, compare and contrast the structural elements of theoretical and conceptual papers, especially identifying where they differ substantially.

6. Why do you think the literature review plays such different roles in these two types of papers?

7. Much like argumentative essays, theoretical papers involve the use of convincing rhetoric. But instead of appeals to logic, emotions, or character, authors are expected to convince readers of the import of their theory. Identify and explain the nine elements of convincing *theoretical rhetoric*.

8. Lynham (2002b) provided an approach that helps authors decide *how much* of their theory to publish in any given paper. Explain her four-pronged approach.

9. Conceptual and theoretical papers also have to meet the criterion of rigor and high-quality scholarship. Explain Robey and Baskerville's (2012) four-quadrant approach to judging arguments used to write theory or conceptual papers (i.e., modes of reasoning and means-end, red thread argument).

10. Compare and contrast analytical versus generative reasoning, which can be employed when writing theoretical or conceptual papers.

APPENDIX

Worksheet for Critiquing
a Journal Article or Research Report

An editable version of this worksheet can be downloaded from **https://study.sagepub.com/mcgregor**.

Particular Research Element of the Journal Article to Be Critiqued	Share your critique in this middle column, applying all of the criteria from the chapter for each research element. It is not enough to just describe what the authors did, *without* critiquing it. Place a full citation for the journal article or research report here:	Did the research element meet the criteria set out in the respective chapter? Indicate Yes, No, Not Sure, or N/A in this cell.
Journal (Chapter 5)	Identify, describe, then critique the journal itself, if a journal article	
Research element	Critique each research element found in your article or research report by applying the relevant chapter content in this middle column; research elements may not appear in this order in your chosen report or paper, and some elements may be missing. If missing, comment on whether its absence is an issue. Don't just say N/A.	
Title of article or research report (Chapter 4)		
Authors' identity and implications of order in which the names are listed (Chapter 4)		

(Continued)

(Continued)

Research element	Critique each research element found in your article or research report by applying the relevant chapter content in this middle column; research elements may not appear in this order in your chosen report or paper, and some elements may be missing. If missing, comment on whether its absence is an issue. Don't just say N/A.	
Abstract (Chapter 4)		
Keywords (some journals do not have any) (Chapter 4)		
Opening points (Chapter 6)		
Kind of research argument (Chapter 6)		
Research questions (perhaps objectives) (Chapter 6)		
Methodological orientation (indicate if explicit or inferred by you) (Chapter 2)		
Introduction (may or may not be separate from literature review, but comment anyway) (Chapter 6)		

Research element	Critique each research element found in your article or research report by applying the relevant chapter content in this middle column; research elements may not appear in this order in your chosen report or paper, and some elements may be missing. If missing, comment on whether its absence is an issue. Don't just say N/A.	
Literature review (may or may not include hypotheses, research questions, objectives and theory, conceptual framework or model) (Chapter 7)		
Theories, models, or conceptual frameworks (may be under a separate heading or part of literature review) (Chapter 3)		
Hypotheses (N/A if not present) (Chapters 10 and 14)		
Research design (Chapter 8)		
Methods (different criteria for qualitative, quantitative, and mixed methods) (Chapters 8, 9, and 10)		
Results if quantitative (comment on statistics) (Chapters 11, 12, and 13) Findings if qualitative (Chapter 13) Both if mixed methods (especially comment on the principle of integration) (Chapter 14)		

(Continued)

(Continued)

IF ARGUMENTATIVE ESSAY, THEORETICAL PAPER, OR CONCEPTUAL PAPER, you cannot critique method, results/findings, discussion, or limitations (unless the author has included them); instead, focus on the research elements in the shaded area below.		
Argumentation style and quality of execution (deductive/inductive) (Chapter 17)		
Thesis-antithesis-synthesis (Chapter 17)		
Type of rhetoric (ethos, pathos, logos) (Chapter 17)		
Extent of theory reported (Chapter 18)		
Conventions for reporting conceptual and theoretical papers (Chapter 18)		
Logical fallacies (Chapter 18)		
Tables and/or figures (if none, could there have been any?) (Chapter 10)		
Discussion (may be stand-alone section or integrated into the Results/Findings or Conclusions section) (Chapter 14)		
Delimitations and limitations (may or may not have separate headings) (Chapters 6 and 13)		
Implications (may or may not have separate heading) (Chapters 14, 15, and 16)		

Conclusions (may or may not have exact heading, but look for wrap-up of sorts; check especially for modal verbs and modal force) (Chapter 15; check Chapter 16 for modal verbs)		
Recommendations (may have exact heading or be buried in text, but try to find and judge them; if none, could there have been any? Check for modal force) (Chapter 16)		
References (in list and in text) (Chapters 4 and 5)		
Acknowledgments (if none, could there have been any?) (Chapter 4)		
Research bios (if none, could there have been any?) (Chapter 4)		
Appendices (judge them; if none, could there have been any?) (Chapter 4)		
Footnotes and endnotes (judge them; if none, could there have been any?) (Chapter 4)		

What is your general assessment of *the scholarship* in the article or research report, given what you discovered while assessing each individual *research element*? To express this judgment, first give the entire paper or report a thumbs-up, thumbs-down, or not sure (use the *icon*). Then, prepare at least four additional paragraphs in the space below, using an extra page if required (*not* just one paragraph). Refer to particularly contentious or well-done research elements of the paper or research report to justify your final judgment on the scholarship.

The following document will be used to assess your assignment:

Scope/range—number of research elements covered in your critique (possible 20–21)		
Appropriateness of your judgment about *not* critiquing particular research elements		
Depth—quality of the analysis of each research element that you did critique (depth *and* correctness)		
Thoroughness when applying material covered in the chapter - Was your application of the chapter material that you *did* use nuanced and sophisticated or just rudimentary? - Also, did you leave out relevant chapter content that *could* have been applied?		
Degree to which your final **judgment** of the scholarship (set out in the four paragraphs above) was **supported** by your overall analysis of each research element	# of thumbs-up # of thumbs-down # of uncertain # not evaluated	Example 1 Although you gave the scholarship a thumbs-up, you gave two key research elements a thumbs-down: methods and discussion. Your final judgment is not supported by your judgment of these key research element judgments. Example 2 You gave a thumbs-down to the scholarship, and this was supported by 15 thumbs-down for separate research elements, especially the Method and Discussion sections.

REFERENCES

Aarons, G. A., Fettes, D. L., Sommerfeld, D. H., & Palinkas, L. (2012). Mixed methods for implementation research: Application to evidence-based practice implementation and staff turnover in community based organizations providing child welfare services. *Child Maltreatment, 17*(1), 67–79.

admin. (2015a, October 7). Difference between model and theory [Web log post]. Retrieved from http://pediaa.com/difference-between-model-and-theory/

admin. (2015b, November 13). Difference between theme and topic [Web log post]. Retrieved from http://pediaa.com/difference-between-theme-and-topic/

African Virtual University. (ca. 2015). *Guidelines for writing & organizing your research paper*. Retrieved from the AVU website: http://conference.avu.org/public/conferences/1/Guidelinesforwritinga_researchpaper.pdf

Agarwal, R., Echambadi, R., Franco, A., & Sarkar, S. (2006). Reap rewards: Maximizing benefits from reviewer comments. *Academy of Management Journal, 49*(2), 191–196.

Alaranta, M. (2006, June). *Combining theory-testing and theory-building analyses of case study data*. Paper presented at the European Conference on Information Systems, Göteborg, Sweden. Retrieved from http://aisel.aisnet.org/ecis2006/175/

Albers, S. (2014). *Conceptual paper development and theory building in management and organization studies*. Retrieved from the University of Southern Denmark (Syddansk Universitet) website: http://static.sdu.dk/mediafiles//A/6/5/%7BA65A5D0A-29A8-4D14-B4F0-D1C9614429D1%7DConseptual%20Paper%20IME%20Sept%2014.pdf

Aliaga, M., Cobb, G., Cuff, C., Garfield, J., Gould, R., Lock, R., . . . Witmer, J. (2010). *Guidelines for assessment and in statistics education: College report*. Washington, DC: American Statistical Association. Retrieved from http://www.amstat.org/education/gaise/GaiseCollege_Full.pdf

American Academy of Family Physicians. (2016). *AAFP definitions for policy statement, position paper and discussion paper*. Leawood, KS: Author. http://www.aafp.org/about/policies/all/policy-definitions.html

American Heritage Dictionary (4th ed). (2000). Boston, MA: Houghton Mifflin.

American Institute for Conservation of Historic and Artistic Works. (2013). *AIC position paper guidelines*. Retrieved from the AIC website: http://www.conservation-us.org/docs/default-source/governance/position-paper-guidelines-(february-2013).pdf?sfvrsn=12

American Psychological Association. (2001). *Publication manual of the American Psychological Association* (5th ed). Washington, DC: Author.

Anderson, G. (2012, October 10). No result is worthless: The value of negative results in science [Web log post]. Retrieved from https://blogs.biomedcentral.com/on-medicine/2012/10/10/no-result-is-worthless-the-value-of-negative-results-in-science/

Anderson, G. (2015). *How to write a paper in scientific journal style and format*. Retrieved from the Bates College Department of Biology website: http://abacus.bates.edu/~ganderso/biology/resources/writing/HTWtoc.html

Anderson, L. W., & Krathwohl, D. R. (Eds.). (2001). *A taxonomy for learning, teaching, and assessing: A revision of Bloom's taxonomy of educational objectives* (Complete ed.). New York, NY: Longman.

Anderson, S. (Ed.). (2014). *Collins English dictionary* (12th ed.). Glasgow, Scotland: HarperCollins.

Anfara, V. A., & Mertz, N. T. (Eds.). (2006). *Theoretical frameworks in qualitative research*. Thousand Oaks, CA: Sage.

Anglika. (2008, October 27). Thread: Axiom vs assumption [Web log comment]. Retrieved from https://www.usingenglish.com/forum/threads/81541-axiom-Vs-assumption

Annesley, T. M. (2010). The discussion section: Your closing argument. *Clinical Chemistry, 56*(11), 1671–1674.

Arena, P. (2012, December 13). The role of assumptions [Web log post]. Retrieved from http://duckofminerva.com/2012/12/the-role-of-assumptions.html

Armstrong, J. S. (1997). Peer review for journals: Evidence on quality control, fairness, and innovation. *Science and Engineering Ethics, 3*(1), 63–84.

Aronson, J. (1994). A pragmatic view of thematic analysis. *The Qualitative Report* [e-journal], *2*(1). Retrieved from http://www.nova.edu/ssss/QR/BackIssues/QR2-1/aronson.html

Ary, D., Jacobs, L. C., & Sorensen, C. (2010). *Introduction to education research* (8th ed.). Belmont, CA: Wadsworth.

Association of Legal Writing Directors & Barger, C. (2010). *ALWD citation manual: A professional system of citation* (4th ed.). Alphen aan den Rijn, The Netherlands: Wolters Kluwer.

Aswar, M. (2011). *STA630: Research methods*. Retrieved from the Virtual University of Pakistan website: http://vulms.vu.edu.pk/Courses/STA630/Downloads/STA630%20-%20Research%20Methods.pdf

Auman, M. (n.d.). *Hints for writing a conclusion*. Retrieved from the Anchorage School District website: https://www.asdk12.org/middlelink/la/writing/stepup/writing_conclusion.pdf

Avison, D., Fitzgerald, G., & Powell, P. (2001). Reflections on information systems practice, education and research: 10 years of the Information Systems Journal. *Information Systems Journal, 11*, 3–22.

Axelrod, R. B., & Cooper, C. R. (1993). *Reading critically, writing well.* New York, NY: St. Martin's Press.

Azar, B. (2006, January). Discussing your findings. *gradPSYCH Magazine.* Retrieved from the American Psychological Association website: http://www.apa.org/gradpsych/2006/01/findings.aspx

Azevedo, L. F., Canário-Almeida, F., Almeida Fonseca, J., Costa-Pereira, A., Winck, J. C., & Hespanhol, V. (2011). How to write a scientific paper: Writing the methods section. *Portuguese Journal of Pulmonology, 17*(4), 232–238.

Babor, T., Stenius, K., Savva, S., & O'Reilly, J. (Eds.). (2004). *Publishing addiction science* (2nd ed.). Essex, England: Multi-Science Publishing.

Bacharach, S. B. (1989). Organizational theories: Some criteria for evaluation. *Academy for Management Review, 14*(4), 496–515.

Back, M. D., Stopfer, J. M., Vazire, S., Gaddis, S., Schmukle, S. C., Egloff, B., & Gosling, S. D. (2010). Facebook profiles reflect actual personality, not self-idealization. *Psychological Science, 20*(10), 1–3.

Bak, N. (2003). *Guide to academic writing.* Cape Town, South Africa: University of the Western Cape.

Baker, J., Brizee, A., & Angeli, E. (2013). *Essay writing.* Retrieved from the Purdue OWL website: https://owl.english.purdue.edu/owl/owlprint/685

Balkin, R. S. (2009). Publishing a conceptual manuscript. *Journal of Professional Counseling, 37*(1), 1–2.

Baltimore County Public Schools. (2015). *Research process steps.* Retrieved from the BCPS website: https://www.bcps.org/offices/lis/researchcourse/steps.html

Balucanag-Bitonio, J. (2014). *Theoretical framework.* Retrieved from the SlideShare website: http://www.slideshare.net/jobitonio/theoretical-framework-37836171

Bamber, V. (2014). Think global, act local in masters scholarship. *Think piece paper prepared for Higher Education Close Up conference*, Lancaster, England. Retrieved from http://www.lancaster.ac.uk/fass/events/hecu7/docs/ThinkPieces/bamber.pdf

Bannister, R., & Monsma, C. (1982). *The classification of concepts in consumer education* [Monograph 137]. Cincinnati, OH: South-Western.

Barrett, C., Reardon, T., & Webb, P. (2001). Nonfarm income diversification and household livelihood strategies in rural Africa: Concepts, dynamics, and policy implications. *Food Policy, 26*(4), 315–331.

Baylorn, R. M. (2008). Writing process. In L. M. Given (Ed.), *The SAGE encyclopedia of qualitative research methods* (pp. 949–950). Thousand Oaks, CA: Sage.

BCS Information Retrieval Specialist Group. (2006). *ECIR draft paper guidelines (Version 1.0).* London, England: Author. Retrieved from http://irsg.bcs.org/proceedings/ECIR_Draft_Guidelines.pdf

Beach L. R. (1990). *Image theory: Decision making in personal and organizational contexts.* New York, NY: Wiley.

Beall, J. (2010). "Predatory" open-access scholarly publishers. *The Charleston Advisor, 11*(4), 10–17.

Bean, J., & Creswell, J. W. (1980). Student attrition among women at a liberal arts college. *Journal of College Student Personnel, 21*(4), 320–327.

Bellanca, P. (1998). *Ending the essay: Conclusions.* Retrieved from the Harvard University website: http://writingcenter.fas.harvard.edu/pages/ending-essay-conclusions

Belli, G. (2009). Non-experimental quantitative research. In S. D. Lapan & M. T. Quartaroli (Eds.), *Research essentials: An introduction to designs and practices* (pp. 60–77). San Francisco, CA: Jossey-Bass.

Bem, D. J. (2004). *Writing the empirical journal article.* In J. M. Darley, M. P. Zanna, & H. L. Roediger III (Eds.), *The compleat academic: A career guide* (2nd ed.) (pp. 105–119). Washington, DC: American Psychological Association.

Bennett, B. (2015). *Logically fallacious.* Sudbury, MA: Archieboy Holdings.

Bentley, M. (2011). *Writing effectively for WHO.* Retrieved from the World Health Organization website: http://www.colelearning.net/who/

Berg, M. J. (2008). Experiential knowledge. In L. M. Given (Ed.), *The SAGE encyclopedia of qualitative research methods* (pp. 321–322). Thousand Oaks, CA: Sage.

Betts Adams, K. (2016, June 21). IX. Manuscripts for qualitative and mixed-methods research [Web log post]. Retrieved from https://arcq.academiccoachingandwriting.org/academic-writing/academic-writing-blog/ix-manuscripts-for-qualitative-and-mixed-methods-research

Biagioli, M. (2003). Rights or rewards? Changing frameworks of scientific authorship. In M. Biagioli & P. Galison (Eds.), *Scientific authorship* (pp. 253–280). New York, NY: Routledge.

Birochi, R., & Pozzebon, M. (2016). Improving financial inclusion: Towards a critical financial education framework. *RAE—Journal of Business Administration, 56*(3), 266–287.

Bishop Library. (2016). *How to write a research paper: Identifying keywords.* Retrieved from the Lebanon Valley College website: http://libguides.lvc.edu/c.php?g=333843&p=2247147

Bitchener, J., & Basturkmen, H. (2006). Perceptions of the difficulties of postgraduate L2 thesis students writing the discussion section. *Journal of English for Academic Purposes, 5*(1), 4–18.

Blackmore, E., & Rockert, W. (2004). *Becoming critical consumers: Research and the media.* Toronto, ON: National Eating Disorder Information Center.

Blaxter, M. (2013). Criteria for the evaluation of qualitative research papers. *Medical Sociology Online, 7*(1), 4–7.

Bleske-Rechek, A., & Fritsch, A. (2011). Student consensus on RateMyProfessors.com. *Practical Assessment, Research & Evaluation, 16*(18). Retrieved from http://www.pareonline.net/getvn.asp?v=16&n=18

Blicq, R. S. (1992). *Technically write!* (4th ed.). Scarborough, ON: Prentice Hall.

Block, P., Brueggemann, W., & McKnight, J. (2016). *Another kingdom: Departing the consumer culture.* Hoboken, NJ: Wiley.

Board, S., & Meyer-ter-Vehn, M. (2014). *Writing economic theory papers.* Retrieved from the UCLA website: http://www .econ.ucla.edu/sboard/teaching/Writing EconomicTheory.pdf

Bohman, J. (2005). Critical theory. In E. N. Zalta (Ed.), *Stanford encyclopedia of philosophy*. Stanford, CA: Stanford University. Retrieved from https://plato .stanford.edu/entries/critical-theory/

Boote, D., & Beile, P. (2005). Scholars before researchers: On the centrality of the dissertation literature review in research preparation. *Educational Researcher, 34*(6), 3–15.

Booth, W., Colomb, G., & Williams, J. (1995). *The craft of research*. Chicago, IL: Chicago University Press.

Botha, M. E. (1989). Theory development in perspective: The role of conceptual frameworks and models in theory development. *Journal of Advanced Nursing, 14*(1), 49–55.

Bothamley, J. (2004). *Dictionary of theories* (3rd ed.). New York, NY: Barnes & Noble.

Boudah, D. J. (2011). *Conducting educational research*. Thousand Oaks, CA: Sage.

Boundless. (2016, May 26). Models, theories, and laws [Web log post]. Retrieved from https://www.boundless.com/physics/ textbooks/boundless-physics-textbook/ the-basics-of-physics-1/the-basics- of-physics-31/models-theories-and- laws-195-6078/

Bowser, D. (2009). *Logic and inquiry: Chapter 1 notes (Lecture notes for Phil 111-51 university course)*. Clarion, PA: Clarion University, Venango College. Retrieved from http://www.thinking shop.com/Clarion/logic/pdf/Clarion_ Logic_CH1_Notes.pdf

Boylorn, R. (2008). Writing process. In L. M. Given (Ed.), *The SAGE encyclopedia of qualitative research methods* (pp. 949–950). Thousand Oaks, CA: Sage.

Bracey, G. W. (2006). *Reading educational research*. Portsmouth, NH: Heinemann.

Brenner, E. (2001). *Developing a research question*. Retrieved from the Skyline College website: http://accounts.smccd. edu/brenner/lsci105/rsrchqus.html

Bronstein, L. R., & Kovacs, P. J. (2013). Writing a mixed methods report in social work research. *Research on Social Work Practices, 23*(3), 354–360.

Brown, A. B. (2014, February 10). III. Writing an effective discussion or conclusion section [Web log post]. Retrieved from http:// www.academiccoachingandwriting.org/ academic-writing/academic-writing- blog/iii-writing-an-effective-discussion- or-conclusion-section

Brown, M. (2009). *Lecture 4: Statistics: Hypothesis testing and estimation*. Retrieved from the Michigan State University website: http://learn.chm.msu.edu/epi/PDF/ EPI546_Lecture_4.pdf

Brown, M., & Paolucci, B. (1979). *Home economics: A definition*. Alexandria, VA: American Association of Family and Consumer Sciences.

Bruce, N. (2001a). *Argumentation*. Retrieved from the Academic Grammar website: http://www4.caes.hku.hk/acad grammar/general/argue/main.htm

Bruce, N. (2001b). *Making recommendations*. Retrieved from the Academic Grammar website: http://www4.caes .hku.hk/acadgrammar/report/repProc/ sections/discuss/reccom.htm

Bryman, A. (2008). On methods and methodology. *Qualitative Research in Organizations and Management, 3*(2), 159–168.

Buchanan, D., & Bryman, A. (2007). Contextualizing methods choices in organizational research. *Organizational Research Methods, 10*(3), 483–501.

Bunton, D. (2005). The structure of PhD conclusion chapters. *Journal of English for Academic Purposes, 4*(3), 207–224.

Burgess, G., & Burgess, H. (ca. 2005). *A general summary of Aristotle's appeals*. Retrieved from the Beyond Intractability (University of Colorado, Boulder) website: http://www.beyond intractability.org/print/25143

Burns, A., & Burns, R. (2008). *Basic marketing research* (2nd ed.) Hoboken, NJ: Pearson Education.

Burr, B. K., Hubler, D. S., & Kuns, J. B. (2017). How much is too much? Investigating time and cost preferences to attending relationship education. *Journal of Family and Consumer Sciences, 109*(1), 26–33.

Bustos Coral, J., Ortiz Jiménez, J. P., & Voetmann, K. (2015). Appreciative inquiry lean. *AI Practitioner, 17*(4), 23–29.

Butchvarov, P. (1960). The concept of possibility. *Philosophy and Phenomenological Research, 20*(3), 318–337.

Cabell's Directories of Journals. (2011). Beaumont, TX: Cabell's International.

Cabrita, E. M., Mealha, I. F., & Queiroz de Barros, R. (2014). Challenges facing pre-service ESP teacher education. In J. de Dios Martínez Agudo (Ed.), *English as a foreign language teacher education* (pp. 339–358). New York, NY: Rodopi.

Caldwell, K., Henshaw, L., & Taylor, G. (2005). Developing a framework for critiquing health research. *Journal of Health, Social & Environmental Issues, 6*(1), 45–54.

Callahan, J. J. (2010). Constructing a manuscript: Distinguishing integrative literature reviews from conceptual and theory articles. *Human Resource Development Review, 9*(3), 300–304.

Callaway, M. (2007). *Resources for writers*. Retrieved from the Arizona State University website: http://www.public.asu .edu/~macalla/logosethospathos.html

Cameron, R. (2011). Mixed methods research: The five *P*s framework. *Electronic Journal of Business Research Methods, 9*(2), 96–108.

Campbell, L. M. (1994, August 4). Some items I look for in a thesis prospectus (Methods section) [Electronic mailing list message]. Retrieved from http:// comm.grad-college.iastate.edu/cce/ resources-database/view.php?id=169

Caracelli, V. J., & Greene, J. C. (1997). Crafting mixed-method evaluation designs. *New Directions for Evaluation, 74*, 19–32.

Casanave, C. P., & Li, Y. (2015). Novices' struggles with conceptual and theoretical framing in writing dissertations and papers for publication. *Publications, 3*(2), 104–119.

Castello, M. (2014). Basic data types. In T. Chaisson & D. Gregory (Eds.), *Data and design* (pp. 20–28). Columbia, MO: Reynolds Journalism Institute. Retrieved from the Amazon Web Services website: http://orm-atlas2- prod.s3.amazonaws.com/pdf/13a07b1 9e01a397d8855c0463d52f454.pdf

Castro-Palaganas, E. (2011). *Conceptual and theoretical contexts*. Retrieved from the Tebtebba website: http://www

.tebtebba.org/index.php/all-resources/category/122-revlit-and-conceptual-framework?

Celce-Murcia, M., & Larsen-Freeman, D. (1999). *The grammar book* (2nd ed.). Boston, MA: Heinle & Heinle.

Centre for Independent Language Learning. (2008a). *Report writing: Guidelines for writing acknowledgements*. Retrieved from the Hong Kong Polytechnic University website: http://www2.elc.polyu.edu.hk/FYP/html/ack.htm

Centre for Independent Language Learning. (2008b). *Report writing: Recommendations*. Retrieved from the Hong Kong Polytechnic University website: http://www2.elc.polyu.edu.hk/cill/eiw/report_recommendations.htm

Chappell, R. (2006, February 25). Concepts of possibility [Web log post]. Retrieved from http://www.philosophyetc.net/2006/02/concepts-of-possibility.html

Chinn, P. L., & Kramer, M. (1998). *Theory and nursing integrated knowledge development* (5th ed). Maryland Heights, MI: Mosby.

Choudhuri, D., Glauser, A., & Peregoy, J. (2004). Guidelines for writing a qualitative manuscript for the Journal of Counselling & Development. *Journal of Counselling & Development 82*(4), 443–446.

Christ, T. W. (2007). A recursive approach to mixed methods research in a longitudinal study of postsecondary education disability support services. *Journal of Mixed Methods Research, 1*(3), 226–241.

Christopher, A. N., Marker, P., & Zabel, K. L. (2015). Becoming a writer about psychology. In D. Dunn (Ed.), *The Oxford handbook of undergraduate psychology education* (pp. 751–768). New York, NY: Cambridge University Press.

Chua, C. N. (Ed.). (ca. 2003). *Publish or perish*. Retrieved from the MRCOphth website: http://www.mrcophth.com/publishorperish/Index.html

Chubbuck, K. (2009). It's a wrap! Writing effective conclusions. In *Brandeis writing program in-class exercises* (pp. 108–109). Waltham, MA: Brandeis University. Retrieved from http://www.brandeis.edu/writing program/writing-intensive/instructors/files/KCconclusion.doc

Cicovacki, P. (2009). Transdisciplinarity as an interactive method. *Integral Leadership Review, 9*(5). Retrieved from http://integralleadershipreview.com/4549-feature-article-transdisciplinarity-as-an-interactive-method-a-critical-reflection-on-the-three-pillars-of-transdisciplinarity/

Claremont College. (2011). *Highschool public debate program judging rubric—2010*. Retrieved from the Claremont College Parliamentary Debate Institute website: https://ccpdi.files.wordpress.com/2011/02/hspdp-judging-rubric-v-jan114.jpg

Clarivate Analytics. (2016, October 3). Press release: Acquisition of the Thomson Reuters Intellectual Property and Science Business by Onex and Baring Asia completed: Independent business becomes Clarivate Analytics. Retrieved from http://ipscience.thomsonreuters.com/news/ip-and-science-launched-as-independent-company

Cline, A. (2012, December 15). *Critiquing arguments*. Retrieved from the About Religion website: http://atheism.about.com/od/logicalarguments/a/critiquing.htm

Clucas, S. R. (1997). *Construction as a curriculum organizer for technology education* (Doctoral dissertation, Virginia Tech University). Retrieved from https://theses.lib.vt.edu/theses/available/etd-9597-162630/

Cockerill, A. W. (2005). *Weighty words vs words of action*. Retrieved from the Delta Tech Systems website: http://www.richardgilbert.ca/achart/public_html/articles/publications/words2.htm

Cofield, S. S., Corona, R. V., & Allison, D. B. (2010). Use of causal language in observational studies of obesity and nutrition. *Obesity Facts, 3*(6), 353–356.

Cohen, J. (1988). *Statistical power analysis for the behavioral sciences*. Hillsdale, NJ: Erlbaum.

Cohen, R. (2014). *The think piece: A guide*. Retrieved from the University of California, San Diego, website: http://profcohen.net/thinkpieceguide.pdf

Colander, D. (2013). *Microeconomics* (9th ed.). New York, NY: McGraw.

Cole, M. (2006). Qualitative research: A challenging paradigm for infection control. *British Journal of Infection Control, 7*(6), 25–29.

Cole, R., & Firmage, D. (2006). *Critically reading journal articles*. Retrieved from the Colby College Biology Department website: www.colby.edu/biology/bi319/GuideReadJour.doc

Collier, D., LaPorte, J., & Seawright, J. (2012). Putting typologies to work: Concept formation, measurement, and analytic rigor. *Political Research Quarterly, 65*(1), 217–232.

Colquitt, J. A., Zapata-Phelan, C. (2007). Trends in theory building and theory testing: A five-decade study of the Academy of Management Journal. *Academy of Management Journal, 50*(6), 1281–1303.

Cone, J. D., & Foster, S. L. (2006). *Dissertations and theses from start to finish* (2nd ed.). Washington, DC: American Psychological Association.

Conitzer, V. (2006). *Computational aspects of preference aggregation* (Doctoral dissertation, Carnegie Mellon University). Retrieved from https://www.cs.duke.edu/~conitzer/thesis.pdf

Cooper, H. M. (1985). *A taxonomy of literature reviews*. Paper presented at the Annual Meeting of the American Educational Research Association, Chicago. Retrieved from ERIC database. (ED254541)

Cooper, H. M. (1988). Organizing knowledge synthesis: A taxonomy of literature reviews. *Knowledge in Society, 1*(1), 105–126.

Corden, A., & Sainsbury, R. (2006). *Using verbatim quotations in reporting qualitative social research: Researchers' views*. York, England: University of York, Social Policy Research Unit. Retrieved from https://www.york.ac.uk/inst/spru/pubs/pdf/verbquotresearch.pdf

Corley, K. G., & Gioia, D. A. (2011). Building theory about theory building: What constitutes a theoretical contribution? *Academy of Management Review, 36*(1), 12–32.

Corti, L. (2008). Data management. In L. M. Given (Ed.), *The SAGE encyclopedia of qualitative research methods* (pp. 193–195). Thousand Oaks, CA: Sage.

Coupe, T., Ginsburgh, V., & Noury, A. (2010). Are leading papers of better quality? Evidence from a natural experiment. *Oxford Economic Papers, 61*(1), 1–11.

Cramer, K. M. (2013). Six criteria of a viable theory. *Journal of Motivation, Emotion, and Personality, 1*(1), 9–16.

Creswell, J. W. (1994). *Research design: Qualitative and quantitative approaches.* Thousand Oaks, CA: Sage.

Creswell, J. W. (2008). Mixed methods research. In L. M. Given (Ed.), *The SAGE encyclopedia of qualitative research methods* (pp. 526–529). Thousand Oaks, CA: Sage.

Creswell, J. W. (2009). *Research design* (3rd ed.). Thousand Oaks, CA: Sage.

Creswell, J. W. (2010, March 26). *How to write a mixed methods journal article for submission.* Paper presented at a University of Manitoba Research Forum, Winnipeg. Retrieved from https://umanitoba.ca/centres/aging/media/Creswell.Workshop_-_How_to_Write_a_Mixed_Methods_Article.ppt

Creswell, J. W., Klassen, A. C., Plano Clark, V. L., & Smith, K. C. (2011). *Best practices for mixed methods research in the health sciences.* Washington, DC: Office of Behavioral and Social Sciences Research. Retrieved from https://www2.jabsom.hawaii.edu/native/docs/tsudocs/Best_Practices_for_Mixed_Methods_Research_Aug2011.pdf

Creswell, J. W., & Miller, D. L. (2000). Determining validity in qualitative inquiry. *Theory Into Practice, 39*(3), 124–130.

Creswell, J. W., Plano Clark, V. L., Gutmann, M. L., & Hanson, W. E. (2003). Advanced mixed methods research design. In A. Tashakkori & C. Teddlie (Eds.), *Handbook of mixed methods in social and behavioral research* (pp. 209–240). Thousand Oaks, CA: Sage.

Creswell, J. W., & Tashakkori, A. (2007). Developing publishable mixed methods manuscripts. *Journal of Mixed Methods Research, 1*(2), 107–111.

Croad, G., & Farquhar, S. (2005). Being a critical consumer of research is important: Consider the political spin and shortcomings of NZCER's Competent Children Study for example. *New Zealand Journal of Teachers' Work, 2*(1), 17–19.

Croft, W. (2003). *Typology and universals* (2nd ed.). Cambridge, England: Cambridge University Press.

Cropanzano, R. (2009). Writing non-empirical articles for Journal of Management: General thoughts and suggestions. *Journal of Management, 35*(6), 1304–1311.

Dallal, G. E. (2001). *Little handbook of statistics.* Retrieved from the Tufts University website: http://www.jerry dallal.com/LHSP/LHSP.HTM

Daniel, R., & De Stavola, B. (2012, July 5). *What is the difference between association and causation?* Paper presented at the ESRC Research Methods Festival, Cambridge, England.

Dash, N. K. (2005). *Online research methods resource: Module: Selection of the research paradigm and methodology.* Retrieved from the Manchester Metropolitan University website: http://www.celt.mmu.ac.uk/research methods/Modules/Selection_of_methodology/index.php

Dauber, D. (2014, January 13). What is the difference between a research article and a concept paper? [Web log post]. Retrieved from https://www.researchgate.net/post/What_is_the_difference_between_a_research_article_and_a_concept_paper

Day, R. A. (1998). *How to write & publish a scientific paper* (3rd ed.). Phoenix, AZ: Oryx.

Day, R. A., & Gastel, B. (2006). *How to write and publish a scientific paper* (6th ed.). Westport, CT: Greenwood.

Deleuze, G., & Guattari, F. (1991). *What is philosophy?* New York, NY: Columbia University Press.

Del Favero, M. (2005). Academic disciplines: Disciplines and the structure of higher education, discipline classification systems, discipline differences. In *Education encyclopedia.* Retrieved from http://education.stateuniversity.com/pages/1723/Academic-Disciplines.html

Dence, S., Iphofen, R., & Huws, R. (2004). *An EU code of ethics for socioeconomic research.* Brighton, England: Institute for Employment Studies. Retrieved from http://www.respect project.org/ethics/412ethics.pdf

Denzin, N., & Lincoln, Y. (Eds.). (1994). *Handbook of qualitative research.* Thousand Oaks, CA: Sage.

Denzin, N., & Lincoln, Y. (Eds.). (2011). *SAGE handbook of qualitative research.* Thousand Oaks, CA: Sage.

Department of Justice. (2015). *Legistics.* Ottawa, ON: Government of Canada. Retrieved from http://www.justice.gc.ca/eng/rp-pr/csj-sjc/legis-redact/legistics/toc-tdm.asp

Derese, S. (ca. 2015). *Introduction to PhD research proposal writing.* Retrieved from the University of Nairobi, Kenya, website: http://nairobi.daad.de/imperia/md/content/aussenstellen/nairobi/introduction_to_phd_proposal_writing_natural_sciences.pdf

DeRose, K. (2009). *The case for contextualism.* Oxford, England: Oxford University Press.

de Vaus, D. A. (2001). *Research design in social research.* London, England: Sage.

Deviant, S. (2010). *The practically cheating statistics handbook.* North Charleston, SC: Createspace Independent Publishing Platform, Amazon.com.

Dewey, A. (2012, May 29). Do questions make good titles? [Web log post]. Retrieved from http://www.investment writing.com/2012/05/guest-post-do-questions-make-good-titles/

de Wit, B., & Meyer, R. (2010). *Strategy synthesis* (3rd ed.). Hampshire, England: South-Western Cengage Learning.

Dickson, J. G., Conner, R. N., & Adair, K. T. (1978). Guidelines for authorship of scientific articles. *Wildlife Society Bulletin, 6*(4), 260–261.

Dillinger, M. (2011). *Writing up the methods section.* Retrieved from the Mike Dillinger website: http://mikedillinger.com/SJSUpapers/WriteupMethodsSection.pdf

Donmoyer, R. (2008). Paradigms. In L. M. Given (Ed.), *The SAGE encyclopedia of qualitative research methods* (pp. 591–595). Thousand Oaks, CA: Sage.

Donovan, P. (2010). *Paradigms and decision-making frameworks*. Retrieved from the Managing Wholes website: http://managingwholes.com/holistic-management-1.htm

Dowden, B. (2004). *Guidelines for writing philosophy papers*. Retrieved from the California State University, Sacramento, website: http://www.csus.edu/phil/req/writing.htm

Driessnack, M., Sousa, V. D., & Mendes, I. A. C. (2007a). An overview of research designs relevant to nursing: Part 2: Qualitative research designs. *American Journal of Nursing, 15*(4), 684–688.

Driessnack, M., Sousa, V. D., & Mendes, I. A. C. (2007b). An overview of research designs relevant to nursing: Part 3: Mixed and multiple methods. *American Journal of Nursing, 15*(5), 1046–1049.

Drotar, D. (2008). Thoughts on establishing research significance and preserving scientific integrity. *Journal of Pediatric Psychology, 33*(1), 1–5.

Drotar, D. (2009). How to write an effective results and discussion for the Journal of Pediatric Psychology. *Journal of Pediatric Psychology, 34*(4), 339–343.

Dryden, T., & Achilles, R. (2004, May 13). *Teaching the reflective massage therapist: How to teach research literacy in the classroom*. Paper presented at the 2nd International Symposium on the Science of Touch, Montreal, QC. Retrieved from http://ccrt-ctrc.org/congres/handsout/13_7d.pdf

Dryer, M. S. (2006). Descriptive theories, explanatory theories and basic linguistic theory. In F. Ameka, A. Dench, & N. Evans (Eds.), *Catching language* (pp. 206–234). New York, NY: Mouton de Gruyter.

Dubin, R. (1978). *Theory building* (Rev. ed.). New York, NY: Free Press.

Dudovskiy, J. (2016). *The ultimate guide to writing a dissertation in business studies*. Retrieved from http://research-methodology.net/about-us/ebook/

Dunkin, M. J. (1996). Types of errors in synthesizing research in education. *Review of Educational Research, 66*(2), 87–97.

Dury, R. (ca. 2000). *A brief glossary of modality*. Retrieved from the University of Bergamo (Italy) website: http://dinamico2.unibg.it/anglistica/slin/modgloss.htm

Eaton, J. M. (1996). *Paradigms*. Halifax: Nova Scotia Department of Health. Retrieved from http://www.chebucto.ns.ca/CommunitySupport/NCC/SCDEFJE.html

Eaton, S. H. (2014, February 19). How many sources do you need in a literature review [Web log post]. Retrieved from https://drsaraheaton.wordpress.com/2014/02/19/how-many-sources-do-you-need-in-a-literature-review/

Edelson, J. (2015). *Writing a good conclusion paragraph*. Retrieved from the Time4Writing website: http://www.time4writing.com/uncategorized/writing-a-good-conclusion-paragraph/

Edinburgh Napier University. (2012). *Report writing*. Retrieved from the ENU website: http://www2.napier.ac.uk/gus/writing_presenting/reports.html

Editage Insights. (2014, January 29). How to interpret journal acceptance rates [Web log post]. Retrieved from http://www.editage.com/insights/how-to-interpret-journal-acceptance-rates

Eftekhar, M. (2015). *Limitations and delimitations in a research*. Retrieved from the IAUHETT WikiSpaces website: https://iauhett.wikispaces.com/file/view/LIMITATION+AND+DELIMITATION+.docx

Elgin, D., & LeDrew, C. (1997). *Global consciousness change: Indicators of an emerging paradigm*. San Anselmo, CA: Awakening Earth Organization. Retrieved from http://www.duaneelgin.com/wp-content/uploads/2010/11/global_consciousness.pdf

Ellinger, A. D., & Yang, B. (2011). Creating a whole from the parts. In T. S. Rocco & T. Hatcher (Eds.), *The handbook of scholarly writing and publishing* (pp. 115–124). San Francisco, CA: Jossey-Bass.

Ellis, R. M. (2015). *Middle way philosophy: Omnibus edition*. Raleigh, NC: Lulu.

Elsevier. (ca. 2009). *How to write a world class theoretical paper*. Retrieved from the University of Texas at San Antonio website: http://www.utsa.edu/lrsg/Teaching/GEO6011/HowToWritePaper.pdf

Emerald Group Publishing. (2016). How to . . . ensure your article is highly downloaded: What to do PRIOR to submission [Web log post]. Retrieved from http://www.emeraldgrouppublishing.com/authors/guides/promote/optimize1.htm

European Health Psychology Society. (2014). *Submissions*. Retrieved from the EHPS website: https://www.ehps.net/ehp/index.php/contents/about/submissions

Evans, D., Gruba, P., & Zobel, J. (2011). *How to write a better thesis*. Victoria, Australia: Melbourne University Press.

Evans, P. (2016, June 14). Debt-to-income ratio ticks down to $1.65 for every dollar Canadians earn. *CBC News*. Retrieved from http://www.cbc.ca/news/business/statistics-canada-debt-income-financial-1.3634166

Ewer, B. C. (1905). The idea of possibility. *Journal of Philosophy, Psychology and Scientific Methods, 2*(1), 5–12.

Fahnestock, J. (2002). *The appeals: Ethos, pathos, and logos*. Retrieved from the Tripod website: http://members.tripod.com/butler_s/f2002-1002/appeals.html

Farrugia, P., Petrisor, B. A., Farrokhyar, F., & Bhandari, M. (2010). Research questions, hypotheses and objectives. *Canadian Journal of Surgery, 53*(4), 278–281.

Fawcett, J., & Downs, F. (1986). *The relationship of theory and research*. Norfolk, CT: Appleton Century Croft.

Fetters, M. D., Curry, L. A., & Creswell, J. W. (2013). Achieving integration in mixed methods designs: Principles and practices. *Health Services Research, 48*(6), 2134–2156.

Field, A. (2013). *Discovering statistics using SPSS*. London, England: Sage.

Fink, A. (2004). *Conducting research literature reviews* (2nd ed.). Los Angeles, CA: Sage.

Firestone, J. (2010). The strategic literature review. *Graduate Student Success Web Article Series, 1*(1). Retrieved from http://graduateschool.utsa.edu/images/uploads/The_Strategic_Literature_Review.pdf

Firth, F. (1967). The anatomy of certainty. *The Philosophical Review, 76*(1), 3–27.

Fischman, G., & Tefera, A. (2014, June 17). Commentary: If the research is not used, does it exist? *Teachers College Record* (Article ID No. 17570). Retrieved from http://www.tcrecord.org/Content .asp?ContentId=17570

Folse, H. (2000). Logical positivism. In J. Fieser & B. Dowden (Eds.), *The Internet encyclopedia of philosophy*. Martin: University of Tennessee. Retrieved from http://www.loyno.edu/ ~folse/logpos.htm

Ford, A. (2009). *Modeling the environment* (2nd ed.). Washington, DC: Island Press.

Foster, M. (2015). *Advanced [English grammar]: Modal auxiliary verbs*. Retrieved from the English Power website: http://www.englishpower.eu/ en/ep-free-lessons/advanced/verbs/ modal-auxiliary-verbs#.VqlSbq32bgo

Fox, N. J. (2008). Post positivism. In L. M. Given (Ed.), *The SAGE encyclopedia of qualitative research methods* (pp. 659–664). Thousand Oaks, CA: Sage.

Fox, N. J. (2013). *The structure of a qualitative paper* [PowerPoint]. Retrieved from the Academia website: https://www .academia.edu/3073153/How_to_write_ and_structure_a_qualitative_paper_ Powerpoint_2013_?auto=download

Freedman, L., & Plotnick, J. (2008). *Introduction and conclusions*. Retrieved from the University College (Toronto) website: http://www.uc.utoronto.ca/ sites/default/files/uploads/intros-and-conclusions.pdf http://www.utor onto.ca/ucwriting/introconcl.html

Fritz, K. (2008). *Writing qualitative research papers*. Retrieved from the John Hopkins University website: http://ocw.jhsph.edu/courses/qualita tivedataanalysis/PDFs/Session9.pdf

Frost, J. (2015, December 10). Why are P value misunderstandings so common? [Web log post]. Retrieved from http://blog.minitab.com/blog/adven tures-in-statistics/why-are-p-value-misunderstandings-so-common

Gal, I. (2002). Adults' statistical literacy: Meanings, components, responsibilities. *International Statistical Review, 70*(1), 1–51.

Gall, M. D., Gall, J. P., & Borg, W. R. (2015). *Applying educational research* (7th ed.). Hoboken, NJ: Pearson.

Galvan, J. L. (2006). *Writing literature reviews* (3rd ed.). Glendale, CA: Pyrczak.

Garbin, C. (2016). *What is meant by "statistical power" and what is the advantage if our research has lots of it?* Retrieved from the University of Nebraska website: http://psych.unl.edu/psycrs/350/ unit2/gallery/sq8.doc

Garfield, E. (2005, September 16). *The agony and the ecstasy: The history and meaning of the journal impact factor*. Paper presented at the International Congress on Peer Review and Biomedical Publication, Chicago, Illinois. Retrieved from http://garfield.library.upenn.edu/ papers/jifchicago2005.pdf

Gay, L. R., Mills, G. E., & Airasian, P. W. (2006). *Educational research* (8th ed.). Upper Saddle River, NJ: Merrill Prentice Hall.

Geletkanycz, M., & Tepper, B. J. (2012). Publishing in *AMJ*—Part 6: Discussing the implications. *Academy of Management Journal, 55*(2), 256–260.

Gephart, R. (1999). Paradigms and research methods. *Research Methods Forum, 4*(1). Retrieved from the Academy of Management Research Methods Division website: http://division.aomonline.org/ rm/1999_RMD_Forum_Paradigms_and_ Research_Methods.htm

Gerring, J. (1999). What makes a good concept? A criterial framework for understanding concept formation in the social sciences. *Polity, 31*(3), 357–393.

Gillett, A. (2015). *Using English for academic purposes: A guide for students in higher education*. Retrieved from the UEFAP website: http://www.uefap .com/speaking/symbols/symbols.htm

Gilson, L. L., & Goldberg, C. B. (2015). Editor's comment: So, what is a conceptual paper? *Groups & Organization Management, 40*(2), 127–130.

Ginsburgh, V. (2012, May 25). Are leading papers in an issue of a journal of better "quality"? [Web log post]. Retrieved from http://voxeu.org/article/are-leading-academic-papers-really-better-quality

Given, L. M. (Eds.). (2008). *The SAGE encyclopedia of qualitative research methods*. Thousand Oaks, CA: Sage.

Glaeser, E. L. (2003). *Economics 2010a Lecture 11: Final notes: How to write a theory paper*. Retrieved from the Princeton University website: http://www.princeton.edu/~reddings/ tradephd/Glaeser_Lecture_11.pdf

Glanz, K. (2016). *Social and behavioral theories*. Bethesda, MD: National Institute of Health. Retrieved from https://obssr .od.nih.gov/wp-content/uploads/2016/05/ Social-and-Behavioral-Theories.pdf

Glaser, B. G., & Strauss, A. (1967). *The Discovery of grounded theory: Strategies for qualitative research*. Chicago, IL: Aldine.

Golash, D. (2005). *What is a conceptual paper?* Retrieved from the American University website: http://www1.american .edu/dgolash/conceptpap.htm

Goldfarb, R. S., & Ratner, J. (2008). "Theory" and "models": Terminology through the looking glass. *Econ Journal Watch, 5*(1), 91–108.

Goodson, P. (2017). *Becoming an academic writer* (2nd ed.). Thousand Oaks, CA: Sage.

Gøtzsche, P. C., Hróbjartsson, A., Johansen, H. K., Haahr, M. T., Altman, D. G., & Chan, A.-W. (2007). Ghost authorship in industry-initiated randomised trials. *PLoS Medicine, 4*(1), 47–52.

Gould, S. (2011). *Study guides: Grammar*. Retrieved from the Birmingham City University website: http://library.bcu .ac.uk/learner/Grammar%20index.htm

Grammarly. (2017). *Grammarly handbook*. Retrieved from the Grammarly website: http://www.grammarly.com/ handbook/

Granqvist, E. (2015, March 2). Why science needs to publish negative results [Web log post]. Retrieved from https:// www.elsevier.com/authors-update/ story/innovation-in-publishing/why-science-needs-to-publish-negative-results

Graybill, F., & Iyer, H. K. (1994). *Regression analysis*. Toronto, ON: Duxbury Press (Nelson).

Greenberg, S. (2006). *How to write a literature review*. Retrieved from the University of Calgary website: http:// saul.cpsc.ucalgary.ca/pmwiki.php/ GradTips/GradTipsLiteratureReview

Gregori, S. (2011). *Modal verbs.* Retrieved from SlideShare website: http://www.slideshare.net/usoasol/powerpoint-modal-verbs

Guba, E. G. (1981). Criteria for assessing the trustworthiness of naturalistic inquiries. *Educational Communication and Technology Journal, 29*(2), 75–91.

Guba, E. G. (1990). *The paradigm dialog.* Newbury Park, CA: Sage.

Guba, E. G., & Lincoln, Y. S. (2005). Paradigmatic controversies, contradictions, and emerging influences. In N. K. Denzin & Y. S. Lincoln (Eds.), *The Sage handbook of qualitative research* (3rd ed., pp. 191–215). Thousand Oaks, CA: Sage.

Guetterman, T. C., Fetters, M. D., & Creswell, J. W. (2015). Integrating quantitative and qualitative results in health science mixed method research through joint displays. *Annals of Family Medicine, 13*(6), 554–561.

Guilford, C. (2015). *Occasions for argumentative essays.* Retrieved from the Paradigm Online Writing website: http://www.powa.org/convince/occasions-for-argumentative-essays

Gutek, G. (2014). *Philosophical, ideological, and theoretical perspectives on education.* Saddle River, NY: Pearson.

Guy. (2012, February 25). Point estimation vs hypothesis testing and interval estimation [Web log comment]. Retrieved from http://math.stackexchange.com/questions/113076/point-estimation-vs-hypothesis-testing-and-interval-estimation

Habermas, J. (1984). *Theory of communicative action, Volume 1: Reason and the rationalization of society* (T. McCarthy, Trans.). Boston, MA: Beacon Press.

Hacquard, V. (2011). Modality. In C. Maienborn, K. von Heusinger, & P. Portner (Eds.), *Semantics* (pp. 1484–1515). Berlin, Germany: Mouton de Gruyter.

Haggan, M. (2004). Research paper titles in literature, linguistics and science: Dimensions of attraction. *Journal of Pragmatics, 36*(2), 293–317.

Hall, S. (Ed.). (1997). *Representation.* Thousand Oaks, CA: Sage

Hallberg, L. R.-M. (2010). Some thoughts about the literature review in grounded theory studies. *International Journal of Qualitative Studies on Health and Well-being, 5*(3), 1.

Halloran, B., & Flores, W. (2015). *Think piece: Mobilizing accountability: Citizens, movements and the state.* Washington, DC: Transparency Accountability Initiative.

Hancock, B. (2002). *Trent focus for research and development in primary health care: An introduction to qualitative research.* Nottingham, England: Trent Focus Group. Retrieved from http://classes.uleth.ca/200502/mgt2700a/Articles/Qualitative%20Research.pdf

Handley, E., & Oakes, S. (2016). *Developing a research question.* Retrieved from the SUNY Empire State College website: https://www.esc.edu/online-writing-center/resources/research/research-paper-steps/developing-questions

Hanson, R. (2011). *What is rhetoric?* Retrieved from the Soft Chalk Cloud website: https://www.softchalkcloud.com/lesson/files/e5yoZPA2mfGr3n/Rhetorical_Triangle_print.html

Hargens, L. L. (1988). Scholarly consensus and journal rejection rates. *American Sociological Review, 52*(1), 139–151.

Harnad, S. (1996). Implementing peer review on the net: Scientific quality control in scholarly electronic journals. In R. Peek & G. Newby (Eds.), *Scholarly publication: The electronic frontier* (pp. 103–118). Cambridge, MA: MIT Press.

Haroldson, A., & Yen, C. (2016). Consumer understanding of nutrition marketing terms: A pilot study. *Journal of Family and Consumer Sciences, 108*(3), 24–31.

Harper, D. (2016). *Online etymology dictionary.* Lancaster, PA. Retrieved from http://www.etymonline.com/

Harris, S. R. (2014). *How to critique journal articles in the social sciences.* Thousand Oaks, CA: Sage.

Hart, D. L., Poston, W. R., & Perry, J. F. (1980). Critically reading a research article. *Journal of Orthopaedic and Sports Physical Therapy, 2*(2), 72–76.

Harvard University. (ca. 2001). *Research methods: Some notes to orient you.* Retrieved from the Harvard University website: https://isites.harvard.edu/fs/docs/icb.topic851950.files/Research%20Methods_Some%20Notes.pdf

Harzing, A.-W. (2016). *Journal quality list* (57th ed.). Retrieved from the Harzing website: http://www.harzing.com/download/jql_journal.pdf

Hashemi, R. H., & Gohari Moghaddam, I. (2016). A mixed methods genre analysis of the discussion section of MMR articles in applied linguistics. *Journal of Mixed Methods Research* [Advance online publication]. doi: 10.1177/1558689816674626

Hatley, T. (2017). A critical review of pre-engagement organizational consulting diagnosis methods. *Integral Leadership Review, 17*(1). Retrieved from http://integralleadershipreview.com/15400-422-critical-review-pre-engagement-organizational-consulting-diagnosis-methods/

Herrnstein, R. J., & Murray, C. (1994). *The bell curve.* New York, NY: Free Press.

Hess, D. R. (2004). How to write an effective discussion. *Respiratory Care, 49*(10), 1238–1241.

Hesson, J., & Fraias-Hesson, E. (2010a, October). Tense of methods section [Web log post]. Retrieved from http://academicenglishsolutions.blogspot.ca/2010/10/tense-of-methods-section-as-previously.html

Hesson, J., & Fraias-Hesson, E. (2010b, September). Writing the method section of research papers [Web log post]. Retrieved from http://academicenglishsolutions.blogspot.ca/2010/09/writing-method-section-of-research.html

Heuerman, T., & Olson, D. (1998). *Pamphlet 2: Worldviews.* Moorehead, MN: A More Natural Way. Retrieved from http://www.thephora.net/forum/showthread.php?t=31678

Hieke, S. (2015, January 29). What is the exact difference between a conceptual paper and a quantitative research paper? [Web log comment]. Retrieved from https://www.researchgate.net/post/What_is_the_exact_difference_between_a_conceptual_paper_and_a_quantitative_research_paper

Hill, A. B. (1965). The environment and disease: Association or causation? *Proceedings of the Royal Society of Medicine, 58*(5), 295–300.

Himma, K. E. (2013). The ties that bind: An analysis of the concept of obligation. *Ratio Juris, 26*(1), 16–46.

Himma, K. E. (2015, November). *Is the concept of obligation moralized?* Retrieved from the SSRN website: http://ssrn.com/abstract=2692283: DOI http://dx.doi.org/10.2139/ssrn.2692283

Hindle, A. (2015, January 23). How to write about your study limitations without limiting your impact [Web log post]. Retrieved from https://www.edanzediting.com/blogs/how-write-about-your-study-limitations-without-limiting-your-impact

Holewa, R. (2004). *Strategies for writing a conclusion.* Retrieved from the Literacy Education Online website: http://leo.stcloudstate.edu/acadwrite/conclude.html

Holland, K., Duncombe, D., Dyas, E., & Meester, K. (2014). *Scopus frequently asked questions: The role of an editor.* Amsterdam, The Netherlands: Elsevier. Retrieved from https://www.elsevier.com/__data/assets/pdf_file/0005/95117/SC_FAQ-Role-of-an-Editor-22092014.pdf

Hollenberg, R. (2017). *Chapter 1—Basic concepts 1.4 Validity, truth, soundness, strength, cogency.* Retrieved from the Long Beach City College website: http://itdc.lbcc.edu/oer/philosophy/rh/1-4/1-4-notes.html

Holloway, I., & Wheeler, S. (2002). *Qualitative research in nursing* (2nd ed.). Malden, MA: Blackwell.

Howard-Jones, P. (2008). *Fostering creative thinking.* Bristol, England: Higher Education Academy.

Howe, K. R. (1992). Getting over the quantitative-qualitative debate. *American Journal of Education, 100*(2), 236–356.

Huddleston, R. (ca. 2010). *A short overview of English syntax.* Retrieved from the University of Edinburgh website: http://www.lel.ed.ac.uk/grammar/overview.html

Huddleston, R., & Pullum, G. K. (2005). *A student's introduction to English grammar.* Cambridge, England: Cambridge University Press.

Hunt, S. D. (1991, June). Positivism and paradigm dominance in consumer research: Toward critical pluralism and rapprochement. *Journal of Consumer Research, 18*, 32–44.

Hunter, A. (2001, May). Taxonomies. *Knowledge Management.* Retrieved from http://www0.cs.ucl.ac.uk/staff/a.hunter/tradepress/tax.html

Hyland, K. (1996). Writing without conviction: Hedging in research articles. *Applied Linguistics, 17*(4), 433–454.

IEP Staff. (n.d.). Deductive and inductive arguments. In J. Fieser & B. Dowden (Eds.), *Internet encyclopedia of philosophy.* Retrieved from http://www.iep.utm.edu/ded-ind/

Ilott, I., Gerrish, K., Laker, S., & Bray, K. (2013). *Naming and framing the problem: Using theories, models and conceptual frameworks* [Starter for 10 Series, No. 2]. London, England: National Institute for Health Research. Retrieved from https://drive.google.com/file/d/0B1On41OBiiu3ZzVvX0N6cFkzaXc/view

Imel, S. (2011). Writing a literature review. In T. S. Rocco & T. Hatcher (Eds.), *The handbook of scholarly writing and publishing* (pp. 145–160). San Francisco, CA: Jossey-Bass.

Imenda, S. (2014). Is there a conceptual difference between theoretical and conceptual framework? *Journal of Social Sciences, 38*(2), 185–195.

Ingham-Broomfield, R. (2008). A nurses' guide to the critical reading of research. *Australian Journal of Advanced Nursing, 26*(1), 102–109.

Ivankova, N. V., Creswell, J. W., & Stick, S. L. (2006). Using mixed-methods sequential explanatory design: From theory to practice. *Field Methods, 18*(1), 3–20.

Iyer, R., & Muncy, J. A. (2016). Attitude toward consumption and subjective well-being. *Journal of Consumer Affairs, 50*(1), 48–67.

Jabareen, Y. (2009). Building a conceptual framework: Philosophy, definitions, and procedures. *International Journal of Qualitative Methods, 8*(4), 49–62.

Jacard, J., & Jacoby, J. (2010). *Theory construction and model-building skills.* New York, NY: Guilford.

Jacob, E. (1987). Qualitative research traditions: A review. *Review of Educational Research, 57*(1), 1–50.

Jacobs, R. L. (2011). Developing a research problem and purpose statement. In T. S. Rocco & T. Hatcher (Eds.), *The handbook of scholarly writing and publishing* (pp. 125–141). San Francisco, CA: Jossey-Bass.

James, K., Bearne, E., & Alexander, E. (2004). "Doggy's dead": Reflecting on a teacher research study about young children's sociodramatic play. *Teacher Development, 8*(2&3), 165–179.

Jammal, E. (2010). *Guidelines for academic writing.* Retrieved from the Heilbronn University website: https://www.hs-heilbronn.de/6553371/academic_writing_2010.pdf

Jarrahi, M. H., & Sawyer, S. (2009). *Contextuality and information systems: How can the interplay between paradigms help.* Paper presented at the i-Conference, Chapel Hill, NC.

Jefferson County Schools, Tennessee: Project LA. (2002). *Action verbs.* Retrieved from http://classroom.jc-schools.net/la/activities/Verbs-action.ppt

Jewell, R. (2016). *Writing for college.* Retrieved from the Writing for College website: http://www.tc.umn.edu/~jewel001/CollegeWriting/home.htm

Jill. (2003, November 2). Mean or median? [Web log post]. Retrieved from http://mathforum.org/library/drmath/view/65606.html

Johnson, B. (2006). *Answers to study questions for chapter 16.* Retrieved from Johnson and Christensen's educational research textbook website: http://www.southalabama.edu/coe/bset/johnson/studyq/sq16.htm

Johnson, B., & Christensen, L. (2012). *Educational research* (4th ed.). Thousand Oaks, CA: Sage.

Johnson, R. B., Onwuegbuzie, A. J., & Turner, L. A. (2007). Toward a definition of mixed methods research. *Journal of Mixed Methods Research, 1*(2), 112–133.

Johnson, R. H. (2000). *Manifest rationality: A pragmatic theory of argument.* Mahwah, NJ: Erlbaum.

Jones, J. (1996). *Statistics: Lecture notes.* Retrieved from the Richmond Community College website: https://people.richland.edu/james/lecture/m170/

Jones, M. (Ed.). (2016). *Writing your dissertation: Results and discussion.* Retrieved from the Skills You Need website: http://www.skillsyouneed.com/learn/dissertation-results-discussion.html

Jonker, G. P. (2015). *Types of conclusions*. Retrieved from the Cabrillo College website: http://www.cabrillo.edu/~gjonker/Conclusions.pdf

Jonsen, A. R., & Toulmin, S. (1988). *The abuse of casuistry: A history of moral reasoning*. Berkeley: University of California Press.

Joshi, Y. (2014, February 27). Why do journals ask for keywords? [Web log post]. Retrieved from http://www.editage.com/insights/why-do-journals-ask-for-keywords

K12 Reader. (2015). *Action verbs*. Retrieved from the K12 Reader website: http://www.k12reader.com/term/action-verbs/

Kallestinova, E. D. (2011). How to write your first research paper. *Yale Journal of Biology and Medicine, 84*(3), 181–190.

Kallet, R. H. (2004). How to write the methods section of a research paper. *Respiratory Care, 49*(10), 1229–1232.

Kaplan, R. M., & Saccuzzo, D. P. (2009). *Psychological testing* (7th ed.). Belmont, CA: Wadsworth.

Kashatus, W. C. (2002). *Past, present and personal*. Portsmouth, NH: Heinemann.

Kastens, K., Pfirman, S., Stute, M., Hahn, B., Abbott, D., & Scholz, C. (2014). *Discussion*. Retrieved from the Columbia University website: http://www.ldeo.columbia.edu/~martins/sen_sem/SeniorSem_Discussion.pdf

Kattiyapornpong, U., Turner, P., Zutshi, A., Hagel, P., & Fujimoto, Y. (2011). Learning to read journal articles. *TMC Academic Journal, 5*(2), 83–96.

Kemerling, G. (2011). Logical positivism. In *Philosophy pages*. Retrieved from http://www.philosophypages.com/hy/6q.htm

Kennedy, M. M. (2007). Defining the literature. *Educational Researcher, 36*(3), 139–147.

Keysrwar, K. L. (2014). *Research methods flashcards*. Retrieved from the Quizlet website: https://quizlet.com/45801305/research-methods-flash-cards/

Khazanchi, D., & Munkvold, B. E. (2003, September). *On the rhetoric and relevance of IS research paradigms*. Paper presented at the 36th Hawaii International Conference on System Sciences. Retrieved from https://www.computer.org/csdl/proceedings/hicss/2003/1874/08/187480252b.pdf

Khoo, S., Ha, H., & McGregor, S. L. T. (2017). Service quality and student/customer satisfaction in the private tertiary education sector in Singapore [Article #592920]. *International Journal of Educational Management, 31*(4). doi: 10.1108/IJEM-09-2015-0121

Kilduff, M. (2006). Publishing theory. *Academy of Management Review, 31*(2), 252–255.

Kim, S. (2003). Research paradigms in organizational learning and performance: Competing modes of inquiry. *Information Technology, Learning, and Performance Journal, 21*(1), 9–18.

Kimmins, H., Blanco, J., Seely, B., Welham, C., & Scoullar, K. (2010). *Forecasting forest futures*. Axon, England: Earthscan.

Klein, D. B., & Romero, P. P. (2007). Model building versus theorizing: The paucity of theory. *Econ Journal Watch, 4*(2), 241–271.

Kline, W. B., & Farrell, C. A. (2005). Recurring manuscript problems: Recommendations for writing, training, and research. *Counselor Education and Supervision, 44*(3), 166–174.

Kling, R., & McKim, G. (1999). Scholarly communication and the continuum of electronic publishing. *Journal for the Association for Information Science and Technology, 50*(10), 890–906.

Knafl, K. A., & Howard, M. J. (1984). Interpreting and reporting qualitative research. *Research in Nursing and Health, 7*(1), 17–24.

Knott, D. (2009). *Critical reading toward critical writing*. Retrieved from the University of Toronto website: http://www.writing.utoronto.ca/images/stories/Documents/critical-reading.pdf

Koch, T. (1996). Implementation of a hermeneutic inquiry in nursing: Philosophy, rigour and representation. *Journal of Advanced Nursing, 24*(1), 174–184.

Konradsen, F. (ca. 2016). *Lesson 3: Research objectives*. Retrieved from the Better Thesis website: http://betterthesis.dk/getting-started/short-synopsis

Kopelman, L. M. (1994). Case method and casuistry: The problem of bias. *Theoretical Medicine, 15*(1), 21–37.

Kosur, H. M. (2012, October 7). English modal verbs: Definitions reference sheet [Web log post]. Retrieved from http://www.brighthubeducation.com/esl-lesson-plans/37641-modal-verbs-in-english/

Kotler, P. (2000). *Marketing management* (10th ed.). Upper Saddle River, NJ: Prentice Hall.

Kratzer, A. (1991). Modality. In A. von Stechow & D. Wunderlich (Eds.), *Semantics* (pp. 639–650). Berlin, Germany: Mouton de Gruyter.

Kretchmer, P. (2008a). *Fourteen steps to writing an effective discussion section*. Mill Valley, CA: San Francisco Edit. Retrieved from http://www.sfedit.net/discussion.pdf

Kretchmer, P. (2008b). *Twelve steps to writing an effective results section*. Mill Valley, CA: San Francisco Edit. Retrieved from http://www.sfedit.net/results.pdf

Kriegeskorte, N. (2012). Open evaluation: A vision for entirely transparent post-publication peer review and rating for science. *Frontiers in Computational Neuroscience, 6*(79). doi:10.3389/fncom.2012.00079

Krueger, R. A. (1998). *Analyzing and reporting focus groups results*. San Francisco, CA: Sage.

Kuhn, T. S. (1962). *The structure of scientific revolutions*. Chicago, IL: University of Chicago Press.

Kuhn, T. S. (1970). *The structure of scientific revolutions* (2nd ed.). Chicago, IL: University of Chicago Press.

Kumar, P. S. (2011). *Causation in epidemiology: Association and causation*. Retrieved from the Health Knowledge website: http://www.healthknowledge.org.uk/e-learning/epidemiology/practitioners/causation-epidemiology-association-causation

Kurland, D. J. (2000). *What is critical reading?* Retrieved from the Critical Reading website: http://www.criticalreading.com/criticalreadingthinkingtoc.htm

Labaree, R. V. (2016). *Research guides: Organizing your social sciences research paper.* Retrieved from the University of Southern California Writing Center website: http://libguides.usc.edu/writingguide

Lai, H. R. (2013, September 21). Writing good results and discussions [Web log post]. Retrieved from https://buckleye cology.wordpress.com/2013/09/21/writing-good-results-and-discussion/

Lambert, V. A., & Lambert, C. E. (2012). Editorial: Qualitative descriptive research: An acceptable design. *Pacific Rim International Journal of Nursing Research, 16*(4), 255–256.

Lamothe, A. R. (2012). Factors influencing usage of an electronic journal collection at a medium-size university: An eleven-year study. *Partnership, 7*(1). Retrieved from https://journal.lib .uoguelph.ca/index.php/perj/article/view/1472/2467#.WCC0L3kzVok

Landry, A. (1982). The auxiliary verbs *must*, *need* and *dare*. *Terminology Update, 15*(6), 5–10.

Landsberger, J. (ca. 1996). *Writing position papers.* Retrieved from the Study Guides and Strategies website: http://www.studygs.net/wrtstr9.htm

Lasley, P. (2008). *Indices, scales and typologies.* Retrieved from the Iowa State University website: http://www .soc.iastate.edu/class/202/power point/indexscalesandtypologies.pdf

Lather, P. (1994). Critical inquiry in qualitative research: Feminist and poststructural perspectives: Science "after truth." In B. Crabtree, W. L. Miller, R. B. Addison, V. J. Gilchrist, & A. Kuzel (Eds.), *Exploring collaborative research in primary care* (pp. 103–114). Thousand Oaks, CA: Sage.

Leckie, G. (2008). Researcher roles. In L. M. Given (Ed.), *The SAGE encyclopedia of qualitative research methods* (pp. 771–776). Thousand Oaks, CA: Sage.

Lee, C. (2010, July 15). Five steps to a great title [Web log post]. Retrieved from http://blog.apastyle.org/apastyle/2010/07/five-steps-to-a-great-title.html

Lee, S. (2013). *Report writing: Introduction.* Retrieved from the SlideShare website: http://www.slideshare.net/orangecanton/report-writing-introduction

Lee, T. W., & Mitchell, T. R. (1994). An alternative approach: The unfolding model of voluntary employee turnover. *Academy of Management Review, 19*(1), 51–89.

Lee, T. W., Mitchell, T. R., Wise, L., & Fireman, S. (1996). An unfolding model of voluntary employee turnover. *Academy of Management Journal, 39*(1), 5–36.

Leech, N. L. (2012). Writing mixed research reports. *American Behavioral Scientist, 56*(6), 86–881.

Leiss, E., & Abraham, W. (Eds.). (2014). *Modes of modality.* Philadelphia, PA: John Benjamin.

Lerner, N. (ca. 2003). *20.109 Writing introductions and discussions.* Retrieved from the OpenWetware website: http://openwetware.org/images/1/16/WritingIntroDiscuss.pdf

Lin, A. C. (1998). Bridging positivistic and interpretivist approaches to qualitative methods. *Policy Studies Journal, 26*(1), 162–180.

Lincoln, Y. S. (1995). Emerging criteria for quality in qualitative and interpretive research. *Qualitative Inquiry, 1*(3), 275–289.

Lincoln, Y. S., & Guba, E. G. (1985). *Naturalistic inquiry.* Thousand Oaks, CA: Sage.

Lincoln, Y. S., & Lynham, S. A. (2007, February). *Criteria for assessing good theory in human resource development and other applied disciplines from an interpretive perspective.* Paper presented at the Academy of Human Resource Development International Research Conference in the Americas, Indianapolis, Indiana.

Locke, L. F., Silverman, S. J., & Spirduso, W. W. (2010). *Reading and understanding research* (3rd ed.). Los Angeles, CA: Sage.

Lindsay, J. (2012). *Think piece.* Retrieved from the Brown University website: https://canvas.brown.edu/courses/202417/pages/writing-assignment-number-1-think-pieces

Lockyer, S. (2008). Qualitative research, history of. In L. M. Given (Ed.), *The SAGE encyclopedia of qualitative research methods* (pp. 706–710). Thousand Oaks, CA: Sage.

Lofland, J. (1976). *Doing social life.* New York, NY: Wiley.

Lund, A., & Lund, M. (2013). *Laerd statistical guides: Hypothesis testing.* Retrieved from the Lund Research (Norway) website: https://statistics .laerd.com/statistical-guides/hypoth esis-testing-3.php

Lunsford, T. R., & Lunsford, B. R. (1996). Research forum: How to critically read a journal research article. *Journal of Prosthetics and Orthotics, 8*(1), 24–31.

Lynch, S. M. (2013). *Using statistics in social research: A concise approach.* New York, NY: Springer.

Lynch, T. (2014). *ELTT course 10: Writing up qualitative research: Unit 3: Methodology.* Retrieved from the University of Edinburgh English Language Teaching Center website: http://www.docs.hss .ed.ac.uk/iad/Postgraduate/PhD_researchers/Writing/3_Methodology.pdf

Lynham, S. A. (2002a). Quantitative research and theory building: Dubin's method. *Advances in Developing Human Resources, 4*(3), 242–276.

Lynham, S. A. (2002b). The general method of theory-building research in applied disciplines. *Advances in Developing Human Resources, 4*(3), 221–241.

MacCleave, A. (2006). Incommensurability in cross-disciplinary research: A call for cultural negotiation. *International Journal of Qualitative Methods, 5*(2), Article 8. Retrieved from https://ejournals.library.ualberta.ca/index.php/IJQM/article/view/4389/3515

MacDonald, D., Kirk, D., Metzler, M., Nilges, L., Schempp, P., & Wright, J. (2002). It's all very well, in theory. *Quest, 54*(2), 133–156.

Macefield, R. (2006). Conceptual models and usability. In C. Ghasoui (Ed.), *Encyclopedia of human computer interaction* (pp. 112–119). Hersey, PA: Idea Group References.

Mack, N., Woodsong, C., Macqueen, K., Guest, G., & Namey, E. (2005). *Qualitative research methods: A data collector's field guide.* Durham, NC: Family Health International.

Mackey, A., & Gass, S. M. (2005). *Second language research, methodology and design.* Mahwah, NJ: Erlbaum.

Mahon, J. (2010a). *A little logic.* Retrieved from the Washington & Lee University website: http://home.wlu .edu/~mahonj/LittleLogic.htm

Mahon, J. (2010b). *Guide to writing a philosophy paper.* Retrieved from the Washington & Lee University website: http://home.wlu.edu/~mahonj/ WritingPaper.htm

Maietta, R. C. (2008). Computer-assisted data analysis. In L. M. Given (Ed.), *The SAGE encyclopedia of qualitative research methods* (pp. 103–107). Thousand Oaks, CA: Sage.

Maimon, E. P., Peritz, J. H., & Yancey, K. B. (2005). *A writer's resource.* New York, NY: McGraw-Hill.

Marradi, A. (1990). Classification, typology, taxonomy. *Quality and Quantity, 24*(2), 129–157.

Martin, R. (2007). *The opposable mind: How successful leaders win through integrative thinking.* Boston, MA: Harvard Business School Press.

Mason, J. (2006). *Six strategies for mixing methods and linking data in social science research* [ESRC National Centre for Research Methods Working Paper 4/06]. Southampton, England: National Centre for Research Methods. Retrieved from http://eprints.ncrm.ac.uk/482/1/0406_ six%2520strategies%2520for%2520mixi ng%2520methods.pdf

Matarrese, C. B. (2006). *Argument.* Retrieved from the Minnesota State University, Mankato, website: https:// www.mnsu.edu/philosophy/pdf/class/ Argument_Info.pdf

Matthews, J., & Matthews, R. (2008). *Successful scientific writing* (3rd ed.). Cambridge, England: Cambridge University Press.

Max Planck Institute of Economics. (2006). *Discussion papers.* Retrieved from the Max Planck Institute website: http://www.mpi-fg-koeln.mpg.de/pu/ discpapersen.html

Maxwell, J. A. (2008). Designing a qualitative study. In L. Bickman & D. Rog (Eds.), *The SAGE handbook of applied social research methods* (pp. 214–253). Thousand Oaks, CA: Sage.

Maxwell, J. A. (2013). *Qualitative research design* (2nd ed.). Thousand Oaks, CA: Sage.

Maxwell, J. A., & Mittapalli, K. (2008a). Explanatory research. In L. M. Given (Ed.), *The SAGE encyclopedia of qualitative research methods* (pp. 324–325). Thousand Oaks, CA: Sage.

Maxwell, J. A., & Mittapalli, K. (2008b). Theory. In L. M. Given (Ed.), *The SAGE encyclopedia of qualitative research methods* (pp. 876–879). Thousand Oaks, CA: Sage.

McAnsh, S. (2002). *Tense use in the results section.* Retrieved from the University of Oulu (Finland) website: http://cc.oulu.fi/~smac/TRW/tense_ results.htm

McGregor, S. L. T. (1993). *Consumer policy: A social network/political economy perspective* (Unpublished doctoral dissertation). Glasgow, Scotland: University of Strathclyde.

McGregor, S. L. T. (2004). Modelling the evolution of a policy network using network analysis. *Family and Consumer Sciences Research Journal, 32*(4), 382–407.

McGregor, S. L. T. (2006). *Transformative practice.* East Lansing, MI: Kappa Omicron Nu.

McGregor, S. L. T. (2007). *International Journal of Consumer Studies* decade review 1997–2006. *International Journal of Consumer Studies, 31*(1), 2–18.

McGregor, S. L. T. (2008). Ideological maps of consumer education. *International Journal of Consumer Studies, 32*(5), 545–552.

McGregor, S. L. T. (2010a). *Consumer education as a site of political resistance: 50 years of conceptual evolutions* [Monograph #201001]. Seabright, NS: McGregor Consulting Group. Retrieved from http://www.consultmcgregor.com/ documents/publications/monograph_ consumer_education_2010.pdf

McGregor, S. L. T. (2010b). Historical notions of transdisciplinarity in home economics. *Kappa Omicron Nu FORUM, 16*(2). Retrieved from http://www.kon.org/ archives/forum/16-2/mcgregor.html

McGregor, S. L. T. (2010c). Integral leadership and practice: Beyond holistic integration in FCS. *Journal of Family and Consumer Sciences, 102*(1), 49–57.

McGregor, S. L. T. (2011a). Consumer education philosophies: The relationship between education and consumption. *ZEP: Zeitschrift für internationale Bildungsforschung und Entwicklungspädagogik, 34*(4), 4–8.

McGregor, S. L. T. (2011b). Home economics in higher education: Pre professional socialization. *International Journal of Consumer Studies, 35*(5), 560–568.

McGregor, S. L. T. (2012). Bringing a life-centric perspective to influential megatrends. In D. Pendergast, S. McGregor, & K. Turkki (Eds.), *The next 100 years: Creating home economics futures* (pp. 24–37). Queensland, Australia: Australian Academic Press.

McGregor, S. L. T. (2013). *Fostering ideological awareness for consumer professionals* [McGregor Monograph Series No. 201301]. Seabright, NS: McGregor Consulting Group. Retrieved from http:// www.consultmcgregor.com/documents/ publications/ideological-reframingfor-consumer-professionals.pdf

McGregor, S. L. T. (2014). Sustainable life path concept: Journeying toward sustainable consumption. *Journal of Research for Consumers, 24.* Retrieved from http:// jrconsumers.com/Academic_Articles/ issue_24/Issue24-2Academic-McGregor .pdf

McGregor, S. L. T. (2015). Framing consumer education conceptual innovations as consumer activism. *International Journal of Consumer Studies, 40*(1), 35–47.

McGregor, S. L. T. (2016). Exploring modality in home economics discourse. *International Journal of Home Economics, 9*(2), 71–94.

McGregor, S. L. T., & MacCleave, A. (2007). Analysis to determine Canadian, American, and Australian agreement about home economics/ family and consumer sciences professional competency domains. *Kappa Omicron Nu FORUM, 17*(2). Retrieved from http://www.kon.org/archives/ forum/17-2/home_economics_profes sional_competency_domains.html

McGregor, S. L. T., & Murnane, J. (2010). Paradigm, methodology and method: Intellectual integrity in consumer scholarship. *International Journal of Consumer Studies, 34*(4), 419–427.

McGregor, S. L. T., Pendergast, D., Seniuk, E., Eghan, F., & Engberg, L. (2008). Choosing our future: Ideologies matter in the home economics profession. *International Journal of Home Economics, 1*(1), 48–68.

McLean, G. N. (2011). Writing theory, conceptual, and position articles for publication. In T. S. Rocco & T. Hatcher (Eds.), *The handbook of scholarly writing and publishing* (pp. 209–221). San Francisco, CA: Jossey-Bass.

Merriam, S. B. (2009). *Qualitative research.* San Francisco, CA: Sage.

Meschede, T. (2010). Accessing housing: Integrating qualitative and quantitative research methods. In B. Thyer (Ed.), *The handbook of social work research methods* (2nd ed., pp. 609–613). Thousand Oaks, CA: Sage.

Messick, R. E. (2015). *Development solutions think piece series No. 1 : When should developing nations borrow policies from other countries?* Seoul, Korea: UNDP Policy Center.

Michael, R. S. (2004). *Treats to internal & external validity: Y520—Strategies for educational inquiry.* Retrieved from the Indiana University Bloomington website: http://www.indiana.edu/~educy520/sec5982/week_9/520in_ex_validity.pdf

Michaelson, H. B. (1990). *How to write and publish engineering papers and reports* (3rd ed.). Phoenix, AZ: Oryx.

Michell, J. (1986). Measurement scales and statistics: A clash of paradigms. *Psychological Bulletin, 3,* 398–407.

Miles, M. B., & Huberman, M. (1994). *Qualitative data analysis* (2nd ed.). Thousand Oaks, CA: Sage.

Miller, J. E. (2015). *The Chicago guide to writing about numbers* (2nd ed.). Chicago, IL: Chicago University Press.

Mitzenmacher, M. (2010). *How to read a research paper.* Retrieved from the Harvard University website: https://www.eecs.harvard.edu/~michaelm/postscripts/ReadPaper.pdf

Monash University. (2006). *Writing literature reviews.* Victoria, Australia: Author. Retrieved from http://www.monash.edu.au/lls/llonline/writing/general/lit-reviews/print-section.doc

Morel, M. (2012). Writing recommendations and executive summaries. *Keeping Good Companies, 64*(5), 274–278.

Morgan, D. L. (1998). *Focus group guidebook.* San Francisco, CA: Sage.

Morrow, D. R., & Weston, A. (2016). *A workbook for arguments* (2nd ed.). Indianapolis, IN: Hackett.

Morse, J. M. (1991). Approaches to qualitative-quantitative methodological triangulation. *Nursing Research, 40*(2), 120–123.

Morse, J., & Maddox, L. (2014). Analytic integration in qualitatively driven (QUAL) mixed and multiple methods design. In U. Flick (Ed.), *The SAGE handbook of qualitative data analysis* (pp. 524–539). Thousand Oaks, CA: Sage.

Moschis, G. P. (1986). *Consumer socialization: A life-cycle perspective.* Boston, MA: Lexington Books.

Mosier, R. D. (1968). From inquiry logic to symbolic logic. *Educational Theory, 18*(1), 32–38.

Mosterín, J. (1996). Philosophy and cosmology. In G. Munévar (Ed.), *Spanish studies in the philosophy of science* (pp. 57–88). Boston, MA: Kluwer.

Motulsky, H. (2009). *Frequently asked questions: FAQ# 1089.* Retrieved from the GraphPad website: http://www.graphpad.com/support/faqid/1089/

Muehlhauser, L. (2009, November 19). Intro to logic: Abductive reasoning [Web log post]. Retrieved from http://commonsenseatheism.com/?p=3703

Munker, D. (2012, December 1). Staying on track: The red thread of the narrative [Web log post]. Retrieved from http://www.storydriven.net/blog.htm?post=885192

Murnane, J. (2008). *Valuing stakeholder knowledge: An interpretive study of knowledge cultivation and enablement in a nonprofit human services organization* (Doctoral dissertation, Iowa State University). Retrieved from http://lib.dr.iastate.edu/cgi/viewcontent.cgi?article=2172&context=etd

Murray, C. (2003). *Writing a position paper.* Retrieved from the St. Francis Xavier University website: http://www.sfu.ca/cmns/130d1/WritingaPositionPaper.htm

Myers, I. B., & Myers, P. (1980). *Gifts differing: Understanding personality type.* Mountain View, CA: Davies-Black.

Nahrin, K. (2015). Objectivity and ethics in empirical research. *International Journal of Scientific and Research Publications, 5*(7). Retrieved from http://www.ijsrp.org/research-paper-0715/ijsrp-p4381.pdf

Nalzaro, L. M. (2012). *Chapter 6: Theoretical & conceptual framework.* Retrieved from the SlideShare website: http://www.slideshare.net/ludymae/chapter-6theoretical-conceptual-framework

National Foundation for Educational Research. (2016). *Developing young researchers.* Retrieved from the NFER website: http://www.nfer.ac.uk/schools/developing-young-researchers/

Nepomuceno, N. V., & Laroche, M. (2016). Do I fear death? The effects of mortality salience on anti-consumption lifestyles. *Journal of Consumer Affairs, 50*(1), 124–144.

Nestor, P. G., & Schutt, R. K. (2015). *Research methods in psychology* (2nd ed.). Thousand Oaks, CA: Sage.

Neuman, W. L. (2000). *Social research methods: Qualitative and quantitative approaches.* Boston, MA: Allyn & Bacon.

Newman, I., & Newman, C. (2011). Increasing the likelihood of publishing quantitative manuscripts. In T. S. Rocco & T. Hatcher (Eds.), *The handbook of scholarly writing and publishing* (pp. 179–190). San Francisco, CA: Jossey-Bass.

Newman, I., Newman, D., & Newman, C. (2011). Writing research articles using mixed methods. In T. S. Rocco & T. Hatcher (Eds.), *The handbook of scholarly writing and publishing* (pp. 191–208). San Francisco, CA: Jossey-Bass.

Newman, I., Ridenour, C., Newman, C., & DeMarco, G. M. C. (2003). A typology of research purposes and its relationship to mixed methods. In A. Tashakkori & C. Teddlie (Eds.), *Handbook of mixed methods in social and behavioral research* (pp. 167–188). Thousand Oaks, CA: Sage.

Newton, P. E. (2013). *Does it matter what "validity" means?* Retrieved from the University of Oxford website: http://oucea.education.ox.ac.uk/wordpress/wp-content/uploads/2013/06/2013-Meaning-of-validity-Oxford-v4-slides.pdf

Nie, K., Ma, T., & Nakamori, Y. (2007). Building a taxonomy for understanding knowledge management. *Electronic Journal of Knowledge Management, 5*(4), 453–466.

Nielsen, L., & McGregor, S. L. T. (2013). Consumer morality and moral norms. *International Journal of Consumer Studies, 37*(5), 473–480.

Niglas, K. (1999, September 22–25). *Quantitative and qualitative inquiry in educational research: Is there a paradigmatic difference between them?* Paper presented at the European Conference on Education Research, Lahti, Finland. Retrieved from http://www.leeds.ac.uk/educol/documents/00001487.htm

Niglas, K. (2001). Paradigms and methodology in educational research. *British Education Index, Education-line.* Retrieved from the University of Leeds website: http://www.leeds.ac.uk/educol/documents/00001840.htm

Nkwake, A. M. (2013). *Working with assumptions in international development program evaluation.* New York, NY: Springer.

Norris, J. M., Plonsky, L., Ross, S. J., & Schoonen, R. (2015). Guidelines for reporting quantitative methods and results in primary research. *Language Learning, 65*(2), 470–476.

Northam, J. (2011, March 29). Thoughts on writing recommendations for a research thesis [Web log post]. Retrieved from http://blogs.bournemouth.ac.uk/research/2011/03/29/thoughts-on-writing-recommendations-for-a-research-thesis/

O'Cathain, A., Murphy, E., & Nicholl, J. (2008). The quality of mixed methods studies in health services research. *Journal of Health Services Research and Policy, 13*(2), 92–98.

Öhman, A., & Löfgren, M. (ca. 2010). *Guidelines for reports using qualitative methodology.* Retrieved from the *Journal of Rehabilitation Medicine* website: http://www.medicaljournals.se/jrm/index.php?option=com_content&view=article&id=27&Itemid=56

Olk, P., & Griffiths, T. L. (2004). Creating and disseminating knowledge among organizational scholars: The role of special issues. *Organization Science, 15*(1), 120–129.

Onwuegbuzie, A. J., & Teddlie, C. (2003). A framework for analyzing data in mixed methods research. In A. Tashakkori & C. Teddlie (Eds.), *Handbook on mixed methods in the behavioral and social sciences* (pp. 351–384). Thousand Oaks, CA: Sage.

O'Toole, M. (Ed.). (2013). *Mosby's medical dictionary* (9th ed.). Toronto, ON: Elsevier Canada.

Otto, A., & Webley, P. (2016). Saving, selling, earning, and negotiating: How adolescents acquire monetary lump sums and who considers saving. *Journal of Consumer Affairs, 50*(2), 342–371.

Owen, W. F. (1984). Interpretive themes in relational communication. *Quarterly Journal of Speech, 70,* 274–287.

Oxford American College Dictionary. (2002). New York, NY: Oxford University Press.

Ozagac, O. (2006). *Argumentative essay.* Retrieved from the Boğaziçi University website: http://www.buowl.boun.edu.tr/students/types%20of%20essays/ARGUMENTATIVE%20ESSAY.pdf

Paley, J. (2008). Positivism. In L. M. Given (Ed.), *The SAGE encyclopedia of qualitative research methods* (pp. 646–650). Thousand Oaks, CA: Sage.

Palmer, F. R. (2001). *Mood and modality.* Cambridge, England: Cambridge University Press.

Panter, M. (2016). Choosing effective keywords [Web log post]. Retrieved from http://www.aje.com/en/arc/editing-tip-choosing-effective-keywords/

Parish, J. D. (2013). *Course syllabus fall semester 2013 TMGT 599 01E.* Retrieved from the Texas A&M University website: http://www.tamuc.edu/academics/cvSyllabi/syllabi/201380/81646.pdf

Parncutt, R. (2015). *Structuring the argument of a theoretical paper in the social sciences.* Retrieved from the University of Graz website: http://uni-graz.at/~parncutt/argument.html

Parncutt, R., & Painsi, M. (2006). *Structuring the argument of a theoretical paper.* Proceedings of the 9th International Conference on Music Perception and Cognition, Bologna, Italy. Retrieved from http://uni-graz.at/~parncutt/publications/PaPa06_argument.pdf

Patidar, J. (2013, May 7). *Nonexperimental research design.* Retrieved from the SlideShare website: http://www.slideshare.net/drjayeshpatidar/nonexperimental-research-design

Patterson, C. H. (1983). *Theories of counseling and psychotherapy.* Philadelphia, PA: Harper & Row.

Patton, M. Q. (2002). *Qualitative research and evaluation methods* (3rd ed.). Thousand Oaks, CA: Sage.

Pattypie. (2017). *Quality improvement chapter 7.* Retrieved from the Quizlet website: https://quizlet.com/22501861/quality-improvement-chapter-7-flashcards/

Paul, R. (1993). The logic of critical and creative thinking. In R. Binker & J. Williams (Eds.), *Critical thinking* (pp. 16–32). Tomales, CA: Foundation for Critical Thinking.

Pearl, J. (2009). Causal inference in statistics: An overview. *Statistics Surveys, 3,* 96–146.

Pearson, H. (2006). Credit where credit's due. *Nature, 440*(7084), 591–592.

Peng, J. (1987). Organisational features in chemical engineering research articles. *ELR Journal, 1,* 79–116.

Pereira, A. G., & Funtowicz, S. (2005). Quality assurance by extended peer review: Tools to inform debates, dialogues & deliberations. *Technikfolgenabschatzung: Theorie und Praxis, 2*(14), 74–79.

Perkins. (2007). *A general summary of Aristotle's appeals.* Retrieved from the East Caroline University website: http://www.ecu.edu/cs-acad/writing/wac/upload/ethos-pathos-logos.docx

Philadelphia University. (n.d.). *Guidelines for writing a literature review.* Retrieved from the Philadelphia University Learning and Advising Center website: http://www.philau.edu/learning/INC/pdf/Writing%20a%20Literature%20Review%20SLA%20%20Arch.pdf

Piantanida, M. (2001). A think piece on "think pieces." In M. Piantanida (Ed.), *Invitation to study group monograph.* Retrieved from the University of Pittsburgh website: http://www.docs-r-us.com/pdffiles/SG%20Piantanida%20.pdf

Pirk, C., de Miranda, J., Kramer, M., Murray, T., Nazzi, F., Shutler, D., van der Steen, J., & van Dooremalen, C. (2013). Statistical guidelines for *Apis mellifera* research. *Journal of Apicultural Research, 52*(4). doi:10.3896/IBRA.1.52.4.13

Plakhotnik, M. S., & Rocco, T. S. (2009). Four components of a manuscript reporting qualitative empirical studies: A brief overview. In M. S. Plakhotnik, S. M. Nielsen, & D. M. Pane (Eds.), *Proceedings of the Eighth Annual College of Education & GSN Research Conference* (pp. 105–111). Miami: Florida International University.

Plakhotnik, M. S., & Shuk, M. B. (2011). Resources: Further reading for scholarly writing. In T. S. Rocco & T. Hatcher (Eds.), *The handbook of scholarly writing and publishing* (pp. 311–323). San Francisco, CA: Jossey-Bass.

Platt, J. (1986). Functionalism and the survey: The relation of theory and method. *Sociological Review, 34*(3), 501–536.

Ponterotto, J. G. (2005). Qualitative research in counseling psychology. *Journal of Counseling Psychology, 55*(2), 126–136.

Possel, H. (2013). *Transition words.* Retrieved from the Smart-Words website: http://www.smart-words.org/linking-words/transition-words.html

Preissle, J. (2008). Ethics. In L. M. Given (Ed.), *The SAGE encyclopedia of qualitative research methods* (pp. 273–277). Thousand Oaks, CA: Sage.

Pruyt, E. (2006, July 23–27). *What is systems dynamics? A paradigmatic inquiry.* Paper presented at the 24th International Conference of the System Dynamics Society, Nijmegen, The Netherlands. Retrieved from http://www.systemdynamics.org/conferences/2006/proceed/papers/PRUYT177.pdf

Psychology Writing Center. (2010). *Summarizing a research article.* Retrieved from the University of Washington website: https://depts.washington.edu/psych/files/writing_center/summarizing.pdf

Pyrczak, F. (2008). *Evaluating research in academic journals* (4th ed.). Glendale, CA: Pyrczak.

Ramakantan, R. (2007). The "discussion" in a research paper. *Medical Writing, 17*(3), 148–149.

Ramalho, R., Adams, P., Huggard, P., & Hoare, K. (2015). Literature review and constructivist grounded theory methodology. *Forum: Qualitative Social Research, 16*(3), Article 19. Retrieved from http://www.qualitative-research.net/index.php/fqs/article/view/2313/3876

Randolph, J. J. (2009). A guide to writing the dissertation literature review. *Practical Assessment, Research & Evaluation, 14*(13). Retrieved from http://pareonline.net/pdf/v14n13.pdf

Raulin, M. L., & Graziano, A. M. (1994). Quasi-experimental and correlational studies. In A. M. Colman (Ed.), *Companion encyclopedia of psychology* (pp. 1122–1141). New York, NY: Routledge, Chapman, & Hall.

Ravitch, S. M., & Riggan, M. (2016). *Reason & rigor: How conceptual frameworks guide research* (2nd ed.). Thousand Oaks, CA: Sage.

Reed, A. (2010, November 3). 8 provocative questions that encourage lateral thinking [Web log post]. Retrieved from http://www.bridging-the-gap.com/asking-provocative-questions-to-encourage-lateral-thinking/

Reilly, K. (2016). Footnotes and endnotes [Web log post]. Retrieved from https://www.sophia.org/tutorials/footnotes-and-endnotes—2

Rennie, D., Yank, V., & Emanuel, L. (1997). When authorship fails: A proposal to make contributors accountable. *Journal of the American Medical Association, 278*(7), 579–585.

Rhode, D., & Packel A. (2011). *Leadership.* New York, NY: Wolters Kluwer.

Richardson, J., Smith, A., & Meaden, S. (2012). *Thou shalt not commit logical fallacies.* Brisbane, Australia: yourlogicalfallacyis.com. Retrieved from https://yourlogicalfallacyis.com/pdf/Logical_Fallacies_on_A4.pdf

Ridner, A., & Wilson, B. (2016). *Research methods in psychology: Tutoring solution course.* Retrieved from the Study.com website: http://study.com/academy/course/research-methods-in-psychology-tutoring-solution.html

Rindova, V. (2011). Moving from ideas to a theoretical contribution: Comments on the process of developing theory in organizational research. *Journal of Supply Chain Management, 47*(2), 19–21.

Ritchie, J., & Lewis, J. (2003). *Qualitative research practice.* London, England: Sage.

Roberts, C. (2010). *Tips on how to write theoretical papers.* Retrieved from the Iowa State University website: http://www.public.iastate.edu/~carlos/soc401/papers/tips.pdf

Roberts, M. (2010, November 10). How to write the results section of a research paper [Web log post]. Retrieved from http://www.firehow.com/2010102620879/how-to-write-the-results-section-of-a-research-paper.html

Robey, D., & Baskerville, R. (2012, March). *Dimensions of conceptual rigor and characteristics in theoretical reviews.* Paper presented at the First Annual Atlanta-Athens Conference on Research in Information Systems, Atlanta, GA. Retrieved from http://www.cis.gsu.edu/rbaskerville/aacris2012/presentations/Robey_AACRIS_2012.pdf

Robson, D., & Gray, R. (2007). Serious mental illness and physical health problems: A discussion paper. *International Journal of Nursing Studies, 44*(3), 457–466.

Rocco, T. S., & Plakhotnik, M. S. (2009). Literature reviews, conceptual frameworks, and theoretical frameworks: Terms, functions, and distinctions. *Human Resource Development Review, 8*(1), 120–130.

Rocco, T. S., & Plakhotnik, M. S. (2011). Increasing the odds of publishing a qualitative manuscript. In T. S. Rocco & T. Hatcher (Eds.), *The handbook of scholarly writing and publishing* (pp. 161–178). San Francisco, CA: Jossey-Bass.

Rodrigues, V. (2013, November 4). How to write an effective title and abstract and choose appropriate keywords [Web log post]. Retrieved from http://www.editage.com/insights/how-to-write-an-effective-title-and-abstract-and-choose-appropriate-keywords

Rohmann, C. (1999). *A world of ideas: A dictionary of important theories, concepts, beliefs, and thinkers.* New York, NY: Ballantine Books.

Rojon, C., & Saunders, M. N. K. (2012). Formulating a convincing rationale for a research study. *Coaching, 5*(1), 55–61.

Rolfe, G. (2006). Validity, trustworthiness and rigour: Quality and the idea of qualitative research. *Methodological Issues in Nursing Research, 53*(3), 304–310.

Royal Melbourne Institute of Technology. (2008). *Writing a report*. Melbourne, Australia: Author. Retrieved from https://www.dlsweb.rmit.edu.au/lsu/content/pdfs/2_assessmenttasks/super_report.pdf

Rundell, M. (Ed.). (2007). *Macmillan English dictionary* (2nd ed.). Oxford, England: Macmillan Education.

Ryan, A. B. (2006). Methodology: Analysing qualitative data and writing up your findings. In M. Antonesa (Ed.), *Researching and writing your thesis* (pp. 92–108). Mace, Ireland: Maynooth Adult and Community Education.

Ryan, G. W., & Bernard, H. T. (2003). Techniques to identify themes. *Field Methods, 15*(1), 85–109.

Ryan, K., & Cooper, J. (2007). *Those who can, teach*. Boston, MA: Wadsworth Cengage Learning.

Ryan, P. (2009). Integrated theory of health behavior change: Background and intervention development. *Clinical Nurse Specialist, 23*(3), 161–172.

Saga, M. (2011). *How to write recommendations for a report*. Retrieved from the eHow website: http://www.ehow.com/how_5847636_write-recommendations-report.html

Salkind, N. J. (Ed.). (2010). *Encyclopedia of research design*. Thousand Oaks, CA: Sage.

Salmani, D., & Akbari, M. (2008). Fuzzy and research paradigms relationships: A mutual contribution. *Online Journal of Academic Leadership, 6*(2). Retrieved from http://www.academicleadership.org/emprical_research/340.shtml

Salomone, P. R. (1993). Trade secrets for crafting a conceptual article. *Journal of Counseling & Development, 72*(1), 73–76.

Samuels, H. (2004). *Writing a conclusion: Tip sheet 18*. Retrieved from the Cambridge Rindge and Latin School website: http://www.crlsresearchguide.org/18_Writing_Conclusion.asp

Sandelowski, M. (1995). Sample size in qualitative research. *Researching in Nursing and Health,18*(2), 179–183.

Sandelowski, M. (2000). Focus on research methods: Whatever happened to qualitative descriptive? *Research in Nursing and Health, 23*, 334–340.

Sanders, M., Tingloo, A., & Verhulst, H. (2005). *Advanced writing in English*. Philadelphia, PA: Coronet Books.

Sauvage, G. M. (1913). Positivism. In *The Catholic encyclopedia* (Vol. 12). New York, NY: Robert Appleton. Retrieved from https://en.wikisource.org/wiki/Catholic_Encyclopedia_(1913)/Positivism

Schafer, J. L., & Graham, J. W. (2002). Missing data: Our view of the state of the art. *Psychological Methods, 7*(2), 147–177.

Schafersman, S. D. (1997). *An introduction to science*. Retrieved from the Stony Brook State University of New York website: http://www.geo.sunysb.edu/esp/files/scientific-method.html

Schield, M. (2010). *Statistical literacy: A short introduction*. Retrieved from the Statistical Literacy website: http://statlit.org/pdf/2010Schield-StatLit-Intro4p.pdf

Schmidt, N., & Brown, J. (2012). *Evidence-based practice for nurses* (2nd ed.). Mississauga, ON: Jones & Bartlett Learning Canada.

Schneider, F. (2014, February 18). What's in a methodology? [Web log post]. Retrieved from http://www.politicseastasia.com/studying/whats-methodology/

Schram, T. H. (2006). *Conceptualizing and proposing qualitative research* (2nd ed.). Upper Saddle River, NJ: Pearson Merrill Prentice Hall.

Scott, J. H. (1998). *The principles of argumentation*. Retrieved from the California State University, Northridge, website: http://www.csun.edu/~hcpas003/argument.html

Scott-Lichter, D., & Editorial Policy Committee, Council of Science Editors. (2012). *CSE's white paper on promoting integrity in scientific journal publications 2012 update* (3rd rev. ed.). Wheat Ridge, CO: Council of Science Editors.

Shah, S., & Corley, K. (2006). Building better theory by bridging the quantitative-qualitative divide. *Journal of Management Studies, 43*(8), 1821–1835.

Shamoo, A., & Resnik, D. (2015). *Responsible conduct in research* (3rd ed.). New York, NY: Oxford University Press.

Shank, G., & Brown, L. (2007). *Exploring educational research literacy*. New York, NY: Routledge.

Sharma, M., Knowlden, A. P., & Nahar, V. K. (2017). Applying a new theory to alter binge drinking behavior in college students. *Family Community Health, 40*(1), 52–55.

Shenton, A. K. (2004). Strategies for ensuring trustworthiness in qualitative research projects. *Education for Information, 22*(2), 63–75.

Shields, P., & Rangarjan, N. (2013). *A playbook for research methods*. Stillwater, OK: New Forums Press.

Shon, P. C. (2015). *How to read journal articles in the social sciences* (2nd ed.). Thousand Oaks, CA: Sage.

Shuttleworth, M. (2015). *How to write a research paper* (2nd ed.). Kristiansand, Norway: Explorable.com.

Silver, A. (2017, January 18). Controversial website that lists "predatory" publishers shuts down. *Nature.com News*. Retrieved from http://www.nature.com/news/controversial-website-that-lists-predatory-publishers-shuts-down-1.21328

Silverman, D. (2000). *Doing qualitative research*. London, England: Sage.

Simmons, A. B., & Michael, R. S. (2002). *Types of variables*. Retrieved from the Indiana University website: http://www.indiana.edu/~educy520/sec5982/week_2/variable_types.pdf

Simmons, R. L. (2016). *The infinitive phrase*. Retrieved from the Grammar Bytes website: http://www.chompchomp.com/terms/infinitivephrase.htm

Simon, M. K. (2011). *Dissertation and scholarly research: Recipes for success*. Seattle, WA: Dissertation Success.

Simon, P. (2013). *The Grammaring guide to English grammar* (2nd ed.). Retrieved from http://www.grammaring.com/the-grammaring-guide-to-english-grammar

Sinclair, M. (2007). Editorial: A guide to understanding theoretical and conceptual frameworks. *Evidence Based Midwifery, 5*(2), 39.

Sisson, A. (2012, October 24). What is considered a good impact factor? [Web log post]. Retrieved from http://libanswers.mdanderson.org/a.php?qid=67547

Sitko, N. J. (2013). *Designing a qualitative research project: Conceptual framework and research questions* [PowerPoint presentation]. Lusaka, Zambia: Indaba Agricultural Policy Research Institute. Retrieved from http://fsg.afre.msu.edu/zambia/Conceptual_Framework_and_Research_Questions.pdf

Skelton, J. R., & Edwards, S. J. L. (2000). The function of the discussion section in academic medical writing. *British Medical Journal, 320*(7244), 1269–1270.

Smith, C. (2010). *Course in Logic 101: Validity, strength, soundness and cogency.* Retrieved from the EditThis website: http://editthis.info/logic/?title=Validity,_Strength,_Soundness_and_Cogency&printable=yes

Smith, C. H. L. (2008). *The use of basic science.* Retrieved from the European Organization for Nuclear Research website: http://public-archive.web.cern.ch/public-archive/en/About/BasicScience1-en.html

Smith, J. K. (1983). Qualitative versus quantitative research: An attempt to clarify the issue. *Educational Researcher, 12*(3), 6–13.

Smith, L. R. (2011). *Eastern versus western logic.* Retrieved from the Lawton's Domain website: http://webpages.charter.net/lrsmith/eastwest.htm

Smith, M. L., & Glass, G. V. (1987). *Research and evaluation in education and the social sciences.* Englewood Cliffs, NJ: Prentice Hall.

Smithey Fulmer, I. (2012). Editor's comments: The craft of writing theory articles—Variety and similarity to AMR. *Academy of Management Review, 37*(3), 327–331.

Smyth, R. (2004). Exploring the usefulness of a conceptual framework as a research tool. *Issues in Educational Research, 14*(2), 167–180.

Social Science & Medicine. (2010). Guidelines for qualitative papers. Retrieved from the SS&M website: http://www.journals.elsevier.com/social-science-and-medicine/policies/guidelines-for-qualitative-papers

Sonnenberg, K. (ca. 2002). *Conclusions and recommendations.* Retrieved from the Paper Masters website: https://www.papermasters.com/conclusions_recommendations.html

Sousa, V. D., Driessnack, M., & Mendes, I. A. C. (2007). An overview of research designs relevant to nursing: Part I: Quantitative research designs. *Latin American Journal of Nursing, 15*(3), 502–507.

Stange, K. C., Crabtree, B. F., & Miller, W. L. (2006). Publishing multimethod research. *Annals of Family Medicine, 4*(4), 292–294.

Steiner, E. (1988). *Methodology for theory building.* Sydney, Australia: Educology Research Associates.

Sternberg, R. J. (2003). Duplex theory of hate: Development and application to terrorism, massacres, and genocide. *Review of General Psychology, 7*(3), 299–328.

Sternberg, R. J., & Gordeeva, T. (1996). The anatomy of impact: What makes an article influential? *Psychological Science, 7*(2), 69–75.

Stockburger, D. W. (1998). *Introductory statistics* [Revised WWW version e-book]. Retrieved from http://www.psychstat.missouristate.edu/introbook/sbk00.htm

Suber, P. (2015, December). Open access overview. *The SPARC Open Access Newsletter.* Retrieved from http://legacy.earlham.edu/~peters/fos/overview.htm

Sugimoto, C., Larivière, V., Ni, C., & Cronin, B. (2013). Journal acceptance rates: A cross-disciplinary analysis of variability and relationships with journal measures. *Journal of Informetrics, 7*(4), 897–906.

Sullivan, A., & Tseng, R. (2002). One for the road. In *Pocket English idioms.* Retrieved from the GoEnglish.com website: http://www.goenglish.com

Suter, W. N. (2012). *Introduction to educational research* (2nd ed.). Thousand Oaks, CA: Sage.

Swales, J. (1990). *Genre analysis.* Cambridge, England: Cambridge University Press.

Swales, J. M., & Feak, C. B. (2004). *Academic writing for graduate students* (2nd ed.). Ann Arbor: University of Michigan Press.

Swanson, C. (n.d.). *A brief guide to writing philosophy papers.* Retrieved from the Vancouver Island University website: https://www2.viu.ca/philosophy/brief-guide-to-writing-philosophy-papers.asp

Swanson, R. (2013). *Theory building in applied disciplines.* San Francisco, CA: Berrett-Koehler.

Swartout, K. (2014). *Analyzing and interpreting mixed methods research.* Retrieved from the Research Talk website: http://researchtalk.com/wp-content/uploads/2014/01/Analyzing-and-Interpreting-Mixed-Methods-Research.pdf

Swedberg, R. (Ed.). (2014). *Theorizing in social sciences.* Stanford, CA: Stanford University Press.

Swinscow, T. D. V. (1997). *Statistics at square one* (9th ed.). London, England: BMJ.

Sykes, A. O. (1992). *The inaugural Coase lecture: An introduction to regression analysis.* Retrieved from the University of Chicago Law School website: http://www.law.uchicago.edu/files/files/20.Sykes_.Regression.pdf

Tamburri, R. (2012). Opening up peer review. *University Affairs, 53*(4), 20–24.

Tashakkori, A., & Creswell, J. W. (2007). Exploring the nature of research questions in mixed methods research. *Journal of Mixed Methods Research, 1*(3), 207–211.

Tashakkori, A., & Teddlie, C. (1998). *Mixed methodology: Combining qualitative and quantitative approaches.* London, England: Sage.

Tashakkori, A., & Teddlie, C. (2010). *Sage handbook of mixed methods in social & behavioral research.* Thousand Oaks, CA: Sage.

Tavallaei, M., & Abu Talib, M. (2010). A general perspective on role of theory in qualitative research. *Journal of International Social Research, 3*(11), 570–577.

Taylor, C. (ca. 2006). *What is "synthesis"???* Retrieved from the University of Manitoba website: https://umanitoba.ca/faculties/nursing/students/What_is_synthesis.pdf

Taylor, D. B. (2007). *A guide to verb tense voice and mood in scientific writing*. Toronto, ON: University of Toronto. Retrieved from http://hswriting .library.utoronto.ca/index.php/hswrit ing/article/download/3340/1476

Taylor, D. B., & Procter, M. (ca. 2009). *The literature review: A few tips on conducting it.* Retrieved from the University of Toronto Writing website: http://www .writing.utoronto.ca/images/stories/ Documents/literature-review.pdf

Teddlie, C., & Tashakkori, A. (2006). A general typology of research designs featuring mixed methods. *Research in the Schools, 13*(1), 12–28.

Teddlie, C., & Tashakkori, A. (2009). *Foundations of mixed methods research.* Thousand Oaks, CA: Sage.

Teddlie, C., & Tashakkori, A. (2010). Overview of contemporary issues in mixed methods research. In A. Tashakkori & C. Teddlie (Eds.), *SAGE handbook of mixed methods in social and behavioral research* (2nd ed., pp. 1–44). Thousand Oaks, CA: Sage.

Tengler, M. (2014). Think piece series: Activists and extractive industries: An alliance against social development. Retrieved from the UNRISD website: http://www.unrisd.org/ystp-tengler

Tenopir, C., & King, D. (2000). *Towards electronic journals.* Washington, DC: Special Libraries Association.

The Learning House. (2016). *Conceptual approaches to nursing* [Online course]. Louisville, KY: Author. Retrieved from http://www.elearnportal.com/courses/ nursing/conceptual-approaches-to-nursing

The Writing Center. (2010). *Conclusions.* Retrieved from the University of North Carolina at Chapel Hill website: http:// writingcenter.unc.edu/handouts/ conclusions/

The Writing Center. (2014a). *Argument.* Retrieved from the University of North Carolina at Chapel Hill website: http:// writingcenter.unc.edu/handouts/ argument/

The Writing Center. (2014b). *Scientific reports.* Retrieved from the University of North Carolina at Chapel Hill website: http://writingcenter.unc.edu/handouts/ scientific-reports/

Think piece. (2016). In *Merriam-Webster's online dictionary.* Retrieved from http://www.merriam-webster.com/ dictionary/think%20piece

Thomas, A. (2008). *Lecture 23: Estimation and hypothesis testing.* Retrieved from the University of Oxford website: http://www.stats .ox.ac.uk/~tomas/html_links/0809/ Lecture23.pdf

Thomas, G. (2011). *Doing research.* London, England: Palgrave.

Thorne, S. (2000). Data analysis in qualitative research. *Evidence-Based Nursing, 3*(3), 68–70.

Toadvine, A., Brizee, A., & Angeli, E. (2017). *Active and passive voice.* Retrieved from the Purdue OWL website: https://owl.english.purdue.edu/ owl/owlprint/539/

Torraco, R. J. (2005). Theory development and research methods. In R. A. Swanson & E. F. Holton III (Eds.), *Research in organizations* (pp. 351–374). San Francisco, CA: Berrett-Koehler.

Trochim, W., & Donnelly, J. (2007). *The research methods knowledge base* (3rd ed.). Manson, OH: Atomic Dog.

Tucker, K., Derelian, D., & Rouner, D. (1997). *Public relations writing.* Upper Saddle River, NJ: Prentice Hall.

Tullis Owen, J. A. (2008). Naturalistic data. In L. M. Given (Ed.), *The SAGE encyclopedia of qualitative research methods* (pp. 550–546). Thousand Oaks, CA: Sage.

Ulrich, W. (2011, November–December). Towards a taxonomy of research practice. *Ulrich's Bimonthly.* Retrieved from http://wulrich.com/bimonthly_novem ber2011.html

UniLearning. (2000). *Report writing.* Retrieved from the University of Wollongong, Australia, website: https://unilearning.uow.edu.au/main .html

University of California. (2011). *Write a literature review.* Retrieved from the University of California, Santa Cruz, website: http://guides.library.ucsc .edu/write-a-literature-review

University of Guelph Writing Services. (2004). *How to write a literature review.* Guelph, ON: Author, Learning

Commons FastFact Series. Retrieved from http://www.lib.uoguelph.ca/get-assistance/writing/specific-types-papers/writing-literature-review

University of Guelph Writing Services. (2006). *Writing your first university paper.* Guelph, ON: Author.

University of Hawaii. (1998). *Writing a position paper.* Retrieved from the Internet Archive website: https://web .archive.org/web/20070316023144/ homepages.uhwo.hawaii.edu/~writing/ position.htm

University of Leicester. (2009). *What is critical reading?* Retrieved from the University of Leicester website: http:// www2.le.ac.uk/offices/ld/resources/ study-guides-pdfs/writing-skills-pdfs/critical-reading-v1%200.pdf

University of Leicester. (2012). *Presenting numerical data.* Retrieved from the University of Leicester website: http:// www2.le.ac.uk/offices/ld/resources/ study-guides-pdfs/numeracy-skills-pdfs/ presenting%20numerical%20data%20 updated%20LD.pdf

University of Richmond. (2010). *Writing effective conclusions.* Retrieved from the University of Richmond Writer's Web website: http://writing2.richmond .edu/writing/wweb/conclude.html

University of Sydney. (2016). *Theoretical article (essay) structure: Rules and common mistakes.* Retrieved from the University of Sydney School of Psychology website: http://www.psych .usyd.edu.au/current_students/writ ing_guides/essayA.shtml

University of Waterloo. (2014). *Guidelines for the reporting of incidental and secondary findings to study participants.* Waterloo, ON: Author.

University of York. (2007). *The meaning of modal verbs.* Retrieved from the University of York website: http://www .york.ac.uk/res/elanguages/index/ Modulecd/cu4s6/cu4s60301.htm

Urbaniak, G. C., & Plous, S. (2013). *Research Randomizer* (Version 4.0) [Computer software]. Middletown, CT: Social Psychology Network. Retrieved from http://www.randomizer.org/

Utting, P. (2013). *Think piece: Social and solidarity economy: A pathway to socially sustainable development?* Retrieved

from the UNRISD website: http://www
.unrisd.org/unrisd/website/newsview
.nsf/%28httpNews%29/AB920B156
339500AC1257B5C002C1E96?Open
Document

VandenBos, G. R. (Ed.). (2010). *Publication manual of the American Psychological Association* (6th ed.). Washington, DC: American Psychological Association.

van den Hoonaard, D. K., & van den Hoonaard, W. C. (2008). Data analysis. In L. M. Given (Ed.), *The SAGE encyclopedia of qualitative research methods* (pp. 186–188). Thousand Oaks, CA: Sage.

Vanderbilt University. (2010). *Reporting quantitative results*. Retrieved from the Vanderbilt University Institutional Research Office website: http://virg
.vanderbilt.edu/AssessmentPlans/
Results/Reporting_Results_
Quantitative.aspx#Tables

van Maarseveen, H., & van der Tang, G. F. M. (1978). *Written constitutions*. Dobbs Ferry, NY: Oceana.

van Zanten, H. H. E., Meerburg, B. G., Bikker, P., Herrero, M., & de Boer, I. J. M. (2016). Opinion paper: The role of livestock in a sustainable diet: A land-use perspective. *Animal, 10*(4), 547–549.

Vine, B. (2004). *Getting things done at work*. Philadelphia, PA: John Benjamins.

von Fintel, K. (2006). Modality and language. In D. Borchert (Ed.), *Encyclopedia of philosophy* (2nd ed., pp. 20–26). Detroit, MI: MacMillan Reference USA.

Wacker, J. G. (1998). A definition of theory: Research guidelines for different theory-building research methods in operations management. *Journal of Operations Management, 16*(4), 361–385.

Wake Forest University. (2011). *List of action verbs for resumes and professional profiles*. Retrieved from the Wake Forest University Career and Professional Development website: http://career
.opcd.wfu.edu/files/2011/05/Action-Verbs-for-Resumes.pdf

Wallace, M., & Wray, A. (2011). Scholarly reading as a model for scholarly writing. In T. S. Rocco & T. Hatcher (Eds.), *The handbook of scholarly writing and publishing* (pp. 44–61). San Francisco, CA: Jossey-Bass.

Walli, B. (2014, August 14). Taxonomy 101 [Web log post]. Retrieved from

http://www.kmworld.com/Articles/
Editorial/What-Is-.../Taxonomy-101-
The-Basics-and-Getting-Started-with-
Taxonomies-98787.aspx

Watts, R. E. (2011). Developing a conceptual article for publication in counseling journals. *Journal of Counseling & Development, 89*(3), 308–312.

Weaver, K., & Olson, J. K. (2006). Understanding paradigms used for nursing research. *Journal of Advanced Nursing, 53*(4), 459–469.

Weaver, P. C., & Weaver, R. G. (1977). *Persuasive writing*. New York, NY: Free Press.

Weber, R., & Brizee, A. (2013). *Logical fallacies*. Retrieved from the Purdue OWL website: https://owl.english
.purdue.edu/owl/resource/659/03/

Webster, J., & Watson, R. T. (2002). Analyzing the past to prepare for the future: Writing a literature review. *MIS Quarterly, 26*(2), xiii–xxiii.

Weick, K. E. (1995). What theory is not, theorizing is. *Administrative Science Quarterly, 40*(3), 385–390.

Westphal, J. (Ed.). (1995). *Certainty*. Indianapolis, IN: Hackett.

What are footnotes? (2014). Retrieved from the Plagiarism.org website: http://www.plagiarism.org/citing-sources/what-are-footnotes/

Wheeler, B. (Ed.). (2005). *Music therapy research* (2nd ed.). Philadelphia, PA: Barcelona.

Wheeling Jesuit University. (n.d.). *How do I write a position/argument essay?* Retrieved from the Wheeling Jesuit University Academic Resource Center website: https://www.wju.edu/arc/
handouts/position_arg.pdf

Whetten, D. A. (1989). What constitutes a theoretical contribution? *Academy of Management Review, 14*(4), 490–495.

Whetten, D. A., & Cameron, K. S. (1995). *Developing management skills* (3rd ed.). New York, NY: HarperCollins.

Wiersma, W., & Jurs, S. (2009). *Research methods in education* (9th ed.). New York, NY: Pearson.

WikiHow. (ca. 2016). *How to write a conclusion for a research paper*. Retrieved from the WikiHow website: http://www

.wikihow.com/Write-a-Conclusion-
for-a-Research-Paper

Wikipedia Encyclopedia. (2016a). *Citation*. San Francisco, CA: Wikipedia Foundation. Retrieved from https://en.wikipedia.org/
wiki/Citation

Wikipedia Encyclopedia. (2016b). *English modal verbs*. San Francisco, CA: Wikipedia Foundation. Retrieved from https://
en.wikipedia.org/wiki/English_modal_
verbs

Wikipedia Encyclopedia. (2016c). *Theorem*. San Francisco, CA: Wikipedia Foundation. Retrieved from https://en.wikipedia.org/
wiki/Theorem#Relation_with_scientific_
theories

Wilfred Laurier University Library. (ca. 2009). *Developing a research question*. Retrieved from the WLU Library website: http://library.wlu.ca/sites/default/
files/pdfs/tutorials/researchquestion
.pdf

Williams, E. (1998, March 26). *Research and paradigms*. Retrieved from the Victoria University of Wellington Department of Interdisciplinary Studies website: http://www.umdnj.edu/idsweb/
idst6000/williams_research+paradigms
.htm#Paradigm

Williams, J., Mulkins, A., Verhoef, M. J., Monkman D., & Findlay, B. (2002). *Needs assessment: Research literacy and capacity amongst complementary and alternative health care providers*. Ottawa, ON: Health Canada, Perspectives on Natural Health Products—Natural Health Products Directorate.

Williams, Y. (2016). *True experiment: Definition and examples*. Retrieved from the Study.com website: http://study
.com/academy/lesson/true-experiment-definition-examples.html

Williams-Jones, B., Pipon, J., Smith, E., & Boulanger, R. (2014). Challenges of ethical open-access publishing. *University Affairs, 55*(2), 40.

Wilson, I. M. (2000). *Sampling and qualitative research: Theme paper 2*. Retrieved from the University of Reading Statistical Services Center website: http://www
.reading.ac.uk/ssc/resources/Docs/
QQA/tp2_samp.pdf

Winsor, H. B. (1986). *Beyond critical thinking: A plea for creative alternatives* [Mimeographed].

Wolcott, H. F. (1988). Ethnographic research in education. In R. M. Jaeger (Ed.), *Complementary methods for research in education* (pp. 187–249). Washington, DC: American Educational Research Association.

Wolcott, H. F. (1990). *Writing up qualitative research*. Newbury Park, CA: Sage.

Wong, P. T. P. (2006). *How to write a research proposal*. Retrieved from the International Network on Personal Meaning website: http://www.meaning.ca/archives/archive/art_how_to_write_P_Wong.htm

Yadav, M. S. (2010). The decline of conceptual articles and implications for knowledge development. *Journal of Marketing, 74*(1), 1–19.

Yin, R. (1984). *Case study research*. Thousand Oaks, CA: Sage.

Yule, G. (2006). *Oxford practice grammar advanced*. Oxford, England: Oxford University Press.

Zammito, J. H. (2004). *A nice derangement of epistemes: Post-positivism in the study of science from Quine to Latour*. Chicago, IL: University of Chicago Press.

Zardo, P., & Pryor, P. (2012). The OHS professional as a "critical consumer" of research. In Health and Safety Professionals Alliance (Ed.), *The core body of knowledge for generalist OHS professionals*. Tullamarine: Safety Institute of Australia.

Zeegers, M., & Barron, D. (2015). *Milestone moments in getting your PhD in qualitative research*. Kidlington, England: Elsevier (Chandos).

Zent, E. S. (2001). *Writing effective purpose statements*. Retrieved from the University of Washington Tacoma website: http://faculty.washington.edu/ezent/imwps.htm

Zuse, H., & Bollman-Sdorra, P. (1992). Measurement theory and software measures In T. Denvir, R. Herman, & R. Whitty (Eds.), *Formal aspects of measurement* (pp. 219–260). New York, NY: Springer Verlag.

INDEX